D0712124

Gropius

FIONA MacCARTHY

GROPIUS

The Man Who Built
the Bauhaus

The Belknap Press of
Harvard University Press
Cambridge, Massachusetts
2019

First published in 2019
by Faber & Faber Limited as *Walter Gropius: Visitionary Founder of the Bauhaus*
Bloomsbury House
United Kingdom

Typeset by Faber & Faber Limited
Printed in the United States of America

First Harvard University Press edition, 2019

Library of Congress Cataloging-in-Publication
data is available from the Library of Congress

ISBN 978-0-674-73785-3 (cloth : alk. paper)

To Richard Calvocoressi

Contents

Contents

THIRD LIFE • AMERICA

Gropius Family Tree

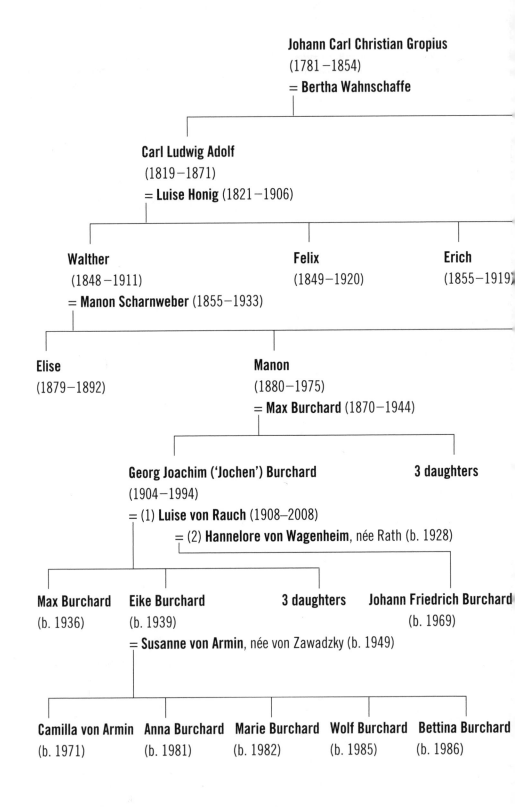

Johann Carl Christian Gropius
(1781–1854)
= Bertha Wahnschaffe

Carl Ludwig Adolf
(1819–1871)
= Luise Honig (1821–1906)

Walther
(1848–1911)
= Manon Scharnweber (1855–1933)

Felix
(1849–1920)

Erich
(1855–1919)

Elise
(1879–1892)

Manon
(1880–1975)
= Max Burchard (1870–1944)

Georg Joachim ('Jochen') Burchard
(1904–1994)
= (1) Luise von Rauch (1908–2008)
        = (2) Hannelore von Wagenheim, née Rath (b. 1928)

3 daughters

Max Burchard
(b. 1936)

Eike Burchard
(b. 1939)
= Susanne von Armin, née von Zawadzky (b. 1949)

3 daughters

Johann Friedrich Burchard
(b. 1969)

Camilla von Armin
(b. 1971)

Anna Burchard
(b. 1981)

Marie Burchard
(b. 1982)

Wolf Burchard
(b. 1985)

Bettina Burchard
(b. 1986)

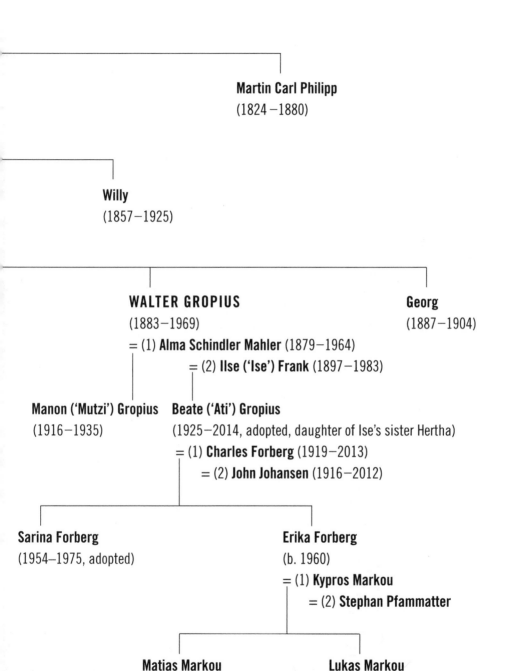

Martin Carl Philipp
(1824 –1880)

Willy
(1857–1925)

WALTER GROPIUS
(1883–1969)
= (1) **Alma Schindler Mahler** (1879–1964)
= (2) **Ilse ('Ise') Frank** (1897–1983)

Georg
(1887–1904)

Manon ('Mutzi') Gropius
(1916–1935)

Beate ('Ati') Gropius
(1925–2014, adopted, daughter of Ise's sister Hertha)
= (1) **Charles Forberg** (1919–2013)
= (2) **John Johansen** (1916–2012)

Sarina Forberg
(1954–1975, adopted)

Erika Forberg
(b. 1960)
= (1) **Kypros Markou**
= (2) **Stephan Pfammatter**

Matias Markou
(b. 1992)

Lukas Markou
(b. 1997)

Preface
The Silver Prince

How do you decide on your subject? This is a question people like to put to writers at literary festivals. I tend to answer that my subjects have always chosen me, the result of a long obsession, as with Byron, the fruits of a chance encounter, as with Eric Gill. They sit there in your mind, sometimes for years, waiting to claim you, like the start of a close friendship or inevitable love affair. In fact the starting point of my search for Walter Gropius was not an encounter with a person but a chair.

It was 1964. I was then a mini-skirted Courrèges-booted young journalist working for the *Guardian*. The place was Dunn's of Bromley, a modern-minded furniture store in a London suburb. The chair was the Isokon Long Chair. It was not designed by Gropius himself but by his close Bauhaus colleague Marcel Breuer and it was created when they were both living in England, taking refuge from the Nazi regime in Germany. I may have been the *Guardian*'s Design Correspondent but this was like no chair I had ever seen before, made of laminated plywood, curvaceous, fluid and poetic. The original advertising leaflet, designed by another Bauhaus Master, László Moholy-Nagy, suggested that anyone reclining on the Long Chair would imagine they were airborne. I tried out the chair and decided he was right.

This was where the chain of coincidence that led me to Walter Gropius began. The occasion at Dunn's was the relaunch of the Long Chair, production of which had been suspended in the war, when plywood parts made in Estonia could no longer be obtained. Among those present was Jack Pritchard, the modernist entrepreneur who had founded Isokon, commissioned Lawn Road Flats in Hampstead and supported Gropius and Breuer while they were in England. He came darting over and I was enchanted by his somewhat risky spontaneity of manner. Within the first two minutes he had invited me to come and spend a weekend at his house in Blythburgh in Suffolk. Over the next twenty years I went there often with my designer husband David Mellor and later with our children. It became a place we could escape to, almost a second home.

That house was like nothing I had ever known before. Jack and his psychotherapist wife Molly presided over a regime of the ever-open door, through which a wonderfully random mix of people – architects and scientists, artists and musicians, academics, surgeons, psychoanalysts, inventors – endlessly thronged. Conversations on art, science and politics raged non-stop. Children were treated as if they were grown up.

The mood, as I came to realise, was a throwback to progressive Hampstead of the 1930s. Jack never failed to emphasise that the house itself had been designed by his architect daughter Jennifer, the proud result of his liaison with the Hampstead nursery school teacher Beatrix Tudor-Hart. The layout of the building had a lovely flexibility which was later to remind me of Gropius's own house in Lincoln, Massachusetts. The routine was self-consciously uninhibited. The early-evening sauna with a little birch-twig beating was followed by the obligatory naked plunge into a fairly freezing Suffolk swimming pool. Supper often consisted of Jack's Ultimatum Salad, an amalgam of any food he could lay his hands on in order to feed the often unexpected multitudes. Conversation, which continued way into the night, included many references back to Gropius and Breuer and that whole lost world of pre-war European modernism. There was much detailed talk about the Bauhaus, its personalities, its ethos. This became familiar territory to me too.

Most memorably at Blythburgh art was all around us. The little Henry Moore on the side table in the dining room; the Calder mobiles in the children's bunkhouse, almost asking to be kicked around. The curtains were designed by the Pritchards' friend Ben Nicholson. Art was not treated as sacrosanct, not given ostentatious attention or respect, certainly not regarded as a commercial commodity. It was there to be enjoyed just as part of normal life. This was the driving force behind the original concept of the Bauhaus as envisioned by Gropius. Responding to the horrifying carnage of the First World War, in which technological advances had been harnessed to the weaponry of destruction, the Bauhaus – literally the House of Building, with its underlying sense of spiritual reconstruction – was Gropius's attempt at a reversal of this process. Biography as I've come to see it is a slow-burning process of the making of connections. My original friendship with Jack and Molly Pritchard brought me in the end to Walter Gropius himself.

In autumn 1968 the Bauhaus exhibition arrived at the Royal Academy in London. It had opened originally in Stuttgart, sponsored by the German government at a time when the achievements of Gropius and the Bauhaus were being celebrated in a somewhat desperate attempt to obliterate the memory of their persecution by the Nazis, who had forced the closure of the school in 1933. The exhibition stressed the concept of democratic art as part of the German tradition of the past. For Gropius himself and for the remaining Bauhaus students and teachers, many of whom came to London for the opening, this was a highly emotional time. The exhibition and the catalogue had been designed by the former Bauhaus Master Herbert Bayer. Jack Pritchard took on a delightedly proprietorial role.

He invited me to come to dinner at the Isobar, the Lawn Road Flats restaurant designed by Marcel Breuer, to meet Bayer. In the 1960s, thirty years after it was first designed, the Isobar still kept its authentic period quality. We sat at Breuer's plywood table, Jack and Herbert Bayer facing me as I perched on an Isokon plywood stool. Bayer was still handsome, debonair and charming. We talked about the past, about the Bauhaus and Berlin in the 1930s, about Bayer's later years of working in New York. What I was only much later to discover was that Herbert Bayer's passionate affair with Gropius's wife Ise had been the one serious threat to their long marriage. One of the fascinations of working on biography is the way in which such submerged histories emerge.

The next day, at a special private viewing of the Bauhaus exhibition, Jack Pritchard introduced me to Gropius himself. He was then eighty-five, small, upright, very courteous, retaining a Germanic formality of bearing, a reminder of how Gropius had once been the glamorous moustachioed officer in the gold-frogged dress uniform of the Hussars.

As he told me, by 1968 he had experienced three disparate lives: first in Germany as a radical young architect and then as the founder and director of the Bauhaus, the flight to England via Rome in 1934, followed by yet another emigration. He had now lived in America for more than thirty years. Gropius had experienced the long life of a wanderer, albeit an especially distinguished one. Though his English had obviously improved greatly since his nervously tongue-tied arrival at Victoria Station, he had never entirely lost his German accent. His face was deeply lined. He was by this time evidently ageing and he died a year later, in July 1969. But Gropius at this point was still valiant and impressive, with a flickering of arrogance. I could see why Paul Klee, one of the first Masters he appointed to the Bauhaus, referred to Gropius in his early Weimar days of authority and glamour as the Silver Prince.

———

Walter Gropius was a man of extraordinary charisma. For more than twenty years, from 1910 to 1930, he was at the very centre of European modern art and design. His Fagus factory building of 1913 and his purpose-designed buildings for the Bauhaus at Dessau, much admired in their time, still strike one as impressively experimental. As the founder and director of the Bauhaus he invented a form of creative education that influenced art schools worldwide. Gropius was a philosopher and thinker who could put his ideas over with conviction and lucidity. He was enormously attractive to women. For those (myself included) who initially viewed Gropius as a driven, formal character his sexual charisma comes as a surprise. He had a glamorous notoriety in his own time through his long love affair with Alma Mahler, Gustav Mahler's wife, the sex goddess of Vienna. But for one reason or another Gropius has more recently failed to register as the fascinating figure that he was in his own time.

Not the least of the myths I have had to contend with in writing his life is the idea that Gropius was doctrinaire and boring. For this we have to blame Tom Wolfe's coruscating satire *From Bauhaus to Our House*, published in 1981, in which Gropius is pilloried unjustly as inventor of the monolithic high-rise buildings in our cities. His later image was certainly not helped by his lacklustre portrait in the memoirs of Alma Mahler, who had her own agenda in denigrating Gropius to justify her sexually volatile behaviour. In Ken Russell's 1974 movie *Mahler* poor Gropius appears as a sadly wimpish figure who never stood a chance. In Percy and Felix Adlon's more recent cult film *Mahler auf der Couch* (2010), in which Gustav Mahler takes a trip to Leiden to discuss his marriage problems with Sigmund Freud, Gropius again appears as a negligible figure on the outer reaches of the composer's tormented sexual history. My own view of Gropius is altogether different. I see him as in many ways heroic, a romantic and optimist, a great survivor. Through the spiritual and physical upheavals of the twentieth century, to which Gropius the architect was especially vulnerable, his life had a peculiar resilience.

By the time he met Alma in the health spa at Tobelbad in 1910 the young Gropius was already established as an architect, at the centre of the Berlin avant-garde. It was a summer of reciprocated passion, as their interchange of letters clearly shows. Nor was this in any sense a fleeting romance. After Mahler's death Gropius and Alma were actually married for five years. They had a child together, the daughter named Manon who died in her teens and to whom Alban Berg's Violin Concerto 'To the memory of an angel' was dedicated. Gropius plays far too important a role in Alma's history to be convincingly written out.

Once they were divorced in 1920 Gropius had further liaisons. New documentation shows him as the ardent – sometimes the absurdly over-ardent – lover of two particularly interesting women, Lily Hildebrandt and Maria Benemann, one an artist, one a poet. Both were still in adoring contact with Gropius decades later. Sexually Gropius was far from negligible.

His second wife Ise, born Ilse Frank, whom he married in 1923, was his equal partner, a sharp and sophisticated woman. Ise provides the riposte to another Gropius legend put about by his detractors: that Gropius denigrated women. It is difficult to see how the Bauhaus could have flourished as it did without Ise by his side as organiser, as adviser. Her detailed Bauhaus diary, from which I quote many extracts in this book, deserves to be published in its entirety for the light it sheds on Gropius's achievements in setting up the Bauhaus in the first place and recruiting such a variously talented body of teachers, including Paul Klee, Wassily Kandinsky, Oskar Schlemmer, Josef Albers, Marcel Breuer, László Moholy-Nagy. These were by no means the easiest of people. Gropius had warring artistic egos to contend with. But a clash of opinion was something he believed in. He viewed argument as part of creativity itself.

As Gropius envisaged it the Bauhaus, first in Weimar then in Dessau, was a place of light and freedom, concentration and experiment. Walter Gropius has often been compared with William Morris, not totally convincingly. But something they certainly shared was a belief in the importance to designers of a knowledge of materials and techniques in evolving new forms of construction. From the start Bauhaus teaching had its basis in the crafts. Although almost all the Bauhaus Masters were men, this was a place in which women, too, would flourish. Recruitment figures for the Bauhaus show that female students frequently outnumbered males. Anni Albers, Gunta Stölzl, Marguerite Friedlaender, Marianne Brandt: all these were star performers who responded to the rigorous yet easy-going ethos of the Bauhaus. For the wonderfully talented textile artist Albers the Bauhaus gave her purpose and direction. Oskar Schlemmer's famous painting, now at MoMA in New York, showing female Bauhaus students crowding up the Dessau stairway, beautifully seizes the exciting aspirational mood.

Any modern biographer of Gropius has the accusation to contend with that he was a Nazi sympathiser, an idea that started to gain currency in the 1970s and which I examine in some detail in this book. He clearly had no sympathy for the local National Socialist factions in Weimar and in Dessau, who opposed and harried him through the Bauhaus years. The increasingly violent and repressive tendencies of German politics appalled him, as his revealing letters to his daughter Manon make absolutely clear. But in 1928 he returned to Berlin, planning to resurrect his architectural practice. He had an office to support. He needed commissions. He needed clients. These were lean years for architects in Germany. He sought work where he could find it, some of it connected with the projects of Nazis. In such circumstances the question we should ask is 'What would we have done?'

Once Hitler came to power in 1933 Gropius's situation was increasingly untenable. The Nazis opposed everything the Bauhaus stood for and the creative freedom that Gropius believed in. In many people's eyes Gropius *was* the Bauhaus. Although he was not Jewish, his avant-garde associations and his connections with 'degenerate' artists made him a marked man. Gropius was not actually forced into exile, but his beliefs and his affiliations left him little choice.

From then on, his was the story of a displaced person. 'Nobody's baby' was how Gropius described himself in London in 1956. He continued to feel himself German but once he reached America he managed to reinvent himself, not so much as an architect but as a theorist, an educator, an architectural sage. He always claimed to have greater rapport with younger people than with his own contemporaries. This had been true at the Bauhaus from the start. Emotionally and intellectually deepened by the experience of exile, Gropius, the respected philosopher and teacher, was to flourish in the States. He spoke up for developing artistic creativity, especially the innate creativity in children. Gropius began to argue with a new conviction, echoing the words of William Morris, for the central importance of beauty in every human life: 'the creation of beautiful proportions and materials is not enough . . . Beauty is an integral element in the whole life and cannot be isolated as a special privilege for the aesthetically initiated; it is a primary need of all.'

Gropius's influence on post-war architecture in America and internationally was enormous. His one-time Harvard students amounted to a global dynasty. They included I. M. Pei, Paul Rudolph, Philip Johnson, Bruno Zevi, Ulrich Franzen, Harry Seidler, Fumihiko Maki, the industrial designer Eliot Noyes. Two young English architects, Richard Rogers and Norman Foster, were later to train with Paul Rudolph at Yale. Without Walter Gropius's broad-based approach to industrial designing, as first developed at the Bauhaus, there might not have been an architect-designer as fluently imaginative as the American Charles Eames.

Gropius found a role in the States, celebrated and bemedalled. But like many of his contemporary exiles he never lost the sense of his European past. When I met him in London in the 1960s he reminded me of Christopher Isherwood's Bergmann, the Austrian émigré film director in the novel *Prater Violet*. 'I knew that face,' says the narrator. 'It was the face of a political situation, an epoch. The face of Central Europe.' This was equally true of Walter Gropius. He still seemed a European through and through.

Who Is Walter Gropius? This was the title of a film made in 1967 by the documentary director Roger Graef. It was the question I eventually decided I must try to answer. That initial meeting with Gropius intrigued me. As a subject for biography he gradually settled in my mind. Was he really so charmingly courteous as he seemed? To some he appeared merely arrogant and grumpy. The architectural historian Joseph Rykwert, for instance, was later to write harshly, 'As a man he seemed to have fewer redeeming features than many of his kind . . . his pinched humourless egotism was unrelieved by sparkle.' Others have detected an element of phoneyness. This was the so-called great architect who remained unable to draw. Was Gropius a lastingly important innovative thinker or, as some would argue, simply a remarkably effective self-publicist?

Such questions continued to waylay me and Gropius remained stored up in my mind for several decades as a possible subject for biography. The urge to define him turned into a quest that for the last few years absorbed my thinking time and working time, research programme and travels. This book is the result. Who indeed is Walter Gropius, a man who has always aroused such strong feelings both of admiration and opprobrium? What interest and relevance does he still hold for us today?

FIRST LIFE · Germany

The ageing Walter Gropius looked back at his childhood, remembering an episode that struck him as significant: 'when I was a small boy
somebody asked me what my favourite colour was. For years my family poked fun at me for saying, after some hesitation, "*Bunt ist meine
Lieblingsfarbe*," meaning "Multicoloured is my favourite colour."' The
colours of the rainbow were what he really loved. Gropius's early yearn-
ings for variety were serious and lasting: his appreciation of completely
varied building styles, from classical Greek to twentieth-century Japanese; a love of music that included both Schoenberg and the Beatles;
the improbable and sometimes inflammatory mixes of creative people
he gathered in around him. As he put it in a speech made in Chicago on
his seventieth birthday, 'The strong desire to *include* every vital component of life instead of excluding them for the sake of too narrow and
dogmatic an approach has characterised my whole life.'

Gropius was born on 18 May 1883 in Berlin, the rapidly expanding imperial capital where variousness had become a way of life. He
was christened Adolf Georg Walter Gropius in the neo-Gothic Fried-
richswerdersche Kirche, of which Karl Friedrich Schinkel was the
architect. Growing up he was exposed to a whole commotion of architectural styles, Gothic and Romanesque, Baroque and neo-classical.
The challenge of the city, as he came to comprehend it, was intriguing
and dementing. What *was* the ideal city? And what were an architect's
responsibilities in the shaping of the city? After victory in the Franco-
Prussian War and the unification of Germany in 1871, Berlin was
emerging as a powerful and thriving European capital, a city on a par
with London, Paris or Vienna. Its population grew from 826,000 in
1871 to 1.9 million in 1900. Alongside the excitements of expansion

there were the inevitable social problems. Berlin, as Gropius watched it through its stages of transition from imperial to modern, was the place of his first loyalty, the city which first taught him that an architect had social obligations. Even when far away from Germany through his years of exile, Berlin was still the city that Gropius came back to in his architectural imagination.

Architecture was in his background. His father's Prussian family was embedded in the solidly respectable high bourgeoisie. Gropius's great-great-grandfather had been a parson in Helmstedt, a town in Lower Saxony. His descendants were predominantly clergymen, teachers, minor landowners and soldiers. But Gropius's family had an entrepreneurial tendency as well. In the early nineteenth century his great-grandfather Johann Carl Christian Gropius became a partner in a Berlin silk-weaving works. Already there were family connections with the intricate skills of making and an intimate knowledge of materials, early precedents for the workshop practice on which Gropius's Bauhaus philosophy was based.

Johann's brother Wilhelm Ernst was the proprietor of a company making theatrical masks and, more ambitiously, acquired a theatre where he put on performances with landscape scenery and moving statuary magically animated and lit. Such entertainments were a popular feature of the city. The writer Walter Benjamin, who grew up in Berlin, described the strange enchantments of these so-called dioramas. A little bell would ring before each moving image was revolved to face the expectant audience: 'And every time it rang, the mountains with their humble foothills, the cities with their mirror-bright windows, the railroad stations with their clouds of dirty yellow smoke, the vineyards, down to the smallest leaf, were suffused with the ache of departure.'

Wilhelm Ernst's two enterprising sons, inspired by Bouton and Daguerre's famous Paris diorama, developed these techniques to create their own spectacular Gropius Diorama in Berlin. This consisted of three huge scenic paintings, each more than sixty foot wide and forty high, revolving in sequence accompanied by four-part choral music. The Gropius Diorama continued until 1850, and again one finds the family fascination with theatre paralleled in Walter Gropius's later interest in performance, for instance his collaboration with Erwin Piscator on the concept of 'Total Theatre' as well as Oskar Schlemmer's theatrical experiments of the Bauhaus years.

A key figure in developing the Gropius Diorama was the architect Karl Friedrich Schinkel. He was a protégé of both Johann Carl Christian and Wilhelm Ernst Gropius, who employed and encouraged him at an early stage of his career. Indeed for a time the young Schinkel was a lodger in a Gropius family house on Breitestrasse, near the silk works, sharing cramped accommodation on an upper floor where the aspiring architect ingeniously used painted folding screens as room dividers. It was Schinkel who provided the sketches, made in Paris in 1826, for the Gropius Diorama. Years later, after Schinkel himself had become renowned as the architect of many of Berlin's great civic buildings – the Neue Wache, the Schauspielhaus theatre, the Altes Museum, Gropius's christening place the Friedrichswerder church, the Bauakademie architectural school – he was to have a potent direct influence on the Gropius architectural dynasty.

Schinkel was certainly the role model for Walter Gropius's successful great-uncle, Martin Gropius. He studied at the Bauakademie and formed one of the largest architectural firms in Berlin, Fa. Gropius & Schmieden. Martin Gropius absorbed the classical influence of Schinkel to design such well-proportioned and grandly urban buildings as the Gewandhaus in Leipzig and the Renaissance-style Kunstgewerbemuseum in Berlin, originally built as a royal art museum and now known as Martin Gropius Bau.

More poignantly, Gropius's own father Walther Gropius, also inspired by Schinkel, started out with ambitions to become an architect. But according to Gropius, his father was too lacking in confidence, too timid and withdrawn for a profession that needed a certain flamboyance in approach. After only a short period of designing actual buildings he retreated into public service. He was working as a civic building official by the time his son Walter was born. However, his own thwarted ambitions never stopped him from supporting his son's architectural beginnings. According to an old friend, the elder Walther Gropius was 'the only really *kind* man' he had ever known.

Walther Gropius assumed that his son would follow family tradition by becoming an architect in the formal urban Schinkel mode. In a sense he would not have been disappointed, for Gropius himself remained a staunch admirer both of Schinkel and of Schinkel's own mentor David Gilly. In spite of the fact that Schinkel himself was stylistically promiscuous, veering from neo-classical to romantically medieval, his buildings had an overriding structural consistency, a mastery of space that Gropius admired. Even Adolf Loos, early-twentieth-century uncompromising modernist and anti-ornamentalist, recommended Schinkel to the newer generation as the exemplar of architectural purity. And for Gropius's contemporary Mies van der Rohe, Schinkel 'had wonderful constructions, excellent proportions, and good detailing'. Gropius's father might have found his son's later architectural work in some ways disconcerting but their shared admiration for Schinkel's architectural mastery was unwavering.

Though it seems that Gropius's father was sweetly ineffectual, Gropius's mother was quite another matter. Manon Scharnweber Gropius, the descendant of French Huguenot émigrés who settled in Prussia in the seventeenth century, was a formidable woman, possessive and ambitious for her family. Young Gropius had three siblings: Elise, who was born in 1879 and who died in her early teens; a second sister, Manon, two years older than Walter, to whom he was devoted; and a younger brother, Georg, known in the family as Orda. Family life was sedate, contained and cultured. Walter Gropius 'had *Kultur* in his bones', as the historian Peter Gay described it. There were theatres and lectures, there was a lot of music, with family outings to operas, concerts and ballet in Berlin. Walter's sister Manon was encouraged by their mother to accompany her brothers in trios and chamber music. Orda was a precociously talented violinist. Walter played the cello, but nothing like so well.

Walter and his mother were always particularly close, locked together in a fondness which would later prove a challenge to his wives. Alma's response was confrontational, Ise's more deviously conciliatory.

Walter with his parents, sister Manon and younger brother Georg, *c.*1892.

The family lived at 23 Genthinerstrasse in the Schöneberg district on the west side of the city. This was a pleasant, highly respectable residential area close to the Tiergarten, the large public park. The Gropius apartment building stood in a leafy area of substantial houses, with the tall spire of the Apostelkirche, built in the 1870s in bright red-orange brick, dominating the end of the street.

Walter Benjamin, born ten years after Walter Gropius, was brought up in a Jewish but otherwise similarly comfortable, settled bourgeois household in the same part of the city. Benjamin's memoir of his Berlin childhood gives an almost dreamlike impression of the area, with its formal mid- to late-nineteenth-century *Gründerzeit* architecture of prosperous, substantial houses with their inner courtyards and their loggias. 'Everything in the courtyard', wrote Benjamin, 'became a sign or hint to me.' Nearby there were hackney carriage stands on which the fascinated child watched the coachmen hang their capes while watering their horses. He remembered how the rhythm of the metropolitan railway and the distant sounds of carpet beating rocked him to sleep.

Walter Benjamin's memoir was written in the early 1930s, before he, like Gropius, was forced to leave Berlin, and it exudes a sense of pending exile. Benjamin is thought to have eventually committed suicide on the French–Spanish border in 1940. There is a strange magic in his account of childhood. The statues in the Tiergarten, 'the caryatids and atlantes, the putti and pomonas', mystify the boy who, 'thirty years ago, slipped past them with his schoolboy's satchel'. He is struck by the curious sights and sounds from the zoo nearby, with its gnus and zebras, elephants and monkeys, accompanied by the distant music of the Tiergarten bandstand. In shopping expeditions to the city with his mother, he glimpses another side to Berlin life, the underworld of poverty, seeing with fascinated horror the beggars and the whores with their thickly painted lips. As Benjamin comments in his book, 'I have made an effort to get hold of the *images* in which the experience of the big city is precipitated in a child of the middle class.' Walter Gropius's own upbringing, exposed to similar enchantments and terrors of the city, was very much like this.

At the age of six Gropius was sent to a private elementary school in Berlin, and then three years later he started a conventional classics-based education at the Humanistische Gymnasium, part of Berlin's publicly sponsored educational system. He attended three of these gymnasia from 1893, finally leaving the Stegliz Gymnasium when he was nearly twenty. He had done so well in his final exams, which included submitting an impressive translation of Sappho's 'Ode', that his proud father took him out to a lavish celebration dinner at Kempinski's restaurant, where he toasted Walter's successes with champagne.

Gropius was at this stage rather withdrawn, shy and solitary. His visual interests were still quite undeveloped. So far there were few signs of Gropius the influential architect. But he later claimed that his obsession with building structures had been fired while still at school by Julius Caesar's account of the construction of the bridge across the Rhine, which Gropius discovered in *The Conquest of Gaul*. He had drawn it up according to Caesar's description and constructed a scale model.

Gropius the architectural student at the Munich Technische Hochschule, 1903.

Not long after, in early 1903, he enrolled in the Munich Technische Hochschule to take an intensive course in architectural studies: history, design, building construction. This was his first time away from home.

Gropius's apartment in Munich was just a stone's throw from the Alte Pinakothek picture gallery and the Bayerische Staatsbibliothek, close to the university, the second-hand bookshops and the ancient courtyards tucked in behind the street facades. The young Gropius had spent his free hours in the museums, studying the Munich collections of German, Dutch and Italian Old Masters and discovering the work of the French Impressionists.

But he was not to stay in Munich long. First of all he was officially summoned to start his compulsory year's military service in the late summer of 1903. Then there was intense family anxiety about the serious illness

Gropius the cadet in the 15th Hussars Regiment, Wandsbeck, 1904.

of his younger brother Orda, who was suffering from what seems to have been the kidney disorder later to be known as Bright's disease. Gropius decided to postpone his military training and returned home to Berlin in July. After months of painful illness, in January 1904, Orda died. This shock affected Walter profoundly. He stayed on in Berlin comforting the family and entered the architectural firm of Solf and Wichards, two Berlin architects who were family friends, as a by then relatively mature apprentice. Although he began as a draughtsman in the office, his true talent for practical construction was quickly recognised and he was soon being sent out on site work, controlling the concept and architectural detailing of buildings. As is well known – a much repeated truth that has almost become a cliché – technical draughtsmanship was never to be Gropius's strong point.

Finally, in the summer of 1904 Gropius reapplied for his military service with the 15th Hussars stationed at Wandsbeck near Hamburg. He wrote home to his mother, optimistically telling her he was living comfortably in a big old rural Gasthof. He added with a characteristic touch of vanity, 'My uniforms fit me well and I shall look very elegant in them.' A photograph of the slim and upright Walter Gropius as a cadet in the Hussars' splendid uniform, staring boldly ahead, definitely bears this out. Probably he looked even better on his horse.

The Hussars' training schedule was focused upon horsemanship: cleaning the stables in the early morning, grooming the horses, polishing the harnesses and saddles. Then afternoon riding lessons, learning how to trot with no stirrups and no bridle, riding side-saddle, backwards and standing up. He boasted to his mother that he outrode his companions in spite of the fact his horse was particularly challenging. This horse's name was Devil. His progress was recognised by the officers, who soon awarded him his spurs. After such intensive training Gropius kept up his love and indeed his need for horses, carrying on riding right into old age.

His regimental social life was far more problematic. Gropius's family had military connections: his father had fought in the Franco-Prussian War; his cousin Richard had served in the army from 1863 and kept meticulous records of the Gropius family's military history, listing his relatives' ranks and decorations. But what nobody seemed to have foreseen as a hazard was that the 15th Hussars was an aristocratic regiment. Gropius, whose background was essentially bourgeois, found it hard to gain acceptance amongst the inner circle of his contemporaries who on the whole came from wealthy families. Interestingly he seems to have made friends with another exception to the regimental rule, a Jew, 'Doctor' Lehman, whom Gropius described in a letter to his mother as 'a very nice person. Inexperienced, naïve, and clumsy, he is not at all ostentatious or profligate. I have not discovered any Jewish trait in him.' It would be wrong to interpret this too strictly. His youthful comments typify the automatic anti-Semitic thinking of his time and class.

Gropius was gradually accepted in the regiment, partly because of his inherent skill in horsemanship and also because he had been assiduous at cultivating useful introductions, a talent he would perfect in his later Bauhaus years. He began to be invited into Hamburg high society, going to musical evenings and dances where he found the atmosphere uncongenial, superficial, snobbish: 'very beautiful girls, but all cold Hanseatic blood.' Gropius now started to find himself in favour with his commanding officer, who took him to the races and invited him to lunch. But the military life was alien to him. He missed being able to cultivate his own special interests in art and architecture. 'After this year', Gropius lamented to his mother, 'I will be mentally completely dull.'

Besides, in this fast-spending regiment he found himself embarrassingly short of money. Expenses in the 15th Hussars were quite enormous, with outlay on horses, tailors, saddlers, shoemakers or the whole extravagant lifestyle thought suitable for officers. Gropius's family was reasonably prosperous but the allowance his father could afford to give him went nowhere near to meeting the bills he had to pay. At one point Gropius was reduced to asking for a loan from his Jewish friend Lehman. It appears to have been a relief both to him and to his parents when after a year in the army Gropius decided to return to his architectural training, enrolling in September 1905 at the Königliche Technische Hochschule in Berlin-Charlottenburg.

For the next two years Gropius was back in Berlin, going through the motions of an architectural training as rigorous and formal as the one he had already experienced in Munich, with as many as seventeen courses to master. Students were expected to work a twelve-hour day, but Gropius was always good at finding his escape routes. He liked to leave Berlin for holidays at Timmendorf, the family summer house on the Baltic north of Lübeck. This house by the sea belonged to his mother, Manon Gropius, a present from her relatively wealthy aunt, and it had been a gathering point for the family since Walter was a child.

He also loved to visit the family estate at Janikow near Dramburg, Pomerania, owned by his father's younger brother Erich. Erich was an ambitious experimental farmer, far more go-ahead in attitude than Gropius's father. He originally bought Janikow in 1883, an estate of fertile fields and woods and trout ponds, developing scientific methods of animal breeding and fish hatching. He was conscious of the need for proper functional standards in his agricultural buildings and in housing for his workers. It was Uncle Erich who gave Gropius his first professional commission, for farm buildings at Janikow.

This commission came in autumn 1905. Gropius was twenty-three and was only just beginning his training at the Hochschule. But the opportunity to design real working farm buildings, including a smithy and a laundry, was too tempting to resist. He set himself up with a draughtsman to assist him, recognising his own technical weakness in this area and inventing the collaborative method he continued all his life, with Gropius originating the architectural concept, delegating the detailed constructional drawings to an assistant but still keeping close control over the progress of the work. After these first farm buildings Uncle Erich commissioned a new granary. Gropius designed a tall fairy-tale building with sloping roofs and high-up windows, a structure that is almost Rapunzel's tower.

At the same time Gropius was designing his first domestic building, a house near Dramburg for the Metzners, who were family friends. This building too has elements of fantasy, with its gables, balconies and low curving roofs. What people forget about Gropius the functionalist is that he had a deeply emotional expressionist side. These very early buildings are in tune with the sentimental-medievalist architecture of the British Arts and Crafts movement, with Ashbee and Voysey, with Mackintosh and Lorimer. Nor in fact are they remote from the later Hitler-period mythology of buildings related to their native German soil. Gropius himself would refer to these first buildings as his youthful sins.

A further commission from his uncle for agricultural housing at Janikow brought out a very different side: that of the socially conscious and rational young man. Uncle Erich, benign landowner, inculcated him with views of the social responsibilities of an architect. Gropius began developing an awareness of the extreme divisions within society, an attitude quite different to the narrow social outlook he had known in the privileged Hussars, whose lifestyle provided such a blatant contrast to the restricted lives of the agricultural labourers. He designed four simple practical buildings at Janikow, each with accommodation for two farm workers' families, with gardens around them and large views across the fields. All his life Walter Gropius would be convinced of the human need for greenery, a yearning for proximity to nature, the reminder of the natural forces of renewal. This was something that sustained him through the years of his long exile. It is already manifest in his designs for Janikow.

Gropius had by now given up on the Hochschule. There had been too many interesting interruptions, time taken out from his studies to design his new buildings and supervise their construction on site. 'I cannot follow the lectures after the long pause,' he told his mother arrogantly. 'They are anyway illusory except maybe for geniuses.' Already he was showing his belief in the practical above the merely theoretical. He resisted the Hochschule's prevalent philosophy of clothing new buildings in historical styles. Gropius made another of the peremptory decisions that were by now becoming a feature of his life. Without completing his course and without taking his final examination he left the Hochschule in Berlin in 1907. He had conveniently received a legacy from a relation which allowed him, as he put it, to 'push forward from the beaten path into unknown regions, in order to know myself better'. He now set out on a year-long expedition to Spain.

Walter Gropius was unusually susceptible to travel. Certain journeys were to leave an indelible impression on his highly tuned visual imagination. His first visit to America in 1928 was one such influential journey. The vast industrial architecture of factories and silos, bridges and conveyors, vista upon vista of functional grandeur, lastingly affected the scale of his ambition. Another expedition that affected Gropius deeply was his tour of Japan in 1954, a journey that put architecture in a new perspective. His Spanish trip of 1907 was the first of these journeys that influenced him for life.

In the autumn of that year he set off with a travelling companion, Helmuth Grisebach, a young aspiring artist he had known for years from seaside holidays in Timmendorf. Helmuth's father, Hans Grisebach, a fashionable Berlin architect, had designed both families' holiday homes. Gropius at first was not pleased with his companion, complaining of his lack of responsiveness: 'not even the most wonderful thing in the world can raise him from his slumber. He has not once said anything interesting.' The lethargic Grisebach left all the detail of their travel arrangements to Walter, behaving like a helpless child. He had hardly even bothered to learn three words of Spanish. But gradually, as they shared such revelatory experiences, the two of them started to get on.

They travelled on a passenger ship, the *Albingia*, stopping off in the harbour at Le Havre, which Gropius found extremely sinister, assuring his mother he had kept his revolver at the ready as they strolled around the port at night. The ship hit a bad storm as they reached the Bay of Biscay and all the passengers were seasick. It was rather a relief when the ship docked at Bilbao and the journey continued across dry

Gropius and Helmuth Grisebach travelling in Spain.

land. A contemporary photograph shows the two young men on horse-back. A little comic drawing by Grisebach shows them riding donkeys through mountainous countryside. Otherwise they travelled on foot. On previous expeditions in Europe Gropius had been *en famille*, guided by his mother with her Baedeker around Italy, Switzerland, Austria, France and the Low Countries. These were carefully planned cultural excursions. Spain in 1907 was a great deal more ad hoc.

Gropius, at twenty-four and having already started his own practice as an architect, had his mind on studying Spain's great architectural structures: the churches, the palaces, the fortified towns. He was an unusually earnest and well-motivated young man. Before they left Bilbao he and Grisebach had viewed the city's churches and cathedrals, including the fourteenth-/fifteenth-century cathedral of Santiago, so named as Bilbao had been a point of transit for pilgrims travelling the route to Santiago de Compostela through northern Spain. Further on, approaching Burgos, Gropius and his companion stopped at the abbey of Santo Domingo de Silos, a Benedictine monastery where they were enthusiastically received by the abbot and the monks.

Here Gropius was not only impressed by the extreme beauty of the cloister with its decorative carvings in Romanesque style, he was also deeply touched by what for him was the new experience of the Roman Catholic Mass. Up to now Gropius had seemed immune to religion, admitting, for example, in a letter to his grandmother that a Rogation Day procession passing beneath his window in Munich in 1903 had left him cold. But now four years later the monks' Gregorian chant especially moved him.

Gropius and Grisebach were now heading south towards Segovia. Gropius was wildly excited by the sight of the Castillo de Coca, the massively turreted late-medieval castle-palace built in brick in the highly decorative Mudéjar style, combining the Islamic with flamboyant Gothic. He described Coca in a letter to his mother as looming up in the barren landscape like a story-book edifice, a fantasy building 'with its thousand pinnacles and towers'. It rose 'wonderful, grand, and monumental in the melancholy desolation of its environment'.

Travelling on he was also much impressed with the architecturally peculiar cathedral of Avila, in the south of Old Castile. The cathedral was actually planned as a cathedral-fortress, its rounded apse having a dual function as one of the defensive turrets of the city walls. The construction of this dual-purpose building apparently began in the late eleventh century within the remains of a previous church which was then in ruins following a sequence of Muslim attacks. For Gropius his Avila visit was an early indication of the vulnerability of buildings, as would become so tragically clear to him when he returned in 1947 to a Berlin devastated by the Second World War.

Besides the architecture of Avila Gropius was also impressed by the women of the city, almost all of whom struck him as genuinely beautiful, with a strength of feature that made northern Europeans look insignificant in comparison. Considering his record of extreme susceptibility to women as he grew older, Gropius seems to have been a surprisingly late starter. There are no signs of earlier flirtations, let alone serious love affairs. But in Spain to some extent he made up for lost time. Arriving in Madrid in late October 1907 he reported to his mother that the women were in general so ravishingly beautiful and well turned out that he dressed in his own best formal clothes, the perfect off-duty Hussar officer, in order to join the evening parade along the street. At an evening party, the result of an introduction from the German embassy, he met 'the two most beautiful girls in Madrid', a pair of young Cubans both so exquisite in face and figure that Gropius almost gasped. He braced himself to escort one of the young Cubans to the dining table and discovered she was also intelligent and amiable. But, as he reassured his always watchful mother, his heart was still intact.

Another new experience for Gropius in Madrid was the *corrida*. This too was unsettling. The Spanish bullfight, with its ferocious element of ritual, struck him at first as absolutely alien. He watched with horror as the matador and *banderilleros* pranced brandishing the *muletas* to enrage the bull. The torn and bloodied body of the horse filled him with such horror mixed with strange excitement he found himself trembling. The twitching picador's horse in its death throes; the spectators roaring; the confidence and skill of the matadors themselves. The whole scene of primitive Spanish passions appalled but fascinated Gropius and he returned to the *corrida* several times.

The Berliner could not help observing that Madrid did not compare for grandeur with Potsdamer Platz, lacking the same quality of monumental buildings. Perhaps he was a little biased about this. But he admired the city for the elegance of its layout, with its beautiful squares and interconnected promenades. He and Grisebach went to concerts and theatres, and Gropius explored the public galleries. He counted up that he had been on nine visits to the Prado, mainly to view the Velázquez paintings he particularly loved.

Their German embassy contacts meant that he and Grisebach had a sociable time. One of their new friends, Josef 'Pepé' Weissberger, a sophisticated bachelor businessman who spoke six languages including Arabic, encouraged the young men to start up a new career in the art market, buying cheap bits and pieces, especially pottery, in the little Madrid junk shops and selling them on at a considerable profit. They became more ambitious in their plans. Helmuth, who had by far the larger income from his family, telegraphed home asking for more money when he thought he had discovered a genuine Murillo. Their idea was to take their treasures back to Germany, where they would be exhibited and sold. Grisebach made an excited expedition to Paris to show what he imagined was a painting by Claudio Coello to the director of the Louvre.

Gropius, initially a little sceptical, got carried away by the possibilities and he too wrote home to beg his mother for more funds, which she sent on condition that his father was not told. It is interesting to see Gropius at this stage growing in confidence in his own judgement in assessing works of art. He claimed that the discipline of picking out and valuing artworks for the market taught him a great deal more than merely viewing paintings as an amateur. However, Gropius proved to be an art dealer manqué. Once they returned to Germany their acquisitions turned out to be at best works by followers of Murillo and disappointingly unsaleable.

In the run-up to Christmas 1908 Pepé Weissberger joined them on an expedition to Segovia, Granada and the southern Spanish coast. It was a delight to emerge from rocky landscapes into the tropical vegetation and sultry air of Malaga, where, according to the now slightly homesick Gropius, it was as warm as a July day in Berlin. Writing home he describes the laden orange trees, the cacti (Gropius was always to be a bit obsessed by cacti), the profusion of chrysanthemums and roses. They feasted on two dozen oysters each in a restaurant in which the table decorations had transformed the room into a bower of beautiful geraniums and they drank far too much of the local sherry, stumbling over the rocks and tiptoeing through the late-flowering Spanish tulips on the way home to their beds. Gropius comments on how alcohol in conjunction with the romantic landscape had affected his companions, Grisebach becoming moody, Weissberger sentimental, while he himself simply grew more quiet and content.

This was the first Christmas he had spent away from home. By now the travellers were back in Madrid. They were swept up into Spanish Christmas celebrations, dining in Madrid's most elegant restaurant and going to a sparkling rococo performance at the Teatro Lara, which Gropius describes as the best theatre in Spain. But in spite of such diversions Gropius was overcome with nostalgia and anxiety, picturing his parents sitting alone beneath their modest Christmas tree. The still quite recent loss of his brother Orda was greatly on his mind. He wrote in a newly affectionate mood to reassure his parents that at Christmas there would be 'a strong thread of love and longing' between Berlin, Alfeld (home territory of his mother's family) and Madrid. Gropius wrote separately to his father, who was on the edge of retirement from his post in the civil service and showing signs of depression and withdrawal from family life. He suggested, perhaps a little overconfidently, that this was the right time for his father to retire since he himself was now set to make his way in life.

One of Walter Gropius's lifelong enthusiasms certainly started on his journeyings through Spain. This was his passionate predilection for traditional Spanish decorative tiles: the *alicatados*, inlaid tiles in Moorish style, and the blue-and-white Catalonian tiles known as *azulejos*. He made sure that he saw the best collections in Madrid, the most impressive being that belonging to de Osma, the Spanish Finance Minister. Presumably the introduction came through the embassy. This private display struck Gropius as much more beautiful than anything comparable in most museums; only the Poldi Pezzoli in Milan could compete with it. De Osma was thrilled by the young German's precocious interest in and knowledge of the crafts.

Through the embassy Gropius met another young German enthusiast, Hans Wendland, and together they set off to Barcelona, where they searched out marvellous examples of traditional Spanish craftwork, textiles and carvings, being especially excited by the decorative tiles of Catalonia. It was here that Gropius hit on the idea of reviving old methods of ceramic tile production to make newly designed wall coverings for contemporary architecture. He managed to be taken on for work experience in a ceramic tile factory at Triana near Seville, working alongside the Spanish artisan-craftsman employees. At Triana he sketched out his designs for some animal friezes, cut them into large tiles, glazed and kiln-fired them and finally assembled them, the first of the glazed ceramic murals which became a feature of his later buildings. Years later, when his new wife Ise first toured the Bauhaus workshops she remembered how Gropius had gone through a craft training in one of the most famous tile-making plants in Spain and how this 'had instilled in him a great admiration for the intricacies of good craft work in any kind of material'.

It was in 1908 in Barcelona that Gropius first encountered the work of Antonio Gaudí. It might at first appear that Gaudí the fantastical futuristic architect and Gropius the rational were polar opposites. This was not completely so. First Gropius visited the Gaudí buildings then finished or in various phases of construction: the Park Güell, the garden suburb on the Montaña Pelada, a glorious kind of Spanish Disneyland with its magical creatures and weirdly inventive ceramic decorations; the Batlló House with its wonderfully undulating roof. He may have seen the Milà House, Gaudí's almost surrealist six-storey apartment block. He certainly saw the Sagrada Família in its early stages, for it was here in the workshop alongside the slowly evolving cathedral that Gropius and Gaudí met.

The meeting itself was a non-event. Gropius found Gaudí, an obsessive and eccentric personality then in his mid-fifties, absorbed in his work and uncommunicative. The vastly ambitious Sagrada Família had been commissioned in the early 1880s. At the time of Gropius's visit the crypt was complete and the Nativity facade was making progress. The construction of its tall encrusted stone towers had been ongoing since 1901. At the time Gropius admitted himself mystified by Gaudí's architectural thinking, with its curious blend of neo-Gothic and art nouveau, although he was impressed by Gaudí's obvious religious fervour and fanatical concentration on the task in hand. It was only much later that Gropius fully understood Gaudí's daring and inventiveness as a structural engineer. 'Some of the Sagrada Família walls are a marvel of technical perfection,' he commented when he revisited Barcelona in 1932.

The idea of the building of the great cathedral by a dedicated group of artist-craftsmen living on the site had been inculcated in Walter Gropius early. While still at the Hochschule in Berlin he had listened to an influential lecture on the *Bauhütten*, the communal dwelling houses for the construction workers of the Middle Ages. It seems likely these ideas were reinforced by his visit to Gaudí on the site of the Sagrada Família, where Gropius was conscious of the sense of dedication and spiritual awakening inherent in such a perfectionist architectural work. The concept of the great Expressionist cathedral, co-operative in its organisation and inspiringly organic in its forms, resurfaced in the early stages of the Bauhaus, symbolising the hoped-for start of a new world.

3
Berlin
1908–1910

In 1908 Gropius returned to a Berlin very different in mood from the city of his childhood. Berlin was now the fastest-expanding manufacturing centre in the whole of continental Europe, with its population swelling accordingly. The great majority of Berliners were crammed unhealthily into large-scale barrack-like tenement blocks, the profitable *Mietskasernen*. Even in the more elegant environment of West Berlin, where Gropius was once again living with his family, there was a growing sense of instability. As described by the journalist Robert Walser, who arrived in Berlin from Switzerland in 1905, 'Everything here is caught up in an endless process of cultivation and change.'

Berlin city centre was by this time lively to the point of frenzy. The hustle and bustle was said to be so great that 'In Berlin you have the impression that an alarm has just been sounded: "Everything races, takes flight."' Already the jostling Berlin streets had the *mouvementé* quality of a Kirchner painting. The palatial coffee houses overflowed with patrons holding secret trysts and guzzling Berlin patisserie. The nature of the metropolis was altered by the overwhelming bulk of new department stores and by shopping arcades, centres of urban pleasures and temptation, futuristic structures built in glass and iron and steel, the materials emblematic of modernity.

Gropius almost immediately found employment in the architectural office of Peter Behrens, thanks to Karl Ernst Osthaus, a contact he had made in Madrid. Osthaus was an influential young German patron of avant-garde art and architecture who had founded the Folkwang Museum in Hagen. He was a friend and admirer of Behrens, and had given him his first architectural commissions. Osthaus had been impressed by Gropius's knowledge of local ceramics and had actually purchased some examples of Spanish pottery which Gropius had shown him. He wrote to Behrens suggesting that he interview the obviously promising young architect as soon as Gropius got back to Berlin.

Behrens's increasingly successful architectural office was then at Neubabelsberg near Potsdam, a large purpose-built studio in the garden of the Behrens family home. Gropius joined a set-up that was busy and optimistic. Behrens had an eye for talent. The young Mies van der Rohe had already been taken on as an assistant. For a while he and Gropius worked side by side on a Behrens housing project. A little later Le Corbusier would also join Peter Behrens at Neubabelsberg.

For a socially conscious architectural practice at the beginning of the twentieth century the challenges of urban development and rampant industrialisation were daunting, but Behrens's cool, systematic approach remained impressive. As Gropius remembered, 'he took a fresh unprejudiced start for any problem of design.' He described him as 'an imposing personality, well dressed and having the cool deportment of a conservative Hamburg patrician. Endowed with will power and a penetrating intellect he was moved more by reason than by emotion.' Gropius was always to acknowledge Peter Behrens as his master, the person who introduced him to the basic working principles of architecture and design.

It was Behrens who gave him 'the first foundation' on which he could build his later development as an architect. Most importantly this lay in Behrens's breadth of vision. He was a designer of enormous versatility, designing not just buildings but the detail within buildings: furniture and textiles, light fittings, cutlery, glass, china. He was just as confident in lettering and type design. As the influential art director for the Allgemeine Elektrizitäts-Gesellschaft (AEG), Germany's largest supplier of electrical equipment, Behrens controlled all aspects of the company's architecture and design. It is possible to view him as the founding father of industrial design and corporate identity.

Previously, Behrens had been a moving spirit in the artists' colony at Darmstadt, developed with the support of the Grand Duke of Hesse in 1899. Hesse, like Osthaus, belongs in the European network of pro-

Portrait of Peter Behrens by E. R. Weiss, 1906

gressive, confident young male connoisseurs who gave twentieth-century modernism its original impetus. The Grand Duke, son of Queen Victoria's favourite daughter Alice, was an anglophile art lover and an enthusiastic patron of English arts and crafts. He had commissioned work for the palace at Darmstadt from both C. R. Ashbee and M. H. Baillie Scott. Peter Behrens's own beautifully detailed, artistically coherent Darmstadt house was not only a marvellous continental exemplar of English Arts and Crafts philosophy, the notion of 'the art that is life', it was also in its way a harbinger of Gropius's architectural imperatives.

Behrens's vision of architectural totality, extending from the structure to the art and design within the building, was an obvious inspiration for Gropius's concept of *Gesamtkunstwerk*, the total work of art.

Years later Ise Gropius pointed out how his years with Peter Behrens, 'who was not only a famous architect but also worked as a designer of utilities', had instilled in Gropius a great deal of 'practical knowledge'. This was in the context of her first viewing of the Bauhaus Weimar workshops, with their hands-on training in techniques of pottery, carpentry, metalwork, weaving, wall painting. Behrens himself respected making both by hand and machine. A few months before Gropius joined his office Behrens had been one of the co-founders of the Deutscher Werkbund, a progressive group of architects, designers, artists, craftsmen, industrialists, academics and interested intellectuals. The Werkbund was concerned with reforming design education; bringing fine and applied art closer together; redefining the role of the artist in society; evolving a new culture 'based on respect for the creative power of the individual personality'. There was a political subtext in the aim of improving the German economy by raising the aesthetic standards of manufactured products. These were central interests to Gropius, who would join the Deutscher Werkbund in 1910.

Gropius modestly defined his starting role within the office as that of 'Professor Behrens's factotum', being given any job that needed doing. His first more formal assignment was that of site manager for two rather extravagant and esoteric private houses, the Cuno and Schröder houses in Hagen, which Karl Ernst Osthaus had originally commissioned. These stood on a hilltop above the town at Eppenhausen, where Osthaus was in the process of developing an artistic colony, much inspired by Darmstadt.

Out of the office Gropius was welcomed into the Behrens family home at Neubabelsberg, where he seems to have been treated as a favoured son. Here he taught the Behrenses' daughter, Petra, to play tennis. He himself was a good player, powerful and agile, but it seems that at this point he overstrained his wrist, developing a tremor that made drawing and writing, a problem since his youth, now even more difficult for him.

Professionally too Behrens took Gropius under his wing. He shared his own knowledge of such specialist subjects as the stereometric constructional secrets of the medieval mason guilds and the geometrics of Greek architecture. Behrens himself was an admirer of Schinkel, whom he too regarded as his architectural ancestor, and he and Gropius made expeditions together to examine Schinkel's buildings in and around Potsdam.

In 1908 Behrens took his young assistant on an architectural study tour of England, Gropius's first visit to the country that in the 1930s would become his place of exile. We have no detailed records of an itinerary which included factories, industrial buildings and historic monuments. It is likely that in planning the trip they took advice from Hermann Muthesius, a power behind the concept of the Deutscher Werkbund. Muthesius, who had been officially attached to the German embassy in London, researched English housing from 1896 to 1903 and returned to Germany to preach the merits of the impetus towards the simple and rational he discovered in English Arts and Crafts architecture and design.

We might assume that on Gropius's initial journey to England he and Behrens viewed Richard Norman Shaw's garden suburb at Bedford Park, which included a remarkable house by C. F. A. Voysey, an architect Muthesius especially admired. They may well have seen such feats of engineering as William Henry Barlow's vast overarching train shed at St Pancras Station and Joseph Paxton's Crystal Palace, by then re-erected at Sydenham, a masterpiece of nineteenth-century iron and glass architecture and a very early example of prefabricated building. Gropius later called it 'a landmark in the history of building, the birthdate of modern architecture'.

We do know that on this visit to England Gropius took the opportunity to see Uncle Willy, his father's youngest brother. Gropius knew his aunt and uncle and their five anglicised children from their holiday visits to Uncle Erich at Janikow. There is a small memento of the 1908 family reunion, a photograph of Gropius and his Tante Wiene sitting together on a bench in Chislehurst, Kent.

When Gropius was working in the Behrens office designs for the new AEG factory in Moabit, Berlin, were already underway. This factory was Gropius's first real experience of a large-scale building under construction. The new Turbine Hall, in which huge turbine engines were produced, was at the time the biggest steel-structure building in Berlin. Artistically, too, it was ambitious, the idealistic Behrens being eager to make the factory 'sing the great song of work' ('*Das hohe Lied von Arbeit singen!*'). The Turbine Hall had something of the monumental quality of a Schinkel building, while its emphasis on good working conditions for its employees brought it unmistakeably into the modern world. Not just good practical working conditions but something more inspiring. Following his experience with Behrens Gropius would argue that the awakening of the sense of beauty lying dormant in every human being was in itself a basic worker's right.

Peter Behrens's AEG Turbine Hall, Berlin, 1909.

He established a particular rapport with Walther Rathenau, son of the founder of AEG. Walther, the lively and literate young industrialist, became the friend of Stefan Zweig, Max Reinhardt and Rainer Maria Rilke, as well as the architect-designer Henry van de Velde. Edvard Munch painted his portrait. He exchanged verse telegrams with Richard Dehmel. He was a modernist, a lover of American architecture, addicted to notions of technology and speed. It was Walther Rathenau, by then AEG President, to whom Gropius made a personal approach in 1910 in order to arrange a meeting to discuss his ideas on factory-produced housing.

Inspired by visiting Krupp's workers' housing initiative in the Ruhr, Gropius presented a paper to Rathenau suggesting that AEG should invest in prefabricated housing. He pointed out that the Americans were already entering the field, citing catalogues produced by Sears, Roebuck and the Hodgson Company of Dover, Massachusetts offering components for houses of various styles, shapes and sizes which could be ordered by mail for erection on site. Rathenau did not in fact pursue Gropius's proposal, but schemes for low-cost, quick-assembly housing remained central to Gropius's thinking for many years to come.

There were by now signs that Gropius was moving out of Behrens's orbit. He had been absorbing other influences, already becoming particularly interested in architectural developments in the United States. His ever-encouraging mother drew his attention to Frank Lloyd Wright, just becoming known in Germany, and they went together to the first exhibition of Wright's architecture in Berlin. The earliest book about Wright's work to appear in Germany was published by Wasmuth in an edition by the English Arts and Crafts architect C. R. Ashbee, whose own mother was German. International cross-currents in design and architecture were evidently speeding up and the highly ambitious Gropius was getting restless.

Problems arose in the Behrens office. Behrens was understandably annoyed when, due to an error made by Gropius, the height of the attic in the Cuno house at Hagen turned out to be incorrect. The client, Dr Willy Cuno, was the Mayor of Hagen, and Frau Cuno was vituperative in her criticism of the faults in design and lack of supervision in construction, leading to problems with the circular staircase and 'the most vexatious dampness of the walls'. There were complaints about technical misjudgements in the Schröder house as well. Gropius in his capacity as site manager was obviously culpable.

It seems probable that Behrens had been irritated by Gropius's independent approach to Walther Rathenau. It has also been suggested that their early closeness had been undermined by Behrens's growing sense of social inadequacy compared to Gropius. Behrens, born out of wedlock and then orphaned early, was brought up by a guardian, whereas Gropius's own family background was relatively upright and secure.

In any case Gropius himself had now begun complaining about conditions in the Behrens office. He resented pandering to affluent clients neglectful of the real needs of the great mass of the populace. He saw the problems caused by Behrens's own inability to control his workload, being always overwrought and in a rush. This may have been self-justification on Gropius's part, although it should be noted that Le Corbusier made similar complaints of an unreasonable and unstable employer and lasted only a few months in Neubabelsberg. The upshot of these tensions between Gropius and Behrens led to what was a perhaps inevitable parting of the ways. Gropius wrote unapologetically to Osthaus, who had brought them together in the first place, that 'latterly differences between Behrens and myself have so escalated that yesterday I was obliged to see that I can do no further work with him'. He left Behrens's office in June 1910. But he realised that his own debt to Behrens was considerable and they remained in touch over the years.

———

In 1910, after leaving Behrens, Gropius set up his own architectural practice, first close by in Neubabelsberg and later in Berlin itself. He already displayed formidable self-confidence for a young architect with so little practical experience. He now took on an architectural assistant, Adolf Meyer, who had coincided with Gropius in Behrens's office, before leaving to work with Bruno Paul, another progressive architect on the Deutscher Werkbund circuit. Meyer, who was just a year older than Gropius, was an interesting man who had trained as a cabinet maker. He had come under the influence of the Dutch architect and Theosophist Johannes Lauweriks as a student at the Düsseldorf Kunstgewerbeschule. Like other progressive architects of the period Meyer had an exploratory spiritual side, a belief in ideal concepts of harmony both on a practical and a metaphysical level. He and Gropius formed a close working collaboration that lasted, with a wartime intermission, until 1925.

Adolf Meyer is the mystery man in Walter Gropius's history. There have been long-running arguments over just who was responsible for what aspects of the office. Gropius himself was always adamant that Meyer was not an equal partner but a paid employee, albeit an assistant whose creative input was important. There was no later clarification from Meyer, who died unexpectedly in middle age by drowning off Baltrum in the North Sea.

But the working methods he first evolved with Adolf Meyer amounted more or less to the modus operandi that Gropius developed into a philosophy. This was a slow process of Gropius outlining his ideas for Meyer to interpret on the drawing board, a toing and froing of creative input that would form the basis of Gropius's evolving theories of architectural co-partnership. The sharing out of responsibilities is arguably the reason why Gropius's buildings lack the sometimes transcendent personal qualities of architecture by his contemporaries Le Corbusier and Mies van der Rohe.

In beginning his own practice at the age of twenty-seven Gropius already had work on hand from his most faithful client, Uncle Erich. His father's ambitious younger brother had now bought a much larger new estate adjoining the original Janikow in Pomerania. This estate, known as Golgenzut and comprising twenty-five acres of fertile land with farm workers' houses and agricultural buildings, provided opportunities for Gropius and Meyer, and they also had commissions from other local contacts of Uncle Erich's. But these were only relatively minor jobs and the flow of work at the start was not sufficient to make Gropius feel secure.

It was from the other side of Gropius's family that his most important new commission came. Gropius was energetic in contacting companies he knew were embarking on new buildings. He was always adept at the dropping of an influential name and had written on spec to Carl Benscheidt, owner of the Faguswerk in Alfeld-an-der-Leine in Lower Saxony, a factory that specialised in making wooden lasts for ortho-paedic shoes. In the letter Gropius mentioned his mother's cousin Max Burchard, a district magistrate in Alfeld. Benscheidt, a progressive, paternalistic industrialist, attended Gropius's talk at the Folkwang Museum in Hagen and was intrigued by his ideas.

The subject of the talk was industrial construction and monumental art, and Gropius used what had become his favourite illustration of the subject: the enormous grain elevators and silos of the United States. He was at this period obsessively collecting photographs of American industrial buildings, in collaboration with his patron Karl Ernst Ost-haus. Shortly before he started work on the Fagus factory he drafted a letter to his then lover Alma Mahler, who was spending the winter in New York with her husband Gustav Mahler, confiding his highly romantic architectural dreamings:

I would like to build a large factory entirely of white concrete, all blank walls with large holes in them – large plate-glass planes – and a black roof. A great, pure, richly structured shape, undisturbed by small colour variations, painterly values, and architectural curlicues. Impact achieved solely with bright walls and shadows. Simple. Egyptian quietude. Increasingly, I am convinced that work is the only true deity of our time and in art we must help find an expression for it.

This was not quite how the Fagus factory turned out. It was not the futuristic white building of Gropius's imaginings. But when he and Benscheidt met in February 1911 they found that they had an imme-diate rapport and Gropius was commissioned to begin work on the new shoe-last factory developments.

The production of orthopaedic shoe-lasts was a very specialist indus-try linked to naturopathy and the cult of health and freedom, popular in Germany in the late nineteenth and early twentieth centuries. Ben-scheidt himself had taken to a naturopathic diet after a chronic illness as a child. He became a vegetarian and all his life he kept to a routine of early-morning barefoot walks across the fields. His consciousness of his mission in life first dawned on him when he went to work as a young man in the well-known naturopathic treatment centres run by Arnold Rikki. It was Rikki who realised that the foot problems he saw in so many of his patients were caused by badly fitting shoes. The remedy was to provide custom-made orthopaedic shoes. The form-fitted shoe-lasts produced by Benscheidt helped shoemakers work more precisely and could differentiate the left foot from the right.

The enterprising Benscheidt, who had connections to the *Lebens-reformbewegung*, the nineteenth-century German social reform movement, first set up his own workshop in Hanover producing both lasts and shoes. He was then appointed general manager for Carl Behrens, whose firm in Alfeld soon became the leading shoe-last manufacturer in Germany due to Benscheidt's technical innovations. By the time Benscheidt and Gropius met, Behrens had died and Benscheidt had resigned after a ferocious quarrel with the Behrens heirs. He was now in the process of forming his own company with American backers, the United Shoe Machinery Corporation in Beverly near Boston. With maximum tactlessness Benscheidt bought a site directly opposite the Behrens factory in Alfeld, with its own private railway line extension linking the new works to the main Hanover–Göttingen line. Gropius's Faguswerk commission was involving him in a bitter exercise in local rivalry. It was Benscheidt's ambitious declaration of intent.

Initially Gropius was not given the job of designing the whole factory. Benscheidt had already taken on Edmund Werner, a Hanover architect experienced in factory design who had previously worked on the Behrens buildings just across the way. Werner had already provided a site plan, floor plans and constructional drawings for the Fagus factory, but Benscheidt was less confident about Werner's involvement in the factory exterior, feeling that he lacked the necessary flair. It was this initial partial commission for a facade for the office block, the public face of the forward-looking new company, that Benscheidt entrusted to Gropius.

The obvious influence on the design for the Faguswerk is Peter Behrens's AEG Turbine Hall. Perhaps it was Gropius and Meyer's connection to that project that secured them the commission. Like AEG the Fagus factory was conceived in modern terms, its architecture branding it a temple of progressive industrial thinking, a palace of beauty for the workers, dozens of whom were being tempted across from the neighbouring Behrens factory by Benscheidt, who needed their expertise. Construction of Gropius and Meyer's spectacular steel and glass facade began in May 1911. Shoe-last-making flourished, additional buildings were needed and by the winter of 1912 Werner had been sidelined. All future architectural contracts went to Gropius, the start of a close relationship between him and the Benscheidt family that lasted until 1925.

Walter Gropius's glass, steel and yellow-brick Faguswerk building (see Plates 1–3), the revised and expanded design for which was finally completed in 1914, has a special place in architectural history as the first European example of curtain wall construction, a self-supporting glazed-wall system in which the outer layer is non-structural, giving the building's exterior the appearance of a total curtaining of glass. It has obvious antecedents, not only in Behrens's AEG Turbine Hall and such earlier experimental glass and metal structures as Hans Poelzig's Werdermühle building in Breslau (now Wrocław in Poland). But the Faguswerk's thoroughgoing use of glass, the 'ethereal material' of Gropius's visions, gives a particular impression of architectural lightness, of a building practically floating in space.

The critic Reyner Banham especially admired the glazed south-west corner of the long facade, within which the inner staircase apparently floats free. He saw this as 'one of the classic locations of the modern sensibility in architecture, possessing the kind of open, limpid, *unbegrenzt* [unlimited] space that would, in due course, become the International Style's most beguiling contribution to the vocabulary of architecture'. He did, however, make the comment that the building might not have acquired its legendary status had it not been so photogenic.

Gropius himself would later view the Faguswerk as his first significant building. He could be combative in defence of his reputation and late in life became embroiled in an argument with the American architectural theorist and critic Lewis Mumford, in which he fiercely defended his own building as the first example of the truly modern architecture, pre-dating anything by André Lurçat or Le Corbusier. Ise Gropius, who visited the factory in 1924, the year after her marriage, was greatly impressed but made the comment in her diary: 'what a pity that this work by Gropius is sitting in such a tiny place and is therefore little known.'

After the Second World War Benscheidt's son Karl, then in charge of the factory, reported to Gropius that occupying American troops had been astounded that a building which struck them as so modern had in fact been designed in 1911, earlier than the First World War. He had to get out the original working drawings to convince them that this was true.

4

Vienna and Alma Mahler
1910–1913

Walter Gropius's momentous first meeting with Alma Mahler took place at the Wildbad Sanatorium, a fashionable clinic in the Styrian mountains set up on the principles of Dr Heinrich Lahmann, pioneer of alternative medicine. The naturopathic regime at Tobelbad focused on exercise, fresh air and a vegetarian diet. As Alma, a reluctant resident, recalled, 'Barefoot, clothed in a horrible nightgown, I meekly took the outdoor exercise in rain and wind that was the hall-mark of the therapeutic faith adhered to at this institution.'

When Alma actually fainted in the hot springs and had to be carried back to bed the German doctor in charge of her regime prescribed sociability and the then fashionable ballroom dancing as an alternative cure. In her memoirs she writes:

Feeling responsible for me, and worried about my dependency and loneliness, he introduced young men to me; one was an extraordinarily handsome German who would have been well cast as Walther von Stolzing in *Die Meistersinger*. We danced. Gliding slowly around the room with the youth, I heard that he was an architect and had studied with one of my father's well-known friends. We stopped dancing and talked.

Gropius and Alma Mahler met on 4 June 1910. Gropius was twenty-seven and exhausted from the stresses of setting up his own practice. Alma was then thirty, wife of the composer Gustav Mahler and well established as the femme fatale of avant-garde Vienna. It seems that within minutes they were totally in love. In her own later account of it her eyes had been opened 'by the tempestuous wooing of the young man in Tobelbad'. Alma's memoirs of course are famously self-serving and she baulks at admitting to her physical unfaithfulness to Mahler. But Alma's diary entries and letters between her and Gropius tell another

The voluptuous Alma Mahler, *c.*1908 • **45**

story of amorous meanderings along the stream after dinner on the night of their first meeting at Tobelbad and passionate sexual entwinings through the night. Even years after, such memories were vivid, mystical in their enchantments: 'I remember one night that was troubled by the coming of the light in the morning and by the sweet singing of a nightingale – but beside me lay a beautiful young man – and on that night two souls met and the body was forgotten.'

For Gropius the meeting with Alma was crucial not just on grounds of his amorous awakening but because it opened up a whole new world of culture. Alma's background was Vienna, in contrast to Gropius's Berlin. 'I am the daughter of an artistic tradition,' wrote Alma, never inclined to play down her credentials, in her autobiography *And the Bridge Is Love*. Her adored father Emil Jakob Schindler was a highly regarded landscape painter, romantic and elegiac in his style. Schindler died in 1892, when Alma was thirteen. Her stepfather, Carl Moll, who had been her father's pupil, was a co-founder of the Wiener Secession, a progressive group of painters, sculptors and architects. Gustav Klimt was the first president of the Secession, which was different in tenor to the Deutscher Werkbund to which Gropius belonged, more subtly self-expressive, more concerned with decoration and texture and the whole spiritual role of art. First members included the architects Joseph Maria Olbrich, who designed the Secession's exhibition building on the Karlplatz, and Josef Hoffmann. Early secret meetings of the Wiener Secession had actually taken place in Alma's family home. In 1901 her family moved into the villa on Vienna's Hohe Warte that Moll had commissioned from Hoffmann. This house, with its beautiful Secessionist interiors, then became the backdrop to Alma's early life.

Where Gropius's background was predominantly visual, with good amateur music-making part of the regime, for Alma music on the best professional level had been the most important element in her upbringing. She herself had been taught and encouraged by Alexander Zemlinsky and, from her teenage years, was composing her own songs and instrumental pieces. She was later to lay claim to more than two hundred musical compositions, but possibly Alma was exaggerating here.

Her marriage to Mahler had immersed her yet more thoroughly in the Viennese musical world. For Gropius his sudden passionate, surprising liaison with Alma brought him new insights, an expansion of his interests and a sometimes painful new depth of understanding of human relations that affected him profoundly from now on.

———

In comparison with Berlin Vienna was historically speaking an old and relatively settled city. The Hapsburg Emperor Franz Joseph, a conservative Catholic, had been on the throne since 1848. The Christian Socialist mayor, Karl Lueger, had run the city since 1897 and exploited the latent anti-Semitic feeling in a city with a relatively high proportion of Jewish citizens. The young Adolf Hitler, living in Vienna from 1908, was presumably already all too susceptible to Lueger's views.

Gropius, through his connection with Alma, was conscious of a very different city, a city in a state of transformation. By 1910 Vienna was becoming a much more fluid place, in which a strong reaction against its old conservatism was evident amongst the intellectual and cultural elite. There was by now a questioning of accepted values in the spheres of art and architecture, literature, theatre and especially human behaviour and psychology. Vienna at this period was undergoing a deep-rooted crisis of identity.

The whole look of the city was changing. As the population expanded, reaching over two million by 1910, the town planner and architect Otto Wagner gave Vienna a new, modern, technological appearance, challenging its former historicist ornamental style. The architect Adolf Loos's powerful series of anti-bourgeois writings expounded values of honesty, rationality and restraint. His design work was brilliantly minimalist. Loos's most controversial building in Vienna, the apartment block and men's tailoring establishment Goldman and Salatsch, was sited with maximum confrontational bravura opposite the ornate gates of the Imperial Palace. It was built in what has now come to seem the magical year of Vienna, 1910.

In Vienna Gropius found a flexibility of outlook that taught him to rethink and expand on what he had previously learned from Peter Behrens on the concept of *Gesamtkunstwerk*. There were frequent cross-overs of discipline. The composer Arnold Schoenberg was a painter whom his friend Wassily Kandinsky made a member of the Blaue Reiter group of artists. The philosopher Ludwig Wittgenstein tried his hand at architecture, designing a radically austere house for his sister. The painter Oskar Kokoschka wrote stories and dramas. Kokoschka's own life story would soon overlap with Gropius's – and indeed with Alma's – in unexpected ways.

The idea of creative cross-currents of discipline, one area informing and expanding another, would be central to Gropius's thinking at the Bauhaus, as would another influential Viennese concept of that period: the idea of the child as an instinctive artist, whose natural creativity should be encouraged rather than damped down by formal training. The ideas of Franz Cižek, Viennese pioneer of children's art education, can be traced in Gropius's own experimental and tolerant approach.

Sex was on the agenda in early-twentieth-century Vienna with a blatancy shocking to the bourgeois population. Freud's studies of the essential importance of infantile and childhood sexuality to later psychological development were deeply controversial. Freud's *The Interpretation of Dreams* had been published in 1900 and his *Three Essays on the Theory of Sexuality* in 1905. Art was becoming more psychologically intense, as in Oskar Kokoschka's and Richard Gerstl's portraits and self-portraits of human beings *in extremis*. Klimt's allegorical paintings and his drawings of nude couplings and masturbating women reflect the fact that at this point in its history Vienna was becoming a highly eroticised city. Egon Schiele's naked self-portraits express both the beauty and the sexual torment that this brought. Child prostitution was then widespread and Schiele's explicit depictions of children and adolescents remind us that in the Vienna of this period, amongst artists and writers, there was a cult of underage sex.

It is obvious from the tone of Gropius's letters that his six weeks at Tobelbad with Alma took him into new realms of sexual experience.

She was then the voluptuous slightly older woman with a considerable amatory back catalogue. Alma's first suitor, when she was seventeen, had been Max Burckhard, distinguished director of the Vienna Burgtheater, who was then in his early forties. Burckhard had wooed her with vintage champagne, partridges and pineapples; he had deluged her with books, fine editions of the classics, which arrived packed in laundry baskets borne in by two porters. 'We had some odd scenes', wrote Alma, 'when I was first intrigued by his strong masculinity, only to turn it aside with a heartless joke.'

Another of the young Alma's serious pursuers had been Gustav Klimt himself, friend and ally of her stepfather, Carl Moll. Klimt was then thirty-five and 'strikingly good-looking'. As Alma analysed it later, 'His looks and my young charm, his genius and my talent, our common, deeply vital musicality all helped to attune us to each other. My ignorance in matters of love was appalling, and he felt and found every sensitive spot.' The masterful Klimt pursued Alma to Italy, where, in 1897, she was travelling *en famille*. Even as a teenager she exerted a magnetic effect on men. Before they reached Genoa Alma's mother had read the entry in her daughter's diary revealing that Gustav Klimt had kissed her, and she put a stop to the relationship.

Alma's next love had been her music teacher, Alexander Zemlinsky, the highly talented musician and composer who was also Arnold Schoenberg's musical instructor. Alma describes Zemlinsky in her memoirs as 'a hideous gnome. Short, chinless, toothless, always with the coffee-house smell on him, unwashed – and yet the keenness and strength of his mind made him tremendously attractive.' It was when Zemlinsky was playing Wagner's *Tristan* that the moment of truth struck them: 'I leaned on the piano,' wrote Alma, 'my knees buckled, we sank into each other's arms.' The music from *Tristan und Isolde* would be a recurring feature, a kind of leitmotif, of Alma's complex love life. In fact Alma never gave herself completely to Zemlinsky but sex-teased and tormented him until, according to her memoirs, she was introduced to Gustav Mahler at a dinner party that included Max Burckhard and Gustav Klimt, her 'childhood crush'.

L. to r.: Max Reinhardt, Gustav Mahler, Carl Moll, Hans Pfitzner in the garden of
Carl Moll's villa in Vienna, 1905.

The dinner party, somewhat overcrowded with Alma's admirers, was
held in autumn 1901 at the house of Berta Zuckerkandl, powerful wife
of an eminent anatomist. Mahler evidently noticed Alma at once and
watched her all through dinner laughing and flirting as she sat between
Burckhard and Klimt. She and Mahler later moved out of the group and,
according to Alma, 'stood in the kind of vacuum that instantly envelops
people who have found each other'. The next morning she agreed to
meet him at the Vienna Court Opera House, the Hofoper, where Mahler
was rehearsing *Tales of Hoffmann*. In January 1902 their engagement
was made public. Alma, already pregnant, married Mahler the following March. She was twenty-two, he was forty-one. It had been a rainy
morning and Mahler arrived on foot at the magnificent Baroque church
of St Charles Borromeo, the Karlskirche, wearing galoshes, a detail that
remained in Alma's mind when she came to write her memoirs. This

unromantic footwear seemed to encapsulate the age difference between them. It was hardly a propitious sign.

Burckhard, Klimt, Zemlinsky, Mahler: there is a certain pattern in the sequence of men with whom the young Alma became sexually connected. All were in their way celebrities, Mahler by this time being the director of the Hofoper as well as an increasingly revered composer and conductor. And the pattern continued when she first met Walter Gropius. Even if he was not famous quite yet, Alma had seen convincing signs of his future architectural reputation. She wrote to him that summer: 'I love in you – your intellect – your artistry – which I *knew* – before I have seen a *stroke* of your drawings – your talents – in regard to living – your charm – and last but not least your beauty – to say nothing of your nobility and kindness??' She added that 'there is not one spot on your body that I would not like to caress with my tongue'.

Alma's marriage with Mahler had begun with high intentions. On the night of their wedding they took the train to wintry St Petersburg for Mahler to conduct Alma's favourite opera, *Tristan und Isolde*. Mahler, although suffering from chilblains, a sore throat and a high temperature, rose to the occasion, giving a superb performance. 'In this strange world', writes Alma, 'I heard the *Liebestod*,' Isolde's final hymn of ecstatic love. Alma was ill too on their arrival in St Petersburg and had been given special permission to stand behind the orchestra, where she could watch her husband's face as he conducted. It became a quasi-religious experience: 'that uplifted face, those open lips! There was divine beauty in his expression when he conducted. I trembled, and felt and *knew* it was my mission to remove all evil from his path, to live for him alone.'

Nine years later such zealous hopes of marriage were dwindling into an onerous and deadening routine. Even before their wedding Mahler had insisted that Alma give up her own composing, ridiculing the marriage of Robert and Clara Schumann with what he saw as Clara's pathetic attempts at competing with her husband. Mahler sent Alma a long letter demanding that she should now live for his music alone. Alma cried all night but she finally agreed. Her married life had become that of the supporter of the egocentric genius. Everything was programmed to Mahler's own work schedule.

Their summers were spent in the country house they rented at Maiernigg in Carinthia, on the shores of Lake Woerther, Mahler rising at dawn to start composing in his isolated little brick hut in the forest. At first Alma, left in the house alone, attempted to play the piano very softly, but Mahler always managed to hear her and objected, even though his workroom was far off in the woods. He would take a midday swim, whistling for his wife to come and join him at the boathouse. Then back to the house. 'The soup', Alma recorded, 'had to be waiting on the table.' After this a long, long walk. 'I climbed fences, crawled through hedges.' Mahler dragged her up almost vertical hillsides. Sometimes she simply felt too exhausted to go on.

Their life back in Vienna would be no less arduous. Mahler's winter schedule was like clockwork too: up at seven, breakfast, work on rechecking his summer compositions, to the Hofoper at nine, lunch at one o'clock sharp, with Alma alerted by a call from the opera to tell her when Mahler was on his way home so that the apartment door stood open for the moment of his arrival. Not a minute lost. After lunch he and Alma went for breakneck walks around Vienna, four times around the Belvedere, the whole way round the Ring. After coffee and cake Mahler would go back to the opera, remaining there for part of the performance. Alma would pick him up but was not allowed to stay any longer than her husband needed to, with the result that she saw a lot of operas 'only in part, never to the end'.

By the time she met Gropius strains were accumulating within the marriage. Serious financial crises: Mahler was incompetent with money. Tensions over music: Mahler's compositions, positioned as they were between the nineteenth century and the modern era, engendered often hurtful controversy. Frequent upheavals at the opera house resulted in Mahler's resignation in 1907. In that same year there had been the terrible anxiety of the Mahlers' elder daughter Maria falling seriously ill with scarlet fever and diphtheria. The child, known as 'Putzi', meaning 'precious', died aged only four at the end of two agonising weeks. Just a few weeks later Mahler himself was diagnosed with a serious defect of the heart.

It seems likely that the sex life of Alma and Gustav Mahler was at this stage far from satisfactory. In spite of his early reputation as a rake, about which her mother had warned her, he had seemed to Alma almost virginal on marriage, having always lived a life of such extreme dedication and austerity. Alma the compulsive flirt was still collecting her admirers, even within the strict boundaries of marriage. These included the young pianist Ossip Gabrilowitsch and the composer Hans Pfitzner. But she could not help lamenting to her diary that she felt as if her wings had been clipped by her marriage to Mahler when she was by nature such a colourful, free-flying bird. By 1910 Alma's doctors decided she was heading for a breakdown. 'I was really sick,' she wrote, 'utterly worn out by the perpetual motion necessitated by a giant engine such as Mahler's mind.'

To help her recover Mahler deposited Alma, little Anna their younger daughter (known as 'Gucki' on account of her penetrating gaze) and the nanny at Tobelbad. He stayed a day or two before returning to the new country home at Toblach in the Dolomites that they had moved to after the death of little Putzi. Mahler was anxious to continue working on his Tenth Symphony.

It is easy to sense the exhilaration and relief for Alma in her meeting with Gropius in this beautiful, discreet, secluded place, the spa being set in a wide valley, carefully landscaped with individual rustic-style villas, each with its own flower garden. Not only was he young, handsome, potentially talented and immediately won over by Alma, he was almost flamboyantly non-Jewish, as her comparison of Gropius in her memoirs to the young knight Walther von Stolzing in Wagner's *Die Meistersinger* shows.

Alma's attitude to Jews is, like many of her traits, ineffably peculiar. On the one hand she shared the anti-Jewish prejudice common to many in Vienna at that period, in particular her virulently anti-Semitic stepfather Carl Moll. She glorifies Gropius for his Aryan qualities. 'Did you ever see Gropius?' Alma was still asking the writer Elias Canetti in the 1930s. 'A big handsome man. The true Aryan type. The only man who was racially suited to me.' And yet Alma had married the Jewish Gustav Mahler, as she was later to marry the Jewish Franz Werfel. As she so candidly observed to Canetti, 'All the others who fell in love with me were little Jews.'

As the passionate affair with Gropius continued Mahler became anxious at receiving only strangely cursory replies to his daily letters or no replies at all. He challenged her, suspecting she was hiding something from him. At the end of June he arrived at the Sanatorium to check up on her. What he found was reassuring. Alma was a good dissembler. Mahler reported back to her mother in Vienna that he had found Alma 'much fresher and stronger' and that he was 'convinced that her cure here has started well'.

Anna Moll herself would soon know about the exact reasons for Alma's miraculous improvement in morale. In early July Gropius travelled to Vienna for a secret visit, during which Alma introduced him to her mother. The meeting was evidently a great success. Afterwards he sent Anna an effusive thank-you letter praising her 'noble humanity'. 'You dear!' exclaimed Gropius. 'My mother couldn't have let me go with more love.' They had evidently made a conspiracy for future communication between Gropius and Alma once she had returned to the Mahler summer house. He would start by sending her a letter through the Toblach general post office, but Anna was to intercept it by telegram if this method seemed too risky.

If Anna Moll's complicity in her daughter's latest love affair seems a bit surprising, we need to remember that her own early life had been sexually mobile. Her second child, Alma's half-sister Grete, was not Schindler's daughter but the result of an extra-marital affair with the painter Julius Victor Berger. Her relationship with Moll, Schindler's student and assistant, had been going on for years before her husband's death and was a cause of great resentment to Alma, who was eighteen when they eventually married. Anna Moll was a natural conspirator and Gropius's arrival brought a certain vicarious excitement to her life.

Alma finally left the clinic on 16 July. Mahler met her at the station at

Toblach and he seemed to Alma suddenly more amorous. In her memoirs she speculates as to whether 'the young stranger's infatuation' had restored her self-confidence, making her more desirable to Mahler. As the desperate post-Tobelbad messages and letters between Gropius and Alma started winging their way to the arranged *poste restante* address three kilometres from the Mahler home, where Alma had to travel to receive and send them, she reassured her lover, 'I feel dreadfully sorry for G [Gustav] – he must feel that I have absolutely no desire to make love to him – on the contrary, that I keep him away from me – which I have so far completely succeeded in doing.' Meanwhile, Mahler had commissioned a specially designed tiara from Josef Hoffmann via Carl Moll for Alma's thirty-first birthday the next month.

What were the lovers expecting to happen? Anna Moll had been enthusiastically encouraging to Gropius, instructing him to hold his head high, telling him that he and Alma had a splendid objective ahead of them. She was evidently envisaging their marriage, signing her letter with a thousand greetings from 'your devoted Mama'. Alma was typically vaguer, telling Gropius how deeply Mahler's music bound her to him still and entreating him to wait. Gropius himself, returning to Berlin, evidently felt a rather arrogant younger man's impatience with these prevarications and it seems he now decided to bring matters to a head.

On 29 July a letter arrived at the Mahler house in Toblach. The letter, in a grey-blue envelope, came addressed in Gropius's handwriting to 'Herr Direktor Mahler'. According to Alma's account of a scene that has now entered legend through its numerous replayings in biographies and films, 'Mahler was seated at the piano when he opened the letter. "What is this?" he asked in a choking voice and handed it to me.' Alma was appalled and mystified, writing back to Gropius, 'Just think – the letter in which you openly write about the secret of our nights of love was addressed to: Herr Gustav Mahler – Toblach – Tirol. Did you really want this to happen?' Or had it been an oversight? In a slightly later letter Alma tells Gropius, 'I am now almost certain that you, in the hurry of departure of the train, forgot to put the address at the beginning. Be that as it may.'

It has sometimes been suggested that Gropius had simply been pre-occupied or careless in addressing this letter to Herr Mahler. Indeed in the 1950s Gropius told Mahler's biographer Henry-Louis de La Grange that he had simply made a dreadful error. But this seems unlikely. Gropius was by nature too precise. Later in life he sought confrontation and discussion with, for instance, the husband of his lover Lily Hildebrandt, as well as the fiancé of his future wife Ilse (later Ise) Frank, and indeed much later with Ise's own lover Herbert Bayer. This suggests Gropius wanted to take charge of any complex emotional situation. It appears that he had a basic instinct for what would be described in modern parlance as talking problems through.

What is certain is that the arrival of the letter unleashed a storm of torment as Mahler felt the shock of his wife's unfaithfulness and Alma in self-defence confronted him with the inadequacies of their married life. He temporarily abandoned composition of the Tenth Symphony and the two of them spent days walking about the countryside in tears, until Anna Moll arrived and attempted to calm down the situation. Although she promised Mahler that she would never leave him, Alma was clearly still hankering for Gropius and his young, lithe, Walther von Stolzing-like physique: 'Gustav', she told him, 'is like a sick, wonderful child. Do write to me *frankly* and honestly, and tell me what you are hoping for the future – how you would arrange things – what would happen to me! If I – decide for a life of love with you, oh – when I think of it – my Walter, that I could be deprived of your *strong* love for my whole life.'

Gropius proposed travelling to Toblach to confront Mahler in person and persuade Alma to leave him. He had written to Alma: 'I'll go out of my mind if you don't call me to come over. I want to justify myself before you both.' The endlessly vacillating Alma was discouraging. But Gropius was determined and it seems that he actually arrived in early August without forewarning her. He was evidently in his most head-strong and obsessive mood. Alma describes in her memoirs how she was out driving through the village when she saw Gropius standing under a bridge. He had apparently been in the neighbourhood for some time. She ignored him, returned home and told Mahler what had happened. It was apparently Mahler who went down to Toblach village and located Gropius. 'Come along,' he said. It was by now night and Alma describes a bizarre scene of Mahler leading the way through the darkness with a lantern, Gropius following behind. Alma had been waiting in her room. Mahler left the two of them together but Alma very quickly broke the conversation off, anxious about Mahler, who had been pacing round his study reading the Bible, with two candles lit and burning on his desk. 'Whatever you do', Mahler said gravely to Alma, 'will be well done. Choose!'

'What choice did I have?' writes Alma. She obviously decided on staying with her husband. Gropius presumably spent the night in the village because Alma describes how the next morning she drove down to see him off from Toblach station, Mahler anxiously coming out halfway to meet her in case she had decided to leave with Gropius after all. The rejected suitor wired her entreatingly from every station on his way back to Berlin. But his banishment was only temporary. Soon Alma was telling him that he must still consider himself as her fiancé, asking him to wait for her, assuring him that she would never look at another man: 'Why should I look for one since I have found you?'

Not surprisingly Mahler evinced extreme reactions to these unexpected dramas. He had been, as Alma puts it, 'churned to the very bottom'. He attached himself to her obsessively, insisting that at night the doors between their two adjoining rooms were left open, so that he could hear her breathing. She often woke up with a start to find her husband standing over her in the darkness 'like a departed spirit'. She was now implored to fetch him at mealtimes from the little building in the forest, where she would often find him lying on the floor weeping, claiming that this brought him nearer to the earth.

Mahler became almost embarrassingly conciliatory. He announced his intention to dedicate his Eighth Symphony to Alma. He made a point of rediscovering her songs, the lieder he had banished in the days before her marriage. 'These songs are good,' he suddenly told Alma. 'They're splendid! I want you to go over them, and then we'll have them published. I'm not going to rest until you start working again.' The score of his Tenth Symphony, once he had returned to it, is annotated wildly with such pleadings as 'Have mercy! Oh, God! Oh, God! Why hast Thou forsaken me!' and 'The Devil is dancing it with me! Madness, take hold of me, the accursed one!' He burst out crazily, 'I feel trapped by carnal lust, and eternal slavery is my desire!'

Alma became anxious about her husband's sanity, telling Gropius of her fears that 'this idolatrous love and adoration – which he is now offering – can no longer be called normal'. It was at this point that Mahler decided to consult Sigmund Freud about the problems in his marriage. After making three appointments and then cancelling them, Mahler finally set out on a long train journey to Leiden in Holland, where Freud was then on holiday.

They met in a cafe in the late afternoon of 26 August and spent the next four hours walking round the streets of the Dutch spa town. As Freud recollected in 1935:

He felt his visit was necessary because his wife was rebelling at the time over the turning away of his libido for her. On a most interesting stroll, we went through his life and uncovered his conditions for loving, and most especially his Mary complex. I was quite impressed with the man's brilliant ability to understand things. No light fell on the symptomatic façade of his obsessive neurosis. It was as if someone were digging a single deep shaft through a perplexing edifice.

It seems from Freud's account to his pupil Marie Bonaparte that the conversation had been reassuring to Mahler. The analyst focused on the fact that Alma had loved her father, Emil Jakob Schindler, and could only seek out and love the same type of small-sized older man with spiritual authority such as Gustav Mahler undoubtedly possessed. In Freud's recollections of the consultation the Gropius factor seems to have been absent or at least played down. But then Alma, self-serving and probably inaccurately, comments in her memoirs that Freud had sternly reproached her husband for unreasonable expectations of their marriage: 'How dared a man in your state ask a young woman to be tied to him?'

The affair of course continued. For her birthday, in blatant competition with the Hoffmann tiara which Mahler had commissioned, Gropius sent Alma the present of a Chinese jacket via Anna Moll. She told him she would cherish it: 'you owned it and you held it in your beloved hands.' Through September the letters between them reached new heights of eroticism. Alma wrote to tell Gropius how much she needed sex: 'I feel that for my heart and all my other organs nothing is worse than enforced asceticism. I mean not only the sensual lust, the lack of which has made me prematurely into a detached, resigned old woman, but also the continuous rest for my body . . . Now I am in bed . . . I am with you so intensely that you must feel me.' She asked him 'when will be the time when you lie naked next to me at night and nothing can separate us any more except sleep?' She signed herself 'Your wife' and told Gropius how urgently she longed to have a child by him.

They plotted secret meetings in Vienna and in early September carefully arranged an assignation in Munich, where Mahler, still very far from well, had arrived to conduct final rehearsals for the first performance of his Eighth Symphony. Alma and Mahler were staying in a luxury apartment in the Hotel Continental where their rooms had been transformed into bowers of roses. While Mahler was rehearsing Alma met her lover at the entrance of the Regina Palast, the hotel Gropius had booked into on his own. She had told him to be discreet in coming to the concert, which took place on 12 September.

Mahler's huge-scale choral work for eight soloists, double choir and orchestra, composed in 1906, was rapturously received, not least by Gropius. So carried away was he by Mahler's genius that he afterwards wrote Alma a solemn letter of self-sacrifice. He told her that 'G's music moved my heart so much that I left the concert with this feeling that we could not hurt him, we must bow down to this man.' Gropius had since been reading Paul Stefan's biography of Mahler and told Alma that his respect for Mahler's extraordinary talents – 'your husband's superb qualities both as a man and as an artist' – prevented them continuing their physical relationship. 'I met you yesterday with the intention of telling you that we must remain pure. Only what you said to me yesterday made it impossible for me to speak.'

This extraordinary letter exists only in draft. Gropius writes in an

evidently agitated state, gearing himself up to raise again this problematic question of their future abstinence from sex. We see him casting
himself as the Wagnerian hero, telling Alma:

I have a Tristan-like faith, I am too much of an idealist, more than I like to admit. I
have got to know my feeling for chastity as something remarkably strong – my hair
stands on end when I think of the unthinkable . . . My love for you is something so
wonderful that I can only hope for your sake, I cancel myself out entirely and let
you go free.

Gropius drafted this letter not just in a heroic mood of self-abnegation
in the face of Mahler's genius, proposing they should separate at least
until Alma was released by Mahler's death. He was also forcing himself
to face the almost unthinkable, the thing that went on haunting him,
asking Alma the 'difficult question' of when her physical relations with
Mahler had been resumed.

What I wanted to believe was that you were following him, watching over him, and
going to protect him until he passed away – but not that you were his beloved . . . for
a person like you the physical presence of a strong-willed person was inevitably
more effective than my bungling scribbling from a long way off. His will was simply
stronger and more mature, and compelled you to surrender. The fact that you did
shows that your passion for me was a mistake. I take the full blame for that.

Most probably this letter, so full of dark imaginings, was never sent
to Alma. They did not give each other up. In mid-September Gropius
wrote to her ecstatically as 'My life's happiness'. He told her he could
see 'a younger, more beautiful life arise from the endured pain . . . There
are absolutely no inhibitions in my feelings towards you . . . There is
a likeness between us, our desires are similar, the fluctuations of our
feelings move in similar ways.' There was now a resumed intimacy,
almost a kind of cosiness, in their relationship. Gropius was reading
Stendhal's *The Charterhouse of Parma* on Alma's recommendation.
'Have you read Novalis?' he asked her. Alma Mahler would later set to
music the texts of two Novalis poems.

In spite of Mahler's continuing suspicions their plottings and plan-
nings continued as before, with clandestine meetings in Vienna. Mahler

was committed that winter to New York, honouring his contract as conductor at the Metropolitan Opera, and was also booked for a series of concert tours around other cities in America. Alma had been hoping these plans might leave a little leeway in pursuing her relationship with Gropius but an increasingly possessive Mahler insisted she should travel out with him.

They were sailing from Cherbourg. Alma had managed to negotiate things so that she travelled on her own from Vienna via Paris, bringing the family luggage with her on the Orient Express. Their daughter Anna would also be going to America, together with the nanny. Alma was planning that Gropius would meet her on the train. She sent him instructions:

Rendez-vous would be Munich. I shall leave Friday 14th October at 11.55 on the Orient Express from Vienna. My coupé-bed Number 13 is in the second sleeping car. I have not been to town and so I don't know your answer yet. I write and hope into the blue. I would advise you (if you are going) to take your ticket in the name of Walter Grote since Gustav leaves two days later and might have the lists of travellers shown to him. Please answer soon.

Her lover Walter Grote joined Alma in her sleeping car in Munich and they travelled on to Paris, where they managed to spend the next few days together, days recollected by Alma in rapturous terms once she and Mahler had arrived in New York: 'The days in Paris, delightful and untroubled. There was never yet a dissonance in our love. Only that you poor chap always had to wait so long for me. That was terrible for me! I was always among people and could be so little with my man!' While she was away she told Gropius not to squander his 'lovely youth', which belonged to her.

Gropius returned to his office at Neubabelsberg. He and Meyer were at this point designing a starch factory in Baumgarten in Kreis Karwitz and continuing their work on the estates of Walter's Uncle Erich. Negotiations for their future work on the Fagus factory began in the winter of 1910.

Gropius and Alma continued to communicate discreetly through the New York Central Post Office, located in a downtown area. She sent him little sketches of their ninth-floor apartment in the Savoy Hotel. Alma, at least at this stage, showed enthusiasm for Gropius's architectural career, already envisaging how his success would make her love the greater. 'The more you accomplish,' she told him, 'the more you will be mine.' He had evidently given her commissions to carry out in New York on his behalf, and she told him: 'I shall try to get the architectural things for you, the only difficulty is lacking the professional vocabulary.' She asked him to send her 'small fotos' of his work. Just before they left Austria she and Mahler had bought a new plot of land at Breitenstein in the Semmering, a romantic mountain area not far from Vienna where they intended to build themselves a summer residence, replacing the now problematic house at Toblach, the place of such desperate emotional upheavals. Alma asked Gropius to advise on the building, telling him she was sending him her plans so that he could inform her mother of what was missing and give her his ideas. Signing her letter 'Your bride Alma', she told him, 'I want something in my house designed by you.'

––––

Alma and Gropius had been separated for three months when Gropius went to hear Mahler's great Seventh Symphony in Berlin, returning as exhausted and agitated as he had previously been by Mahler's Eighth. He said he now felt like someone who needed 'to cling to his own identity, who doesn't want to be thrown out of his own course, who enters a foreign land in amazement'. This stupendous one-and-a-quarter-hour-long symphony, which has often been described as an artistic milestone, the first beginnings of musical Expressionism, for the moment totally disorientated him.

He remembered how when he first heard Mahler's music in Munich in September, when Alma had also been present at the concert, too many 'streams of feelings' crossed his mind to allow his intellect to form a conscious understanding of the work. This time the situation was different. The 'striving, the lonesome search for God in this work has moved me . . . but I fear this alien strength because my art rises from a different soil.' He reminded Alma he had written to her recently about the ideal synthesis that he had become aware of in Greek philosophy, 'the beautiful mind and the beautiful body and of my reverence for the duality. You understand the transferred meaning for the arts.' Here Gropius was echoing, perhaps unconsciously, the Apollonian–Dionysian dichotomy that was a central tenet in the then fashionable Nietzsche's thought.

It is an especially significant letter since it shows Gropius's developing perception of artistic and intellectual connection, the relationship between the theoretical concept and the physical presence of the artwork. Such ideas would be important to his later belief in breadth and experiment in education. In understanding the roots of creativity Mahler's Seventh had deep personal significance. 'For me', he told Alma, 'this evening has brought new insights into Gustav and you and me.'

Meanwhile, Mahler's schedule in America was exhausting. Problems arose within the orchestra. He drove himself on, insisting on performing even when obviously ill. Finally he collapsed with a streptococcal infection, endangering his already weakened heart. As Alma wrote to Gropius on 25 March 1911, 'It is a recurring endocarditis – in other words a severe illness and very dangerous for a heart like his.' She claimed to be longing more than ever for her glamorous young lover: 'My dear Walter – I implore you, you must also be a completely healthy, strong and physically young man, so that we, when we see each other again, can have endless joy in one another and our love . . . I want you!!! But you? Do you want me, too?'

It must have been absolutely clear to Alma that Mahler was dying. His doctor and close friend Joseph Fraenkel, another of the men who came under Alma's spell, was holding out no hope for him. Alma was now forced to spoon-feed her husband and to sleep in his room at night. Anna Moll was summoned to New York. The whole family left America in April to make the crossing back to Cherbourg and from there to Paris, where Alma and Gropius had only recently spent such irresponsible days of bliss. From the Elysée Palace hotel Mahler was transferred to a sanatorium, and from there, as he continued to deteriorate, he was moved on to Vienna. He and his entourage arrived by train at the Westbahnhof and were transported to the Loew Sanatorium. He fell into a coma on 17 May and died towards midnight on the 18th, a night of the most terrible stormy weather. Alma construed it as a hopeful sign for her future life with Gropius that Mahler had died on Walter's twenty-eighth birthday. In spite of her apparently devoted ministrations to her ailing husband in New York, was there a sense that Alma had wanted, even perhaps willed, her husband's death? She confessed retrospectively in her diary in July 1920, 'Gustav's death, too – I wanted it. I once loved another man, and he was the wall I couldn't climb over.' Was Alma Mahler merely blithely irresponsible or were her instincts more reprehensible?

Alma claimed to be too ill to go to Mahler's burial at the cemetery in Grinzing. She had vowed not to attend a funeral again after the shattering experience of being at her father's. Over the next weeks she spent much time collapsed in bed but continuing to write her daily love letters to Gropius, who had reacted solemnly and sympathetically to Mahler's passing: 'I knew him still too little as an artist, but as a human being he met me in such a noble way that the memory of those hours is inextinguishable to me.'

———

The glorious vision that the lovers kept expressing in their letters of an immediate reuniting after Mahler's death inevitably proved impossible. They could not be together so instantly without causing a scandal. Alma herself was now a well-off widow, in receipt of a good pension from the Vienna Court Opera as well as the money she inherited from Mahler, whose incompetence with finance Alma herself had managed to reverse. The name Mahler gave Alma her own kudos, a position in society she went on exploiting all her life. There were clearly advantages for her in remaining Mahler's widow rather than signing up for a new life with a still relatively obscure young architect.

From Gropius's own viewpoint the relationship had problems. His architectural practice, still in its early stages, needed more attention than his recent hectic lifestyle, with Alma's continuing demands and dramas, had allowed him to give. In addition Gropius was shaken by the death of his much-loved father in February that year. There were also his lingering suspicions that Alma's sexual ministrations to her husband had continued through Mahler's final illness, a rumour that is still current, although it seems unlikely considering the condition he was in.

Gropius became evasive, avoiding meeting Alma, telling her in late September 1911:

A hot feeling of shame is welling up in me which tells me to avoid you. I want to go away for a while and test whether I shall really be able to put my love into such a beautiful form that it would be worthy of you if you would want it. Only this would balance the suffering I have caused Gustav and you on account of my lack of mature precaution. Today I do *not* know it and feel deeply saddened about myself.

Through the autumn he was evidently in a state of collapse, suffering from a tooth infection and general exhaustion. In December he went into the sanatorium at Weisser Hirsch on the outskirts of Dresden, another institution founded by the famous Dr Lahmann. Here his pattern of life was sadly different from the enraptured weeks with Alma at the Tobelbad clinic. He told his mother he was taking lonely walks.

When he returned to Berlin Alma arrived to join him and, for the first time, to meet his mother. The introduction went badly. Alma, used to the intellectual chatter and emotional fluidity of the Moll house in Vienna, found Gropius's mother settled in her ways, with the formality and stiffness of the Berlin upper bourgeoisie. She registered and resisted Manon's extreme possessiveness of her son.

After that visit the relationship became increasingly fractured. Alma continued writing and demanding. But the letter she sent Gropius on 18 May 1912, recalling the fact that this was the anniversary of Mahler's death, did not mention that it was also Gropius's birthday, mystical in its importance as the convergence had appeared the year before. Through that summer she reproached him for not replying to her letters. She asked him why he wasn't coming to see her in Vienna. By the end of November she was asking him to return some magazines that she had lent him, asking him accusingly, 'Aren't we human beings who had understood each other fully?' It seemed the great love affair was winding down.

Early in December Gropius replied:

I was glad that you thought of me with love. But I didn't really understand the meaning of your words. You have drifted too far away from me and therefore the intimacy of mutual understanding has suffered. And you seriously wonder and ask 'Don't these things grow?'. No, it cannot be as it used to be; everything has become basically different now. Is it possible to change very strong feelings of togetherness arbitrarily into feelings of friendship? Would these keys sound for you if I played them? No. Too little time has passed since the days of most painful realisation. I don't know what will happen; it doesn't depend on me. Everything is topsy-turvy, ice and sun, pearls and dirt, devils and angels.

Mahler, before his death, had forbidden Alma to wear mourning. He had encouraged her to see people, attend concerts, go to the theatre. She took him at his word and, through that year of 1912, as her love affair with Gropius was waning, she reverted to her favourite form of entertainment. As she tells us in her memoirs, 'Soon I was surrounded by outstanding men, as before.' The secret of Alma's magnetic effect on men of fame and talent was her combination of deference and knowing-ness. She understood their world. There was also the fact that apparently she wore no brassiere or corset. Alma's soft and increasingly curvaceous body sent out a promise of accessibility.

An early suitor was Dr Joseph Fraenkel, Mahler's devoted doctor in New York, who now turned up in Vienna and entreated Alma to marry him 'after a decent interval'. In the United States the Viennese-born Fraenkel had become a great hero. As personal physician to many millionaires he got huge fees, which enabled him to treat the poor on the East Side free of charge. But to Alma Joseph Fraenkel appeared merely 'an elderly, sick little man quite unheroically nursing a fatal intestinal ailment. I did not want to tie myself to him.' After two fruitless visits across the Atlantic Fraenkel was finally dismissed.

Next on the agenda in Alma's newfound project for 'roaming in souls' was the 'immensely gifted composer' Franz Schreker. But one of his recent operas, *Irrelohe*, had shown him to be 'already on the down-grade' while his latest, *Der Schmied von Gent*, which Alma had seen at the Charlottenburg Opera House, was a positive fiasco. Alma could be ruthless. She writes of Schreker, 'I walked beside him for a stretch and left him at the right time.'

A closer involvement it seems was with Paul Kammerer, the eminent experimental biologist, with whom Alma had happened to travel on the train back from Munich where Mahler's great admirer Bruno Walter had just been conducting the first performance of *Das Lied von der Erde*. To her surprise Kammerer had offered her a job as his assistant in his biological laboratory in the Vienna Prater. Intrigued, she had accepted. 'When I reported for work', Alma recorded, 'Kammerer showed me a box full of squirming mealworms which I was to feed to his beloved experimental reptiles. I felt a twinge of nausea. "What's wrong?" Kammerer asked, surprised. "They're not bad." And he reached into the wriggling mass, brought out a handful, and stuffed the worms into his mouth!' For some time afterwards Alma was put off eating noodle soup.

But it was not the mealworms that finally determined Alma against Kammerer, nor even the lizard eyes and the axolotls kept in the basement of the laboratory. The problem was the fact that Kammerer, a married man, fell seriously in love with her. 'I did esteem him as a friend,' wrote Alma, 'but as a man, I always found him disgusting.' His behaviour was so outré. Every other day he would run out of her house threatening to shoot himself – preferably on Gustav Mahler's grave.

But if Fraenkel, Schreker, Kammerer were minor entertainments, Alma's next relationship was altogether different. It was an affair that outdid even Alma's complex life with Walter Gropius in the wildness of emotion and the passion of its sex. She looked back on her next three years with Oskar Kokoschka as 'one fierce battle of love', maintaining that never before had she experienced 'so much tension, so much hell, such paradise'.

The initial connection had come through Alma's stepfather. Koko-schka had been commissioned to paint a portrait of Carl Moll. The sittings took place in the Josef Hoffmann house on the Hohe Warte, where

Kokoschka, a newly fashionable young artist with highly sophisticated visual taste, had appreciated the now slightly passé aura of oriental magnificence, with its Japanese vases, great sprays of peacock feathers and Persian carpets on the walls. He would often be asked to stay to dinner and it was on one of these evenings that he met Alma. Writing in 1921 he was still able to recreate the drama of that first encounter: 'I loved a woman from the moment I first set eyes on her, with my whole existence, even unto death for love's sake.'

After dinner Alma took him through to the next room and sat down at the piano, where she played and sang Isolde's 'Liebestod' for him, using her well-practised seduction techniques. According to Alma, Kokoschka then pressed forward, locking her into an embrace of a ferocity she had never experienced before.

He and Gropius were of the same generation – Kokoschka at the time was twenty-six – but they came from very different backgrounds, Kokoschka having been born at Pöchlarn, a small town on the Danube not far from Vienna. His father came from a Prague family of goldsmiths but was then employed as a travelling salesman for a firm of jewellers. Kokoschka had won a scholarship to study at the progressive Kunstgewerbeschule, the school of applied art, in Vienna. Compared with Gropius's privileged upbringing Kokoschka's early years were a struggle and, according to Alma, when she first met him his appearance was strikingly uncouth. 'He was tall and slender, but his hands were red, tending to swell. His ears, though small and finely chiselled, stood out a little. His nose was rather broad and inclined to swell, too. His head was carried very high. He walked sloppily, as though shoving himself forward.' But for her this uncouthness was part of the attraction, in contrast to Gropius's uprightness and polish: 'I loved the ill-bred, stubborn child in him.'

There are signs of a sexual uncouthness too. Alma recorded how Kokoschka could only make love in the context of the most peculiar game-playing. He told her, 'I shall never let you go away again except riding on my back, so that no one can take you away from me. I sleep in your coat, so that at least I have your smell.' He evidently had sadomasochistic tendencies. As he wrote longingly to Alma: 'I would so much like you to be at least cross with me, but here and hitting me with your dear, beautiful little hands!'

Where Kokoschka and Gropius certainly converged was in their artistic ambition and talent. Both passed the test of incipient star quality Alma looked for in her lovers. Where Gropius was being regarded in Berlin as a progressive young architect of promise, by this stage receiving important new commissions, most notably for the 1914 Deutscher Werkbund exhibition, Kokoschka had acquired a reputation in Vienna as one of the most promising artists of the avant-garde.

In 1909 he had given up his commercial graphic work for the relatively conventional Wiener Werkstätte, the design workshop run by Josef Hoffmann. He became part of that close network of writers, intellectuals, composers and artists opposed to the artistic and social conventions of the time. Kokoschka's great friend and patron, the architect Adolf Loos. encouraged him to take the financially riskier path as a painter of portraits in a modern Expressionist idiom, resisting easy flattery in favour of a penetrating, often painful psychological truthfulness.

By the time he met Alma the alarmingly shaven-headed young artist had become a notorious figure, an object of fascination in the city. He was known for the lurid poster he designed for his own violent Expressionist drama *Mörder, Hoffnung der Frauen (Murderer, the Hope of Women)* and his frightening self-portrait as a suffering Christ. He had the reputation of being the *Oberwildling*, the super-wildman. Kokoschka's iconoclastic persona in early-twentieth-century Vienna was roughly equivalent to that of the later young British artist Damien Hirst.

The satirist Karl Kraus, the modernist writer and poet Peter Altenberg and his prime supporter Adolf Loos had already had their portraits painted by Kokoschka. Once he had completed the portrait commissioned by Carl Moll, Kokoschka turned his attention to Alma, who had demanded he should paint her.

He found the request both pleasing and unnerving. He had never before painted a woman who appeared to have fallen in love with him at first sight. Over the next three years of their rapturous–tormented relationship Kokoschka drew and painted Alma innumerable times. 'He painted me, me, me – he no longer knew other faces,' Alma wrote. Kokoschka also painted her a series of decorative fans (see Plate 5). He viewed these as his love letters, their own passionate story spelled out in picture language. Six of the seven fans are still in existence: for such small, intimate objects, they overflow with incidental detail and high drama.

After the death of Mahler, Alma's relations with Kokoschka could be freer than her behaviour had been with Walter Gropius. This was no nerve-racking semi-clandestine affair. Alma was now living independently in her own garden flat in north Vienna, near the Vienna woods. She and Kokoschka were able to travel together. In August 1912 they took a working holiday in Mürren in the Bernese Oberland. Here Kokoschka painted the view across the valley of the three great looming mountains, the Eiger, Münch and Jungfrau, which might be seen as standing for Gropius and Kokoschka, with Alma in between them. He started on the portrait that she had demanded, a painting slightly reminiscent of the *Mona Lisa*, depicting Alma Mahler with a faint mysterious smile.

The stay in Switzerland was extremely problematic. Kokoschka was now desperate to marry Alma, who suspected she was pregnant, and he travelled to and from Interlaken in the valley trying to make arrangements for a wedding. Alma was resistant to the whole idea of marriage, and describes herself awaiting his return upstairs in her room in the Grand Hotel and Kurhaus, trembling with anxiety in case he should succeed. When negotiations to obtain a licence failed she returned to Vienna in a highly nervous state. The pregnancy was now confirmed and Kokoschka reluctantly agreed to an abortion, carried out in mid-October. In the clinic he removed the blood-stained cotton dressing from Alma and took it home with him, insisting that this was his only child and always would be. 'Later', wrote Alma, 'he perpetually carried around this old, dried-out piece of cotton.'

In 1912 Kokoschka embarked on the *Double Portrait of Oskar Kokoschka and Alma Mahler* (see Plate 4) that has now become so famous, showing him and Alma standing close together, clasping hands as if in a symbolic giving of a ring. Kokoschka described this as an engagement picture, and it has a delicate solemnity. He was still viewing Alma as his future wife, and indeed Carl Moll had agreed to the proposed marriage, saying that he saw no particular difficulty. Alma herself had written encouragingly from Nice, where she was then staying with her great friend Lili Lieser, promising to marry him as soon as they were reunited in Vienna. It would not be long before she changed her mind.

In the *Double Portrait* Alma is wearing the jacket of the pair of 'fiery red pyjamas' that she says she disliked because the colour was so piercing. The red pyjamas were taken over by Kokoschka, who habitually wore them while working in his studio, where he would 'receive his shocked visitors in them and stood more in front of the mirror than his easel'.

Alma and Gropius were virtually incommunicado through 1912 while she and Kokoschka were travelling abroad. It was as if she had totally exhausted him. Evidently Gropius had no idea of the recent developments in Alma's life. Indeed it seems he was only just aware of Kokoschka as an artist, having seen but not particularly registered his graphic work in the newly opened Berlin Expressionist gallery Der Sturm. It was not until early in 1913, coming face to face with Kokoschka's *Double Portrait* in the twenty-sixth Berlin Secessionist exhibition, that Gropius realised painfully and precisely what had been going on.

5

Gropius at War

1914–1918

Through the winter of 1913–14 Gropius was working on his next important commission: the factory and office building for the Deutscher Werkbund exhibition in Cologne. This was a central feature for the large-scale exhibition of arts and crafts and industrially manufactured products. Gropius's remit was to design a complex of buildings which would demonstrate convincingly 'the architectural elements and dimensions of a modern machine factory'.

The commission had reached him via his faithful supporter Karl Ernst Osthaus. It was a rushed job, taken over from the previous architect, Hans Poelzig, who had resigned in the summer. Though he complained that his workload was inhuman, he was feeling confident that his Cologne factory would be 'something quite good. Everyone whose judgement I value congratulates me spontaneously.' He had the support of other Deutscher Werkbund members, including his ex-employer Peter Behrens and Henry van de Velde.

Gropius was compelled to use an existing building for the Machine Hall. This had been a feature of the Leipzig Building Trade exhibition the previous year. But although he was disappointed not to be able to design his allotted group of buildings coherently from scratch, he managed to make some amendments to the Machine Hall, which he then formed into an impressive architectural complex containing a large new office building and a courtyard. The office block was a consciously monumental building, with Assyrian-style columns flanking the front entrance and with echoes of ancient Egyptian structures. It stood at the same time as a temple of modernity in its structural poetry of glass and iron. With this emphasis on bringing civilised values to early-twentieth-century factory production Gropius's Werkbund exhibition building was

Gropius's office building and factory for the Deutscher Werkbund exhibition in Cologne, 1914.

Sleeping car interior designed by Gropius, shown at the Deutscher Werkbund exhibition, Cologne, 1914.

in its way symbolic of a hoped-for future for Germany itself. Sculptures, paintings and stone reliefs were specially commissioned from contemporary artists including Georg Kolbe and Gerhard Marcks. An ambitious integration of art with architecture was always to remain central to his thinking. It was the 1914 Werkbund building that, following the Fagus factory, confirmed Walter Gropius's growing reputation.

Gropius had moved to Cologne in April to oversee the final stages of construction. The exhibition, which opened in May, attracted over a million visitors in three months. There were forty-eight restaurants, tea houses and food stalls. There was live entertainment from orchestras and bands as well as puppet plays. Puppets were a craze in Germany at that period. Theatrical performances took place in the purpose-built new theatre designed by van de Velde. Gropius himself had been diversifying the scope of his work and exhibited designs for domestic interiors, automobiles and a beautiful luxurious railway sleeping car which must surely have reminded him of travelling with Alma on the Orient Express.

Gropius had now been elected to the board of the Deutscher Werkbund, then at thirty-one its youngest member. He became embroiled in the now legendary altercation that took place in Cologne at the time of the Werkbund exhibition. Looking back on it Gropius described his role in the row between the two respected grandees van de Velde and Hermann Muthesius as that of the 'enfant terrible'. His intervention shows his growing confidence. The crux of the argument, which took place in public with an audience of a thousand, lay in the developing conflict in the Werkbund between the arts and crafts and mass production. Muthesius argued a strong case for a more rigid and disciplined approach to architecture and design, in which artistic flights of fancy and self-indulgence would be banned, while van de Velde defended passionately the personal inspiration of the artist and the greater value of originality and individualism.

In view of Walter Gropius's later reputation as champion of clean lines and rationality he might have been expected to support Muthesius, but in fact he allied himself with van de Velde, not only because – as is so often forgotten – Gropius had a strongly spiritual side but also because he disliked Muthesius personally, describing the Prussian civil service architect as 'an unpleasant man who used tricky methods to get into the lead. His mind was also much too rigid and "unartistic".' Interested as Gropius already was in the potential of standardisation in building and design he believed above all else in the creative freedom of the artist, the slow processes of 'inwardness' which allowed architects and designers finally to reach the heights.

———

Gropius's burgeoning professional career would soon be interrupted. The Austrian Archduke Franz Ferdinand and his wife were assassinated in Sarajevo on 28 June 1914. War was declared on 1 August and Gropius as a military reservist was immediately called up. He reported to the 9th Wandsbeck Hussars on 5 August, was appointed sergeant major and sent straight into action in the Vosges mountains in Alsace, where the Imperial German Army were to be locked into long battles with the French. Back in Berlin his architectural office was left to be run by Adolf Meyer. When Meyer himself received his summons for war service the office was closed for the remainder of the war.

We get a clear idea of Gropius's war service via the detailed letters he sent home from the front. These are now in the Bauhaus Archive in Berlin, long scrawled accounts of setbacks and triumphs, advances and retreats, vividly recreated with many underlinings. Little annotated postcards with pictures of bleak military outposts and military comrades are also included among these poignant personal mementoes of Walter Gropius's war.

At first, in the Vosges, Gropius was assigned to field reconnaissance duties. It was his job to ride out through the countryside, with half a dozen accompanying soldiers on horseback, to establish exactly where the enemy troops were. One of his early expeditions was to Mount Aubry, which overlooked a valley near Senones. Here he had to climb a densely wooded hill to check if a crossing point was clear of enemy troops so that the German machine guns could be safely brought up. He arrived at the summit, found the route clear, posted sentries and then crawled on his belly up a slope nearby.

Below him he could look right down the valley of the Meurthe. All

Gropius saw military service
from 5 August 1914
with the 9th Wandsbeck
Hussars.

the roads in the valley were jammed with enemy troops. He only just had time to make an accurate count when he was suddenly aware of firing from the bushes and two enemy soldiers appeared. Gropius quickly retreated and waited with the horses for another hour. Remounting, he tried again to look down into the valley, making certain the French army had not altered its position. But at this point a whole line of enemy riflemen emerged from the woods and started giving fire. Gropius and his troops rode off fast and escaped without suffering casualties; the French soldiers were apparently shooting very badly. It was a nerve-racking episode. But as a result Gropius was able to relay to headquarters troop-movement reports of such importance that, as he boasted to his mother, 'they decided the day and perhaps more'.

One gets the impression from Gropius's accounts of these often desperate days in the Vosges mountains that he was both terrified and stimulated by such new experiences, drawing on resources he hardly knew that he possessed. Rides out in pouring rain. Nights spent on muddy roads, shivering with cold. No sleep at all. Early on there is a kind of zest in these descriptions. But as the war continues in such treacherous terrain his reports become overlaid with indignation at the widespread loss of human lives and the sheer incompetence of his superiors.

During the night of 21 September 1914 Gropius was woken up and given orders to leave immediately with fifteen men for a reconnaissance ride from Senones towards Celles. As he told his mother, he already knew this terrifying forest and arrived there with a trembling heart. The French troops were so well hidden that they were invisible. After the initial shooting Gropius gave orders for the horses to be removed to safety. He then fought forwards with his troops in the first infantry line. In the first hour they lost eighty of the original three hundred men.

They lay there in the forest for the whole day without moving, receiving reinforcements in the evening, which allowed them to dislodge the French from their entrenchments. Then Gropius received 'an insane order, totally unworkable' to ride behind enemy lines to establish communication with General Neubert at headquarters near Celles. After only ten minutes on this mission they arrived at an entrenchment of felled trees, a massive barrier which the horses could not pass. Gropius requested infantry help. A sergeant arrived with a body of soldiers who managed to remove the trees. Despite having explicit orders to advance, the sergeant, who was shaking with nerves, refused to go further. So Gropius, although in theory a ground observer, was forced to put himself at the head of the infantry troop, with the horses now bringing up the rear.

They marched on for an hour through the night. Then a voice called out from twenty feet away. They had marched straight up to the enemy sentries. Shots were fired at their column. Gropius's nerve-shattered sergeant disappeared. Gropius attempted to bring the detachment of soldiers back into line and spent the remainder of the night standing in the road in pouring rain.

Next morning he was able to restore communication with his horsemen on the road. He and his troop were constantly being shot at by enemy marksmen in the trees and bushes. Finally that night reinforcements arrived and the French were routed. At last, wrote Gropius, 'we could finally leave this terrible forest . . . But what losses. I got out of it alive after two dreadful days and nights without sleep, steadily buzzed by bullets, and cries of the wounded and dying in my ears.' The horror of these war experiences affected him for life. After his return to the regiment, where the colonel had been touchingly relieved to see him, Gropius was once again summoned in the night. He expected that this meant another call of duty, but instead he was ceremonially presented with the Iron Cross in recognition of his courage, the first to be awarded to his regiment.

In November 1914 Gropius was promoted to lieutenant. This was a quicker promotion than was usual for reserve officers in the German army. But Gropius's record had so far been impressive. The war was dragging on more slowly than expected. The early impetus of the German offensive through Belgium and across the Marne was now halted. A general retreat had been ordered in September. Meanwhile, the casualty rate among German officers was high. Gropius was pleased with his new status. He found it 'much pleasanter' to rank as an officer. There were rumours that he might be sent to Belgium. But he and the regiment were soon directed back to the Western Front entrenchments, with orders to retake a hilltop position at Ban-de-Sapt from the French.

Once again Gropius judged this despairingly as a 'totally mismanaged situation', the French trench at Ban-de-Sapt being more or less impregnable. Realising this they set off with heavy hearts. For four days and nights without sleep they moved slowly uphill through enemy artillery. On 1 January 1915 a 15 cm mortar grenade exploded right in front of Gropius. He remained unconscious for some minutes and then, as he describes it, he 'got up, oh miracle, only covered with dirt. The shock was terrible.'

The next day they attacked. The French soldiers had dug through to a point that brought them only seven metres away. Sending a shell into the enemy trench was the beginning of what Gropius calls a 'hellish dance'. The German officer in charge chose the youngest of his soldiers to jump first into the enemy trench. Gropius himself led the left wing of the company. Four different artilleries began shooting.

Machine guns bombarded them from both sides as well as rifle fire.

Their captain was shot in the heart directly in front of Gropius. There were no reserve troops so he and his men had to keep going for another day and night. They forced themselves to stay awake by smoking and had to beat the soldiers to prevent them from going to sleep on their feet. When they eventually buried their captain in Laître they almost collapsed in exhaustion and misery. 'Much honour', writes Gropius, 'but how dear this glory! From 250 men we are now down to 134.'

Gropius's nerves were shattered. At night he suffered what he calls 'the screaming jeebies'. The field hospital's doctor diagnosed this as 'insomnia caused by nervous tension', maintaining that it would be cured by a few days' rest away from the front. He was moved to a hospital in Strasbourg. But in fact the screaming jeebies that started in the First World War never really left him. His second wife Ise described how the insomnia triggered by the grenade that exploded next to him in the Vosges mountains remained with him for years. She had tried hard to develop relaxation techniques to help him through the problem but she failed to prevent 'the nightmares that disturbed Gropius's sleep even when he was beyond middle age'.

Writing to his mother from the hospital he told her how much he had been missing her and that he had been especially longing for the children of his married sister, Manon Burchard: 'I try to visualise their little personalities.' He saw these children as the harbingers of better times to come. In January 1915 he was moved from hospital in Strasbourg back to Berlin on convalescent leave.

This is the point at which Alma resurfaces after her turbulent two years with Oskar Kokoschka, during which her relations with Gropius were almost broken off. She had in fact written at least once before, in July 1913, a kind of warning letter in which she informed Gropius she might get married to Kokoschka, describing him as 'a kindred spirit of ours', but at the same time reassuring Gropius that she would still continue to remain connected with him through all eternity. 'Write to tell me whether you're alive – and whether this life is worth living,' she implored him. There is no record that Gropius replied.

In May 1914 Alma tried again. This time it was Gropius's well-publicised buildings for the Cologne Werkbund exhibition that excited her. She had been alerted to his growing fame by Berta Zuckerkandl, international journalist and patron of the arts, at whose dinner table she had first met Gustav Mahler. Berta had told Alma, 'There is a young architect in particular who has had an enormous success, a certain Walter Gropius.' As Alma records in her deliberately obfuscating memoirs, 'My brief, earnest relationship of Tobelbad had been lost in the grey fog of time; but I had made no mistake about his talent. I sat down and wrote him a letter of congratulations.' Alma suggested meeting in July.

She received no personal response to this proposal, just the formal official information that Lieutenant Gropius of the Wandsbeck Hussars was then in a field hospital recovering from his experiences of battle. Alma still claimed to have had an intimation that this shocked and wounded soldier was destined to mean something in her future life.

Alma's liaison with Kokoschka had meanwhile been suffering accumulated strains. The series of fans in which he depicts their amatory history reflects his growing fears of losing her, its imagery increasingly turbulent and doom-laden. The four-metre-long mural painted by Kokoschka in the music room of Alma's new house at Breitenstein in the Semmering shows her in a ghostly light pointing heavenwards, while Kokoschka stands in hell below her, consumed by deathly flames.

Alma at one stage promised Kokoschka that she would marry him once he had painted a masterpiece. In 1913 he completed *Die Windsbraut* (*The Bride of the Wind* or *The Tempest*), which shows the lovers lying entwined in ecstasy and torment in a boat on a stormy sea. This painting is generally considered Kokoschka's greatest work. (Its original title had been the Wagnerian *Tristan und Isolde*.) But Alma had evidently gone back on her promise of marriage by the time the painting was exhibited in Munich in August 1914.

Through 1914 relations between them had deteriorated further. Kokoschka began scaring her. One day when she went round to his studio she found that he had painted it completely black, the black walls being covered with white crayon sketches. Alma claimed it was in self-protection that she now decided to distance herself from him. However, they were both at Breitenstein for New Year 1915 and apparently spent the night together lovingly. But Alma that same evening wrote to Walter Gropius reminding him of how he too had come to Breitenstein, her architect of choice and also her devoted lover, pacing out the floor for her in the early stages of the house's reconstruction, when Gropius had designed a long fireplace wall for the living room constructed of massive granite blocks. Alma tells him in her letter how greatly she is longing for his safe return from battle. Once he returns she will need to wish no more . . .

Gropius's heroism on the battlefield had been reported in the papers. Alma wrote to the field hospital in Strasbourg suggesting a reunion. He replied from Berlin, where he was on convalescent leave, and in February 1915 she arrived to see him. Meeting the recently wounded Gropius again she found him overwhelmingly attractive: 'In his early thirties he was still the perfect Walther von Stolzing, one of the most civilised men I know, besides being one of the handsomest.'

Alma's fortnight in Berlin began with Gropius's recriminations over her relations with Kokoschka. 'Days were spent in tearful questions, nights in tearful answers.' But finally in Borchardt's luxurious restaurant, with fine wine to assist their reconciliation and the sense of the excitements and exigencies of war, Gropius fell in love again with Alma. There was only an hour left before he was due to catch the train to see his mother, who was then in Hanover. Alma went with him to the station and Gropius dramatically pulled her up to join him in the already moving train. She tells us in her memoirs that she didn't have her nightgown with her, had made no preparations whatsoever for a journey, but that in this new mood of elated rediscovery she didn't mind at all.

Gropius was soon back fighting at the front. He had now received another decoration, the Bavarian Military Medal Fourth Class with Swords, for his courage as a ground observer in deliberately drawing enemy fire upon himself. One bullet had penetrated his fur cap, another had shot through the sole of his shoe, there were bullets through the left and right sides of his coat. With his regiment Gropius took part in the battle for Nancy-Epinal near the German–French border, on the Moselle River line. He and Alma were exchanging passionate letters. They were now writing to one another daily. She was calling him 'husband', signing herself 'your wife', wondering whether she was pregnant, reliving the detail of their lovemaking. 'Our wildness makes me tremble,' she told Gropius; it had been 'so heavenly'.

In fact Alma was not pregnant. But she had now become fixated on their marrying just as soon as Gropius could get leave, repeating her new name like an effusive little chant: 'Alma Gropius! Alma Gropius! Look at that! Isn't it lovely. Gropius! Do write this name again in one of your letters. Want to see it written by you! Foreign name – lovely fantasies on a moonlit night. I am glowing and cannot sleep.'

In the run-up to the wedding there were problems. The first was Manon Gropius, still hostile to a woman she had identified as flighty and from an alien culture. To Gropius's mother Vienna seemed a foreign land. She told her son that there was no hope whatsoever that she and Alma would reach an understanding. Assuming that Alma would be moving to Berlin she now considered leaving to avoid an almost certain rift. An attempted reconciliatory visit from Gropius and Alma did nothing to improve the situation. Manon wrote wearily that 'the embattled days passed here with you and Frau M. were like a whirlwind roaring over me. I was left bowed and exhausted.'

Gropius himself counter-attacked, reminding her of his own inner need to free himself from stultifying family conventions, telling her how he had 'tried in a *young* life, to test their present-day value, to discard the flawed and short-sighted, to expand their limits and, in short, to adapt them to our *new* day and therefore to our justified way of life'. He argued that marriage to Alma, 'a woman who possesses the greatest inner freedom', should have struck her as a logical symptom of her son's own necessary development.

Manon caved in. As Gropius entreated she sent Alma a grovelling conciliatory letter, asking permission to call her 'this beautiful name' Maria, the name for Alma that Gropius preferred: 'Walter writes so much about his dear Maria, that it appears unnatural to me to address you formally.' For the time being these overtures were effective. Less easily quenched were the doubts arising at the prospect of her marriage in Alma's own mind.

Did she really love Walter Gropius? This was the question candidly put to her by her old admirer, reptile specialist Paul Kammerer, who was convinced that she did not. Alma's own inner doubts keep recurring in her diary. She begins suspecting that 'this person is not what my life is about'. His intense jealousy of the notoriously flamboyant Kokoschka proved irritating. By the spring of 1915 Alma had started seeing the liaison with Gropius as a dead end, a mismatch of temperament: 'he is just tepid, and I am not – that will never work.' And certainly Gropius could be intensely focused, whereas Alma was volatility itself.

Alma had now moved from her Vienna garden flat to a much more spacious ten-room apartment on the fourth floor of Elisabethstrasse 22 in Vienna's first district. Here she would lie in bed and cry, upsetting and bewildering her little daughter Anna. Her mood swung and she would write hysterically to Gropius on the battlefield, saying she was kissing his 'beloved name! The name of my lord and master.' Alma was going just a little mad and indeed it seems amazing that the clandestine wedding actually happened. It took place hurriedly on 18 May 1915 at Registry Office 3 on Parochialstrasse in Berlin. No members of either family were present. Two witnesses, a self-described mason called Richard Munske and a young army pioneer named Erich Subke, were brought in from the street.

Gropius had been given a two-day leave of absence from the regiment. On the day after the wedding Alma wrote in her diary of her determination to make it a good marriage: 'my desire is pure and clear, I have no other wish but to make this talented man happy!' No doubt she meant it at the time.

———

Oskar Kokoschka, with encouragement from Alma, had volunteered for the armed forces. Vouched for by Adolf Loos, he joined the 15th Imperial

Oskar Kokoschka volunteered for military service with the
15th Imperial Dragoons in 1915.

Dragoons, a crack cavalry regiment. Like Gropius, on first joining the Hussars he found the financial demands on him exorbitantly high and had to use the proceeds from the sale of his painting *Die Windsbraut* to buy the necessary horse and his own extravagant uniform. Photographs of Kokoschka in his curving golden helmet show how much his military uniform became him, as indeed Walter Gropius's had suited him.

He had an eventful war, volunteering for the Eastern Front and being sent to the Ukraine. In February 1915, when Alma was reconciled with Gropius and planning to be married to him, she took the precaution of writing to Kokoschka, asking him to send her the key to his studio. She was evidently worried that if he did get killed, the many love letters she had written him would jeopardise her standing as the bride of Gropius.

Towards the end of the summer Kokoschka was badly wounded, first by a bullet in the head and then by a bayonet piercing his lung. Rumours started circulating in Vienna that he had been killed, so Alma rushed round to his studio, with the key, retrieving 'sackfuls' of the letters she had written to him, letters whose arrival he had once awaited with such a pounding heart. While she was about it Alma also took away the hundreds of sketches and drawings Kokoschka had left behind.

In mid-October 1915 the wounded Kokoschka was moved back to an infirmary in Vienna. It was the following July before he was judged fit to serve again, this time as a non-combatant liaison officer for war artists on the Isonzo Front, in the Slovenian–Italian theatre of war. In late August 1916 a grenade exploded close beside him and Kokoschka was brought back to Vienna suffering from shell shock. He had been totally out of touch with Alma, who had not answered any of his letters. But he had heard that she was married and pregnant with Gropius's child. He asked Adolf Loos to contact Alma for him, entreating her to come and sit by him in hospital. Alma refused. Kokoschka felt this refusal with some bitterness. He admitted in his autobiography, 'Really, I knew that any attempt to recapture the past must be in vain.'

In a curiously typical desperation fantasy he was later to commission a life-size doll formed in Alma Mahler's image from the Munich doll

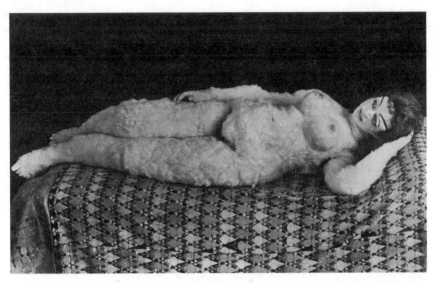

Life-size doll in Alma's image, commissioned by Kokoschka from
Munich doll maker Hermine Moos, 1919.

maker Hermine Moos. He told her, 'If you are able to carry out this task
as I would wish, to deceive me with such magic that when I see it and
touch it I imagine that I have the woman of my dreams in front of me,
then dear Fräulein Moos, I will be eternally indebted to your skills of
invention.' He wanted the doll to reproduce his lost lover's actual meas-
urements, providing Hermine Moos with an accurate life-size sketch.
He also asked her to make it possible that his sense of touch would 'be
able to take pleasure in those parts where the layers of fat and muscle
suddenly give way to a sinuous covering of skin'. But Alma proved too
much for even Hermine Moos's skilfulness. The doll was an enormous
disappointment when it came.

Through the war years Kokoschka had been working on a drama,
Orpheus und Eurydike. The idea had first come to him in hallucinatory
form as he lay wounded in the field hospital at Volodymyr-Volynskyi,
just north-west of Lutsk in the Ukraine. He started the first outline
in the military hospital in Brunn. The bullet through his skull had
impaired Kokoschka's vision but his recall of past events was now all
the more intense. He put into the play, as close as he could come to it in
words, the experience of his joyful/agonising years with Alma Mahler,

recreated through the myth of Orpheus and Eurydice. If Kokoschka was Orpheus and Alma was Eurydice, then the role for Gropius, the purloiner of his lover, obviously became that of Hades, king of the underworld in which she was now captive. In Hades there are also elements of Mahler, whose posthumous reputation and enduring hold on Alma Kokoschka much resented, while the Furies can be seen as the sycophantic circle of her Viennese admirers.

Kokoschka reworked the idea, which Alma quickly recognised as their own story, to form the basis of a painting and then a series of etchings. There is an extra frisson of coincidence in that *Orpheus und Eurydike* was first performed in Frankfurt in 1921 with music by Ernst Krenek, the Viennese composer whose marriage to Alma and Gustav Mahler's daughter Anna took place three years later, lasting only a few months. Gropius and Kokoschka were never to be close. But from now on there is a sense of them continually winding in and out of one another's lives through their connections with avant-garde Vienna and their later rather parallel experience of exile, as well as their complex inter-relationships with Alma. Kokoschka enquired of Loos in 1918 from Dresden, sarcastic at the thought of her marriage to Gropius, 'What is my idol doing in her bourgeois married bliss?'

Three years later, when the *Double Portrait*, their so-called engagement picture, was about to be exhibited in Dresden, Kokoschka wrote to Alma himself. 'Alma,' he told her, 'I have in front of me the picture that I once painted of the two of us, in which we both look so exhausted, and you are giving me back the ring.' Impossible not to think of Gropius too and remember the shock of recognition that he felt when he first saw this all-too-revelatory painting in the Berlin Secessionist exhibition back in 1913, before the war began.

———

On 31 August 1915, just a few days after the secret wedding in Berlin, it was the bride's birthday. Alma was thirty-six and Gropius, now back with his regiment, had ordered the present of an onyx necklace, which Alma found 'so wonderfully beautiful' she had kept it on all night in bed and promised her new husband that she would always wear it as the token of their love.

Things of course were not so simple. There were tensions in the marriage right from the beginning. 'My marriage to Walter Gropius was the oddest I could imagine,' Alma wrote later. The suspicions and rows over Kokoschka still surfaced. Once in a frenzy of jealousy Gropius seized one of the seven fans Kokoschka had painted for Alma – the fourth in the series, apparently inscribed with a passionate poem Kokoschka had written – and threw it on the fire.

Besides Gropius's smouldering resentment of Kokoschka, relations between Alma and Gropius's mother were now more problematic than ever. Manon had been let into the secret of their marriage, which she greatly disapproved of, unconvinced by Gropius's argument that Alma was such a celebrity in Vienna that the news that she had now remarried would result in more publicity than anyone so sensitive could bear. Manon once again attempted conciliatory overtures, but these were arrogantly repulsed by Alma. 'She is very greedy for power and very passionate,' Alma told Gropius, 'but this word does not come from passion but from vehemence, because everything in her person is too small . . . Tell her that the doors of the whole world which are open to the name Mahler will fly shut to the totally unknown name Gropius.' Alma was an intrepid insulter, even of her newly acquired husband: 'I know who you are and who you are for me, but for the world you are an unwritten page. She should go and hear a symphony and that may make her understand more, though I don't trust her judgement.' Manon Gropius must see that 'there was only one Gustav Mahler and that there is only one Gropius'. Had Manon Gropius ever considered what Alma had sacrificed in marrying her son?

To add to these tensions there was the simple fact of separation. Alma became restless in Gropius's absence, unable to sympathise with his own privations on the military front. 'You wrote today about *December*!' she lamented soon after the wedding. 'So that will mean *4 months*!' She, the greedy connoisseur of rich Viennese cooking, complained of being unable to remain 'content with eating bread soup'. Sometimes it seemed to her that she knew nothing about her husband any more, could not even remember the detail of his face. Then she would suddenly be overcome with longing:

The first time we see each other again, I shall sink down on the ground before you, remain on my knees, and, kneeling, beg you to take your sacred appendage in your hands and place it in my mouth, and then I will use all the finesse, all the refinement I have learned with you . . . Then you will go wild, clutch me in your arms and with all tenderness lay me down on the bed, which is as wide as the two of us are long – there are flowers in the room, and candles burn, and you will lay me down and afflict me with hideous tortures, because you always make me wait – until I burst into tears and implore you! Please!!

She asked Gropius to send her his own sexual fantasies in reciprocation. We have no record of whether on the Moselle battle front he managed to obey.

Four months after the wedding, in December, Gropius returned to Alma in Vienna on Christmas leave. It was a short but contented time. Gropius was welcomed with great warmth and friendship, eleven-year-old Anna appearing especially infatuated with her mother's handsome new husband as she had previously idolised Kokoschka. But apparently her keen interest in Gropius diminished once he shaved off his spectacular moustache. In the euphoria of the reunion Gropius tried once again writing to his mother to bring about a reconciliation with Alma. He still could not resist criticising Manon's resistance to the element of originality, wilfulness and paradox which, he argued, was 'the mark of Cain' in all people of true talent. His mother, he argued, failed to acknowledge him as the iconoclast he was.

———

It was at this point, in the early years of the war, that Gropius became involved in plans for the school that evolved into the Bauhaus. He was summoned from the Vosges to Weimar in Thuringia, a cultural oasis in eastern-central Germany, to meet the Grand Duke and Duchess of Saxe-Weimar and local government officials. He arrived straight from the front, still in his military uniform of the Hussars, to be guided from the gatehouse through the corridors and chambers of the ornately decorated Schloss, to discuss the ideas still forming in his mind for a new school, with the workshop as the basis, a visionary meeting point of art and industry.

The new appointment as director of the Kunstgewerbeschule, the Grand Ducal School of Arts and Crafts in Weimar, had been brought about by the enforced resignation of Henry van de Velde. In 1908 the former Hochschule für Bildende Kunst, the local academy of art, combined with the Kunstgewerbeschule as part of a plan for a single Grand Ducal Saxon school of art. Buildings for the two institutions, both purpose-designed by Henry van de Velde, were sited close to one another in the town.

Over the years van de Velde's position became untenable as local animosities against the Belgian architect intensified. Weimar opponents and officials demanded his expulsion and van de Velde was finally driven to hand in his resignation a week before the outbreak of war. He struggled on alone in Weimar and then took refuge in a psychiatric clinic in Königstein before managing to travel on to Switzerland. He was by this time in a very shaky mental state.

Before leaving the Kunstgewerbeschule van de Velde had proposed three possible successors. One was Walter Gropius, another was the sculptor Hermann Obrist, and the third was the architect August Endell, the latter two distinguished practitioners in the Jugendstil tradition. Walter Gropius was of a younger generation and still relatively unknown. It seems likely that van de Velde saw Gropius as an ally since he had supported him in the acrimonious Werkbund debate with Muthesius the year before.

Gropius was initially doubtful, but after some reflection he decided that such an official position would give him authority and bolster his career. He would have scope for building up good architectural contacts around Weimar, as van de Velde himself had done. Alma, when she heard about the suggestion, was realistic and constructive, giving him the benefit of her worldly advice. 'This position', she told him, 'is not so grand. You should enter into it only if they give you all the authority you ask for in *writing*. Not to speak about money and title is Aryan super-*noblesse* which will be a drawback later on.' It was Alma who put pressure on her husband to speak to the Grand Duke personally before he committed himself to make the move.

Once he returned from the ducal interview he sent a telegram to Alma from the front. She replied enthusiastically, telling him the telegram had put a ray of happiness into her heart. 'Weimar! I would like that *best*! A small house to rent there and to *begin*, away from relatives and friends.' Perhaps inspired by these visions of domestic bliss with Alma, Gropius corresponded with the Grand Duke through his chief of staff, Freiherr von Fritsch, setting out his ideas for the sort of school he now envisaged, a school for an ideal future in which art, craft and technology were fused.

Gropius's proposals were well received. But the pressures of war intervened. The Kunstgewerbeschule was closed from October 1915 and the building was used as a military hospital. The Grand Duke and his staff in Weimar were preoccupied. Gropius was back with his troops in the Vosges. Any plans for the future Bauhaus were on hold.

Gropius now became involved again in one of his most challenging architectural projects: the redesign of the Villa Mahler at Breitenstein. He was remodelling the terrace, adding a new porch to give a better vista of the nearby Schneeberg mountain. Alma was now pregnant and that perhaps explains why she was more caustic and querulous than ever. In the spring of 1916 she sent a long lament from Breitenstein to Gropius on the battle front in answer to his queries on the progress of the work.

'Has the porch been enlarged to the dining room windows?' This is written by an architect – or one who would like to represent himself as one – to his pregnant wife, during the war, and for my house located at a height of 1000 metres . . . In peacetime and if I were in full health, such a reinforced concrete terrace would be a fatiguing enterprise because everything is more difficult here and I can get workmen only with great effort – but now! This thoughtlessness makes me wonder. *Such inconsiderateness!* If I were so foolish as to try to do such a thing, you should do everything to prevent me from going ahead with it. Open doors, draughts, dirt, strange men in the house – but mainly danger of getting overtired. And this you never realized.

She suggested sarcastically that his next commission should be the conversion of a jailer's house.

Rather than being irritated by her tone, Gropius tried to keep her calm. He was delighted by the news of her pregnancy, news that would now make their marriage public. He decided to keep from her the episode in which he only just managed to escape from a military reconnaissance plane that had crashed, killing its pilot. He attempted to pacify Alma when she continued to complain about his mother, who had made a special visit to Breitenstein when she heard about the pregnancy. Manon intended to bring about a final reconciliation with the woman she now optimistically described as 'a rare and fine human being with rich inner resources . . . even if many of her ideas, habits and views are foreign and strange to me'. This visit started well but ended acrimoniously, with Alma criticising her mother-in-law's extravagant shopping habits and tasteless vulgarity in keeping up her large home in Berlin.

In her letters to the front, Alma taunted Gropius on the subject of her continuing attractiveness to other men while admitting to suspicions about his own unfaithfulness. She had heard about the very high proportion of men fighting who were now suffering from venereal disease. At the same time she unleashed to him her own sexual longings at a time of deprivation: 'I am very sensual, long always for unheard things. Want to suck you in from all sides like a polyp . . . pour your sweet stream into me.'

In summer 1916 the war was entering an excruciating period, with battles grinding on around Verdun on the Meuse and now the Allied offensive on the Somme. Writing from his regimental field headquarters in the Vosges in August Gropius confessed to feeling 'livid with rage, sitting here in chains through this mad war which kills any meaning of life'. He foresaw that the war would ruin the German people spiritually and economically too. He confided to his mother, 'The mood on the front against the government is becoming dangerous, thank God, and may these miserable writers of notes become bankrupt before all of us.' Beyond all this Alma's laments from Vienna caused him great anxiety: 'I don't know what to do, my nerves are shattered and my mind darkened.' On 1 September Gropius was promoted to adjutant of the regiment and his military responsibilities were increased.

He was allowed a fortnight's leave to be with Alma for the birth of their child. But the baby was late. 'This child has no wish to appear in this world gone mad,' he wrote. After seventeen days' waiting he had anxiously gone back to the front. Their daughter, Manon, finally arrived on 5 October 1916 after a problematic labour. He heard the news by telegram. A letter followed in a few days' time telling him that all was well with both the mother and the baby. His joy was overwhelming. Gropius felt so proud and happy that he wanted to 'embrace the world', especially since Alma had euphorically told him that she now planned for them to have a son.

As soon as he heard the news Gropius excitedly made plans to buy a lavish present for Alma in celebration of the birth. He wrote from the front to Carl Reininghaus, one of the leading modern art collectors in Vienna, to negotiate the purchase from his collection of Edvard Munch's oil painting *Summer Night by the Beach* (see Plate 6), a picture that Alma particularly loved. On the very same day that Gropius's request reached Reininghaus the latter despatched two servants with the picture and a flattering letter telling Alma that in fact it had been hers for years – 'he just had not found the right occasion to send it'. As we shall see, the present from Gropius had a tortuous later history.

Always unpredictable, Alma behaved strangely when Gropius finally arrived to see his daughter, having travelled all night from the French front to Vienna. He had negotiated another two days' special leave and hurried home directly from the station. Alma was appalled by his appearance: 'When I saw him grimy, unshaven, his uniform and face blackened with railroad soot, I felt as though I were seeing a murderer.' She refused to let Gropius get close to the baby, standing defensively in front of the swaddling table where the infant lay and, after his entreaties, only allowing him to view little Manon from across the room. Twenty years later Gropius was still remembering that scene of Alma like a lioness defending her cub from somebody determined to wrest it from her. As Alma herself later explained it, 'I would not let him share possession of the child because my fears had come true – because my feelings for him had given way to a twilight relationship.' Sustaining a

Gropius, Alma and their daughter Manon, born on 5 October 1916.

relationship at long distance was alien to her nature. The marriage to
Gropius was over almost as soon as it had begun.

Gropius returned to Vienna for the christening at Christmas 1916.
He and Alma were temporarily reconciled. Alma, originally Catholic, had converted to Protestantism like her husband and the baptism
was held in Vienna's main Evangelical Church. Their small daughter
was now named Alma Manon Anna Justine Caroline Gropius. In the
family she was known as Mutzi, a diminutive from *mutzig*, meaning
small and cat-like. Gropius's stepdaughter Anna was a godmother, as
were both his and Alma's mothers, although Gropius's own family was
not represented at the christening itself. There were masses of white

lilies, candlelight, a Christmas tree, and Alma herself had dressed in white.

Once again, Gropius's leave was only brief and it was three months before he saw Manon again, reporting to his mother with delight: 'she is lying next to me and sings endless songs, like a little twittering bird. She is a cheerful child and full of vivacity. And very pretty though she looks so very much like me.' Gropius had a particular affinity for children and his relationship with Manon was to be a mixture of anguish, the agonies of separation, and an exceptional *tendresse*.

In his new appointment as regimental adjutant Gropius's responsibilities were onerous. He was shifted to the Somme, to other western battlefields and then to Namur on the Meuse in Belgium, now a designated headquarters of military communications. Here he was appointed as instructor in a communications training school for generals and other top military personnel. He and his team were initially billeted in an abandoned castle near Namur. The interior of Château Flaurinne had been devastated by marauding soldiers but the exterior, with its gardens and terraces still intact, seemed to Gropius the most beautiful and impressive architectural ensemble that he had ever seen. But by summer 1917 conditions were worsening and Gropius was now reduced to sleeping in a local peasant's house and living on 'turnips and so-called liverwurst'. War was wearing on the nerves. He felt a real desperation. 'Surely', he wrote, 'there *has* to be an end of it all this year.'

Gropius's own work in integrating military communications was varied. Mainly he was running a dog training school, perfecting the uses of canine message carriers in battle. Alma was caustic about the dog training, telling him that she was 'totally unable' to reconcile herself with the idea of seeing him in such an unworthy position: 'It is too repulsive for you – and for me.' She maintained that dogs were unclean animals and was especially revolted by the thought of Gropius holding their mouths open with his fingers and looking down into them. She repeatedly reminded him that Alma Mahler's husband had to be 'first class'.

Of course Alma was most unjust to Gropius, whose responsibilities, besides dog training, covered the co-ordination of all forms of military

communication: homing pigeons, signal throwers, light signal appara-
tus. It was an assignment well suited to his technological interests and
the range and precision of his mind. As he boasted to his mother in
November 1917, writing from the Somme: 'My school has become a
very big thing and we have to stand up to the critique of the whole army
from West, South and East.'

Gropius returned to Vienna to spend Christmas 1917. He arrived
from Italy, where he had been training Austrian soldiers in the use of
dogs as message carriers. This was not an easy visit. Gropius himself was
battle-worn and nervy. He was still making jealous scenes about Kokoschka, demanding that Alma should give away the *Mona Lisa* portrait,
all of his drawings and the six remaining fans. She presented the portrait
and drawings to the museum founded in Hagen by Gropius's patron Karl
Ernst Osthaus, but she was too attached to the deeply meaningful fans
to part with them. And in the end she also took Kokoschka's enigmatic
portrait back.

Gropius's lingering resentment of Kokoschka in fact was out of date.
Alma now had a new love, Franz Werfel, the Austrian–Bohemian poet
and playwright, whom she met in November 1917. There had been a
strange early intimation of Werfel the summer before, on the day after
her marriage to Gropius. Before he returned to the front Alma went
with him to a military equipment supplier, where she waited impatiently while he carefully selected the leather for a new pair of riding
boots. 'The strong odour of Russian leather numbed my senses,' Alma
recalled. 'I fled into the open, to the cab we had waiting outside. Then
it happened that I saw a book peddler's cart, bought a magazine, and
opened it to the poem "Man Aware" by Franz Werfel.' Looking back at
this episode she recognised Werfel as her destiny. Alma, as we have
seen, had a convenient belief in fate.

When they met in her Elisabethstrasse salon, introduced by the esoteric writer and editor Franz Blei, Alma was already familiar with Werfel's poetry. Indeed she had set one of his poems, 'Der Erkennende', to
music. She was immediately impressed by the unpredictable and charismatic Werfel. Werfel was then twenty-six, eleven years her junior. He

had been born in Prague, then part of the Austro-Hungarian empire. He had served in the army, taking part in the Austrian advance in Italy before being sent to the Russian front. He was now back in Vienna, attached intermittently to the Army Press section but with time on his hands for meeting his fellow iconoclasts in cafes and paying court to Alma. He knew and loved Mahler's music. He also impressed Alma by reading Arnold Schoenberg's *Die Jakobsleiter* (*Jacob's Ladder*) to her with full dramatic effect, telling her, 'I know the entire conflict of this man. He is a Jew – the Jew who suffers from himself.'

Werfel himself was of course Jewish. It was Alma who described him in her diary as 'a bowlegged, fat Jew with thick lips and floating slit eyes!' In that sense he was the very opposite of Gropius, once her Aryan ideal and the father of their little daughter Manon, about whom Alma had once written that everything good about herself and Gropius, their supremely Aryan characteristics, had come together in this sacred child. But Alma was infinitely changeable. She had now moved away from worship of the Aryan into a state of besottedness with Werfel. And one has to remember Gustav Mahler had been a Jew as well, unimposing in physique.

Alma and Gropius struggled uneasily through Christmas. His presence was getting badly on her nerves. There was a curious evening which Werfel, Blei, Gropius and Alma spent together, playing and singing from *Meistersinger* and Charpentier's *Louise*. Werfel recited his poem 'Der Feind'. When a blizzard descended Werfel and Blei had to stay the night, sleeping on two sofas covered in rugs. Alma, now so preoccupied with Werfel, did her best to hide it, smiling at her brightest when the time arrived for Gropius to rejoin his regiment on 29 December 1917. He left in the early morning. Alma was looking forward to attending that evening's concert of Mahler's *Das Lied von der Erde*.

To Alma's horror Gropius returned suddenly, ringing the bell violently. He had missed his train. He now had to stay in Vienna for another day. This was the moment, confessed Alma in her diary, at which she reached the full realisation that her love for Gropius was now completely over, replaced by something approaching 'a bored loathing'. As she and Anna travelled to the concert in a horse-drawn carriage, Gropius walked along beside them, begging Alma to take him to the concert. But she said she had no ticket for him. Gropius went home alone.

When he finally left Vienna the next day he sent Alma a telegram as he crossed the border from Austria into Germany. It took the form of a quotation from a poem by Werfel. 'Splinter the ice in your features,' it said.

Gropius had now been diverted to the battle lines between Soissons and Rheims in central France. He was feeling appallingly depressed by his return to 'the grey world' of the war zones, conscious of becoming 'mentally reduced'. He told his mother that his nerves were getting worse. He embarked on a bitter outburst against the iniquities of wartime economics, rampageous inflation and especially the profiteerings of the Jews:

We can fight battles as much as we want to but the weaklings and the pigs at home will destroy everything we achieved. The Jews, this poison which I begin to hate more and more, are destroying us. Social democracy, materialism, capitalism, profiteering – everything is their work and we are guilty that we have let them so dominate our world. They are the devil, the negative element.

This is a surprisingly virulent attack from a man whose later views were far from being anti-Semitic. Many of Gropius's closest friends and colleagues at the Bauhaus would in fact be Jews. But it has to be remembered that such anti-Semitic feeling was then common in Gropius's upper-bourgeois Berlin milieu, sharpened by the exigencies of war. Were these the signs of Gropius's now rising suspicions and resentment of Franz Werfel, who ostentatiously embraced his own Jewish inheritance?

He did not allow himself to feel enthusiastic when Alma informed him she was pregnant early on in 1918. He couldn't yet feel any joy, he told his mother, about the arrival of another baby in such desolate wartime conditions. Manon Gropius responded generously, inviting Alma to Berlin to see her. But Alma, the salon hostess, was too busy with her social plans.

Through late spring and early summer Gropius began feeling relatively optimistic about the progress of the war. As observation officer he had taken part in the entire battle of Oise and then returned to base to hear reports of German success at Arras. Having previously felt that his career as an artist was doomed and that he would be 'entirely forgotten by the world', he now envisaged an eventual resurfacing as the director of a school, 'one where I myself give the direction', a school that would be run 'in a contemporary spirit'. Here in the midst of battle a glimmer of the future Bauhaus was beginning.

In May 1918 Gropius was elated by his experiences in the battle of the Marne. 'I was in the middle of it right from the beginning. Everything turned out so well as we couldn't have dreamed it. I was in front of the thousands of cannons and the night of the 27th was indescribable . . . I am well, though I do not have the nerves of 1914. Sleep is luxury, we eat day or night whenever possible.' He was wounded again and hospitalised, receiving the insignia for wounds received in combat. But this was a time of fake optimism. For the German fighting forces the summer of 1918 was the beginning of the end.

Alma's latest pregnancy was now advancing. From the military hospital in Vienna Gropius had been able to visit Alma and Manon; they had also managed short encounters in Berlin. Gropius was becoming increasingly anxious about further family responsibilities, particularly worried about family finances with Vienna now in the hands of the black market. He was driven to rent out his own Berlin apartment. He could not bear the thought of being dependent on Alma and the money that Gustav Mahler had bequeathed.

In June 1918 Gropius was recalled to the Soissons–Rheims front line. Almost straight after rejoining the forces he was buried alive in the collapse of a so-called German stronghold. It was a terrifying experience. He was the only one of his companions to survive once a flue allowed a little flow of air down to the rubble. He lay trapped there under stones and timber for three days, shouting for help until finally the German troops combing the battlefield for signs of survivors rescued him. He was taken to a field hospital where his injuries were treated, and then moved, at his request, to a military hospital near the Mahler House at Breitenstein where Alma was now staying, waiting for what had already been predicted to be a difficult birth.

Alma and Franz Werfel had been lovers since Gropius's uneasy Christmas visit to Vienna. Now in July 1918 Werfel went to visit Alma in the Semmering, where she was ensconced with Anna and the baby Manon. As he admitted in his diary, he failed to control himself when they made love. As he wrote, 'I did not spare her.' Alma reiterated, 'Werfel and I lived our intoxication further and unfortunately paid very little attention to the unborn child inside me. We carried on with total thoughtlessness in our drunken stupor.' The result was that during the night of 27/28 July Alma haemorrhaged badly. She woke up, turned on the light and found that she was standing in a pool of blood. Anna hurried into Breitenstein to send Gropius the news. An alarmed and guilty Werfel left the station just as Gropius arrived on an emergency military train from Vienna, accompanied by a gynaecological specialist.

Her condition was alarming. It was recommended that Alma should be moved to Vienna. Gropius, the midwife and the doctor carefully transported the fragile, bleeding Alma, who had to be carried lying head down on a cart which seemed more like a bier. They travelled on by train, first in a normal railway carriage, but since Alma needed to lie down she was moved into a cattle wagon, a *Leichenwagen*, such as was used to transport corpses in the war. When they finally arrived at the Loew Sanatorium, the very hospital where Gustav Mahler had died, the baby was induced. From the beginning this was a sickly child.

Gropius heroically stayed by Alma's side, his presence only serving to increase her guilt. 'She has a great magnificent heart', he told his mother, 'and it is no accident that people love her so much. She deserves it.' At the time he did not seem to register what was clear to Werfel when he saw the baby just a few days later. Quite unmistakeably this was not an Aryan but a Jewish boy.

The baby was born on 2 August 1918. On 26 August Gropius discovered the truth by overhearing a telephone conversation in the morning between Alma and Werfel in which they called each other by their first names. He had come into the room and heard her call him Franz. Gropius 'crumpled as though struck by lightning'. Although he had registered Alma and Werfel's mutual attraction, he clearly had not realised the full extent of it.

That same afternoon Gropius called to see Werfel, who was asleep and did not hear him knock. Gropius left him an extraordinary message: 'I am here to love you with all the strength at my command. Spare Alma! The worst might happen. The excitement, the milk – if our child should die!' Werfel was overcome by his nobility. Certainly the response was generous, with Gropius accepting the paternal role. But it was also confrontational. As we have seen before in his relations with Mahler, Gropius liked to get the upper hand in any emotional situation.

In late October Alma and Gropius made love again, apparently 'without the least sensation' on her part. She claimed that she gave herself to him out of sympathy and that she came to view this as a mortal sin. In early November 1918 Gropius sent Alma a letter asking her to give him custody of their daughter Manon. He proposed that Alma herself should live with Werfel, Anna and the now seriously ailing baby Martin. This suggestion so upset her that she broke down and cried all day.

Gropius and Werfel together went to see her. She announced she had decided to end her relations with them both and go her own way, a single parent in Vienna leading a completely independent life. In a state of high emotion Gropius fell down on his knees to ask Alma's forgiveness for the clearly impossible demands he had been making. Werfel said 'a few thoughtful, unpretentious words' to counteract the melodrama of the situation.

Meanwhile, the First World War was coming to its end. The United States had now become involved and American troops had reinforced the Allies. The finale came suddenly on 28 and 29 October, when the German generals admitted defeat, asking for an armistice. Kaiser Wilhelm II abdicated on 9 November and the Sozialdemokratische Partei (Social Democratic Party) declared a republic, with Friedrich Ebert as its provisional chancellor. Germany, like Gropius's domestic life, was in turmoil. What would be the aftermath?

6

Bauhaus Weimar and Lily Hildebrandt
1919–1920

Revolution started to break out in many German cities in the winter of 1918–19, the result of increasing social tensions following the ending of the war. Berlin saw a general strike and an attempted communist revolutionary coup, the so-called Spartacist Uprising. This was brutally suppressed by a mercenary army of anti-communist ex-soldiers assembled by the government. The leading Spartacists Karl Liebknecht and Rosa Luxemburg were imprisoned and then murdered.

Gropius was all too conscious of the incipient violence. Released from military service on 18 November, he was swept up into the mood of desperation of the time. His despair at the chaos and destruction of his country galvanised him into action. He was later to describe how 'as in a flash of lightning' it dawned on him that 'the old stuff was out'. In that sense Gropius's pre-eminent achievement – the concept of the Bauhaus – evolved from the ruins of the First World War.

'I am here to participate in the revolution,' he wrote to Osthaus from Berlin on 23 December. 'The mood is tense here, and we artists have to strike while the iron is hot.' Following the November revolution of 1918 he had been involved in the highly political Novembergruppe, an offshoot of the avant-garde magazine and art gallery Der Sturm, formed with the aim of creating a new progressive cultural climate. Its members included the artists Gerhard Marcks and Lyonel Feininger and the architects Erich Mendelsohn, Hans Poelzig, Mies van der Rohe and Bruno Taut. In Berlin Gropius joined an associated group, the Arbeitsrat für Kunst, the Work Council for Art, a radical collective of progressive architects, painters and sculptors of which he was soon elected chairman. The Arbeitsrat put a particular emphasis on building houses for the people, which would create new democratic, life-enhancing

possibilities. The mood within the Arbeitsrat was emotional, supportive. Gropius told his mother that 'all come to the meetings and that is
incredibly beautiful and animating . . . This is the type of life I have
always had in mind, but the cleansing effect of the war was necessary
for it.'

His connections with the Arbeitsrat gave Gropius the impetus to
pursue the idea he claimed to have been turning over in his head for
many years. This was the idealistic concept of the Bauhaus, a modern
version of the medieval stonemasons' guild, the *Bauhütte*. It would be
a collaborative group of artists of all disciplines united in constructing
a new and better world.

His relations with his fellow artists in the Arbeitsrat gave Gropius
hope and consolation at a time when his personal life was in total disarray. In theory he and Alma were still together, and indeed under the
law they were still married. Gropius had returned to Berlin 'to build us
a new life', wrote Alma in her memoirs. But back in Vienna she was
still intermittently with Werfel and increasingly anxious over their son
Martin, born so prematurely. 'The little boy is very large and strong
but the head has grown too fast and he is mentally retarded,' Alma
wrote to Manon Gropius. Martin suffered from a severe dropsy of the
brain, which caused his head to swell alarmingly. As far as his mother
was concerned Gropius kept up the pretence that the now dangerously
malformed child was his own. Werfel's son Martin had been christened
Martin Johannes Gropius. Meanwhile, to his anguish Gropius's own little daughter Manon was with Alma in Vienna, far away.

Far from finding the means in Berlin of providing for his complicated family, his architectural work had now totally dried up. In
December 1918 he told Karl Ernst Osthaus how for the past fortnight he had been 'storming through Berlin, looking for some job or
another', but without success. 'After 4½ years most of the footprints
one left behind have been wiped away.' His frustration and anger
spilled out in diatribes against the outdated bourgeois values of his
own extended Gropius family. Even his once valued patron Uncle
Erich came under fire. He had gone to Matzdorf for his uncle's funeral

and returned feeling completely alienated by his inward-looking Pomeranian relatives: 'They are excessive in their country landowners' resentments, obstinately prejudiced and full of arrogant political megalomania, without ever looking at their own faults. They see only what is coming down, but not what is growing up.' This was the bourgeois complacency and blindness which Gropius would have to contend with as he established the Bauhaus.

Early in 1919 Gropius reopened negotiations over his future role at the Weimar Kunstgewerbeschule, the arts and crafts school, which had been suspended through the war. He had originally been approached to be director of the Kunstgewerbeschule only, not of the Hochschule für Bildende Kunst, the Weimar academy of art. 'But', as Gropius recollected later, 'I wanted both, suggested that to the Provisional Government, and got the assignment of Director of both Institutes.' The experience of war and its bitter aftermath had evidently sharpened his ambition.

His appointment started from 1 April 1919. Gropius now, at the age of thirty-five, had a grand reformist concept for his institution. This was to be an art school in which emphasis was placed not on easel art or 'salon art', as Gropius termed it, the self-regarding art of a bourgeois elite, but on a truly democratic art allied to architecture, art for the people in which everyone could share. The Bauhaus Manifesto and Programme radiates the vigour and conviction of his vision:

The ultimate aim of all creative activity is the building!

The decoration of buildings was once the noblest function of the fine arts, and the fine arts were indispensable to great architecture. Today they exist in complacent isolation, and can only be rescued from it by the conscious co-operation and collaboration of all craftsmen. Architects, painters and sculptors must once again come to know and comprehend the composite character of a building both as an entity and in terms of its various parts. Then their work will be filled with the true architectonic spirit which, as 'salon art', it has lost.

Gropius's emphasis in his ideas for the Bauhaus was on a literal process of rebuilding. The slow process of craft became a rallying point in his radical vision of a new understanding of materials in terms of their properties and their potential. This would be a species of atonement for the widespread outrages of an increasingly mechanised form of warfare:

Architects, sculptors, painters, we all must return to the crafts! For art is not a 'profession'. There is no essential difference between the artist and the craftsman. The artist is an exalted craftsman. In rare moments of inspiration, transcending the consciousness of his will, the grace of heaven may cause his work to blossom into art. But proficiency in a craft is essential to every artist. Therein lies the prime source of creative imagination. Let us then create a new guild of craftsmen without the class distinctions that raise an arrogant barrier between craftsman and artist! Together let us desire, conceive, and create the new structure of the future, which will one day rise toward heaven from the hands of a million workers like the crystal symbol of a new faith.

The four-page leaflet which contained this rousing manifesto had a woodcut on the title page (see Plate 7), the work of Lyonel Feininger, one of Gropius's new staff appointments to the school. The woodcut illustrates the skyward-pointing architecture of the great cathedral, its spires symbolising the hopes and aspirations of the new regime.

The choice of Feininger's Expressionist image of the great cathedral had not been accidental. Gropius was always more of a romantic than he superficially appeared. He shared the fascination felt by his fellow members of the utopian-socialist Arbeitsrat für Kunst, in particular by Bruno Taut and Adolf Behne, for the concept of the abstract inspirational glass building, of which the tower of the medieval Gothic cathedral stood as the ultimate example. Taut had designed a wondrous Glass Pavilion for the 1914 Deutscher Werkbund exhibition. Later, in blatant opposition to the war, he envisaged a huge garden city for three million inhabitants, with a 'City Crown' crystal building in the centre, consisting of just one symbolic glass room.

Ideas of such spiritually powerful glass buildings had been promulgated by Der Sturm, the revolutionary Berlin gallery and publishing house with which Gropius was closely connected. Der Sturm's publication of the futuristic novelist Paul Scheerbart's book *Glasarchitektur* in 1914 had a profound effect on Gropius and his visually radical Arbeitsrat contemporaries. As Scheerbart himself expressed it so succinctly:

> Glass brings in the new Age:
> Brick-culture does us nothing but harm.

We can see the fascination with *Glasarchitektur* in Gropius's own romantic pairing of glass turrets placed at the entrance to the model factory for the Cologne Werkbund exhibition and, just a little later, in his competition entry for the design of the *Chicago Tribune* Tower. Certainly his ambitious plans for the Bauhaus, as expressed to the Weimar theatre director Ernst Hardt, show Gropius in an architecturally visionary mood: 'I imagine Weimar building a huge estate around the Belvedere hill with a centre of public buildings, theatres, a concert hall and, as a final aim, a religious building; annually in the summer great popular festivals will be held there.' Now at last in post-war Germany he saw himself as laying 'the foundation stone of a republic of intellects'.

In many ways Weimar seemed the ideal place for such a venture. This historic city 150 miles to the south-west of Berlin clung to the memory of its intellectual past to such an extent that it was sometimes called 'the German Athens'. Goethe, Schiller and Nietzsche had been residents, and indeed Nietzsche's imperious sister Elisabeth Förster-Nietzsche was still living in Weimar, tending to behave as if she owned the city. She had commissioned Henry van de Velde to design and furnish the Nietzsche Archive she established in the ground floor of the house in which her brother died.

By the time that Gropius arrived there Weimar had acquired a new identity. In January 1919, after Germany had been declared a republic, elections for a new Republican National Constitutional Government took place, and from the autumn of that year Weimar became the official seat of the German government and capital of the state of Thuringia. The Bauhaus, officially known as the 'Staatliches Bauhaus in Weimar', came under the jurisdiction of the Thuringian Ministry of Education. Gropius was paid a salary of ten thousand marks and provided with a rent-free studio and the possibility of interesting architectural commissions from the state. At this early stage he was already dreaming of a total Bauhaus settlement in the environs of Weimar. He envisaged a new kind of art school, an experimental community of artists free of the old academic hierarchies. Gropius declined the title of Professor on ideological grounds.

In setting up the Bauhaus Gropius was virtually starting from scratch. The new school formed by the amalgamation of the original Kunstgewerbeschule with the Hochschule occupied the two adjacent Weimar buildings Henry van de Velde had originally designed. The Hochschule had continued to operate in wartime but the Kunstgewerbeschule building, used as a reserve military hospital, was now in a desolate state, with no teaching equipment. The building had been looted during the war and the workshops emptied out of tools. Hardly a planing bench remained. Though Gropius inherited some of the teaching staff from the academy, these were artists rooted in the academic tradition and inimical to his new ideas.

His priority was now to recruit staff who combined a modern artistic sensibility with an underlying respect for craftsmanship. These new Bauhaus teachers were to be known as 'Masters' rather than 'Professors', emphasising the element of workshop practicality Gropius saw as crucial to the role. To begin with he drew on his close connections in the Berlin Expressionist circles of Der Sturm and the Arbeitsrat für Kunst. Gropius's first appointments were of Gerhard Marcks, the sculptor who had made reliefs in terracotta for the 1914 Werkbund factory building, and Lyonel Feininger, whose woodcut of the crystalline cathedral on the cover of the Bauhaus Manifesto was soon popularly known as 'the Cathedral of Socialism'.

Marcks was appointed Master of Form in the pottery workshop and Feininger Master of Form in the print workshop. Feininger, an American born in New York who had moved to Germany to study art, had been recruited by Gropius in Berlin, travelling with him to Weimar on the train on 18 May 1919, the date that Feininger was always to remember as 'the beginning of the finest adventure' in his artistic career. Every year for the next thirty-seven years Feininger sent Gropius a commemorative letter remembering 'that day full of wonder and enchantment'. That journey had marked 'the decisive turning point' in his so far quiet, rather solitary artistic life: 'something unforgettable, quite amazing to contemplate: Weimar – *das Bauhaus*'. Gropius had a remarkable capacity to inspire loyalty even among those whose artistic outlook did not totally coincide with his.

To start with, the organisation of the Bauhaus verged on the chaotic. There was no possibility of regular systematic instruction as teachers and students were feeling their way. But things began to change with Gropius's appointment of Johannes Itten, the intellectually charismatic figure who soon became established as the most influential of the Bauhaus Masters, with his own devoted following. Itten, initially appointed Master of Form in the stained-glass and cabinet workshops, took the initiative in evolving the Preliminary Course, the *Vorkurs*, attended by all students entering the Bauhaus. The course not only gave training in basic manual skills but raised awareness of colour, form, texture, composition, the properties of different materials, the whole spectrum of artistic sensibility. This was the foundation course eventually adopted in one form or another by art schools all over the world.

The mystically minded Swiss abstract painter Itten was a former elementary school teacher who had studied colour theory with Adolf Hölzel in Stuttgart before opening his own private art school in Vienna in 1916. In Vienna he became a protégé of Alma's, who admired Itten's 'finely modelled face' and his 'eloquent, somewhat Egyptian mouth', as well as his intense profundity of thought. Itten had become attached to Alma's salon and indeed was present at her very first meeting with Franz Werfel. She later claimed that there had been 'an oddly fraternal' and (for once) 'unerotic bond' between herself and Itten. It was Alma who introduced Gropius to him. With his interest in psychoanalysis and his close involvement in Franz Cižek's work on the creative education of children, Itten brought to the Bauhaus an important element of Viennese thinking of the time.

The Bauhaus year was divided into two academic terms: a summer semester running from April to June and a winter semester from October to March, with a three-month summer recess. The first summer semester had been relatively disorganised and tentative; Gropius was anxiously preoccupied with trying to establish a viable financial basis for the Bauhaus. It was autumn 1919 before the school started to get properly into its stride with a student enrolment of 119 men and 126 women, the highest it would ever be.

Where did these students come from? According to Helmut von Erffa, one of the early arrivals at the Bauhaus, Gropius's Manifesto was a call to action, rallying 'young men and women from all walks of life, from all over Germany and even a few from abroad'. A contingent of students had followed Itten from Vienna. Of the rest, some were art students dissatisfied with conventional academic teaching methods, others were seriously interested in the experimental approach to creative education which had been developed by Friedrich Fröbel in Germany, pioneer of imaginative learning through play, as well as by Cižek in Vienna. Some had only recently been discharged from the army, arriving at the Bauhaus still in their old uniforms and with shaven heads. Others of course, as von Erffa reminds us, 'were just dreamers, poets and mystics who were attracted by the idealistic and, in some ways, otherworldly atmosphere of group endeavour'. Some of the people arriving at the Bauhaus struck one observer as a horde of seekers from the pages of a Dostoevsky novel.

This was a time of social disruption in which the *Wandervogel* movement flourished and self-styled apostles were trekking through the countryside gathering support among the disaffected young. One of these bearded, black-robed prophets, Louis Haeusser, arrived at the Bauhaus searching for recruits, and some of the students disappeared to join him. Gropius posted a warning on the noticeboard that anybody leaving in mid-term would not be readmitted to the school.

At this early period of creating the Bauhaus Gropius was ubiquitous. He interviewed prospective students himself. He gave an introductory talk to new students at the start of every term, explaining the ideas that had brought the Bauhaus into being and enthusing them about their work programme ahead. Anni Albers, a student from 1922, remembered all her life the experience of 'a gradual condensation', during the

Gropius in the early
Bauhaus period in Weimar,
1921.

hour that Gropius spoke, 'of our hoping and musing into a focal point, into a meaning, into some distant, stable objective. It was an experience that meant purpose and direction from then on.'

Gropius would go out walking with the students. He ate democratically in the canteen. He took part in their mind-expanding evening entertainments, in which Gerhard Marcks the sculptor might read a story by Heinrich von Kleist and Gropius an extract from Karl Scheffler's *Das Gesims* (*The Cornice*), exploring the spiritual significance of the building arts. At the first Bauhaus Christmas, in 1919, Gropius took a central role in the great feasting organised for staff and students. He carried round the food himself, presenting it symbolically to each guest individually. To one of the participants, the weaver Gunta Stölzl, it seemed like the biblical washing of the feet.

Alma had agreed to take their daughter Manon to visit Gropius twice a year. After multiple excuses she and Manon arrived in Berlin in the middle of May 1919, having made a protracted train journey from Vienna to Berlin through the newly formed nation of Czechoslovakia. In Berlin she heard the not unexpected news that little Martin had died in the clinic in Vienna where he had been receiving care for the past few months. The effects of his congenital disease had left no hope. It was Gropius who announced Martin's death to Alma, who seemed virtually unaffected by it. 'If only I had died instead,' he said.

Martin's father Werfel wanted Alma to return to Vienna, but instead she now agreed to travel back to Weimar with Gropius. This was her first visit to the Bauhaus and what she called her husband's 'grandiose plan for a new form of art education'. Prejudiced against his vision of a technological future as she was, even Alma could not fail to be impressed by the scope and ambition of his Bauhaus schemes. As she was later to admit, 'There was a new artistic courage abroad in those days, a soaring passionate faith. I noticed it even in Gropius, whose own work was alien to me, whose charts and graphs and calculations left me baffled.'

The responses of the Bauhaus towards Alma were mixed. In late May a Weimar cultural grandee, Richard Klemm, a professor of the former academy of art, held a tea party to welcome Gropius and Alma, as well as new staff members of the Bauhaus, among them Lyonel Feininger, who reported back favourably in a letter to his wife: 'In him and her we are facing two completely free, honest, exceptionally broad-minded human beings who don't accept inhibitions, characteristics of great rarity in this country.' But there were other more critical reports of a spoilt, demanding woman who was visibly bored in an environment she found unsympathetic. Many of the Bauhaus students resented Frau Gropius with her sophisticated Viennese manner, who all too clearly considered them as outré and unkempt.

Alma's first visit to the Bauhaus was marred by constant quarrels over Manon, now aged two and a half. Alma wanted to leave Gropius at any cost but that of giving up her daughter. On the day that Alma fainted from all the pent-up anguish Gropius finally sent a telegram to Werfel asking him to meet her in Dresden and take her back to Vienna to recover. She had now become abusive towards Gropius, vilifying him in her diary: 'What do I care about the elegant gentleman with the brightly coloured spats who just happens to be married to me?' She piled on the insults: 'I am not a Gropius and so I cannot call myself Gropius either. My name is Mahler for all eternity.' Finally, in July 1919, Gropius lost patience and wrote to Alma proposing a divorce.

He sent her legal documents to be signed, partly blaming Werfel. 'Your splendid nature', he told Alma, 'has been made to disintegrate under Jewish persuasion which overestimates the word and its momentary truth. But you will return to your Aryan origin and then you will understand me and you will search for me in your memory.' He also upbraided Alma herself, saying: 'This is your tragedy which brought great harm to us and which forces you again and again into new passions while the old ones are not yet exhausted.' For her, feeling 'extends only to the short time of passion and sexual fervour'. At first Alma demurred, making the preposterous suggestion that she should spend half the year with Werfel and the other half with Gropius. But she finally gave in and negotiations for the terms of the divorce began.

Alma's own analysis of the basic reasons for the breakdown of the marriage was just a little different from Gropius's. She accepted that her husband had many ideal assets, being strikingly handsome, a highly gifted artist, racially speaking a man of Alma's kind. They even had common relatives in Hamburg. So 'was it Lady Music, not his element', Alma now asked herself in her private diary, which had driven them apart? 'Or was it my indifference to his mission, my lack of interest in his architectural and human goals?'

Certainly Alma's initial enthusiasm for Gropius's interests and talents had dwindled over time. Her Viennese family background was rooted in the fine and decorative arts, and Gropius's workshop philosophy as it now developed at the Bauhaus was fundamentally alien to her. She maintained that in 'their impassioned modernism' the Bauhaus people went too far. Her next visit to Weimar, another long-delayed one, took place from late February to mid-March 1920. Since Gropius's apartment was still being completed she and Manon at first stayed at the Hotel Elephant in the town. This was another problematic visit, with continuing rows over sharing custody of Manon, the tensions being exacerbated by the nationwide general strike called on 13 March in response to the Kapp Putsch, an attempted right-wing coup which had started in Berlin, named after one of its leaders, Wolfgang Kapp and Walther von Lüttwitz. The unrest had now spread to other cities.

Alma and Manon watched from the hotel window as the opposing forces took up positions just below them in the market square. 'Workers spat on the helmeted, motionless young men of the Kapp forces, and the mob howled.' The account that Alma gives of it shows her quite clearly on the side of the Kapp militia.

On 21 March, by which time they had moved into Gropius's still unfinished flat in Empress-Augusta-Strasse 32, they watched the funeral for the nine local Weimar workmen who had been shot and killed in the fighting. 'An endless procession, carrying banners with inscriptions such as "Remember Liebknecht! Remember Rosa Lux-emburg!" now passed by.' Many Bauhaus staff and students had joined in the procession; some of the banners had in fact been assembled in the Bauhaus workshops. Gropius later regretted that he had let Alma persuade him not to join in the procession. He was always nervous about jeopardising the position of the Bauhaus by taking an active part in local politics. But he was to make amends later when he won the competition held for Weimar artists to design a memorial to the workers who died in the Kapp Putsch (see Plate 10).

By the spring of 1920 it was obvious that not only were Alma and Gropius opposed aesthetically, they were at odds politically too. But were these the only causes of their final estrangement? Or was there something more? Were they a sexual mismatch too? As with Koko-schka, Alma's relations with Werfel were based on a certain kind of sexual fantasy, in this case a fixation with cripples. She had poured out in her diary in September 1919:

Franz first admitted his perversities to me and then very skilfully deployed them as phobias. I was so excited I couldn't sleep last night. I kept seeing cripples and him, and intoxicated myself on them. A one-legged person – lying down. He and I. I as a spectator, boundlessly excited, so powerfully that I had to lay a hand on myself. Now I am lying down and envisioning myself in such a situation.

In May 1920, still awaiting the divorce, she returned to Weimar to fetch Manon, who had been staying with her father. Alma dismayed Gropius by confessing what he called the 'horribly dissolute trait' she had acquired. Writing in her diary Alma now implies that Gropius's consternation gave her second thoughts: 'My imagination, out of love for Franz, is full of the most perverse images and an addiction to crippling. In the happiest moments I have blended in more and more ugly ideas that excited him. I love him and that is why I will guide him back, not allow myself to be pulled down. Thank you, Walter – thank you!' Possibly for Gropius Alma's confessions of collusion in Werfel's 'addiction to crippling' were the final straw.

By this time the terms of the divorce settlement had been agreed. Gropius accepted the role of guilty party, going to a hotel room with a prostitute, with detectives in attendance to provide the evidence. On 11 October 1920 Gropius's marriage was at an end, custody of Manon being finally awarded to Alma. In spite of his anguish at surrendering his daughter, maybe in a sense Gropius felt relieved by the finality of this. He had written in all honesty to Alma, 'I long for a companion who loves me and my work.'

Gropius now embarked on a consoling new relationship. His passionate liaison with Lily Hildebrandt, which had started in the autumn of 1919, no doubt encouraged him to co-operate with Alma's demands for the divorce. Lily was five years younger than Gropius, an artist of versatility and talent. Photographs show her as vivid, graceful and intense. She was then living in Stuttgart with her husband, art and architecture critic Hans Hildebrandt. She and Gropius had met at the Stuttgart convention of the Deutscher Werkbund. Because of the distance separating them their snatched encounters were boosted by constant letters, telephone calls and telegrams. There are more than 130 communications from Gropius to Lily dating from 1919 to 1922 now in the Bauhaus Archive, and it is through this correspondence that we get the clearest picture of Gropius at the Bauhaus in those first formative years.

Lily Hildebrandt with fellow students of Adolf Hölzel, Dachau, c.1919.

Lily was Jewish, born Lily Uhlmann. She had studied painting at Adolf Meyer's private art school in Berlin, and had then been a student of Johannes Itten's mentor Adolf Hölzel in Dachau. Lily had connections with the Blaue Reiter association of abstract-leaning Expressionist painters founded in Munich by Wassily Kandinsky and Franz Marc. By the time she met Gropius she had begun to develop techniques of *Hinterglasmalerei*, reverse painting on glass. Lily also illustrated children's books. She and Hans had a son, Rainer, born in 1914, but Lily was always a free spirit in her attitude to marriage. As Rainer said later, his mother was not cut out to be faithful in the conventional sense. 'She did not want to go to heaven, she said, it would be too boring.' She could rely on meeting her best friends in hell. According to Rainer, Hans too had his diversions: '"I was not the only one for him, but always the one," said my mother.' Gropius, typically, determined from the start to make friends with Lily's husband, who struck him as a free, unbourgeois person. Hans Hildebrandt became a respected commentator on Walter Gropius's work.

The first assignation between Gropius and Lily took place on 21 October 1919 in Frankfurt, Gropius travelling south from Berlin. He had written to Lily wild with excitement, saying he had booked rooms both at the Frankfurter Hof hotel and at the Carlton. Lily, who knew Frankfurt better than he did, was to choose the one she liked best. He ridiculed her idea that she should pretend to be his sister: 'Nobody will believe that your little nose belongs in the same family as my monster nose.' Gropius instructed Lily to meet him from the train, and then he imagined how impatiently they would 'rush into each other'. 'Darling,' he tells Lily, 'my whole warmth shall caress you. My hands search for the sweet naked skin, the ravishing young limbs which are longing for me . . . Put a flower between your lovely thighs when you are hot from thoughts of me and send it to me in a letter.' In the aftermath of his domestic rows and recriminations with Alma this new affair with Lily Hildebrandt gave Gropius a glorious sense of irresponsibility.

He loved the freedom of it, the *mouvementé* quality. 'Our union', he told Lily, 'is not focused on peace and rest – only on movement and encounter. Two meteors kiss each other in the universe.' In Gropius's first love affair of this new period he glories in a conscious lack of commitment, adopting the self-image of the wandering star. 'My darling, my glittering darling', he calls Lily. 'Lilychen my darling', 'My Lily-cat'. He sends her absurdly ardent letters signed '*dein W*'. 'I have a great longing for you this morning. Am so thirsty for tenderness as I haven't been for a long time. I would like to penetrate you with the sword of love – and enveloped by your sweet body and we should stay this way for hours not knowing where the *I* ceases and the *you* begins.' He revels in exchanges of domestic detail: 'Your hair lotion hasn't arrived yet, my darling, otherwise I would have thanked you for it.' He ends this letter to Lily 'I kiss your sanctuaries'.

After the loneliness and turmoil of the war years and almost a decade of embattlement with Alma, Gropius looks at Lily with 'enchanted eyes'. He has an almost mystical vision of her soul standing before him 'in sweet nakedness', telling her, 'I see you as if you were made of glass and behind you float the mists of multicoloured sensibilities.' It is an artist's image. Gropius could have been visualising Lily's own abstract compositions in stained glass. Once the divorce with Alma becomes final he informs Lily that although he will miss little Manon very much, he is filled with relief and joy at the new freedom. 'Now I am more than ever a nomadic star in the firmament and stand bondless towards the other sex.' As the sensitive Lily would have registered, her lover's joyous hymn of freedom contained a warning too.

———

Through 1919 and 1920 the Bauhaus gradually established a particular identity. Students and staff soon came to appreciate the charms of Weimar: the English-style park with the monument to Goethe, the Belvedere, the Tempelherrenhaus, an ancient little house built for the Knights Templar in which Itten had his studio. It was pleasant to wander in the woods nearby and the cafes in the town provided good meeting places for discussions. The atmosphere of Weimar was relaxed and rather sleepy, described by one ex-student as 'full of traditions, museums and retired officials, a Stratford-on-Avon and Cheltenham rolled into one'.

The Bauhaus students were already forming a cohesive group, united by the feeling that they were fighting for the same ideals in opposition to the largely uncomprehending world around them. They dressed in a kind of Bauhaus uniform, partly for reasons of poverty, partly as a sign of rebelliousness. These early women students wore their hair loose and descending to the shoulders in defiance of the norms of feminine respectability. The young men took to wearing rather picturesque shirt-blouses, adapted from uniforms left behind in Weimar by Russian prisoners of war. To make these look less military the students dyed them in different colours, deep reds and blues and greens. The long hair with which many of the male students arrived, legacy of the *Wandervögel* movement, would now be cut short or shaved off completely. The resulting bald scalp gave scope for imaginative decoration, such as painting the smooth skull in black squares for a party.

Party near Weimar, 1924. One of a succession of elaborate parties for which the Bauhaus became famous.

The spectacular parties which became such a legendary facet of life at the Bauhaus were already beginning. The weaver Gunta Stölzl recorded in her diary the 'wonderful party' held on her first evening at the school, describing the large hall with white-clothed tables and green walls, cheerful music, a marvellous free dinner. Shadow plays were performed, one depicting the actual construction of the dining hall in a 'fabulously witty and imaginative' way. Then, as at all later Bauhaus parties, there was dancing. 'It wasn't beautiful dancing, but wild and frolicsome, like dancing on a colourful meadow.' This was a very early introduction to one of the basic tenets of the Bauhaus: the creative overlapping of work and play.

From then on every weekend a party would be held. To begin with these informal Bauhaus parties took place, for reasons of economy, in little village inns in the hills of Oberweimar. Music would be played by Bauhaus members, Ludwig Hirschfeld-Mack on the concertina, Andreas Weininger ('Andi') on the piano, Joost Schmidt on the violin. This was the beginning of the famous Bauhaus band. Then everyone joined in the Bauhaus dance, that kind of passionate stamping, in couples, male and female not entwined but facing one another. A later development was the monthly themed Bauhaus ball, for which elaborate décor and costumes were created. Kite Festivals were held in which fantastically coloured decorative kites were launched into the skies, watched with fascination by the local Weimar children. Lantern Festivals, with lanterns glowing in the twilight, were invented too. Not only were these Bauhaus community events in themselves magnificent examples of abstract design and theatricality, they were also a means of concentrating energy, diffusing inevitable discontents and tensions in the school.

There were many internal ceremonies too, the marking of important personal occasions which brought the generations together. Lyonel Feininger's son, T. Lux Feininger, came from Berlin to the Bauhaus with his father as a boy of nine, finding the atmosphere 'delightfully different from the musty disciplines' of the Berlin Gymnasium where he had been a pupil. He immediately responded to the mood of welcoming spontaneity he discovered at the Bauhaus, the element of play and the special celebration of the birthdays of the Masters. A paper-lantern-lit serenade by Bauhaus students on his father's birthday under the windows of their house in Weimar remained an unforgettable experience for him.

There is often a sense of marvel in descriptions of these first years of Gropius's Bauhaus. People look back at them as a species of lost paradise. For Lydia Driesch-Foucar, a ceramics student who in 1920 had joined the Bauhaus pottery at Dornburg, an outpost of the community twenty miles from Weimar, one of her happiest memories was of

Teaching staff and students at the Bauhaus Weimar, including Oskar Schlemmer,
Gunta Stölzl and Josef Albers, bottom right waving.

bathing parties in the River Saale on Saturdays and Sundays, as well
as on warm summer evenings after work. The river flowed through the
valley with many loops and meanders, one of which had formed what
was virtually an island of tall trees where the ground was covered with
sand and high grass. The students and Masters from Weimar would
come to join the potters in this secluded area. 'As though in paradise',

writes Driesch-Foucar, 'the strong handsome young men and women disported themselves in the water, the sun and the green surroundings. They were truly dionysian scenes and pictures which repeatedly dominate the memories of my entire earlier life.'

It was just this sort of memory of days of such joy and hopefulness that would keep those who had once been at the Bauhaus almost uncannily united over future decades. Separated by political differences, by deprivations and sufferings in the Second World War and then, for many Bauhäusler, by life in exile, there was a strange sense of enduring love between them. 'When we meet under the sign of the Bauhaus or see each other for the first time we are one – we agree,' wrote Lothar Schreyer the stage designer, who taught at the Bauhaus from 1921. And one of the continuing memories that joined them was of Gropius himself at the centre of activity, so full of ideas and dedication, driving himself on with great determination, often overstretched and anxious but very rarely showing it. His eyes were like stars, as Lyonel Feininger once said.

Early in the 1930s Nikolaus Pevsner, the German art historian whose book *Pioneers of the Modern Movement: From William Morris to Walter Gropius* was already on his mind, went to visit Gropius in Berlin. He got out a photograph he had brought with him, the well-known portrait of Morris with high broad forehead and flowing hair and beard taken by his friend Emery Walker, and showed it to Gropius. 'So that is Morris,' said Gropius. 'I have never seen a picture of him. And yet I owe him so very much.'

Gropius's debt to Morris is obvious in his idea of the Bauhaus at Weimar being based on workshop practice. He shared Morris's view of the essential role of crafts in arriving at a true and exact knowledge of materials and techniques, a prerequisite of all designing. He would have known and approved of the initiative of Morris's protégé W. R. Lethaby, founder of the London Central School of Arts and Crafts, whose craft-based curriculum had been influential in Deutscher Werkbund circles. Gropius found Morris's championing of art for the people close to the democracy of creativity that he himself espoused. As Morris had expressed it in an Arts and Crafts statement of 1896, 'in order to have a living school of Art, the public in general must be interested in Art; it must be a part of their lives; something which they can no more do without than water or lighting.'

But though Gropius had many overlaps with Morris in his view of craftsmanship, he was setting up the Bauhaus in a very different period. He had endured the horrors of the First World War. He believed in workshop practice, the perfecting of techniques, the beauty of hand-finishing, the human satisfaction in creative control of all aspects of the work. Gropius, however, went much further than Morris or his English Arts and Crafts followers in aiming at a fusion of art and technology for the transformation of the modern world.

The workshops, instruction at the Bauhaus in this early period covered six main areas: sculpture in stone, wood, ceramics and plaster; metalwork; cabinetry; painting and decorating; printmaking; weaving. Each workshop had its Master of Form, responsible for the artistic direction, and its Workshop Master, a craftsman or (in rarer cases) a craftswoman who provided technical expertise. In 1920 Gropius made three important new appointments. Georg Muche, a painter from Der Sturm circles in Berlin, became Master of Form in the woodcarving and weaving workshops. Oskar Schlemmer, the stage designer and painter who, like Lily Hildebrandt, had studied with Adolf Hölzel in Stuttgart, was initially appointed Master of Form in the wall-painting workshop, gravitating to the theatre workshop later on. Paul Klee was the new Master of Form in the bookbinding workshop, as well as being made responsible along with Itten for teaching part of the Preliminary Course.

Klee, by then forty-two, was already well known as a member of the Expressionist Blaue Reiter group and also through his connections with Der Sturm. His flat was on the hill above the park in Weimar, furnished with very comfortable well-used furniture. There was a grand piano in the centre of the living room, watercolours on the wall, Klee's black cat on the sofa. According to a friend, the Swiss lawyer and collector Rolf Bürgi, Klee especially loved cats, 'their calm, their philosophical adaptation to their owners' homes and work'. Routinely after supper he would fetch his violin and he and his wife Lily, a

Paul Klee in Weimar.

former music teacher, would play pieces by Bach or by Mozart, his
favourite composer.

Paul Klee was an object of mystery and veneration at the Bauhaus.
The student Hans Fischli described a visit to his studio, which was
through the park along the winding paths past Goethe's garden house:

We were permitted to observe the fish in his large aquarium; he switched the light
on or off, he carefully drove some of them away from where they were so as to see
concealed ones better. His pictures, both finished and unfinished, stood and lay

about . . . Many called and call Paul Klee a magician, but he was not. He never performed conjuring tricks. He was an inventor who discovered magical things.

In the year after Gropius recruited Klee he persuaded Wassily Kandinsky to join the Bauhaus staff. Kandinsky had by this time left Russia, disillusioned with the revolutionary Soviet regime which he had at first supported, and returned to Germany to resume his painting in Berlin. He now taught on the Preliminary Course and became Master of Form in the wall-painting workshop, forming a kind of double act with Klee, allied yet contrasted in their attitudes and practices.

Kandinsky, at fifty-six, appeared much older than Klee when he first joined the Bauhaus and of another generation. A former student, Georg Teltscher, later known as George Adams, described Kandinsky's 'old world politeness. He was always very neatly and conventionally dressed in contrast to us students.' His input at the Bauhaus was relatively informal and detached. 'He came sporadically to set his students' projects and criticise their work.' His mind was more focused on continuing his painting, which, after its early period of organic abstraction, had now entered a largely geometric phase. The students admired him for his power and dedication, his clarity and logic. Both Klee and Kandinsky were considerable additions to the teaching staff. It was extraordinary that Gropius managed to attract and to retain for the Bauhaus artists of such calibre.

———

Gropius was mostly in a mood of great self-confidence, boasting to Lily about his evident attractiveness to other women. 'No,' he reassured her, 'I am not in love with another woman, didn't kiss anyone even at the big party the other day. It seems that I am at an age and in a state of mind which attract women. Many invite my advances. But that should not trouble you, on the contrary.' It was not only these predatory women; people in general were now adoring Gropius to an almost embarrassing extent. 'What is it that makes me suddenly so lovable?' he asked Lily. 'It is astonishing and I don't understand it. Even people who used to hate me suddenly like me.' No doubt it was the aura of commitment and success with the early stages of the Bauhaus that was drawing people to him. His war record was impressive and his connection with Alma had given him a certain notoriety and glamour. But this glow was not to last.

Just a few months later Gropius was telling Lily that the Bauhaus was cracking at the seams. Part of the basic problem was financial. The Bauhaus was drastically underfunded by the Thuringian government in relation to Gropius's ambitious schemes, and as the value of the German mark began falling, partly as a result of war reparations leading to a period of hyperinflation, the Bauhaus's financial situation could only become worse. Writing to Lily, Gropius lamented the terrible conditions of the students, most of whom had no financial resources. Some were housed in the dismal Prellerhaus, a still war-damaged building behind the main teaching block. Others had to find their own accommodation. Gropius blamed the lack of resources for the failure to provide specific architectural training at the Bauhaus, a blatant omission in a school focused on building arts, as some of the students were beginning to complain.

In a state of sudden desperation he told Lily, 'Everywhere I try to secure some money but I am not gifted for that. Can't you help to find capitalists?' And in fact not only did the energetic Lily assist him in forming a Bauhaus Circle of Friends to raise morale and support fund-raising, she also helped him to sell off his own family antiques and properties to help finance the school. Among these family heirlooms inherited by Gropius was a silver table service once owned by Napoleon, which had been abandoned in the course of war and retrieved from the Belle Alliance battlefield by one of his military ancestors. Much to the indignation of his family Gropius sold the silver to subsidise the purchase of the plot of land in Weimar on which vegetables were grown for the Bauhaus canteen.

As we saw in the episode of the Kapp Putsch funeral in Weimar and Gropius's reluctance to join in the procession for the victims, he had been determined at the outset to keep the Bauhaus out of politics. He maintained that once the school became a playground for political games, it would collapse like a house of cards. But independence from politics was increasingly difficult for him to achieve in such a volatile period in Germany as a whole and in the particular political situation in the state of Thuringia itself. The new state parliament was socialist and in theory supported the Bauhaus. But there were right-wing factions within the parliament and opposition to Gropius from within the fundamentally conservative city of Weimar itself. Particular criticism of the Bauhaus and its experimental attitude to art and design came from the artists of the former Weimar Hochschule, the academy of art, and their local supporters, an antagonism only partially resolved when the school was removed from Gropius's aegis and set up independently in 1921.

A final local irritant was the demand from Friedrich Nietzsche's sister, Elisabeth Förster-Nietzsche, old friend and past patron of Henry van de Velde, that the Bauhaus should provide van de Velde with a house and studio in reparation for his cold-shouldering in Weimar in the war. Gropius, not himself a great admirer of Nietzschean philosophy, resisted this suggestion, pleading that his own position as Bauhaus director was still not established. He did not feel secure. By 1920 he was increasingly beleaguered. 'I am in the terrible vortex of dangers,' he told his Lilychen in early February, apologising for postponing a planned visit to Frankfurt. He hoped she would manage instead to come to him.

Gropius tried valiantly to improve the local image of the Bauhaus and defend the ideas which underlay its teaching. He invited local citizens' groups to visit the school and meet the students. He addressed public meetings. He described 'a big Bauhaus battle' in the town, a heated meeting on the theme of 'The New Art in Weimar', which many of the Bauhäusler themselves attended. As he explained to Lily:

I knew that this would be a call to arms against the Bauhaus – and this is what it became. The speakers, narrow-minded dilettantes of the city, caught themselves in a net of the most stupid, furious, and unobjective attacks. The hall was overflowing with people. I let them all talk first and then I spoke myself, sharp and witty, and my words played such havoc with the speakers that under a continuous endless applause the case was dismissed in my favour. It was the best propaganda for the Bauhaus.

But hard as Gropius tried to overcome local resistance this was a losing battle. For many conservative citizens these strangely dressed groups of Bauhaus students wandering through Weimar seemed alarming. Many spoke in foreign accents. There were few local recruits. At a time of escalating anti-Semitic prejudice it was suspected that a high proportion of these students were Jewish, although in fact there were relatively few Jews at the Bauhaus at that time. In reactionary Weimar the outlandish appearance of the Bauhäusler signified potential immorality, and indeed a strong local complaint was sent to Gropius from the Director of the Second Administrative Area. This focused on the Bauhaus parties on the River Saale, where males and females could be viewed 'without any bathing costumes whatsoever and in places accessible to everyone. People walking past have taken objection and this infringement of decency has caused public annoyance and represents a danger to morals, especially for young people.' At the same time gossip about Gropius's relationship with Lily, a married woman, had begun to spread.

On 18 December 1920 a celebratory gathering, one of the great parties at which the Bauhaus so excelled, was held to mark the topping out of the Sommerfeld House on Limonenstrasse in the Dahlem suburb of Berlin. The ceremony involved a bonfire, a procession and a chorus celebrating the building arts, a programme inspired by the ideas of the Anthroposophists. It culminated in a ritual in which six Bauhäusler dressed as carpenters drew a garland up to the rafters of the house. The carpenters' costumes of Manchester brown suits, shirts and ties were donated by the client, Sommerfeld himself.

Adolf Sommerfeld was one of the most enthusiastic if financially unreliable of Gropius's early clients, drawn into his orbit by a real fascination with the Bauhaus and its aims. He was a romantic entrepreneur, one of six children of a forgemaster, who himself had a practical training as a carpenter. Like Gropius, Sommerfeld had been excited by modern possibilities of structures and techniques and had founded his own increasingly successful large-scale construction firm. He had now commissioned Gropius to design him an artistically perfect new home.

Gropius's own private architectural office was by this time incorporated in the Bauhaus. It was becoming busier. His original Berlin partner Adolf Meyer had joined him in Weimar and a number of Bauhaus
students assisted informally in the Gropius office, partly deflecting
the criticism that the Bauhaus offered no official architectural training. Gropius and Meyer designed for Sommerfeld a block construction
house to be built out of the timber which Sommerfeld had salvaged
from a now redundant German navy battleship and had cut to size in his
own sawmill. The building, constructed in teak, with its atmospheric
overhanging roof, projecting beam ends and central entrance porch,
had obvious antecedents in Frank Lloyd Wright's early Prairie houses,
and indeed Gropius and Meyer had been spotted in the early stages of
the concept studying the large Wasmuth portfolios of designs by Wright.

The Sommerfeld House, Limonenstrasse, Berlin, 1920.

The Sommerfeld House was a visionary building, developed as a truly
collaborative work. 'This was the first opportunity', wrote Gropius, 'to
give the students in the workshops the possibility to show their hands in
coloured glass windows, sculptural reliefs in wood, metal screens and
lighting fixtures.' It was the Bauhaus version of the *Gesamtkunstwerk*,
the total work of art. The great prismatic stained-glass windows were

the work of Josef Albers, then still an apprentice at the Bauhaus; the furniture was designed by the young Hungarian Marcel Breuer, who arrived at the Bauhaus as a student in 1920. Joost Schmidt was responsible for the extraordinary 'jagged style' teak carvings for the doors and staircase. Sommerfeld had asked for as many carvings as possible on every conceivable surface inside and outside the house. The critic Robert Hughes was later to comment that the building was 'so Teutonic, so redolent of trolls and forest with its notched log walls and pitched timber roof, that Goering could well have approved it as a hunting lodge'.

In later years Gropius attempted to distance himself from the Sommerfeld House, seeing it as having been at odds with his later architectural rationality. But this was silly of him. Its Expressionist fervour reflects his high-flown aspirations for the Bauhaus at that time.

7

Bauhaus Weimar and Maria Benemann
1920–1922

In early 1920 the handsome, charismatic director of the Bauhaus acquired a new lover, the poet Maria Benemann. Maria, an aficionado of modern dance, had come to Weimar to promote a performance in the local theatre by Mary Wigman, whose dance school in Zurich Maria had attended. Wigman, a disciple of Emile-Jaques Dalcroze and Rudolf von Laban in developing techniques of Expressionist dance, was still relatively unknown in Germany. It was an article by Maria Benemann published in the local paper that persuaded the director of the Weimar theatre to book her for an experimental evening of dance.

Modern dance was very much on the agenda at the Bauhaus. The middle-aged, white-haired Gertrud Grunow, a revered figure at the Bauhaus who became its only female Master of Form, shared Johannes Itten's concepts of spiritual wholeness. Her courses derived from rhythmic gymnastics and the relation of the body to the mind. Grunow had been profoundly influenced by the early-twentieth-century *Lebensreform* movement and ideas of the relationship between free movement and spiritual harmony. At the Bauhaus she worked closely with Lothar Schreyer in developing the stage workshop. The emphasis given to performance at the Bauhaus reflects Gropius's own enthusiasm for the concept of what became known as Total Theatre, the amalgam of music, movement, costumes and scenery, dialogue and poetry, involving a total immersion of the senses. As Gropius grew to see it, theatre becomes a mirror of life itself.

He was receptive when Maria Benemann approached him for help in supporting the Weimar debut by the Expressionist Mary Wigman, which at that point had no bookings at all. He listened to her pleadings carefully and then promised to send the whole Bauhaus, including all the craftsmen with their wives, to that night's performance.

Maria arrived to find the theatre full. Gropius himself was sitting at the front and nodded to her, smiling. Wigman's performance varied in its rhythms and moods, slow and solemn, fast and whirling, then dignified and statuesque again, with the dancer now wearing sweeping robes as if in ancient mourning. 'In the classical sense', as Maria put it, 'neither her face nor her body were beautiful, but her expressive force set new standards.' Finally she disrobed and danced again, by this time almost naked. Maria's little daughter Inge, enraptured, watched every move that Wigman made. Inge was later to embark on a similar career.

In the excitement of the moment Gropius seemed to have forgotten Lily Hildebrandt. After Wigman's performance he was waiting outside the theatre. Maria stammered her thanks. It turned out that the jealous resident ballet mistress at the theatre had bribed the ticket office not to sell a single seat.

They met again soon afterwards at a costume ball held at the Bauhaus, a fundraising event to which members of the public had been invited. Maria was seated at a different table when one of her neighbours, the wife of a Dr Adler from Vienna, had suddenly jumped up on the table and started dancing. Gropius looked startled as the reckless Mrs Adler cavorted perilously on the small round table. He moved his chair to sit beside Maria, saying confidentially, 'I too am married to a Viennese.' This was just before Gropius's divorce from Alma became final. He added, after a pause, 'It is like two circles that do not close.'

Maria was, thankfully, very unlike Alma, less extreme in temperament, less overpoweringly sexual. Her background was in literature rather than in music. Maria was five years younger than Gropius, from a well-off, cultured Dresden Jewish family. She appears long-faced, delicately beautiful, with a rather melancholy look. She had been married to a poet, Gerhard Benemann, and besides their daughter Inge they had a younger child, a son named Joachim. Gerhard had been killed fighting with his infantry regiment in the very early weeks of the First World War.

Before the war Maria had already established herself as a promising young poet. She had had three of her poems published in the avantgarde monthly magazine *Die Weissen Blätter*, edited by Franz Blei, and

The young poet Maria Benemann, 1914/15.

had been encouraged by none other than Franz Werfel. When Blei and Werfel suggested she should publish a collection of her poetry Blei wrote the subtly persuasive advertising copy: 'Maria Benemann speaks her soft prayers from the devotion of a timid heart.'

It was her husband who had given her the present, in autumn 1913, of the recently published three-volume collection of poems by Richard

Dehmel. Gerhard suggested she send Dehmel one of her poems, and this introduction erupted into a highly romantic love affair. It was from Dehmel that Maria later took the title of her memoirs, which include an account of her relationship with Gropius: *Leih mir noch einmal die leichte Sandale*, 'Bestow on me once again the light sandal'. The light sandal stands for the onset of poetic inspiration.

From 1915 onwards she had also been in touch with Rainer Maria Rilke. Again the correspondence started with a fan letter from Maria, burgeoning into an affectionate correspondence in which they exchanged news of progress on their poetry. Rilke wrote to Maria from Hamburg to tell her of the responses of a small group of literary enthusiasts to a reading of some of her poems. 'It suddenly brought back the whole nameless spell which touched the surface of things and made us listen.'

In 1916 Maria had moved to Zurich, one of the group of artists and intellectuals in exile while the war raged on in Germany and France. It was here that Wigman began giving her first solo performances, dressed only in a minimal skirt and brassiere. Maria, at first a little shocked, came to see this abandonment of conventional costume as a welcome sign of liberation.

Maria found Zurich a stimulating city, with its continual comings and goings of people and ideas. She acted as a kind of secretary to Werfel, noticing with interest how carefully he hoarded the many letters that reached him from Vienna, all in the same characteristic scrawly handwriting. Alma's of course. It was through this connection with Werfel that Maria first became aware of Walter Gropius and his whole troubled history.

Before she and Gropius actually met in the spring of 1920 Maria had her own connections with Weimar. She was on visiting terms with Henry van de Velde and attended Elisabeth Förster-Nietzsche's soirées. But she had recently moved with her two children further away to Blankenheim, a town south-west of Bonn. In Gropius's first affectionate communication to Maria, replying to what he describes as her 'dear letter', he suggests he might come and visit her in Blankenheim quite soon.

By the time he writes again, on 19 April 1920, relations between them have changed dramatically. 'MARIA', he addresses her, surrounding her name in an Expressionist explosion of comets and stars. In the letter Gropius reaches for his most dramatic language of passionate non-commitment:

I am a wandering star in this universe, I know no anchor, no chains, I go into hiding when I am suffering and only seek out others when I am fulfilled and have something to give, I tie myself nowhere and to no one. I leaven things wherever I go and thus generate *life*; I am a *thorn* and hence a powerful, dangerous tool!!! I love. Love without any object – high, eternal intensity.

You wanted me and I gave myself to you and it was beautiful and pure, two stars united their burning flames, but

make no threats!

make no demands!

expect nothing!

for everything that people give each other is a *gift*. I know nothing, I promise nothing, I gratefully imbibe your warmth and one day I will wield my sword again. But now I am seated in 1000-fold suffering in ashes, am restless and torn and need quietude and solitude. Love! Write poetry! Take pleasure in your new surroundings. I hold you closely into my arms. Your shooting star.

Their meetings were erratic not just because of Gropius's continuing involvement with Lily Hildebrandt and his bitter confrontations with Alma over Manon, but also because he was so constantly in transit, travelling the country to give lectures to generate interest and support for the Bauhaus, going to Berlin meetings of the Arbeitsrat für Kunst and other revolutionary groupings with which he was connected. His next communication to Maria two weeks later was a rushed one: 'In a flash the wandering star hied him hence to Berlin – with greetings to you and au revoir.'

Although it appears that Maria attended one or two of the newly established open evenings at the Bauhaus Gropius was wary of her presence, his anxiety about her possible over-familiarity of manner perhaps exacerbated by the rumours flying round already concerning his relationship with Lily Hildebrandt, not to mention fascinated speculation over his divorce from Alma. He told Maria not to be upset if he appeared to be indifferent to her in public, explaining that in the context of the Bauhaus his personal relations with others needed to be kept very private. Certainly Gropius's correspondence with Maria is different in tenor from his communications with Lily, less domestic, with many fewer insights into the developing conflicts at the Bauhaus, more philosophical and literary. In July 1920 we find him assessing Maria's poetry:

The two poems were a joy, firstly because they arise from genuine experience and then because they contain within them the core of feminine life and narration, that is to say, the right premise for poetry by a woman and that is in itself the most important thing. The form is not yet mature and not distinctive enough . . . There is nothing to be said against a loose, rhymeless form, but it has to be consistent! . . . A work of art *always* demands a concisely executed form, however paradoxical its contents, because therein speaks the character of the human work of art as opposed to the abandon of nature. I am penning this critique because you *responsibly* expect it of me, and therefore I have read your lines very carefully and repeatedly and have absorbed them.

It is a thoughtful and intelligent critique, from one artist to another, even if Gropius tends to view her writing with something of the male bias of his time. But already in this letter there are signs of Gropius finding Maria's emotional dependency becoming onerous. He complains about her way of making demands which render it 'all but impossible' for him to help smooth the path for her: '*That is no way to behave, Maria!*' 'I am not a sleek salonnier,' he tells her, 'I am a sharp thorn that speaks out against platitudes and convention.' He reminds her that in his first letter back in April he told her that 'for me there is only *one* standpoint for human beings: *make no demands, expect nothing, just give!* You didn't understand me, this is the only wisdom that I have acquired in a strong life. I will not stray from that, it has become my compass and my yardstick.' We can see just how different Gropius has become since the naively passionate encounter with Alma in Tobelbad. Years of terrible turbulence have altered him. His affections and ambitions have now become much broader, almost all-encompassing. He ends his letter to Maria, 'I have great love, love without object, which also enfolds you in my arms.'

As Maria becomes sadder and more desperate, Gropius does his best to soothe her:

You are suffering greatly, and I am sorry it should be so. But, for the lord's sake, try to become *simple*. You will find no happiness in exaggeration, in adoration. Go away for a while, regain your calm in the countryside. Do only that which is closest to hand and do it simply, well, and sensibly, then you will be better and you will learn to recognise your own limits. The steadier you become, the more you will mean to strong, worthy individuals.

In another letter Gropius tries once more to reason with Maria:

You shy away from plunging the thorn of realisation into your chest, in a way you are still at play with yourself, not yet taking yourself entirely seriously, as yet not able to find the courage to stride towards the hard, pointed arrows of reality, the pain of which is so welcome until we in due course recognise that pain is the same as pleasure. Just dare to use your own feet and you will suddenly be able to walk.

Here Gropius is no longer the romantic lover but the worldly realist. 'You will be shutting yourself off from my harshness and implacability as you read this, but one day you will understand.' He sent Maria over twenty cards and letters during 1920, after which there was a parting of the ways. She moved far away from the big cities, working for a time as the head of a children's home, then studying the medieval salt water repositories of the North Frisian Islands. She was a strange woman, original and elusive. It was 1967 before they were in touch again.

However, Gropius's concurrent correspondence with Lily Hilde-brandt continued, as did their hectic assignations in Frankfurt, in Munich, wherever they could manage and despite many emotional vicissitudes. Perhaps partly because of his involvement with Maria their affair had lost its original magic. In 1921 Gropius told Lily that in spite of his wish to be able to feel just as intensely for her as he had done a year ago, he could not quite achieve it: 'I am striving for it, but one cannot force the flames.' She was in ill health and it seems that she had some kind of nervous breakdown in 1922, the year that Gropius wrote to her suggesting they begin to develop 'a firm bond of friendship beyond our loving twosomeness that will be independent of passions and will therefore have eternal value'. This was more or less what they achieved. Unlike his correspondence with Maria, Gropius's exchange of letters with Lily Hildebrandt continued for a lifetime, only breaking off for an anxious interval of non-communication during the Second World War.

————

In one of the letters written to Lily in October 1920 Gropius lamented about serious upheavals at the school: 'The Bauhaus peels one skin after another off in mad crisis.' These problems were demanding 'breathless exertion' from him. 'Itten is now fire's flame.'

Johannes Itten, whose Preliminary Course all incoming Bauhaus students now attended, had succeeded in establishing a power base in competition to Gropius's own. He particularly influenced the younger painters in recognising the importance of the unconscious in creative work and in the way he introduced previously unregarded objects, even the rubbish collected from scrapheaps, as having an intrinsic interest. When Itten asked his students to contemplate the texture of the thistle the more susceptible among them regarded this as a deep spiritual insight. He became increasingly involved in Mazdaznanism, a cult derived from ancient Persian Zoroastrianism which attracted a sizeable following in America and central Europe before and just after the First World War.

Itten's attempts to convert the Bauhaus to Mazdaznanism were thorough. He shaved his head and took to wearing a quasi-monastic robe. 'He looked like a priest to me,' wrote Paul Klee's young son Felix, impressed with 'his red-violet, high-buttoned uniform, his bald, shaven crown and his gold-rimmed glasses'. The more fanatical students shaved their own heads in emulation. Itten's closest disciple on the staff was the artist Georg Muche. The students composed a Bauhaus chorus, 'Itten, Muche, Mazdaznan', whistled to the tune of the Bavarian jingle 'Und dann kommt der Prinzregent mit der Kerzen in die Hand'.

The basis of the cult was purification. Itten's Bauhaus disciples followed a rigorous regime of gymnastics, breathing exercises, ferocious

Johannes Itten, Weimar, 1921.

The effects of the Mazdaznan diet, *Régime Mazdaznan*. Cartoon by Paul Citroen, 1922.

laxatives and purging, followed by a period of fasting and spiritual contemplation. The prescribed Mazdaznan diet was strictly vegetarian, consisting of vegetables grown in the school allotments. Some of the students became so undernourished they defected to the soup kitchen in the town. Alma, in spite of her original championing of Itten, was unimpressed by Mazdaznan. Reading through a pile of pamphlets on the night that she arrived on one of her reluctant Bauhaus visits, she was horrified to note the now obligatory diet of 'uncooked mush smothered in garlic'. She found Itten's disciples 'recognisable at a distance, by the garlic smell'. When she asked Gropius for Itten's telephone number she was told he was out of action: '"You can't see him now," said Gropius. "He's had one of his bilious attacks."'

> he was in his office
> at the van de velde bauhaus building in weimar
> when I first met him,
> presenting my work
> to become a student at the bauhaus.
> above his desk in the spacious high-ceiling'd room
> hung a cubist léger.
> there was also a medieval architectural drawing.
> gropius wore black trousers, white shirt, slim black bow tie,
> and a short natural-coloured leather jacket
> which squeaked with each movement.
> his short moustache, trim figure, and swift movements
> gave him the air of a soldier
> (which in fact he had been until recently).

The composer of these lines, designer Herbert Bayer, graphic artist and pioneer of the capital-free typeface, first met Gropius in the director's office when a prospective student in 1921. The contrast at this point between formal, precise, still soldierly Gropius as described by Bayer and shaven-headed Itten in his monkish sandals could hardly have been greater. Their differences were ideological as well. Just as Gropius felt that Mazdaznan practices – the exercises, the purgings, the lengthy meditations – were a distraction from the real goals of the Bauhaus, Itten had no interest in practical handcrafts. Gropius's philosophy of work-shop practice and his underlying concept of design for industry were anathema to Itten and the students who were his overawed disciples. Gropius now began to lay down the law, reining Itten in, attempting to confine his influence to formal teaching programmes on the Prelim-inary Course. Bauhaus Master Oskar Schlemmer, an interested and perceptive observer of the conflict, noted in his diary: 'so Itten and Gropius are duelling it out, and we others are supposed to play referee.'

Itten resigned under mounting pressure and finally left Weimar in the spring of 1923. Gropius never lost his respect and admiration for Itten as a teacher or for the imaginative dedication with which he invented the Preliminary Course at the Bauhaus. 'He was certainly a strong per-sonality,' Gropius wrote of Itten in 1946, the year after the war, explain-ing that they separated finally because 'he mixed up his teaching with Mazdaznan and as I did not want to have that half-religious approach incorporated in our education I caused him to leave'.

———

Gropius was becoming well practised in the holding of the line, assailed as he soon was from the opposite direction by the Dutch Constructivist Theo van Doesburg, who first arrived in Weimar early in 1921. Where Itten and his followers criticised the Bauhaus from their Mazdaznan point of view as being too concerned with the functional and rationalist, van Doesburg regarded it as self-indulgently concerned with roman-tic individualism. He reported to a Constructivist colleague soon after his arrival in the town: 'At Weimar I have turned everything radically upside down. This is supposed to be the most famous Academy with the most modern teachers! Every evening I have talked to the students and spread the *vermin* of the new spirit.' Already the formidably articulate van Doesburg was busy fomenting discord.

Van Doesburg was a painter and an early admirer of Piet Mondrian, impressed by ideas of the significance and discipline of the linear in art. In 1917, with Mondrian, Bart van der Leck, J. J. P. Oud and others, van Doesburg had co-founded the art, architecture and design movement De Stijl, which aimed to arrive at a universal language that would 'manifest itself in all objects as a style born from a new relationship between the artist and society'. This style was geometric, minimalist, boldly coloured, doctrinaire.

Gropius had first met van Doesburg in Berlin at the house of Expressionist architect Bruno Taut, a sociable gathering which included Gropius's partner Adolf Meyer and several Bauhaus students. Van Doesburg regaled them by showing a multitude of photographs of work by De Stijl members, after which Gropius invited him to visit the Bauhaus in January 1921. It was later put about that Gropius had suggested he should join the staff but this was strenuously denied by Gropius himself, who was later to describe van Doesburg as 'an arrogant and narrow man. He would have wrought havoc in the Bauhaus, so I did not want to have him as a teacher although his philosophy interested me and many others in the Bauhaus.' In fact it seems to have been Meyer who encouraged van Doesburg to install himself in Weimar, where he gave inflammatory anti-Bauhaus lectures and stirred up discontent.

Van Doesburg's philosophy, as well as his appearance, was the very opposite of Itten's. He dressed not in monkish robes but in his own fairly sinister Constructivist uniform of black shirt, white tie and a monocle, which caused great surprise to the citizens of Weimar as he walked around the town. Photographs show his intense and brooding look.

Van Doesburg held solemn intellectual evenings at his home, during which he indoctrinated visitors in the values of geometric purity in architecture. Helmut von Erffa recorded a lecture on Constructivism given by van Doesburg 'while his wife played De Stijl music – practically all in octaves as I remember, but with a definite affinity to squares and rectangles'. This was powerful stuff. Van Doesburg attracted the most discontented Bauhaus students, some of whom actually went to work for him. He and his De Stijl colleagues attacked the concentration on individual artworks, the pictures, graphics, single works of sculpture. They were cynical about the quality of Bauhaus works. Feininger's attempts at Cubist painting were better done in France ten years earlier; Klee merely 'scribbles sickly dreams'; 'Itten's emptily pompous daubing aims only for superficial effect'; 'Schlemmer's works are experiments familiar to us from the work of other sculptors'. Even Gropius's Expressionist monument to the fallen in Weimar cemetery was castigated as 'the result of a cheap literary idea'. Van Doesburg was caustic about any form of art unrelated to architecture, the machine and mass production. His doctrine was entirely that of collectivism, 'art as the collective expression of a nation and a style'.

In October 1922, in a move that challenged Gropius on his own home base, van Doesburg organised a Constructivist Congress in Weimar. El Lissitzky, Hans Richter, Hans Arp and Tristan Tzara were among the European avant-garde adherents of Constructivism and Dada who attended. The tenor of the Congress was the glorification of the collective as opposed to the 'tyranny of the subjective' in art. As Lissitzky put it in his address to the gathering, 'The new art is formed, not on a subjective, but an objective.' Traditional social relations were upended. In the new evolving culture, 'The artist is companion to the scholar, the engineer and the worker.' Bauhaus workshop training in the arts and crafts was out.

For Gropius, van Doesburg was not only deeply irritating as a contentious presence in the town but too doctrinaire, too rigid in the views he was espousing. One of Gropius's deeply held beliefs was in variousness, the concept of *all* colours being of equal interest, which he had spoken up for as a child. His great strength as director of the Bauhaus was, in the words of Lothar Schreyer, his 'enchanting, sympathetic attitude especially to the younger generation', along with his genuine tolerance for other opinions. He deliberately aimed to let the students' work develop from within, without outside interference. Consciously he encouraged them to make detours. 'The Bauhaus philosophy was not to be preconceived.' All the same it is clear that the incursions of van Doesburg and his wide-ranging criticism of the Bauhaus had a lasting effect on Gropius's future planning for the school once, to his relief, van Doesburg left Germany for Paris in 1923.

———

142

Gropius's own architectural work had been developing in a style quite different to that of his earlier Expressionist buildings: distinct from the Sommerfeld House with its marvellous complexity of handmade components and rich surface decoration; distinct from the overt symbolism of Gropius's *Monument to the March Dead of the Kapp Putsch* in Weimar cemetery, with its upward-thrusting sculptural dynamic of the bolt of lightning suggesting the rising power of the proletariat.

It is with the remodelling of the Jena theatre that we first become aware of a new architectural thinking. In the unornamented cubic design of the exterior there is an incursion of rationality, even of severity. The foyer is a highly disciplined linear construction. The workshops of the Bauhaus made the purpose-designed, sleekly upholstered geometric seating. This move back to unadorned clarity continued with Gropius's design, in collaboration with his architectural assistant Fred Forbat, for a large-scale ferro-concrete warehouse for the farming equipment manufactured by Kappe and Co. near Gropius's earlier Faguswerk building at Alfeld-an-der-Leine.

The new mood of architectural functionalism is most wonderfully and convincingly expressed in Gropius and Meyer's competition entry for the *Chicago Tribune* office building. This was an international competition with the brief that the new building should not only enhance the civic beauty of Chicago, it should be the most beautiful office building in the world, as befitted the world's most widely circulated newspaper. Gropius was emphatic that this should be a building which 'definitely would not use any historical styles, but express modern times with modern means'. He arrived at a design for a towering steel, glass and iron structure, a stepped-up building which at its tallest would stand thirty floors high, with pairs of protruding balconies rhythmically placed. This was an aspirational building, a symbolic crystal tower in the centre of the city. *Glasarchitektur* yes, but a building of a most contemporary kind.

The *Chicago Tribune* competition was a stitch-up, biased as it was towards American competitors. The deadline for Americans was set at 1 November 1922, that for foreign competitors 1 December. The jury had already met on 13 November and drawn up a preliminary list of winners. Once the foreign entries came in only one, from Finnish architect Eliel Saarinen, was added to the list. He was awarded second prize. The winner was a Gothic-style skyscraper, not dissimilar to the New York Woolworth building, designed by the New York firm of How-ells and Hood. The thirty-seven German entries, including designs by Gropius's modernist architect colleagues Bruno and Max Taut and Ludwig Hilberseimer, got nowhere. Nor did the somewhat lunatic giant Doric column by the Austrian Adolf Loos.

After the war, when Gropius was living and working in the States, he maintained that he had attempted to bring modern architecture to America in 1922 but no one understood it. An exaggeration maybe, but partly true.

8

Bauhaus Weimar and Ise Gropius
1923–1925

The Bauhaus Week has begun! Posters on all railway buffet cars! The President is coming to the opening. The hotels are packed with foreigners. 1,000 flats had to be evacuated to make way for the art writers. In every square the Bauhaus Internationale is played. The only thing to smoke is Bauhaus brand. Huge hard currency speculation is shaking the money markets.

And the reason for this? There are a few cupboards full of little bits of cloth and pots in the museum, and all Europe is excited. Poor Europe! That, with due deference, is my view of the 1923 Bauhaus Week.

This was Gerhard Marcks's ironic internal response to Gropius's ambitious plans for a large-scale public exhibition of work by teachers and students. The exhibition was promoted under the slogan 'Art and Technology – A New Unity' and it represented a conscious reorientation of the Bauhaus, a move away from the original emphasis on handmaking and the concept of the artist as 'an exalted craftsman' towards a new ideal of design for industrial production. The early romantic phase was over. There was now pressure on the Bauhaus to move visibly into a technological new world.

Gropius himself had been reluctant to stage a big public exhibition so early in the Bauhaus's development. But the Thuringian government as well as the local authorities in Weimar were anxious to see evidence of what the school they were financially supporting, albeit reluctantly, had been achieving. Gropius himself was hoping to secure the Bauhaus's own internal source of revenue by marketing Bauhaus products and by encouraging industry to commission designs. Besides, he was ambitious for the international reputation of the school itself. Already, in 1922, a Bauhaus exhibition had been held in Calcutta, instigated by the Indian poet, philosopher and cultural ambassador Rabindranath

Tagore, who had been impressed by what he had seen of the Bauhaus on a visit to Germany the year before.

Gropius inaugurated Bauhaus Week in Weimar on 15 August 1923 with a slide lecture, 'Art and Technology – A New Unity', the first public proclamation of the new philosophy. Bauhaus Week had been timed to coincide with a Deutscher Werkbund conference in Weimar and photographs show a large, formally dressed crowd gathered in the workshop-wing entrance hall, listening respectfully. Paintings and sculptures by the Bauhaus Masters were exhibited in the local Landesmuseum, while paintings and graphic works by students were shown in the former Hochschule building. Products by students were spread around the different workshops. New signage redefined the Bauhaus buildings, much of it designed by Herbert Bayer, a student at that time.

Oskar Schlemmer designed a decorative scheme for the hallway of the Bauhaus workshop wing. This included a Schlemmer mural and relief sculptures by Schlemmer and Joost Schmidt. The Bauhaus Week decorations remained in situ until 1930, when the Nazi director of the school that took over from the Bauhaus ordered the works to be destroyed.

Gropius's own office on the second floor had been redesigned for Bauhaus Week, with furniture and textiles made in the school workshops (see Plate 11). It was opened to visitors, one of the most purist of whom, Mies van der Rohe, expressed his disappointment that the decoration was so fussy. It struck him as a throwback to the Wiener Werkstätte style. For the future of the Bauhaus – the school which Mies himself would eventually inherit – the director's office made him fear the worst.

Gropius organised an exhibition of work by international architects, a collection of drawings, photographs and models in the now advancing modern style. Gropius's own architecture was included, as was that of Le Corbusier, which Gropius had already registered and admired, having read his articles *'vers une architecture'* published in Le Corbusier's periodical *L'Esprit nouveau*. He had written to 'Corb' to ask him to send examples of his work for the Bauhaus exhibition. This was the beginning of a lifelong friendship and an international camaraderie of architects that led five years later to the first Congrès Internationale d'Architecture Moderne (known familiarly as CIAM).

Visitors to Bauhaus Week also saw an example of living architecture, the experimental Haus am Horn. This was a small residential building on Am Horn Strasse in Weimar, the site originally earmarked by Gropius for his much larger-scale Bauhaus settlement (see Plate 8), a hoped-for utopian development in which the whole Bauhaus community would work to rediscover a lost unity of work and life. In fact funding just this single experimental dwelling had been problematic. Early on in 1923 an appeal was sent out to Henry Ford, William Randolph Hearst and other potentially susceptible American millionaires. In the end the financing of the building was undertaken, once again, by Adolf Sommerfeld. The house was constructed between April and August 1923, with furnishings designed and made in the school workshops. It was seen as a prototype for housing that could be mass-produced.

Haus am Horn was not designed by Gropius himself. The architect had been selected by open competition, judged by a Bauhaus collective which included students. The painter Georg Muche won, the young Bauhäusler having considered Gropius's own architecture too conventional. The perils of democracy! Gropius clawed back overall responsibility for the positioning and site development. The Haus am Horn as built attracted much attention for its innovative practicality and compactness, taking the form of a central living area with a number of small rooms splaying out around it. The minimal kitchen, designed to simplify the housewife's life by saving space, time and energy, contains standardised elements similar to those of Margarete Schütte-Lihotzky's better-known 'Frankfurt Kitchen' of 1926. The art critic Paul Westheim, in a jokey article about the Bauhaus mania for squares, comments that 'the Cubist idol, the Maggi stock cube' was all that was missing from the clean-lined kitchen of the Haus am Horn.

Surrounding Bauhaus Week there was a packed programme of lectures and performances. Theatre was becoming an increasingly important part of the Bauhaus curriculum since Oskar Schlemmer, with his sense of light and movement and belief in theatrical performance as a total work of art, had taken over full responsibility for the stage workshop. Schlemmer's ground-breaking *Triadisches Ballett* was recreated for Bauhaus Week. Schlemmer envisaged a triadic unity of dance, costume and music. In its early versions three dancers performed its architectonic structure of three parts in coloured three-dimensional costumes which are themselves evolved from basic mathematical shapes. Schlemmer acknowledged the influence not only of Dalcroze, Laban and Mary Wigman but also of Negro jazz, tap dancing, music hall and circus.

Oskar Schlemmer's *Triadisches Ballett* (Triadic Ballet), 1927.

On the night following the *Triadisches Ballett*, at Gropius's own remodelled Stadttheater in Jena the *Mechanisches Kabarett* was performed. This was designed by two talented students, Kurt Schmidt and Georg Teltscher. Teltscher subsequently recorded the excitement of the weeks before the opening, when they were all working at fever pitch. He himself had been the main dancer in the cabaret. 'Abstract shapes were attached to our bodies, which were clad in black tricot against a black back-cloth, so that strange, abstract shapes were seen moving in slow or quick rhythm across the stage.' The music was specially written by Hans Heinz Stuckenschmidt. Postcards, leaflets, posters were sent out internationally, 'to attract the widest possible range of visitors'.

As Teltscher realised, Bauhaus Week was 'a most ambitious and precarious undertaking' just four years after the establishment of the school, 'which itself had to take place under such difficult and frustrating conditions'. But once again 'we were carried by the enthusiasm which Gropius was able to provoke'. There were many foreign visitors, so that Gropius himself was swallowed up in interminable explanations and discussions, showing them around and experiencing for the first time international responses to the concept of the Bauhaus. He told his mother proudly that Bauhaus Week had attracted a mass of distinguished visitors, including Igor Stravinsky, who arrived for a performance of his own recent theatrical composition *L'Histoire du soldat*, with Carl Ebert reciting and Hermann Scherchen conducting. The Italian composer Ferruccio Busoni had also visited Weimar to hear six of his piano pieces performed by Egon Petri. Official representatives from the Soviet Union had come to assess this revolutionary enterprise. In all, over fifty thousand people travelled to Weimar for the exhibition. The Bauhaus was now definitely on the map.

Not all the responses were enthusiastic. The architect Adolf Behne was critical of an exhibition which showed clearly that the Bauhaus was in a period of change, stranded unconvincingly between its old allegiance to the handicrafts and its embrace of new technology. But it seems that many more of the visitors were both excited and impressed. The young architectural critic Sigfried Giedion, arriving on the night train from Munich to Weimar, had been carried away by the Bauhaus exhibitions, the performances of music by Stravinsky, abstract ballets by Schlemmer and Kandinsky. He said he had a glimpse of a whole new modern culture, of 'a world that was being reborn'.

At the end of Bauhaus Week, on the Sunday evening, a lantern parade was held. It started at the Bauhaus, processing round the edge of Goethe's beautiful romantic park until it reached the hall in the Schützengasse, right in the centre of Weimar old town. The lanterns, fantastic in their form and colours, had been made by the students as a tribute to Johannes Schlaf, the naturalist poet. Schlaf himself was in Weimar and went marching in the midst of the students in procession. Finally a coloured screen-play was performed, a reflective-light performance by Ludwig Hirschfeld-Mack. Successive waves of colour accompanied by fugue-like music ebbed and flowed through Weimar into the night.

————

With Gropius's new emphasis on 'Art and Technology' the balance of power in the Bauhaus workshops changed dramatically. The Hungarian-born Constructivist László Moholy-Nagy had taken over from Itten as director of the Preliminary Course in spring 1923, assisted by Josef Albers, the first of the Bauhaus students to be promoted to a teaching post.

There could hardly have been a greater contrast in outlook and appearance than that between the shaven-headed, ruminative Itten and Moholy, self-styled man of tomorrow, habitually dressed in an industrial boiler suit. Moholy's ideas on art and society had, in parallel to Gropius's, been formed by his bitter experiences of war. He had fought with the Austro-Hungarian army and been seriously injured. He instigated his own style of abstract geometric art signifying the new rational post-war society, breaking completely with the destructive, hidebound errors of the past. Moholy was a co-founder of the Hungarian Activist journal *MA* (*Today*) and in fact had taken part in the Constructivist conference held in Weimar in 1922.

In the following year Gropius met him in Berlin. He was immediately impressed by his work and his vitality and offered him a post at the Bauhaus straight away. Moholy's great preoccupation as an artist was with space, and with movement within space. He was to follow through these interests not just in painting, sculpture, architecture and industrial design but also in photography and film, advertising and typography. Gropius described his power and versatility as 'Leonardian'. They became close allies and lifelong friends.

Moholy helped to create the new mood at the Bauhaus. As a teacher he brought dedication and freshness. He was completely unselfcon-

László Moholy-Nagy, director of the Preliminary Course from 1923,
in his customary technician's dress.

scious, totally absorbed in the idea of the moment. 'With the attitude of an unprejudiced, happy child at play,' as Gropius described him, 'he surprised us by the directness of his intuitive approach.' Moholy's wife Lucia, already a photographer, came with him to Weimar. Here she worked with Moholy on developing the photogram technique and was to become more or less the Bauhaus's official resident photographer, recording the buildings, the people and the atmosphere in a sequence of images that came to define the Bauhaus, and indeed still do.

For Gropius the problems in changing the emphasis within the Bauhaus workshops from the handmade and romantic to the clean-cut and mechanistic often appeared daunting. The weaving workshop, for instance, had up to now been strongly influenced by folk art. The woodcarving workshop, so active in the decoration of the Sommerfeld House, had perfected a fantastical Expressionist style. A highly elaborate 'African Chair', a painted oak throne for a mythic tribal chief, was (now almost unbelievably) designed by the modernist architect Marcel Breuer when a Bauhaus student in 1921.

Converting the outlook in the ceramics workshop to industrial production seems to have been an especially hard task. In April 1923 Gropius wrote severely to the workshop Master, Gerhard Marcks:

Yesterday I looked at the many new pots you have all been making. Almost all of them are unique objects, and it would be quite wrong if you were not to look for ways in which the good work in them could be made available to more people . . . We have to find ways of reproducing some pieces with the aid of the machine.

The greatest progress towards mass production would be made in the metalworking workshop under Moholy-Nagy as the new Master of Form. It was Moholy's students Marianne Brandt and Wilhelm Wagenfeld who designed the smooth-lined, restrained, subtly geometric metalwork that became almost symbolic of Bauhaus design in later years (see Plates 13 and 14).

Gropius's preoccupations were by no means simply artistic. Inflation was turning to hyperinflation in Germany. In 1923 Herbert Bayer was called on to design three emergency banknotes for the government of

Thuringia, in denominations from a million to five million marks. With local support becoming increasingly problematic Gropius was actively pursuing possibilities for marketing the Bauhaus in the wider world. A business manager, Emil Lange, was appointed. Bauhaus products were exhibited at the Leipzig Fair in September 1923, their first commercial showing, and then in the Werkbund exhibition in Stuttgart.

Gropius always rose to the occasion. Crisis seemed to energise him. Lyonel Feininger described meeting him by chance in early August. It was seven thirty in the morning: 'he approached me affectionately, took me by the arm and wanted to say a few things to me – so I went with him to the Bauhaus. He never complains, never seems exhausted or embittered. He works until 3 in the morning, hardly sleeps at all.' Feininger was sceptical about Gropius's new 'Art and Technology' directive. But his personal admiration for 'Gropi', as he called him, was intense. 'One can feel sorry for anyone who cannot, somehow or other, take heart from this man.'

———

We remember Gropius had once told Alma of his longing for 'a companion who loves me and my work'. Finally he found her in the early summer of 1923. On 28 May Gropius was giving his 'Art and Technology' lecture in Hanover, invited by his friend and supporter Alexander Dorner, director of the Hanover Landesmuseum. Sitting in the front row and listening attentively were two young women in their twenties, Ilse Frank and her younger sister Hertha. Ilse was strikingly attractive with light brown hair and a tiny, perfectly formed nose that gave her a gamine look, an easy confidence. She had dressed elegantly for the occasion in a swirling black rayon cape and black silk hat. Gropius watched through a slit in the curtain as the audience assembled. He told her later that he had instantly fallen in love and knew then that he would go to any lengths to meet her. She too was impressed both by the lecturer and by the lecture. 'The Bauhaus idea had captured me totally,' she wrote. She asked Alexander Dorner if she and her sister could join them for dinner afterwards, but Dorner explained that no guests had been invited since

Gropius needed to leave early in the morning to return to Weimar. Bauhaus Week was already in full preparation.

The next morning, however, Ilse heard a taxi drive up to the Frank family house in the prosperous suburbs of Hanover. She and her sister were in the process of selling the house following the recent death of their mother and imagined this was a prospective purchaser. In fact it was Gropius spying out the land. She was curious to know whom he might have been visiting and telephoned a neighbour, the painter Kurt Schwitters, whom the girls had often visited while he was constructing the famous Merzbau installation in his house. But Schwitters had not seen Gropius since the night of the lecture. She then contacted Dorner, who told her that Gropius had left as planned early in the morning; she must have had a hallucination.

The episode lingered in her mind over the next few days while she was in Dillenburg. This industrial town in Hesse, for centuries an iron-mining centre, was where the Frank family ironworks, the Frank Eisenwerke, was based. For the past two years Ilse had been engaged to a cousin, Hermann Frank, a manager at the works, and with the marriage imminent she was immersed in wedding plans. When she returned to Hanover the maid reported that a boy had come round to the house and asked her many questions about the two Frank sisters. He had seemed a well-educated, affable young man and she had replied as best she could. This turned out to be Gropius's nephew Joachim ('Jochen') Burchard, sent by Gropius on a reconnaissance mission.

Meanwhile, he had written to the two sisters directly, saying, 'Unfortunately, through my own fault, I have failed to make your acquaintance. I wish you could have spent the evening after my lecture with us. I shall pass through Hanover again next week, coming from Cologne. May I make good then on what I missed this time?'

Back in Hanover they invited him to dinner. It later turned out that Gropius had in fact stayed on for several days in a Hanover hotel awaiting their return, making excuses to his Bauhaus colleagues that he had gone to visit the Fagus factory. Ilse described 'a very enjoyable evening during which I became more and more entranced by his personality

and his ideas'. When Gropius left she went with him to the door and lingered there to watch him walk down the steps and through the garden
to his taxi waiting in the street. 'This was something no well-educated,
engaged girl could do' in Germany at this period, and such a blatant
abandonment of protocol gave Gropius hope.

Ilse was the eldest of four sisters, all of them destined in some way
to rebel against the conventional values of their solid bourgeois Hanover family. The youngest daughter, Ellen, was to become a fairly well
known actress. Ilse herself had acquired a new perspective through
being sent to an English boarding school in Oxford in 1913, in the
year before the war; she had then been a Red Cross nurse in army
hospitals, in charge of a station for thirty wounded soldiers. In defiance of the mores of the time she had already been living with her
fiancé. She had worked for a newspaper in Munich and was always to
have great journalistic aptitude. More recently, back temporarily in
Hanover, she had taken a job in an avant-garde bookshop where Kurt
Schwitters was an enthusiastic customer. Her greatest obsession was
literature.

A week or so after the dinner Gropius wrote to implore her not to
go ahead with the wedding. He knew instinctively that they belonged
together. Ilse was torn by a sense of obligation towards her cousin
Hermann, a rather lost and ineffectual character for whom she felt
a kind of sisterly love and responsibility, and her sudden attraction
towards Gropius and his ideas. 'You have come to me like a comrade
from childhood days who has also not forgotten how easy and simple
it is to get together when there is trust . . . now you came and you
said that everything is good and ever since a beautiful rainbow shines
within me in all colours.' As if by instinct she had alighted on the
image of the rainbow of all colours that had so enraptured Gropius
when young.

In June she went to visit him in Weimar, spending two or three days
there looking round the school, which was seething with activity in
preparation for the Bauhaus exhibition. In the evenings they managed
quiet conversations, exchanging their past histories, discussing future

plans. She was suddenly seized with feelings of anxiety about her own ability to enter this completely new environment, worried about her standing in relation to the Masters and the students. But Gropius was not to be deflected when she suggested that after all the turmoil she would create by abandoning Hermann she might only disappoint him in the end. 'He looked at me with his beautiful, penetrating eyes and said: "I am totally immune to disappointment because I have trained myself to look at people or situations not for what they seem to be right now but for what they might become."' As Ilse came to realise, this was Gropius's policy with his students too.

Soon afterwards she travelled to meet him in Cologne. They stayed in a hotel together and 'as if this were all happening in another star, we were completely united', Ilse wrote. But she was still reluctant to commit herself, still embroiled in a whole network of love and obligation to her family, to Hermann, as well as the sheer fear of creating a scandal. She delayed and prevaricated. She was also afraid she might be pregnant, whether by Gropius or Hermann is unclear, but was relieved to discover she was not.

In July Gropius sent her a tirade of impatience:

I am not a man who can wait! I storm through life and whoever cannot keep pace will remain at the wayside. I want to create with my spirit and with my body, yes – also with my body and life is short and needs to be grasped . . . When we met I felt I had come home as never before with any woman. Without reservation I gave you my inner and outer possessions, but it has made you perplexed and you began to divide it up in parts. But I comprehend the world as unity and this feeling suffuses my entire consciousness. Your wish is impossible, because it is senseless to separate body and spirit. The soul forms the body, but the body cannot create a soul. As often as we become lovers the *whole* of life, birth and death revolves in our hearts . . . Ours was no play. We had formed a holy bond in blessed nights . . . but you leave me in uncertainty and my humility changes into anger when I find my most sacred gift disdained. Strong people feel great tensions, their heart is never indolent, it dissolves in love and can immediately harden into steel again. You forced the tenderness of my heart to change into sharpness. But one thing remains – your veracity is radiantly beautiful! You creation of my heart, how should I not know also about your darkness! . . . The miraculous and painful grace of a great love is still unknown to you, but it is going to be part of your fate and it may come soon when grief and longing will break out for unknowingly discarded values.

Do you understand me, my beloved, do you understand my being hard and un-relenting? But I stand at the threshold and I must speak to you without restraint: in you slumber *wonderful* forces whose essence I had meant to develop into mean-ingful reality and I wanted to fight for you with all I have. But your attitude is still determined by half-heartedness and so I refrain . . . You are standing at a crucial turning point of your life and whatever you choose, seize it and live it *fully*. Only total dedication counts, everything else is weak. Make a clean break, liberate your-self . . . Goodbye . . . I believe in you!

Gropius was now in a new mood of complete determination, quite different from his altercations with Lily and Maria. He was committed, no longer viewing himself as the wandering star.

But Ilse still demurred. Two days before she and Hermann planned to leave for Munich for the wedding, where a great family gathering would be taking place, Gropius apparently lost hope and sent her a farewell present, an almost complete set of *Le Charivari*, the nineteenth-century French magazine illustrated by Daumier. Ilse tells us that this 'gener-ous and noble gesture by someone who thought he had lost his battle' overwhelmed her to such an extent that she finally gave in. On the eve of the wedding she broke the news to Hermann, who had half expected it. He made it easy for her, not uttering a single word of reproach. But it had obviously been the greatest disappointment to him, as she reported back to Gropius, who, with his strange tendency to intervene at times of emotional crisis, asked her whether he himself should go and talk to Hermann. Ilse's sister Hertha wisely advised that this would only make an agonising situation worse.

A final stipulation made by Gropius was that Ilse should change her name to Ise. Perhaps this was a final rejection of her formal Hamburg upper-bourgeois background. The name Ise had a more pared-down Bauhausian feel. Although it was never a legal change of name it was as Ise that she now came to join him in Weimar in August 1923. 'I arrived at his door', she recollected, 'with a little suitcase in my hand and dis-appeared for all those who had known me before into a new world that had no equal anywhere and that gave me the chance to develop my own personality, according to my own lights, within its framework.' Ise's own impact on the Bauhaus was to be considerable.

Bauhaus Week was in progress when Ise moved finally to Weimar. At first, to prevent gossip, she stayed as the guest of Paul Klee and his wife. Gropius was anxiously fending off Lily Hildebrandt, not having told her of the advent of Ise, pretending to have been away on building sites and suggesting that Lily find lodgings far afield for Bauhaus Week rather than staying in Weimar itself.

Ise and Gropius both attended the Mask and Costume Ball held in the evening of 19 August, one of those legendary Bauhaus celebrations that continued on till sunrise. They left early in the morning to catch an express train from Jena to Verona and then on to Venice, where they stayed in a little Italian hotel looking out over a small piazza. 'We were left free to explore each other,' Ise remembered. This was an early honeymoon. They were still travelling incognito, having left it too late to obtain a marriage licence. Gropius had mislaid his divorce certificate and had had to write off to Vienna to obtain a duplicate. But he had already told his mother and asked her to spread the news around their friends. After years of agitation and insults from Alma, Manon Gropius was delighted at the prospect of an amenable daughter-in-law from a similar well-to-do bourgeois background to her own.

The marriage between Direktor der Staatlichen Bauhauses Walter Adolf Georg Gropius and Frieda Paula Julie Ilse Frank finally took place in Weimar on 16 October 1923. It was a civil ceremony at which Klee and Kandinsky were witnesses. The registrar at first refused to accept Kandinsky's signature, insisting there was no such name as Wassily. At the time of the wedding Gropius was forty, Ise twenty-six. The age difference between them was parallel to that of Gustav Mahler and Alma Schindler on their wedding day.

After the wedding they left again for Paris on what amounted to a second honeymoon. The object this time was a visit to Le Corbusier for an exchange of views on architecture and for Gropius to see Corb's most recent works: the studio-house in Paris he had designed for his friend,

Ise and Walter Gropius a few years after their marriage on 16 October 1923.

the painter Amédée Ozenfant (1922), and the La Roche-Jeanneret double house (1923), for the Swiss banker and collector of modern art Raoul La Roche and Albert Jeanneret. The two architects met for the first time in the Café Les Deux Magots. Le Corbusier elaborated on his vision for a *ville contemporaine* of three million inhabitants. They discussed standardisation and prefabrication of houses, a shared enthusiasm at the time, and Gropius brought out a graph demonstrating how while the cost of living had doubled in the USA, the cost of the mass-produced Ford car had actually halved. In the Deux Magots he and Le Corbusier pored over the pictures of American grain silos which Gropius had brought with him as examples of the new industrial monumentalism. The mood of the meeting it seems was in stark contrast to the dinner some years later in Corb's Paris apartment, when his wife, the rather crude and outspoken ex-mannequin Yvonne, turned to Gropius and asked him whether he had seen it. Gropius, mystified, asked her what she meant. 'Vonvon', as Corb called her, slapped her bottom. *'Mon cul!'* she said.

Ise was now officially installed in Gropius's apartment on Kaiserin-Augusta-Strasse. Her life as 'Frau Bauhaus' was beginning. She met with some initial resistance from the older generation of her family. Her godfather was bemused by a visit to Weimar a few days after the wedding, when Gropius gave him a copy of the newly published first book about the Bauhaus, *Staatliches Bauhaus in Weimar* (see Plate 9) He told Ise that she must have been 'inspired by madness' in joining such a set-up and all communication between them ended. Alma was apparently 'beside herself with anger and disappointment' when she heard that Gropius had remarried, writing to tell him that she would never allow Manon to visit him in Weimar again.

Gropius was now also beset by former lovers. Ise describes in her memoirs how three of them arrived in Weimar to confront him when they heard news of the marriage. She does not give names but these women were presumably Lily Hildebrandt, Maria Benemann and another conquest he had made, the photographer Margarethe Fellerer, who lived in Ascona with the painter Ernst Frick. A formidable older lady, a leader of Weimar society, had also arrived at the flat in Kaiserin-Augusta-Strasse to tackle Gropius angrily about his lack of wisdom in marrying a much younger woman, so unsuitable a consort for the director of the Bauhaus. Gropius, beleaguered, at this point asked Ise to take over his problematic personal correspondence, and letters to and from his former lovers were in effect censored from now on.

But at the Bauhaus itself Ise was welcomed. Gropius took her on a full tour of the workshops, carpentry, metalwork, weaving and the rest, including the ceramics workshops in their outpost at Dornburg. Unlike Alma, Ise, of a different generation, more intellectually flexible in outlook, immediately felt attuned to the direction the Bauhaus was now taking. With the arrival of the relatively youthful László Moholy-Nagy, who was only twenty-eight when he first came to Weimar, the balance was shifting. Ise was not only of the same generation as the younger Bauhaus Masters but also as some of the most talented of the students: Herbert Bayer, born in Haag in Austria-Hungary in 1900; Breuer, born in Pécs, Hungary, in 1902; Alexander 'Xanti' Schawinsky, born in 1904 in Basel. These three were to form a lasting bond with Ise which continued through the years of their exile in the States.

Ise modernised the Bauhaus. She encouraged Gropius to buy a gramophone, which they played with great enjoyment at their home in Kaiserin-Augusta-Strasse, where Klee loved to accompany it on his violin. Her experience in journalism made her an effective Bauhaus publicist, drafting and editing Gropius's statements, reports and articles, which she typed up with tremendous expertise. She recollected, 'My ability to type proved a godsend, and for most of our married life my little typewriter was a steady companion on all our trips.'

Most importantly Ise's role within the Bauhaus was in forming connections between the generations and acting as arbiter between the men and women. Gropius wrote to her gratefully not long after their marriage, 'I believe finally that the great desire of my whole life to find a real comrade who is ready to walk with me through thick and thin has become possible with you.' As personal and political attacks on Gropius and the Bauhaus worsened, Ise became indispensable to him.

Public and critical acclaim for the 1923 Bauhaus exhibition had served to increase local opposition to Gropius. His new emphasis on industrial production enraged the guilds of craft workers, who saw this as a threat. In 1923 a new national government took power in Berlin, leading to a surge of demonstrations by radicals throughout Germany. Right-wing Reichswehr forces were sent to Weimar in November to repress socialist–communist influences in the government. Thuringia was placed under martial law. Not only was the Bauhaus itself investigated, soldiers arrived to carry out a search of Gropius's own home. The one-time officer of the Hussars wrote in a fury to the military commander: 'Yesterday morning at half past ten I was summoned home from my office by a soldier because there was a search warrant. The house was searched by a deputy officer and six men in a sensational manner . . . I am ashamed of my country, your Excellency, ashamed of being apparently without protection in my own country, in spite of my achievements.' State elections now put the conservative factions in power in Thuringia, ending the pro-Bauhaus socialist government. Auguries for the future of the Bauhaus were not good.

———

Early in 1924 Ise became seriously ill. She was now two months pregnant but, taken into hospital in Weimar, she lost the baby. She blamed the incompetence of the doctor. Suffering agonising pain she was moved to the more specialist Sanatorium Königspark at Loschnitz near Dresden where, as she describes, she 'learned a lot about the chemistry of nutrition, was massaged, sunbathed and given a lot of rest so that I finally appeared to be knitted together again'. During those six weeks of Ise's absence Gropius was distraught, sending flowers, visiting, writing her the forty-five letters now in the Bauhaus Archive, telling her, 'I am already so tightly connected with you that I feel absolutely halved without you.' In the sanatorium Ise was translating articles from Le Corbusier's *L'Esprit nouveau* from the French for Gropius and was reading Henry Ford.

Meanwhile problems with Alma once again erupted. Gropius had been invited to lecture in Vienna and was eager to accept since this would give him a chance to see Manon. Ise, all too conscious of Alma's hostility to her and the marriage, was reluctant for Gropius to go. He offered to cancel the trip in deference to her. On one of his visits to the sanatorium, they discussed the possibility that they might go together, but this appears to have ended in a bitter argument.

Ise wrote apologetically to him afterwards: 'you know whenever I am confronted with the "complex", it always brings disaster. And there we face its innermost core and its name is: Alma . . . She is *not* kind and one feels an inclination to be *against* her unless one is completely *for* her.' Ise was reluctant to risk a meeting. As she put it to Gropius, 'would you approach Vesuvius with confidence after you have just seen it in flames?'

Ise's fundamental problem was her feeling that Alma had had so strong an influence on Gropius in what she saw as his 'decisive years', the years between twenty-five and thirty-five, that his whole being was 'impregnated by her':

That is her possession. If you had *only* loved her! But no, you owe her more than just a beautiful human experience. Each person meets the moment in his life when his whole essence is suddenly stimulated by another human being, or a book, or an experience, and that remains the most *important* moment in his life. You have received that from her and I shall envy her for that as long as she lives.

Ise was astute in her acknowledgement that Gropius's feelings for Alma were irrational, belonging as they did to the realms of their past passion. Gropius responded:

I am happy that finally you talk about it! We must be quite frank and open with each other. I have told you without holding back what I think of Alma, what I received from her . . . You are right, these are things of passion, but to become human – oh, how difficult – means to master these passions by consciousness. I want us to be wise and to guard ourselves because our passions are terrible powers which suddenly overtake us. I know this all too well and I want to prevent by all possible means that our sweet, beautiful, hopeful, pure marriage is not going to suffer from the shadows of my past.

Ise herself provides an interesting insight into their sexual relations. Her doctor at the Sanatorium Königspark gave her his opinion that she was 'erotically still quite dormant and girlish'. He could see nothing 'animal-like' in her disposition. Ise made no comment at the time but suggested to Gropius, 'maybe you could enlighten him some day that I do not exactly live next to you as a passively tolerant sexual partner'. However, the doctor was right 'in so far as a spiritual experience has to precede any physical one with me'. In the end they made a pact, agreeing that they should travel together to Vienna. But her doctor forbade it and Gropius made a brief visit to Alma and seven-year-old Manon on his own.

Ise returned to Weimar in late May 1924, in time for Walter's forty-first birthday celebrations, when they stayed up dancing till four in the morning and Gropius was deluged with presents from the Masters and the students. She described to his mother how the Bauhaus band was 'in a fantastic mood. Gropius was carried on the students' shoulders with deafening cheers.' This was a Bauhaus birthday ritual, during which Gropius continued smoking his cigar. By coincidence the local minister of state, Friedrich Schultz, happened to visit: 'he was amazed and pleasantly disappointed to see the ill-reputed Bauhaus in such spirit.'

After this they left Weimar for a summer holiday with Gropius's family in the house by the sea in Timmendorf. But before long Gropius had to hurry back to Weimar. There was mounting crisis at the Bauhaus. Back in March he had been summoned by the right-wing Völkische Partei leader in charge of education in Thuringia, whom Gropius described as a man with no cultural interests whatsoever, to be told that official financial support for the Bauhaus would not be renewed in future.

In late April Gropius had been viciously libelled in the so-called Yellow Brochure. In this inflammatory pamphlet the Bauhaus was attacked for being anti-German. Its community activities were Bolshevist and Spartacist. Foreign Masters and students were given preferential treatment. It turned out that the scurrilous pamphlet was composed by three ex-members of the Bauhaus staff who had been dismissed for intrigue in 1922. Hans Beyer had been an accountant at the Bauhaus, Josef Zachmann a master craftsman in the cabinet-making workshop and Carl Schlemmer, brother of Oskar, a master craftsman in the wall-painting workshop.

Carl Schlemmer, known as Caska, was in Ise's view 'a bad character but a splendid technician and quite indispensable when it came to putting together the costumes Oskar had designed'. Lily Hildebrandt too had warned Gropius about Caska. When the Yellow Brochure was distributed in Weimar and beyond, the students printed posters in support of Gropius and the Masters issued a public statement attacking the pamphlet for obscenity.

On 6 July 1924 an announcement was made in the local newspaper, the *Weimarische Zeitung*, by the Association for the Protection of German Culture in Thuringia, protesting at the continuing existence of the Bauhaus:

All the mechanical games, the arrangements of materials, the colour effect, each distorted idiot's head and bizarre human body, all the schizoid scribblings and experiments in embarrassment which we find in exhibitions and publications of the State Bauhaus in Weimar are decadent values . . . They have nothing to do with genuine art.

This focus on what were viewed as stylistic aberrations of the Bauhaus was a premonition of the Nazis' later campaigns against 'Degenerate Art'.

To add to Gropius's mounting anxieties over the summer Emil Lange, the Bauhaus's business manager, had resigned, apparently defeated by the complications of accounting in a business enterprise that was also part of a complex and unorthodox educational establishment. The Bauhaus was attempting to do too much at once. Lange's successor, Wilhelm Frederick Necker, had only been appointed very recently. Meanwhile, on 18 September 1924, the new right-wing Thuringian government, having considered the report of the official audit office which assessed the State Bauhaus as unprofitable, gave a 'cautionary warning' to the director and the Masters of potential termination of their contracts with effect from 31 March 1925. This was indeed 'a black morning!' in Gropius's increasingly pessimistic view.

In response to what was viewed as victimisation there was an upsurge of support for Gropius and his school. The Friends of the Bauhaus enlarged its membership impressively, assisted by Ise's genius for networking. The prestige governing body now included Arnold Schoenberg, Albert Einstein, Marc Chagall and the architects Josef Hoffmann, Peter Behrens, Hans Poelzig and H. P. Berlage, as well as, more surprisingly, Alma's past and current lovers Oskar Kokoschka and Franz Werfel. All the same, Gropius was now reluctantly deciding that his future in Weimar was increasingly uncertain. It was time for the Bauhaus to find a new location. Cologne, Frankfurt, Essen, Düsseldorf and Dessau were among the cities now being considered as alternatives.

In September 1924 Ise sounded out the ground in Cologne. Here she met the then mayor, Konrad Adenauer. Ise had achieved the introduction through her old connections with Adenauer's wife Gussie. Gussie was smiling and welcoming but so totally unable to latch on to the ideas behind the Bauhaus that Ise was discouraged. With Adenauer himself

Ise Gropius – 'Frau Bauhaus' – photographed by Lucia Moholy in 1924.

it was quite a different matter. Almost as soon as she was shown into his office he expressed real interest in the Bauhaus and its problems.

She was with him for an hour and a half, during which Adenauer read an article by Gropius on the Bauhaus which she had brought with her, and pored over the Bauhaus book which, as Ise reassured her husband, she 'showed to him in strict selection'. This was a technique she had by now perfected, 'picking out only those things which the various people might be able to assimilate'. Adenauer had shown a special interest in the Bauhaus 'Bogler' teapot, responding to its underlying concept of standardised parts and economy of means. He expressed the hope of meeting Gropius next time he came to lecture near Cologne. Ise diagnosed that Adenauer stood politically to the left of the Zentrum Partei (Centre Party) and, as she told Gropius, 'he is just as fed up with Germany as you are, but, just as you yourself, cannot bring himself to part with it.' An interesting view of the man who became the first Chancellor of the newly founded Federal Republic of Germany in 1949.

Ise made good use of her time in Cologne working on the marketing of Bauhaus products. A second showing at Leipzig Fair the previous February had not been a success, with sales proving disappointingly slight. Not only had there been a reaction against the pared-down, functional Bauhaus style in a context of overwhelming bourgeois kitsch, there had also been resistance on grounds of cost. The simple Bauhaus lamp designed by Marianne Brandt had been admired but considered too expensive, the basic problem being that the Bauhaus lacked resources for investing in mass production. There were failures in fulfilling even the few orders they had received, with complaints of saucers being supplied without cups. The commercial structure behind the Bauhaus products had not inspired confidence up to now.

Ise courageously tried again, calling on Alfred Tierz, the owner of a large Cologne department store, in the hope of interesting him in Bauhaus textiles and carpets. She invited him to Weimar. Ise also drummed up interest in Gropius's lectures. Her letters radiate a newfound energy and purpose. She spent several weeks away, also visiting Düsseldorf and Essen, and wanted to spend longer, to keep going. She suggested that if Gropius allowed her to travel round for a year, the Bauhaus would manage to do better business. But Gropius was desperate to have her back at home.

Through the autumn and winter of 1924 there was a further deterioration in relations between the Bauhaus and the Weimar and Thuringian governments. Things became so desperate financially that Ise had a dream in which she left Walter to marry an American millionaire. She dreamed she was waiting for the marriage, wearing her white wedding dress, when she was startled to notice that her sister was busily making up Gropius's face. When she questioned this he said, 'Well, I simply cannot go with my own face to your wedding.' Conditions at the Bauhaus were indeed becoming just a bit surrealistic. Ise comments in her diary, 'What ingenious solutions dreams provide that would never occur to a rational mind!'

The political situation was now threatening as the Nationalsozialistische Deutsche Arbeiterpartei (National Socialist German Workers' Party or Nazi party) became a serious force. National Socialist attacks on the Bauhaus increased to such an extent that Gropius was forced into taking the initiative. On 26 December 1924 he and the Bauhaus Masters sent a letter to the government of Thuringia announcing the dissolution of the Bauhaus on 1 April 1925, after their official contracts expired. The letter of resignation ended pugnaciously: 'We accuse the Government of Thuringia of having permitted and approved the frustration of culturally important and always non-political efforts through the intrigues of hostile political parties.' The letter was signed 'by all the Masters'.

This was followed, on 13 January, by a letter from the Bauhaus students: 'We notify the Government of Thuringia that we, collaborators at the State Bauhaus at Weimar, shall leave the Bauhaus together with the leaders of the Bauhaus because of the actions of the State government.' There had been 127 students – forty-five women and eighty-two men – at the Bauhaus for the winter term. The dissolution of the Bauhaus was reported in all the national papers, together with a good deal of angry comment. Ise noted in her diary, 'Nobody will believe that the Bauhaus has really come to an end.'

––––

After all the tensions and upheavals Gropius was exhausted. In late February 1925 he and Ise set off on an extended trip to Genoa. Gropius was always easily revived by fresh visual excitements. Genoa, with its dramatic changes of scale, fluctuations of level, its sudden deep ravines, its contrasts between the simple little houses and magnificent huge palaces, delighted him and Ise. They both became addicted to what Ise calls 'the charms of the Italian jewellery stores'. They ate in the most ordinary little trattorias, a habit they continued for the rest of their eight weeks in Italy.

From now on it was Ise who kept travel diaries for herself and Gropius, recording their journeys and their joint impressions of people and surroundings. One of Gropius's most valuable traits was his ability to distance himself from the problems of the moment, of which there would be many, and immerse himself in new scenes and new surroundings. Back in Italy for a more protracted visit than their 'secret honeymoon' in 1923, Ise found him a wonderfully relaxed companion, retracing the Italian sightseeing journeys he had made with his parents as a child.

They went by boat from Genoa to Naples, travelling down the country's west coast to arrive at what Ise describes as 'this teeming, lively, dirty and tremendously attractive city'. No other town had so impressed them with the impact of humanity. Gropius has often been viewed as a rigorous architectural technocrat, impervious to human needs and feelings. This was certainly not so. In Naples he and Ise were thrilled by the way that so much of human life took place right in the streets: 'all happenings, all passions are demonstrated in view of everybody'. Significantly too it appeared that Neapolitans had none of the servility which they were becoming so accustomed to in Germany in 1925.

Gropius was impressed by the way that southern Italian architecture seemed to have evolved so naturally. Taking the train from Pugliano to the top of Vesuvius they saw how even the new houses were built 'according to tradition and apparently without an architect'. They were aware of sophisticated rural people who had almost unthinkingly 'stuck to this beautiful way of building'. Approaching Positano Gropius marvelled at a town almost 'glued against the rocks of the mountain, very beautiful and very strange in its architecture', showing its Saracenic influence.

The architectural high point of their trip was reached at Taormina in Sicily, the little town built high above the sea, with the silhouette of

Etna looming large and ominous behind it. They arrived in late February to find the town already a mass of purple flowers, while the smouldering volcano was still half covered in snow. Gropius, at the time so immersed in the theory of theatre in terms of both architecture and performance, was carried away by the view at sunrise from Taormina's classical Greek theatre on the cliff edge, the spectacle described by Ise as 'the most perfect, grandest drama thinkable!'

But there was another spectacle to come, and this was the sudden, completely unexpected appearance in Taormina of Alma. She had been on travels in Egypt and the Holy Land with Werfel and they were on the way back home to Venice, where Alma had recently bought herself a three-storey palazzo, now known as the Casa Mahler, in the San Tomà area near the Grand Canal. A meeting face to face with Alma continued to be the thing Ise most dreaded: 'Oh, you don't know', she had once confessed to Gropius, 'how often I worriedly compared myself to her and how I looked for, and naturally found, her superiority in every photo and every letter.'

Painful wrangles over access to Manon still continued. Alma was obsessed with keeping the child to herself. Gropius had an additional reason for anger, dating back to a malicious plot Alma had perpetrated at the Bauhaus in the spring of 1923, when Kandinsky had suggested that Arnold Schoenberg, a mutual friend of his and Alma's, should apply for the vacant directorship of the music academy at Weimar. Alma was antagonistic to Kandinsky and had spread the rumour that he and Gropius were anti-Semitic. Appalled at hearing this, the Jewish Schoenberg had instantly withdrawn his application. Kandinsky was upset and mystified; Gropius was horrified and furious, knowing all too well Alma's capacity for complicated plotting. So a meeting between Alma and the Gropiuses in Sicily did not augur well.

But it turned out to be surprisingly successful. Gropius and Ise were packed for departure, having loaded up the shawls, necklaces, tortoise shells and other acquisitions of their travels. The rather hectic circumstances had, in Ise's words, 'made this fortuitous encounter easy and casual and a lot of the tension that had built up between us simply melted away because we were both surprised on foreign ground and quite unprepared for battle'. After this relations between Gropius's wife and his ex-wife would be civil though still wary all their lives.

———

Gropius's stay in Taormina was cut short by a telegram from Georg Muche at the Bauhaus informing him that the city of Dessau had made a promising new offer to take over the Bauhaus. In Gropius's absence Muche and Feininger had been left in charge of these first negotiations, rather regretting that they had encouraged 'Gropi' to take such a protracted Italian holiday. He and Ise now hurried back to Weimar, a three-day train journey, arriving exhausted but exhilarated too.

There was last-minute panic when the scurrilous Yellow Brochure appeared in Dessau too, and Carl Schlemmer wrote an inflammatory anti-Bauhaus letter to the city. 'The devil has entered the scene again,' wrote Ise. 'If characters like Carl Schlemmer, Beyer, Zachmann, de Fries and who else should succeed in bringing down the Bauhaus, we might give up hope for the next artistic development in Germany, because it would prove that the reactionary spirit was victorious and will decide everything in the future.'

The decision on whether the Bauhaus came to Dessau was finally set for 23 March. Gropius had travelled over for the day and telephoned Ise that evening to tell her that the local parliament had voted in favour of the Bauhaus by twenty-six votes to fifteen. Gropius's local lecture had re-assured many. A telegram of support from other leading architects – Peter Behrens, Bruno Taut, Hans Poelzig, Erich Mendelsohn and Mies van der Rohe – had been influential too. There had also been encourage-ment from Prince Aribert of Anhalt. Most crucial had been the backing for the Bauhaus from the directors of the Junkers factory, hoping for future co-operation. 'Big relief', writes Ise, 'and final relaxation of the unbearable tension of the last months.'

Once Dessau had been definitely decided on as the new destination for the Bauhaus there was much coming and going, planning, decision-making, anguished discussions over who would make the move with

Gropius to Dessau, who might stay behind in Weimar, who would find new work elsewhere. By the end of May Gropius and Ise had vacated their apartment. Ise wrote, 'The apartment is empty and I pulled off the tiny little calling card which I had found so surprising and touching when I first appeared in Weimar.' She found it horribly ironic that a major of the repressive right-wing Reichswehr would be replacing Gropius as tenant of the flat with immediate effect.

There was a pervasive sense of winding down. The majority of products of the Weimar workshops now became state property, though some were purchased by Gropius and the Masters. In late March, at the end of the last Bauhaus winter term, a *Letzter Tanz*, the final celebratory farewell party of the Weimar Bauhaus, was held in the Ilmschlösschen castle. Herbert Bayer's design for the invitation incorporated a condolence card from the Bauhaus's friends and families in Weimar, announcing themselves as being deeply moved at the departure. The Bauhaus band played. The mood was bittersweet.

There were many more farewells and Weimar reminiscences. A massive bathing party of Bauhäusler of all the generations was held on the banks of the Elbe. And then in late June there was 'a lovely get-to-gether' of the Masters in a *Weinstube* in Weimar attended by the Muches, Moholy-Nagy, Klee, Gunta Stölzl, Oskar Schlemmer. 'Klee very lively, which is rare for him,' writes Ise. In mid-July there were final Weimar goodbyes between the Masters' families. The Masters' wives kissed one another fondly: 'Nina Kandinsky had a cold but Frau Feininger did not let that bother her.'

Then and later the Bauhaus generated such mixed feelings. The best summing up of those early Weimar years comes from Xanti Schawinsky, stage designer, writer, dancer, who first came to Weimar as a student in 1924. He writes of how the very first art school of this particular experimental sort had been full of 'experiences of the stormy but also of the quietest kind', with all imaginable nuances in between – 'of thought, of discovery, of resignation, of madness, of reason, of doubt, of friendship and devotion, of the consciousness of human worth, of joy and of pain too'.

As far as Gropius was concerned the Weimar years reveal his incredible resilience in the face of internal tensions at the Bauhaus added to virulent local opposition. In spite of many setbacks he held fast to his vision of the central role of art within society and of the true meaning of community. This became the future pattern of his life. His powers of endurance would be tested further in the politically supercharged years that lay ahead.

9

Bauhaus Dessau
1925–1926

'If one regarded Weimar as the so-called childhood, the period of storm and stress, life for the Bauhaus started in Dessau in all seriousness.' This was how it seemed to Tut Schlemmer, wife of the painter and theatre workshop Master Oskar Schlemmer. For Gropius Dessau brought a kind of culmination of all he had hoped for after the horrors of the First World War.

Dessau as a city was quite different from Weimar. It was over twice the size, with a population of seventy thousand in comparison with Weimar's thirty thousand. It was further north than Weimar, two hours' journey from modern, cosmopolitan Berlin. It was predominantly industrial, dominated by the huge Junkers engineering and aircraft company. The city was administered by the Sozialdemokratische Partei (Social Democratic Party) and its liberal mayor Fritz Hesse championed the move of the Bauhaus to Dessau. The enterprising Hesse envisaged a return to the cultural glory days of Dessau, as it had been when Prince Fritz of Anhalt ruled the city more than a century before.

For Gropius the great attraction of Dessau was the opportunity to design a whole complex of new buildings for the school. This came at a time when his private practice was in a problematic state, with several commissions on hold for lack of funding. Fighting off local opposition to the Bauhaus in Weimar had prevented him from focusing on his own architectural work. So the prospect that Mayor Hesse now held out to him of large purpose-designed workshops and studios, houses for the director and the Masters and a student accommodation block, all funded by the city of Dessau, was irresistible. On that first visit to Dessau Hesse had taken Gropius and Ise on a tour of the future building site on the outskirts of the city, an area of greenery set partly in

The Masters on the roof of the Dessau Bauhaus, 1926.
L to r: Josef Albers, Hinnerk Scheper, Georg Muche, László Moholy-Nagy, Herbert Bayer, Joost Schmidt, Walter Gropius, Marcel Breuer, Wassily Kandinsky, Paul Klee, Lyonel Feininger, Gunta Stölzl, Oskar Schlemmer.

pinewoods and opposite a park. Ever since childhood he had dreamed of living in a pinewood, Gropius exclaimed.

Gropius was eager to get started and to resurrect the Bauhaus in its new setting and in its new technological image. Once again this was a time of hope.

The faculty remained more or less intact. Kandinsky agreed to go to Dessau, and so, after a great deal of dithering, did Klee. Oskar Schlemmer too had been very undecided but finally arrived in the autumn of 1925. The inspiring but always rather otherworldly Feininger, once described by Gropius as 'more of an ivory tower artist than the others', had pleaded to be relieved of teaching commitments. He came to Dessau with no contract and no salary but was still considered as integral to the community. Of the former Masters only Gerhard Marcks, the ceramics workshop Master, now moved elsewhere.

With the transfer of the Bauhaus to Dessau the teaching structure altered. The two-tier system of Form Master and Technical Master was abandoned in line with Gropius's current emphasis on art and technology. The two functions from now on were combined in an overall

Master with exceptional breadth of interests and experience, of whom Moholy-Nagy was the prime example. And it was significant for the future of the school that the most talented former Bauhaus students – Josef Albers, Herbert Bayer, Marcel Breuer, experimental colourist Hinnerk Scheper and sculptor and stage designer Joost Schmidt – were now promoted to being junior Masters. Another ex-student, the weaver Gunta Stölzl, would soon join them. ('*Meister*', she wrote boldly on her identification card, rejecting the female '*Meisterin*'.) The sense of the Bauhaus as an almost sacred dynasty was important to its image as the century progressed.

The start of the summer term was delayed by the exigencies of moving. Term finally began on 13 May 1925. Recruitment had been poor and student numbers dwindled to twenty males and forty-two females. Classes were held in makeshift accommodation: crammed into the storerooms of a defunct mail-order company and into corners of the buildings of the local Kunstgewerbe und Handwerkschule. The Masters' studios were temporarily housed in the Dessau art museum. But Gropius's hopes and energies were focused on plans for his new buildings and final fruition of the utopian schemes he had already formulated but never achieved while the Bauhaus was in Weimar. This was his great aim for a free-thinking community in which art was not considered as a luxury or adjunct but as a necessary element of life itself.

In Gropius's plans for a living, working community of artists it is easy to trace the influence of his mentor Peter Behrens and the artistic colony at Darmstadt in which Behrens had been such a force. It is possible to look back further and to link his ambitious schemes with the utopian ideals of William Morris and his followers in the English Arts and Crafts movement. There are traces of *News from Nowhere*, Morris's futuristic novel, in Gropius's ideas of creating a community harmonious in its self-sufficiency, with the pursuit of beauty at its core.

There are obvious parallels with C. R. Ashbee's colonisation of the village of Chipping Campden in the Cotswolds, with its sequence of craft workshops and its ambitious educational programme. Gropius in fact was to visit Chipping Campden later in his life. But the important difference of course is that whereas Morris and the Arts and Crafts idealists were consciously backward-looking in their thinking, romantically recreating an imagined past, Gropius was consciously moving forward at the Bauhaus into a modern world of linked-up thinking, in which art and science, technology, psychology as well as advanced studies in visual perception were combined. The Bauhaus workshops were no longer simply workshops: Gropius had begun describing them as laboratories of art in which the Bauhaus would be training 'an entirely new kind of collaborator for industry and the crafts who has an equal command of technology and design'.

In developing his plans for the new Bauhaus building Gropius was influenced by two of his own architectural projects of this period. One was the commission for the Friedrich Fröbel House in Bad Liebenstein, a complex of kindergarten, daycare centre, workshops and residential children's home which embodied Fröbel's thinking on the creative education of the child. Gropius was disappointed when this project eventually foundered for want of international funding. The other related educational scheme was the design of an international philosophical academy at Erlangen-Spandorf, a wonderfully high-flown project evolved by Professor Rolf Hoffmann of the University of Erlangen and supported by a number of eminent philosophers including Bertrand Russell. This scheme evaporated when Hoffmann absconded to the United States, taking with him the donations he had collected.

Some of Gropius's ideas for the spatial organisation of these buildings, both intended to be icons of progressive educational thinking, are reflected in his designs for the Bauhaus, which he consciously envisaged as an architectural showstopper, a glamorous public statement of intent.

As early as June 1925 Gropius submitted drawings and a model of the proposed new Bauhaus building to the Dessau authorities. The buildings consisted of a teaching and workshop wing, a theatre, a canteen, a gym and twenty-eight studio apartments for student accommodation, specific rooms for students being an innovation for the time. Originally it had been proposed that the local Kunstgewerbeschule should be accommodated in one wing of the school, but to Gropius's relief this plan was abandoned and the Bauhaus building developed as its own independent architectural entity.

Gropius's long-term working partner Adolf Meyer had decided not to make the move to Dessau. He stayed on in Weimar, working freelance before moving to Frankfurt to become director of the municipal building council. There was no animosity in the parting. Indeed Gropius recommended Meyer for the post. His young chief assistant, Ernst Neufert, was now promoted to run Gropius's new office, which with so much urgent work on hand was now enlarging, totalling around twenty employees. Ise was hopeful about Neufert's appointment, having taken him on a Sunday-afternoon bicycle ride in order to sound him out. 'He is such an able, dear person', she concluded, 'and will probably develop well. Since Meyer left and he has taken over a totally different tempo has come over everything.' Of Neufert's blatantly Germanic wife she comments, 'Visit with Frau Neufert. Her broad, blond, motherly type is very enjoyable; maybe a little too "teutsch"?'

Once plans for the new Bauhaus building had been officially accepted, foundations were laid during the summer of 1925 and construction was already beginning by July. Meanwhile, designs had been progressing for the little colony of houses for the director and the Masters on a site in the pinewood ten minutes' walk from the main building. Gropius himself was very much in charge of this whole concept, assisted by Neufert as chief planner. Neufert was said to be running the office 'under thunder and lightning', working enormously hard and at great speed.

Ise describes in her diary how the wives of the intended occupants of the three double houses for the Masters – Moholy-Nagy and Feininger, Kandinsky and Klee, Muche and Schlemmer – could not resist giving their own views on the planning: 'Ground plans! All women in the Bauhaus are busy playing now the new game "The women as creative person". Frau Nina [Kandinsky] wants a fireplace; Frau Klee wants a coal cooking stove; Frau Muche would like everything electrical; Frau

Schlemmer wants nothing electrical.' Gropius handled this by saying yes to all suggestions before going ahead and designing what he had already decided on. At this stage he was working every evening until eight thirty. He abandoned plans for riding every morning through the summer because the pressures of work, in simultaneously designing the new building and restructuring the teaching at the Bauhaus, although exhilarating, were also exhausting.

His post-war insomnia remained a constant problem. But Gropius had remarkable determination, an inner resourcefulness, an almost childlike cunning in the way that he resisted all attempts to deflect him from his aims. Ise writes:

In reality, and in spite of all his experience and knowledge of the practical world, he lives like a child who, unperturbed by obstacles of all sorts, wants to carry out a certain plan. He only deals with 'grown up' things to realise his ideas in the world of reality and he has learned very well to put on the bourgeois mask.

By the autumn of 1925, after its rather tentative beginnings, the Bauhaus in Dessau appeared a lot more settled. The organisation of the teaching was now rationalised: the workshops for stained glass and pottery closed, cabinet making and metal were combined. The printing workshop was refocused with a new emphasis on layout, typography and advertising. A new photography workshop would soon be introduced. In the following year the Bauhaus was redesignated a Hochschule für Gestaltung, an institute for design, formalising Gropius's aims for closer links with industry. The Masters were now officially known as Professors, although the designation of 'Master' persisted in the community. A limited company for marketing Bauhaus products, Bauhaus Gmbh, was incorporated in Dessau in October and the *Katalog der Muster*, a catalogue including details of prototype designs of Bauhaus products, was brought out. Ise noted in her diary that a request from England to reproduce Bauhaus designs had been received.

A project dear to Gropius's heart, but postponed by the upheavals of the move, was finally realised in October 1925, when the first eight

Portrait of Gropius by Lucia Moholy, 1927.

1. Fagus factory, Alfeld-an-der-Leine, 1913–25.
Photographed by Helen Mellor in 2016.

2. Facade of the Fagus factory.
3. Internal staircase, Fagus factory.

4. Oskar Kokoschka, *Double Portrait of Oskar Kokoschka and Alma Mahler*, 1912–13. Oil on canvas. This was the portrait which, seen by Gropius at the Berlin Secessionist exhibition in 1913, revealed the truth of their relationship.

5. Sixth of the series of decorative fans painted by Oskar Kokoschka for Alma, one of which was destroyed by Gropius in a jealous rage.

STAATLICHES
BAUHAUS
IN WEIMAR

6. Edvard Munch, *Summer Night by the Beach*, 1902–03. Oil on canvas. The painting was given by Gropius as a present to Alma on the birth of their daughter Manon.

7. Lyonel Feininger, preliminary design for the programme of the State Bauhaus in Weimar, 1919. Woodcut with letterpress on green paper.

8. Walter Determann, site plan for Bauhaus-Siedlung, the Bauhaus housing settlement, showing Gropius's ambitions for establishing a self-sufficient artistic community, Weimar, 1920.

9. Herbert Bayer and Lásló Moholy-Nagy, cover of the book *Staatliches Bauhaus in Weimar 1919–1923* (State Bauhaus in Weimar 1919–1923), published for the Bauhaus exhibition in 1923.

10. Gropius, *Monument to the March Dead of the Kapp Putsch*, Weimar cemetery, 1921. Destroyed by the Nazis but restored after the Second World War.

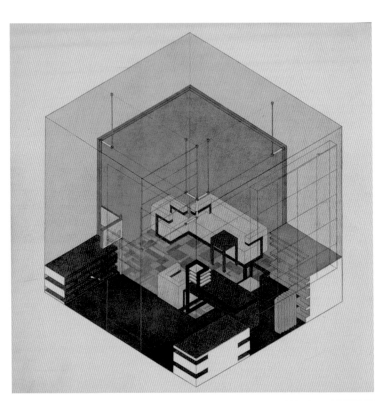

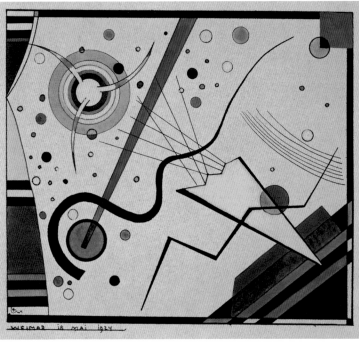

11. Isometric projection by Herbert Bayer of Gropius's office in the Bauhaus, displaying the skills of the various workshops, 1923.

12. Wassily Kandinsky, card for Gropius's forty-first birthday, one of a series of drawings and paintings presented to Gropius by the Bauhaus Masters.

13. Tea Infuser MT 49, 1924, by Marianne Brandt, showing the design principles of the Bauhaus workshops at their purest.

14. Table Lamp MT 8, 1924, by Wilhelm Wagenfeld, which soon acquired the status of a Bauhaus classic.

15. Isometric projection of design for the Törten housing estate on the southern edge of Dessau, by Gropius's architectural office, 1926–28.

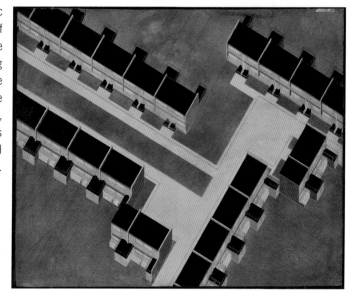

16. Four of the Bauhaus Books, edited by Walter Gropius and László Moholy-Nagy, 1925–30.
Published by Albert Langen Verlag, Munich.

volumes of the *Bauhausbücher*, the series of Bauhaus Books, appeared (see Plate 16). These were masterminded by Gropius and Moholy. Ise's editorial input was substantial. She records on 10 October: 'The first Bauhaus books arrived lovely and gay-looking. We are really persuaded that they will be a great success.' In the prospectus for the series the editors explained that these books would publicise the teachings of the Bauhaus, volume 2, for example, being on Paul Klee. The series reflected Gropius's breadth of involvement in modernism generally. Volume 1 was entitled *Internationale Architektur* and included work by Le Corbusier. Volume 5 was on Mondrian and the new artistic movement of Neoplasticism.

Bauhaus Books, of which there were to be fourteen, were strong on research and quasi-scientific discoveries in art. In spite of Gropius's personal antipathy to the author, Theo van Doesburg's *Grundbegriffe der neuen gestaltenden Kunst*, defining the new Constructivist principles, was volume 6. The jackets were designed by a variety of artists: Schlemmer, for example, designed the cover for his book on Bauhaus theatre, illustrating one of his own Triadic figures. But the series was visually unified by internal typography and layout by Moholy. Bauhaus Books were not simply 'lovely and gay-looking'. Their experimental graphics made them an astonishing achievement. Their unity in diversity summed the Bauhaus up.

Herbert Bayer's concept of 'universal' lettering was another important factor in creating public recognition of the Bauhaus. Bayer, the ex-student who was now a junior Master, was encouraged by Gropius to expand the former printing workshop into a fully fledged design studio, creating advertising material, exhibition posters, catalogues and letterheads both for the Bauhaus and for external clients. The 'universal' alphabet evolved by Bayer dispensed with capital letters altogether. He put the argument that the distinction between upper and lower case served no phonetic purpose: it should be abandoned for the sake of rationality and modern-day efficiency. Life needed speeding up, said Bayer: 'we write everything small in order to save time', a message he actually spelled out on the letterhead he designed for Gropius at

Dessau. It became the Bauhaus rule, Ise noting in her diary: 'The Bauhaus has now decided that for typographical and time-saving reasons it will only use small letters from now on.' At such a blatant statement of modernity many of the citizens of Dessau were appalled.

Herbert Bayer emerges as one of the most brilliantly engaging figures at the Bauhaus. He and Ise Gropius appear already to have had a particular rapport. She recollected how the two of them had been sent together in these early days in Dessau on a mission round the town to search out lodgings for new arrivals. 'Like wandering journeymen we knocked at many doors and rang innumerable bells to find quarters for students.'

Marcel Breuer too was proving himself, at the age of twenty-three, as a force to be reckoned with, the most intellectually powerful of the young Masters, though he could also be belligerent and moody. Writes Ise: 'he struggles to keep his soft heart and his great sensibility in check'. The Hungarian-born Breuer, although married to former student Martha Erps, was an intrepid womaniser. At one point he had to leave Dessau temporarily after complaints he had seduced a neighbour's wife.

The talented but volatile Breuer was entrusted with designing the furniture for Ise and Walter Gropius's new house. In spite of many pressures, this was still a time of optimism and excitement, with the Bauhaus buildings underway and potentially important new relationships being formed. 'We advance now in all directions,' writes Ise. 'I think we may experience the best time of our life.'

Ise became ill again over the summer. She had been suffering agonising back pains. She returned to the Sanatorium Königspark near Dresden and remained there all through August. Adhesions had been diagnosed, the result of her earlier miscarriage. After weeks of treatment but with no improvement Ise insisted on an investigative operation. This revealed a new and unexpected problem. Her appendix had formed itself into a cocoon with her ovaries and one of her Fallopian tubes. 'The whole mess was taken out,' wrote Ise, 'and my husband suffered agonies when the operation took so much longer than he had expected.' At the time her doctors held out the hope that Ise might still be able to get pregnant since the left side of her reproductive organs had not been affected. But a further exploratory operation ten years later proved that this area too was damaged by adhesions and she and Gropius had to accept that having children would never be a possibility.

While Ise was in the sanatorium and the hospital, Gropius, left alone in Dessau, was feeling increasingly bereft. At the time he was suffering additional worries as a building strike stopped work on the construction of the Bauhaus. He was writing long letters to Ise, the longest she had received in her whole life. Their interchange of letters during this separation is wonderfully touching, reflecting the deep and wide-ranging love of literature they shared.

She had only just discovered the German Romantic poet Friedrich Hölderlin and had been enraptured. Gropius replied, 'My dearest heart, your sweet letter just now with the kind of insights into your soul which I love. You have such a wonderful, rich inner life and I understand completely what you write about. Yes, Hölderlin must affect you very much. Your soul substances are akin to one another.' He told her that he owned a precious copy of Hölderlin's composition 'Abstrakt Lyrik' in a specially printed edition by Bruno Adler. He added that he felt he and Ise had now been separated for a year: 'when you are back I shall never let you go anymore.'

The bond between them strengthened through Gropius's sympathetic involvement in the problems of Ise's sister Hertha. In April 1925 Hertha had told Ise she was pregnant. Fuldes, the father, was a young trainee physician described by Ise as 'a man of extraordinary beauty and ability'. He was clearly on the brink of a promising career, which would be jeopardised by early parenthood, and he had rejected all ideas of marriage. His reluctance was encouraged by his devoted and domineering mother, whose only other son had been killed in the First World War.

Hertha made the bold decision to keep the child and, as Ise put it, 'face its illegitimacy', which of course would attract considerable opprobrium at the time. She travelled to Dessau to discuss the situation with Gropius, who might have been expected to disapprove of Hertha's independent attitude because of his own conventional background and his public status as director of the Bauhaus. In fact, convinced that Hertha's child had been conceived in what she had seen as genuine love rather than temporary dalliance, Gropius supported her plan for single parenthood, assuring her he would not consider it 'a blot on his own reputation'.

His attitude was unfailingly constructive. He travelled several times to Hanover in an attempt to sort out Hertha's affairs. He even tried to persuade Fuldes's parents to let their son get married after all, at least temporarily, the wedding to be followed by a quick divorce. Ise felt a little guilty that this burden was added to her husband's many other problems, but the intervention certainly paid off in terms of lasting trust and fondness between Hertha and Gropius. The whole episode was to have important consequences within the Gropius family.

——

It looked like being an anxious Christmas 1925, with the birth of Hertha's baby imminent. Gropius's mother, formerly comfortably off, was worried that her money was now running out. Ugly little rumours about Alma's hostility to Ise were circulating amongst the theatrical community in Dessau: 'They try to persuade Alma against me and I shall probably have to make an end to this nonsensical gossip,' Ise complained.

Gropius himself, increasingly overstretched, had been suffering from an attack of flu, missing a performance of Schubert's 'Unfinished' symphony followed by Mahler's *Lied von der Erde*. Ise and Breuer sat next to one another and were surprised to discover how little they now related to the Mahler. The music seemed so tortuous to Ise she would have preferred to go home in the middle. 'We do not respond any more', she judged, 'to this subjectively centred tragicality and, in spite of our respect for the greatness of this lovely spirit, we turn away because it has lost its validity for us.' For those who knew Stravinsky, Mahler now seemed foreign. There had been a similar sense of alienation a few days earlier when Karsavina, the classical ballerina, had performed.

In mid-December Gropius and Ise returned to Italy, feeling in need of a total change of scene. They decided to spend Christmas in Rapallo. Here it poured for three days, on the first of which news reached them of the safe arrival of a daughter for Hertha, named Beata Evelina, 'a very healthy, pretty little person'. Fuldes the father remained determinedly uninvolved.

They were staying at the Hotel Bristol in Rapallo, a haunt of the well-heeled English, who, to Ise's surprise, were very friendly to the Germans, encouraging the Gropiuses to play bridge and join in ballroom dancing. The English contingent included Joseph Chamberlain, the Foreign Secretary, and his family. Chamberlain was in Rapallo to meet the Italian Fascist prime minister Benito Mussolini in advance of an international conference in Locarno. The Locarno Treaties of 1925 guaranteed the western borders of Germany as they had been first drawn in 1919.

The Gropiuses viewed the arrival in Rapallo of such a controversial figure as the Italian leader with great interest. Ise commented, 'His influence does not seem to recede as people here want us to believe. He did look rather miserable and his impaired state of health may explain the frequently rash tempo of his actions. He wants to accomplish a tremendous task in a limited time.' Just a few months later, in April 1926, the first of several attempts would be made to assassinate Mussolini.

The building of the Bauhaus had been progressing well. Soon after the Gropiuses arrived back from Italy preparations for the topping-out ceremony, marking the completion of the first phase, had begun. This was preceded by the *Weisse Fest*, one of the archetypal Bauhaus celebration parties. This time all participants were told to wear white costumes. A few days before, the female students from the weaving workshop had assembled at the Gropius apartment to start baking preparations for a feast in which all the food would be uniformly white. On the evening itself the party was judged to have reached the high standard of the early, very beautiful Bauhaus parties in Weimar. The students not only made the ravishing decorations and costumes, two thirds of them all-white, with the rest patterned in chequers, polka dots or stripes, they had also installed surrealistic altars and waxworks in the galleries. The theatre workshops, not always to be totally relied on, excelled themselves that night with superlative performances produced by Oskar Schlemmer and Joost Schmidt.

The next day the actual topping out took place. Ise describes this as a radiantly successful occasion with speeches by the building works foreman and by Gropius. All the workmen were invited to a celebration supper and a repetition of the previous evening's *Weisse Fest*. The workmen entered into the spirit of the entertainments, making valiant attempts to dance to the music of the Bauhaus band.

The only downside, which made Gropius angry, was the virtual boycott of the celebrations by his own architectural office, a separate entity within the school. Here tensions had arisen. The recently appointed office manager, Ernst Neufert, who had made such a good impression to begin with, had already decided to leave, having received an offer to return to Weimar and take over the day-to-day running of the Bauhochschule, the teaching institution that had succeeded the Bauhaus there. This created a serious dilemma for Gropius since, apart from his valuable years of experience in the office, Neufert had provided useful architectural training for the students. Gropius had been relying on Neufert in his long-planned development of experimental standardised housing too.

This defection turned out to be more damaging than anyone had at first realised when it was discovered that during the year in which the super-efficient Neufert was in charge, the records of Gropius's early projects, all the sketches and proposals as well as finished drawings of completed buildings, had been cleared out and presumably destroyed. This was at the time when Gropius and Ise were on holiday in Italy. Neufert later refused to take responsibility, maintaining that the drawings had been left around in piles and that visitors had no doubt felt free to help themselves.

Construction of the Bauhaus building continued through the year of 1926. By October Ise reported that work was now at fever pitch. Early in November everything was 'in hottest preparation' for the opening, planned for 4 December. There were almost daily conferences about the inaugural ceremonies, with Mayor Hesse taking part 'as though this were his own personal affair'. By the middle of November it was estimated the Bauhaus must prepare for at least a thousand visitors to the inauguration. Press interest was rising, with so many requests for photographs of the new building that Lucia Moholy was working day and night to fulfil demand. A social evening was held for the local Circle of Friends of the Bauhaus, including a concert: Klee and his wife Lily played the violin and piano, and Lou Scheper sang.

3 December 1926 was press day. Sixty reporters turned up to view the buildings and the mayor gave a big evening reception at which music by Alban Berg, Schoenberg and Mussorgsky was performed. Everyone was in celebratory spirits and many interesting foreigners had now arrived in Dessau, among them André Lurçat from Paris, two architects from Russia, and also the architect Mart Stam from Holland, with whom Gropius was especially impressed.

4 December was Inauguration Day itself. The estimate of a thousand visitors was far exceeded. At least 1,500 people crowded into the new building. Mayor Hesse worked with almost superhuman energy to organise the throng and to keep people informed about the day's programme. 'What a difference to the situation years ago in Weimar!' Ise writes. There were good official speeches of welcome. Gropius himself was so overwhelmed by the great crowd and by the huge interest in the Bauhaus from all sides that he was almost silenced. He led a tour of the building, then returned home for a brief interval to eat, totally exhausted, before setting off again to show visitors the early beginnings of his new experimental housing development in the nearby village of Törten. The Dessau council had given him the contract for sixty low-cost houses using standardised construction units and, after considerable panic, the first two of these had been finished just in time (see Plate 22).

Press reactions to the Bauhaus started to appear in early January. 'The interest is astonishing,' Ise comments; 'Gropius is quite stunned by the success.' What impressed people so much about the Bauhaus buildings? To start with, the sheer spectacle, the great expanse of glass in the workshop wing connected to the main teaching and administrative block, the two buildings linked by the long stretch of a bridge set on pillars spanning the approach road (see Plates 17–19). The bridge contained Gropius's own architectural studio on its upper floor.

A central section of the workshop wing contained the stage and auditorium, with the communal canteen for students and professors at the back. For the first time the Bauhaus could mount its own theatrical productions and invite the most avant-garde performers from elsewhere. In those early Dessau days Kurt Schwitters gave his famous eccentric recitations; the dancer Gret Palucca, Mary Wigman's student, performed on the Bauhaus stage. Béla Bartók came to play there: 'such a dear, enchanting person that he won over everybody right away'. The whole space could be opened out for festivals and parties. The concept of the building provided opportunities for creative experiment never before envisaged in an art school.

Béla Bartók on a visit to Dessau, 13 October 1927, flanked by Gropius and Paul Klee.

In the six-storey residential building known as the Prellerhaus, named in memory of the much shabbier Prellerhaus in Weimar, were twenty-eight studio-bedrooms, with shower rooms, baths and a gymnasium in the basement. These were occupied by junior teaching staff and students. The gym, which was fitted with a large soft carpet, provided useful overnight accommodation for students too poor to afford to pay for lodgings in the town. The architecture of the Prellerhaus encouraged uninhibited behaviour. According to Marianne Brandt, a Prellerhaus resident, even Gropius was shocked when he discovered students using the flat roof and studio facade 'for balancing exercises' and to gain access 'as a cat burglar'. She herself got used to perching on the railing of her balcony, overcoming her occasional attacks of dizziness. Brandt explains that the Prellerhaus created a true spirit of community: 'How well we lived in those studios and how pleasant were the conversations back and forth from one balcony to another!'

The interior design and decoration throughout the Bauhaus building was the wall-painting workshop's responsibility. The lighting fixtures were provided by the metal workshop, while the tubular steel furniture, then the epitome of modern design thinking, was designed by Breuer. The concept originated when he was living in a room at the Bauhaus in Weimar and the milkman arrived every morning on his bicycle. Breuer had become fixated on the elegance of the milkman's chromium-plated, tubular steel handlebars. His tubular steel chair developed from this vision of ideal functionality. In just so many senses the Bauhaus building was homemade. It was part of Walter Gropius's visionary concept of communal endeavour that the students and the Masters worked together in creating their own world within the world.

For new students arriving their first sight of the building was inspiring. The first English Bauhaus student, Wilfred Franks, described how he arrived in Dessau after dark, 'and there was this beautiful glass-fronted building, all lit up, with people walking about inside. If you can imagine, a fifty-foot-high area of glass with the lights shining through and the steel girders of the construction four feet back from the glass. You can't imagine what an experience that was.' Franks later became an actor and dancer and the composer Michael Tippett's close associate.

Werner David Feist, a nervy, disaffected young Jewish boy from Augsburg who came with his parents on a first visit to the Bauhaus,

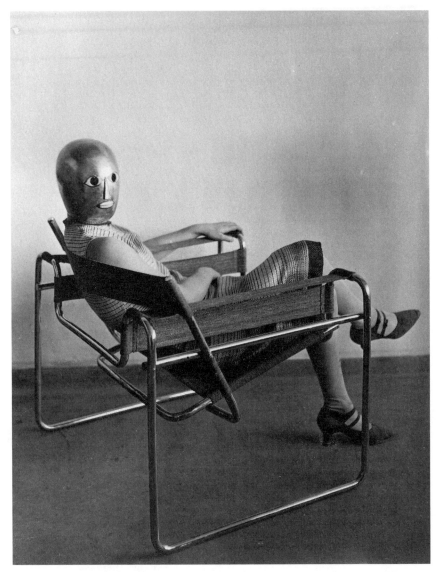

Ise Gropius or Lis Bayer in an Oskar Schlemmer mask,
sitting on Breuer's 13-3 Club chair, 1926.

experienced a similar reaction of amazement mixed with hope. Gazing
across at Gropius's building, Feist recalled,

I was overawed and elated, puzzled and anxious all at the same time. This con-
figuration of cubic units standing starkly isolated in an open space bordered by a
tree-lined avenue on the far side was unlike anything I, or my parents, had ever

seen. But for me it was the first document of a new spirit and a new reality that I hoped to become part of.

Feist became a distinguished graphic artist and art director, first in London, then in Canada.

The Bauhaus building acted as a beacon. Student numbers started rising, from twenty-one male and sixty female students in the summer of 1926 to forty-three male and 110 female a year later. Feist described the atmosphere as being like that of a large family, with students and Masters living side by side. Most people knew one another at least slightly. There was a great diversity within the student body. Germans formed the core but there were also Swiss, Polish, some Italian, Hungarian, Czech and Austrian students and even an officially sponsored Bauhaus student from Japan. Their social backgrounds were more varied than had been the case in Weimar.

Xanti Schawinsky leads an open-air dance and movement class on the beach between the Elbe and the Mulde.

There were several girls from well-to-do families: for example, smart ginger-haired Lies (Elisabeth) Henneberger and her friend, tiny freckle-faced Lo (Lotte) Rothschild, both identified by Feist as 'not outstanding talents', as well as Grit Kallin, a mature woman of great worldly charm to whom Josef Albers was clearly attracted, and 'two near menopausal Swiss ladies' whom Feist liked to imagine as 'running an arty shop in some Alpine spa'. Student life was now more varied, easy-going, more casually flirtatious. The Bauhaus was becoming a fashionable place.

The Bauhaus building in Dessau was a high point of Gropius's architectural achievements. It was by no means technically perfect. The flat roof began to leak, cracks started to appear in its prefabricated concrete walls, and the spectacular glass frontage of the workshop wing meant that the building could be stifling in the summer, much too cold in winter. But the triumph of the building was the life of the community that it created, its fluency and beauty, the way that it held out new possibilities for art.

Not only was the building effective in expressing the ideals of the Bauhaus, it was Gropius's statement of belief in the power of the modern. The Bauhaus was a truly original contribution to the developing International Style of architecture. The mid-twentieth-century critic Reyner Banham saw the Bauhaus as a visionary building in its almost three-dimensional quality of planning, with those two main structures bridged across the road. Indeed he maintained that this central, bridged section of the Bauhaus building 'casts light on aspects of Gropius that are at variance with the commonly held view of him' as an architect lacking in imagination and romance. Seeing it now it is hard to comprehend that this building was designed almost a century ago.

10

Bauhaus Dessau

1927–1928

The Polish poet Tadeusz Peiper visited the Bauhaus in 1927 and was excited to see the little colony of Masters' Houses:

They are located in a secluded avenue away from the school building and separated from it by a large suburb of the town. Their walls form a white light, surrounded by the green light of the lawns and trees. Flat roofs – a horizontal line – press them to the ground. Windows search for light where they can. Projections catch the shadows. Platforms and terraces deliver air and warmth. I saw the new architecture for the first time, not as an illustration, but in its entire inspiring existence.

Like the Bauhaus building, the three pairs of Masters' Houses and the larger single house for the director were conceived as demonstrations of a new, simpler, more creative way of living. They were Gropius's prototypes for homes of the future, using industrialised components. With their flat roofs, their assemblages of cubic building elements, their sense of floating within space, these were houses of immense originality and confidence. They bear a clear relation to the slightly earlier Auerbach House in Jena, designed by Gropius in 1924 while he was still working in collaboration with Adolf Meyer. But the Bauhaus Masters' Houses in Dessau go further in clarity of concept and rigorous organisation of activities (see Plates 21, 22).

In arriving at these sparse, calm and highly disciplined house plans, Gropius was determined that life should be 'freed of unnecessary burdens' in order to 'unfold more freely and richly'. The fittings and the furnishings came from the Bauhaus workshops. Walk-in wardrobes were provided, ventilated linen closets, ingenious rotating cupboards that opened from both sides. Compared with the houses for the estate in Törten that Gropius was then developing, these were highly sophisticated dwellings and Gropius's supreme achievement in private house design.

Construction took place through 1925 and the Masters moved in during the summer of 1926, a few months before the opening of the new school building. Moholy-Nagy and his wife Lucia lived in the first house, with the Feininger family alongside. Oskar and Tut Schlemmer moved into the second semi-detached house, where their neighbours to begin with were Georg Muche and his wife; in 1927, when Muche left the Bauhaus, having been more or less ejected by his students in the weaving workshops, Hinnerk and Lou Scheper moved in. The third semi-detached house was Kandinsky's and Klee's. They were friends but their views on interior colour were quite different, Kandinsky's colour scheme being cool and purist in contrast to Klee's more earthy tones. Gropius's designs for the Masters' Houses allowed for such variants, and this was their great strength.

Paul Klee and Wassily Kandinsky outside the Masters' Houses, Dessau, 1929.

The Masters' Houses were not just family homes but work spaces. The Bauhaus artists had their own studios included. These were productive houses. Felix Klee recalled that one wall of his father's almost square studio was black and he painted many of his big paintings there.

'The size of the room was probably an indirect cause of the new tack that Klee's art took at this period.' Most of the Masters' wives were themselves creative. Julia Feininger was a painter, Lou Scheper was an illustrator and a specialist in colour. Lucia Moholy was not only a photographer, she was also the close working partner of her husband in the pursuit of 'cameraless photography'. The Bauhaus children were

Master's House, Dessau. Oskar and Tut Schlemmer on the top floor, Georg Muche and his wife El in the centre, Josef and Anni Albers and their three children on the bottom balcony, 1926.

involved in the projects of the moment through their families and colleagues. Growing up in such a tightly knit community they saw art as a part of their everyday lives.

'I'm sitting on our terrace which is simply blissful,' wrote Lyonel Feininger to his wife Julia soon after moving in.

The overhang and the short south wall that, on the plans of the house, we were so unhappy about, give just that comfortable light – without these projections everything would be bathed in the sun and mid-day heat. It's true of all the rooms – they are nicer to live in and almost always larger than we imagined from the plans and without furniture in them . . . There is real *space* here and one has the impression of being out in the open. I would not have believed that I could get over the loss of our balcony so easily – on the contrary, it's a thousand times more beautiful here.

Walter and Ise Gropius in the living room of the Director's House,
with Marcel Breuer's tubular steel chairs, 1927.

Gropius's own house was on a larger scale, a detached villa. Ise had regarded it as the 'longed for, dreamed of vision' in which she and Gropius could enjoy a more settled and comfortable married life than had ever been possible in Weimar. She confided in her mother-in-law Manon, 'We have of course a lot of fantasies about our new house,' telling her how she had begun working out the ground plans, which Gropius then went over in order to eliminate the impossibilities his wife had been suggesting. Even more than the houses for the Bauhaus Masters he envisaged his own home as a show house, a perfect exemplar of new attitudes to living: rational, convivial, sun-worshipping, healthy, focused on a free and easy lifestyle and on art.

In order to publicise the house they allowed it to be filmed by Humboldt-Film Berlin. Ise brought in her actress sister Ellen and Ellen's beautiful, vivacious Russian friend Shifra Offsejewa to help her demonstrate the practical effectiveness of the furniture and lighting and other Bauhaus household products. Ise was a talented publicist. The educationalist Konrad Wünsche commented admiringly, 'When Frau Gropius poses on the double sofa in the living room of the Master's House or stands at the writing desk for the photos in the Bauhaus book about the Dessau buildings you could be convinced by her manner that she was showing an aesthetic, ergonomic example of a building.' Her earlier training in domestic science meant that Ise was especially convincing in demonstrating Gropius's labour-saving kitchen.

All this effort resulted in numerous visits of inspection. Lily and Hans Hildebrandt, the French, the Dutch — 'there was no end of it,' notes Ise. She and Gropius guided round the press and early sightseers. The Gropius house and the Dessau Masters' Houses were essential elements in the Bauhaus's burgeoning reputation.

But in relation to the Bauhaus there was always opposition. Its very nature made the Bauhaus confrontational. There was hostility towards the architecture from less enlightened members of the Dessau public. Ise overheard 'some very indignant exclamations by the public in front of the faculty houses'. Some of the junior Masters — Marcel Breuer and Josef Albers being amongst the most vocal — were resentful that the older staff members were receiving such preferential treatment. The students were critical of buildings which in their view provided no radical solution to the national housing problems. Ise comments unsympathetically, 'They have probably dreamed about a housing block for *all* of them to move in without considering that too much inbreeding would follow.'

Misgivings even came from the resident Masters themselves. Lyonel Feininger was embarrassed by the crowds of sightseers goggling at the Masters' Houses and trespassing in the gardens to stare in through the windows. Schlemmer was bitterly critical of the luxurious facilities of Gropius's house in particular, with its basement flat for a caretaker, guest apartment and provision for a maid. Schlemmer confided in his wife, 'I was shocked when I saw the houses! I had a vision that some day people without apartments would stand here, while the artist-gentlemen sunbathed on the roofs of their houses.' When the Gropiuses came back from a holiday visit to the Baltic coast they found so many windows smashed in their new house that they were forced to acknowledge the extent of local hostility.

———

Relations with Alma had become marginally easier since their surprise encounter in Taormina, and Gropius was hoping to arrange for his daughter Manon to visit Dessau on her own. His beloved Mutzi was now almost eleven. Apart from his few rushed expeditions to Vienna she had hardly seen her father since the short, tense stay in Weimar with her mother in February 1920, at the time of the Kapp Putsch demonstrations. Ise, now firmly in control of her husband's personal correspondence, took over negotiations with Alma, who was obsessively possessive of her delicately beautiful daughter. Alma had always had a curious penchant for photographing the child naked. She was reluctant to allow Manon out of her own near-suffocating close control into what she called the 'strange surroundings' of the Bauhaus in Dessau.

Urged repeatedly by Ise she finally agreed to deliver Manon for a four-week visit to her father in early November 1927, at a time when she and Werfel had their own commitments. Gropius met mother and daughter in Berlin and Alma spent a night in the Director's House in Dessau before leaving to join Werfel in Hamburg. According to Ise,

Manon Gropius
photographed at
Atelier Fayer, Vienna,
1926/7.

Manon Gropius
posed in
historical costume,
1925.

'Alma acted as friendly as possible,' while Manon greeted Gropius ecstatically, 'as if they had never been separated'.

This was indeed a very new environment for Manon. Her upbringing, partly in Vienna, partly at the Mahler palazzo in Venice, had been one of sophisticated theatricality. Her pale face, long dark hair and greenish eyes – the colour of her father's – made the child appear almost other-worldly. A carefully staged photograph which Alma sent to Gropius from Venice shows Manon in the heavy brocade costume of a Spanish infanta, clearly modelled on portraits by Velázquez in the Kunsthistor-isches Museum. The girl was very shy and introverted. In the autumn before she visited Dessau she had been enrolled in a boarding school in Geneva. Gropius had arranged to meet her there the morning after her arrival but found to his surprise that mother and daughter had already left for Venice. Manon had found the environment so alien she had apparently implored Alma to take her home.

Manon found it difficult to make friends with the other children at the Bauhaus. This was not a new problem. Back in 1920, when she had come to Weimar on a visit to her father, Maria Benemann's daughter Inge had been imported to keep her company. It was not that children of the Bauhaus were neglected. They were absolutely integral to Dessau life. Art at the Bauhaus was very much child-centred, as we know from Lou Scheper's fantastical illustrated children's books, Paul Klee's puppets, the whole emphasis on creative play. Children appear in many Bau-haus photographs, grouped along the balconies of the Masters' Houses. But although they paid dutiful visits to Manon, they were not used to strangers. They operated in little gangs. Used as she was to conversing with her mother's and Werfel's adult friends, Manon found it easier to make connections amongst the Bauhaus teachers, becoming especially attached to the brilliantly wayward theatre designer and performer Xanti Schawinsky. Although only eleven she already showed precocious talent as an actress, encouraged by Werfel and Alma's theatre friends.

'We are getting along beautifully with Mutzi,' Ise writes in her diary for 15 November, when the girl had been with them for a week. 'In her exterior as well as in her character she is the image of her father. As

Manon with her father on a long-awaited visit to Dessau in November 1927.

he has great tensions in his nature, so has she, changing between the most sensitive gentleness and being quite headstrong . . . With us she is serene and trusting and extraordinarily tactful.' Particularly striking to Ise had been Manon's natural creative skills: she designed an adjustable chair and table almost as soon as she arrived. 'She is totally visually orientated and has an abhorrence of ugly people.'

Gropius had recently acquired an Adler car of which he was inordinately proud. (Erwin Kleyer, owner of the Adlerwerke, was one of the Bauhaus's new clients.) Father and daughter went out on expeditions, and he and Ise took Manon to Hanover one day in a wild snowstorm to introduce her to her grandmother and aunt. Ise noted, 'Walter is completely enamoured of his daughter and he is right – anybody would love this dainty, loving, serene child.' She and Manon became closer. Manon began addressing her as 'Ischen'. The Gropius dog, Nuschi, also became her friend.

On 1 December they regretfully returned Manon to Alma and Werfel in Berlin, going on to see *Rasputin* at the Volkstheater. Gropius had been recently commissioned by Erwin Piscator, the politically orientated Volkstheater director, to design a radical new building reflecting his concept of Total Theatre, a flexible space that did away with the barrier between actors and audience created by the conventional proscenium stage.

Over the following months he missed little Mutzi painfully, but the visit on the whole had been happy and constructive. Gropius had extraordinary powers of recovery. In creating the Bauhaus he had to some extent obliterated the horrors and disasters of the First World War. Now this new closeness with his daughter seemed to him symbolic of what he might retrieve from his own tumultuously troubled emotional past.

In his Bauhaus Manifesto the building arts had been absolutely central: '*The ultimate aim of all creative activity is the building!*' Gropius had originally exclaimed. Once the Bauhaus came to Dessau the need for a fully fledged architecture department to replace the ad hoc system of students working in his own office became urgent. Ise commented in April 1926, 'The introduction of an architectural class at the Bauhaus, which could independently take on commissions without having to rely on the Gropius office, is a necessity.' In spring 1927 a department of architecture was finally established, becoming a permanent fixture of Bauhaus teaching from then on.

The Swiss architect Hannes Meyer was recruited by Gropius to run the new department after Mart Stam declined. Gropius had admired Meyer and his partner Hans Wittwer's proposed architectural scheme for the Palace of the League of Nations in Geneva. Meyer, like Stam, had made a good impression on his visit to Dessau for the inauguration of the Bauhaus building. The proposed appointment was discussed at a meeting of the Masters and Mayor Hesse in January 1927 and was approved by all except Kandinsky, who voiced doubts about Meyer's practical abilities, judging him as more of a theoretical thinker. According to Ise, Kandinsky 'also pointed to Meyer's outspoken communistic tendencies. Gropius thinks, on the other hand, that these are quite unpolitical.' In this view of the rigid doctrinaire socialist Hannes Meyer he was being astonishingly naive.

Hannes Meyer, second director of the Bauhaus, with students
on the terrace at Dessau, *c.*1929.

Meyer, then living at Mentone in Switzerland, came to Dessau in February to discuss the appointment. Ise judged that 'Personally he is very nice though, like a true Swiss, somewhat wooden. Very clear, open and definite, no great tensions and contradictions in his characters.' In this assessment of the deeply devious Hannes Meyer she was to be proved wrong too.

He took up the appointment in April 1927. To begin with all was smiles. 'Hannes Meyer and family arrived. Lively, nice people with delightful children. We shall get along well together and the students have high hopes of Meyer.' By June tensions were showing. Ise heard from Lou Scheper that there were troubles between Hannes Meyer and his wife. 'Meyer seems to force his wife too much into his own life style and proceeds too dogmatically and theoretically. His view that one should not have a housemaid goes too much at his wife's expense.' The modern-minded Ise Gropius pointed out that in America household aids were making the housewife's burden lighter. 'Besides this', she reported, 'there also seem to be other women involved and Meyer shows too little tact and is too inflexible.' Within the close community of the Bauhaus intrigue and gossip surfaced fast.

Antagonisms arose between the tactless, confrontational Meyer and the other Bauhaus Masters. Even Oskar Schlemmer, who had welcomed Meyer enthusiastically, calling him the new flower in Gropius's buttonhole, turned against his manipulative traits. More seriously Meyer soon began to prove himself opposed to the whole spirit of the school. Looking back he defined his horrified unease on assessing the situation in Dessau:

What did I discover at the time of my appointment? A Bauhaus whose reputation exceeded its achievements many times over, and within which an unparalleled self-promotion was conducted. A 'school of design' in which a problematic-constructive entity was made out of every tea glass. A 'cathedral of socialism' in which a medieval cult was engaged in by revolutionaries of pre-war art with the assistance of a youth that squinted towards the left . . . One lived within the colourful sculptures of the houses. On their floors lay the emotional complexes of young women. Everywhere art strangled life.

Gropius came to regret his appointment of Meyer, saying he had not recognised the mask over his face. 'I believe', he wrote much later, 'that Hannes Meyer's downfall was his denying art as such.' For the Bauhaus as Gropius originally conceived it Meyer's arrival in Dessau was to be the beginning of the end.

Even before Meyer's arrival many other problems had been piling up. Within weeks of the opening of the Bauhaus buildings it emerged that the construction budget had been exceeded by one hundred thousand marks. The most serious miscalculation had been made by the now departed Ernst Neufert, who had not included charges of thirty-five thousand marks for bricks. Gropius was 'quite beside himself about this, since he knows that this will cost the Mayor a hard battle and diminish his trust'. He blamed himself for the oversight, attributed by Ise to his overwhelming workload.

There were rows within the faculty at this anxious period of increasing financial stringency, caused by disagreements and delays over industrial contracts and rising costs in general. The now cash-strapped city of Dessau was unable to bail the Bauhaus out. When Gropius proposed that full-time teachers should take a ten per cent drop in salary Kandinsky and Klee were both incensed. Gropius wrote self-pityingly to Kandinsky, 'You are uninformed as to the superhuman burden I have to carry here . . . I can only continue to work if I receive the direct assurance of the Masters to support me more than up to now. Otherwise I have to withdraw, because it is of no use to wear oneself out for nothing.' A temporary five per cent reduction was finally agreed.

Klee and Kandinsky also complained about Ise bringing in an instructor from Berlin to give classes in the Charleston and other modern dances that were eagerly attended by the younger, more frivolous members of the faculty. These classes took place in the Director's House, to the accompaniment of Ise's gramophone.

Mayor Hesse, originally Gropius's enthusiastic champion, was finding it increasingly difficult to defend the Bauhaus against its critics in the municipal government. In June 1926 Ise had observed that he was 'looking wan and tired. The worries and struggles about the Bauhaus have cost him a lot.' Just a few months later relations between Hesse and Gropius considerably worsened, with Hesse complaining that Gropius was only using the Bauhaus to further his own career. He had extravagantly bought the Adler car. He was making too many trips away. Gropius countered by accusing Hesse of a lack of understanding for 'the artistically inclined person', whom he treated as if he were just another municipal employee. Pettily, Hesse closed down the Bauhaus canteen in the evening as an economy measure, a ruling that Gropius immediately reversed.

The rift between them widened further when on 26 November 1927 the Sozialdemokratische Partei (Social Democratic Party), to which the mayor belonged, lost half its seats on Dessau city council. He and Gropius had a very hostile meeting. Ise observed, 'Hesse now strikes a note towards G. that is hardly bearable. He is terribly overburdened right now and personally holds it against the Bauhaus that the election had ended with a loss for the democratic party.' Already at this stage Gropius had the impression that the mayor was anxious to get rid of him and replace him with Hesse's new ally, Hannes Meyer.

Hesse's anxieties vis-à-vis the Bauhaus have to be seen in the wider context of the country as a whole. The political situation was darkening. As long ago as the winter of 1925, travelling back from Italy to Germany, Gropius and Ise had been conscious of the grimness of the atmosphere: 'Cold weather, cold people, the nearer we got to Germany . . . we returned from the serenest humanity into the grey inhumanity.' There had been hostile responses to the Bauhaus in Weimar. Prejudice was now increasing in Dessau too, where the Bauhaus was regarded by many as a Jewish–Bolshevistic enclave, artistically crazy and racially impure.

Matters came to a head in January 1928, when a politically motivated article was published in a local newspaper questioning the fees Gropius's private office had been charging for the Törten housing project. He threatened to resign if there was no retraction of the falsely malicious accusations. Receiving no apology he first requested the municipal council to release him from his contract as director of the Bauhaus and then, in early February 1928, wrote an official resignation letter to Mayor Hesse and issued a public statement. He proposed that Hannes Meyer should succeed him. According to Ise, Hesse was 'beside himself' on receiving Gropius's notice and quickly began 'trying through great amiability to make up for the neglect of many months'.

The news that Gropius would be leaving was given to the students at an evening dance in the Bauhaus canteen. They were so shocked that at first the band refused to go on playing and Gropius had to insist on the

Weaving-workshop students on the Bauhaus staircase, *c.*1927.

dance continuing. One of the students, Fritz Kuhr, gave an emotional speech, telling Gropius that although they had not always agreed with him, he remained their guarantee that the Bauhaus would not develop into a one-sided, stereotyped school: 'For the sake of an idea we have starved here in Dessau. You cannot leave now. If you do, the way will be opened for reactionaries . . . Hannes Meyer as director of the Bauhaus is a catastrophe.' The evening ended with the near-hysterical Bauhaus students processing round the cafe carrying Gropius on their shoulders. Some of the older students were heard to call him '*Du*'.

Why did Gropius persist in supporting Meyer as his successor at the Bauhaus against growing hostility from the Masters and the students? Joost Schmidt from the theatre workshop suffered a nervous breakdown, crying for several hours when he heard the news. 'He suffers more than I can say from G.'s leaving,' writes Ise, 'and since the main motive for his work was his love for G. and his Bauhaus, he does not feel rooted in Hannes Meyer's ideas.'

But it seems that Gropius had had the intention of grooming Meyer as his successor when he first appointed him. It was in his nature to keep faith with all those he recruited to the Bauhaus, however awkward or, as with Oskar Schlemmer, positively hostile to the regime they proved. Creative dissidence was a part of the whole ethos of the Bauhaus. As Gropius wrote in retrospect: 'Everyone except Moholy-Nagy was at one time or other in opposition to me, but they all stayed on.'

Besides, Meyer himself could be plausible and cunning. In spite of the general suspicions and misgivings about the new appointment Gropius managed to convince himself that Meyer would still be the best man for the job. It was only years later that he came to describe Meyer as 'a treacherous character, which I did not recognise early enough'.

What were the reasons for Gropius deciding to leave the Bauhaus at this juncture? He had been its creator, its director, its chief spokesman for the past nine years. In many people's view Gropius *was* the Bauhaus. At a time of growing political hostility towards it he sensed himself becoming the Bauhaus's liability. He felt the time had come to make an independent move. After a period of relative stagnation his own architectural work was increasing and his reputation in the eyes of the critics was improving. A rise in the value of the mark led to an upsurge in architectural commissions. Gropius had been invited by Mies van der Rohe to design two houses for the experimental Weissenhof settlement near Stuttgart, in which fifteen other of Europe's most avant-garde architects were involved. The now desperately conciliatory mayor confirmed

Gropius's continuing involvement with the Törten housing project and with a new building for the Employment Office in Dessau. According to Ise, 'The longing and joy about being able to work on his problems again after so many years of administrative work is great.'

He also had his mind on wider horizons. Ever since the First World War Gropius had been ambitious for a rebirth of German society in which all classes would enjoy better living conditions. While preoccupied with the running of the Bauhaus and fending off opposition in Dessau he had been unable to develop larger, more comprehensive plans at a time when other German cities, particularly Frankfurt, were making important new developments in modern housing. Since the implementation of the international rescue plan for Germany, the Dawes Plan of 1924, foreign investment had hugely boosted the country's economy. The resulting architectural boom in German cities had favoured the modern style, the *Neues Bauen*. Gropius now grasped new possibilities in signing a contract with his enthusiastic patron Adolf Sommerfeld to design a major housing development of five thousand units, to be occupied by twenty-five thousand people, with its own schools and civic buildings, in Berlin.

In any case Gropius by this time was exhausted. The writer Grete Dexel summed up the situation perceptively in a newspaper article entitled 'Why Is Gropius Going?' She observed: 'Gropius, the organiser on the grand scale, has grown tired. He prefers to devote his energies to his own work instead of weakening them in the ceaseless battle against hostile forces and in the fruitless attempts to put the Bauhaus on a firm financial footing. That is why he is going.'

1 March 1928 was Ise's birthday. Gropius gave her a collection of the most beautiful of the Bauhaus products. They were anxious to keep as many as they could. Three weeks later, on 25 March, a farewell party for Gropius was held at which a play commemorating his nine years as director was performed. After this there was dancing and wild shouting, and Gropius was lifted on high and carried round the room to a chorus of acclaim. The students and teachers presented him with a portfolio, *9 Jahre Bauhaus: Eine Chronik*, a collection of humorous, nostalgic drawings, photographs and collages in which they recorded

their impressions of the Bauhaus since Gropius first invented it. One of the most touching of the presentation images is Edmund Collein's photographic collage of the Prellerhaus, with the residents overflowing from the building, crammed into the corners, perched along the roof. This last party for Gropius celebrated the end of a unique community. Moholy, Breuer and Bayer would now be leaving too.

The distinctively coloured world of the Bauhaus would fade, as Lou Scheper remembered it: 'Clear light and clear dark shades, pure white and pure black, and a variety of clear, clean stages of grey – this was the world of colour that the evil brown and blighted red of the Third Reich broke into.'

The Prellerhaus studio and accommodation block at Dessau becoming overcrowded. Montage by Edmund Collein.

11
America
1928

To lessen their anguish at leaving the Bauhaus Ise and Gropius now travelled to America. This was a serious study tour for him. The United States was the country where many of the architectural ideas which interested him most were making headway, particularly the latest developments in engineering structures and mass-produced components which allowed housing to be assembled rapidly in many different ways. Gropius had already lectured on the subject, citing the latest American experiments in his talk 'The House in Eight Days'. Not only was this visit to the States architecturally inspiring, it was important to Gropius's history, acting as a bridge between the old world and the new.

Their voyage was partially sponsored by Adolf Sommerfeld, who had a vested interest in Gropius's findings. He and Gropius were then immersed in visionary schemes for building a colossal factory, in the American efficiency style, to mass-produce building components and transform the whole housing industry, taking Henry Ford as their inspiration. Sommerfeld's wife Renée, who had brothers in the States, made the journey with Gropius and Ise, though Sommerfeld himself was too busy to go. Their travels were officially supported by the Reichsforschungsgesellschaft, the German research institute for housing construction.

'Sommerfeld has a plan to make the departure of G., myself and Frau Sommerfeld to the US a big affair,' Ise tells us. This was an opportunity to publicise their schemes. 'He will ask some important German politicians and bankers and also some American journalists to his house.' Berlin Minister-President Otto Braun was invited to the tea party, as was the city's chief planner, Martin Wagner, and Gropius was instructed by the avid self-promoter Sommerfeld to make a farewell speech.

They sailed from Bremen on the new German liner the SS *Columbus* on 28 March 1928. It was an eleven-day crossing, well documented in the many hundreds of photographs taken by the Gropiuses to record their travels. This was a time when photography was entering the public sphere and as well as more serious architectural pictures the records of the trip included numerous informal snapshots. We glimpse Ise and Renée stretched out on lounge chairs on deck, wearing cloche hats and snuggled beneath rugs. Walter, in a jaunty flat cap, tweed jacket and diamond-patterned V-neck jumper, poses on-board ship, ocean stretching far beyond.

On 7 April 1928 Prof. and Mrs Walter Gropius are on the list of notable arrivals from overseas published by the *New York Times*. They were in New York for the next three weeks, staying at the Plaza Hotel on Fifth Avenue. (In the early 1930s the art patron Solomon R. Guggenheim opened his modern collection to the public by appointment in his own suite at the Plaza, showing work by, among others, Klee and Kandinsky, which Guggenheim had acquired when he visited the Bauhaus himself.)

On that first New York visit Gropius was busy following up letters of introduction to American architects, engineers, contractors and government planning authorities. He studied New York high-rise buildings and their methods of construction indefatigably, as Ise remembered in an interview given in the 1970s: 'I think every single skyscraper of that time I've seen before it was finished. Gone up with these dreadful elevators which ran outside the building – quite dangerous. But my husband had to be up on every single one and I was the only one who could speak English. So I had to be along on all these trips.'

Gropius's great preoccupation of the time was with steel frame construction, which he had used himself in the experimental housing he designed for the Weissenhof estate. The photographs of Brooklyn Bridge taken on his journey show his awe and fascination on viewing one of the great New York structures of the past, with its steel cable construction supported by massive sandstone and granite pylons. These New York pictures have a strangely visionary, almost surrealistic quality. The Flatiron Building, shot at a steep angle, seems set to topple over,

Gropius in 1928 with his entry for the *Chicago Tribune* Tower competition of 1922.

crushing the crowds below. The great bulk of the French Building on Fifth Avenue has an element of threat. A vertiginous view of the bridge at Grand Central Station contains a premonition of Gropius's most controversial structure, the New York Pan Am skyscraper of 1958.

Ise Gropius on Brooklyn Bridge, photographed by Walter Gropius in 1928.

He and Ise were also overwhelmed by the rush, noise and commotion of the New York traffic. New York was even more frenzied than Berlin, but there were compensations. They tried out the entertainments: Barnum's Circus, the Roxy Theatre and the Ziegfeld Follies, where it

214

struck them that 'the nakedness of the girls was not nearly as prominent as compared to that on the German stages'. Nudity in Berlin was almost *de rigueur*.

On 29 April they travelled on to Washington by train. They had time for only a quick tour of the city. Gropius met with federal committees on construction materials and building regulations. He called on the German ambassador and visited the Lincoln Memorial. He was unimpressed by Washington. Although it had the reputation of being a 'planned city', Gropius was highly critical of its inherent inconsistencies. It attempted to be both a capital city and a federal district. It had 'separate standards for the political and social elite, for government employees and the middle class, and for Negroes'. The American attitude to black people shocked and alienated him.

Two days later the three travellers took the train to Chicago. There was much to thrill them there. The Great Fire which devastated the city in 1871 had in some ways proved a blessing, allowing the rebuilding of Chicago as a planned, coherent entity. Gropius admired the orderly layout of the suburbs and he was impressed by the efficient substructure of the city: the centralised heating and power plants, the Chicago city tunnel, the basement shipping system and the way in which the flow of the Chicago river had been reversed in order to drain away pollution from Lake Michigan.

Gropius was of course especially delighted with Chicago's simple industrial structures, the pioneering concrete construction of the Sears, Roebuck building, the massive silos and grain elevators he had venerated right from the start of his career. He tracked down Frank Lloyd Wright's architecture in Chicago. He'd admired the illustrations; now at last he saw the real thing. He and Ise found and photographed the exquisite Robie House of 1908–10 and Unity Temple in Oak Park, Illinois. Gropius was always aware of his considerable early debt to Wright, not only in the details of individual buildings but also in his concept of architectural wholeness, his dazzling imaginative stretch.

Besides the Wright pictures in the Gropiuses' album is a perhaps wistful photograph of the recently completed *Chicago Tribune* Tower, a castellar edifice, a neo-Gothic skyscraper, which had been selected in preference to Gropius's own 1922 Chicago competition design.

Gropius, as we have seen, was exceptionally responsive to changes of place, to new experiences of landscape. New Mexico and Arizona excited him more than anywhere he had been before. They were there in early May, taking the Santa Fé train through New Mexico to the Arizona border. In an article written in 1934 Ise vividly describes how the train clattered westward:

The closer we get to the Arizona border, the stranger the image that surprises us each morning when we awake. The Prairie extends interminably before us, a strange scent comes through the cracks of the sealed windows of the compartment, which still contains the well-conserved city air we've brought with us, and the seats gradually become coated with a fine layer of sand. Our wide Pullman berths, set up alongside the window, finally fulfil our marvellous childhood dream of gliding through a strange landscape lying down and taking everything in without effort. Dark Mexican faces peer in at us at the stations, it gets oppressively hot and ever larger clouds of sand swirl after the last wagon. The New Mexico ground is poor and infertile; shaggy, gaunt horses foraging for their beggarly feed between hills of sand look up at us and corpses lying around intensify the impression of a merciless barren land.

The travellers took a spectacular route, passing through Yuba City, the Rio Grande and the Painted Desert, which Gropius maintained gave them 'the most overwhelming impression' they had ever had. Reaching the strange inverted landscape of the Grand Canyon, Gropius described it as a 'negative mountain'. There are photographs of Gropius posed at the Grand Canyon, a frontiersman dressed in dungarees and Stetson, and of Ise sitting elegantly on a boulder beside a waterfall. The party hired a guide at the El Tovar Hotel, a dashing young American named Jack who, in Ise's view, made it explicable that rich young American women ended up marrying poor cowboys from Arizona.

Travelling through these strange landscapes gave Gropius the opportunity to pursue his passion for cacti. He had assembled a formidable collection during his days at the Bauhaus in Dessau. This craze became well known, and Gropius's friends indulged it. At one of his birthday parties the staff and students gave him a collection of artificial cacti they had designed and made. A cucumber shaped as a cactus, with carved radishes as blossoms, was remembered as being the most beautiful of these. Gropius's enthusiasm for the phallic and prickly cactus plant, a favourite motif of the Surrealists, may appear at variance with his belief in the disciplined and smooth. But this again is an example of his ability to hold apparently conflicting views at the same time.

The high point of the Arizona trip was the excursion they made with Jack as guide to visit the Hopi, Navajo and Havasupai Indian reservations. They started off in a Packard car, then continued the journey on Indian ponies, an arduous eight-hour ride over the mountains in the heat of summer. As soon as they arrived there was a sudden rainfall,

Gropius, Grand Canyon, Arizona, 1928.

which the Havasupai Indians, suffering from drought, gratefully attributed to the white foreigners, believing they had brought rain from their
native country. The villagers quickly organised a race in honour of the
Germans, involving the lassoing and breaking of wild horses, and performed a ceremonial dance of joy. Jack and the visitors then rode on to
a waterfall. A photograph shows Gropius having plunged into the water,
a tiny figure immersed in a vast pool.

He wrote to tell his daughter Manon of his visit to the Arizona Indians.
She was already fascinated by Native Americans, having devoured Karl
May's *Winnetou, the Red Gentleman*, the first volume of the well-known
trilogy based on the adventures of the Apache chief. 'My dear Mutzi,'
Gropius wrote on his return to the El Tovar Hotel, 'for 10 days I have
actually been among Indians! We travel by horse and wagon through
this God's country and praise the descendants of Winnetou.' He told
her that 'nowadays they are peaceful with the whites, but they still very
much have their dress, dwellings and customs of old!' Gropius had also
loved May's book since boyhood and he now sent Manon a de luxe
edition of the whole *Winnetou* trilogy. He observed that with her two
long pigtails Manon looked like an Apache Indian herself. For Gropius
Arizona never lost its magic. It became his favourite place of escape.
He returned there frequently later in his life.

From Arizona they went west to California. Los Angeles brought
a total change of scene. The mid-1920s was a time when a number
of highly individualistic architects – Frank Lloyd Wright, Rudolph
Schindler, Richard Neutra in particular – were bringing new forms of
architecture to Southern California. Arriving in Los Angeles on 14 May
Gropius made immediate contact with Neutra, who gives an account
in his memoir *Life and Shape* of the surprise phone call he received:
' "Gropius here. I don't know whether you remember my name." '

Neutra remembered it very well indeed. He too was an architectural émigré, intensely European in his background, having come from
a wealthy Jewish-Hungarian family. He arrived in the United States
in 1923 and worked briefly for Frank Lloyd Wright before moving to
Southern California to join Schindler and then developing his own

architectural practice in Los Angeles. He had only recently visited the Bauhaus in Dessau, where Mies van der Rohe had now taken over from Meyer as director. Neutra now answered Gropius, ' "For heaven's sake! What do you mean, whether I remember! Where are you? I'll come right away to pick you up." ' This was the beginning of an important friendship between Gropius and Neutra, which endured for life.

On Gropius's first visit to Los Angeles he grasped something of the energy of a movement in modern architecture which was both international and local, rooted in the Californian way of life. Neutra took him to see his own recently completed Jardinette Apartments, a luxury block of flats in Hollywood. They viewed buildings by Wright, presumably visiting his Los Angeles concrete block houses, clearly influenced by Mayan and Aztec architecture. They saw buildings by Schindler, whose famous Lovell Beach House for the pioneering health physician Dr Phillip Lovell was designed in the mid-1920s, the exemplar of architecture that encouraged an optimum, healthy, well-balanced mode of being. Neutra also took Gropius and Ise to the Hollywood motion picture studios. Southern California was another high spot of their travels in America. Both of them responded to the pervasive energy and optimism, the glamour, the belief in the modern. They were impressed by the sheer drama of the towering steel structures of the oil rigs that they photographed massed along Long Beach.

After LA, Detroit. Again a total change of scene. Here Gropius was greeted by the engineer–architect Albert Kahn, who arranged a formal dinner in his honour and took him on a tour of the Ford factory he had designed at Dearborn. Gropius, who had so frequently cited Henry Ford as the high priest of mass production from whom Germany should learn, was amazed by the efficiency of the River Rouge Plant, as the Ford factory was known. But he expressed misgivings at the extent to which the workers had become more or less subsumed into the production line. For Gropius the human factor was increasingly important. Within mechanisation he could see inherent threats. He was not alone in his misgivings. After all this was the decade in which Fritz Lang's dystopian movie *Metropolis* was made.

With only three days remaining before the homeward journey Gropius, Ise and Renée were back in New York. Here they had a busy programme of social events: a soirée given in their honour by the owner of the sumptuous Astor Hotel, lunch with the critic Lewis Mumford, dinner with the banker Felix Warburg, a memorable meeting with the writer H. L. Mencken and, especially significant in view of Gropius's return to America a decade later, an encounter with the erudite young art historian and collector of Chinese porcelain Alfred Barr, who was to be an important influence on the reputation of the Bauhaus in the States. Barr had visited the Bauhaus in 1927, but Gropius had apparently been absent. Now in New York they met and bonded, with Gropius judging Barr's ceramics collection as 'fabulous'.

In those final days Gropius and Ise still packed in new experiences, finding whole new areas of New York to explore. They discovered Chinatown, the Italian district, the Jewish Lower East Side ghetto, the last of which they rated as squalid, in stark contrast to the more spacious and salubrious Yorkville, centre of the New York German community. A particular excitement for Gropius was Harlem, where the Cotton Club became his favourite entertainment place. The club was restricted to white patrons but promoted the best black entertainers. He raved about Duke Ellington's band and the wonders of the floor show. 'Everything original and artistic comes from the Negro' was his and Ise's view.

The visit to America represented something of a turning point for Gropius. The photographs he took there give us an indication of his thrill at the stupendous, the glories of the landscape, the long tradition of architectural energy which sharpened his own ambitions. On Sunday 26 May they set sail again, back to Berlin and what was to prove a whole new stage of life.

Berlin was now a progressive, restless city at the centre of surprisingly rapid German economic recovery and industrial expansion. Real incomes, production and export volumes were already reaching pre-war levels by 1926. This growth in confidence generated the architectural revival that had encouraged Gropius's return from Dessau to the city of his birth.

'The ideas of the new architecture were victorious across the whole front,' wrote the critic Max Osborn in 1929.

The city today is surrounded by an enormous sweep of industrial buildings, which result from the functional way of thinking, the sense of space, and the new monumentality of modern architecture. Nowhere has the new beauty of the technological era found freer expression than in this unmissable development of machine halls, fortresses of production, storehouses, and pounding workshops, which with their administration buildings, internal circulation systems, fantastic steel structures, chimneys, mobile cranes, and soaring landmark towers spread in all directions far and wide across the formerly calm lands of the March of Brandenburg.

Gropius's hopes for a fusion of art and technology seemed to be taking tangible shape.

At the same time Berlin in the late 1920s was experiencing what has rightly been described as a golden age of culture, a sudden creative juxtaposition of radical and experimental talents. Architects and artists; novelists, poets and literary journalists; composers and musicians; actors and theatrical producer-impresarios: all energised by the communal experience of working and socialising in the capital. It was now the view amongst sophisticated Europeans, of whom Count Harry Kessler is a prime example, that 'Paris has become boring and Berlin is now the city where true amusement is to be had'.

1928 was the first time Gropius had lived in Berlin in any settled way since the upheavals of the First World War. He and Ise now took a spacious twelve-room flat on the third floor of an apartment building in Potsdamer Privatstrasse, a traffic-free street near the Potsdamer Platz. This had originally been the site of the Botanical Garden and rare trees and shrubs still grew in the front garden. Two tall cedars of Lebanon, Ise's pride and joy, flanked the entrance to the building. A huge gate isolated the street from the busy Potsdamerstrasse nearby, allowing the Gropiuses to live what they looked back on as 'a secluded, quiet life in the middle of the turmoil of the great city'.

The building itself, designed thirty years earlier by Berlin architects Cremer and Wolffenstein in an ornate neo-Gothic style, standing in blatant contrast to the architecture Gropius himself espoused, was easily able to accommodate the Gropius architectural office, which at its busiest employed twenty staff. Unusually for the time, one of Gropius's employees in Berlin was a female architect-engineer named Hilde Hartke. The entourage included two maids, a cook, a secretary, a female archivist and a house and office boy. These were days of optimism, when Gropius was living and working on a considerable scale.

The interior of the Gropius apartment was strikingly modern, furnished with the Bauhaus furniture and objects the Gropiuses had now had transported from Dessau. There was also the gramophone and their growing collection of phonographic recordings, which besides their old staples of Stravinsky, Krenek and Bartók had been broadening out to include jazz by Louis Armstrong, Spanish guitar music and recordings of music from Asia and China, rarities in Europe at the time.

The Gropius flat became a gathering point for friends from many disciplines, people of many different nationalities speaking in a variety of foreign accents while Gropius, correct, urbane and quietly charismatic, held centre stage. At this period he wore his hair brushed forward into a thick fringe, a style which Nikolaus Pevsner, meeting Gropius in Berlin, found disconcerting. 'Discipline and integrity,' Pevsner remembered later: 'I have never in my life met these two qualities united in one man so powerfully, so intensively as they are in Walter Gropius.'

Gropius's fringe. Photograph taken by Hugo Erfurth in Dresden, 1928.

In Berlin Gropius and Ise remained closely connected to the Bauhaus designers who had moved from Dessau with them: Herbert Bayer, Marcel Breuer, Lázsló Moholy-Nagy. Records of gatherings at the Gropius flat give an indication of their large network of acquaintances including, for example, the sculptor Naum Gabo, the playwright and novelist Ödön von Horváth, the composer Kurt Weill. Gropius and Ise were in the audience at one of the earliest performances of Brecht and Weill's *Threepenny Opera*, which opened in Berlin in 1928. Years later Ise still had a vivid memory of Brecht himself 'sitting forlornly in the front balcony watching the performance, dressed in what looked from far like a dark workman's shirt – no tie – but, on closer inspection, turned out to be of black silk. This alone was enough at that time to utterly confuse people, as he kept on confusing them at every turn of his life.'

Friendships between the Gropiuses and other progressive Berlin architects of his generation remained central to their lives. The city was unique at this period for the number and sheer quality of forward-looking architects – Bruno Taut, Erich Mendelsohn the designer of the streamlined Universum cinema, Mies van der Rohe, besides Gropius himself – whose work, although by no means uniform, combined to bring about the revolution in style, the sheer exhilaration of the move towards the modern to be seen in Berlin in 1929.

Gropius did not believe in the concept of the solitary genius, the 'starchitect', as it would later be termed. In this he was of course the opposite of Frank Lloyd Wright, whose position as America's most important architect was sustained by his considerable self-belief. 'G. is always dissatisfied with himself and his talent,' wrote Ise; 'he is convinced that his main gift is his power to envision everything in its total context.' He believed implicitly in the creative grouping as a means to bring about wide-ranging social change. In response to the devastation and disaster of the First World War Gropius, as we have seen, had been closely involved with the foundation of the Berlin-based Arbeitsrat für Kunst, an association of progressive architects and artists, and had kept up this connection through the Bauhaus years.

More recently, from 1925, he had been a founder member of a new radical group of architects, the Zehnerring, the Ring of Ten. Here the membership again included Taut, Mendelsohn and Mies van der Rohe, as well as younger architects Hans Scharoun and Hugo Häring. The idea was between them to develop an architectural culture fit for a new era, the concept of an architecture that went far beyond the design of individual buildings into the economic planning of whole cities. The mid-twentieth-century architect needed a broad remit covering the whole spectrum of social concerns: health and welfare, work and leisure, creating the optimum conditions for the leading of well-balanced human lives. The Ring organised wide-ranging exhibitions and published controversial articles designed to alter public thinking about architecture. For Gropius these architectural groupings were not only professional networks but the basis of important personal connections. Even more so without his day-to-day interchanges at the Bauhaus, he needed these friendships emotionally.

Gropius was never instantly gregarious. As Ise noted in her diary, 'He isn't a great conversationalist and it takes a certain measure of readiness on the side of the listener before he warms up.' But once formed his attachments tended to be deep, affectionate and lasting. They expanded considerably from 1928, when CIAM, the Congrès Internationaux d'Architecture Moderne, was formed, bringing Gropius into close contact with all the major modern European architects, founding fathers of the so-called International Style.

The organisation was inaugurated in June 1928 at a three-day meeting at the Swiss château of La Sarraz near Lausanne, where the formidable chatelaine, Hélène de Mandrot, herself an art collector and interior designer, was an enthusiastic patron of the modern spirit in architecture and design. The main impetus in forming CIAM was Gropius's friend and great supporter Sigfried Giedion, the learned and eccentric Swiss art historian said to be 'a compelling speaker with a delivery like no one else's. He intoned his sentences with his eyes closed as though in a trance induced by intense concentration.' Giedion was appointed secretary general of the organisation. Papers were given by Le Corbusier, the German town planner Ernst May, the French modernist architect André Lurçat and the Dutch architect H. P. Berlage. Gropius was absent from this inaugural CIAM meeting, having only just returned from his visit to America. But his controversial views on minimum dwellings and on high-rise buildings dominated the next two CIAM congresses, held in Frankfurt in 1929 and in Brussels in 1930.

These were serious, sometimes combative conferences, attended by the leading international practitioners, concerned with the need for architecture to respond imaginatively to the social and political pressures of the time. But they were convivial occasions too and Gropius's new contacts with Alvar Aalto from Finland, Sven Markelius from Sweden, Josep Lluís Sert from Barcelona, Farkas Molnár from Hungary and other influential figures were important in establishing his position at the centre of the international scene. He and Le Corbusier were from now on CIAM's acknowledged leaders. The British architectural critic J. M. Richards gives a little portrait of them both on the platform of a CIAM congress, viewing Corb as 'the indubitable bird' alongside Gropius 'the quintessential horse': Le Corbusier as the free flier and Gropius the more grounded and hard-working.

Gropius's considered pronouncements on housing at this period will come as a surprise to those who unfairly hold him responsible for a twentieth-century proliferation of soulless housing blocks, accusing him of being grimly inflexible and doctrinaire. His proposals are in fact consistently humane. As he viewed it, 'The *basic requirements* for the general planning of a large residential development are: *daylight, fresh air, sunshine, tranquillity, limited population density, good accessibility, rationally designed, convenient apartment interiors, pleasant overall ambience.*'

Existing woodland should be largely left intact. 'The natural accidents of terrain, the way it is accommodated in the design, the spacing generated by the thoroughfares, the interspersing of trees and other vegetation among the buildings to open and close the sightlines – all these features generate agreeable contrast, relax and enliven the grid plan, mediate between buildings and humans, create dialogue, and land scale.' Architecture, he maintained, 'emphatically does not begin and end with its functional value, with mere fulfilment of a purpose – unless it be our psychological need for a harmonious living environment.' Here Gropius is already speaking in the future language of the Greens.

In Gropius's speeches and writings of this period another unjustly held impression is refuted: that Gropius was anti-feminist. Here he is lecturing in 1929 on 'The Sociological Foundations of the Minimum

Dwelling', making the case for 'new forms of centralized master house-holds which partially relieve the individual woman of her domestic tasks'. In this concept of a modern community building, with communal facilities, day care for the children, cafeterias and roof gardens, ideas Le Corbusier was also exploring, Gropius was sympathetic to the needs of the modern woman in 'gaining more free time for herself and her children while participating in gainful occupations and liberating her-self from dependence upon the man'. Perhaps the experience of Ise's sister Hertha had influenced his thinking. He had a clear idea of the role of the architect in making possible 'the intellectual and economic emancipation of women to an equal partnership with men'. Gropius also insisted that every adult needed to have his or her room, 'small though it may be'.

Eight of the rooms in the Gropius apartment in Potsdamer Privat-strasse were given over to the architectural office. Otto Meyer-Otten was the office manager, Carl Fieger and Franz Möller the principals. We do not have any detailed description of the actual office but some-thing very close to it is vividly described by the writer Franz Hessel in his 1929 collection of essays, *Ein Flaneur in Berlin*:

The architect takes me into his spacious, light-filled studio. He leads the way from one table to the next, showing me plans and three-dimensional models for site land-scaping; workshops and office block; laboratories for an accumulator factory; he shows me designs for an aircraft exhibition hangar, and drawings for one of the new, light, and airy housing projects that will rescue hundreds and thousands from housing shortages and squalid tenements. He goes on to tell me of all that Berlin architects are now planning and – in part – about to execute.

Hessel's busy architect might well have been Gropius. Certainly his office at this point, in the years following his move back to Berlin, was very fully occupied with large-scale housing projects. He continued to be involved with the low-cost housing developments at Törten. He was also in close collaboration with the indefatigably ambitious Adolf Sommerfeld on the 'Gropius City', a visionary co-operative settlement planned to house five thousand families at very low rents alongside the Potsdam railway line on the outskirts of Berlin.

A further Sommerfeld project was a settlement of one thousand apartments in Bad Dürrenberg. In 1928 Gropius was involved, again with Sommerfeld as the developer, in a huge programme for the reconstruction of a still war-torn Paris. In connection with this project the Gropius office developed prefabricated housing systems and apartment block designs, as well as replanning whole areas of the capital. Early in 1929 Gropius won first prize in a competition which attracted three hundred entries for a housing development on a large site in Spandau. None of these grand schemes ever saw the light of day. The most tangible result of all his hopes and efforts in returning to Berlin is an apartment block at Siemensstadt, on the west side of the city, a salubrious estate designed for middle-income families. Ironically this beautiful and decorous four-storey building is far from being a high rise, and certainly not a solution to the problem of rehousing Berlin's working population, Gropius's great preoccupation of the time.

All of these optimistic plans and schemes were crushed by the global economic collapse at the end of 1929. As Gropius's progressive views took centre stage at the second CIAM congress in Frankfurt, the New York stock market was in freefall. The effects of 'Black Thursday', 24 October, the day the New York stock market collapsed, were felt globally. In Berlin the impact was dire, taking the form of increasing unemployment, drastic cuts in pay, the closing down of well-established German companies, widespread cancellation of civic projects. Politics became more polarised, more violent, with outbreaks of fighting between National Socialists and Communists in the Berlin streets. Nearby, Potsdamer Platz became a favourite place for Nazi demonstrations, where crowds would gather shouting 'Germany awake!', 'Death to Judah', 'Heil Hitler'. Political extremism was coming close to home.

In 1930 the office started working on what might have been the most impressive and convincing of Gropius's high-rise architectural projects, two eleven-storey apartment blocks on a cliff-side site on the shore of Lake Wannsee, Berlin, looking across to Lindwerder Island and linked by a one-storey circular pavilion. This project was also cancelled due to lack of funding. For Gropius it was the beginning of a disappointing and disorientating time.

There was, however, a brief respite when, in the spring of 1930, the German Foreign Office commissioned the Deutscher Werkbund to carry out the German contribution to the exhibition of the Société des Artistes Décorateurs Français, to be held in Paris. This was a significant overture since Germany had been excluded from the Paris 1925 *Arts Décoratifs* exhibition. The Werkbund appointed Gropius to be artistic director of the German section, held in the Grand Palais. He embraced the opportunity of creating an exhibit which, as he explained it in the catalogue, would 'bear witness to the contemporary and modern creative spirit in Germany. It shows methods and results of the organic connection with today's social and technological world.'

To demonstrate this new, modern, clean-lined Germany Gropius assembled his old team from the Bauhaus. Moholy-Nagy, Marcel Breuer and Herbert Bayer were each given a section to design. Moholy showed lighting fixtures, a redesigned post office and his own photo-essay on Germany. Breuer contributed interior designs for a new hotel. Bayer selected a display of 'German standard goods', Bauhaus-designed or Bauhaus-approved examples of modern furniture and textiles, household appliances, stage designs and architectural projects. In a way this was an early version of the legendary Bauhaus exhibition which would be held at the Museum of Modern Art, New York, in 1938.

Gropius's own contribution to the Paris exhibition took the form of his current favourite architectural concept of the multi-purpose communal space, the gathering point for the inhabitants of one of his high-rise housing blocks (see Plate 24). As he saw it, 'we need casual and non-committal ways of being together in rooms', an informal, almost accidental proximity 'which develops a new and easier form of human contact'. His communal areas designed for the 1930 Werkbund exhibition took the form of a bar and a dance floor, with secluded little lobbies for listening to the radio, playing records, reading, playing games. Upstairs was a library and a noticeboard for community bulletins and messages. A swimming pool and gym were provided for the residents.

This vision of modernity was completed by Marcel Breuer's svelte steel frame furniture.

The whole ensemble had a glamour and sophistication visitors found thrilling. The critic of the *Journal des débats* saw Gropius's sequence of communal rooms as 'space and light' governed by reason, but which also showed 'a magic of precision', a 'mysterious beauty in the exact forms'. The widely travelled connoisseur Count Harry Kessler made the entry in his diary: 'In the afternoon, I visited the Gropius exhibition in the Salon des Artistes Décorateurs. It has caused a considerable sensation here. There is no doubt whatever that it is more interesting than the French arts and crafts exhibition which is set alongside it.'

Walter and Ise Gropius with Le Corbusier in Paris, 1930.

Back at the Bauhaus itself yet another crisis had been developing. Gropius had been consciously keeping his distance since his departure from Dessau in 1928, but inevitably reports soon started reaching him of how Meyer, once installed, had lost little time in putting his policies into reverse. 'As I recognized too late,' Gropius maintained in a letter to a colleague in America, 'he was scheming to keep his intentions to himself until he was in the saddle. He sacrificed his personal integrity for his hidden political intentions. Not only myself, but everyone else in the Bauhaus was completely surprised when his communistic leanings came into the open after he was installed as Director.'

We do need to be aware that these words were written in 1963, when Gropius himself was living in America; at the tensest phase of the Cold War he was wary of acknowledging Bauhaus connections with communists. However, it is clear that Meyer, almost pathetically conscious of being seen as 'the insignificant follower of a great predecessor', drastically altered the curriculum, putting greater stress on collectivist theory and scientific working methods while diminishing the fine art, abstract, individualistic content of the courses. Gropius had striven for a balance between art and technology. From now on there was far more technology than art.

Hannes Meyer's championing of design for social relevance in opposition to abstract art naturally antagonised the fine artists on the faculty, Kandinsky and Albers emerging as particularly hostile to the new regime. Oskar Schlemmer was resentful of the way his theatre productions had been denigrated by Meyer and a group of communist students as 'irrelevant, formalistic, too personal'. He left the Bauhaus in October 1929, bitter in his dislike of Meyer. 'Gropius', maintained Schlemmer, 'was a man of the world, after all, capable of the grand gesture, of taking risks when it seemed worthwhile. The other fellow is petty-minded, a boor – and most important, not up to the job.'

By no means all the moves Meyer made were detrimental. On the positive side he greatly strengthened the teaching of architecture at the Bauhaus, bringing in Mart Stam and Ludwig Hilberseimer, the latter a radical theorist of cities who introduced the first student course in city planning. Meyer and his architectural partner Hans Wittwer won a competition for a new building for a school for the German trade union federation in Bernau, involving Bauhaus students in a real live architectural project. Meyer's regime was more successful than Gropius's had been in generating sales of Bauhaus products. The annual income from production almost doubled in the two years while Meyer was director and a contract for the now well-known Bauhaus wallpaper was signed with the manufacturer Emil Rasch in 1929.

However, by this time Meyer's days were numbered. Whereas Gropius as director of the Bauhaus was politically circumspect, as we have seen, Meyer was much less cautious. Marxism and Leninism were introduced into the Bauhaus as official subjects, along with lectures on scientific studies, philosophy, psychology and sex education. Political activities and arguments were positively encouraged by Meyer, for whom politics was central to his outlook. 'I remember three students coming to me and giving me a copy of the Communist Manifesto,' the English student Wilfred Franks remembered. 'They put it on the bench where I was working and said, "Read that Wilf and then you'll know what we are all about."' Bauhaus students at the time could hardly help being politicised, polarised between Meyer's brand of Marxism and the Nazis, whose influence in Dessau was making itself felt.

In summer 1930 Mayor Hesse, panic-stricken, telephoned Gropius in Berlin to tell him of his worries that Meyer's communistic policies had become a serious danger to the Bauhaus. Gropius encouraged Hesse to dismiss him. On 29 July the mayor demanded Meyer's resignation, accusing him of encouraging political activities at the school and of promoting 'Marxist teaching methods that undermine the civic conception of *Bauwesen* [construction] and infect youth'. Meyer protested in a long defensive open letter to Hesse that he circulated to the newspapers. He took legal action against the Dessau authorities. A financial settlement was finally agreed. In 1930 Meyer left Germany, taking half a dozen Bauhaus students with him, to settle in the USSR, where he believed, as it turned out naively, 'a true proletarian culture is being formed'.

Mayor Hesse pleaded with Gropius to come back to the Bauhaus. Gropius refused and recommended Mies van der Rohe, his early colleague and now to some extent his Berlin rival, to become the new director. Mies had in fact rejected the position when he was originally offered it, in preference to Meyer, in 1928. But now he accepted and the Bauhaus altered in atmosphere and outlook yet again.

The authoritarian, formal Mies took over in autumn 1930, determined to restore order and discipline to the school, clamping down on the activities of militant communist students, reversing Meyer's emphasis on mechanisation and standardisation, introducing his own concepts of architecture, planning and interior design. But local political opposition to the school was now increasing.

Wilfred Franks was haunted all his life by a Nazi demonstration in the main square in Dessau. The police arrived on horseback and drove the Bauhaus students back into the side streets. The police action was clumsy and crude. 'Then we heard the sounds of a brass band in the distance and it came nearer and nearer. Very soon the brown shirts came into the square, which we had filled a short time before. It was packed full of brown shirts and the police. This was the first time I had seen them.' The omens for Mies's tenure at the Bauhaus were becoming increasingly alarming as Nazi opposition in Dessau was stepped up.

———

Gropius had hoped to see more of his daughter after moving to Berlin. He promised her a couple of pleasurable days out driving in the Adler, reminding her of their expeditions in Dessau. But circumstances had altered. Manon was now at the Institut Hanausek in Vienna, the boarding school Alma had once attended. Alma, on reaching the age of fifty and in poor physical shape, had finally given in and agreed to marry Werfel. The ceremony was held at the Rathaus in Vienna on 6 July 1929. Instead of an 'Onkel Werfel' Manon now had an official stepfather and a rival to Gropius himself.

He was painfully aware of a new distance between himself and Manon. On 26 February 1930 he wrote complaining,

My dearest Mutzi, do you know it's been *six* months since your last little letter to me? You outdo me considerably in my letter-writing aversion and now I must once more give you a loving little push in writing you – how are things going, what are you up to, who do you go around with – everything interests me that concerns you. I only see you from very far away, through upside-down opera glasses, and my entire papahood goes up in smoke if your little hand doesn't write at least one letter soon.

Following the marriage Alma and Werfel moved into a new house in Vienna, the impressive and beautiful Villa Ast, designed in 1911 by Josef Hoffmann for the rich construction engineer Edvard Ast. This mansion was on the Hohe Warte, around the corner from the house where Alma's mother was still living with Carl Moll. Gropius asked Manon to send him an accurate floor plan of her room in this 'fancy chateau' so that he could give her a complete set of bedroom furniture including a bed and dressing table. He had recently designed a whole range of modular furniture for the Feder department store in Berlin, a predecessor of the popular post-war 'flat pack' furniture designs.

In another sweetly confidential letter, written in 1931, Gropius tells Manon of his triumph in designing a new cabriolet sports car for the Adler factory in Frankfurt, one of a series of car body designs commissioned by Erwin Kleyer (see Plate 25). He boasted that the Sport-Reise Cabriolet, with fold-down front seats that converted into beds, 'won top prizes in all the big beauty contests: in Wiesbaden the golden ring, in Berlin the prize for the most beautiful German car'. The Berlin accolade was at an international auto show held in February 1931. It is proof of Gropius's remarkable resilience that he was able to diversify with such enthusiasm at a period when his architectural commissions were dying down.

The mood in the country was worsening. According to László Moholy-Nagy's soon-to-be second wife, Sibyl Pietzsch, then working in Berlin as a motion picture scriptwriter, 'Hitler's power, which had been a provincial buffoonery, acquired an unexpected reality in 1931.' Over the next two years millions of unemployed men were to join his private army, the Sturmabteilung, the so-called Storm Troopers. Sibyl goes on, 'Newspapers and radio commentators became increasingly sympathetic to the Weltanschauung, the new world view. Big industry picked up the scent of a potential rearmament boom, and economists spared no mental acrobatics to reconcile Hitler's liquidation of capital interest with the mouth-watering promise of annihilation of the labour unions. Life started to be obscured by miasmic clouds of cowardice and treachery.'

Gropius, the architect and the employer, was painfully aware of these developments, telling his now fourteen-year-old daughter of his secret fears for the future:

> ... you can hardly imagine the difficulties that have beset me in the last few months in this battered and impoverished Germany. Being true to my plan to only live and work for things that seem important to me and worth my effort, I have fought hard to exist, for a 'decent' living, the kind we all would love to have, but I can tell you that it's more satisfying in the end to live by one's ideas, to be a pioneer, than to only consider what makes money. I am writing you about terrible grown-up things, but I remember you're so smart, I feel I'm more a friend to you than a father, and I already think you will follow after me.

His confidence in his beloved Mutzi is poignant, especially when one is conscious of the fact that her health was already precarious and that she was suffering from back problems. Alma sent Gropius an X-ray showing Manon's alarmingly delicate spine. At this stage they rarely saw one another. Gropius was surprised to hear his daughter had suddenly left school and was taking a course in foreign language translation. Manon was already fluent in Italian and French. In November 1931 she stayed briefly with her father in Berlin, but the visit was cut short by the news that Alma and Gustav Mahler's daughter Anna, now on her third marriage, this time to Werfel's publisher Paul Zsolnay, had attempted to commit suicide after a problematic love affair. Alma needed Manon back at home.

———

In the early 1930s Gropius was pushing forward with proposals for high-rise housing as the means of solving the social problems in big cities, the subject on which he had become so messianic since his extended travels in the States. In a whole series of lectures, broadcasts and articles Gropius extolled the benefits of multi-storey apartment blocks in giving city dwellers the amenities of living in a healthy green environment, while good communication systems could rapidly bring country dwellers to the city. Gropius's vision for this ideal future was graphically presented at the German Building Exposition in 1931 in a series of explanatory panels designed with his one-time Bauhaus colleague

Xanti Schawinsky. The Jewish Schawinsky had taken a post as director of the graphic art studios in the municipal government of Magdeburg. But the local increase in racial persecution forced him to leave and he was now working freelance in Berlin.

As well as high-rise housing Gropius continued to develop fast-assembly prefabricated homes. He designed an ingenious prefabricated copper house for the Hirsch Copper and Brass Works of Finow in Brandenburg. Forty of these houses were built on an experimental basis, but further development was halted when the Hirsch-Kupfer company, originally under Jewish ownership, was handed over to new management after the National Socialists came to power.

Gropius's office was still attempting to diversify into product design. Ise's family firm, the Frank ironworks in Dillenburg, helpfully commissioned him to redesign and modernise their range of cast-iron and wood-burning stoves. His 'Oranier' design became the company's best seller. But of course in a sense this was desperation work for an architect with a vision as ambitious as Gropius's. The drawing in of opportunities in Germany as a result of the economic downturn now made him more dependent on possible commissions abroad and he opened an office in Buenos Aires in partnership with a former employee, Franz Möller, who had moved to Argentina. One of their joint projects was a small house of very minimal construction which could easily be enlarged or altered. This was known as the 'Gropius Standard' home.

It is at this point that Gropius became occupied with two large-scale speculative designs for the Soviet Union, entering the international competitions for the Ukrainian State Theatre in Kharkov in 1930 and the even more massive and symbolic Palace of the Soviets in Moscow in 1931. Gropius already had links with the Soviet Union. His achievements at the Bauhaus were well known there since the Russian writer Ilya Ehrenburg had attended the opening of the Bauhaus in Dessau in 1926 and viewed the early beginnings of the Törten estate. Ehrenburg had been followed by other delegations of architects, engineers and government officials from the Soviet Union, which at that time was still to some extent espousing modernism.

Gropius's design for the four-thousand-seat Kharkov theatre 'for musical mass-productions' was a variant on his earlier Total Theatre concept for Piscator, a space that would encourage the complete involvement of the audience, using a system of projectors with which the stage, ceilings and side walls of the auditorium could be 'flooded' by changing lighting effects or films. Gropius's mechanised stage was 'designed like an industrial manufacturing hall or a switching yard with possible moves in every direction'. His flexible new theatre was put over as an 'inexhaustible large space machine' covered by a glass skin. However, this futuristic concept did not find favour with the judges, who failed to consider it a good solution for 'a theatre of mass events', a building that also needed to cater for sporting fixtures, circus shows and political demonstrations. When the results were declared Gropius came eighth. He does not appear to have been too disconcerted. The entering of major international competitions was (and still is) part of an architect's accepted way of life.

The Palace of the Soviets was another grandiose architectural project, this time for a ceremonial hall in Moscow near the Kremlin, on the site of the recently demolished Cathedral of Christ the Saviour. Well-known architects, including Le Corbusier, Hans Poelzig and Erich Mendelsohn as well as Gropius, were invited to submit proposals in the second stage of an international public competition. This was Gropius's initial concept, put over in enthusiastic terms: 'The Soviet Palace a new pole! A monument to the idea of the USSR. Therefore: a single powerful spatial body entirely visible at a glance, over a circle as the symbol of the connection of the masses of the people of a huge human and political unity.'

Gropius's design took the form of two circular auditoria, with one hall large enough to accommodate fifteen thousand people placed opposite a smaller hall with a capacity of six thousand. There was scope for mass marches and demonstrations in the open spaces between the two. The radical orientation was symbolic of communal activity, a unity of purpose, and provided easy access so that thousands of people could easily throng in. Like the theatre for Kharkov Gropius's design for the Palace of the Soviets was technically sophisticated, with screens and mobile stage equipment. But there was no chance whatsoever it could win.

For a modernist architect the timing was disastrous. This was the moment in which the Soviet concept of art for the people had taken a distinctly different turn from the freedom of expression of the years that followed the Russian Revolution, when avant-garde art had been allowed to flourish. By the 1920s the Soviet regime was distancing itself from these radical beginnings and in 1932 the governmental central committee announced the formation of the Artists' Union of the USSR, which ruled that Socialist Realism was the only acceptable style.

The competition for the Palace of the Soviets was adjudicated by 'a jury whose most noteworthy member was Dictator Stalin', as *Time* magazine caustically commented. Three finalists were then announced, reactionary architects all working in a neo-classical style. In May 1933 the Russian Boris Iofan was declared the winner, with a gigantic wedding cake design 415 metres tall, to be topped by a seventy-metre statue of Lenin. As with Gropius's earlier experience in entering the *Chicago Tribune* competition, this had been a put-up job. The Palace of the Soviets was never built. The Second World War intervened and in 1958 the site was cleared for the construction of the open-air civic swimming pool.

———

Worsening political conditions in Berlin made Gropius and Ise all the more anxious for changes of scene. In late spring 1930 they discovered the esoteric pleasures of Ascona on the shore of Lake Maggiore in the Swiss canton of Ticino. Since the German *Lebensreform* and *Wandervogel* movement of the early twentieth century, Ascona had been a place of pilgrimage for idealists in search of a better way of being, not unlike the 'mindfulness' movement of today. On a hill known as Monte Verità a primitive socialist colony had been formed, rejecting the conventional values of society, espousing vegetarianism, nudism, its own specialist code of morality and endless speculative argument. The colony attracted members and visitors from many disciplines – for instance Hermann Hesse, Carl Jung, Erich Maria Remarque, Rudolf

Steiner and Henry van de Velde. Rudolf Laban set up a school for the performing arts in Ascona in 1913. Isadora Duncan and Mary Wigman developed their theories of dance, movement and ritual there.

It was well known to the Bauhäusler. Paul Klee was an enthusiast. Oskar Schlemmer, staying in Ascona in 1927, mentioned in a letter to a friend that other visitors included Moholy-Nagy, Marcel Breuer and their wives,

the poet Nebel of the 'sturm', various singers, barons, dancers, dancing countesses, painters male and female, native Asconians and Ticinese, fishers and boatsmen, chauffeurs (do you get the picture)? . . . The freedom and mobility one has in Ascona are unique for this area; the Asconians are used to everything, thanks to the eccentrics, saints, nature worshippers and painters, so that no one causes so much as a raised eyebrow.

The rich collector Baron von der Heydt was then in the process of building a hotel on Monte Verità designed by the modernist architect Emil Fahrenkamp.

Herbert Bayer, Xanti Schawinsky and Gropius, 1933.

It is surely an indication of Gropius's deteriorating financial situation that in 1930 he and Ise chose to stay not in the baron's new modern hotel but in the cheaper and homelier Casa Hauser. They returned to Casa Hauser later in the summer with Xanti Schawinsky, Marcel Breuer, Herbert Bayer and his wife Irene, a close-knit and convivial Bauhaus house party, Schawinsky describing Ascona as 'the place where brows reached the sky and bottoms travelled Third Class!' There was beach life and *bocce*, at which Gropius proved himself an expert bowler. The Bauhaus friends went walking up the hill to Bosco, the village just above Ascona, looking down on Lake Maggiore from above. But apparently Gropius, who suffered from weak ankles, was not a great walker and often stayed behind.

Gropius and Shifra Canavesi
photographed by Josef Albers in Ascona, 1930.

The mood on the whole was carefree and romantic. Photographs taken during that summer in Ascona suggest a heightened sexuality. Shifra, the glamorous actress friend who had taken part in the filming of the Gropius house in Dessau, turned up. She was now married to the musician Bruno Canavesi but that by no means cramped her style. A sequence of pictures taken by Josef Albers shows Gropius and Shifra in a whole succession of flirtatious poses, entwined with one another. Gropius appears delighted. This was a brief period of irresponsibility, a complete change of surroundings, a release from the worries of Berlin, and it was the summer in which Ise and Herbert Bayer fell in love.

The love affair between Ise Gropius and Herbert Bayer was not just a fleeting Monte Verità flirtation. Ise's adopted daughter Ati wrote later that 'the attachment held great significance for her and was to influence her and her marriage for many years to come'. Ise at the time was thirty-five. Herbert Bayer was three years younger, married to the photographer and graphic designer Irene Hecht, whom he had first met when she visited the Bauhaus exhibition in Weimar in 1923. She became a Bauhaus student and they married two years later. The Bayers had a daughter, Julia, who was three at the time of the Ascona summer. But the marriage had not been easy and there was already a history of trial separations.

Bayer, the brilliantly experimental graphic designer, had a reputation as a Bauhaus playboy. 'Oh zatt Hehr-bert,' Anni Albers would exclaim whenever she thought back on him. According to the Dessau Bauhaus student Werner David Feist, 'Bayer was an immaculate dresser, sported a small moustache, and seemed to me a somewhat vain body beautiful overlooking the scene quietly with his large dark eyes.' But there was something more interesting too in Herbert Bayer's subtle, complex make-up, a certain detachment and aloofness. 'Bayer's cool and his total lack of an easy smile made me feel uncomfortable in his presence,' Feist tells us. Perhaps it was this balance between Bayer's superficial cosmopolitan aura of vanity and glamour and his sense of solemn inner purpose that Ise found so irresistible in him.

On making the move from Dessau to Berlin Bayer set up his own successful office as a graphic and exhibition designer, becoming artistic director of the Berlin office of the Dorland advertising agency and working on *Vogue* magazine's Paris edition, as well as collaborating with Gropius on exhibition design. His practice was now becoming more complex in its elements, working as he was for these new fashion-conscious clients. His advertisements and posters, which often incorporated photography, were increasingly surrealistic at this period, with a growing element of the erotic, appealing to the subliminal desires of a sophisticated international public. From Ise's point of view the love affair with Bayer brought a wonderful release, a sense of fresh horizons. Her arduous and dutiful 'Frau Bauhaus' years were over, and now she was living in Berlin Ise was feeling in need of new excitements, a new role.

Gropius was still unsuspecting of the liaison between his wife and Bayer when he took a short midwinter holiday late in 1930. He had not been to Spain since the 1907 visit made with Helmuth Grisebach. He reported back to Manon of the pleasures of this 'brief but delightful' return to Spain with Ise: the wild storms in the Bay of Biscay followed by beautiful sun in the interior; the 'raw and very manly' language of the Spanish people, straightforward and sincere, 'without empty phrases'; the 'remarkable and beautiful' Spanish music, in which the 'so-called *cante jondo*' – he tells Manon – 'oddly enough arose from the synagogues, from Jewish hymns'. From Madrid Gropius and Ise took 'the most beautiful train in Europe', travelling along the Riviera and 'the Côte d'Argent in a proper *Schlaraffencar*', a luxury carriage of fantasy and ease.

At Easter 1931 Walter and Ise were joined by Herbert Bayer and his wife for a skiing holiday in the Czech resort of Marchendorf. Ise was already a good skier, having learned as a young girl, when she lived within easy reach of the Bavarian alps. Gropius, at the age of forty-eight, found skiing hard to master. During that year Ise took to going on her own independent holidays, skiing with Bayer while Gropius was left working in Berlin. He began complaining at the lack of letters from her: 'Shocking! Tonight no letter from you, and that after your last one, which already sounded somewhat faint.'

Pathetically, Gropius complains of her neglect of him at a time when he is 'in need of warmth and tenderness as never before'. He attempts

to arouse Ise to jealousy by telling her of a potential rival, a beautiful twenty-three-year-old divorcée: 'I drove her in my car when she
left, but unfortunately I had too little time; but it was fun to see that
women still fully react to me, very much so, even when they are beautiful.' We see him pleading with her to respect their marriage: 'don't
let anything enter our ring. It closed so well and safely up to now, and
my feelings for you are just as tender as on the first day. These are not
just words . . . We have lived well together, and I miss you very much.'
He had no proof of Ise's unfaithfulness but he certainly had a sense of
danger. Here are echoes of the letter sent by Gustav Mahler to Alma at
Tobelbad when her passionate liaison with Gropius first began.

Through 1932 Herbert Bayer wrote Ise a sequence of loving and agonising letters, all of which she kept. He wrote to her early on in January,
saying that 'perhaps it is not right for me to write, but I cannot keep
everything to myself'. Irene did her best to make the family Christmas
agreeable and their little daughter's excitement helped the days along.
Bayer, like Gropius, calls his daughter 'Mutzi'. But he confesses that he

Ise Gropius photographed by Herbert Bayer in Montana, 1932.

already has great longings for Ise and does not know how he is going to bear up under the strain.

Bayer was torn between his physical attraction towards Ise, together with the feeling that she would be able to assist him in developing his work, and his admiration for and loyalty to Gropius. He respected the close partnership between the woman he called 'Pia' and the man he knew as 'Pius', the familiar inner-circle Bauhaus names for Ise and Walter. 'You know that we want to do everything not to destroy your marriage,' he told her. But it was a struggle: 'My dear Pia,' Bayer wrote in turmoil, 'I am trying to clear my head, but I am not succeeding.' He was drawn back to the places that connected him with her:

I live as in a dream which has mixed the most beautiful and the saddest things together. But everything I observe meantime I bring into relation to you. Everywhere I see only you. Weimar was the place where I saw you for the first time quite unsuspecting, but the moment was clear and precise in my memory when I stood at the door of the canteen last night . . . I know now that I cannot shut you out and that my love for you will be part of me for all my life.

In March 1932 Gropius went to Barcelona for the CIAM congress. Ise did not go with him. The journey would have been expensive and she and Herbert went skiing instead. A few weeks after Gropius returned they finally braced themselves for the confession.

Gropius was apparently taken by surprise when Ise first began to tell him the truth. He had not guessed. And he even then imagined that if Ise was indeed unfaithful, the more extrovert Schawinsky was the likely candidate. Gropius tried hard not to be judgemental, comforting himself and Ise by remembering his own past liaisons with Alma and then Lily while both of them were married to older husbands. He told Ise, 'I know how you feel . . . I have done the same.'

Then, following his usual confrontation pattern, Gropius contacted Herbert Bayer and arranged to meet him in Berlin. The meeting took place in Potsdamer Privatstrasse, on Gropius's home ground. 'I let him go ahead in his own way', Gropius explained, 'and only saw to it that an atmosphere without nightmarish quality prevailed and that we had some good talks. We sat up until 5.30 am in very lively conversation. You floated like an invisible presence in our minds.'

Bayer himself reported back to Ise more emotionally, evidently shaken: 'Pius was deeply concerned and generous and noble and everything a man can possibly be. He has prevented that I should feel ashamed before him. It is so painful that I should give such grief, to him of all people.' All the same Bayer held on to the illusion that he and Ise might resolve the situation: 'an absurd idea recurs to me all the time if there existed the possibility that we could really follow and live out our feelings and that you might then return to Pius. But I'm afraid a lifetime would be too short for this.'

Gropius could not let the situation go. Obsessively, a few days later, he met Bayer again. 'Yesterday we had a real stag party,' he told Ise. 'We went to our small lake near Ferch, swam in the rain, picked water-lilies and ploughed up the world in words . . . we had a naked picnic and then went to Ferch for a cup of coffee. Your spirit was among us, my dear.' We can sense in Gropius at this juncture a kind of desperation in not blaming and alienating Bayer. Emotional ties to the Bauhäusler remained so strong in him. There is a sense of submerged eroticism in this episode, a reverence for brotherhood, an almost sacred charge. At the same time he was anxious to keep his marriage going, imploring Ise, 'I know that our mission to each other is by no means fulfilled as yet.'

These meetings between Gropius and Bayer continued. Later in July, when Gropius was in Frankfurt, Bayer called on him unexpectedly one morning, confessing his regret that he had not told Gropius many months before, at the very beginning of the affair: 'his feeling of guilt had prevented this'. Gropius, still in his super-magnanimous mode, 'tried to free him from this feeling because it should not become a hindrance to our understanding'. They drove together amicably to a charming little inn on the Rhine, 'just the right ambience for us', and from there they wrote Ise a joint postcard. 'You yourself, my dear,' Gropius told Ise, 'are still the big unknown in my equations, I know too little about your inner self. We have been separated for four weeks now and the essential things one cannot put in a letter. But I still have a hopeful feeling about our mutual relationship and its promises for the future.' Ise retreated, taking refuge with her sister Hertha at Murnau on the edge of the Alps, south of Munich. Bayer followed her there and the love affair went on.

Gropius continued trying to resolve the situation. Adler was now one of his few remaining clients. Kleyer, the owner of the Adlerwerke, remained confident that the Depression in Germany was temporary. His policy meanwhile was to expand and diversify his product range, and Gropius was commissioned to design less expensive cars, trucks and other vehicles. Only a year later the whole Adler factory would be concentrated on vehicle production for the Third Reich. But for the moment, while he was working as Adler's chief designer, Gropius rented an apartment at Wiesbaden, convenient for the Adler factory in Frankfurt, and insisted that Ise move there with him. Commuting between Wiesbaden and Frankfurt in his own Adler Cabriolet, Gropius applied for and received permission to carry a gun, a small-bore pistol. As the Nazi party edged its way to power in Germany these were increasingly tense times.

Shortly before Christmas 1932 Gropius and Ise were invited by their Swiss friends Sigfried and Carola Giedion to go skiing in the mountains at Arosa. They loved Arosa and returned quite often, together or, more frequently, Ise on her own with Bayer. After Ise implored him – 'will you let us have our fling?' – Gropius reluctantly gave his permission for their liaison to continue on the ski slopes. Ise at first requested a month alone with Bayer. On this first quasi-official holiday together he allowed them just a fortnight. Confiding in Gropius's biographer Reginald Isaacs decades later, Ise recollected how 'she adored the mountains, the air, the skiing, and being romantically in love with an attractive and passionate young man'. At the end of the fortnight Bayer left Arosa. Immediately Gropius arrived to take over. The situation was obviously painful but he was still in control.

——

1932 had been an increasingly depressing year for Gropius. On Christmas Day he wrote sadly to his mother from Berlin, apologising for not being able to come to give her a Christmas embrace. 'But things are so difficult

246

these days,' he said. He was feeling his age. 'Sometimes I am annoyed with myself that I am almost fifty years old and have not earned enough to allow me to help to ease and extend your life.' Manon Gropius had not been well. She was suffering from bronchitis and her financial situation continued to be worrying. But Gropius tried to comfort her by saying that the situation was even worse for others: 'when one walks through the city to visit relations or when we get the latest news of our friends from Russia and see how people are suffering today we have no option but to be glad without sentimentality that we are still doing so well.'

Considering what Gropius says of Russia it is perhaps surprising that we find him embarking on a trip to the Soviet Union in the second week of 1933. Only weeks before, the German Expressionist architect Hans Poelzig, Gropius's associate since early Deutscher Werkbund days, had come under fire in nationalist circles for taking a post as Soviet government adviser on the construction of the Palace of the Soviets, the original competition for which the designs of both Poelzig and Gropius had failed to win.

But in accepting an invitation to lecture in Leningrad on 'High, Middle and Low Buildings in City Planning' Gropius was still showing signs of his usual self-assurance. He was a loyal German. He had seen distinguished service in the First World War. He could not be suspected of harbouring communist leanings. When later he was asked whether he had not at this juncture, having little work in Germany, been sounding out the possibilities of emigrating eastwards, he denied this strenuously. And in any case his view of the Soviet Union became the more critical the longer that he spent there, travelling around the countryside from Leningrad by train, becoming increasingly aware of the mistrust and political chicanery surrounding any Soviet architectural project. Moisei Ginzburg, the Russian modernist architect Gropius most admired for his communal apartment block buildings, had now fallen out of favour as a result of the Stalinist directive towards a historicist architectural style.

An architect who saw Gropius on this Russian visit described him as looking 'grey, depressed and frustrated'. Erich Mendelsohn, meeting him just after his return, said that Gropius was 'horrified and shaken by what he has seen and experienced. The great idea has been ground down by democracy, the great surge of energy has been directed along a false trail.' Originally Ise had been planning to go to the USSR with him and they had obtained two visas. But their funds were now so low and Gropius's lecture fee so meagre that in the end he travelled on his own.

The start of 1933 was not encouraging. Just before he left for Leningrad news reached him that his mother, his unwavering supporter, had died suddenly. He had planned a New Year visit. 'I am very sad of course,' Gropius told his little Manon, named after her grandmother. Manon Burchard Gropius was seventy-eight years old, 'when life naturally makes its way towards the end, but knowing this is of no help. She was so alive inside, affectionate and full of love . . . she was made of some rare, human superabundance.'

On 4 February he was back in Berlin.

'I suffer very much under the circumstances that are now in Germany, I am ashamed of what is happening here and to my personal work where every possibility seems to be blocked for now.' Gropius wrote this melancholy letter to his daughter Manon on 17 May 1933, on the day before his fiftieth birthday.

What were these new circumstances in Germany of which Gropius was now so despairingly aware? Hitler's election as Chancellor, a panic-stricken move by the beleaguered German President von Hindenburg, came as a surprise to many. On the day of the election, 30 January 1933, the writer Klaus Mann, eldest son of Thomas, commented in his diary, 'News that Hitler has become Reich Chancellor. Never thought we would see the day.' Hitler spent the next few months consolidating his position, pursuing a policy of *Gleichschaltung*, getting the nation into line with Nazi thinking. On 27 February, in suspicious circumstances, the Reichstag was set on fire. Hitler announced the emergency decree which suspended many civil liberties and led to mass arrests of Communists and Social Democrats, allowing him to consolidate his power within the parliament. There was an escalation of violence on the Berlin streets to which Gropius and Ise, even in the seclusion of Potsdamer Privatstrasse, could not have been oblivious.

The powers of the Nazis were ruthlessly extended through the spring of 1933. An Enabling Law, the *Ermächtigungsgesetz*, was passed by the Reichstag on 23 March, a measure that altered the German constitution, overthrowing all vestiges of parliamentary democracy. The purge of all Jews and anti-Nazis from official positions in the civil service began and trade unions and workers' organisations were forcibly disbanded. The authority of local governments was reduced as the Nazis seized power in the German regional states. In May 1933 the now notorious book burnings, held in many German cities, started with a conflagration in Berlin, carried out by a group of Nazi students with the implicit support of Joseph Goebbels, Hitler's Minister for Propaganda. The bonfires were of books considered 'un-German' in their tenor, including the works of Sigmund Freud. For any future form of freedom of expression – political, literary, artistic – as Gropius was already realising bitterly, prospects were becoming dramatically worse.

The Nazi policy of purging the professions of Jews and political opponents made it impossible for architects to practise unless they officially signed up to conform. Even before Hitler's advent as Chancellor the Kampfbund für Deutsche Kultur, the Fighting League for German Culture, had openly attacked modern German architecture and art on both stylistic and racial grounds, denigrating its practitioners as decadent if not actually communists or Jews.

Nazi artistic censorship extended to architects whose work was considered 'un-German' in its character, purist and functional in appearance as opposed to traditional and countrified, in tune with the Nazi mythology of nationhood. Gropius may not have been Jewish but his views on architecture were becoming increasingly unacceptable. 'Whether Gropius is a Jew or not is entirely irrelevant here,' wrote the right-wing commentator Rudolf Paulsen in a particularly virulent attack on Gropius's architecture in the newspaper of the National Socialist party, the *Völkischer Beobachter*, in March 1932. The heading was 'Culturally Bolshevik Attacks'. The article continued, 'The people find the new style of building so foreign that they speak of the Palestinian style. And that is entirely justified. For those smooth and insipid garages for people to live in, these bench-assembled dwellings are, in our German landscapes, simply a mockery of all natural connections with the soil.' The sneering reference to 'Palestinian style' refers to Tel Aviv, which German Jewish emigrants to Palestine were now transforming into a modern garden city by the sea, favouring the white-box cubic architecture that had come to be associated with the Bauhaus.

In Nazi Germany Gropius's long connection with the Bauhaus, as its inventor and protector, made him a marked man. Inevitably he was identified with everything in the modern style that was being vilified.

Once Hitler became Chancellor the prospects for modernist architects in Germany were very bleak. The Jewish Erich Mendelsohn left straight away for England: 'I flee Germany the day Hitler takes over, March 1933, forty five years old. The door to the European continent closes behind me.' Hitler's Germany was no longer tenable for him. For Gropius the situation was more complex. He still counted himself a patriotic German. As an architect he needed to keep his practice going. He needed a continuing substructure of clients and commissions. Architecturally speaking Gropius had always had very big ideas of re-establishing the grandeur that had been Berlin in the days of Schinkel, though in a different idiom.

And Nazi aesthetics were not straightforward; there was never a complete eschewing of the modern. Joseph Goebbels had sophisticated breadth of taste. He claimed to be supporting architecture and art that reflected a new and modern Germany, an attitude progressive architects found encouraging. In Italy Mussolini's Fascism was aesthetically avant-garde in outlook. Perhaps the Nazi regime could be persuaded to come around to Gropius's own way of thinking. He persisted, with what now looks like naivety.

This is Gropius's account of Nazi attempts to prevent him, as a politically controversial figure, from fulfilling his commission to design a section in an important commercial exhibition:

A uniformed Nazi patrol came to my house and told me I would regret it if I participated in a large exhibition called 'German People, German Work' in which I was building a good-sized department for the non-ferrous metal industry. Furious, I went immediately to the Goebbels Ministry, to the Department Chief in charge, pounded a table and complained about the impertinence of such a Nazi patrol. He promised to protect me, but things became worse, particularly in connection with the press, which attacked the Bauhaus and me personally. The fight became hopeless for an individual alone.

After his outburst the objections died down and Gropius and Mies van der Rohe, who had also been commissioned to co-design the exhibition, were permitted to proceed.

Gropius was driven to make a further protest. Alfred Rosenberg, the violently anti-modernist leader of the Kampfbund für Deutsche Kultur, now demanded the exclusion of Jewish members from any organisation seeking the approval of the Nazi party. This applied to members of the Deutscher Werkbund, who debated the issue early in 1933. Twenty-seven of the thirty members at the meeting remained silent. Only Gropius, his friend the Berlin planner Martin Wagner and the Bauhaus alumnus Wilhelm Wagenfeld objected. In March Gropius resigned from the board along with Wagner, who was promptly ousted from his Berlin architectural post. Membership of the Kampfbund now became obligatory for all architects practising in Germany.

As he had been in his Bauhaus years Gropius was scrupulous about keeping politics separate from work. When the new office manager Hans Dustmann, successor to Otto Meyer-Otten, revealed his political sympathies by coming to the office in his Nazi uniform, Gropius immediately dismissed him. This episode, inevitably reported to party officials, did not improve relations with Hitler's new regime.

There is a strange symmetry in Gropius's story and that of the Bauhaus. After Weimar, after Dessau, the school eventually followed him to Berlin. Under Mies, as we have seen, the Bauhaus in Dessau became predominantly an architectural training school, newly disciplined and orderly, with Meyer's communist element expunged. Nevertheless he did not succeed in deflecting continuing attacks from National Socialist members of the local Saxony-Anhalt parliament. These worsened once the Nazis took control in 1932 and were determined to clamp down on the so-called Jewish Bauhaus culture. Nazi officials carried out an inspection of the school and declared its work un-German. The Bauhaus at Dessau was closed and the teaching staff discharged from 1 October 1932. Storm Troopers moved into the building, smashing windows and throwing school equipment down into the street. Not long afterwards Gropius's building housed the training of Nazi party officials. A photograph shows them assembled outside the workshop wing, wearing Nazi insignia. The Bauhaus sign had already been torn down.

Mies van der Rohe made a brave decision to move the Bauhaus to Berlin. The school opened two weeks later as a private institution, occupying a large disused telephone factory in Steglitz, a quiet suburb

Student Ernst Louis Beck outside the Bauhaus building in Berlin-Steglitz, c.1933.

Mittwoch, 12. April 1933   **Berliner Lokal-Anzeiger**

Haussuchung im „Bauhaus Steglitz"

Kommunistisches Material gefunden.

Auf Veranlassung der Dessauer Staatsanwaltschaft wurde gestern nachmittag eine größere Aktion im „Bauhaus Steglitz", dem früheren Dessauer Bauhaus, in der Birkbuschstraße in Steglitz durchgeführt. Von einem Aufgebot Schutz-

war jedoch verschwunden, und man vermutete, daß sie von der Bauhausleitung mit nach Berlin genommen worden waren. Die Dessauer Staatsanwaltschaft setzte sich jetzt mit der Berliner Polizei in Verbindung und bat um Durch-

Alle Anwesenden, die sich nicht ausweisen konnten, wurden zur Feststellung ihrer Personalien ins Polizeipräsidium gebracht.

polizei und Hilfspolizisten wurde das Grundstück besetzt und systematisch durchsucht. Mehrere Kisten mit illegalen Druckschriften wurden beschlagnahmt. Die Aktion stand unter Leitung von Polizeimajor Schmahel.

Das „Bauhaus Dessau" war vor etwa Jahresfrist nach Berlin übergesiedelt. Damals waren bereits von der Dessauer Polizei zahlreiche verbotene Schriften beschlagnahmt worden. Ein Teil der von der Polizei versiegelten Kisten

suchung des Gebäudes. Das Bauhaus, das früher unter Leitung von Professor Gropius stand, der sich jetzt in Rußland aufhält, hat in einer leerstehenden Fabrikbaracke in der Birkbuschstraße in Steglitz Quartier genommen. Der augenblickliche Leiter hat es aber vor wenigen Tagen vorgezogen, nach Paris überzusiedeln. Bei der gestrigen Haussuchung wurde zahlreiches illegales Propagandamaterial der KPD. gefunden und beschlagnahmt.

Newspaper report of a raid on the Bauhaus in Berlin by police and Storm Troopers, 12 April 1933. Students without papers were arrested.

in the south-west of the city. Of Gropius's old Masters Albers and Kandinsky are listed on the teaching staff, along with Mies's collaborator and lover, the interior and furniture designer Lilly Reich. A fundraising party with a raffle was held for the school on 18 February 1933, a throwback to the famous parties held in Weimar and Dessau. One of the new students described the carnival as 'glorious, a great success, and obviously something special even by Berlin standards . . . The rooms in the basement made an incredibly distinguished impression, furnished and decorated as though for a great social occasion. One's not used to that kind of thing at other parties in Berlin.'

The Bauhaus still clung on to its marvellous élan. But on 11 April, at the start of the summer term, Berlin police and Storm Troopers armed with rifles moved in to seal off the building. A search was carried out for communist propaganda allegedly hidden in the school. The action was in theory directed against the mayor of Dessau, Gropius's one-time bosom friend Fritz Hesse, now completely out of favour with the Nazi government. The Bauhaus students were herded together in the entrance hall. According to one witness, 'Mies also stood there at the door of his office. The powerfully built man filled the door frame completely and appeared unwilling to move. Not far from him stood a member of the Gestapo with his finger on the trigger of his carbine.' Any students unable to produce identity papers were arrested and taken to police headquarters. Newspaper photographs show them being carted off, loaded in a lorry. The papers claimed that Mies had fled to Paris, while Gropius, the previous director of the Bauhaus, was in Russia. In fact they were both still in Berlin.

Although Gropius was certainly aware of these escalating problems at the Bauhaus, he seems to have remained silent and detached. He does not appear to have attended the fundraising party, nor even to have donated a prize for the raffle, as many of his former Bauhaus colleagues did. There are no records of Gropius having had any contact with Mies. Was this because there was still a residue of ancient rivalry between them, dating back to the time when they both worked in Behrens's office? Was he tactfully respecting the fact that Mies was director of the Bauhaus now and needed no intervention from him? Was Gropius simply being cautious in view of the precarious political position of a modernist architect in Berlin at the time? Or, probably more likely, was the gradual demise of the Bauhaus just too painful for him to contemplate?

Soon after Hitler became Chancellor he started on a programme of large-scale building projects. In part this was a policy intended to counteract the effects of the Depression, an initiative to improve rapidly the prospects for Germany's six to seven million unemployed. Hitler recognised that the building industry was a key to improving the nation's economics. In explaining this policy years later, in summer 1938, he said that the planning for the new construction work followed two directions: utilitarian buildings such as houses, roads and waterways, and on the other hand noble and consciously monumental building projects. 'In other states', maintained Hitler, 'the leaders are always somewhere in a palace: in the Kremlin in Moscow, the Belvedere in Warsaw, in the Royal Palace in Budapest, or the Hradschin in Prague. I now have the ambition to raise buildings for the new German people's state that will bear comparison, without any hint of shame, with these formerly royal edifices.'

From 1933 Hitler, who had had his own early ambitions to become an architect, inaugurated a sequence of architectural competitions for palatial new buildings in Berlin. Gropius managed to steer clear of the competition for an advanced school for the training of Storm Troopers, but he was amongst thirty German architects invited to submit designs for a huge new building for the Reichsbank, now expanding rapidly as it became more crucial in supporting the Nazi party's development. Mies van der Rohe was also included. In May, when the jury announced the results, Mies was one of six prize-winning architects, his designs receiving the highest accolade. Hitler, however, personally intervened and the job was given to the run-of-the-mill director of the Reichsbank's building department, Heinrich Wolff.

Gropius's proposal was for a large, dignified, steel frame building, a five-storey perimeter structure enclosed within four nine-storey wings.

The facade was to be finished in cream-coloured glazed ceramic tiles. Because his office was by no means busy he went far beyond the brief in submitting detailed plans, elevations and renderings. To some extent this was Gropius's attempt at a compromise building. His Reichsbank design has an element of formality, almost a pomposity, absent from any of his early work. All the same it was not lavish or palatial enough to please the Nazis. The jury rejected his submission, maintaining that its plainness 'gave the impression of a large factory'. But Gropius had never had any chance of winning. Having resigned from the Werkbund board in protest against the exclusion of Jewish members he was by this time a target of Nazi hostility.

In mid-June 1933 he wrote despondently to Manon: 'the outlook is bad here, there's no work anywhere, and for several months now I've been taking so many long walks like no other time in my life.' At this period he had only two private commissions: a house for the industrialist Johannes Bahner at Kleinmachnow and another for a lawyer, Dr Otto Heinrich Maurer, in Dahlem, both relatively modest cubic buildings with overhanging porches. The roof of the Maurer house, originally a flat one, was altered in the planning stage to make a more traditional hipped roof in line with the new Nazi planning rules. Depressed by such restrictions and the lack of possibilities for work in Germany, Gropius was now actively seeking opportunities abroad. 'On Tuesday or Wednesday', he told Manon, 'Ise and I go to Dartington Hall, Totnes, S. Devon, England. A wealthy Englishman, who wants to partition and eventually build on his estates, seeks my advice and has invited Ise and me to stay for three weeks at his country seat.'

———

The wealthy Englishman was Leonard Elmhirst, idealistic son of a Yorkshire clergyman and landowner. Leonard was now in his mid-forties. As a young man he had worked in India with Rabindranath Tagore in setting up the Institute of Rural Reconstruction in West Bengal. It was probably through him that Elmhirst first heard of the Bauhaus, since Tagore had sponsored the Bauhaus exhibition in Calcutta in 1922. In

1925 Elmhirst married Dorothy Straight, an American widow five years older than himself. She was seriously cultured and immensely rich, the daughter of William Collins Whitney, the lawyer, politician and successful business entrepreneur. On their marriage the Elmhirsts bought the Dartington estate in rural Devon, a run-down tract of land of almost a thousand acres with a dilapidated medieval manor house. Here they embarked on an ambitious rural reconstruction project. Unusually for English country landowners at that period the Elmhirsts, particularly Dorothy, were addicted to the modern and Dartington became a byword for the artistic avant-garde.

The Elmhirsts knew about the forced closure of the Bauhaus in Dessau through Nancy Wilson Ross, an American friend of Dorothy's. Nancy's son Charles had been a Bauhaus student and she wrote to the Elmhirsts to plead for their financial support for the school in its new incarnation as a private institution in Berlin. Mies van der Rohe had put his entire capital into keeping the Bauhaus going, 'but it seems quite plain that he cannot carry the load alone. I'm probably not making you see the tragedy of the Bauhaus destruction at all, but if you were in Germany for a time and realised how disastrously super-nationalism is rooting out all that really admirable spirit which the Germans displayed after the war', the Elmhirsts would surely feel impelled to help. In spite of the eloquence of Nancy Ross's plea Leonard replied that they were not in a position to offer much support, but he and Dorothy, as an expression of their sympathy with the ideals of the Bauhaus, were sending an anonymous gift of five hundred dollars via Charles Ross to Mies van der Rohe personally.

The invitation to Gropius to visit Dartington came a few months later. The Elmhirsts had by this time made a brief trip to Berlin, seeing Nancy Ross and investigating the architectural scene. They were anxious to commission the world's best modern architects to work on the new buildings they had in mind for Dartington. In May 1933 Gropius was invited to survey the scene at Dartington himself. He had apparently already dropped a hint via Henry Wright, an American architect who was working on a Dartington project at the time and whom Gropius met when Wright was briefly in Berlin, that he would like to take a holiday in England 'and to spend the time somewhere where experimental work was being carried on.'

A definite proposal to Gropius came via Dartington's managing director, William Slater. A letter addressed to 'Herr Professor Dr. Gropius' arrived in Potsdamer Privatstrasse suggesting a visit of three weeks to a month. He was offered hospitality and a contribution to travel expenses. Slater told him, 'We at Dartington are doing a considerable amount of building, in particular in the development of land and the building of houses.' Interesting as this prospect sounded Gropius saw he had a communication problem. 'My knowledge of the English language is very insufficient,' he warned Slater. 'I understand fairly well, but I am very awkward in talking. I ask you therefore if there is any possibility to take my wife with me, she speaks English almost fluently, and is very good acquainted with my work and my ideas, besides that I would rather not separate from her during my holidays.' Marcel Breuer, who at this stage did not even attempt to communicate in English, was invited to Dartington at the same time.

They took a ship to Harwich, arriving on 26 June 1933, then travelling by train south-west to Devon. This was Gropius's first visit to England since his 1908 architectural tour, when he visited his Uncle Willy in Chislehurst. The scene they found at Dartington was like nothing he had experienced before:

An ancient gothic palace erected by the bastard brother of the English king in the 14th century. A vast park with trees as I have never seen. Fantastic wealth, 60 motorcars albeit rather plain, one saw no servants apart from the classic butler, the lord served himself at the table! The wife is an American and has an enormous fortune, thus they are determined to spend 600,000 pounds annually, earmarked primarily for educational purposes. Two research institutes, a dance school, model farms, sawmills, laundry, weaving mill, etc., all of it planned to solve modern production problems. A large section of the coast has been purchased to establish a bathing resort.

This was the description Gropius sent to Manon, excited by and admiring of the scene he found at Dartington but understandably bemused.

The architectural project Gropius had hopes of was a large new housing development planned by the Elmhirsts along the Devon coast at Churston Ferrers. He was disappointed to discover that the job had already been given to the American architect William Lescaze. This was one of the hazards of working for the Elmhirsts. They tended to have too many irons in the fire. Gropius had little to do on this first visit except give his views on modern architecture to the Elmhirsts and lie on the beach with Ise in the sun.

All the same his stay at Dartington had been exhilarating. He could relate to the developments he found there: the utopian combination of workmanship and husbandry; the conviction of the central importance of creativity; the links between education and the arts. The Elmhirsts had set up a progressive school in Devon with an emphasis on children's freedom of expression. He felt he was back on familiar ground, explaining in a thank-you letter in his halting English that 'many details and the kind of human relationship between the members of your staff remembered to me the first times of the "Bauhaus" in Weimar. Likewise the junction of all parts and details and their bringing them into relation to the whole life was my principal aim.'

On his return to Germany he sent Leonard a copy of Moholy-Nagy's Bauhaus essay 'The New Vision', commending it to him as an exemplary explanation of 'the spiritual roots of the new imagination of space in modern art'.

Returning to Berlin in late July 1933 Gropius must certainly have been aware of a final crisis at the Bauhaus. After the arrest of a number of the students the school remained shut down for three months while Mies negotiated with the authorities and pleaded with Alfred Rosenberg himself. On 21 July the Gestapo agreed to the school reopening under certain conditions, one of which was that the unacceptably avant-garde Kandinsky should be dismissed. But it was too late. Two days earlier the Bauhaus faculty had voted to dissolve the school because after so protracted a closure, with no fees coming in, it was no longer economically viable. Mies said he would in fact have agreed to the conditions but the Bauhaus simply had no money left.

The affair between Ise and Herbert Bayer continued with ecstatic little holidays together in Swiss mountain villages. Earlier in the year Bayer sent 'Pius' a letter, not this time from Arosa but from the nearby ski village of Davos. He writes semi-apologetically, referring to 'the harsh reality of me and Pia being together'. He is still clearly anxious to keep Gropius's friendship:

I was all the more filled with desire to see you here because, without exaggeration, I miss you. A strange quirk of fate has seen to it that I, too, have hurt my leg, so we could have lounged around in each other's company. I do wish you were here, not only because the three of us need that at some point but also because I would like to be here with you . . . It weighs me down terribly that again and again I cause distress and diminish happiness.

All the same he can't help saying that 'the joy of spending some days in the snow with Pia puts everything else into the shade'. With maximum tactlessness Bayer encloses postcards showing seductive ski tracks criss-crossing the mountains and skiers swooping down the slopes.

Was Ise being ruthless? But then Gropius's dismissal of Maria Bene-mann and distancing himself from Lily Hildebrandt at the time of Ise's first arrival at the Bauhaus were perhaps ruthless too. It appears he was seriously suffering at this point. He was by now too depressed and over-wrought to attend the August CIAM congress to which he had looked forward, having told Manon he needed to be there because he was now CIAM vice-president.

This was the famous CIAM 4, the Functional City congress, which took place on board the cruise ship the SS *Patris II*, sailing from Marseilles to Athens and back. A hundred delegates, guests and spouses attended to discuss the shaping of the modern global city. László Moholy-Nagy's film of the shipboard congress gives the mood of it: hugely wide-ranging, argumentative, convivial. Gropius must have been much missed.

Meanwhile, his own local anxieties increased. By mid-September, because he had had no commissions for so long, he was contemplating selling his Adler Cabriolet. He could see that he would soon have to close down his office, laying off his staff and moving to a smaller apartment. In this despondent mood we find him writing to his new English supporter William Slater in Devon, describing the current situation in Germany, almost nine months after Hitler's election as Chancellor: 'Unfortunately the present state of conditions for the modern architecture does not show the slightest improvement. It will take a very long time to extinguish all the false prejudices and to advance a more objective view on the whole development.' There was a galling little episode that summer when threats were made to demolish one of his best buildings of the period, the circular Employment Office in Dessau, now denounced by the Nazis as a 'circus-like building in a very Bolshevist style'.

He was in a very problematic situation. What in the circumstances could Gropius have done? He could have emulated Albert Speer, an architect of a younger generation whose career flourished once he joined the Nazi party in 1931. Speer was recommended to Goebbels to assist with renovating the party's Berlin headquarters. His designs for the 1933 Nuremberg Rally led to his official post as Commissioner for the Artistic and Technical Presentation of Party Rallies and Demonstrations. By the end of 1933 Hitler appointed him to manage the rebuilding of the Reich Chancellery. Speer ingratiated himself so much that Hitler was soon entrusting him with plans for rebuilding the new Germany in a manner that reflected the Führer's grandiose ambitions. This was the architect who embedded himself right at the centre of the Nazi regime.

There were of course many opportunities for architects in a regime reliant on visual expressiveness to develop party loyalties and over-awe opponents. Former members of Gropius's office defected to the Nazis. The already shifty Ernst Neufert became Speer's commissioner for issues of standardisation; Otto Meyer-Otten, once the Berlin office manager, would later be appointed chief construction supervisor for the crucially important Rimpl factories, designated the Reichswerke Hermann Goering ('National Factories of Hermann Goering'); Hans Dustmann, the architect ejected for arriving in the office in his Nazi uniform, became official architect for the Hitler Youth. But Gropius was not, and could never be, a Nazi. It was not in his nature to kow-tow, whereas Hitler soon came to regard the oily and obsequious Speer as a kindred spirit. Gropius always retained the habit of command.

Besides, the ideology of racism appalled him. Living in the centre of Berlin he was well aware of the Nazi persecution of the Jews. In one of his letters to Manon, written in September 1933, he asks her to give a message to Franz Werfel, the Jew whose pro-Jewish ideology enraged the Nazis. Werfel's writings were included in the Nazi book-burnings and in 1933 he was forced out of the Prussian Academy of Arts. Gropius's message says: 'I feel a special kinship with him right now and have half a mind to get myself circumcised out of sympathy.'

But horrified though he was by Nazi outrages Gropius was still unwilling to leave the country to which he felt his deepest loyalty. He was at this point settling for a policy of limited co-operation with the new regime, while still retaining his integrity. This was the mood in which Gropius, on 12 December 1933, signed up for membership of the Reichskulturkammer (RKK), the State Chamber of Culture. The RKK was the organisation in overall control of German cultural activities. It was set up by Goebbels in his role as Propaganda Minister in the autumn of 1933. All members of the Bund Deutscher Architekten (BDA), the architects' professional body, which included Gropius, were virtually forced to join. Without RKK membership they would be unable to practise. Gropius signed up on 12 December 1933, becoming architect-engineer member 706. In applying he had to submit proof of Aryan ancestry, and he presented his family tree. An official photograph on his membership card shows him looking aged and grim.

———

By December 1933 Gropius's finances were so bad that he and Ise had to rent out the majority of their apartment and move into just two remaining rooms. In an attempt to cheer themselves up they took two short holidays over Christmas, first returning to Arosa with Sigfried and Carola Giedion and then making a final expedition in the Adler to the Riesengebirge mountains. Here Gropius had set up a Bauhaus reunion, renting a ski hut for a curious kind of rerun of that previous carefree summer in Ascona. Breuer was there again, and so was Schawinsky. Gropius braced himself for Bayer to be invited too, still attempting to control the situation vis-à-vis Ise and keep his important male friendships intact. This time Bayer came without Irene, from whom he was now living more or less apart. They were finally divorced in 1945.

Besides inevitable emotional tensions there were multiple political anxieties. Breuer, born in Hungary to Jewish parents, renounced all religion in 1926 when he filed papers with the Official Provincial Rabbinate in Dessau stating that he did not wish to be considered Jewish. But his position remained uncertain as the Nazi regime became more doctrinaire. Schawinsky, Polish-Jewish but born in Switzerland and possessing a Swiss passport, hoped he was immune. After his ejection from his teaching post in Magdeburg in 1932 he worked as a graphic designer in Berlin, partly alongside Bayer in the Dorland studio, but after being arrested by the Gestapo and interrogated earlier in 1933 he had now fled Germany to take refuge in Italy.

Herbert Bayer, a non-Jewish Austrian working in Berlin for an international advertising agency, might have seemed to be relatively safe, but the Nazis were now making inroads into Austria as the forces of the Social Democrats challenged the Fascist government of the Chancellor Engelbert Dollfuss. Among his other jobs Bayer was undertaking typographic work for Nazi clients, designing the graphics for official propaganda exhibitions in Berlin including *Deutsches Volk – deutsche Arbeit* ('German People, German Work'), and designing the prospectus for the 1933 German *Century of Progress* exhibition in Chicago. Cooped up together in the mountain ski hut on that uneasy Christmas holiday, both he and Gropius must have been aware of the ambivalence of their situation.

In the year since Hitler became Chancellor not only had the remnants of the Bauhaus in Berlin been summarily closed down, many of the former Bauhaus Masters had been dismissed from their posts and were now dispersed. Wassily Kandinsky emigrated to France. Paul Klee left Dessau in 1931, taking a post at the Düsseldorf Kunstakademie. He had kept on his Master's House in Dessau, commuting from there to Düsseldorf. In 1933 the house was raided and searched while Klee was absent and three washing baskets of documents were confiscated. The Nazis suspected him of breaking currency regulations. In April of that year Klee was dismissed from his teaching position on the false grounds that he was a Galician Jew. He left Germany and went back to live in his native Switzerland.

In what amounted to a purge of former Bauhäusler the painter Georg Muche, once Johannes Itten's great ally, designer of the Haus am Horn in Weimar and an experimental steel house in Dessau, was removed from his post as professor at the academy in Breslau (now Wrocław, Poland). The sculptor Gerhard Marcks, one of Gropius's original appointees to the Bauhaus back in 1919, was relieved of his position as director of the school of arts and crafts at Burg Giebichenstein near Halle after he protested against the dismissal of Jewish colleagues. He withdrew into what he called 'inner emigration' from 1933.

The brilliantly experimental Oskar Schlemmer, always a law unto himself, had left Dessau for Breslau in 1929 after Hannes Meyer and some of the students had demanded that the Bauhaus theatre department should be politicised. Once the Breslau teaching post evaporated when the academy closed for a lack of funds Schlemmer moved on to a position in Berlin. By the spring of 1933 he was already under attack, along with fellow teaching staff of the Vereinigte Staatsschulen für Freie und Angewandte Kunst, the Unified State Schools for Fine and Applied Art, on grounds of being a 'destructive Marxist-Judaic element'. He complained to Gunta Stölzl that all his connections were under investigation: 'ancestors, party, Jew, Marx, Bauhaus'.

These attacks coincided with a new Nazi policy to remove and pillory works of art in public collections on aesthetic grounds of being anti-German. This was a preliminary to the notorious 'Degenerate Art' exhibitions of 1937. Schlemmer sent a boldly worded letter of protest direct to Joseph Goebbels saying:

Deeply shaken by what I hear from numerous cities in the Reich, including Dessau, Mannheim, and Dresden, where the museums' collections of modern art are to be placed in 'chambers of artistic horrors', each picture labelled with the sum paid for it, exposed to the mockery and indignation of the public, I take the liberty of appealing to you with an urgent plea that you call a halt to these measures.

He made the point, which Gropius would have in theory agreed with, that 'Artists are fundamentally unpolitical and must be so, for their kingdom is not of this world'.

In August 1933 Schlemmer was fired summarily from his Berlin teaching post. But, by some process of double-think, he still managed to convince himself that his own art corresponded to National Socialist principles. And within the next few months Schlemmer's entry for a mural competition for the Congress Hall in the Deutsches Museum in Munich took the form of an abstract composition of row upon row of military figures making what looks like the Nazi salute. For artists and designers, both Jewish and non-Jewish, this was a time of growing desperation. Schlemmer was just one of many artists at this period in Germany who showed signs of being morally confused.

What was going on in Gropius's own mind? Member 706 of the RKK was still the convinced modernist, arguing as best he could that the new ideals of architecture and town planning were too crucial to be jettisoned. To him, modernism and nationalism, in the sense of architecture that reflected a new progressive Germany, could coexist. In arguing these views Gropius clearly hoped he had found an ally in Eugen Hönig, President of the Reichskammer der Bildenden Künste, the Reich Committee for Fine Arts. Hönig was an architect and professor of architectural history at the Munich academy of art. In writing to Hönig, having heard him lecture in March 1934, Gropius appealed to his sense of historical continuity:

Shall this strong new architectural movement which began in Germany be lost in Germany? Must we be forced to stop our work, when the entire world has begun to accept our initiative and to carry further our inspiration? . . . The new architecture offers opportunities for creative development. But above all I myself see this new style as the way in which we in our country can finally achieve a valid union of the two great spiritual heritages of the classical and the Gothic traditions. Schinkel sought this union, but in vain. Shall Germany deny itself this great opportunity?

Gropius ends this letter not with the approved Nazi sign-off, '*mit deutschem Gruss*', but with a non-committal 'I greet you . . . yours'. He was desperately trying to keep his professional options open whilst still preserving, as best he could, his personal integrity.

In these early months of 1934 Gropius and Martin Wagner became involved in a protest against a planning proposal for East Prussia. They objected to a scheme that took the form of piecemeal industrial development along existing transportation routes. They put forward a counter-proposal for industrial expansion based around towns and cities, a blueprint for future urban development in Germany as a whole. Their statement of protest, addressed to the president of the province of East Prussia but sent via Hans Weidemann, a sympathetic contact in the Propaganda Ministry, is blatantly nationalistic in its argument for a city-region prototype for Germany 'which would eclipse the attempts of other countries . . . [and] successfully answer the challenge of the coolie work of Japanese men with the coolie work of German machines, the challenge of the ruthless exploitation methods of the Russians with the precision of German engineers, and of American work for self-interest with the German people's work for the common good'. This time the letter ended in Nazi style, '*mit deutschem Gruss*'. Gropius and Wagner were evidently hoping for a much-needed commission, but this did not materialise.

Following his unsuccessful entry for the Reichsbank Gropius braced himself to enter another competition, this time for a prototype Haus der Arbeit ('House of German Labour'). This scheme, initiated by the Deutsche Arbeitsfront, the German Labour Front, was intended to be the first of a nationwide series of community buildings incorporating sports clubs, cultural centres and spaces for community events, celebrating the German work ethic. The idea was inspired by similar schemes already initiated by the Dopolavoro, the workers' recreational organisation, in Fascist Italy. It was part of the German Labour Front's nationalistic policy of 'Strength through Joy'.

Gropius was one of 692 architects who entered the competition, collaborating with his former student and draughtsman Rudolf Hillebrecht. Gropius wrote to his ally Hans Weidemann in the Propaganda Ministry outlining his ideas: 'The Houses of German work should be a temple to the German spirit of work. They should be a permanent and impressive embodiment of the newly recognisable conception of community – one without class distinctions. The form of the Houses of German work will be an expression of the Nationalist Socialist worldview.' Gropius's plan was for a large sports complex in the Berlin Tiergarten, including a theatre and a large site for official parades. Hillebrecht's architectural drawings show flags with swastikas descending from four flagpoles on the edge of the huge sports ground. The swastika emblem was *de rigueur* for German public buildings at this period. It should perhaps be noted that Mies van der Rohe's swastikas in his designs for the German pavilion at the 1935 Brussels World Fair, unfurling in triumph at the exhibition entrance, were far more ostentatious.

Gropius's public reputation made it extremely unlikely he would win the competition for the House of German Labour. In any case the contest was abandoned on Hitler's instructions. His design for the non-ferrous metals section of the *Deutsches Volk – deutsche Arbeit* exhibition, which opened in Berlin in April 1934, was his final completed work in pre-war Germany.

Deutsches Volk – deutsche Arbeit was a blatantly propagandist exhibition glorifying the German work ethic and the strength and purity of the German race. There were six exhibition galleries in all in the Hall of Honour, of which one – the section boosting the non-ferrous metal industries – was allotted to Gropius and another to Mies van der Rohe. Gropius's Bauhaus devotee Joost Schmidt, the young designer who had broken down at his departure, worked alongside him on the exhibition and illustrated the presentation boards, one of which depicted muscular workers pouring molten metal into great containers. Herbert Bayer designed the cover for the exhibition catalogue, a triumphalist design incorporating the victor's laurel wreath.

Judging from the photographs and isometric drawings (see Plate 26) Gropius's section, trumpeting the virtues of the German magnesium, nickel, aluminium, copper, tin, lead, zinc and plastics industries, shows a predictable competence and flair. The *pièce de résistance* was a slowly revolving staircase, a metal tower symbolic of metalworking prowess. But Gropius's name was never even mentioned in the publicity for the exhibition. The architect of the once so celebrated Faguswerk factory, the 1914 Werkbund exhibition building, the Dessau Bauhaus building had become *persona non grata* in Nazi Germany.

The *Deutsches Volk – deutsche Arbeit* exhibition pushed Gropius to his limits. Ise was terrified he might explode into fury and repeat the episode of his challenge to Goebbels. Gropius could collude only so far and she was convinced they needed to leave Germany: 'I could see that he would not submit and would be in constant danger.' She realised that if he had stayed on in Nazi Germany, he might easily have ended in a concentration camp.

SECOND LIFE · England

14

London, Berlin, Rome

1934

In April 1934 a polio epidemic was raging in Venice, though the local authorities were censoring reports. Manon, Alma and Franz Werfel were staying there over Easter in the Casa Mahler. Manon was already unwell when her mother and Werfel went back to Vienna for a gala performance of Mahler's *Das Lied von der Erde*. The next evening news reached them that she was seriously ill. By the time Alma, alarmed, returned to Venice poliomyelitis had been diagnosed. Paralysis started in the legs and soon Manon was paralysed from the neck down. She had difficulty breathing. Once her condition stabilised it was decided she should go back to Vienna for specialist treatment. Alma had important friends in the neo-Fascist Austrian government and now, at her urgent request, the government provided the former Emperor Franz Joseph's ambulance car, in which Manon travelled home like an invalid princess.

Gropius was as usual kept short of information. It was 6 May before he sent this letter to his daughter in the house on the Hohe Warte:

Dearest Mutzili, finally you are close enough and I could telephone at last and get details about how you are and how wonderfully you have come through this ordeal . . . for all that you have endured, my sweet Mutzi, our human nature is admirably adapted, especially if one is young, such that I see you rising from this insidious illness like a beautiful phoenix . . . I strove in vain for that Hitler series you wanted, it doesn't exist. So I can only send you the Wagner series.

The reference is to a series of collectibles, stamps or possibly cigarette cards. Although his now invalid daughter was seventeen, she was in some respects still a child.

Gropius, although so evidently anxious, was preoccupied with plans for a visit to London for an exhibition of his work at the Royal Institute of British Architects. He was leaving four days later. It was Ise who wrote to Manon next, explaining that he had accepted this English invitation 'with a heavy heart', but he could not reject it 'because little by little he has had to rely on whatever foreign work there is. For us here every path is blocked to him and we stand before a vast field of rubble.' We can see from this letter how precarious the situation had become.

———

Gropius travelled to England on his own. Once again Ise stayed behind because they could not afford the extra fare. The exhibition of Gropius's architectural work was held at RIBA's premises in Conduit Street. He was by no means a well-known figure in the England of that period but he was to the specialist taste of a very small group of cognoscenti, aware of the reputation of the Bauhaus. A few had even ventured to Dessau to visit it. The RIBA exhibition was promoted by Philip Morton Shand, a rare British enthusiast for German functional architecture and design.

Morton Shand was an idiosyncratic character, a tall balding figure, 'ex-Etonian with some private income, extremely well read, rather supercilious, difficult to get on with, but with an intensive enthusiasm for modern architecture'. As well as being an architecture critic, writing for the *Architectural Review*, he was a wine expert, a food writer, a connoisseur of women. He was on his fourth marriage by the time that Gropius came to London. He was also anti-Semitic, making jokes about the Jews in a schoolboyish manner his architectural colleagues found repugnant. His enthusiasm for the work of Gropius might be seen as a facet of his contrariness. Morton Shand was the key figure in bringing Gropius to England in 1934.

Persuaded by Morton Shand, RIBA secretary Ian MacAlister helped organise the exhibition, which was opened by the president, Sir Raymond Unwin, on 15 May 1934. The now elderly Unwin, who had been a follower of William Morris and a leading light in the English garden city movement, was not a natural supporter of Gropius's views on prefabricated buildings and communal apartment blocks, but he was a generous man and did his best.

He made what was reported as 'an entertaining contrast' between the more 'personal and emotional' work currently to be seen at the London Royal Academy and the rigorous logic of the RIBA exhibition, gallantly suggesting, 'It is, perhaps, owing to the failure of English architects to appreciate the theories of Philip Webb and Lethaby, which correspond very closely to those of Professor Gropius, that the modern movement is so little understood in this country.' Unwin's citing of Morris's disciple W. R. Lethaby was perspicacious since Lethaby, founder and first Principal of the London Central School of Arts and Crafts in 1894, had introduced workshop training into art schools. Lethaby had indeed been the precursor of Gropius's educational ideals.

On the evening after the exhibition opened Gropius was invited to give a talk to the Design and Industries Association, drawing a crowded audience to its London basement premises. The DIA, as it was familiarly known, was founded in 1915 by a group of forward-looking designers, manufacturers, educationalists and architects aware of the need to improve national standards of design. It was a conscious riposte to the Deutscher Werkbund in the early months of the First World War. Now, in an ironic twist of loyalty, the British DIA was Gropius's great supporter. 'During the late twenties and early thirties we looked towards the Bauhaus at Dessau and Walter Gropius as a source of inspiration,' R. D. Best, a leading light of the Birmingham DIA branch, recollected. 'So great was our enthusiasm that his name was even introduced into a DIA charade.' Gropius became 'Grow Pious'.

The London talk had been a great anxiety to Gropius, whose English, according to Ise, was practised mainly by reading Edgar Wallace mystery stories out aloud to her. His prepared script, translated by Philip Morton Shand, was sent over to Berlin and in the weeks before departure he and Ise read it through and through. The occasion was an inspiration for much of the audience. The young architect Maxwell Fry presided and remembered all his life the scene of 'this highly nervous lion of a man reading Morton Shand's translation of his dense German script to an electrified audience filling every corner of the small hall'. It was obvious Gropius could barely understand what he was reading but he valiantly kept going, holding the audience with 'a level and commanding glance'.

Gropius's subject was 'The Formal and Technical Problems of Modern Architecture and Planning'. He spoke on his favourite theme of the need for a broad view of architecture, an architecture that was all-embracing in its scope. He argued for the place of art and design not as an optional esoteric extra but as a necessary part of every human life. Gropius spoke out against art for art's sake and the equally dangerous philosophy of commerce as an end in itself. In the mid-twentieth century industrialisation had to be accepted, but the machine must always be controlled by human understanding and careful moral judgement. Machines must not take over. Machines must not run wild.

In London in 1934 such a broad, impassioned view of architecture was quite new. According to Maxwell Fry, Gropius 'filled us with a fervour as moral as it was aesthetic. When the applause ended the meeting broke up in a state of wild excitement and Gropius was shaking with emotion as he turned to thank me.'

Also in the audience, and even more affected, was the young art historian Nikolaus Pevsner, who had known and hero-worshipped Gropius back at home in Germany. Pevsner had been summarily dismissed from his post at Göttingen University in the Nazi purge of Jewish academics. He had only recently arrived in England and was now starting research for a survey of design in British industry, later to be published as *An Enquiry into Industrial Art in England*. For Pevsner both professionally and personally this was a precarious time, and late that night at Euston Station, waiting for a train that would take him back to Birmingham, he wrote to his wife Lola to tell her of the impression Gropius made on him: 'I have such a wild veneration for this man – the way he holds himself, what he has achieved, and his manner of speaking . . . Someone who really belongs to your "Deutschland", with the very greatest creative gifts as well. My head whirls with it. Everything else seems so petty – the worries, the prospects, everything.'

During his brief visit in England Ise was writing to Gropius anxiously and fondly, hoping that the talk had gone better than expected. 'I can imagine that you are dead tired,' she tells him. 'Do you remember the days in New York when we were so dead beat from speaking English?'

Ise gives him her own news. She has been keeping herself busy in his absence, writing magazine articles and beginning reading Werfel's novel *The Forty Days of Musa Dagh*, his intrepidly partisan account of the Armenian genocide at the hands of the Ottomans, which she has found depressing in relation to the current situation in Berlin. She has cheered herself up by lunching with her friend, the designer Irene von Debschitz, going to the theatre with her sister Ellen and spending an evening with her other sister Hertha and her niece Ati, who was now reaching school age.

Ise gives Gropius a touching account of the Mother's Day picture Ati painted for Hertha, showing a child sitting in a beautiful small garden and holding out her hand to her mother. The still childless Ise comments poignantly that she has never in her life seen 'such a philosophical representation of the relationship between mother and child'.

It is clear from Ise's letters to Gropius in London that the love affair with Herbert Bayer, if not completely over, has entered a new phase. She tells Gropius that Herbert telephoned to offer her the job of writing the text for a calendar he is designing for his clients the Berthold Company. She is tempted, although worried that the fee offered is a derisory 200 RM. (Under Hitler the German mark had been transformed into the Reichsmark.) But she argues that in their current state of poverty perhaps she ought to take it in order to get further commissions as a copywriter.

She and Bayer met for lunch to discuss the pros and cons. He was in a good mood, excited over plans for an expedition with Breuer: a trip down the Danube into Hungary. He invited Ise to go with them, but she decided not to, aware of his new mood of hedonism and flirtatiousness, about which he was frank. She reported back to Gropius that Herbert had decided 'never to get involved in human relationships again', adding her own rather acerbic comment, 'I think he forgets that then all development may stop. Lajkó [Breuer] and he have put up a philosophy together on this score that appears to me to be somewhat sterile, but *chacun à son goût.*'

Her once passionate affair with Bayer seems to have calmed down into a teasingly intimate close friendship. She even asks Gropius to buy a pair of sandals for Bayer while he is in London, drawing a diagram and giving him the length of Herbert's foot as 30.5 cm. Whether Gropius carried out this commission we shall never know.

He was on his way home on 18 May, his fifty-first birthday and, as Ise reminds him, the only one of his birthdays since their first meeting which they were spending apart. Gropius travelled back via the School of Architecture at the University of Liverpool. Its professor, Charles Reilly, an architect and the co-designer of the Peter Jones department store in Sloane Square, had created another little pocket of modernity in the largely anti-progressive England of the time. Reilly had just retired but his influence in Liverpool lived on and plans were now being made for Gropius's London RIBA architecture exhibition to travel on to Liverpool, Leeds, Birmingham and Manchester.

Ise sent her birthday telegram to greet Gropius in Liverpool. She was clearly missing him. 'Every morning Ali' – the Gropiuses' dog – 'joins me in bed, sniffs around and finds it unsatisfactory! So do I!' She was anxious to know of his impressions of England. 'How much happier one could be there,' she suggested, 'something you cannot say about us here.'

This brief visit to London in May 1934 was decisive in his later move to England. He was also getting offers from America: encouragement from the editor of the *Architectural Record*, A. Lawrence Kocher, for Gropius to set up an architectural office; the possibility of a teaching post at Columbia University. But the fact that at the time he favoured England was partly the result of the warmth of his reception at the RIBA, where proposals were underway to have Gropius nominated for the RIBA Gold Medal, and most importantly because his new contacts made in London brought the hope of new architectural commissions. There was also the question of Manon, whom he already saw so rarely. The news of her illness was another source of anguish. If he moved to America, his daughter would be still further away.

In the audience for Gropius's talk was a young entrepreneur, Jack Pritchard, 'a Puck-like figure from the furniture industry', as Maxwell

Fry described him, 'but with the true blood of patronage in his veins'. Like the Elmhirsts, though with less resources, Pritchard was a committed modernist. He studied engineering and economics at Cambridge and long before he knew, or even knew of, Gropius he had an instinctive feeling for a fusion of technology with art. In 1925 Pritchard took a job with the Venesta Plywood Company and put his mind to finding new uses for plywood, exploiting its lightness, strength and curviness. 'Plywood Pritchard', as he became known, was committed to developing plywood as a material for the modern world.

While working for Venesta in Paris Pritchard visited Le Corbusier's buildings. In 1930 he and the architect Wells Coates went to view the experimental settlement at Weissenhof in Stuttgart, now a place of modernist pilgrimage. This was where he first saw Gropius's architectural work. In that same year Pritchard commissioned Le Corbusier with Pierre Jeanneret and Charlotte Perriand to design the Venesta stand at the Building Trades exhibition at Olympia: a startlingly enterprising idea for Britain at the time. In 1931 his investigative travels took him to the Bauhaus. Pritchard arrived in Dessau with Wells Coates and Serge Chermayeff, a Russian-born architect practising in London.

Pritchard was by now aware of the impressive record of the Bauhaus's new thinking as applied to existing materials, ideas that had shaped his own philosophy. He was disappointed that three years after Gropius's resignation the building appeared more or less deserted. 'All the same', wrote Pritchard later, 'the Bauhaus looked fine amid the unkempt grass, and at least we could look round the building, which, in itself, had a very powerful impact on me.' And, as it turned out, from the time of his first brief meeting with Gropius at the RIBA exhibition opening, their lives, their work, their families would be intertwined.

Gropius was back in Berlin on 7 June 1934, when he wrote to Morton Shand, sounding out the ground:

I am very pleased that my stay in England was clearly not in vain and that, despite the difficulties of language, we were able to have some kind of understanding, as I must presume from the numerous people who talk to me about success . . . Meanwhile I have seriously been thinking about looking for work in England. The difficulties which oppose this are however considerable, mainly for material reasons. I must at least count on living there for ½ to 1 year without earning, even if all other questions can be settled, because one cannot get accustomed to a completely changed working life too quickly. Without definite prospects I cannot resolve anything but I shall be forced to undertake something because here there are no prospects of work.

Morton Shand was ahead of him, having had discussions the previous evening with Maxwell Fry about the possibility of Fry and Gropius going into partnership. A prearranged architectural partnership would be a condition of Gropius's entry into Britain. There was already a build-up of resistance to the arrival of émigré architects in a country where employment prospects for architects in general were dwindling in response to the depression in the building industry.

The RIBA itself was becoming nervous at what it regarded as potentially unfair competition from foreign architects. In 1933 the RIBA Council sent a letter to the Minister of Labour asking for more stringent entry regulations, proposing that the admission of foreign architects should be limited to 'those with special qualifications who are in a position to establish themselves in independent practice' and who would genuinely add to 'the technical abilities and culture of the profession'. The ultimate authority for entry lay with the Home Office. Erich (later Eric) Mendelsohn, who had now arrived in London and indeed attended the talk given by Gropius, fulfilled these conditions and was working in partnership with Serge Chermayeff.

A few days after Gropius returned to Germany Maxwell Fry himself contacted him to say, 'I feel very honoured and glad to be able to work with you.' Not only had Fry chaired Gropius's talk, Gropius had actually stayed with him and his family in their house in Lower Mall in Chiswick, by the Thames. Fry's letter told Gropius the June weather was so hot that he and his family were 'all lying about with few clothes on. The river outside is very low and looks burningly hot, the boat crews rowing with bare backs, and avoiding with difficulty the crowds of boys bathing from the river banks and the bridge.' His little daughter Ann 'is happily playing in her house in the garden dressed in nothing but a hat and a pair of red shoes'. It is clear that there was already a good rapport between them. Fry now wrote delightedly to Gropius, 'I had never dared to hope that I might work with you.'

The hyperactive Morton Shand had already identified a potential architectural commission for Gropius to start on after he arrived. This was a new Isokon scheme for a block of flats at Didsbury in Manchester ,on a suburban hillside site owned by a friend of Jack Pritchard's, DIA stalwart A. P. Simon. The Isokon company, formed by Pritchard, his wife Molly, the architect Wells Coates and others in 1931, was involved in property development of the most idealistic kind: the construction of 'dwellings for modern people'. The name Isokon itself was ostentatiously progressive, standing for 'Isometric Unit Construction'. In 1933 Isokon's ambitious project for Lawn Road Flats in Belsize Park, a rare beacon of modernity in London, later to be known as the Isokon building, was nearing completion, and part of the offer to Gropius entailed accommodation in a studio flat in this brand-new building, with service and meals provided for six months 'or whatever time is needed for the job'.

Gropius accepted these proposals delightedly but a little anxiously when it came to detail. 'Do you think it will be possible to lend some furniture? And what is the average salary for a maid?' Gropius was planning to rent out his Berlin apartment with furniture included, giving the German authorities the impression that he intended to return. Jack Pritchard offered to lend furniture and Fry assured Gropius that because Lawn Road Flats were designed to be service flats, he would not need a maid.

———

While Gropius was away Ise was preoccupied with making arrangements for him to visit Manon in Vienna as soon as he returned. Vienna had been in a state of upheaval since February 1934, following the violent uprising by the Social Democrats against Chancellor Engelbert Dollfuss's ultra-conservative government. Because of the political tensions border restrictions for travellers between Germany and Austria were stepped up and the fee for a travel permit from Berlin was 1,000

Manon Gropius photographed by Lily Hildebrandt in 1933.

RM, a dauntingly large sum for the Gropiuses in their state of penury. Ise first went to the police station to enquire about the regulations. She was told she needed to apply to the Ministry of the Interior, who required a letter from Alma to certify the seriousness of Manon's condition. Ise asked Gropius to telephone Alma from London in the hope of organising this since Manon still showed no signs of recovery. He was in Vienna by 8 June 1934, having borrowed the money for the permit and booked into the Hotel Bristol. He told Mutzi he would call her as soon as he arrived. He could not wait to see her. He and Manon had not actually met since December 1931, on that all too quickly curtailed visit to Berlin.

There were phases of her life Gropius had totally missed out on: for example, Manon's ambitions to become an actress, encouraged by the prominent director and friend of the family Max Reinhardt, who had actually offered Manon the part of First Angel in his and Hugo von Hofmannsthal's adaptation of Calderón's *El gran teatro del mundo* (*The Great Theatre of the World*) for the Salzburg Festival in 1934. Such suggestions were frowned on by the anxiously possessive Alma and Franz Werfel.

Gropius had also been unaware of Manon's conversion to Roman Catholicism, no doubt stimulated by Alma's new liaison with the rather sinister priest Johannes Hollnsteiner, a rising star in Austrian Roman Catholic and Fascist political circles. Alma, now in her fifties, had fallen wildly in love with the thirty-seven-year-old Hollnsteiner, who, although short, balding and bespectacled, made her feel that the long night of winter had given way to a balmy springtime. Hollnsteiner evolved the convenient belief that the rule of chastity only applied when the priest was wearing vestments and he took to staying overnight at the Hohe Warte.

When Manon sent news of her change of faith Gropius responded: 'Your becoming Catholic surprised me, I myself am totally unchurchlike, but every visually and sensually talented person naturally prefers the Catholic Church with the pomp and circumstance of its ceremonies to Protestantism's arid austerity.' He was doing his best to understand.

Alma was still pursuing her old policy of keeping father and daughter apart. At this period Gropius was hauntingly reminded of the scene that followed Manon's birth, when he returned from the front to see his baby daughter, and Alma behaved like a lioness possessively defending her cub. She had already lost one daughter, little Putzi, and probably this made her more obsessively protective of the third. Even on the occasion of Gropius's fiftieth birthday in 1933 Manon, not allowed to telephone congratulations from home, had been reduced to attempting to reach him from a phone box in the local post office. Frustratingly she had been unable to get through. Manon suspected that her mother intercepted and destroyed her father's letters. At one point Gropius had even been reduced to tucking little secret messages into the magazines he sent to Manon, knowing that Alma never looked at these.

Now that Gropius was actually so close by in Vienna, Alma made reluctant overtures. She invited him to dine at the Hohe Warte and he was taken to see Manon in her sick room, on the upper floor of the house in what had previously been Franz Werfel's study. According to her nurse-companion Ida Gebauer, Gropius was speechless, taken aback by the scene before his eyes.

The sick room had been decorated like a shrine, hung with paintings by Alma's father Emil Schindler and piled high with flowers. Manon herself was enthroned in a large wing chair said to have been occupied by Talleyrand himself at the Congress of Vienna in 1814. An ornate oriental rug disguised the worst effects of her illness: she was more or less immobilised below the waist. The invalid was loaded with her mother's jewellery. Alma sat regally beside her daughter, possessively clutching Manon's hand.

Gropius was permitted only a short visit before Alma despatched him back to his hotel. Over the week he was in Vienna his time with Manon was limited to half an hour a day. Insisting on seeing Manon's doctors, he seems to have accepted their optimistic view that his daughter was improving and was likely to be able to walk again. How much was this wishful thinking? Alma's mother Anna Moll commented after Gropius's departure that he was deceiving himself: Manon was already an incurable cripple. Carl Moll went further in congratulating Alma for managing the spectacle so well.

Once he had returned to Berlin in mid-June Gropius wrote to Alma himself, saying he was pleased that Manon was making such good progress, due to Alma's unstinting care. His careful conciliatory behaviour towards Alma, in such contrast to his usual decisive professional demeanour, suggests how fearful he was of having access to Manon limited still further. After his departure Manon herself was particularly restless. She sent a few more messages, trying to sound hopeful. But she seems to have sensed she was not going to see her father again.

———

Gropius came back to a Berlin of increasing violence. On 30 June – 1 July 1934 Ernst Roehm, leader of the Storm Troopers, General Kurt von Schleicher and others high up in the Nazi party or the military were executed for allegedly plotting against Hitler. Gropius's office had so little work that the staff was reduced to one draughtsman and the secretary.

Definite arrangements for the Gropiuses' move to London were underway. Plans were now made for Gropius to attend an international theatre conference in Rome as an official delegate from Germany, and then proceed to London. Meanwhile, Philip Morton Shand was busy making preparations for Gropius's arrival, including writing an article on his work. Herbert Read, the fervent champion of European modernism and admirer of the Bauhaus, optimistically predicted that Gropius would be settled in Britain within six months.

Gropius had been invited by the Fondazione Alessandro Volta in Rome to take part in the theatre conference. This was at the instigation of Dino Alfieri, Italian Minister of Culture, Goebbels's equivalent in Fascist Italy, who was trying hard to establish closer ties between Mussolini's Italy and Hitler's Germany. Alfieri was already an admirer of Gropius's work. Gropius was invited to give a talk, which he entitled 'Building Theatres', a summary of his ambitious concept of an architecture for the future modern theatre. A crucial consideration at this juncture was that his and Ise's expenses would be generously paid.

Gropius needed official permission to travel outside Germany. On 19 September 1933 he wrote to his supporter Professor Eugen Hönig for authorisation to attend the Volta conference. At the same time he requested an official permit to work temporarily in England on a modest housing commission. He stressed the fact that he was still maintaining his Berlin practice, left in temporary charge of former Bauhaus student Wils Ebert, and that he would be keeping his Berlin apartment too. He was given permission to go to the conference, and on 4 October 1933 Hönig granted him authorisation to remain in England until 30 April 1935. He expressed his personal trust in Gropius's integrity: 'I regard you as a straightforward man with the emotions and reliability of a German, whose artistic efforts cannot be doubted in terms of seriousness of your goals.'

Hönig was not a member of the Nazi party but as president of the Reichskulturkammer he was officialdom. We can be aware of Gropius treading very carefully, anxious for a multitude of reasons – professional caution, a still enduring loyalty towards Germany, responsibility towards his and Ise's families – to leave the country with a minimum of fuss. His 'Leave of Absence' permit left open the prospect of an imminent return.

Besides, like other German intellectuals of the period, he and Ise were not convinced of the permanence of the Hitler regime: 'It is difficult to understand with hindsight', Ise wrote later, 'what was in our minds at that time: we firmly believed that this whole hokus pokus (that's what most of those we knew called it) could not last beyond a few months.'

Just before he left for Rome, on 1 October, Gropius wrote again to Manon to tell her 'we sit in a dreadful disarray of packing'. The Potsdamer Privatstrasse apartment had to be cleared in preparation for its tenant, Käthe Riesler, the daughter of Max Liebermann the painter. If it appeared that the Gropiuses had left the country permanently, the apartment would have been confiscated by the state. On the way to Rome, still surprisingly eager for a new experience, Gropius and Ise planned to make a detour to Assisi. He had never seen the Giotto frescoes there. In Rome he and Ise would be staying grandly in the Hotel Palazzo e Ambasciatore on Via Vittorio Veneto. The mood was set when, on the first day of their arrival, Ise collided in the revolving door of the hotel entrance with the King of Spain.

The Volta Theatre Conference of 1934 was an intellectually glittering affair, a final gathering of many of the giants of European culture before the outbreak of the war. The delegates were not only architects and stage designers but also writers, critics and composers: Maurice Maeterlinck, André Maurois, W. B. Yeats, the Dutch architect H. Th. Wijdeveld, the English stage designer and theorist Edward Gordon Craig, Ashley Dukes, founder of the Mercury Theatre in London, as well as the Futurist Filippo Tommaso Marinetti and Luigi Pirandello. Mussolini devotee Pirandello had just been awarded the 1934 Nobel Prize in literature for 'his almost magical power to turn psychological analysis into good theatre'. Werfel had been asked to participate in the conference but partly because of Manon's illness had declined.

The German star actor and producer Gustaf Gründgens, who was soon to be notorious for ingratiating himself with the Nazi regime, was also invited. Hitler had vetoed Gründgens's invitation because, in Ise's later view, he already had great plans for him in Germany and did not yet want to identify himself with the Mussolini regime. 'Walter, on the other hand, was expendable.' So the Gropiuses arrived at the conference hoping but still not certain that they would be able to arrange to travel on to England from Rome.

As the only Germans at the conference they were given preferential treatment, although Ise indiscreetly confided to Alfieri that they did not intend to return to Germany since they disapproved of Hitler's regime. Undeterred Alfieri arranged for them to see the Exhibition of the Fascist Revolution, which displayed the most modern Italian design: 'To our horror, he appeared for this occasion in his black Fascist uniform, had the military guard present arms for our entrance and put us altogether in the most embarrassing position.' At the official conference reception in the Capitol Ise was led down the line of guests on the arm of Achille Starace, secretary of the Fascist Party. When the delegates assembled for a performance of the Franchetti opera *La figlia di Iorio* (*The Daughter of Iorio*), at which Mussolini was expected, Gropius and Ise were seated on their own in a box in the opera house alongside Il Duce, while the rest of the delegates

were seated below them in the stalls. At the glittering party afterwards Alfieri made a point of introducing Ise to Count Ciano, Mussolini's son-in-law. The next day, while Gropius attended one of the
many sessions of the conference, Alfieri took Ise on a tour of Rome,
trying hard to charm her. He was a practised seducer. But she made
it clear she was not available.

The theatre conference had its own moment of drama on 9 October 1934 when proceedings were interrupted by the news that King
Alexander of Yugoslavia, together with the French ambassador, had
been murdered in Marseilles. The political implications were complex: 'Everybody had to think very fast how to respond to this event.
The French did very badly,' judged Ise. 'Alfieri, on the other hand,
was very skilful when announcing the news which tore the conference
members into different directions. During one of the meetings Marinetti
made the famous statement of the *"poetica di guerra"* which drove the
French wild and drew a furious riposte from Maurois.' Marinetti was
already controversial as author of the Futurist Manifesto. His concept
of a theatre that encouraged audience participation in themes of exag-
gerated violence and eroticism could be guaranteed to cause commotion amongst conference delegates of such wildly opposed views. This
was an address which expressed in extreme and vivid terms a Fascist
viewpoint of the glories of self-sacrifice in war.

Gropius was the third of three principal speakers at the Volta conference. His address, 'Building Theatres', drew on his own personal
experience of theatre at the Bauhaus and his work on the theatres for
Jena and Krakow, besides his proposals for the Palace of the Soviets
and the recent House of German Labour project. These last two were
political theatre, sites of power politics, involving audience participation on a giant scale. Most of all Gropius's address emphasised his
concept of Total Theatre, evolved with and for the highly politicised
Berlin director Erwin Piscator. 'The theatre of the future must become a
spiritual centre for the masses,' as Gropius now expressed it, 'fulfilling
its social and dramatic role.' At a time of vastly increased competition
from the movies live theatre needed to justify its place.

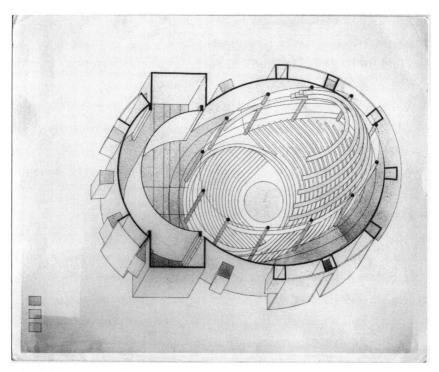

Isometric projection of Gropius and Piscator's 'Total Theatre' concept.

His Total Theatre concept was coherent and inclusive, encouraging the utmost audience involvement. Gropius aimed at what he termed 'an architectural totality . . . The public must be rooted from its intellectual apathy, assaulted, and forced to participate in the play.' The architecture itself would be a part of the performance. Gropius envisaged Total Theatre as 'a tremendous demonstration of everything that our age has created in new construction techniques and new materials. Glass, concrete, steel, and other metals will be used, harmonized by the laws of proportion, rhythm, and the colour and the structures of the materials.'

Unfortunately these heady visions of the theatre of the future fell on mainly deaf ears. Few of the delegates understood German, and in any case the structural aspects of the theatre were of minimal interest to the literary grandees in the audience. Even some of Gropius's fellow designers were unconvinced. No sooner had Gropius finished speaking than Edward Gordon Craig rose to his feet. Gordon Craig, then in his sixties, very much the grand old man of British theatre, had a considerable pedigree. He was the illegitimate son of Ellen Terry and the architect Edward Godwin. He had been the lover of Isadora Duncan. He was a director as much as a designer, still famous for his 1911 production of *Hamlet* at the Moscow Arts Theatre commissioned by Stanislavsky himself. Gordon Craig was of the old school of director as dictator. He was unimpressed by Gropius's address, finding his democratic view of theatre soulless. Prospects of new theatres of steel, glass and concrete were lost on Gordon Craig.

Gropius was able to argue back next morning to the delegates who had spoken out against his concept. 'Why this hysterical fear of the machine? This is only a question of secondary importance. The machine does not create the New Theatre; it only gives new ways of expression, provided that *subject matter* is there.' He was later permitted, in a written rejoinder included in the published conference report, to defend himself more specifically:

I believe I can dispel easily the apprehensions Mr. Gordon Craig has expressed. The very idea of the plan for this theatre is increased adaptation to very different scenic concepts. It opposes the rigid establishment of space used up to now in the theatre and makes available a variety of space for different producers . . . It is exactly the opposite of Mr. Gordon Craig's fears.

Even at this moment of crisis in his life Gropius was still passionate in holding firm to his artistic principles.

Gropius and Ise now had to negotiate their journey to England since at this point they only had permission for the return trip from Rome to Berlin. This they arranged through the Volta conference offices. According to Ise, 'The crucial moment for us came when we, with casual mien, asked the secretary whether she would order us a ticket to London instead of Berlin and she immediately and innocently answered "yes, why not". We were trembling inside what the answer would be.' They were only just in time as two months later, once relations between Italy and Germany grew closer, they would probably have needed official permission for this London detour.

They had been allowed to bring only 20 RM out of Germany between them, less than £100 today. They wired their Dutch friend C. H. van der Leeuw, enterprising owner of the Van Nelle factory in Rotterdam, and he managed to transfer money for the journey. They now travelled from Rome to Zurich, where Gropius was booked to give a lecture. En route they stopped briefly in Milan, where they managed a brief reunion with Xanti Schawinsky. Here Gropius, deeply ashamed to have missed Manon's eighteenth birthday in all the commotion of departure from Berlin, bought her an antique jade pendant which he said he trusted would endow his daughter with radiant health. This proved to be a sadly forlorn hope. In Zurich they found the Giedions were depressed about the exodus of many of their friends from Germany and anxious about the politics of Switzerland, where the Nazis were already 'beginning to knock at the doors'.

Gropius had his own particular fears about the future. He was continually anxious that starting a whole new professional life in another country would be very hard for him. He explained these misgivings to Manon: 'I am not only too attached to Germany, I also have this feeling that the emigrant quickly loses his roots that nourish him from within; and only a young tree can survive being transplanted.' He was clearly afraid of the effects his arrival in an unfamiliar country might have on his powers of creativity.

There were other niggling worries. These again he confided to his daughter, giving her his temporary address c/o Maxwell Fry's office in Westminster. 'I am curious about how to survive in this inartistic country with unsalted vegetables, bony women and an eternally freezing draught!?'

15
London
1934

Ise wrote later: 'We had come from environments where every stone was shaking and where emotions ran high and it was suddenly as if the whole world around us was standing still, completely oblivious of what was brewing abroad and happily explaining to questioning foreigners that England was planning to muddle through no matter what.'

Around two thousand refugees arrived in Britain in the first year after Hitler took power in January 1933. Many of these refugees were Jewish. Gropius was not technically an exile: he had not actually been forced to go. Nor was he sure he would be staying. As we have seen, he kept his options open. He had come to Britain so to speak officially. He still hoped against hope that Hitler could be ousted and that he would be able to return home to Berlin. But certainly at this point he was a displaced person. He had broken completely with all he had built up professionally in Germany, his hopes of future work there, his roots, his culture, his huge array of contacts, his whole familiar, absorbing way of life. Arriving in a London that he hardly knew, still speaking embarrassingly broken English, he was faced with a painfully difficult adjustment. Even English weights and measuring systems were mysterious. But as Ise pointed out, 'we were used to difficulties, having felt as aliens at home'.

He and Ise arrived at Victoria station at 3.20 p.m. on 18 October 1934. There to greet him was the small reception committee of Philip Morton Shand, his future architectural partner Maxwell Fry and a young and nervous Jack Pritchard, overawed at the prospect of the arrival of an architect of such great reputation in the only just completed Lawn Road Flats. Pritchard had not even realised that Gropius was married and had allocated only a single person's flat. When Gropius and Ise both got off the train Pritchard made a panic telephone call from the station to his wife Molly, asking her to quickly change the single to a double.

Pritchard drove the Gropiuses across London particularly slowly in order to give time for the move to the double accommodation. When they eventually arrived at Lawn Road Flats, in the area on the edge of Hampstead known as Belsize Park, Pritchard stopped the car at one of the very few modernist buildings in London at the time, a looming apartment block constructed in monolithic reinforced concrete and rendered dazzlingly white. This seems to have been the first use of reinforced concrete for a domestic building in Britain. The sculptural structure gave Lawn Road Flats a certain 1930s glamour. Agatha Christie, a later Lawn Road resident, compared the building to a giant ocean liner beached along the street. The critic J. M. Richards viewed it as a structure in which the architect, Wells Coates, improved on Le Corbusier, approaching more closely to a *machine à habiter* than Le Corbusier ever did himself.

Wells Coates, Lawn Road Flats (the Isokon Building), 1934.

For Gropius, arriving in London that October, Lawn Road Flats must have seemed reassuringly familiar, except that these communal service flats were built not for the workers but for left-wing London intellectuals. In Ise's retrospective view it was hard to think of any shelter in London that would have made them quite so happy. 'After having experienced an initial success of Modern Architecture in Germany we had been forced to leave everything in the destructive hands of Nazism and at this moment of defeat it was of inestimable value to us to become right away part of a bold venture in the architectural development.' The Gropiuses themselves viewed Lawn Road Flats in terms of 'an exciting housing laboratory, both socially and technically', which they were fascinated to observe.

Lawn Road Flats had been ceremonially opened only three months earlier, in July 1934, by the local Conservative MP, Thelma Cazalet. The ladies all wore hats. Photographs show them ranged along the terraces of the concrete building, images as atmospheric and as telling as any of the Bauhaus's evocative group pictures. In arriving at Lawn Road Flats at just this juncture the Gropiuses were thrown into a milieu of progressive English life of which Jack and Molly Pritchard were particular exemplars. These were children of the stolid professional classes determinedly resisting the expectations of their upbringing in terms not only of politics and culture, especially the arts, but also in the detail of the way they lived their lives, challenging preconceptions in domestic arrangements, sexual behaviour, upbringing of children. Lawn Road Flats itself was the visible expression of mid-twentieth-century English progressive attitudes.

Jack and Molly Pritchard were also in that sense very Cambridge people. Jack had studied engineering as an undergraduate at Pembroke College, veering off into economics. Besides his job at the plywood firm Venesta and his great enthusiasm for modern architecture he was now involved in planning a whole new, efficient and socially equitable Britain. The urgent need for systematic long-term national planning was very much a part of left-wing thinking at the time. Pritchard was a founder member of PEP, short for Political and Economic Planning, an

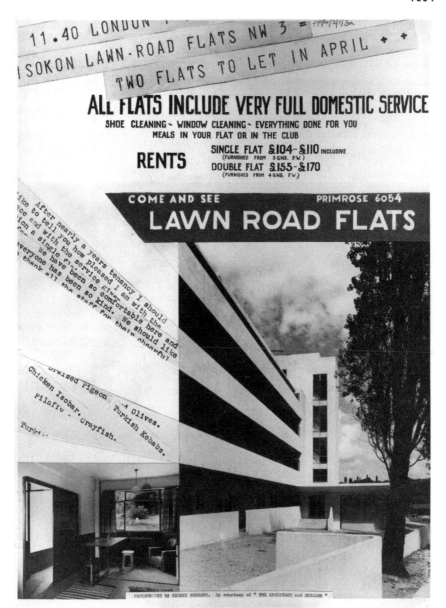

Early advertisement for Lawn Road Flats.

early version of what would now be called a think tank, and chairman of its offshoot known as TEC PLAN, set up to investigate the social changes that could be brought about by modern technology. Pritchard's aspirations already overlapped with Gropius's own.

Molly had studied science at Girton, then a women's college. After working originally as a biochemist her interests shifted to psychology and she trained as a psychotherapist. Molly Pritchard was a highly articulate woman interested in patterns of human behaviour and emotional responses and it was she who drew up the original brief for Lawn Road Flats. The building was envisaged as providing accommodation for young professional men and women with very few possessions. These would be people with an income of around £500 a year (£33,000 in today's money). They would need only minimum facilities for sleeping, cooking, eating and clothes storage. Right from the beginning Lawn Road Flats were seen as service flats with cleaning and even shoe polishing provided and simple meals delivered as required by the resident housekeeper to individual flats.

By the time Gropius and Ise arrived there the Pritchards had two children, Jonathan, then aged eight, and Jeremy, aged six. Jack and Molly Pritchard were implicit believers in progressive education and both boys were sent as boarders to Beacon Hill, the famous experimental school set up in Sussex by Dora Russell with her husband the philosopher Bertrand Russell. Since the break-up of their marriage, Dora was now running Beacon Hill on her own. She and the Pritchards had become close friends. Many of their shared ideas of creative education, deriving from the teachings of Fröbel and Cižek, would have been familiar to Gropius too.

Ideals of non-possessive sexual relationships, at one time a clarion call for both the Russells, were current in the Lawn Road circles. Jack had fathered a child with Beatrix Tudor-Hart, a nursery school teacher described by Pritchard as 'a fine tall girl, handsome and intelligent'. Beatrix was sister-in-law of Edith Tudor-Hart (née Suschitzky), an Austrian Jew who had studied at the Bauhaus and an avid communist who was to become well known as a photographer of scenes of British social deprivation. Beatrix and Jack's daughter, Jennifer, was born in 1929. By the time Lawn Road Flats were under construction Molly Pritchard herself was in the midst of an affair with Wells Coates.

Before his arrival in London Gropius certainly knew Coates, who was one of the international brotherhood of architects, a committed and gregarious member of CIAM and co-founder of its English branch, the MARS group. He had in fact been nervous that Coates might feel he was treading on his territory in living at Lawn Road, but these anxieties now receded. Indeed his friend and supporter J. M. Richards claimed that the arrival of Gropius 'must have warmed Wells's cosmopolitan heart'.

Wells Coates himself was internationalist in origin and outlook, born to Canadian parents in Tokyo. He studied engineering in Canada, fought on the front lines in France and Belgium in the First World War and worked in Paris as a journalist on the *Daily Express* before coming to London to set up his own practice as a designer-architect. For Coates being footloose was a way of life. J. M. Richards describes him as:

A compactly built man with a Ronald Colman moustache and crisply waving hair, well dressed for all occasions with a way of switching on social charm as though it was a beacon from an electric torch; a voluble conversationalist whose talk was spiced with services terminology and avant-garde jargon; ingratiatingly attentive to women, with a line of talk about places he had been.

But beyond all this those who knew him were aware of 'an intensely serious personality, with unswerving integrity about the things he regarded as important (which meant chiefly architecture) and a fighter'.

The concept of Lawn Road Flats was as much Wells Coates's as it was the Pritchards'. Coates believed as they did in the untrammelled existence. Indeed his affair with Molly Pritchard was a feature of the lifestyle he felt should be *mouvementé*. Architecture should express their shared ideals of personal freedom, a shedding of complex obligations and possessions, as Coates himself expressed it in a letter to Jack Pritchard:

. . . this idea of property – so much of this little garden is for you m'dear and this tweeny little wishy bit is for me so there! – is *dead*, dead, dead . . . My scheme provides a place which every actor in this drama can call his own place and further than that my idea of property does not go. This is the room where I sleep, this is where I work and this is where I eat. That is the roof garden where everyone can turn out and enjoy the sun . . . This is the garden where everyone goes. It's like a park. It's our little play ground and not so many legal acres to you and so many to me.

For Gropius, whose own architecture of this period encompassed pleasurable healthy communal activity, such ideas had a ring of familiarity.

When the building was completed, the five-storey Lawn Road Flats, consisted of twenty-two 'Minimum Flats', each of which had a main bed-sitting room, a dressing room linked to a bathroom and a kitchenette. There were also four south-facing two-room flats divided by sliding panels, three studio flats with big north-facing windows and a large penthouse on the fifth floor where the Pritchards themselves lived. Because the building was so new, when the Gropiuses arrived few of the flats were occupied. After the initial panic at the station they were allocated No. 15, one of the slightly bigger flats on the third floor of the building.

Writing to Manon from London Gropius enclosed a little sketch of their accommodation showing the minimum kitchen and the bathroom, the smallish double bed protruding right across the living space, the sofa, the armchair and a little dining table. Compared with the apartment in Potsdamer Privatstrasse or the beautiful, expansive Director's House in Dessau, No. 15 Lawn Road Flats must have seemed extremely cramped. It is not surprising that at this juncture Gropius became engrossed in the writings of Jonathan Swift and his explorations in *Gulliver's Travels* of the phenomenon of changing scales in relation to conventional concepts of normal human size. He and Ise felt shrunk to Lilliputians themselves in one of Wells Coates's Minimum Flats. The Gropiuses had a telephone in Belsize Park of which the number was PRImrose 0226. Obviously missing Manon, Gropius told her that the first ever public television phone had just been introduced, holding out the hope that they would soon be able to speak to one another face to face.

On their first weekend in England the Pritchards suggested a drive out to the country. The Gropiuses said they would like to see the Neolithic structure of Stonehenge. Driving west out of London towards

The Gropiuses' apartment, No. 15 Lawn Road Flats.
Standard kitchen at Lawn Road Flats.
Standard dressing room at Lawn Road Flats.

Wiltshire they passed large billboards on the road. One of these read 'You are now entering the Strong country'. Jack noticed Ise whispering nervously to Walter. A little further on there was another notice which read 'Take Courage'. Another expression of alarm. 'Why did England need all this propaganda?' asked Gropius. The Pritchards were able to reassure their visitors that the hoardings were simply advertising Courage beer. The little episode shows that Gropius and Ise, just arrived in England, were still jittery and puzzled. But compared with the experiences of other 1930s émigrés from Europe their arrival at Lawn Road Flats was relatively painless.

This was partly a matter of the Pritchards' own personalities and interests, the warmth of their welcome, their extensive range of contacts. A later brochure for the Flats lists the many occupational categories residents were drawn from. These were artists, authors, soldiers and economists, even archaeologists and Egyptologists. Residents of Lawn Road Flats in the winter of 1934 included the American economist Philip Sargent Florence, the painter and critic Adrian Stokes, the writer Nicholas Monsarrat, later to be well known for his best-selling Second World War novel *The Cruel Sea*. Another arrival was the Jewish Arthur Korn, Berlin architect and planner, a one-time member of the Ring of Ten who had been expelled from membership of the BDA, the German architects' professional body, when the Reichskulturkammer took it over and forbidden to work as an architect in Germany. Gropius of course already knew Korn well. Lawn Road Flats was to be the place of many such emotional reunions.

Jack Pritchard's generous sociability comes over in some verses written by John Betjeman, also middle-class in background and himself brought up nearby in Highgate:

> We're giving a little party –
> Not exactly lowbrow, not exactly arty,
> For us functional folk who like beauty stark
> And decorate our rooms with it in Belsize Park,
> To know Craven Pritchard is a pretty good scoop:
> He's the live-wire behind the Twentieth Century Group.

Besides Jack Pritchard's ties to the modernist architects of the Twentieth Century Group, precursor of the MARS group, his friendships were
unstoppably broad-based. Living at Lawn Road Flats brought Gropius
into contact with the biologist Julian Huxley and the pioneer of X-ray
crystallography J. D. Bernal, a lifelong communist. Molly Pritchard had
her own professional contacts in the medical and psychoanalytic worlds.

Especially important to Gropius at this juncture were connections he
made with the critic Herbert Read and the painters and sculptors Ben
Nicholson, Barbara Hepworth and Henry Moore. The ' "nest" of gentle
artists', as Read himself described it, referring back to Turgenev's *Nest of
Gentlefolk*, lived in proximity to one another in Mall Studios and Parkhill
Road, very close to Lawn Road Flats. These artists were all members of
a further progressive grouping, Unit One, founded in 1933 by Paul Nash
– another Hampstead resident. Unit One aimed to do away with false divisions between artists and architects, claiming that there was a common
bond between painting, sculpting and building in that each stood for 'the
expression of a truly contemporary spirit'. This was of course a sentiment
with which Walter Gropius felt an immediate sympathy.

Of this group of modernist or abstract artists working close to Lawn
Road Flats Henry Moore impressed Gropius the most. He considered
Moore 'the best of the living English artists' and their friendship continued through the years that Gropius was living in the States. Gropius's
rapport with Herbert Read was even stronger, based as it was on the
belief in art as the dominating factor in any human life. Gropius was
impressed by Read's book *Education through Art*, published by Faber
& Faber in the year of his arrival at Lawn Road. He later wrote: 'When
I left Hitler's Germany in 1934 and settled for a new life in London, I
found in Read a kindred soul who was wide open to the problems of
art and architecture which had occupied my life.' Both agreed that the
key to achieving artistic totality, putting art at the forefront of human
experience, was the creative education of the child.

Hampstead had a history of cultural cross-currents that made it
especially attractive to émigrés from Europe. Once a hilly village
on the northern edge of London, Hampstead had been a gathering

place for intellectuals, writers and artists since the eighteenth century. Defoe considered Hampstead as very close to Heaven. It was a place associated with Hogarth and Constable, Gainsborough, Coleridge and Keats, Wilkie Collins and Charles Dickens. In the mid-twentieth century Hampstead was a centre of alternative thinking and left-wing ideology. The Left Book Club, founded in 1931, was a feature of Hampstead life, with vigorous branch meetings held in a house in Keats Grove. The original Everyman Theatre in Hampstead was reopened as a cinema on Boxing Day in 1933, inaugurating an ambitious programme of the latest films from international sources. Intellectually Hampstead was a stimulating place and in the 1930s, besides the Gropiuses, the area attracted several thousand German-speaking refugees.

Sometimes this seemed like a kind of invasion. As described by J. M. Richards, 'Europe, in the shape of political refugees of many nationalities, travelled to London, introducing a babel of tongues into the lift at Belsize Park underground station and turning eminent names from the art manuals into Hampstead neighbours.' To Richards this influx from Europe seemed distinctly ominous, serving as 'a warning that the oppression of culture which the politics of power had brought was real: we English were not necessarily immune'.

The fast-enlarging influx of 1930s Hampstead refugees from Nazism was to some extent encouraged by Fred Uhlman, an émigré from Germany himself, and his English wife Diana, who together founded the Freie Deutsche Kulturbund (Free German League of Culture) and the Artists' Refugee Committee. Sigmund Freud came from Vienna to live in Maresfield Gardens at Swiss Cottage in 1938, the year of the Nazi invasion of Austria, or *Anschluss*. Oskar Kokoschka, Gropius's long-running rival in love with Alma, now branded a degenerate artist, left Prague that same year to live in an overcrowded lodging house at 2A King Henry's Road in Belsize Park. The Expressionist dramatist Ernst Toller, outspoken in his criticism of the Nazis, had already made his way to Hampstead. In 1938 Alma and Gustav Mahler's daughter, the sculptor Anna Mahler, fled Vienna to live in Hampstead too.

For the Gropiuses, the break with Berlin was inevitably traumatic but in retrospect, Ise saw the experience as important in broadening their view of human nature and in giving them a new zest for foreign travel: 'how immensely it helps to see places develop a sense for the interrelationship of countries and people . . . Lawn Road Flats was our first step in this direction and remains unforgettable.' This was a good way of putting it. For Gropius himself Hampstead in the 1930s was full of past and future emotional reverberations.

———

Gropius was now working with Maxwell Fry in what was for the moment a loose partnership arrangement. As an architect Fry was in a stylistically interim phase, making the move away from the classical tradition in which he had been trained towards the thoroughgoing modern, encouraged by his links with the DIA and the MARS group and his close friendship with Wells Coates. Fry had joined the office of Adams and Thompson, specialist town planners, in 1930 but he now found his ideas so divergent from theirs that he broke away, moving into his own small independent office at the far end of Victoria Street, where he employed a very tiny staff, working on a block of flats and several private houses. Fry's now best-known London building of the period is the Sun House in Frognal Lane in Hampstead, constructed in 1935–6. The north London modernist connections continue.

Fry's modest office in Victoria was a far cry from Potsdamer Privatstrasse in its heyday with Gropius's entourage of architectural draughtsmen and assistants. But Fry wrote movingly about his lack of grandeur. Their difference in age and stature did not matter. Indeed Gropius seemed positively to enjoy Fry's youthful agility, although 'it was foreign to his more ruminative mind'. As architects Fry and Gropius complemented one another, playing what Fry describes as a Prospero and Ariel game, the father figure and the mischievous ethereal attendant. He felt an immediate sympathy for Gropius, 'a great man driven from the country that bore him and that perforce he must love as I my own'. Fry gives the most vivid of descriptions of Gropius at this period, soon

Maxwell Fry, self-portrait at work.

after his arrival in London: 'His face bore the marks of suffering and of the agitations of his departure. It was deeply serious, but unlike Corbusier's, accessible, interested and with an inclination to smile; and when he smiled the deep-set luminous eyes softened in an expression of complete candour, that of a man without a particle of subterfuge in his nature.'

Architecturally of course he was now faced with a very different scene from the one he had known in continental Europe. As Count Harry Kessler had remarked so cuttingly back in 1930, after a visit to London's recently rebuilt Savoy Theatre, where theatre architecture was concerned London and Paris were both at least half a lifetime behind Berlin, Hamburg, Frankfurt and Stuttgart. The same could be said of architecture in general. 'We do not understand the modern movement and we do not like it,' a British journalist commented after visiting the Leipzig Fair. By 1934 there were just a few recognisably modernist buildings in London besides the Lawn Road Flats, almost all of these designed by émigré architects. For instance, the Russian Berthold Lubetkin's early commissions were for the futuristic Gorilla House and Penguin Pool at London Zoo and in 1934 Highpoint I in Highgate. On the Sussex coast Mendelsohn and Chermayeff had won the competition for their beautiful, translucent De La Warr Pavilion at Bexhill-on-Sea. But in general British taste was all too comfortingly retrospective. As Jack Pritchard caustically observed, even in 1930 the British government exhibit at the Buenos Aires exhibition took the form of a Norman castle with a Tudor barn, while the main hall of the Union-Castle Line's new ocean liner, the *Winchester Castle*, was designed in full-blown Flemish Renaissance style.

When Gropius joined Fry there were already commissions being planned for Isokon, Pritchard's architectural development company. Besides the block of flats in Manchester on land owned by A. P. Simon there would soon be schemes for a development in Birmingham. This was another block of modern flats on land owned by Professor Philip Sargent Florence, the American economist whose lectures had greatly influenced Jack Pritchard when he was a Cambridge undergraduate.

Sargent Florence was a design enthusiast who had first suggested and supported Nikolaus Pevsner's survey *Industrial Art in England*. Pevsner took a predictably dim view of British achievements in this area in comparison with Germany, maintaining that 'when I say that 90% of British industrial art is devoid of any aesthetic merit, I am not exaggerating'. Sargent Florence, Professor in Birmingham University's Department of Commerce, had a large house with plenty of land, including a lake. Here it was proposed to build a single block of twenty-four flats. For both these Isokon projects sketch plans were produced by Gropius.

In coming to England Gropius had made a conscious decision to abandon, or at least postpone, his major interest in low-cost housing for the workers and to concentrate on what appeared more immediately feasible: homes for wealthy and discriminating clients. A grandiose project was for a luxury development of sixty-nine flats on St Leonard's Hill near Windsor. Gropius was working on this scheme through the autumn of 1934. The thirty-three-acre site was magnificent, overlooking Windsor Great Park, with a view of Windsor Castle in the distance. King George V was prevailed upon to give his permission for a new building in such close proximity to a royal residence. The total cost was estimated at £225,000 (around £17 million today).

Though these centrally heated flats and apartments were in some respects the opposite of his plans for mass housing in Berlin, they still exemplified many of Gropius's visionary architectural ideals. This was still community living of a kind, with a communal restaurant, residents' lounge and ballroom, a cinema, a swimming pool with Turkish bath. As at Lawn Road Flats domestic service was included in the rent and there was a supervised play space for the children. The scheme for Windsor exemplified Gropius's deeply held principles of conserving amenities by building upwards instead of outwards. This was the antithesis of suburban sprawl, hailed as such by an article in the *Architectural Review* entitled 'Cry Stop to Havoc or: Preservation by Development'. A single large structure as opposed to a whole series of smaller housing blocks meant there was no need to cut down existing trees or destroy gardens and lawns.

Gropius's scheme at Windsor was for a large, impressive mansion set in parkland, the modern equivalent of the historic English country house.

Jack Pritchard, at first rather overawed in Gropius's presence, very soon became his most devoted friend and ally, putting effort into finding him independent clients apart from the Isokon architectural schemes. One important introduction was to Henry Morris, secretary to the Cambridgeshire Education Committee. Morris was a determined innovator, deeply committed to education and the arts. Already in 1924 he had produced a memorandum entitled 'The Village College' which he submitted to the County Council. This argued persuasively for the provision of a central community building in every Cambridgeshire village, a focus for local activities and services, a cultural gathering point which provided villagers with an education for life. 'There would be no leaving school,' wrote Morris. The village college would even provide prenatal classes, after which 'the child would enter at three and leave only at extreme age.' The report was unanimously accepted in 1925.

One of Morris's provisos was that Village Colleges should give opportunities for creative architecture, reflecting his ideas of introducing high artistic standards into local rural villages. But when Sawston, the first of the Cambridgeshire Colleges, was opened in 1930 by the Prince of Wales its neo-Georgian reality fell far short of these idealistic aims. Now, with three more Village Colleges in train, Jack Pritchard planned to remedy the situation. He hero-worshipped Henry Morris, as he had now begun to hero-worship Gropius, and he was determined that the two of them should meet.

Their first encounter took place at Lawn Road Flats. The result was 'orgasm!' according to Pritchard, their ideals of education so completely coincided. He then took both Gropius and Ise to stay with Henry Morris in his rooms in Trinity Street, Cambridge. The visit was clearly a success and Gropius sent Morris a copy of his *Internationale Architektur*, published at the Bauhaus, in appreciation. The introduction eventually led to Gropius's appointment as architect of Impington Village College, the most impressive and substantial of his English architectural works.

In those early months in London Gropius renewed contact with

Leonard and Dorothy Elmhirst. They were eager to employ him now he was a resident in England, and at the start the situation seemed hopeful. Gropius wrote rather boastfully to Martin Wagner, 'They have offered me a leading position and, like all Englishmen, respect highly previous achievements.' However, the Elmhirsts' contract with William Lescaze still had two years to run and the best that they could do for Gropius at this juncture was to ask him to advise on two farm cottages on the Dartington estate. In November 1934 Gropius drew up his 'Abridged Specification of Work and Materials required in the creation of proposed Manager's House and Farm Cottage at New Piggery, Yelland'. For an acknowledged maestro of European architecture this must have seemed a rather lowly job.

On 14 December Gropius and Ise took the train to Paignton, invited by the Elmhirsts for further discussions at Dartington itself. Gropius was still viewing Dartington as 'a sort of English "Bauhaus"' in the energy of its commitment to the arts and its concept of building a community in which art, craft, design, music and theatre could flourish. Dartington in fact was more Bauhaus-like than ever since the arrival earlier that year of Kurt Jooss, the German avant-garde choreographer and dancer, with the whole Jooss–Leeder school of dance from Essen. Jooss was a master of free expressive dance in the tradition of Laban, with whom he had trained. He was now notorious for his satiric ballet *Der Grüne Tisch* (*The Green Table*) and had come under mounting pressure from the Nazis. The generous and sympathetic Elmhirsts had offered a home to him and to his troupe, including its distinguished designer Hein Heckroth. The Jooss approach to dance and theatrical performance – abstract, visually powerful, psychologically intense – was very much that of theatre at the Bauhaus. For Gropius at this juncture the parallels must have seemed agonisingly close to home.

While Gropius was at Dartington there was some discussion of future possibilities. He was asked to consider converting a former barn and smithy into a small theatre. Gropius had already sent the Elmhirsts a copy of his Rome paper on Total Theatre, but this was homemade theatre on a rather different level. There was also the suggestion that Gropius might be appointed a consultant to advise on design of furniture to be manufactured at Dartington and sold in Dartington's London shop in Mount Street. But on the whole it was a disappointing visit, with no large architectural commissions being proposed.

On their return to London the Elmhirsts sent the Gropiuses a cheque with Christmas greetings, telling them this was an expression of warm welcome to their new country. In practice it was more of an apology.

———

By Christmas 1934 Gropius was feeling increasingly dispirited. Christmas had always been an emotional time. On Boxing Day he wrote to Martin Wagner lamenting that 'the mills in England grind very slowly' and that immense patience would be needed before he was able to get properly established. 'People in Germany have no idea of the wealth that exists here, of the good intentions of people to do something sensible with it, and of the general cluelessness and lack of artistic ability. An a-cultural country.' His visit to the ancient university town of Cambridge earlier that year had convinced him that the fundamentally conservative attitude of Englishmen made it impossible for them to appreciate anything new.

Gropius's growing frustration was increased by his inability to communicate. Although he was taking English lessons from a private tutor at the Anglo-German Academy and was simultaneously studying its English-language course for German students, progress was quite slow. Even nearly a year later he felt at a disadvantage in sitting beside H. G. Wells at a formal London dinner, embarrassed into silence: 'with my three words of English, I dare not yet have interesting conversations with such fastidious personalities'.

He was also embarrassingly short of funds, not having been permitted to bring money out of Germany. The travel allowance advanced to him in Rome by his Dutch supporter van der Leeuw was soon used up. Jack Pritchard could not afford to give Gropius more than a minimal fee for work in advance planning of Isokon projects. Ise reminded Pritchard later of how they were sometimes at desperation point:

Don't you remember the little tricks we used in London when we were invited to glamorous dinners and people asked politely where our car was and we said we loved a brisk walk through the fresh air and sneaked off towards the subway . . . And invitations to English country houses where the butler nonchalantly pocketed all our spare money. Oh golly.

Keeping up appearances in line with their perceived status was evidently a considerable strain.

The sense of dislocation felt by both Gropius and Ise in those first few months in England was acute. Gropius never quite forgot the closed-in feeling of a foggy London Sunday. His initial bafflement was similar to that of Fred Uhlman, to whom England seemed as puzzling and remote as China when he first arrived in Hampstead in 1936.

Another close comparison is with the writer Stefan Zweig, who, in February 1934, left Vienna to reach Victoria Station a few months ahead of Gropius. In a sense Zweig too was relieved to be in England, 'a guest of this kindly island', but like many other European exiles he was never fully integrated. During those years Zweig lived in England, from 1934 to 1940, he describes himself existing in a kind of vacuum, 'only spatially and not with his own soul, endlessly anxious about the close friends and family he had left behind in Europe to be kidnapped and humiliated and worse'. Gropius, with so many vulnerable associates and friends in avant-garde European circles, many of them of Jewish ancestry, was haunted by just those fears.

Gropius and Molly Pritchard, Ise and Jack Pritchard on the roof celebrating
the first anniversary of Lawn Road Flats, 1935.

In early February 1935 Gropius sent Manon a determinedly upbeat letter describing his attendance at the inauguration of the new RIBA headquarters at 66 Portland Place. This restrained neo-Swedish edifice designed by Grey Wornum was despised by the MARS group of modernists in London. Gropius, surprisingly, calls it 'a magnificent building', clearly thrilled by the occasion, at which he was well placed beside King George V, who was opening the building accompanied by

Queen Mary: 'he a somewhat stooped and ill-looking papa, she quite regal in bearing'. His greatest enthusiasm was reserved for the Prince of Wales, the future Edward VIII, whom Gropius found remarkable in his informed attitude to architecture, having heard him speak at a dinner at the RIBA: the prince 'functions like a true revolutionary in his circle of English architects and I could subscribe to his every word. As a solution to London's slum problem, he called for high-rise housing with open green spaces and for the assistance of industry in the manufacturing of such housing. Exactly my program for years now.'

This was the last letter Gropius ever wrote to Manon. On 22 April, Easter Monday, he received a telegram giving him the news that her condition had suddenly worsened and his daughter was now dangerously ill.

It was getting on for a year since he had seen her in Vienna. He had little idea of her day-to-day existence. As described by the writer Elias Canetti, a frequent visitor to the house on the Hohe Warte, for the past twelve months Manon 'had been presented in a wheelchair, attractively dressed, her face carefully made up, a costly rug over her knees, her waxen face alive with false hope. Real hope, she had none.' Her enthusiasm for the theatre continued and she was now encouraged by Alma to give little private performances at home. Werfel even took time off from his work to coach her in the lead of his German version of La forza del destino. According to Alma, Manon 'looked quite regal in black tights, doublet and hose, and spoke from her wheel chair like a consummate actress'.

Her mother encouraged troops of visitors, admirers and suitors to visit the sick room, and almost unbelievably, with Alma's connivance, Manon had got engaged to a young Austro-fascist, Erich Cyhlar, a bureaucrat in the office of the Patriotic Front and a protégé of Alma's priestly lover Johannes Hollnsteiner. Alma, possibly aware her illness would be terminal, appeared anxious to fulfil her daughter's hopes and expectations. Evidently Gropius was not informed.

In the week before Easter in April 1935 Manon started having breathing problems, headaches and vomiting. It seems this could have been brought on by an aggressive form of X-ray treatment aimed at controlling the paralysis. On Easter Saturday she seemed to be improving but during the night she began deteriorating. On Easter Sunday morning, sensing she was dying, Manon asked for a priest. Alma summoned Johannes Hollnsteiner from far away in Upper Austria. He arrived in his fast car, driving across country at a quite unpriestly speed. At this point a consortium of at least five doctors had been gathered around Manon. Most of them left at 10 p.m., still feeling generally optimistic, leaving just one doctor, two nurses and Alma at the bedside. But by the early morning the situation was obviously hopeless. It was only at this point that her father was alerted.

The cable Alma sent him arrived at Lawn Road Flats. Alma gave him no details of Manon's worsening condition, only saying he must take the first plane to Vienna. Alarmed, he and Jack Pritchard started desperately trying to make travel arrangements and organise official documents and visas, no mean feat on an English Easter Sunday afternoon. They had succeeded by the early evening, only to receive another telegram from Vienna. Manon had died at 3.40 in the afternoon. The cause of her death was officially given as acute gastrointestinal paralysis.

Gropius was still being kept at arm's length. This second telegram told him that because of regulations the funeral was taking place immediately. He sent an urgent message back imploring Alma to postpone the funeral in order to give him time to get there. Alma did not reply to his request, later claiming to have been in too distraught a state. It was Hollnsteiner who sent Gropius the detailed report on Manon's final days and told him that it had been impossible to delay the funeral, which in any case had been announced in the Vienna newspapers. He managed to blame Gropius for not visiting his daughter any earlier. Not much point now in arriving for her funeral. He had left it far too late.

Gropius and Ise flew to Berlin the day after Manon died, on Tuesday 23 April. They spent the next two days visiting Gropius's sister Manon in Hanover, then stayed on for another week in Berlin, finally moving their belongings out of the apartment in Potsdamer Privatstrasse to a smaller flat in Clausewitzstrasse and packing up the contents of Gropius's office, to be stored until their future plans became more certain.

At this point a return to Germany still seemed a possibility and Gropius arranged to sell off his family properties, including his mother's seaside house at Timmendorf, in order to fund an eventual return. He planned to continue from Berlin to Vienna to visit his daughter's grave, but because of the border restrictions now in force between Germany and Austria permission was refused.

In missing Manon's funeral Gropius was missing out on the process of sanctification that immediately followed Manon's death. She began to be perceived as almost otherworldly, not only within Alma's inner circle but more generally in Vienna and beyond. In Canetti's malicious account of the occasion, 'All Vienna was there, or at least everyone eligible to be received on Hohe Warte.' The mourners who crowded into the church included members of Vienna's political establishment: the entourage of Chancellor Kurt von Schuschnigg, who attended the funeral himself. Alma's lover Hollnsteiner was von Schuschnigg's priest. An object of sympathy was Manon's fiancé Erich Cyhlar, 'the impeccably dinner-jacketed secretary who followed the funeral service leaning on a column in the Heiligenstädter Church. That was the end of his engagement to Manon Gropius; she died as had been foreseen and instead of a wedding he had to content himself with a funeral.'

In the course of Canetti's account Alma makes her own statuesque appearance standing at the graveside, 'a voluptuous but aging penitent, a Magdalen rather than a Mary, equipped with swollen tears rather than contrition, magnificent specimens such as no painter had yet produced'. While her adored Hollnsteiner delivered the oration Alma's tears went on gushing 'until at length they festooned her fat cheeks like clusters of grapes'. Canetti's account may strike one as authentic. But was it a figment of false memory? In fact Alma, with her old horror of funerals, had not attended Manon's funeral at all.

Hollnsteiner's emotional oration delivered at the graveside in Grinzing cemetery dwelt on Manon's special qualities of innocence and grace: 'She blossomed like a wonderful flower. She went through the world as pure as an angel. She was joy and love to many.' A long, fulsome obituary by the musicologist and Alma admirer Ludwig Karpath which appeared a few days later in a Vienna newspaper described her thus: 'a wondrous creature with pure, chaste sensibilities, Manon wandered among us like an angel, adored by all the friends of the family, nurtured and cared for like a tender young shoot that is to be protected from all harm.' It is unlikely that the girl was quite so perfect. Her half-sister Anna's one-time husband Ernst Krenek found her mistrustful and deceitful. Manon's own piano teacher called her a spoiled brat. But the image of the sacrosanct child was now established. The legend of Manon had begun.

The most famous memorial to Manon is Alban Berg's 1935 Violin Concerto dedicated 'To the memory of an angel'. Not only has this two-movement concerto been regarded as a deeply moving tribute on the early death of a loved child, the composition has gathered extra poignancy from the fact that Berg himself died just a few months later as the result of a wasp or bee sting or (less romantically) an infected boil on the posterior. The Bergs' friendship with Alma dated back several decades. They had met very soon after Mahler's death and Berg's wife Hélène became one of Alma's closest companions, so much so that she had helped to look after the then tiny Manon while Alma was in hospital giving birth to Martin, Werfel's son. According to Alma, it was Berg himself who suggested that he should take time off from *Lulu*, the opera he was then composing, to write a new concerto in her memory. Berg had already accepted a commission from the American violinist Louis Krasner for a violin concerto, which up to now was making little progress, so this timing was convenient to him.

As so often in connection with Alma, the ramifications built up in complexity. For the past ten years, with Alma's connivance but unknown to Hélène, Berg had been having an affair with Franz Werfel's married sister Hanna Fuchs-Robettin. Berg was now forced to accept that the love affair was ending. It has been well argued from internal evidence in the concerto's composition, in particular the repeated use of the number twenty-three (associated with Berg himself) in conjunction with the number ten (indicating Hanna), that Manon was not the sole dedicatee of Berg's concerto. There was another angel: Berg's former lover Hanna.

The intricacies of the situation have rightly been compared to Arthur Schnitzler's play *Reigen*, the roundabout of love.

Gropius took Berg's memorial to Manon at face value. In the archive of family correspondence at Harvard we find that he kept the programme for the first British performance, held in the BBC Concert Hall in London on 1 May 1936. There is no definite proof that Gropius attended, but when a year later the Boston Symphony Orchestra performed the Berg concerto dedicated 'To the memory of an angel', he and Ise, by then living in America, were definitely in the concert hall.

There is a further echo of Manon in the Harvard archive: Gropius's belated specification for a monument to Mutzi in Grinzing cemetery. Alma had not wanted a tangible memorial to the daughter she, as a Theosophist, believed still remained with her in spirit. It was left to Manon's nurse, Ida Gebauer, to organise and pay for a simple cross, erected in 1942. By the end of the war the cross had been removed. It was only in 1955 that Gropius heard from Alma's nephew, Wilhelm Legler, himself an architect, about the dismaying condition of the grave. The tombstone Gropius designed takes the form of a triangle made in light grey granite, 10 cm thick, 144 cm long, that rests across the rectangular borders of the grassy plot. Manon's grave has a monumental simplicity, like an ancient Egyptian burial chamber. Eventually Alma was buried there as well.

'For my husband the death of his only child was a terrible blow,' Ise tells us. Gropius felt the loss of Mutzi deeply. He never quite got over it. His earlier biographer Reginald Isaacs, who had numerous conversations with Gropius in his final decades, remembers that thirty years after her death he still could not speak of Manon without pain.

She had been the child lost to him right from the beginning. Manon was inextricably bound up with his history of love and war with Alma, who, soon after Manon's death, attempting to be gracious, had thanked Gropius for his part 'in bringing Mutzi into the world although her road was short. There was incredible inner growth in the last six months of her life.' But, typically, Alma wrote in her private diary that Walter Gropius, 'the father of this angelic child, a brilliant architect', had nevertheless 'bored his own child to tears'. Was this remotely true? Almost certainly not. Gropius's letters to his daughter glowed with affection and amusing detail as he described his travels and his work, and the photographs we have of the two of them together indicate a very close rapport.

———

The early months of 1935 were altogether worrying for Gropius. Hoped-for Isokon architectural projects were collapsing. The block of flats in Didsbury in Manchester, the promise of which first brought Gropius to England, had now fallen through for lack of financial backing. By April Gropius was writing apologetically to Jack Pritchard, whose original offer of six months' free board and lodging was now expiring: 'I am ashamed not to be on my own legs yet after six months' work, but since Manchester had to be cancelled, my budget collapsed and new jobs had to be looked for. In two or three weeks, however, say from the first of May, I shall be able to pay at least board.' He asked if payment of his rent could be postponed until Isokon's major architectural project, the grand scheme for luxury housing at Windsor, was confirmed. But the Windsor scheme itself soon foundered. Because of the scale of the investment it required funding to be raised on the financial markets. A company was formed. Pritchard took a six-month option on the project. At a meeting of prospective supporters in London Gropius and Fry explained their model of the building. All seemed hopeful, but through this crucial period of fundraising Pritchard himself fell seriously ill and the project lost momentum, finally failing to meet financial deadlines. He wrote to Gropius sadly: 'You will think me a broken reed. You will think we asked you to London for nothing.' The Isokon scheme for modern flats at Manchester would eventually be abandoned too after virulent local opposition.

Work for Gropius at Dartington fared little better. Faced with Gropius's arrival on the scene William Lescaze, the American architect already under contract, wrote from New York to his ally W. B. Curry, headmaster of the school at Dartington, in some alarm: 'You, no doubt, know that Gropius has been at the hall, and I do realise that, what with his charm, his Bauhaus reputation and his friendship with Jooss, the situation may be very dangerous for me.' Lescaze also wrote an emotional letter to Leonard Elmhirst, reminding him and Dorothy of the amount of work and hope he had put into commissions for Dartington. Surely they would not let him down.

The result was that Gropius's scheme for the rebuilding of the Barn Theatre, which occupied him through the summer of 1935, was only a very small-scale job. He introduced new seating, an orchestra pit and a revolving stage backed by a plaster dome that formed a cyclorama, a feature that must have brought back family memories of the popular Gropius dioramas of early-nineteenth-century Berlin.

But the Barn Theatre commission at Dartington was far from the scope and scale of architectural work that Gropius had hoped for in travelling to Britain. The suggestion of his possible appointment as overall Dartington design consultant proved a disappointment too. Building on the experience of Bauhaus products Gropius suggested gradually assembling a collection of standard Dartington-made furniture designs of a unified character, developed by a group of young architects under his direction. The range could be extended into light fittings, metal door furniture, textiles and so on. These new products would be exhibited in London in room sets under the name of each designer. It was an imaginative scheme with great potential.

When William Slater, the Dartington managing director, suggested a derisory fee of one hundred guineas a year Gropius replied that he had been thinking in terms of 'a bigger work, both in point of size and in time' than had evidently been in Mr Slater's mind. As a compromise he offered to act as an adviser, but this proposal was never taken up.

Why was Gropius's arrival in England professionally speaking such a non-event? Why was he not more enthusiastically greeted? There are many obvious reasons, among them the predominantly Francophile aesthetic then ruling in British artistic circles, originally promoted by Roger Fry and the Bloomsbury Group. As described by Madge Garland in her survey of 1930s taste *The Indecisive Decade*, the *machine à habiter* ideas 'advocated by Walter Gropius and Mies van der Rohe at the Bauhaus in Dessau and preached by Le Corbusier in Paris were never popular in England where they appealed only to a few intellectuals: the work of such modernists was likened by Wyndham Lewis to a bitter pill in "the nature of paregoric or cod-liver oil to the over-sweet Anglo-Saxon palate".' Or as Anthony Blunt put it in a *Spectator* article, 'The Englishman in general dislikes functional architecture – the buildings of Le Corbusier, Gropius, Mendelsohn and the rest – because they are not *homey*.' The general consensus of opinion in mid-1930s Britain was that the Bauhaus style was rather grim.

'Bauhaus balls' was how Osbert Lancaster defined it. In the jokily complacent atmosphere of literary London the European architect was easily transformed into a comic character, the prime example being the austere, dogmatic Professor Otto Friedrich Silenus in Evelyn Waugh's novel *Decline and Fall*. He is brought in by the fashionable socialite Margot Beste-Chetwynde to demolish and rebuild her historic country house, King's Thursday, in a thoroughgoing modernist style.

Professor Silenus, an amalgam of Gropius and Moholy-Nagy, first attracted his new patron's attention 'with the rejected design for a chewing gum factory which had been reproduced in a progressive Hungarian quarterly'.

His only other completed work was the *décor* for a cinema film of great length and complexity of plot . . . 'The problem of architecture as I see it', he told a journalist who had come to report on the progress of his surprising creation of ferro-concrete and aluminium, 'is the problem of all art – the elimination of the human element from the consideration of form. The only perfect building must be the factory, because that is built to house machines, not men.'

The disbelieving giggle of the superior classes was an indication of what Gropius was up against in England.

He had other, broader prejudices to contend with. He was German, in a country where anguished memories of the Great War were still present. He was an alien in an architectural profession in which British architects themselves were short of work, sensitivities exploited by an article in *Fascist Week* reprinted in the *Architects' Journal*:

At a time when so many of our young and vital architects are in desperate positions, the Royal Institute of British Architects chooses to welcome alien architects and to encourage them in professional practice within this country . . . we have been affronted by the spectacle of prosperous British architects lavishing on these aliens, at big professional functions, encouragement which they conspicuously withhold from the younger architects of their race.

One target of this diatribe is obviously Gropius's 1934 exhibition and reception at the RIBA.

His lack of fluency in English remained a handicap in securing an official posting. In the early months of 1935 he was summoned for discussions about his possible involvement with the Royal College of Art. The part-time principal, the artist William Rothenstein, was resigning and the Board of Education was eager to restructure Britain's 'National College' of art and design training. Since the Gorell Committee Report of 1932 the British government had officially acknowledged the importance of design in relation to trade and the hope was now to reorganise the college in a way that would train designers specifically for future employment in British industry.

The idea of Gropius being brought in as adviser to the college was first suggested by Frank Pick, convinced that a possible role for the famous Dr Walter Gropius in reforming design education in Britain was too good an opportunity to pass by. Pick, a solicitor by training, was a well informed, meticulous and ambitious man, more focused than the majority of amiable, tweedy British design aficionados of the time. Pick was chief executive of the newly formed London Passenger Transport Board and had embarked on a huge exercise to modernise the London Underground, commissioning new architecture for the stations, new posters and maps, a new typeface designed by Edward Johnston. He believed implicitly in design for public good.

The ubiquitous Frank Pick was also chairman of the Council for Art and Industry, a body recently set up by the Board of Trade as part of the mission to improve design standards, and it was in this capacity he contacted the appointments committee for the RCA, setting out Gropius's credentials:

He was one of the leaders in the reform movement in Germany, and he started half a school half an industrial institution at Dessau, called the Bauhaus. It has been taken as a model for the organization of German art schools. As he is a refugee in this country at this present time, I am inclined to think we ought to make use of him in connection with the problems of the Royal College of Art.

Gropius and Pick met in January 1935, with Ise brought in as translator. The scheme didn't get much further. Gropius was never seriously considered as a future principal of the RCA, or even as a permanent director of design with a remit for design training along quasi-Bauhaus lines. The arguments against such an appointment focused not only on his difficulties with communication but also on his advanced age, Gropius being already in his early fifties, and the Treasury's probable reluctance to finance the employment of an alien. Alternative possibilities discussed were appointing Gropius as a nebulous general adviser to the RCA or, failing that, a giver of demonstration classes or, as a last resort, sending him out as a travelling inspector of the network of English trade-based art schools – the pottery school in Stoke-on-Trent, the textile school in Manchester – that the Council for Art and Industry was planning to set up.

Once Percy Jowett, a fairly well-known English Impressionist painter with no strong views on reforming design in industry, was appointed as Rothenstein's successor at the RCA he was encouraged to bring Gropius in to lecture. Jowett arranged a meeting, in the course of which Gropius interrogated him about his future plans and ambitions for the college, 'but of course this I could not tell him'. After this Gropius heard no more.

The only official use made of Gropius's wide European experience and knowledge was the evidence he gave to the Hambledon Committee appointed by the government to propose new guidelines for art and technical education. The whole episode shows how Gropius's arrival placed the 1930s British design establishment, such as it was, in a bit of a dilemma. The more enlightened, Frank Pick in particular, recognised his stature, but they could not work out precisely what to do with him.

Nor did Gropius himself improve the situation by his lack of commitment. One of the arguments given by the Board of Education against employing him to transform the RCA into an English Bauhaus was that he was in England probably only on a temporary basis. And indeed through this first year in England he was still being cautious, sending his annual statement to the German Finance Office, maintaining his official links with Germany, making it clear in press interviews that he was still a German citizen. He was careful to avoid any comment on politics, including the increasing Nazi vilification of modern art. He insisted on this condition of neutrality in agreeing to interviews, telling the American critic George Nelson, who was working on a study of European architects:

As I explained to you when we met in London, I am anxious to be certain that no political hints whatsoever should be given as to the general German attitude to the art I am an exponent of. Since all cultural things in Germany are not at all settled, every statement from outside would be premature and infringe my personal position.

Any statement from Gropius would of course also be likely to endanger his artistic associates, including many Bauhäusler. But in distancing himself from the art he had in the past so determinedly supported this was a kind of selling of his soul.

There were reasons for such wariness vis-à-vis the Nazis. He had written to Martin Wagner in December 1934, 'After the Fürtwangler affair I have a specially bitter taste in the mouth. Our crew is too known so that a whole clique would immediately rise against us, when we would be sanctioned.' Wilhelm Fürtwangler, an outspoken critic of Hitler and the Nazi party's racial and artistic policies, had defended the composer Paul Hindemith, branded by the Nazis as degenerate, going so far as to include a banned composition in a Berlin Philharmonic Orchestra programme he conducted. In the subsequent storm of protest by the Nazis Fürtwangler was forced by Goebbels to resign from his artistic positions. Gropius was well aware of how politically vulnerable he still was.

Cautiously he kept up his links with Eugen Hönig, still president of the Reichskulturkammer, the State Chamber of Culture. On a visit to London Hönig came to share a meal with Gropius at home at Lawn

Road Flats, accompanied by his colleague Carl Christoph Lörcher, a member of the Nazi Storm Troopers. Presumably the food was ordered up as usual from the Lawn Road communal kitchen. Ise recalled that all three of them had got on very well.

From all points of view, in relation both to Germany and England, Gropius's situation was painfully unsettled. He was still in the precarious position of attempting to reconcile two discordant worlds.

17

London

1935–1936

In spite of the disappointments and frustrations of Gropius's initial year in London there was a very gradual shifting of perceptions, a dawning recognition of the aims and importance of the Bauhaus and the achievements of Gropius himself. Herbert Read's groundbreaking study *Art and Industry: The Principles of Industrial Design* was published by Faber & Faber in 1934, with a cover design by Herbert Bayer, and went through several editions over the next two years. In it Read quoted at length from the paper Gropius gave to the Design and Industries Association on that early visit to London in May 1934. He concluded:

I have no other desire in this book than to support and propagate the ideals thus expressed by Dr. Gropius; ideals which are not restricted to the written word, but which have been translated into action . . . In every practical activity the artist is necessary to give form to material. An artist must plan the distribution of cities within a region; an artist must plan the distribution of buildings within a city; an artist must plan the houses themselves, the halls and factories and all that makes up a city; an artist must plan the interiors of such buildings – the shapes of their rooms and their lighting and colour; an artist must plan furniture of those rooms, down to the smallest detail, the knives and forks, the cups and saucers and the door handles.

Read transformed Walter Gropius's early halting words into a model of lucidity.

This process of familiarisation with Gropius and his ideas continued with a series of pro-modernist articles in the *Architectural Review* in 1934 and 1935 generated by Gropius's maverick supporter Philip Morton Shand and entitled 'Scenario to a Human Drama'. In charting the evolution of twentieth-century architecture Morton Shand makes grand claims for Gropius, comparing him in stature to the eighteenth-century English neo-classical architect Sir John Soane as 'a great man, as well as a great pioneer and a great teacher'. Illustrating the article with photographs of both the Fagus factory and Gropius's own Director's House at Dessau, Morton Shand traces a pedigree from Soane to John Ruskin to Gropius's mentor Peter Behrens, claiming Gropius as the major influence on modern architecture.

This reverence for Gropius as part of an apostolic architectural succession reached new heights in Nikolaus Pevsner's *Pioneers of the Modern Movement: From William Morris to Walter Gropius*, then in its gestation and published in 1936. Evelyn Waugh's depiction of Professor Otto Friedrich Silenus, the comic continental functionalist architect, was now being at least marginally undermined.

Gropius's own book *The New Architecture and the Bauhaus* was published in London by Faber in July 1935. The commission had been brought about by Herbert Read, himself a Faber author, and Morton Shand undertook the translation of Gropius's German text. The book gives an account of Gropius's architectural philosophy, illustrated with examples of his work in Germany, from the Fagus factory to the aborted scheme of 1931 for high-rise apartments on the Wannsee shore. Gropius tells his own story of the beginnings of the Bauhaus, when he was summoned in his military uniform to an audience with the Grand Duke of Saxe-Weimar, and the subsequent development of the institution he virtually invented. His book includes photographs of what Gropius describes as 'typical products of the Bauhaus which were adopted as models for mass-production by German manufacturers and which also influenced foreign industrial design': spherical glass and metal light fittings; china tableware designed by Otto Lindig; the prototype minimum kitchen installed in the Haus am Horn; Otti Berger's textiles; Marcel Breuer's tubular steel chairs. A constant theme for Gropius is the way that new materials and technologies open out fresh opportunities in living human life. An architecture of glass and steel and concrete allows new flexibilities, enchanting new amusements. Gropius waxes lyrical in descriptions of glass, 'its sparkling insubstantiality, and the way it seems to float between wall and wall imponderably as the air'. These are passages in which Gropius reminds the reader of his youthful involvement in the utopian *Glasarchitektur* movement. Even now in middle age and in another country he is still attracted to the mystic architecture of the floating world.

Gropius's wide-ranging and at times philosophically complex book caused Faber considerable problems in production. His editor was Richard de la Mare, son of the poet Walter de la Mare. A rather plodding introduction was contributed by Frank Pick. Gropius himself had originally undertaken to design the jacket but at the last minute he pulled out as a result of Manon's death, and the job was handed over to László Moholy-Nagy, who at the time was still living in Berlin.

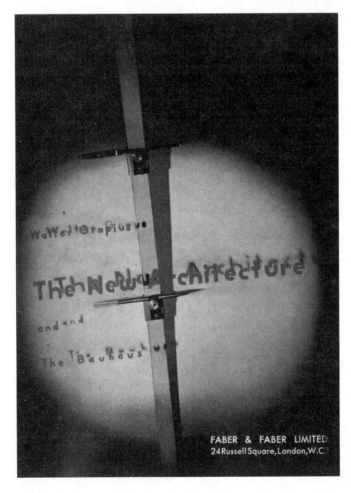

László Moholy-Nagy's jacket design for Gropius's *The New Architecture and the Bauhaus*, published by Faber & Faber in 1935.

Morton Shand, having agreed to translate Gropius's text, discovered he had taken on far more than he had bargained for as the book increased in length and Gropius's thought processes became more convoluted and harder and harder to translate. In Faber's archive there are poignant letters from Morton Shand's wife Sybil saying that the strain of disentangling Gropius's worst passages of 'metaphysical abracadabra' was now making her husband ill. Morton Shand himself lamented, 'Quite between ourselves, I think we may have some trouble with the author who has made attempts to include a wholly incomprehensible passage which effectively mars such unity as I have been able to give to the book.' He was laid low with bronchitis in December 1934 and in March 1935 he was ill again, apologising for delays in delivery and telling Faber, 'I may say that I have never had a more difficult job in the whole course of my life, and it has been the strenuousness of it which has led to this temporary breakdown.' To add to the upsets Morton Shand, who had originally been paid £15 5s for the translation, was later sent a bill for £6 14s for his own corrections, which, understandably, he refused to pay.

The New Architecture and the Bauhaus was finally published on 19 July 1935, with a print run of two thousand copies. Undoubtedly it raised Gropius's public profile and did something to increase understanding in Britain of what the Bauhaus was and the extent of what he had achieved. Gropius was desperate for maximum exposure, fussing when the review he had expected in *The Times* failed to appear and complaining that the book had not been mentioned in the *Times Literary Supplement* or *The Listener*: 'I should like to discover why they have not dealt with it so far.' But on the whole review coverage was generous. Philip Morton Shand rose to the occasion, undertaking to make sure that 'the best man gets the first chance of reviewing it'. He had corralled the usual suspects, the known Gropius supporters and admirers. He also, possibly less usefully, suggested that Faber should distribute copies to libraries in far-flung places such as Iceland, Estonia and Lithuania, where exposure of the book might well result in sales.

The ever-reliable J. M. Richards provided Gropius with a double accolade, with reviews appearing both in the *Architectural Review* and in the *Burlington Magazine* in which he claims: 'Professor Gropius, with the humility that belongs to greatness, hardly gives himself credit in his book for the degree to which he was personally responsible for the architectural regeneration of Europe during the years after the war.'

The hoped-for review in *The Listener* finally appeared, in which the architect Raymond McGrath praised Gropius's concept of 'the new spatial vision', comparing the agility and discipline of the Bauhaus building in Dessau with the lumbering Shell-Mex House in London, completed in 1931.

In the *Sunday Express* John Betjeman wrote effusively about Gropius's achievements at the Bauhaus in introducing standardised design of 'everyday objects such as lamp fixtures, teacups, fabrics and chairs':

These were made with an eye to mass production. German manufacturers bought Bauhaus designs and the result is that most modern flats and houses in Germany have nothing so repulsively pretentious to show as the various modernistic designs which glisten in many a British parlour, the artistic inspiration of some purely commercial workshop. Would that Professor Gropius would re-found a Bauhaus in England!

But Betjeman was then an all-purpose journalist veering in his tastes from the Victorian-nostalgic to the modern and his praise of Gropius's championing of prefabricated housing and ten- or eleven-storey office and apartment blocks does not ring quite true.

It was Anthony Blunt's review in the *Spectator* that was the most enthusiastically convincing. He began by pointing out the problems for Gropius in being understood in an English visual culture still dominated by French influence and perversely neglectful of the German. In painting Picasso and Matisse had been the names to conjure with; in architecture Le Corbusier, to the detriment of Gropius, who in the view of Blunt 'has to his credit an achievement of greater importance than that of any other living architect. Other people have built good buildings or written good books about architecture, but Professor Gropius is the only architect who has attempted a practical solution of the fundamental problems presented by the new relation of art and industry.' The invention of the Bauhaus was Gropius's important and indeed unique achievement.

In his thoughtful, well-argued, even passionate review Blunt praises the inclusion of so many illustrations of Gropius's architectural work, suggesting that 'it will be a revelation to some English readers to see how far Professor Gropius had already advanced along new paths by 1911, when he was putting up buildings which would look reckless in England at the present day. It is perhaps worth adding that the book is admirably produced and has a brilliant photomontage jacket by Professor Moholy-Nagy.' Blunt was the only reviewer to point this out.

Review coverage of *The New Architecture and the Bauhaus* was by no means limited to London. Interest was wider. 'Why Not a City of Leafy Housetops?' was the heading for an article in the *Glasgow Evening News* which optimistically applied Walter Gropius's ideals of light, airy, spacious development of cities to Glasgow's 'stony desert' of claustrophobic tenements. The Liverpool Professor of Architecture, Charles Reilly, reviewed the book enthusiastically for the *Lancashire Guardian*.

In the end this relatively small-scale book had more exposure than Faber or perhaps even Gropius expected. All the same, when the *New English Weekly* described Gropius as 'one of the most remarkable men of genius', this was still a far from widely accepted view.

———

Gropius himself still felt a strong attachment to the Bauhaus and to individual Bauhäusler, and working on the book can only have intensified these memories. The whole experimental ethos, the sense of art and life being joined in symbiosis, remained with many Bauhaus students all their lives.

When Gropius came to London he brought with him a neatly typed address list covering the contacts he had left behind in Germany, from Adlerwerke to Wagner. This touching little document remains among his papers. Many of the names listed are those of Gropius's former Bauhaus associates and colleagues, with whose histories he stayed emotionally entwined. Already there were haunting stories of the intimidation and dismissal of ex-colleagues, many of them Jewish, whom Gropius knew well.

The weaver Gunta Stölzl, who was married to the Jewish-Palestinian architect Arieh Sharon, was victimised by communist students at the Bauhaus after Gropius's departure. They piled up anti-Semitic accusations against her and even fixed a swastika on her door. In 1931 Stölzl resigned and left Dessau, emigrating to Switzerland.

The ceramicist Marguerite Friedlaender had gone on to design standardised ranges of tableware for mass production by the KPM (Imperial Porcelain Manufacture) or, as it became under the Nazis, the StPM (State Porcelain Manufacture). Once the Nazis came to power Friedlaender was dismissed from her teaching post and she fled, first to Switzerland, then Holland. Her porcelain designs continued to be made by the StPM but the name of the designer was now censored.

Margarete Heymann (later known as Grete Marks) set up her own factory, the Haël Workshops for Art and Ceramics, with her husband. At its busiest the factory in Marwitz employed 120 people. But once Jewish-owned businesses started to be taken over by the Nazis the Haël workshops were vulnerable. On 1 July 1933 she took the decision to close the workshops down, and ten months later she was forced to sell the business for the derisory sum of 45,000 RM. She was threatened with imprisonment by the Gestapo but escaped to Bornholm before finally arriving in England in 1936.

The story of Marianne Brandt affected Gropius more closely. She was the design star of the metal workshop. Once Gropius left the Bauhaus, Brandt joined him in Berlin, working in his architectural office; she looked back on this as 'a happy, if all too brief, time'. When work in Potsdamer Privatstrasse evaporated Gropius helped her to find alternative employment at Ruppel, a metalwork factory in Gotha. But this job petered out as well and in 1932 Brandt, a sensitive and melancholic personality, retreated to her parents' house in Chemnitz. Brandt's well-publicised connection to the Bauhaus, besides the highly disciplined and consciously non-*gemütlich* style of her design, made her an object of suspicion to the Nazis, in addition to the fact that she had married a Norwegian. Through much of the 1930s and beyond there was a long period during which the woman described by

Moholy-Nagy as his best and most gifted student simply disappeared.

For Gropius, too, these were students he had nurtured. In a sense he still considered them his people, successors imbued with something of his own idealistic artistic aspirations. As he was later to painfully discover, there were even sadder stories of Bauhäusler to come.

———

Two of his closest Bauhaus friends and colleagues joined Gropius in London in 1935, László Moholy-Nagy in May and Marcel Breuer in October. Both started life in England in the Pritchards' ever-welcoming Lawn Road Flats. Moholy travelled to England from the Netherlands, where he had been living temporarily, working as a commercial artist after leaving an increasingly hostile Berlin. In the previous October he received a summons from Goebbels's headquarters to make a personal submission of three of his abstract paintings for assessment by the jury of the Reichskulturkammer. His departure for the Netherlands and from there to London was only just in time. On arrival at Lawn Road, Moholy was welcomed by a five-guinea payment cheque from Faber for his work in designing the photomontage jacket for Gropius's *New Architecture and the Bauhaus*. His now ex-wife, the photographer Lucia, had already moved to London. Moholy's own move was encouraged by his new love Sibyl Pietzsch, the writer and ex-actress, whom he had married on a brief visit to London in January 1935.

Moholy considered English tolerance, an inbuilt love of understatement and self-deprecation and above all widespread English amateurism to be the perfect antidote to the 'heavy German cult of professionalism'. He blamed rigid specialisation for the dangerous direction German politics had taken. 'England was the country of the amateur – it was his country,' Moholy now felt.

He and Sibyl and their eighteen-month-old daughter Hattula were allotted the flat next to the Gropiuses, No. 16. They lived there for about three months before moving on to Golders Green. But their time in Lawn Road made a lasting impression. Sibyl's later memories included the surprise of arriving at a block of flats 'where all the doors looked the same and had NUMBERS instead of apartment entrances'; the dinner at the Gourmets' Club, a gathering of foodies that later generated the *Good Food Guide*, when the *'pückler'* ice cream dessert on the menu turned out to be made of Roquefort cheese; the disconcerting showing of a ciné film of the Pritchards with their boys and Henry Morris 'frolicking over the hills and dales of England in the stark nude, and we were somewhat shocked, this being 1935 and not 1969'.

On that same evening at Lawn Road Flats Moholy showed the first rushes of *London Zoo*, a film he was making with the evolutionary biologist Julian Huxley. Many of Moholy's professional commissions during his time in England came through his connections on the Hampstead circuit. He worked with the documentary director John Mathias on a film about the sex life of the lobster. The graphic artist and art director Ashley Havinden landed him the post of designer of shop interiors and shop windows in the traditional men's outfitters Simpson's of Piccadilly, where he wittily subverted the whole sartorial image of the English gentleman.

John Betjeman introduced him to Penguin publisher Harry Paroissien, who commissioned Moholy's edgily observant photographs for three books on traditional English life, *The Street Markets of London*, *Eton Portrait* and *An Oxford University Chest*. Jack Pritchard alleged that it was Betjeman who took Moholy to a party 'at the end of which he said to the hostess in his strange pronunciation; "Thank you for your hostilities." She was a little taken aback, and when Moholy told John Betjeman what had happened, Betjeman said: "oh don't worry – she is hostile to everyone."'

While he was in London Moholy tried to galvanise support for creating a British Bauhaus. This was by no means a new idea. As early as 1931 Herbert Read, then Professor of Fine Art in Edinburgh, had attempted to arouse interest and raise money for a centre of modern art in Edinburgh modelled on the Bauhaus, a project intended to restore the city to the position it had once held at the centre of late-Georgian intellectual life. This scheme foundered. Now, with Gropius himself a resident in Hampstead, the Bauhaus idea was resurrected, with meetings between Moholy, Pritchard, Richard Carline, the surrealist painter

Peter Dawson, Henry Moore, Roland Penrose, Peggy Guggenheim and others. Carline, a painter and a central figure in 1930s Hampstead, living in a house on Downshire Hill, later felt that 'alas, the project never had much prospect, owing to the lack of funds, and, more important, the absence of support in the art circles of London of that time'.

Nor is it certain that Gropius, who attended at least some of these meetings, was altogether sold on the idea. His experiences with the Royal College of Art may have acted as a warning. After so many upheavals was even the optimistic workaholic Gropius now simply running out of energy? When the graphic designer Ashley Havinden said to him, 'Walter, how marvellous for us that you are now in England, because you can start a much needed Bauhaus in this country,' his reply was 'Ashley – I couldn't do it again.'

Throughout the early 1930s Marcel Breuer had been rootless and depressed, travelling in Europe and Morocco, sending frequent letters back to Ise – '*liebe pia, pia mia*' – with whom he was on very affectionate terms. In May 1934 he wrote to her from Zurich, bemoaning the political climate: 'there is a fog over everything,' he told her, including what he saw as the inevitable next European war. On Christmas Day he wrote from Budapest, having heard the Gropiuses' news from England: 'Your letter sounds like a fairy tale.' Already in his mind was the possibility of making a move to join them there, and presumably at Gropius's suggestion Breuer had already been in contact with the English modernist architect F. R. S. Yorke to sound out a possible partnership. He could not come to London without definite prospects of architectural work.

In the Lawn Road residency list for 1935 the name 'Herr Breuer' is registered as occupying Flat 16, the flat next to the Gropiuses which Sibyl and Moholy had recently vacated. Breuer's arrival was in itself a drama, in that he smuggled money out of Germany by secreting banknotes between the pages of a paperback edition of Hitler's *Mein Kampf*, addressing the packet to Carola Giedion. She and her husband Sigfried were also then staying with the Pritchards at Lawn Road. Carola, horrified by the arrival of Hitler's 'hated diatribe' in Hampstead, threw the book straight away into the communal rubbish bins. Once Breuer arrived, dismayed to find his money gone, there was a desperate hunt through the decaying rubbish until the banknotes were eventually retrieved.

Like the Gropiuses Breuer became integral to life at Lawn Road Flats, present at the Pritchards' celebrations and parties, exuding his Hungarian flirtatiousness and charm. Afterwards he looked back fondly on Lawn Road and its ambience, writing about the flats as if they were a person in a letter from America: 'I always liked that girl . . . She is a generous wench, a friendly and hospitable one – not careful with what she has. I wish all pretty girls were the same.'

Another ex-Bauhaus arrival at Lawn Road, perhaps not such a welcome one, was Herbert Bayer. The Gropiuses's adopted daughter Ati later had the theory that one of Gropius's motives in moving to England had been to bring about a decisive final separation of Bayer and Ise. But Ashley Havinden, himself greatly influenced by Bayer's work, vividly remembered meeting him at a party at Lawn Road. It seems that Bayer was in London for only a few weeks, returning to Berlin to resume his practice. He had deep misgivings about the regime in Germany, writing to tell Ise in November 1935 that the devil was 'altogether on the loose there'. But Bayer's policy was discreet accommodation with the Nazis and at this juncture he was designing the prospectus for the now notorious 1936 Berlin Olympic Games.

Towards the end of 1935 Gropius's finances were once again in crisis and he was writing sadly to his host, taking some of the blame for recent failures in getting Pritchard's Isokon architectural projects off the ground: 'Gropius is a bad job for Isokon . . . You and I we both have risked and I hope to be as good a loser as you are, making a new start.' Things were so desperate he was now endeavouring to borrow some stopgap money from a friend, the ever-accommodating C. H. van der Leeuw. Pritchard too was generosity itself, telling Gropius, 'You must not worry about the risk I took and lost. The risks you have to take are so much bigger than mine, which are in the ordinary way of business.' He insisted that Gropius should stay on at Lawn Road without paying any rent and, more constructively, invented a new job for Gropius as design consultant to a furnishing company he was now forming, the London Aluminium

Company Ltd. Gropius was to carry out designs himself and to help in selecting a staff designer, for which he would be paid a consultancy fee 'somewhat the equivalent' of the rent for 15 Lawn Road Flats. On the strength of this generous offer Gropius decided to refurbish and redecorate the flat, specifying a new colour scheme in beige and white.

He embarked on designing a whole range of products for the London Aluminium Company, among them folding chairs and tables, teapots and coffee pots, trays and wastepaper baskets. Of these it appears that only the anodised aluminium wastepaper basket ever saw the light of day. Pritchard then formed a subsidiary company, the Isokon Furniture Company, of which Gropius was appointed Controller of Design in January 1936. Gropius proposed that Marcel Breuer should be appointed Isokon's designer and that the first product should be a reclining chair made of plywood. While they were on a trip to Zurich Jack and Molly Pritchard had already seen and much admired an earlier long chair designed by Breuer in lightweight aluminium and had ordered one for their Lawn Road penthouse. They eagerly agreed to Gropius's idea. Breuer's Isokon Long Chair in laminated plywood still stands as a rare and very beautiful example of the 1930s British spirit of modernity.

From the Bauhaus years onwards Breuer's furniture designs had a particular quality of flexibility and freedom. He developed the theory that furniture needed to be 'free in space': 'that any object properly and functionally designed should "fit" into any room as does a living object, like a flower or a human being'. And indeed the architect Clive Entwistle maintained that the Isokon Long Chair had an economy of form and flowing line comparable with that of an orchid or a leopard. Its surrealist quality was emphasised in publicity material commissioned from Moholy, a photomontage showing a contemporary couple both sitting in Long Chairs facing one another, separated by a streamlined light fitting and a table, a scene that had actually been staged in the Pritchards' penthouse flat. The leaflet included Moholy's little drawing of a figure floating in a bath, suggesting that reclining in the Long Chair would seem similarly, pleasurably weightless. The experience would be that of a strangely delicious sensual dream.

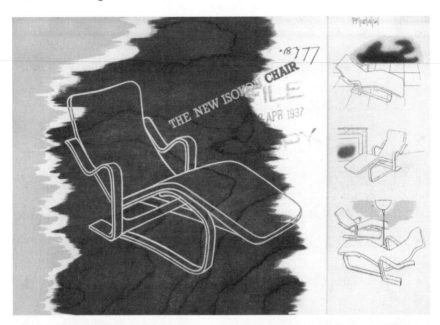

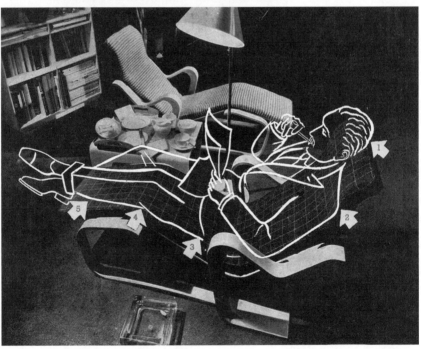

Sales leaflet for the Isokon Long Chair
designed by Marcel Breuer.
Graphics by László Moholy-Nagy, 1937.

Amongst a small sophisticated section of society the Isokon Long Chair became a cult object. Ten of them were ordered to be ranged around the swimming pool in the new luxury flats in Dolphin Square in Westminster. Breuer also designed Isokon plywood dining chairs and tables. Isokon furniture was sold at Heal's, Dunn's of Bromley and John Lewis and exhibited by the MARS group in the New Burlington Galleries. And needless to say it was essential to the scene in Molly Pritchard's own professional consulting rooms in Upper Harley Street.

———

In January 1936 there was a new arrival at Lawn Road Flats. This was Ati, Ise's niece, daughter of her sister Hertha. Hertha, an epileptic who was always delicate, had recently become seriously ill. She had died on New Year's Day. Ise went to fetch the now ten-year-old Ati from Berlin. For a bereft, bewildered child it was a terrible experience. She was desperately seasick on a stormy Channel crossing, sick again on the train journey to London. She felt still worse when Ise gave her her first strange bowl of porridge, hoping to calm her down. Gropius and the Pritchards met her and drove her across London to Lawn Road. She remembered, 'The sky was leaden, and the air was cold and damp even inside the large white apartment house where we finally arrived, and where I was tucked into a room.' This was a small room, 'a cubicle of white walls and a bare floor' on the floor above the Gropiuses, part of the Pritchards' own penthouse. Ati's little cell had been cleared of the toys belonging to the Pritchards' own children, Jonathan and Jeremy, who were now away boarding at Beacon Hill, Dora Russell's school.

Ise had been ill all through the previous autumn, finally going to recuperate at Dartington at the Elmhirsts' invitation. The immediate cause was a recurrence of the gynaecological problems that had dogged her since the early days of her marriage, and now specialists in England had established, contrary to hopes held out to her previously in Germany, that she would never be able to have children. An exploratory operation revealed that the whole reproductive area was 'hopelessly clogged by adhesions'. The arrival of her niece was now a kind of compensation. For Gropius too, still grieving for the recent loss of Manon, Ati became the substitute daughter, the replacement. Their plan now was to adopt Ati officially and bring her up as a daughter of their own.

Ise made great efforts at integrating Ati, organising language lessons, swimming lessons, reading books in English with her. Art lessons for Ati, which she later suspected were subsidised by Pritchard, were laid on too. All the same Ati was evidently lonely, feeling stranded, tending to stare longingly out of the big windows at the many cats which wandered through the greenery behind the flats. Though pets at Lawn Road Flats were against the rules, Ise secretly brought in a little dormouse which entertained Ati by sipping sherry from a glass until, having ventured out onto the balcony, it was finally demolished by an owl.

Jack Pritchard was endlessly jovial and kindly, indoctrinating Ati into the strange experience of swimming in Hampstead Pond once the boys returned from boarding school. 'Jack and the boys took off their clothes and, white-skinned as fillets of sole, jumped in. I was as frozen by the sight of them as by the touch of the pond. This, however, was only the beginning of my English education.' They went for rambles, with rucksacks on their backs, through the English countryside, and it was Pritchard who decided that Ati too must go to Dora Russell's school.

He took her on a visit to Beacon Hill school, having cunningly shown her around several more traditional English boarding schools en route which Ati considered as alien and grim as the Nazi schools she had left behind. Arriving there Ati was immediately thrilled:

Shrieking and giggling half-naked children raced randomly over the lawns, paying no attention to our presence, or that of any adults. There was a swimming pool somewhere behind the overgrown hedges of roses, and the sound of splashing and wild cavorting filled the air. There appeared to be no discernible discipline or order of any kind, and I knew instantly that I loved the place.

Beacon Hill was one of a small group of radical boarding schools in 1930s Britain, which also included A. S. Neill's Summerhill and W. B. Curry's school at Dartington. These schools set out to challenge conventional views of education. 'My own belief', Bertrand Russell wrote, 'is that education must be subversive if it is to be meaningful.' At Beacon Hill attendance at classes was voluntary. The school had a council in which the children were free to make their own mistakes. Ati took to Beacon Hill immediately, finding it 'a child's garden of earthly delights'. There was constant encouragement for children's creativity, in drama, art and craft. For Ati the art room was a centre of activity. Beacon Hill's view of the importance of young people's self-discovery, finding their own direction perhaps as an artist or designer, of course reflected Gropius's own deeply held ideals.

———

For Gropius's own architectural work the following two years brought further setbacks. He had been particularly pleased when he and Maxwell Fry were invited to submit designs for a new building at Christ's College in Cambridge, hoping that this prestige commission in a historic university city, bringing links to the intellectual elite, would help him to establish his position in Britain as an influential architect. The commission was for a student dormitory block with adjoining staff accommodation. Gropius and Fry evolved a modern building that faced inwards to form part of the traditional Cambridge college quadrangle and outwards into Hobson Street in Cambridge town, at which point the building included ten commercial shops. The design was for a steel construction with a natural stone facade which, Gropius argued, would reconcile the modern with its historic setting. In stressing to the mainly hidebound Cambridge dons that he was following the architectural precepts of the old masters Gropius was evidently trying hard.

Christ's College's internal supporters of the scheme were biologist C. H. Waddington, the physicist J. D. Bernal and the scientist and writer C. P. Snow. The meeting at Christ's on 2 March 1937, when Gropius made his presentation to the college, would have made a good scene in one of Snow's novels of university life. The motion to appoint Walter Gropius as 'architect of the new building forthwith' was rejected by the assembled college fellows by thirteen votes to eight. A neo-Georgian design by the traditionalist architect Sir Albert Richardson was eventually built. This episode was more or less repeated at Oxford at this same period over Maxwell Fry's proposals for a new building at All Souls.

In 1936 Gropius and Fry had started an architectural project for Denham Film Processing Laboratories which at first seemed hopeful but which turned out to be another disappointment. The Denham Film Studios were founded by Alexander Korda, originally Sándor László Kellner, who was biased towards his fellow émigrés and as well as Gropius employed his Hungarian compatriot László Moholy-Nagy to provide weirdly wonderful special effects for a film based on H. G. Wells's *The Shape of Things to Come.*

In theory the Denham project should have been ideal for Gropius, drawing on his expertise in industrial architecture in a way that no British commission had yet done. But in fact it gave him very little scope. The steel frame for the building was already in place. There were technical restrictions in that the laboratories needed to be fully air-conditioned and conform to strict fire and safety regulations. It was such a rushed job that Gropius found to his frustration that the clients gave instructions directly to the builders without stopping to consult the architect. He was so discontented with the final result he refused to allow the building to be publicised and refused to accept any further commissions from such problem clients. But at least the Denham Film Processing Laboratories yielded a much-needed £750 fee.

Gropius's most showy and in that sense least characteristic English building is a house in Old Church Street in Chelsea completed in 1936. The commission came from a well-known couple in show business: Benn Levy, the playwright and scriptwriter for the movies, and his wife, the actress Constance Cummings. Cummings remembered Gropius as 'a charming man'.

The site was bought jointly by the Levys and their close friends, the publisher Dennis Cohen and his wife. The Cohens commissioned their own house from Eric Mendelsohn and Serge Chermayeff and the friends planned to share the large garden in between their two new houses of luxurious modernity.

Left to himself Gropius's choice would have been for a house faced in natural brick. He was, as we have seen, very much conscious of historical context, seeing himself as the descendant of Schinkel in Berlin and, now he was in London, as the natural follower of Soane. Already Gropius was attuned to the quiet discipline of London eighteenth- and early-nineteenth-century brick terraced housing and many of the houses in Old Church Street opposite the Levy site were in fact brick-faced. But the Cadogan Estate, owner of the freehold, insisted that the house should be rendered in 'Snowcrete', a sparkling white finish applied to two nearby houses by the fashionable architect Oliver Hill.

Gropius employed another recent German émigré, Albrecht Proskauer (later known as Aubrey Edward Prower), as his draughtsman on the Levy House, planned as a family home on a large scale with accommodation for a butler and three maids. Facilities for glamorous entertaining included a special curved window seat for musical evenings and huge sliding

Gropius, house in Old Church Street, Chelsea, for Benn Levy and Constance Cummings, 1936.

windows which could be thrown open for guests to exit to the terrace. The house has a whiff of Hollywood. Originally Gropius himself designed the furnishings for what he envisaged as a complete ensemble, but the Levys brought in their own antiques. However, he devised a beautiful sweeping central staircase and also provided a special heated stand for exotic plants and cacti. The Levys evidently shared his own cactus mania.

Gropius's curvaceous building was admired in its day by the few British aficionados of the modern and included in his book *The Modern House in England* by Marcel Breuer's then partner F. R. S. Yorke. But tastes change and by 1969 the post-modernist architect Theo Crosby called it 'a perfect example of the failure of early 30s architecture'. The house was by now showing serious signs of wear, which Crosby proposed combating by cladding the building with black slates and rough-cast stucco. This might be seen as the post-modernist's revenge.

Walter Gropius's only other commission for a private house in Britain was the Wood House at Shipbourne in Kent. The commission came from clients of a rather different kind: the young left-wing Jack Donaldson, who became a leading Labour Party politician in James Callaghan's government, and his wife Frances, a writer and biographer best known for her life of Edward VIII. Admittedly Frances Donaldson, like the Levys, had theatrical connections in that her father, Freddie Lonsdale, was the writer of popular drawing-room comedies. But the Donaldsons, who had only recently got married, were a serious, socially conscious left-wing couple and the house they commissioned from Gropius was practical and pleasing rather than *grand luxe*.

Jack Donaldson already had a close connection with modern architecture and with social experiment. He was a supporter of the Pioneer Health Centre set up in the 1920s in Peckham, a deprived area of London, to investigate the social context for diseases and provide a new remedial environment. Donaldson had already been involved in plans for a new purpose-built structure for the Peckham health centre designed by Owen Williams. He had friends amongst the many émigré intellectuals moving into London, and hearing that Gropius badly needed work he paid £400 in advance for the commission. Although the Wood House has sometimes been attributed to Gropius and Fry, the work was carried out by Gropius alone, though assisted, once again, by Albrecht Proskauer, whose initials appear on many of the blueprints.

The house was built on a three-acre sloping site with long views across the fields and woods. The Donaldsons had bought the site from the landowner, Peter Cazalet, a friend. Unusually for Gropius this is a timber building, a calm, coherent house very different in style from his exuberantly Expressionist Sommerfeld House of 1921. His interest in wood had no doubt been revived by his attendance as the guest of honour at the prize-giving lunch for the Timber Development Association's 'All Timber House Competition'. In his speech Gropius urged that 'the modern form of a building is only conditionally dependent on the newness of the construction material . . . The really creative architect does not tie himself up with only some special materials.' The Wood House was clad in an uncreosoted Canadian cedar, a material which changes colour with the seasons, and lined throughout with 'Herocliffe', a non-inflammable pressed reed imported specially from Yugoslavia.

Gropius's plans were refused permission by the local council on grounds that the house would be 'inharmonious with the general development of the district and that by reason of its design it would be injurious to the amenities of the district'. Only an appeal to the Ministry of Health, then the body finally responsible, allowed building work to go ahead. In spite of its distinctively 1930s modernist elements – the steeply angled canopied entrance, the open-air sleeping porch with its own exterior stairway – Gropius's Wood House has now acquired something of the quality of permanence William Morris so admired in buildings: the feeling that it had never not been there.

Maxwell Fry was lucid in describing what it was like to work with Walter Gropius: his modesty combined with his 'sort of lion-like approach . . . I would say that when it comes to design mine comes from my wrist, while Gropius's was more in his head.' Fry considered that as working architects they fitted well together and that Impington Village College was 'a very perfect collaboration'. And he felt that in Henry Morris they had a client who was not only a genius but 'one of the most delicious English eccentrics' Fry had ever met. This was a man who was erudite, poetic, loved architecture and appreciated the historic beauty of Oxford and Cambridge, having been an undergraduate at both. Morris was also a wonderful iconoclast, scornful of both the sterility of British communists and the iniquitous complacency of those he called 'capitalists with faces like plates'. He was the romantic homosexual who revered family life and had a deep respect for education. Fry suggested that collaboration with Morris was especially valuable for Gropius, 'who began to see through him what kind of country this was'.

The indefatigable Jack Pritchard undertook to fundraise to pay the initial fees for the Impington commission, amounting to around £1,200. Henry Morris foresaw that it would be impossible to persuade his Education Committee to appoint an unknown German architect. Pritchard galvanised support from W. G. Constable, Slade Professor of Fine Art at Cambridge, Charles Holden, vice-president of the RIBA, the Cambridge economist John Maynard Keynes and others to write Morris an official letter of support for the 'powerful combination' of Fry and Gropius in designing the new Cambridgeshire Village College: 'Mr Fry brings to the partnership feeling for the English tradition and a highly developed practical sense, while Professor Gropius possesses one of the most original architectural minds of our time, deeply interested in the social aspect of building and most accomplished in using all the results of modern research.'

However convincing this accolade, the total sum required was never fully raised and the scheme ran into further financial crises once it was discovered that Gropius had specified standardised components not being manufactured in Britain at the time. £20,000 was allocated for construction, but as it became clear this was nowhere near enough Gropius himself wrote to Maynard Keynes to ask for his advice in financing an additional minimum £15,000 cost. Keynes was less than helpful, replying from King's College:

I am afraid that I have no useful advice to give you. For your letter only tells me that you are, after all, just like other architects. That is to say, unable to work within the figure prescribed, though fortunately, it seems, superior to some of them in at least warning your clients beforehand rather than bankrupting them after the event!

Even though Gropius and Fry's original concept in the end was watered down, Impington was still a triumph (see Plate 27). When Henry Morris saw the revised plans he wrote to a friend, 'Gropius's plans are superb, a veritable architectural seduction.' This was the fourth in the sequence of Cambridgeshire Village Colleges and it was the one in which Morris's educational concept achieved its fullest visual expression, the long wide corridor providing a great space where the pupils, young and old, would meet and interact. In the relationship of the component areas – classrooms, art and craft rooms, lecture rooms and library, recreation areas, an auditorium – the sense of the developing family was potent and one of Morris's disappointments was that the *Family Group* sculpture by Henry Moore, originally envisaged as an Impington commission, could not be afforded in the end. This was a disappointment to Moore too as he had found the concept of Impington inspiring: 'I think from that time dates my idea for the family as a subject for sculpture,' he later said. However, a version in bronze was installed at Barclay School in Stevenage after the war.

Gropius left England before the building of Impington began. It was carried out under the supervision of Jack Howe as site architect. The college was not finished and occupied until 1939. It is certainly the most impressive and most meaningful of Gropius's English architectural works. His staunch admirer Nikolaus Pevsner was later to rate it as one of the best buildings of its date in England, if not the best. Impington was to be influential in establishing the character of progressive school architecture in the 1950s. It was also important as a prototype for a newly revitalised form of rural life as envisaged in the wartime Scott Report on land utilisation in rural areas. In its unassuming beauty and in the coherence of its planning, the use of simple brickwork in a harmonious country setting, the building is totally convincing. It reminds us of the importance that Gropius attached to art at all the stages of every human life.

Well into his second year in England Gropius showed signs of feeling relatively settled. On 19 June 1936 he wrote to the Undersecretary of State in the Aliens Department requesting permission to stay in England permanently, an application officially supported by Sir Ian MacAlister, secretary of the RIBA. In August Gropius and Ise's residency permits were extended indefinitely. Meanwhile, Gropius entered into a more formal partnership with Maxwell Fry.

The wisdom of these moves to stay in England out of probable harm's way was later reinforced by his degrading treatment by the German authorities during a trip he reluctantly made to Erfurt in Thuringia in November of that year. He had been obliged to return to Germany to testify at the trial of a friend, Wilhelm Guske, the district magistrate of Merseberg, who had been charged with accepting bribes. Guske was let off, but as soon as Gropius emerged from the court building he was seized by the Gestapo and taken to headquarters, where he was searched and questioned. Only when he presented the official letter from the Reichskulturkammer which confirmed that he had permission to carry out an architectural job in England was he released. But the next morning, on the way back to London, he was hauled out of the train at the Dutch border to be questioned again while the train went off without him. Going through the address list of his friends and contacts which Gropius always carried with him, his interrogators alighted on the suspect name Lion Feuchtwanger, author of the virulently anti-Nazi novel *Jew Süss*. Feuchtwanger had fled to France three years before. However the name Feuchtwanger was luckily outweighed by that of the Fascist Dino Alfieri, Mussolini's culture minister, whom the Gropiuses had met in Rome.

Gropius was finally allowed to continue with his journey, returning by the night boat, having had to telegraph van der Leeuw for yet more money. It was a bitterly humiliating experience. Back at Lawn Road Flats, he made a strong complaint to the German court authorities: 'I ask you to realise what impression this degrading treatment has made upon me – a treatment generally reserved for criminal or political suspects. As a loyal German citizen, I feel this unjustified and unwarranted intrusion has denigrated my honour.' The court replied casually that the action must have been taken by police of another jurisdiction.

László Moholy-Nagy experienced a different sort of German nightmare. He was commissioned by a British picture agency to cover the 1936 Olympic Games. Initially Moholy was keen on the idea, interested in the brief to capture the spectator psychology, the contrast in physiognomy between an international audience and the rabid German nationalists. But once he arrived in Berlin in July a succession of events quickly discouraged him. First there was the meeting with his friend, a doctor, who had become a professor at the Nazi-dominated university. Then on the first day of the Olympic Games, when he entered the stadium, he was greeted warmly by an officer in SS uniform. This was a former Bauhaus student who was now a political commissar. Finally Moholy went to visit his old landlady, planning to reclaim the thirty paintings and metal constructions he had left the year before. These paintings were examples of Moholy's early work, his period of transition from representational to abstract painting. But his once protective and devoted former landlady now told him she had cut them up for kindling wood. When Moholy protested she had no right to destroy his property her husband threatened to call the police and have him arrested for *Kulturbolschewismus*, 'cultural Bolshevism'. Those first two days unsettled him completely. On the third morning he called the picture agency to say he wouldn't take a single shot of the Olympics. He and Sibyl rarely talked about Germany again.

Generally speaking the art scene in London, affected by the influx of émigré artists, architects, designers, art historians and publishers during the 1930s, was becoming more receptive to the modern. Gropius began to find a niche in these new networks of progressive artistic activity. An especially important admirer and friend was Peter Norton, a remarkable woman who co-founded the London Gallery in Cork Street in October 1936. The wife of a diplomat, Clifford Norton, her real name was Noel but she was always known as Peter because of her resemblance to Peter Pan, and she had an endearingly optimistic spirit of eternal youthfulness.

Cork Street in Mayfair was becoming something of a centre for contemporary and specifically European art. The Mayor Gallery, relaunched in 1933 with a modernist interior designed by Brian O'Rorke, was especially committed to German art and its opening exhibition showed Paul Klee's work in London for the first time. Peter Norton's London Gallery had an abstract and Constructivist bias. She had her own career as a copywriter at Crawford's, a leading London advertising agency, of which Ashley Havinden was art director. Through Crawford's she had contacts with both Marcel Breuer and Herbert Bayer. She later claimed it had been Breuer and Bayer between them who inspired her to open the London Gallery. She was also a close friend of Moholy-Nagy's. When Gropius was appointed to Norton's Advisory Council this was a coming together of his German past and London present. The interior design was by Breuer and Bayer, while Havinden was responsible for the graphic identity of the gallery.

Gropius was clearly influential on the London Gallery's exhibition programme. The opening exhibition of the work of Edvard Munch, an artist then virtually unknown in England, was followed by an exhibition of Moholy's work, with a catalogue essay by Sigfried Giedion. Gropius himself was much involved in the planning of an exhibition of the work of Bayer, with a catalogue introduced by Alexander Dorner, the museum director who first brought Gropius and Ise together in Hanover back in 1923. Gropius went to the gallery to receive the works that Herbert Bayer had sent to London from Berlin, finding Peter Norton in a sudden state of panic about possible protests from her liberal supporters over showing the work of a designer still co-operating with the Nazi regime. 'She is a little nervous because of the "left" direction of their gallery,' Gropius reported back to Bayer. 'We must try everything to keep them at bay.' He comments that such problems of keeping a balance between art and politics will be new to Bayer, though all too evidently not to him.

Through his friendship with Peter Norton Gropius was able to organise an exhibition in London of his former lover Lily Hildebrandt's paintings. Since Lily was Jewish her husband Hans, the academic and critic, was finding all avenues of paid employment now closed. However, it appears that the Cork Street showing of Lily's abstract *Hinterglas* paintings was less than a success. After it closed she wrote to ask Gropius to make sure that her pictures were returned to Stuttgart in the case and the box with corrugated paper they arrived in. She added, 'I asked Mrs. Norton at the same time that she send me the small amount from the sale of the image as a cheque from London: this will be very useful to me.'

It was the indefatigable Peter Norton who had the idea of holding a large exhibition of modern German art in London as a riposte to the 1937 Munich *Degenerate Art* show. This took place at the New Burlington Galleries in 1938.

There is a sad postscript to Gropius's involvement with the London Gallery. From 1938 Clifford Norton was transferred to the British embassy in Warsaw, where he was notably sympathetic to the Polish cause. The London Gallery was sold to the surrealist impresario and artist Roland Penrose. When Poland fell to the Nazis in September 1939, the Nortons and staff were hastily evacuated via Romania. Peter always regretted that in the panic of departure at only two hours' notice she left behind all her paintings, lithographs and rugs. She especially grieved for the complete set of the French artistic and literary journal *Cahiers d'art*, from the earliest 1926 issue onwards, that Gropius had given her when she opened the London Gallery. How easy it would have been, she lamented later, to have picked up these great treasures and flung them in the car. But at the time her priorities were different, people being obviously more important than personal belongings, and instead of her paintings, modern rugs and Gropius's *Cahiers*, she drove away to safety several Polish employees of the embassy.

In a small but increasingly vocal sub-section of the London art world there was a growing sense of the need for a fuller integration of art and life. One of Peter Norton's aims in setting up the London Gallery had been to convince the British public of the absolute necessity of the visual arts. The opening statement for the gallery bemoaned the absence of pictures in so many modern rooms, 'or worse, the presence of pictures which do not harmonise with the room and the life of those who live in it'. In 1936 Gropius's new London friend John Duncan Miller, the furniture designer responsible for the interiors of the Wood House at Shipbourne, organised the exhibition *Modern Pictures for Modern Rooms*. This included works by not only Moore, Nicholson and Hepworth but also Moholy, Giacometti, Brancusi, Mondrian and Gabo, the Russian Constructivist artist who had now arrived in London, making a strong case for the relationship of abstract art to modern architecture and interior design. Such ideas of course came close to the Bauhausian ideal of the *Gesamtkunstwerk*.

This was a time for a multitude of groupings, small, reformist, argumentative. Gropius was drawn into several of these. Living in Belsize Park in such close proximity to Read, Nicholson and Hepworth he was, as we have seen, connected to Unit One and the artists and writers contributing to *Axis*, a quarterly review committed to spreading knowledge and appreciation of abstract art. From 1936 Gropius was also involved with the more substantial publication *Circle: International Survey of Constructivist Art*. This was a book co-edited by the architect Leslie Martin, Ben Nicholson and Naum Gabo. Artists, architects, writers, scientists were invited to submit proposals for inclusion. Certainly there was a preponderance of Hampstead residents, but there were international contributions too, resulting in an extraordinary gathering of talent. The generously illustrated book was published by Faber & Faber, Gropius's own publisher, in 1937. Faber was at this point the publisher most closely committed to the British avant-garde.

Circle embraced a whole range of disciplines, from Léonide Massine on 'Choreography' to J. D. Bernal on 'Art and the Scientist', from Breuer on 'Architect and Material' to Jan Tschichold on 'The New Typography'. It amounted to a total manifesto for the modern, a new concept of the unity of emotion and intellect, of science and art. Gropius's own contribution was a reprint of his essay on 'Art Education and the State', written originally for the 1936 *Year Book of Education*, in which he argued strongly for making artistic training obligatory in all schools, citing the experience gained from Fröbel and Montessori. Included in the illustrations in *Circle* are Gropius and Fry's designs for Papworth School, a specialist education centre for children suffering from tuberculosis, a carefully planned building not dissimilar to Impington, with special attention paid to light and ventilation. As with many other of Gropius's English architectural projects the job did not proceed beyond initial design stage.

Would his situation in Britain have improved if only Gropius had stuck it out for longer? Certainly by 1936 there were signs that the British were starting to catch up with the experimental European outlook. In the summer of that year Ronald Penrose organised the *International Surrealist Exhibition* at the New Burlington Galleries, with a committee that included Henry Moore, Paul Nash and Herbert Read. Of an ebullient international cast, Salvador Dalí was the star performer. There seems to be no evidence that Gropius attended, but it is difficult to imagine he was absent from an exhibition that showed that the London art scene was at last developing in a more enterprising way. There had of course been connections between Dada, Constructivism and the Bauhaus in its early, less strictly rational incarnation.

A further connection was the modern toyshop opened by Paul and Marjorie Abbatt in Wimpole Street in 1936, in a shop designed by Ernö Goldfinger, an émigré architect originally from Hungary who had arrived in London two years earlier. The Abbatts were progressive educational thinkers who recognised the importance of education through play. They acted as designers, manufacturers and retailers of a whole range of modernist toys and children's furniture. Finished in primary colours, in simple shapes that stimulated a child's creative instincts, the Abbatts' products were almost Bauhaus toys.

Publication of Nikolaus Pevsner's *Pioneers of the Modern Movement: From William Morris to Walter Gropius* was a further step towards consolidating Gropius's public image in a country in which Morris was still loved and admired. On the title page of Faber & Faber's handsomely designed hardback edition portraits of the two men – Morris bluff and bearded, Gropius lean-faced and ascetic – appear alongside one another as if on equal terms. In a closely argued thesis Pevsner makes his claim for William Morris as the founding father of European modernism, tracing a long lineage of artistic innovation from Telford and Brunel, the nineteenth-century engineers, to Morris, Voysey, Mackintosh and Ashbee, viewed by Pevsner as the masters of the arts and crafts in Britain who exerted a strong influence in Germany on Behrens, and from Behrens to Gropius himself.

Pevsner ends with a paean of praise to Gropius as architect of the 1914 Werkbund exhibition model factory:

PIONEERS OF THE
MODERN MOVEMENT

FROM WILLIAM MORRIS
TO WALTER GROPIUS

BY NIKOLAUS PEVSNER

LONDON: FABER & FABER

Title page for Nikolaus Pevsner's *Pioneers of the Modern Movement: From William Morris to Walter Gropius*, published by Faber & Faber in 1936.

There is something sublime in this effortless mastery of material and weight. Never since the Saint-Chapelle and the choir of Beauvais had the human art of building been so triumphant over matter. It is the creative energy of this world in which we live and work and which we want to master, a world of science and technique, of speed and danger, of hard struggles and no personal security, that is glorified in Gropius's architecture.

As a number of critics have commented since, Pevsner's accolade to Gropius verges on absurdity.

In writing this book Pevsner had his own agenda. He was a German refugee as well, with vivid memories of meeting and admiring Walter Gropius as a young man back in Berlin. Gropius was a part of his own past. In aligning Gropius and William Morris, so generally revered on account of his love of the English countryside, the beauty and fluency of his design, his idiosyncratic and trenchant views, Pevsner was not only making manifest his strong dislike of a National Socialist regime towards which he had shown signs of earlier support, a regime that had removed him from his teaching post and finally ejected him from his native land, a regime that had rejected Gropius himself and his modernist aesthetic. He was also rather desperately trying to make a role for himself in the country he had fled to, a strategy that eventually achieved a remarkable success with his masterful forty-six-volume survey of *The Buildings of England*, which validated Pevsner as an English national treasure. He was knighted in 1969.

———

On 28 November 1936, having lunch with Jack Pritchard, Gropius broke the news that he had finally decided to leave England and accept an offer from Harvard University to take over as chair of the Department of Architecture in the Graduate School of Design. Pritchard had seen this coming, later writing understandingly that the news 'was not entirely a surprise. I had indeed made a note that I would have a talk with you about America in view of my feelings about developments there in comparison with here.' He remained angry that the general deep-rooted resistance to the modern prevented Gropius from flourishing in Britain.

His and Ise's departure was a lasting shame and sadness to him and to Molly Pritchard too.

The American pursuit of Walter Gropius gathered pace during his years in London. He attributed his growing reputation to attentive reading among the cognoscenti in the States of his mission statement *The New Architecture and the Bauhaus*. In this he acknowledged the part played by Philip Morton Shand: 'The same man who first made the English public acquainted with my work has unintentionally helped now to lure me out of the country . . . It was Morton Shand who translated my small book on modern architecture so splendidly that it has certainly contributed to bring about my appointment at Harvard University.'

Joseph Hudnut, the newly installed dean of the Harvard Graduate School of Design, met Gropius in Rotterdam and also J. J. P. Oud and Mies van der Rohe. Oud was not interested in the post. Though Hudnut felt instinctively that Mies would prove the more inspiring teacher and that any architectural work he carried out in America would be superior in quality to Gropius's, Mies's links with the National Socialists told against him, as did his irregular relationship with his co-designer, the fiercely independent Lilly Reich. His domestic circumstances seemed unstable. Hudnut was also suspicious that Mies, vain and intransigent, would be difficult to control at Harvard. Gropius won out with his greater affability and eagerness and his potentially broader, steadier and more statesmanlike influence in the United States as a whole. The appointment was confirmed on 13 November.

For Gropius in many ways the decision was nerve-racking. Neither he nor Ise knew what to expect and this was yet another major disruption in their lives. But he was no doubt swayed by the good experience of his Bauhaus colleague Josef Albers, who had emigrated to America with his wife Anni in 1933. Albers was now installed as Professor of Art at Black Mountain College, the experimental arts community in North Carolina. As Breuer reported, 'Albers appears to be doing very well (Black Mtn. College), he wrote very content and feels as if he were back in the old Bauhaus . . . young, fresh and very interested.' Gropius proposed to Hudnut that Albers should now be invited to join the faculty at Harvard, an appointment Gropius would welcome 'for professional as well as personal reasons. For it would make my own work more promising right from the beginning.' He was ever anxious to surround himself with people he already knew and who appreciated his achievements. Hudnut prevaricated over this proposal, saying it should wait until Gropius himself arrived in the States.

Gropius now had the tricky problem of altering the terms of his permitted absence from Germany. He applied first to Ernst Jaeckh, an old Deutscher Werkbund contact who was working in London at the New Commonwealth Institute. He cannily suggested that Jaeckh should intercede on his behalf with the German authorities, arguing that the appointment of a German to the chair at Harvard in succession to a distinguished Frenchman, the Beaux Arts-trained Jean-Jacques Haffner, could only reflect well on Germany.

Jaeckh's approach to Goebbels's propaganda ministry, backed up by Gropius's reliable supporter Eugen Hönig, was successful. Goebbels's ministry accepted the idea that Gropius's appointment could be seen as aggrandising German culture, although the authorities were well aware of his personal ambivalence towards the Nazi regime. As he himself expressed it, they had him on their list as a 'cultural Bolshevist'. Self-protectively he took the precaution of writing to Hönig to assure him that he would always remain loyal to his country, seeing his mission at Harvard as serving German culture, nothing less.

The appointment was made public in January 1937. Among many letters of congratulation he received a bittersweet response from Herbert Bayer saying that while spending Christmas with his family in Austria and thinking about Gropius and Ise 'as I do so often', he had gone into a restaurant where he heard by chance the Bauhaus whistle tune 'Itten Muche Mazdaznan', a coincidence that brought him close to tears. He told Gropius, 'The news about your exodus from this worm-eaten continent I have received with real sorrow . . . The "nearness" of you both up to now was of course an illusion, but at least it was that.' Bayer added he was disappointed that the exhibition of his work that

Gropius had organised at the London Gallery would now open just a few days after Gropius himself had left.

The Gropiuses' final English weekend, Saturday 6 and Sunday 7 March, was spent on farewell visits. They needed to say goodbye to Ati, who remained stranded in England at Beacon Hill school, awaiting the arrival of her adoption papers from Berlin. She would not be joining them in America until later in the year. Over that weekend they also paid a visit to Knole, the Sackville-Wests' gargantuan country house at Sevenoaks in Kent, with its hundreds of rooms, its staircases and turrets, entrances and complex interlocking courtyards, mainly Elizabethan and late Stuart.

It seems likely that the Gropiuses' invitation to the wonderfully English and romantic house came from the modern-minded Edward Sackville-West, the novelist and music critic who was an early enthusiast for Benjamin Britten. Eddy was also a considerable fan of Weimar Germany, having lived in Dresden in 1927 and spent a wild Christmas in Berlin, described in a letter to his fellow homosexual E. M. Forster as being 'triumphantly, aboundingly ugly – so ugly that the mind is left quite free to pursue its own fantasies, unhindered by Beautiful Buildings . . . I was dragged about at night from one homosexual bar to another. The behaviour is perfectly open.' It is also possible that the introduction to Knole was made through the Donaldsons, Gropius's Wood House at Shipbourne being less than thirty miles away. There is something very touching in the idea of Gropius on his last weekend in England being exposed to English architecture at its most magically grandiose.

Gropius's farewell dinner was held on Tuesday 9 March at the Trocadero restaurant off Shaftesbury Avenue. It was a meeting of his old world and his new world, with a Bill of Fare designed by Moholy-Nagy which included a horseshoe-shaped seating plan with a number for each guest, reaching round from Mrs Ise Gropius at 1 to Dr Walter Gropius at 135 (see Plate 28). The guest list included, predictably, the Pritchards, Wells Coates, the Morton Shands, Ashley and Margaret Havinden, the Duncan Millers, Peter Norton and her husband, Professor Charles Reilly and his young son Paul, who was destined to become director of the Council of Industrial Design. Nikolaus Pevsner of course was in attendance. Also present was the émigré architect Ernst Freud, son of Sigmund, who had arrived in London from Berlin in 1933.

The Bill of Fare was English formal. Turtle soup with cheese straws; boiled Scottish salmon; Aylesbury duckling with apple sauce; iced nectarine Melba with petits fours. Julian Huxley was in the chair, presiding over seven after-dinner speakers amongst whom were Maxwell Fry, Henry Morris and Herbert Read. Gropius himself was called on to reply with a tactfully worded speech of affection and gratitude to the friends who had helped and encouraged him while he was in England. He could not, however, resist a few words of admonition to the English for hanging on too much to the past: 'this feature', he said in partial excuse, 'is perhaps more conspicuous in England than in other countries because its peaceful development through centuries has preserved all the old beauty and made people very much aware of the fact that mere progress does not necessarily produce culture.'

For Gropius it was a highly emotional occasion. He remembered later how his heart was bursting with all sorts of different feelings: sadness at leaving England, deep worry about Germany, apprehension about his new responsibilities in the United States.

It was a time of inevitable confrontation with his past. Was he reassured, one wonders, or yet more agitated to receive a letter from his old friend Martin Wagner, who had left Berlin in despair at the outlook for the architectural ideals that he believed in and was now working unhappily in Istanbul? Wagner, hearing news of Gropius's farewell dinner, imagined himself sitting there 'as a ghost emptying not just a glass but a whole bottle for those who have the courage not to bow to the rabble'.

It was now time for Gropius and Ise to depart. They left England on 12 March.

Gropius was to look back on his years in London with a kind of exasperated fondness. He had been welcomed with great generosity and bonhomie and had made many interesting friends. As Ise had commented, for them both it had been an expansion of experience. But generally speaking, over those few years Gropius's influence in Britain had been minimal. It was only after the war that Britain began officially 'going modern', with the work of the Council of Industrial Design and the Festival of Britain of 1951. Nor was it until the 1950s that Gropius's ideas on art education started to take hold. Bauhaus influence was fundamental to the development of the so-called Foundation Course, a freeing of students' creative imagination that became an essential factor in art education in Britain from then on.

Gropius's paucity of architectural commissions during the time he was in England was of course his deepest disappointment. Maxwell Fry remained convinced it was the rejection of the new building for Christ's College in Cambridge that finally decided him to go.

Walter and Ise Gropius leaving England in March 1937.

THIRD LIFE · America

19
Harvard
1937–1939

Gropius was evolving a new sense of perspective, seeing his life unfolding in three episodes: half a century in Germany from his childhood
onwards, followed by a brief experimental stay in England. Now he
was beginning a new life in the States. He wrote thoughtfully to Adolf
Sommerfeld, who had fled from Germany to Palestine, reviewing his
own past history:

This will then probably be the last and final stage of life after the many various lives
one has started. So I begin to draw a line under my English balance and gear myself
to the new thing. So one moves through the different levels of life with some longing
for the old Germany and the friends there who are scattered to the winds.

Gropius himself was now very nearly fifty-four.

Their ship, the *Europa*, docked in New York harbour on 17 March
1937. There to greet Gropius and Ise were Josef and Anni Albers and
Xanti Schawinsky and his wife Irene, who were now living in the States.
On their first evening Schawinsky took the Gropiuses out for a celebration at the Cotton Club, a favourite haunt from their visit to New York in
1928. Duke Ellington was playing and Walter Gropius was once again
enraptured by the 'gorgeous half-castes' performing in the floor show.
They were both conscious that New York was changing its appearance
to such an extent they felt they hardly knew it: 'there were more and
higher towers now and everything is bigger and taller and wider.' Such
changes seemed more marked in comparison with London. It was an
arrival into a new setting in which optimism and uncertainty combined.

Compared with England America of course had a long history of
receptiveness to immigrants. During the weeks following their arrival
the Gropiuses were given several books about the first settlers who came

over in the *Mayflower*. Now, in the mid-twentieth century, America's indigenous spirit of enterprise and openness made it more welcoming to the avant-garde. Many former leaders of progressive European movements in music, popular theatre, abstract or socially critical art, modernist architecture and design chose to take permanent refuge in the United States as opposed to Britain. The job opportunities were that much greater and what amounted to colonies of talented European émigrés collected in Hollywood, centre of the film industry, as well as in already cosmopolitan New York. Bertolt Brecht, another émigré from Berlin, expressed the American capacity for absorbing European talent:

> This inexhaustible melting-pot, so it was said
> Received everything that fell into it and converted it
> Within twice two weeks into something identifiable.

Or as Walter Cook, founding director of the Institute of Fine Arts at New York University, expressed it much more crudely, 'Hitler is my best friend; he shakes the tree and I collect the apples.' The 1930s influx of European exiles enriched American culture immeasurably.

Gropius had been preceded to the States by Mahler's great admirer Otto Klemperer, who left Germany in 1933 to become musical director of the Los Angeles Philharmonic Orchestra. Alma's one-time son-in-law, the composer Ernst Krenek, settled in America in 1938. New York in particular was welcoming to avant-garde and abstract artists. An exhibition of the work of the French painter and sculptor Fernand Léger, held at the Museum of Modern Art (MoMA) in 1935, encouraged him to visit New York and then to settle there. By 1938 we find him decorating Nelson Rockefeller's apartment, already absorbed into the American arts establishment.

The regime at MoMA, which had opened in 1929 with Alfred Barr as its first director, was sympathetic to the European modern movements in architecture and to the Bauhaus in particular. The museum had co-published Gropius's *The New Architecture and the Bauhaus* with Faber & Faber. Once Philip Johnson joined Barr at MoMA as the museum's first director of architecture in autumn 1930 they worked closely together in promotion of the modern, with a sequence of persuasive exhibitions focusing on international modern architecture and the burgeoning profession of industrial design. Soon after Gropius arrived in America detailed plans for a Bauhaus exhibition at MoMA were already underway.

Chicago was another of America's great cities where an understanding of the modern was endemic. Mies van der Rohe, with whom Gropius's career developed in such uneasy symbiosis, followed him to the States and became director of the Architecture School of the newly established Armour Institute of Technology, later Illinois Institute of Technology (IIT), in 1938.

Joseph Hudnut sent a radio telegram to greet the Gropiuses on their arrival on the *Europa*: 'Welcome to America where happiness and success await you'. Hudnut had organised a busy sequence of lunches and dinners in Gropius's honour, such as a lunch at the top of Radio City Music Hall and a dinner at the St Regis hotel at which Alfred H. Barr of MoMA would be present. Gropius's Dartington rival William Lescaze invited them for cocktails. The leading industrial designer Henry Dreyfuss asked Gropius to luncheon at his office in Madison Avenue. There would be a similar high-level introduction programme once the Gropiuses travelled on to Boston. Hudnut had invested a great deal in the appointment of Gropius to the chair at Harvard and he was determined to give it a good start.

Joseph Hudnut was a new appointment to Harvard, having been brought in by its president, James B. Conant – another relatively new arrival with great ambitions for modernising the university. Hudnut had previously been responsible for reforming the architecture programme at Columbia University in New York. He was now entrusted by Conant with restructuring the teaching of architecture at Harvard, shifting it from its previous classical Beaux Arts emphasis towards a broader curriculum more relevant to modern life, allied with engineering, economics, social planning. Gropius was heading a newly formed department, a Graduate School of Architecture, of which the intake was largely of mature students at Master's degree level. Gropius envisaged a Bauhaus-style Basic Design Course as an integral part of the curriculum. In fact this remained a distant dream.

To start with at Harvard all was smiles. Gropius and Ise began life close to the university in Cambridge, staying at the Continental Hotel until they sorted out more permanent accommodation. Gropius wrote gratefully to Joseph Hudnut, using the name by which his friends addressed him: 'Dear Vi, I know what courage it needs to overcome the general stupidity and laziness of hearts and brains in order to change the ordinary beaten track. So I feel very happy about the good luck of having become your companion in this fight for preparing a better architecture in this country.' Ise wrote appreciatively to the Pritchards, telling them that Dean Hudnut and his wife were taking immense trouble to move every impediment out of their way: 'we could not be better cared for as by him and his wife. It is almost like Jack and Molly.'

Hudnut was remembered later by a colleague as 'the least modern individual you could find'. He was short and rather fat, bespectacled and shuffling, habitually wearing an ill-fitting tweed suit. He was clever and ambitious but by no means a through-and-through modernist in outlook. He was an architect by training but his own architecture veered towards colonial revival. He had scholarly interests in history. His wife Claire was an eccentric, perhaps just a little crazy, as described by a former colleague of Hudnut's: 'She fell in love with people. All the time. And she composed music . . . Dyed her hair. And she was in love with the bassoonist at the symphony. And Vi Hudnut just adored her.' He allowed Claire to indulge all her romantic instincts. Compared with the Pritchards, and indeed as it soon turned out the Gropiuses themselves, Vi and Claire Hudnut were basically people of a very different style.

In those early weeks at Harvard Gropius invited all his students for a Bauhaus-style *Bierabend* in the hotel. Here is Gropius in the new world already recreating the rituals of his old world, reaching for the reassuringly familiar.

Hudnut was adept at publicising the arrival of his distinguished new recruit. He himself arranged to write the introduction to the American edition of *The New Architecture and the Bauhaus*. He saw to it that excitable news stories appeared in the university newspaper, the *Harvard Crimson*, quoting Gropius's enthusiastic comments on the architecture of Harvard's University Hall and the 'characteristic old American style' of the Harvard Yard buildings. Harvard Yard must have reminded Gropius, perhaps a little bitterly, of the formal quadrangles of Cambridge, England, too.

Gropius was also lined up at an early stage to give an address to the formal dinner of the Harvard Visiting Committee held at the Harvard Club in Boston on 30 March 1937. He rose to the occasion with a lucid and impassioned argument for a flexible approach to architecture. His powers of expression had improved since his agonisingly hesitant delivery at the RIBA in London three years before. He expressed his deep belief that a young architect should be encouraged to find his own way forward, 'to create independently true, genuine forms' out of the particular conditions that surround him. 'It is not so much a certain readymade dogma I want to teach, but an attitude towards the problems of our generation which is unbiased, original and elastic. It would be an absolute horror for me if my appointment would result in the multiplication of a fixed idea of "Gropius architecture".' He was adamant that the least of his intentions was to introduce 'a so to speak cut and dry "Modern Style" from Europe'.

Altogether it was a hopeful beginning for Gropius in a country in which 'the often primitive, naïve quality', as he saw it, stood in such contrast to frequently discouraging English common sense. The 'undestroyed, untamed' New England landscape around Cambridge delighted him, with its elegant white-painted wooden houses in traditional American colonial style. He viewed New England romantically as a land in which the tradition of welcoming foreigners was second nature, a place of instant friendships and open hospitality dating back to America's old pioneering days. Memories of the Native American stories of his childhood were seeping back into his mind. In a letter to Breuer written soon after his arrival Gropius assured him that the girls in America would flock around him. Quite unlike the girls in England, they look you in the eye, so open and so free. Already Gropius was encouraging Breuer to come and join him in the States and was negotiating with Hudnut at Harvard on his behalf.

A joint portrait taken soon after their arrival shows Ise looking *soignée* in a black dress, black cap and necklace in Bauhaus modern style, Walter upright, handsome and distinguished in his formal suit with waistcoat and the signature bow tie. Through those early months in Cambridge and in Boston formal welcoming dinners and receptions still continued. Ise recalled that their English introductions had placed them immediately at the heart of distinguished, highly cultured Bostonian society, the Henry Jamesian enclaves around Beacon Hill. She remembered the social life as hectic:

Oh my God. We were absolutely killed alive. People at that time would invite us by telegram to come to the North Shore, to the places we'd never heard of, because this was the famous professor, the new man in Harvard, and you can't imagine what Boston would do to make him feel good. Well we were out every single night, and all the other nights we had to give parties to all these people.

Walter and Ise Gropius at Planting Island near Cape Cod, summer 1937.

After what she calculated as sixty-three parties since their arrival they decided they needed a break and took a summer holiday on the shore of Planting Island at Marion in Massachusetts, near Cape Cod.

It was a joyous time, a kind of rerun of previous holidays in Ascona or skiing in the Alps, a gathering of Gropius's now scattered friends. Alexander Dorner, who came to Planting Island with his wife, called it a 'Summer Bauhaus'. The first to arrive were Breuer and Bayer, one from London, the other travelling from his home in Germany. They were followed by Schawinsky and Moholy-Nagy. A holiday routine evolved, with daily swimming in the nude in Buzzards Bay and nostalgic starlit evenings along the shore. For hosts and guests this brought a temporary release from professional and political anxieties.

For Breuer, on his first transatlantic visit, America came as a pleasant surprise. He saw the possibilities now opening out. Bayer too had his mind on working in the States and would soon be involved in curating and designing the MoMA exhibition on the Bauhaus. On Gropius's recommendation Moholy-Nagy was appointed first director of the New Bauhaus in Chicago, taking up his post in the autumn of that year. Gropius was also instrumental in securing for Alexander Dorner the directorship of the Rhode Island School of Design in Providence. He had a vested interest in keeping these familiar Bauhäusler around him. These were people who validated his own history.

There was another arrival in Planting Island. Ati joined her adoptive parents now that the official papers had been cleared. Although Ati had been tearful at leaving the stimulating atmosphere of Dora Russell's school, she found immediate compensations in the summer cottage at Cape Cod, settling in with her new parents, Walter and 'Isi', as she called her, and their Bauhaus friends. Schawinsky and Breuer were her favourites because they took the trouble to play with the now eleven-year-old Ati. 'The meals were merry, Isi was very pretty, and everyone's spirits were high.' She was infected by the fun they were all having. For Ati too this was a good beginning to a completely new structure for her life.

Returning to Harvard in the autumn the family moved into a rented house, an old colonial building on Sandy Pond Road in the countryside at Lincoln, with a beautiful view over forests and fields. Hudnut, ambitious for his protégé's social reputation, would have preferred him to be living in Boston or at least in the relatively fashionable Brattle Street in Cambridge, but Gropius preferred the remoter and more restful countryside environment. Soon, almost miraculously, a building site became available nearby, the property of an altruistic and wealthy Bostonian widow, Mrs James Storrow. The elderly but still enterprising Mrs Storrow, a founder of the Girl Scouts of America and supporter of settlement houses for American immigrants, knew little about modern architecture but was curious about the possibilities. She took up the suggestion from Henry Shepley that she should provide Gropius with a site on her considerable New England property and commission him to build there. Shepley was a local Boston architect, a Gropius supporter who, with Hudnut, sponsored Walter and Ise's application for American citizenship.

Ise could hardly believe their good fortune, writing to Jack and Molly Pritchard that November:

Some generous old lady has had the idea of offering us a beautiful building site on top of a hill and almost no house in sight. Walter is going to design the house and then rent it from her. It seems a fairy tale, but since Walter has been beginning even to discuss the location of the lavatories I am beginning to think it is real.

The five-acre site was pleasantly situated in an apple orchard on a gentle hillside, in partly open and partly wooded country with a view of Mount Wachusett, a melange of the wild and tamed. One of the attractions for Gropius was its close proximity to Walden Pond and its connections to the New England transcendentalists. The wooden hut constructed on the water's edge for the contemplative writer Henry Thoreau, a fine example of architecture without architects, was only a few minutes' walk away. Planning of the house was started that autumn. Ati remembered family weekends being spent walking out over the site, picking out the trees to be transplanted and endlessly discussing how the rooms should be arranged. The newly arrived Breuer, now appointed to an assistant professorship at Harvard and

Walter and Ise having breakfast on the screened porch at the Gropius House.

embarking on his architectural partnership with Gropius, was also involved in early planning of the building that soon became known as the Gropius House.

The house was already under construction through the summer of 1938. The Gropiuses moved in during the autumn, into a form of exist-ence that Ati had never known before, only distantly glimpsed during her childhood in Berlin. She now found herself part of a way of life in which attention to the visual was fundamental, imbued with what had 'an almost moral meaning . . . this was not a focus on appearances, but rather on a way of acutely observing and valuing every form, manmade or natural, in one's environment. What they expressed mattered.'

The Gropius House (see Plate 29), No. 68 Baker Bridge Road, was a relatively modest building but every detail had been carefully thought through. In some ways the house was typically New England in the choice of materials and simplicity of form: the white-painted wood frame structure, the brick chimney, the screened-off porch, the stone retaining walls. There were echoes of Gropius's Wood House at Shipbourne in the use of weatherboarding, which was also applied here internally. But with its simple flat roof, the inevitable object of some local opposition, its expanses of plate glass, its fluency of layout, its use of the most functional industrial materials the Gropius House at Lincoln memorialised the Bauhaus Masters' Houses at Dessau. The critic Lewis Mumford saw the precise point of it, writing in the Visitors' Book, 'Hail to the most indigenous, the most original example of the New England House! The New England of a new world.'

Almost all the furniture came originally from the Bauhaus workshops. After the negotiations with Goebbels the Gropiuses had been permitted to take their possessions out of Germany. Everything except money was allowed to go. Not only did this mean they brought over to America all the records of the Bauhaus, the articles, reviews, critiques and correspondence, they arranged the transportation of their furniture as well, including the desk designed by Gropius for his own use in the director's office at the Weimar Bauhaus. He had also used this desk in Dessau until 1928, when he took it to Berlin. It was now installed in Ati's Lincoln bedroom. The large double desk in the Gropiuses' study was designed by Breuer in 1925 and handmade in the metal workshop. At this desk they worked alongside one another, as if in demonstration of their indissoluble working partnership.

Besides the Bauhaus furniture the Gropiuses brought over two Isokon Long Chairs from London, in which Ise liked reclining at the end of a particularly stressful day. 'The family lives in them,' she told Jack and Molly Pritchard: the Isokon chairs were the centre of the house. She doubted whether the average Englishman was 'willing to relax in so luscious a way, or should we better say licentious?' All the furniture reached them in terrible condition and Ise had to search round the hardware shops in Boston to find the nails and screws that would enable them to renovate these precious remnants of their past.

In settling in New England we see Gropius intent on recreating the family life that had evaded him for decades: the settled existence

Gropius and his adopted daughter Ati in Lincoln, 1938.

he had not achieved with Alma, the life with the loved daughter he had so far been deprived of. The new house was to some extent purpose-designed for Ati. He changed the height of a window sill to please her. Looking forward to her coming teenage years Ati's room on the first floor was relatively independent, with its own external deck and spiral staircase leading down into the garden. She was sent to a local school in Concord, a school much more conventional than Dora Russell's, where Ati found herself welcomed and petted and admired for her ability at drawing and her recently acquired authentic English accent. She had been instructed by her new parents to say nothing of her past history in Germany. Hertha's name was not mentioned ever again.

Gropius threw himself into his new role of fatherhood, waking Ati in the morning before she went to school with little joke expressions remembered from his army days and teasing her at dinner about her work at school. 'My father was no disciplinarian,' she remembered, 'he was a gentle and charming man. I was never taken to task for any failure or pressured to perform at school. Instead, there was warmth, attention and support given to any small project of mine.'

In the evenings he would read to her and Ise in his sonorous and sombre voice, choosing selections from the classics translated into German: Dostoevsky's *The Idiot* and *The Brothers Karamazov*, plays by Schiller, works by Kleist, the great German poets, Shakespeare. He took her skating, taught her riding: he was still the expert horseman of his days in the Hussars.

But however hard he tried to be the loving, carefree father he was never quite convincing. Ati was aware of a certain deep detachment, a residue of experience that set him apart from other grown-up people. 'The expression in his eyes was not like those of others. It was far deeper and more searching.' Later on she came to recognise the wisdom and the sadness of Gropius's demeanour. Nor did she ever really feel herself his daughter. Ati felt no legitimate claim to him.

——

Breuer had returned to London in winter 1937, tying up his affairs. His final farewell to Hampstead took place on Christmas Day. A goodbye dinner was held in the newly completed Isobar at Lawn Road Flats. 'What is Isobar?' a mystified Ise had asked Jack and Molly Pritchard. 'You never mentioned the word before. I suppose it is something to eat.' The Isobar in fact was a club restaurant for Lawn Road residents and friends, designed by Breuer, on the ground floor of the flats. It was called the Isobar because of Molly Pritchard's interest in the weather and Breuer made a feature of a barograph mounted behind glass at one end of the Club Room. All the furniture of course was Isokon. It remained for many years the most moving and most tangible reminder of Gropius and Breuer's London residency and the scene of further emotional reunions between friends who had been parted through the years. It was in the Isobar that Naum Gabo and Naum Slutsky, a goldsmith and former Bauhaus student, encountered one another for the first time after leaving the USSR. Both were small men. They rushed forward, embracing one another in that Hampstead modern setting in amazed delight.

Once Breuer came to live permanently in America a kind of Gropius–Breuer double act evolved. The enterprising Mrs Storrow was so pleased by the progress of the Gropius House she made three further sites nearby available for houses in a similarly modern style whilst allocating a fourth site for a building in the more traditional colonial manner, so that the two approaches could be intelligently compared. She offered one of the three modern sites to Breuer, offering to provide finance for the building of a house for him to occupy. He wrote: 'The newest excitement is the opportunity to build a house for myself . . . in any way I like, without having to pay for it.' Breuer's site was very close to the Gropiuses, lying slightly lower across a grassy slope. They could almost see into one another's houses. Gropius and Breuer would once again be living in near-familial proximity.

In those first years in America the two of them formed a close professional liaison, teaching at Harvard alongside one another and working together in their new architectural partnership. In the Masters' Class at Harvard Gropius and Breuer, the latter in his role as an associate professor, were both in regular attendance for two or three days each week, going round the students' drafting tables, examining the work in progress and starting up discussions. Their approaches were quite different. Gropius was the quieter and more closely focused. A student remembered, 'He was tireless and moved from person to person in the drafting room taking every problem and proposal apart layer by layer, until almost the whole world became involved in our decisions.' He occasionally took a stubby pencil out of his waistcoat pocket and marked a student's drawing or asked a little penetrating question. But his approach was largely cerebral, inspiring, philosophical. 'I like the human body, I like breasts, I like buttocks,' he would tell attendant students in his introductory sessions, still smoking his cigar. 'And I'm for freedom of expression.' Gropius was all for the stretching of the mind and the emotions, for personal intellectual development. He insisted that at Harvard the last thing he intended was to turn out little imitation Gropiuses.

Compared with Gropius's deliberation of manner Breuer was more volatile, ebullient and jokey, moving around the tables, getting easily diverted into conveying to the students in his still shaky English his own more subjective architectural ideas. Some of the students responded more easily to Breuer than to Gropius, maintaining it was 'Lajkó' who actually taught them how to design buildings while Gropius provided the theoretical and philosophical underpinnings. Their students in these early years included Paul Rudolph, I. M. Pei and the industrial designer Eliot Noyes. To this younger generation Gropius was already something of a grand old man. According to Philip Johnson, who entered Harvard as a relatively mature Masters' Class student at the age of thirty-four, it was Breuer who was really the influential teacher. He learned more from Breuer than from Gropius.

One of Gropius's main doubts in accepting the appointment at Harvard was the effect of his new responsibilities on his own still huge architectural ambitions. He wanted to *build*, not simply to teach. Joseph Hudnut was sympathetic, seeing that a prestige architectural practice would bring reflected glory to the Harvard Graduate School, and assisted Gropius with his application for professional registration, allowing him to practise in America. At first he was able to run his architectural practice on the Harvard campus, as he had done at the Bauhaus, but once a former student complained that this was against the regulations, he and Breuer moved their office out to Cambridge, renting space in a former cinema.

These were still the years of the Depression in the States and the practice was slow in getting going. There were at first just two private houses: the Ford House in Lincoln, another of the projects Mrs Storrow had supported on land close to Gropius's and Breuer's own houses, and the Hagerty House, a beach house designed for John Hagerty, who had first been inspired by hearing Gropius lecture, and for John's mother Josephine on a site south of Boston on the Atlantic coast.

Architecturally the Hagerty House combines sophistication of planning with a seashore ruggedness. Its inner courtyard is enclosed by high natural stone walls. The house is dramatically sited right beside the shore. It seems to be connected to nature's very elements. This is a building that shows Gropius veering from European modern to American indigenous.

A more ambitious house evolving at this period was the Frank House in Pittsburgh, Pennsylvania. Here the clients were connected to the wealthy Kaufmann family, owners of the dominant department store in Pittsburgh. The Kaufmanns, who had originally commissioned Frank Lloyd Wright's Fallingwater, may well have encouraged this commission too. The brief given by Cecilia Frank and her husband to Gropius and Breuer was for a very lavish house indeed, containing an indoor swimming pool, a rooftop dance floor, eight bathrooms and multiple service rooms. The house was designed to be fully air-conditioned. The most rarefied materials were specified. Photographs show a luxury interior with Hollywood-style stairway. American streamline curves are everywhere. Did Gropius and Breuer get carried away?

Certainly the Frank House came to be much criticised as an example of extravagant individualism, so contrary to Gropius's previous moral rectitude. His more militant students at Harvard attacked this apparent sudden loss of conscience and even Sigfried Giedion took Gropius to task in *Space, Time and Architecture* for not keeping his clients under control. But by 1941 the Frank House was defended in *Architectural Forum* for its imaginative use of natural materials, combining random ashlar, stone veneer, travertine and natural wood, seeing this as 'new and impressive evidence that contemporary architecture is entering a new phase, richer, more assured, and more human'. Breuer himself defended the mix of curves and angles and the richness of materials, and indeed the Frank House gives us an indication of the way in which Breuer's architecture was developing. He always maintained that a house was not intended to be a contest in rationality but a flexible building constantly evolving, 'a background for human and natural forms – for persons, flowers, books, etc – for the countless varying forms and colours of daily life'.

The Frank House remains a fascinating mystery, owned as it has been by the Franks' reclusive son, who fends off any visitors. I was myself unable to gain entrance when I visited the house in 2015. My guide, the architectural collections director of the Pittsburgh History and Landmark Foundation, had by then been pleading to see inside the house for the past fourteen years.

The Frank House did, however, generate a further commission for Gropius: the Pennsylvania Pavilion at the World's Fair in New York in 1939, a building celebrating the power of democracy and Pennsylvania's role in achieving it. Gropius and Breuer designed the building's structure and Xanti Schawinsky the interior, a dramatic abstract assemblage of the symbols of democracy set – controversially – within a replica of the historic Independence Hall.

———

After a great many discussions and delays the exhibition *Bauhaus 1919–1928* opened in New York on 6 December 1938. It was held in the Museum of Modern Art's temporary accommodation on the lower level of the Time-Life Building at Rockefeller Center, since MoMA's new building on West 53rd Street was then a work in progress. For Alfred Barr, the director and prime mover behind the exhibition, it brought back emotional memories of his first visit to the Dessau Bauhaus as a young modernist enthusiast, still in his mid-twenties, and the formative experience this was for him. In that sense the exhibition was the paying of a debt, given extra edge by the later disastrous sequence of events: the closing down of the Bauhaus by the National Socialist regime, the victimisation of many of the Bauhäusler. The fact that the MoMA Bauhaus exhibition followed on so closely from the Nazi *Degenerate Art* exhibition which opened in Munich in 1937 was by no means a coincidence. Barr, in his introduction to the MoMA Bauhaus catalogue, makes it clear that he views the exhibition in New

York as an expression of continuing solidarity and support. Is the book and exhibition of 1938 'merely a belated wreath laid upon the tomb of brave events?' Barr answers his own question: 'Emphatically, no! The Bauhaus is not dead; it lives and grows through the men who made it, both teachers and students, through their designs, their books, their methods, their principles, their philosophies of art and education.' The message, across another continent, is one of continuity.

The MoMA exhibition was by no means the first showing of the Bauhaus in the States. As far back as 1930 the Harvard Society for Contemporary Art had staged a show entitled *Bauhaus, Weimar, Dessau* in Cambridge, curated by the energetic Lincoln Kirstein, the future American cultural supremo. Kirstein's fellow Harvard student Philip Johnson, already something of a Bauhaus expert, had been involved in fundraising as well as supplying many of the loans. Once Johnson joined Barr at MoMA as first curator of architecture his exhibition programme focused on the European modern and, increasingly, on industrial design. Johnson's *Modern Architecture: International Exhibition* of 1932 included a model of Gropius's Dessau building and photographs of other Gropius architectural projects. The *Machine Art* exhibition two years later showed Breuer's tubular steel furniture, developed at the Bauhaus, and MoMA's later sequence of shows called *Useful Objects* took up and Americanised the Bauhaus message that mass-produced objects could be things of beauty, making the case for truly democratic art.

By the time of the 1938 MoMA exhibition the Bauhaus was not unknown. But there was still a certain vagueness about the exact aims of it, the mood of it, the details. In setting out to explain the Bauhaus history and theories, the people who created it, the content of the courses, the intention was to show the public in America what the Bauhaus was actually *like*.

Coming at a time of such political disruption this was a complex exhibition to organise. Gropius himself, assisted by Breuer, was in charge of the general concept and direction. Ise was involved in editing *Bauhaus 1919–1928*, the accompanying book-catalogue, which Herbert Bayer was designing. Bayer was also in overall control of the selection and installation of exhibits, working with MoMA's new curator of architecture, John McAndrew, who sent out innumerable letters to former Bauhäusler in the hope of locating exhibits and negotiating loans. This was the great problem. The Bauhäusler were so scattered, Bauhaus artefacts were scarce. 'Bayer got the commission to make the first Bauhaus exhibition in the Museum of Modern Art, which he had great difficulties putting together because we could show only what we had brought in our suitcases,' Ise regretfully explained.

Oskar Schlemmer, when first contacted in October 1937 at his studio in Schringen near Badenweiler, had been optimistic about taking part, excited at the prospect of performing his *Triadisches Ballett* at the exhibition opening. 'I shall leap at the opportunity of doing it in New York. Thanks to Gropius and Moholy the whole Bauhaus business has taken on a new immediacy, and the prospects for finally getting to the United States now look good.' But by the time Herbert Bayer was in touch to firm up these plans the situation had altered for the worse. Schlemmer's work was included in the *Degenerate Art* exhibition. His paintings were now officially banned. Dreams of New York were over. Though his work was represented in the MoMA exhibition, Schlemmer was reduced to taking a job at a paint works in Stuttgart, carrying out run-of-the-mill commercial decorating jobs.

Through 1938 Bayer made extended trips to Germany, tracking down former Bauhäusler and asking them for loans. Some of these approaches were successful. Marianne Brandt in her Chemnitz retreat agreed to lend items which, after the exhibition, were either to be purchased or returned. Other overtures were less successful. As Josef Albers had already warned, many of the Bauhäusler who still remained in Europe would be wary of participating. The architect Fritz Schleifer, then living in Altona in Hamburg, pleaded that he was a teacher in the Landeskunstschule, the local fine arts school, and his work was being published so, for political reasons, he preferred not to participate.

Wilhelm Wagenfeld claimed that he did not want his work to be shown in America for fear it would be copied. From 1934 Wagenfeld was in charge of the Vereinigte Lausitzer glass works. He would also be involved as designer for the government-supported Porzellen Manufaktur Allach, the Allach porcelain factory, producers of the Nazis' favourite giftware, which from 1940 onwards operated within the concentration camp at Dachau. Wagenfeld, we might remember, was a Deutscher Werkbund member who had resigned in 1933, along with Gropius and Wagner, in protest against the Nazi ruling that Jewish members should be expelled. It seems that by this time he had changed his tune.

The problems of acquiring loans from Europe meant that the exhibition was dependent on the Bauhaus members and supporters living in the States. Breuer, Anni and Josef Albers, Schawinsky and Alexander Dorner, as well as the Gropiuses themselves, contributed, depleting their own houses. Albers and his students at Black Mountain College and Moholy at the New Bauhaus in Chicago were involved in making reproductions of the Preliminary Course work they had directed at the Bauhaus back in Germany. The final months of preparation were quite frenzied. Bayer only arrived back from his European travels on 22 August 1939. Gropius was too preoccupied to put in more than fleeting appearances at Rockefeller Center, where the exhibition was being assembled, though he managed to rerun his now familiar background essay on 'The Theory and Organisation of the Bauhaus' to provide an introduction to the catalogue, tracing back to John Ruskin and William Morris his belief in art for the people in the broadest modern terms.

Ferdinand Kramer, one of the first students who enrolled at Weimar in 1919, was amongst the now ageing Bauhäusler assembled for the exhibition opening. He too had emigrated from Germany, having been denounced as a degenerate architect. Kramer described the scene, a little bit bemused:

In 1938 the Museum of Modern Art on New York's Fifth Avenue displayed the familiar Bauhaus artefacts – somewhat dusty and slightly frayed . . . Frank Lloyd Wright came with a stunningly beautiful girl on his arm and wearing his big sombrero and a white carnation in his buttonhole. Gropius made a speech – I had heard it in Germany more than once.

Across the street from the museum, Dalí had designed the window displays for the fashionable department store Bonwit Teller: angels with black raven-feather

Frank Lloyd Wright with Walter and Ise Gropius at the opening of the Bauhaus exhibition at the Museum of Modern Art, New York, 1938.

wings in transparent nightgowns. But, dissatisfied with the arrangement, Dalí shattered the store windows and caused a mêlée, into which police cars and fire engines arrived with great fanfare. This marked the opening of the representative Bauhaus exhibition in the United States. I didn't know whether I was awake or dreaming.

Once inside and insulated from these wild New York distractions, what did these early viewers of the exhibition see? The show was divided into six main sections: 'The Preliminary Course', 'The Workshops', 'Typography', 'Architecture', 'Painting' and 'Work from Schools Influenced by the Bauhaus'. It was a mix of photographs, documentation and objects, put together with Bayer's surrealistic touches and teasing directional signage. The colour scheme was predominantly off-white, black and grey with touches of scarlet and deep blue. The exhibition was intentionally only a partial history of the school. Gropius himself suggested that the exhibition should be titled *Nine Years Bauhaus 1919–1928* and Barr agreed on grounds that the school's fundamental principles were established in those first years while Gropius was director. His successor Hannes Meyer, who was by this time living in Geneva having been ousted from the Soviet Union, was totally omitted from the MoMA Bauhaus story. It appears that Meyer, who in fact had joined the Bauhaus at Gropius's instigation in 1927, was not contacted at all during the preparations for the exhibition.

Mies van der Rohe, the final director of the Bauhaus, was approached by Gropius at an early stage. At this point Mies was still practising in Germany. At first he considered participating, but finally, nervous of the possible consequences, he refused. By December 1938, when the exhibition opened, Mies had accepted his appointment in Chicago but, again, it does not seem that Gropius or anyone at MoMA attempted to make him change his mind again. Although Mies's arrival in America was briefly mentioned in the catalogue, this was emphatically the Walter Gropius show.

Bauhaus 1919–1928 had only a short run in New York. The exhibition ended on 30 January 1939. Attendance had been remarkably good, but responses were mixed, ranging from enthusiasm from signed-up modernist enthusiasts such as Lewis Mumford to puzzlement to out-and-out hostility. With so many vested interests involved such polarised reactions were predictable. Barr put the hostile criticisms into four main categories: pro-Nazi and anti-modern; pro-French and anti-German; more general American resistance to the foreign; those who saw the Bauhaus as so far back in history that it had no relevance to America today.

Also, sadly and predictably, in more bigoted circles the exhibition was decried as being Jewish: 'Many Americans are so ignorant of European names that they conclude that, because the Nazi government has been against the Bauhaus, the names Gropius, Bayer, Moholy-Nagy etc. are probably Jewish Communists.' Barr proposed publishing a bold public statement refuting the accusation. Gropius, ever careful of responses within Germany, suggested that he tone the statement down:

It might be well to make a statement as to the Nazi Government of today, but we should try to make it somewhat less aggressive against the Nazis so that it will look like a very objective statement. I think we should not, in any case, defend ourselves against the Jewish question . . . we have had only one Jew among seventeen artists on the Bauhaus faculty throughout the years, and not one on the technical staff, which comprised about twelve people all together . . . I see no reason why we should have to defend ourselves . . . against this foolish point of view of Hitler's.

Once again Gropius was being defensively protective. Barr's idea of a statement was now dropped.

The Bauhaus exhibition travelled on through 1939 and early 1940 to Springfield, Milwaukee, Cleveland and Cincinnati. For Gropius's reputation in the United States it has to be counted a success, raising his public profile as an architect-educator of significance, not just on a European but from now onwards on an international stage. But for Barr himself the experience had been fraught. When Gropius contacted him in an attempt to get an additional payment for Bayer for his work on the catalogue, Barr replied that he felt under no obligation to add to 'the already terrific expenses of both the catalogue and the exhibition', both of which had gone well over budget: 'when I consider the extraordinary confusion and delays involved in getting the catalogue ready, causing incidentally the virtual nervous breakdown of our chief of publications, I must tell you that whatever debt the Museum may owe Mr. Bayer has in our opinion been fully paid.'

Barr could not resist adding a reprimand to Gropius:

While we are speaking frankly about the Bauhaus exhibition I want to assure you that, although it was one of the most expensive, difficult, exasperating and in some ways unrewarding exhibitions we ever held, we do not in the least regret having had it. At the same time I think that we should learn from it as much as we can. I would like to suggest to you that after all our press clippings are in you should take some time to go through them carefully. I am under the impression from your previous letters and from conversations that you were inclined to ignore or belittle the adverse criticisms, somewhat as you did in Germany fifteen years ago. To be perfectly frank, this seems to me rather unwise.

While reminding Gropius of his own deep-rooted admiration for the Bauhaus Barr warned him not to underestimate culture in America, where, after all, the elements of so-called 'progressive education', the emphasis on developing creative instincts, belief in the importance of learning through doing, which Gropius was claiming that he himself invented, had been in existence for the past quarter of a century.

When years later, in 1957, Gropius wrote to Philip Johnson suggesting another Bauhaus exhibition, Johnson, perhaps not surprisingly, declined, telling Gropius he had talked the matter over with Barr and René d'Harnoncourt, one of MoMA's trustees. 'We all feel that the big Museum exhibition and book of 1938, done at great cost to the Museum and with such great love and effort on your part, was a worthwhile and important venture, but that to continue the story with a second exhibition at this time would not have comparable interest and importance.'

Links between MoMA and the Bauhaus always remained close. In 1933 Philip Johnson, then in Stuttgart, was encouraged by Alfred Barr to buy Oskar Schlemmer's most important and atmospheric Bauhaus painting from his exhibition which was summarily closed down by the Nazis. *Bauhaus Stairway* shows a little line-up of crop-headed female Bauhaus students in balletic sequence as they ascend the stairs (see Plate 23). Johnson brought the painting to the States. A 1934 photograph shows it on the wall of his apartment in New York. The idea was that he should donate it to MoMA, and Schlemmer's painting was eventually installed on the staircase of the museum's West 53rd Street building, where this powerful memento of Gropius's Bauhaus at Dessau still hangs.

In his concept of the 1938 New York exhibition Gropius was indeed desperate to make connections between his past associations and his new ones. The New Bauhaus in Chicago and Black Mountain College were brought in as examples of the continuing influence of Bauhaus teaching methods. When Moholy's New Bauhaus opened on the South Side of Chicago in October 1937 with its first twenty-eight students,

Gropius himself was present, giving a speech after the celebration dinner on 'Education Towards Creative Design'.

In evolving his training programme for the school, which was initially sponsored by the Association of Art and Industries, Moholy took as his starting point the Bauhaus Preliminary Course, with its close analysis of materials, but developed the training in a new direction by putting greater emphasis on scientific methodology, film and photography, display and publicity. This was Bauhaus thinking expanded and adapted for a materialist, design-conscious, psychologically astute America. By the time the MoMA exhibition opened the New Bauhaus was already running out of money. But supported by Moholy's own commercial earnings and having acquired local Chicago backers, a new incarnation, renamed the School of Design, opened in Chicago in February 1939.

Black Mountain College in southern North Carolina was a rather different case in that it was founded before Gropius came to Harvard and was not so consciously developed from the original Bauhaus training course. The famous experimental arts college was founded in 1933 by an imaginative classics professor, John Andrew Rice. He was influenced by the ideas of the pioneering American educationalist John Dewey in evolving a curriculum based on personal observation and experiment. Education should not be simply intellectual training. It needed to embrace a much broader creativity in which the eyes and ears, manual dexterity, bodily movement, total human responsiveness must also be involved. With a faculty membership that included John Cage, Merce Cunningham, Willem de Kooning, Buckminster Fuller and Robert Rauschenberg before Black Mountain College eventually closed down in 1956, this was the place where more than anywhere else in mid-century America indigenous progressiveness and European modernism combined. Following the arrival of Josef and Anni Albers at Black Mountain in November 1933 the connection with the Bauhaus became increasingly pronounced.

To start with Josef Albers, much like Walter Gropius when he first arrived in London, was anxiously aware that he spoke very little English. But when a student asked him what his aim was at Black Mountain College he was able to reply, 'To open eyes.' The multidisciplinary approach, with teachers drawn from many different areas of expertise, attracted him. It was what he had become attuned to at the Bauhaus. Albers based his classes on the original Bauhaus Preliminary Course, opening them out into advanced new areas of research into materials and visual perceptions.

Anni Albers's contribution was equally important. She set up the weaving workshop at Black Mountain College, making it a principal area of study while developing her independent career as an artist. Again this replicated the former Bauhaus pattern. She wrote cogently about the importance of the crafts and the spiritual significance of materials as a bastion against the political uncertainties that she and Josef had already so painfully experienced.

Once Xanti Schawinsky joined Black Mountain's faculty in 1936, at Josef Albers's suggestion, there was what amounted to an ex-Bauhaus team. Schawinsky taught classes in illustration and colour theory and initiated a stage studies course, drawing on his experience with Oskar Schlemmer to produce his own programme of multimedia works combining space, movement, light, sound and colour. The arrival of Schawinsky brought something of the unpredictable and effervescent lifestyle of the Bauhaus to North Carolina. Gropius himself became an honoured visitor and lecturer at Black Mountain College. Photographs show him and Ise with faculty members at convivial gatherings. Black Mountain College emulated the Bauhaus in its programme of seminars and lectures by distinguished avant-garde practitioners and its informal, quasi-spontaneous social events. Its remote situation and its emphasis on rural self-sufficiency gave it a special atmosphere of radical experiment. Like the Bauhaus, Black Mountain was a world within a world. When the college planned a move from its original rented premises to a new purpose-built campus on the edge of the nearby Lake Eden, Gropius and Breuer were commissioned to carry out the design.

It is difficult to disentangle Gropius's work from Breuer's during these years of their architectural partnership. When it came to Black Mountain it seems likely Breuer was the partner most concerned with the detail of the work. But Gropius was certainly involved in the ambitious and potentially beautiful concept of the sequence of buildings stretched along the lakeside surrounded by woodland, with the North Carolina mountains looming in the distance. As originally planned, the buildings would have allowed for a completely self-sufficient communal life with residential accommodation, a cafeteria and student recreation rooms, as well as auditoria and workshops for music, drama, art and craft. However, with Black Mountain College in a state of constant

Gropius at Black Mountain College.

financial crisis, plans were repeatedly cut back. The eventual cancellation of the project and its replacement by a smaller, simpler building constructed partly by the college staff and students was another of Gropius's disappointments of this period. But his links with Black Mountain College continued through the years.

————

In spite of the scarcity of architectural work Gropius was now feeling relatively settled with his prestige salaried appointment at Harvard and his family life in New England beginning to open out. Compared with those he had left behind in Europe he was more and more aware of his own good fortune. He wrote to Arthur Korn in 1937, 'I'm on the luckier side of those who left.' This made him the more sympathetic to the many calls on him for help. He had, as we have seen, assisted Breuer, Bayer and Moholy in finding employment in the States. He was also sympathetic to the plight of Martin Wagner, whose experiences as a town planner in Turkey had been so disappointing, intervening on his behalf with Joseph Hudnut. In 1938 Wagner was appointed to teach city planning, now working alongside Gropius at the Harvard Graduate School of Design.

He was less successful in answering the call for help from Otti Berger, one of the most talented of all the Bauhaus weavers. Berger, who was Jewish, was refused membership of the Reichskulturkammer in 1936. This made her unemployable in Germany. In 1937, at Gropius's suggestion, Berger moved to England, where she hoped to find employment in the textile industry. Disappointingly, her only contract was a five-week job at Helios, a contemporary textiles firm. Her prospects were not helped by the fact that she suffered from deafness. Berger wrote again to Gropius in the autumn of 1937, by which time she had moved to Yugoslavia. She now hoped that Gropius could help her to travel to America, where her lover, the architect Ludwig Hilberseimer, would be joining Mies van der Rohe in his office in Chicago. But Gropius was unable to organise a permit, and it later transpired that Otti Berger was murdered in Auschwitz in 1944.

Nor did Gropius succeed in assisting his own one-time lover Lily Hildebrandt, who had written soon after his appointment to Harvard begging for his support for her husband and herself. Would he find the necessary sponsors for them to join him in America? He was not over-hopeful, warning Lily not to expect too much: 'there is such a rush, especially from the German side, that the interest is beginning to ebb, and for that reason one has to proceed carefully.' Evidently Gropius tried. Lily, after all, had at one stage meant so much to him, and Hans was his most loyal of supporters. He made provisional arrangements for the Hildebrandts to lecture in the States. But this scheme was eventually allowed to peter out and by 1939, after further pestering from Hans himself, Gropius wrote a little crossly, 'I realise that something has to be done and I will do what I can. Last year it was much easier.' The Hildebrandts remained in Stuttgart. After this, communication with them ceased, not to be resumed until after the Second World War.

On 3 September 1939 Britain and France declared war on Germany. Gropius's sense of consternation must have been mingled with relief that he and Ise were no longer in England. As German nationals and therefore now considered enemy aliens, they would have been liable for internment, as Nikolaus Pevsner was in 1940. Similarly, Kurt Schwitters was interned in various camps after his arrival in Edinburgh from Norway, finally being incarcerated on the Isle of Man.

In a poignant letter to Jack Pritchard written just before Christmas 1939 Gropius expresses his own sense of the catastrophe now overtaking Europe: 'I think democracy will be victorious in the end, but it is unthinkable what horrible sacrifices will be necessary to achieve that . . . I know that my poor disturbed country will have to pay the most.'

17. The Bauhaus building in Dessau, 1925–26.
Photographed by Helen Mellor in 2016.

18. Auditorium in the Bauhaus building.

19. The six-storey Prellerhaus, designed to accommodate students and young Masters.

20. Anni Albers, Wall Hanging WE 493/445, 1926. Cotton and synthetic silk.

21. House for the Bauhaus Masters, 1925–26, built in pairs in the pinewood.

22. Interior stairway in the house where Wassily Kandinsky lived alongside Paul Klee.

23. Oskar Schlemmer, *Bauhaustreppe* (Bauhaus Stairway), 1932. Oil on canvas. Painted in response to a Nazi decree to close down the Bauhaus in Dessau.

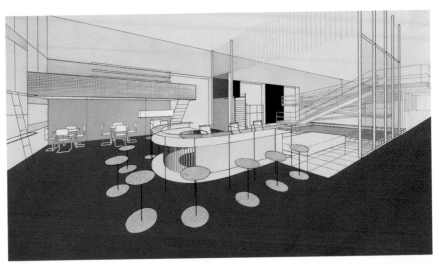

Adler „Standard 6" „Modell Gropius"
Höchstgeschwindigkeit, 110 km/h, 6 Zylinder

Adler „Standard 6" „Modell Gropius"
6 Zylinder, 110 km/h, 6 Zylinder

der neue ADLER

Beim Kauf eines Automobils spielt die Gestalt
des Wagens, sein ästhetischer Gesamteindruck
eine bestimmende Rolle. Welches sind nun
die Mittel, die einen schönen Wagen ent-
stehen lassen?

Das Maß an Schönheit eines Autos hängt von
der Harmonie seiner äußeren Erscheinungsform
mit der Logik seiner technischen Funktionen,
nicht von der Zutat an Schnörkeln und Zierrat ab. Der vollendete technische Organis-
mus muß also seine würdige Ergänzung in einer
ausgereiften, wohlproportionierten Form
finden, die in ästhetischem Sinne genau so
funktioniert, wie der technische Apparat
selbst.

Die reine, edle Form der Adler Wagen ist das
Ergebnis einer planmäßigen Harmonisierung
aller seiner Teile unter Vermeidung alles
unnötigen Aufwandes an Energie, Maße, Gewicht
und Zierrat.

Die hier abgebildeten Adler-Wagen nach Mo-
dellen und Ideen von Professor Dr. e. h.
W. Gropius, Dipl. Ing. M. Rathls, Bildhauer
D. Paulus und Professor R. Liskar sind auf
der „Internationalen Automobilausstellung
Berlin 1931" ausgestellt.

Adler „Standard 8"
„Modell Gropius"

herbert bayer, dessau

der neue ADLER

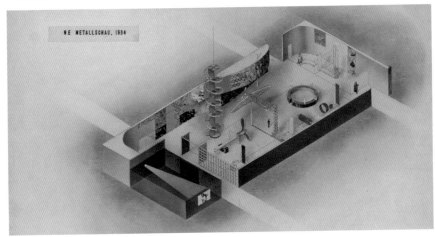

NE METALLSCHAU, 1934

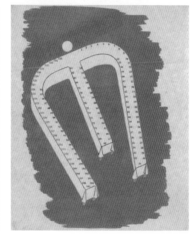

24. Gropius's design for a communal entertainment space for the Deutscher Werkbund section of the exhibition of the Société des Artistes Décoratifs in Paris, 1930. Drawing by Herbert Bayer.

25. Gropius's car design for Adler, 1931.

26. Gropius's design for the non-ferrous metal section of the *Deutsches Volk – deutsche Arbeit* (German People, German Work) exhibition organised by the National Socialist government in 1934. Drawing by Gropius's collaborator on the exhibit, Joost Schmidt.

27. Impington Village College, Cambridgeshire, designed by Gropius and Maxwell Fry, 1936–37.

28. Menu and seating plan designed by László Moholy-Nagy for Gropius's farewell dinner at the Trocadero, London, 9 March 1937.

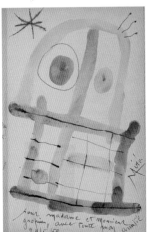

29. The Gropius House, Lincoln, Massachusetts, 1938. Ise Gropius seated in the porch.

30. Gropius House Visitors' Book, entry by Joan Miró, 1959.

31. Ise's traditional lobster dinner at the Gropius House, Christmas 1952. Ise, Gropius, Ati and Gropius's niece Almut Burchard (bottom right).

32. The Pan Am Building, New York, 1958–63. Gropius was the TAC partner in charge, working in collaboration with Emery Roth and Pietro Belluschi.

33. Josef Albers's formica mural *The City*, commissioned for the Pan Am Building.

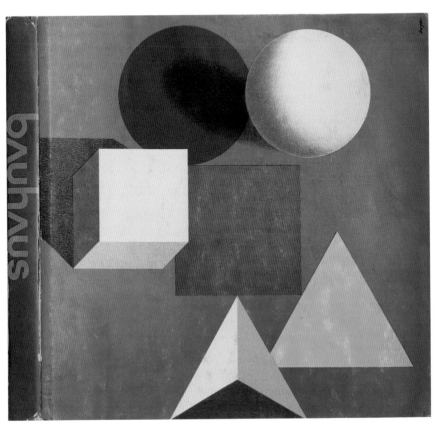

34. Herbert Bayer's design for the dust jacket of the catalogue for the 1968 Bauhaus exhibition at the Royal Academy, London.

20

Harvard and the Second World War
1940–1944

Since the annexation of Austria by Hitler in March 1938 Alma had spent an agitating few years almost constantly on the move. As we have seen, she could be virulently anti-Semitic. Nor was she positively anti-Hitler, referring to him admiringly from time to time as a genuine Teutonic zealot and inclined, according to her daughter, to wear a swastika badge beneath her collar. Alma's stepfather Carl Moll, his daughter Maria and her husband Richard Eberstaller were openly supportive of the Nazis. Alma herself was torn. Her priestly lover, Johannes Hollnsteiner, would soon be arrested by the Gestapo and sent to the concentration camp at Dachau. Alma's own situation was definitely perilous since her husband Franz Werfel was not only Jewish but already an outspoken opponent of the Nazi regime.

Such complexities of loyalty put strain upon their marriage. Alma and Werfel spent much time apart. Alma even reverted to corresponding wistfully with Oskar Kokoschka, wondering why she had ever left him, remembering him as the strangest, most beautiful of all her lovers. She now began to realise that remaining in Vienna was impossible. Alma had already rented out the grandiose villa on the Hohe Warte. She never felt settled there after the death of Manon. She withdrew all her funds from her bank account in hundred-schilling bills, which she and the faithful Ida Gebauer spent the day stitching into Sister Ida's underclothes in order to smuggle the money out via Zurich. On 12 March 1938, the day after German troops entered Austria, she said goodbye to her mother, sensing she would never see Anna Moll again, and set off with her reluctant daughter Anna, planning to join Werfel in Italy.

She and Anna had a nerve-racking journey by train from Vienna to Prague, and were stopped at the border to show their certificates of baptism. All Jews were immediately transported back. The remaining passengers were taken one by one into a curtained-off compartment where they were stripped and searched. Hours later the train was permitted to continue. Alma and her daughter were finally reunited with Werfel in Milan. In May the three of them travelled on to London, where Werfel, entertained and feted, was anxious to settle. But Alma felt completely stranded in London. She found it a relentlessly cold and unsympathetic city and complained of being bereft of German books, without a piano and, worst of all, without German-speaking people. The English seemed complacent. No one understood what was happening in Austria. The atmosphere was so bad that Alma had a nervous breakdown. She and Werfel set off again for Paris. This was just over a year after Gropius left London for the United States.

For the next two years it was a wandering existence. Alma and Werfel first rented a house, an old Saracen tower, on the French Riviera at Sanary-sur-Mer. Then, with the German invasion of France in May 1940, German-speaking emigrants came under suspicion. Werfel was investigated by the local police. They no longer felt safe and were anxious to move on to America. In June 1940 they left Sanary and spent the next fortnight in Marseilles trying unsuccessfully to organise visas to travel to the United States. After many false starts and a chaotic journey, Alma lost her luggage containing, besides other musical scores by her first husband, the valuable manuscript of Bruckner's Third Symphony adapted by Gustav Mahler. They finally reached Lourdes, village of pilgrimage where Bernadette, the miller's daughter, had been visited by the Virgin Mary. Here Werfel, carried away, made the promise that if he and Alma could get to America, he would write his own story of Bernadette.

Finally they struggled their way back to Marseilles, where they were rescued by a young American journalist, Varian Fry, an enterprising Quaker who was a leading light in the Emergency Rescue Committee formed in New York to help especially deserving individuals escape from France. Fry, ingenious, brave and necessarily unscrupulous in this black-market rescue operation, became an almost legendary figure in the mass movement of intellectuals and creative people from continent to continent in the Second World War. Viewing Werfel and Alma as obvious candidates he went to call on them at their hotel, where Alma welcomed him with one of the many bottles of Benedictine she kept conveniently at hand.

Varian Fry organised the details of their flight, made along with the writer Heinrich Mann (elder brother of Thomas), Heinrich's wife Nelly and nephew Golo. He recommended that, in order to avoid the border controls enforced by the pro-German Vichy regime in France, they set out on a journey on foot across the Pyrenees and into Spain. This was a considerable struggle. Heinrich and Nelly Mann were both ageing and infirm. Werfel and Alma herself were hardly agile, both being considerably overweight. However, they made it across to Barcelona. Alma's lost luggage had miraculously been recovered and she carried the Mahler and Bruckner scores across the mountains in her personal baggage. She was relying on the precious manuscripts to finance her new life in America.

From Barcelona they took a train to Madrid, and from there a plane to Lisbon. They reached New York at last by boat on 13 October 1938 and then in December moved on to Los Angeles, taking a house in the Hollywood Hills. Hollywood by then housed a considerable enclave of European émigrés, the world explored so wittily by Christopher Hampton in his 1980s play *Tales from Hollywood*.

In their new life in America Alma and Werfel were reunited with many people from their Viennese and Berlin past. As well as both Heinrich and Thomas Mann they were back in contact with Bertolt Brecht, Max Reinhardt and the conductor Bruno Walter, protégé and devotee of Mahler. Compared with London, where she was so conscious of being a nonentity, Hollywood was a place where many of her neighbours understood precisely who Alma Mahler was. And Werfel himself found fame in fulfilling his vow made in Lourdes to write his own version of Bernadette's visions. Werfel's novel *The Song of Bernadette* was sensationally successful and was made into a film in 1943. It was obvious to those who knew about the illness and early death of Manon Gropius that the saintly Bernadette was partly based on her sacrosanct persona.

In the autumn of 1942 they moved to the glitzier environment of Beverly Hills. Here they lived in what Alma called 'a small select circle' that included Arnold Schoenberg and his wife Gertrud, Fritzi Massary, once the queen of German light opera, both the literary brothers Mann, Lion and Marta Feuchtwanger, the writer Alfred Neumann and the Austrian composer Erich Korngold, who had once been, like Alma, a prize pupil of Zemlinsky. In this network of now elderly European émigrés Alma was regarded with a mixture of deference and disbelief. A new intimate friend, the younger German writer Erich Maria Remarque, famous for his novel *Im Westen Nichts Neues* (*All Quiet on the Western Front*), described Alma after their first meeting as 'a wild, blond wench, violent, boozing. Has already put Mahler under the earth. She was with Gropius and Kokoschka, who seem to have escaped from her clutches. Werfel won't.' In fact contact between Alma and Gropius continued, though very intermittently, through the decades when both of them were living in the States.

————

In New England through the early 1940s Gropius was slowly and anxiously absorbing the progression of the war in Europe. Ise describes him as increasingly fixated on the daily news bulletins on the radio. Hearing of the first wave of German bombardments of London he wrote anxiously to Maxwell Fry, hoping that Fry's wife and daughter were now staying in the country, 'safe from German presents from the air'. Herbert Bayer shared the Gropiuses' horror at the rapid escalation of the war, with the German forces so successfully advancing on many of the places they themselves revered. 'Now the heavenly islands in Greece are getting their turn,' Bayer wrote. 'It is simply grotesque what is going on and the chances of stopping this murderous wave are getting even smaller.' The United States was still remaining neutral, but they began to wonder how long this could last.

As Alma in Los Angeles surrounded herself with European exiles, a comforting entourage of people from her past with inexhaustible resources of shared memories, Gropius in New England was dependent on assembling his inner core of Bauhäusler, the people he was easy with, whose attitudes he shared. Here in a new country these long-familiar faces, the in-jokes and the jollity boosted his self-confidence. Ati remembered how during the war years their house became the meeting point for people from the Bauhaus: 'There was a close inner circle: the artists Herbert Bayer, Josef Albers, Lyonel Feininger, and Xanti Schawinsky and our neighbour Marcel Breuer. They all called my father "Pius" and my mother "Pia", as they had done at the Bauhaus.' Included in this group were Alexander Dorner and Sigfried Giedion, now working in America, and both their wives. 'They seemed like family to me,' wrote Ati, 'for in their presence my parents seemed most relaxed, and there was much laughter, as well as endless talk.'

Ati especially loved it when Gropius became a little drunk and almost playful, as uninhibited and funny as Schawinsky, 'that beloved clown figure' of Ati's childhood back in Germany. 'Sailing out into the garden, glass in hand, one stormy night, he was admonished by Isi who called "Walla, Walla, come in! it's raining!" He replied without hesitation "it's all right, I'll turn it off."'

For New Year 1940 they were all assembled for a celebration party: Marcel Breuer with his new wife, Constance Crocker Leighton – who had been a secretary in the Gropius–Breuer office – the Schawinskys, Herbert Bayer and Gropius's friend from the CIAM congresses in Europe, the Spanish architect Josep Lluís Sert. Ise wrote to Jack Pritchard in London saying what a miracle it was that their bunch of close friends was still sticking together, adding that they already loved Lajkó's new wife Connie *very* much.

From summer 1940 onwards there were three more permanent visitors to the Gropius House. The Blitz was causing Londoners to panic. Thousands of London children were being evacuated into the relative safety of the English countryside. Others were sent much further afield, often to the United States and Canada.

In May 1940 Jack Pritchard wrote to Gropius from Lawn Road asking him to help with his and Molly's plan to send their sons, thirteen-year-old Jonathan and eleven-year-old Jeremy, to live in America. He needed Gropius to write officially inviting the boys to be educated for a year, and he made it clear there would be no question of expenses until after the war. 'I am sorry to have to burden you with these problems as you have had enough worries of your own, but I know of no one whose point of view I could trust better than yours . . . We know we are asking a hell of a lot.' The request in fact was something of a *quid pro quo* since Jack and Molly Pritchard had been so welcoming when Walter and Ise arrived as refugees in London, and Gropius unhesitatingly agreed to have the Pritchard boys to stay.

Jack was preoccupied in London with his war work. As a statistician he was allotted to the Ministry of Supply. It had originally been the plan that Molly should see the boys settled in America and then return to London. In the end she stayed as well, managing to find herself temporary work at Harvard. Ise appeared glad to have her in the house, reporting back to Jack a few months after their arrival, 'We get along very well with each other and with the Breuers next door. There is always something up for Saturdays and Sundays, even if it is only some ping-pong playing.' Molly was able to help Ati with her homework and joined in the family evening reading sessions. Ise realised that Molly soon picked up a great deal of German, although she did not venture to talk.

Between Ati and the adolescent Pritchard boys the chemistry was evidently more problematic. She was particularly hostile to Jonathan and wary of males in general. The Gropiuses put this down to her solitary upbringing by Hertha and lingering resentment of her absent father. An uneasy, suspicious attitude to men continued through Ati's teenage years and on into adulthood.

Molly finally left Lincoln in August 1942. Gropius was evidently sorry to see her go. She had become 'a definite part' of their family life, he told Jack. 'She has been very courageous and we admire her fortitude.' Jonathan and Jeremy stayed in the States and the Gropiuses continued to house them and support them. It was a generous repayment of the debt.

From 1940 onwards the guest room at the Gropius House was never empty. Fortunately the house was planned in such a way that visitors were easily absorbed. Beyond the entrance porch the rooms opened out into an easy sequence from hallway to living room and dining room, these two areas being separated only by a curtain. The living room was planned around the open fireplace, comforting in cold New England winters. In summer a screened porch led out onto the terrace, creating an additional sunny living space.

The Visitors' Book, still kept on exhibition at the Gropius House, with its signatures and photographs, its enthusiastic comments, its witty little drawings, gives fascinating proof of the non-stop influx, containing so many of the famous names of European and American art and architecture (see Plate 30). With its Miró watercolour inscribed 'Pour Madame et Monsieur Gropius', its photo of Hans Arp on his first visit to New England, its humorously cryptic inscription by Wells Coates, its fond words from Le Corbusier to his 'cher *ami*' Gropius 'avec toute mon amitié', the sketch of a curled-up fox by Gropius's fellow émigré György Kepes (now calling himself Georg) 'with old but not aged friendship', the Visitors' Book is a precious document, amounting to a kind of collage in itself.

Soon after the completion of the Gropius House we see evidence of a visit on 24 January 1940 by Frank Lloyd Wright, photographed in his flamboyant winter greatcoat, hat clamped down firmly over his wavy silver locks. If we sense a somewhat belligerent expression, this is not surprising. The grand old man of American architecture had been building up resistance to Gropius's arrival in the New World.

Gropius, who had admired Wright's architecture for so many decades, wrote to congratulate him after visiting Fallingwater in 1938, while he was working on the Frank House in Pittsburgh. Wright's return visit to Gropius at Lincoln had followed on from there. Gropius described the encounter later:

When Wright had dinner with me in my house in January 1940, and we had a few hours of quiet conversation, I found him very bitter about the treatment he had received in his own country, and he referred particularly to the fact that I had been chairman of the Department of Architecture at Harvard while he himself had never been offered such a position of influence when he was younger.

Wright at the time was all too conscious of falling out of favour with the newer generation of American architects, who considered him passé and grandiloquent. He also of course felt a more general resentment about the warm welcome given in America to Gropius and other Bauhaus members. We might see a rather desperate attempt at self-assertion in Wright's dramatic entrance at the opening of the MoMA Bauhaus exhibition, with the glamorous young woman on his arm. Formally Frank Lloyd Wright and Walter Gropius remained on good terms. They had so many overlapping interests: in education and community living, in unit construction, in the beautification of the workplace, in the parameters of the ideal city. Just a few years later Gropius was prevailed upon to sign a petition supporting Wright's plans for non-political constructive social research, which resulted in his concept of Broadacre City.

Gropius never stopped admiring the 'romantic and explosive handwriting' which characterised all Wright's architecture, acknowledging that his 'superb, if somewhat upsetting, showmanship had helped to bring the cause of architecture into public consciousness'. The Robie House in Chicago and the much later Larkin Building in Buffalo were both 'fundamentally new architectural milestones'. But there was always an edginess between Frank Lloyd Wright and Walter Gropius.

In 1948 Sibyl Moholy-Nagy visited Wright at his Taliesin estate and they talked of Gropius. Wright sighed and said, 'A fine man – as most Germans' (Sibyl tells us that Frank Lloyd Wright was a Germanophile); 'too bad that he isn't an architect – just an engineer.'

The most touching of the entries in the Gropius House Visitors' Book is the one for Igor and Vera Stravinsky, dated 2 May 1940. Stravinsky and Vera de Bosset, his beloved companion of twenty years' standing, had been married two months earlier nearby in Bedford, Massachusetts. They had at last been freed to marry following the death of Stravinsky's first wife from tuberculosis in 1939. Stravinsky then moved from Paris to the United States to take up the Charles Eliot Norton lectureship at Harvard, on Gropius's recommendation, and Vera travelled out to join him. Their pictures in the Gropius album show them still in a cel-

Igor and Vera Stravinsky's entry in the Gropius House Visitors' Book
soon after their wedding in 1940.

ebratory mood, Stravinsky now very bald and owlish in round spectacles, Vera in a beautiful black Cossack-style hat with flowing scarf and striped silk shirt with a big pussycat bow. While Stravinsky was at Harvard Gropius resumed the friendship that had started at the Bauhaus. They now had a new reason for closeness: a shared relief in being welcomed in America. As Gropius acknowledged, 'We both owe a debt to our adopted country for a new chance at life at a time when the European continent was darkened, and its cultural life was running in ever narrower channels.'

Ise enjoyed the influxes of visitors, resuming the role she had back at the Bauhaus leading admiring crowds round the Director's House. Here too she was always elegantly dressed, her hair immaculately done, make-up carefully applied. She believed in spending time in making up her face, with an attention to effect that Gropius encouraged, taking the view that women's make-up was itself an art form. But he was less innately sociable than Ise. Sometimes as more and more visitors arrived he would take refuge in the bedroom. Ati often escaped as well.

Behind the scenes a regime of relative frugality took over. These were anxious years in which, as Ati wrote, 'the spirit of economising was much in evidence'. In the Gropius House the lights were religiously switched off when not needed, 'running hot water, frowned upon; heat and fuel, always rationed'. She could remember her parents huddled in shawls in the living room. Gerdy, the massive young black cook, was now dismissed and Ise herself took over the cooking. Alvar Aalto, at the time a visiting professor at Massachusetts Institute of Technology (MIT), was apparently astonished to find Walter Gropius doing the washing up. Ise darned all Walter's socks: none were simply thrown away. Sheets and pillow slips were mended, turned edge to edge and then sewn up again. Ise was adept at remodelling her clothes to reflect the latest fashions. According to Ati, to make do with a minimum was as much an ethic as the ethic of visual perfection prevailing at the Gropius House.

To some extent this frugality reflected the post-Depression mood of America itself, changed times in which financial security was no longer taken for granted and caution and saving were becoming *de rigueur*. But for the Gropiuses there were deeper fears. Ise felt convinced that the Americans were kidding themselves that the war would soon be over and the US could stay out of it. They didn't understand the persistence of dictators as she and Walter did.

———

Early in 1941 Gropius and Breuer, now working in their joint office in Harvard Square, received a commission for a tourist centre at Key West in Florida, an extended sequence of buildings for holiday recreation, including a swimming pool, club rooms and a library. This idea of the waterside development had fascinated Gropius since his visions for a sequence of high-rise apartment blocks along the Wannsee shore. The project at Key West was continued by Gropius alone after he and Breuer had a sudden dramatic and, for Gropius, very painful rift. The background to the row was almost comically trivial. On 23 May 1941 Breuer turned on Gropius as chairman of a jury judging Harvard students work for starting a meeting fifteen minutes late, at 4.15 rather than 4.00. Breuer first complained to Gropius in front of the assembled jury members, then wrote two decisive and for Gropius startlingly aggressive letters. The first, addressed to Gropius in his official Harvard role, with a copy to Dean Hudnut, set out Breuer's basic accusations. 'During our jury meeting of today, you handled the school business in a manner which I feel is below the level of the University and which I personally am not willing to accept. I strongly feel that you mis-used your authority and am deeply offended.'

The second letter, sent to Gropius at home, ended their many years of close collaboration. 'Dear Pius,' Breuer wrote: 'I am now convinced that our partnership is objectively and personally possible no longer. As to the reasons, we each certainly have our own ideas, which I feel it would not help to analyze.' He suggested that their joint office should close on 1 August and that any commissions they received before the closure should be handled privately. 'This in effect would mean that our partnership ceases immediately.'

Gropius replied two days later: 'Dear Lajkó, this is to tell you that I accept your suggestions regarding the dissolving of our partnership. Nothing more can be said after your two amazing letters of May 23.' On a separate sheet, headed 'Facts about a collision between Breuer and myself in Robinson Hall on Friday 23 May at 4:15pm', Gropius set out the facts of the episode as he now viewed it. Indignantly he defended himself against Breuer's accusations: 'The only event which "has been below the level of the University" was Breuer's rebuking me twice in an offending tone in presence of members of the faculty . . . I cannot allow anybody to talk to me as rudely as he did.' Gropius claimed to be surprised and mystified: 'The event itself being but a trifle in my opinion, his outrage was all the more ununderstandable.'

Though Gropius now wrote to express shock and dismay, it seems that in fact he had seen a rift with Breuer coming. He told Bayer in confidence that what he had feared for some time had now happened: 'a bust-up between Lajkó and myself. The reason for it was a petty little thing, but suddenly I had to realise that I was associated in partnership not with a friend but with a foe. He is too deeply in love with himself, and the *"Kleinmeister* complex" against the Bauhaus Director has brought him to commit betrayal towards me.'

And indeed if one looks back through Bauhaus history, these resentments at playing a subsidiary role had been fermenting for decades. As far back as December 1924 Breuer and Albers were threatening to leave the Bauhaus in Weimar to set up on their own in Berlin. Two years later Breuer attempted to resign from his position as Master of the carpentry workshop at Dessau in order to concentrate on training as an architect. 'He feels hampered in his personal development and would like to work in a wider field of activity,' Ise had written in her diary at that time. In 1927 Breuer was demanding to take over the direction of the building department. 'His ambition grows almost alarmingly,' said Ise. Gropius, considering him too young and inexperienced, turned the idea down.

Since then Marcel Breuer, now almost in his forties and becoming increasingly successful and self-confident, had clearly grown increasingly impatient at playing second fiddle to the maestro. In London his furniture for Isokon was admired by the London cognoscenti and his architecture had developed in a highly original direction. Breuer's 1936 Gane Pavilion, a temporary exhibition building designed for the Bristol furniture manufacturer and retailer Crofton Gane and shown at the local Royal Agricultural Show, broke new ground. With its massive Cotswold stone wall slabs, combined with large glass windows and a light wood roof, this was a modernist building that was quite unlike a Gropius work. It had an architectural authority that was becoming increasingly Marcel Breuer's own.

Now that he was working in the States the buildings designed by Breuer alone – his own house at Lincoln, the highly original Chamberlain Cottage on the Sudbury River at Wayland, the first of his woodframed buildings, apparently suspended in mid-air – show how far he was detaching himself from Gropius's influence. Breuer was forging on in his own independent direction. Gropius saw the situation clearly, maintaining that 'he doesn't need me any more since he has had enough personal success now'.

The Bauhäusler's need to separate themselves at some point in their lives from the powerful personality of Gropius did not apply to Breuer alone. Xanti Schawinsky shows signs of feeling similarly oppressed and needing to break free. The photo-collage portrait he made of Gropius, *Theme and Variation on a Face* in 1943, showing Gropius both as a benign and as a dictatorial figure, is startling in its ambiguity. And certainly Gropius to some extent still clung to his old Bauhaus habit of command.

As far as Breuer's bid for freedom is concerned there may have been another influence at work. He was newly married. His wife Connie, who had worked in their joint office and knew Ise well, might have been wary of the continuing influence of the woman, Breuer's 'Pia mia', to whom he had for many years been close, in a complicated part-brotherly, part-amorous relationship.

Angered as he was by Breuer's crude attack Gropius was still desperate to keep his inner core of Bauhäusler around him. His longer-term response to Marcel Breuer's outburst reminds one of his determination to remain conciliatory when Herbert Bayer and Ise first confessed to their affair. Despite the break-up, Gropius and Breuer, although working separately, continued at their office in Harvard Square. Both carried on their teaching at the Graduate School of Design and remained as neighbours for the next few years in Lincoln, until the Breuers made a move to Cambridge and then, in 1946, settled in New York. Amicable correspondence between Breuer and the Gropiuses resumed. There were visits to and fro. Gropius had worked with Marcel Breuer in close proximity for more than twenty years. Now more than ever he could not afford to let such long associations drop.

One of many begging letters Gropius received on behalf of European émigrés came from Albert Einstein. He and Einstein had known one another since the 1920s, when Einstein had been a supporter of the Bauhaus, a member of the Circle of Friends. He too was now living in the States and he wrote from Princeton University telling Gropius of the plight of the German architect Konrad Wachsmann, a protégé of Einstein's who had designed a summer house in Caputh, Potsdam, for him.

Wachsmann, a modernist who trained with Hans Poelzig, left Berlin for Paris in 1938. He had fought with the French against the Germans but, being Jewish, was now in a French internment camp. With the German forces making inroads towards Vichy Wachsmann was in considerable danger. Einstein asked Gropius to help him to emigrate to the United States. Gropius wrote to an old friend of his parents, a former French ambassador to Germany, asking him to organise Wachsmann's release and successfully obtained a visa. Wachsmann finally arrived at the Gropius House in September 1941, frail, undernourished, weary after his long travels, with no means of support. He too was found a room there and he lived in the Gropius household for the next three years.

Konrad Wachsmann with Ise and Walter Gropius in 1946.

Wachsmann and Gropius now collaborated on developing the prefabricated housing structures that had interested both of them for many years. To see Wachsmann at this point as a substitute for Breuer would not be accurate. They were very different personalities. In contrast to the humorous, self-confident Breuer, Wachsmann was more solemn and withdrawn, short, Germanic and intense with a heavy accent, rendered almost incomprehensible by what seemed to be a deep-rooted adenoidal problem. He was described by the critic Peter Blake as an 'introverted technologist, a very private person, single-minded in his pursuit of narrow and highly disciplined objectives'.

Isometric drawing for Packaged House, Walter Gropius and Konrad Wachsmann, 1942.

But certainly the technological visionary Wachsmann could be said to have arrived at the right time to refocus Gropius's ambitions. As Wachsmann gradually recovered from his terrible experiences, they worked together closely on the Packaged House System, as they called it, a fast-assembly concept for wood construction prefabricated housing based on standardised parts that were exchangeable for different types of dwelling. It was claimed that a Packaged House could be assembled in less than nine hours. The project, for which Wachsmann and Gropius entered into partnership, would be of great interest to the military authorities during the coming escalation of the war.

The worst – or the best – had now happened, as Gropius described his mixed reactions to Jack Pritchard after the United States declared war first on Japan and then on Germany and Italy after the Japanese bombing of Pearl Harbor in December 1941: 'Pearl Harbor has speeded up the process of adaptation of our inner and outer skin.'

The new complication for Gropius was that now, being still classed as a German, he was categorised as an alien, the fate he had avoided by leaving England. He was allotted registration number 1885751 and identity card reference 2356. He had to report regularly to the authorities and needed to apply to the relevant office in order to travel outside Boston. His pattern of life was not seriously altered. There were a few irritating incidents such as the bombardment of the Gropius House with tomatoes, apparently the work of a band of local youths, or the rumour being spread that Gropius's morning ride through the woods on Colvin, his horse, had a hidden purpose and that he was sending coded messages to the enemy on a secret radio transmitter. But day-to-day life continued as before. There was very little wartime hardship in New England, only some rationing and shortages of meat. The effects for Gropius were much more psychological. He and Ise had already applied to become American citizens. But now America officially rejected him. This was the third country he had lived in within a single decade. Where did he actually belong?

There was the added problem of scarcity of work. This had been a difficulty for an obvious foreigner, even for a foreigner as distinguished as Gropius, in the years before war was declared. Gropius, for instance, had been in the running as architect for MoMA's new building in New York, only to be rejected by the powerful museum patron Abby Aldrich Rockefeller on grounds that so prestigious a job must go to American architects. With Gropius now officially an alien such prejudice against him was increased. He was permitted to retain his post at Harvard, but the politically cautious Dean Hudnut instructed him to keep a low profile when it came to seeking architectural work. 'Hudnut wants me under a cloak!' Gropius complained.

The war, however, led to one constructive development within the Harvard architectural department. To the delight of Gropius, who was already pushing for opening the department up to women, citing the achievements of women at the Bauhaus, the absence of male students who were now away at war meant that for the first time women were enrolling in the Graduate School of Design, transferred from Smith College architecture school in Cambridge. 'Here are quite some changes,' he wrote to tell Moholy. 'The boys at Harvard drop out rapidly into the Army and Navy but the school is going on through the summer after we have decided to take women . . . maybe out of this will develop a co-education in our school.'

In many ways the Graduate School of Design was actually energised by the United States entering the war. Though most current architectural projects were paralysed, this was regarded as only temporary and there was now an opportunity to focus on planning for better living conditions once peace was finally achieved. Gropius and Martin Wagner, with so much shared experience in rethinking Berlin, were now involved in this.

Wagner had come to join the teaching staff at Harvard at Gropius's original instigation, but there had been recent clashes between the two. Perhaps he felt resentment at his need for Gropius's patronage. No doubt such an uncompromising character as Wagner experienced his own inner anxieties about his future in the United States. In any case Wagner hurtfully suggested that since he had left Germany Gropius's priorities had changed. He accused him of abandoning his original principles of democratic modernism, of selling out to American capitalism. He lamented Gropius's turnaround in viewpoint: 'I found a pretty great difference', Wagner told him all too frankly, 'between my 41 and my 57 aged friend.' He accused Gropius of having turned away from the world's 'most urgent social, economical and artistical problems . . . A museum, a dance pavilion, a "gentleman farm" etc. may be very nice objects and projects, but they are rare trees in the forest of our present urban and rural and social life.'

Coming as it did from so close a friend and colleague this was a formidable attack. But the new priorities of wartime, besides their shared anxieties about the fate of those they had left behind in Germany, at least temporarily reunited them. Wagner was now put in charge of Harvard's regional planning studies and he and Gropius worked together closely in developing a master plan for the improved development of cities in the USA in the post-war years.

Two of Gropius's most promising students at this juncture were Paul Rudolph and I. M. Pei. Rudolph, who was born in Kentucky and whose father was a travelling Methodist preacher, joined the Graduate School of Design in autumn 1941, leaving three years later to serve in the Navy. He was evidently a favoured pupil, allotted one of the best spots in the studio where Gropius himself came to supervise his students. Rudolph was later to acknowledge Gropius as the person who gave him his first real sense of direction in architecture. 'I found in his teaching a base on which one could build, not merely a formula, as so many others have . . . Gropius's strength lies in his ability to analyse and make precisely clear the broad problems of our day.' He regarded Gropius as a great teacher, a theorist, an entrepreneur, who was remarkably articulate, focused and approachable. In Rudolph's opinion he was *not* a good architect but as an educator he was unsurpassed.

I. M. Pei was briefly Gropius's student from December 1942. He was born in China into a successful banking family, moving from Shanghai to the University of Pennsylvania in 1935. His girlfriend Eileen Loo, a landscape architect studying at Harvard, persuaded him to enter the Graduate School of Design. His studies there were almost immediately interrupted when he joined the National Defense Research Committee set up to co-ordinate American research into weapons technology in the Second World War. But, already impressed by Gropius's teaching, I. M. Pei returned to Harvard in 1945. 'When I first came to Harvard', he remembered, 'Gropius did not understand my language. Gropius's contribution to the American architectural scene was that he brought us a common language.' Again Gropius's breadth of outlook was a formative influence.

Two very different architects: Paul Rudolph, the radical exponent of neo-Brutalist concrete structures, the most famous of which is the New Haven Yale Art and Architecture Building; I. M. Pei, in complete contrast, the architect of angularity, transparency and mystery, as seen in his Musée du Louvre Pyramid in Paris, the Bank of China skyscraper in Hong Kong, the Deutsches Historisches Museum building in Berlin, the exquisite and poetic Miho Museum in Japan. Both of these architects give convincing proof of the effectiveness of Gropius's idea of teaching in allowing individual freedom of development rather than imposing a doctrinaire approach. In the slow evolution of architectural teaching at Harvard from historicist to modern, Gropius's breadth of vision brought about a fundamental change.

———

With the United States entering the war, life in the Gropius House at Lincoln became more tense and muted. Ati at sixteen had already left home and was now studying at Black Mountain College, under the eye of Josef Albers. Walter and Ise were inevitably focused on the progress of the war, Gropius concerned not to miss the latest bulletins as the Allied forces battled across Europe. With all communication from the continent cut off they felt desperately worried about all their relations. Gropius's sister Manon was still thought to be living in Berlin, his many Burchard relations in Hanover. At this point the uncertainties surrounding day-to-day conditions in Germany were very hard to bear.

At last on 12 June 1944 Gropius became a US citizen. This was a considerable relief, giving him much more freedom of manoeuvre. He was no longer so much a displaced person. But it is questionable whether he ever felt American. His original sense of being German was too deeply ingrained.

Later in the year, with the end of the war now appearing imminent, he wrote to Maxwell Fry in London:

The horizon looks brighter now, fortunately, and it may be that by the time this letter reaches you there, the last phase of the war in Europe will have arrived, although the last run may be bloody and hard for both sides. It is really pathetic to think what will be left of Europe after this war — I mean not only the visible destruction but that which has been destroyed in the human mind.

There is a deep sense of ambivalence in Gropius's letter. He was terrified to contemplate the fate of the country he still considered as his homeland. Germany finally surrendered to the Allied forces in early May 1945.

As war raged in Europe the Gropiuses' life in New England had been relatively insulated. The quiet rural landscape, the rhythms of nature, their plants, birds and animals were a source of comfort when, as Gropius put it, the world was tearing itself apart. But once the war ended a different mood took over, a process of discovery and retribution as news from Europe came percolating through. 'A lot of my past acquaintances from Italy, France, Poland have either been killed, are missing, or living in miserable circumstances. I fear the coming year will lift the veil on the fate of my acquaintances.' 1945 was a year of an often grief-stricken untangling of the past.

Gropius continued to be desperate for news of his family and in particular his sister Manon Burchard, to whom he had always been close. He tried to trace her through the Red Cross, the US State Department Special War Problems Division, the American Friends' Service Committee of the Catholic Church. The last Berlin address he had for Manon was in Charlottenburg, now under Russian occupation.

Finally, with immense persistence, lines of communication were opened up through the commandant of the American armed forces stationed in Germany. Military searches in Berlin discovered Manon with her daughter Evelina (known as Ine). They were in poor health, living not far from their old home. There were long delays in Gropius's letters arriving. He wrote to her twice in the autumn and winter of 1945. Manon finally replied to him on 18 January 1946, a long detailed letter that told him the story of her war.

Her husband, Max, had died after a stroke in 1944. Manon decided to go back to Hanover, but finding it too lonely there without him she returned to join Ine in Berlin at the beginning of November. Until

Christmas 1944 Berlin was still quiet, but then the air raids started, as many as three times a day. On the final day of the bombardment, on 20 April 1945, the first Russian troops entered Berlin. A number of soldiers burst into the cellar of the house in which Manon and her daughter had taken refuge, offering cigarettes and chocolates. Many of their neighbours, according to Manon, were convinced that the kingdom of heaven had begun on earth. But then the plundering of Berlin houses and the raping of German women started. Manon and Ine managed to escape upstairs and from then on the house was kept locked.

Through 1945 Manon's life was appallingly laborious. Conditions in Berlin immediately worsened. No water, no electricity, no gas, no cooking facilities except for the occasions when she and Ine negotiated to put a little cooking pot on a coal-fired hotplate belonging to the shoemaker who worked on the ground floor of the building. Things only very gradually improved, with electricity returning intermittently on 13 July. She could hardly imagine an existence without shortages and struggles. For Manon this sudden reconnection with her brother and with Ise, secure in their new country of relative plenty, brought her an almost indescribable feeling of relief.

Gropius started to send her regular food parcels via the United States Europe Corporation. The first of these included bacon, cheese, salami, butter, milk and liver pâté. Manon sent him lists of the things she and Ine needed most: a raincoat, a nightdress, a cardigan, cotton stockings and nylons, two pairs of panties in artificial silk, detergent, soap and hand cream. Not all her specialist requirements could be met. Gropius was, for instance, unable to send over any boots, which were unobtainable in America in summer. Nor could he and Ise locate the fabric-covered buttons and linen pillow ties that Manon wanted, considered a necessity by the German *Hausfrau*. Ise wrote to explain, 'There are no linen ties, because people don't use that sort of thing here. They just let the covers hang loosely on the pillow without buttons and button holes, which simplifies life somewhat and looks very good.' Gropius hoped that Manon would now join them in the States, but she saw that this would be too much of an upheaval and refused.

Gropius suddenly found he had a large extended family. Manon's son Georg Joachim, known as Jochen, had briefly been a British prisoner of war. After his release he and Gropius began to correspond. There was so much shared history between them. Jochen's father Max, Gropius's brother-in-law, had been the Prussian *Landrat*, the district administrator, at Alfeld-an-der-Leine, and had helped negotiate the Faguswerk commission for him. Jochen and his sisters had been excited by the Bauhaus and its new ideas, Jochen taking part in Bauhaus events and parties both in Weimar and in Dessau. Most significantly, it had been Jochen whom Gropius sent in pursuit of the beautiful young Ise after he first fell in love with her in Hanover, and he had lodged with the Gropiuses in Berlin in 1928 while he was studying law. When they decided to leave Germany Jochen and his wife Luise raised the money to pay the obligatory *Reichsfluchtsteuer*, the flight tax, on their behalf. Through the war, when Jochen kept a low profile as a marine driver, communication ceased, but once the war ended Gropius sent his nephew long, informative and confidential letters. To some extent Jochen filled the place of the son Gropius had never had. As we shall see, the search for a son-substitute was a recurring pattern in his life.

To Gropius's delight letters also began arriving from Jochen's children. There were five of them: Almut, Max, Anna Manon, Eike, little Sibylle. The whole family was living in Hanover, parents and children squashed into two rooms. They were all extremely musical and kept their morale going by playing quartets. The letters they sent to '*Lieber Onkel Walter*', written in a childish script, decorated with little coloured drawings of fairy tales and flowers, are collected in the Gropius archive at Harvard. These are immensely moving documents, reminding us of Gropius's strong sense of the dynastic. His post-war rediscovery of this large, lively, affectionate young family in Hanover brought him a longed-for reconnection with his past.

But of course reports from Germany brought him new anxieties as he pondered more on what the prospects for his country had been pre-Hitler and what had now become of it. How could Germany ever emerge from such a debacle? His fears pour out in a letter to his sister written in October 1946:

Whenever I read the letters I received from old friends and Bauhauslers who were in concentration camps or in the hands of the Gestapo I was thankful that our families escaped unscathed. But rest assured, I don't underestimate the collective burden that you now all have to bear. The hatred that the Nazis amassed is a terrible negative force that can only gradually dissipate with time. For the present Germany is politically dead, but I do certainly hold out the hope that interest in Germany will reawaken as soon as the process of denazification has come to a conclusion of some kind.

As the Gropiuses realised, it would take years for the search for lost friends and contacts to subside. One of the earliest reappearances was that of the Polish architects Szymon and Helena Syrkus, Gropius's great friends and allies from the pre-war meetings of CIAM. In October 1945 Ise wrote excitedly to Jack and Molly Pritchard that they were looking forward to a visit from the Syrkuses, who had 'quite miraculously emerged from concentration camp, starvation and other nightmares. They are the last people we expected to see again.'

After Gropius's unsuccessful attempt in the years before the war to organise employment for the Syrkuses at Harvard, he discovered to his horror that in 1942 Szymon had been arrested and taken to Auschwitz. Gropius sent an urgent telegram to Pope Pius XII in Rome asking him to intervene to get Syrkus released. No action was taken. There was a long silence. In June 1945 a telegram arrived from Helena in Warsaw. It said, 'Still waiting for Syrkus arrested 1942. Sent to concentration camp Oswiecim.' This was Auschwitz. Her last news of him had been in December 1944. She gave Gropius the number tattooed on Szymon's arm – 77165 – and begged him to help her find him. Gropius immediately sent off letters of enquiry to the organisations set up to deal with the tracing of displaced persons in the aftermath of war.

Early in October 1945 Gropius received an unexpected letter from a stranger, a Mr C. R. Mathewson, recently returned from Germany and now staying at the American Hotel in Brookville, Pennsylvania. He reported a brief sighting of Szymon Syrkus, who wanted Gropius to know he was alive and well. Mathewson added that the only thing that had kept Syrkus from being killed at Auschwitz was the fact that he was an architectural engineer. 'He was forced to work for the Germans in the designing of buildings and gardens for the S.S.' In explaining his survival there was also the factor that he had initially been registered as a Pole and not a Jew. Almost simultaneously with this report from Mathewson Gropius heard from Helena herself. She gave him the news that Szymon was back in Warsaw and that they were hoping to come to America for a few months, a plan that Gropius pursued delightedly, inviting them as delegates to the International Congress for Modern Building. The sudden reappearance of Szymon and Helena in the lives of the Gropiuses was indeed a little miracle of war.

In 1946, after years of wartime silence, Lily Hildebrandt came back into Gropius's life with a letter from Stuttgart which she arranged to be delivered via the American architect Gordon Chadwick, who had served in the US army in Germany as an inspector of German monuments and fine arts and was now returning to the States. Lily's letter is dated 30 January. Gropius finally received it in July.

Lily tells him that during the war years she and Hans had been through 'a *great* many difficult experiences' and had learnt 'more than enough about human nature'. Professionally Hans the art historian had been completely sidelined, dismissed from his post at the Technische Hochschule and banned from publishing any further books, being now regarded as 'a degenerate for his attitude to art, which he uncompromisingly remained true to'. Lily, lying low in Stuttgart, had managed to conceal her Jewish background. She would otherwise almost certainly have perished, like so many other Jewish people that they knew. But continuing to work had been impossible because of wartime privations and her own poor health. In a pathetic scribbled footnote to her letter she explains that she suffered from painful joint disorders as a result of lack of heating in their flat.

'Still we have survived the "Third Reich" and the war,' Lily writes, 'the horror of which you cannot imagine, and even saved our apartment, even if it was frequently damaged.' Many of their precious artworks had been pilfered. Most of their large pre-war entourage of friends and contacts had deserted them. But desperate as the Hildebrandts' experiences had been, there are still traces in this letter of the pre-war Lily, Gropius's 'Lily-cat', his 'Lilychen', who as a young woman had shown such a great eagerness in making her way in the world of modern art.

In her first post-war letter she begs him to send her 'some intellectual nourishment, photographs and publications about buildings by you and others in your circle, about modern painters, about exhibitions etc . . . I would be especially interested in anything about Surrealism.' Gropius was evidently deeply moved to hear from Lily. 'Your letter', he told her, 'seemed to be like news from another world.'

———

Gropius's attitude towards the Bauhaus remained proprietorial. The address list he took with him to America had its separate section for Bauhäusler, as opposed to family and more general friends and contacts. As more and more news of suffering and destitute ex-Bauhaus staff and students emerged from post-war Germany his and Ise's anxieties and efforts to assist them became the more intense.

For example, reports of sightings reached them in a letter to Gropius sent in October 1946 by Margaret Leischner, who had been a student in the Bauhaus weaving workshop and later head of the dye workshops and Gunta Stölzl's assistant. In 1938 she emigrated to England not because she was Jewish but because she could not tolerate Hitler's regime. She was by this time becoming established in London as a textile designer and a teacher and she had returned to Germany as part of a working party set up by the Council of Industrial Design to investigate post-war prospects for design of manufactured goods. She had managed to make contact with Georg Muche and Joost Schmidt. Of the two Muche had survived the best, working at the Krefeld Textilschule, where 'in spite of the trying and difficult times' he had kept his spirit, 'creating a sane oasis around him'. However, 'poor Schmidtchen has aged very much and looks worn, unhappy and lost. No small wonder when one sees how Berlin looks now. I cannot think of a more depressive place in every respect.' She enclosed a letter from a still devoted Schmidtchen to Gropius in America.

Lyonel Feininger, now living with his wife Julia in New York, was also being made painfully aware of the wartime histories of his past colleagues at the Bauhaus, referring to 'the misery and unspeakable sufferings we are constantly made aware of through the letters we receive from abroad'. He described how these letters had an emotionally paralysing effect: 'we dread every new mail and are almost incapable of formulating our distress in words.' The fact that the Bauhaus since its first conception had been seen as such a place of optimism, of high spirits, of the building of a new world of democracy and beauty made these recent cruel reversals hard to bear.

Perhaps the most poignant of all these Bauhaus stories is that of Friederike ('Friedl') Dicker-Brandeis, who had been a pupil of Johannes Itten in Vienna, following him to the Bauhaus in Weimar, where she excelled as a student in textiles, bookbinding and printing. As an artist she was strongly influenced by Klee. In 1936 she married her cousin Pavel Brandeis. In 1942 Friedl and her husband were both deported to Theresienstadt in Bohemia, which was operated cynically by the Nazis as a kind of model camp, the *'cité ideale des Juifs'* as Nazi propaganda termed it. Theresienstadt had a public image as a centre of liberality and culture, although in reality it was a concentration camp. Here Friedl made herself a role teaching art and design to the imprisoned children, drawing on the inspirational teachings of Itten, focusing especially on those who were traumatised and infirm, the extreme casualties of war. She at first refused to leave the children when the Nazis began the forcible evacuation of Theresienstadt but, when Pavel was transferred to Auschwitz in September 1944, she volunteered for the next transport to join him.

Before leaving she secretly entrusted to the care of the supervisor of Girls Home 410 at Theresienstadt two suitcases containing 4,500 drawings, paintings, collages and sculptures done by the camp children. These were only discovered after the war. Meanwhile, in October 1944 Friedl had been murdered in the extermination camp at Auschwitz-

Birkenau. Her husband Pavel survived. Gropius remembered Friedl Dicker-Brandeis when a student as having a rare multifaceted talent and extraordinary energy and dedication. Collective artistic work was one of the basic tenets of the Bauhaus, as was the belief in the innate creativity of children. Friedl's devoted work with the children of Theresienstadt shows these Bauhaus principles enduring in the least propitious circumstances on earth. The rediscovered drawings are now in the Jewish Museum in Prague.

During those first few years after the war ended Gropius could not help being haunted by the past. Mourning for the dead. Continually anxious for those still in Germany in terrible conditions. 'Our desks are piled high with letters from Germany from all those miserable people who, apart from needing physical comfort, ask so desperately for information. That takes up all the weekends,' Ise told Maxwell Fry. Old friends were still suffering 'that terrible sense of isolation from the world which has come over them since Hitler came into power and we feel it a real duty to do whatever we can to answer most of that mail.'

What amounted to a Gropius House industry was now in operation from Lincoln, Massachusetts. Gropius organised a fund for the support of former Bauhaus members in the United States and he and Ise were now sending regular parcels to former Bauhäusler in Germany and Austria, in addition to the food and clothes sent to members of their families. This was a laborious and frustrating task since the post-war delays and regulations meant that these parcels often failed to arrive and had to be re-sent.

When the Bauhaus fund ran low it was Ise's task to drum up support from potential sympathisers. One of these begging letters went to Philip Johnson. Ise wrote to him on 8 September 1947, 'Don't you think there might be quite a few people in this country who would feel themselves indebted to the pioneer work the Bauhaus has been doing and who would be willing to help out at this task?' Johnson sent a friendly letter back. He had indeed been a Bauhaus enthusiast for decades and he enclosed a cheque for $100 as his contribution to the Bauhaus fund. But did Ise realise that in the 1930s Johnson had in fact been a supporter of the Nazis, an enthusiasm he no longer chose to publicise? Denazification was not a purely European phenomenon. Americans too were going through a complicated process of reviewing and editing the past.

As the Bauhäusler re-emerged after the war, what of the Bauhaus itself, Gropius's much lauded building in Dessau? In 1946 Gropius wrote to tell his nephew Jochen that the Bauhaus was still standing because it had been on the Allied list of notable buildings not to be bombed. All the same the main school building, which was occupied by the Junkers works in wartime, had been damaged in the course of an air raid on Dessau in March 1945. The nearby Director's and Masters' Houses had fared worse. Gropius's own house was destroyed almost completely, only the garage and basement still remaining. The portion of the double house originally occupied by Moholy-Nagy and later on by Albers was also obliterated in the Allied bombing raids.

In 1947 the architect Margarete Schütte-Lihotzky was travelling by bus to attend a congress of former prisoners of the Nazis and concentration camp victims. The driver of the bus took a route via Dessau, stopping briefly at the site of the once resplendent Bauhaus. The experience was dismaying. 'I got out', she wrote, 'and stood before a pile of rubble.' The damage was evidently worse than Gropius had thought.

The three-power occupation of Berlin by Britain, the USA and the USSR took effect on 3 July 1945 and the reputation of the Bauhaus became enmeshed in Cold War rivalries. Early in 1946 Gropius was approached by the military governor of Germany, General Lucius D. Clay, to take on responsibility for planning the reconstruction of the American Sector. He received but rejected a similar request to advise the Soviet forces occupying Berlin.

To begin with Gropius was reluctant to agree to the Americans' offer. In a letter to his nephew Jochen he explained his reasons for demurring. 'My post at Harvard is for life' (Gropius was in fact to be proved wrong about this supposition), and 'the school has the best reputation in the country, which is reflected in the fact that we are overrun with applications. My private practice is also very busy. I have completely

The Bauhaus building in Dessau damaged by an air raid in 1945.

restructured it.' Gropius had joined with seven much younger partners to form The Architects Collaborative, the Cambridge-based practice known as TAC. 'At my age', he explained, 'I can see no sense in suddenly abandoning these roles and taking on a new one again, which would consist more of administration than physical planning.' Another possible reason for his hesitation may have been a simple fear of the emotional complexity of returning as an American citizen to the Germany he still regarded as his home.

In the end Gropius compromised. He accepted a more limited advisory appointment and flew with some trepidation in a DC4 military cargo plane to the city he had last seen in 1935.

The flight was not an easy one. After quarter of an hour one of the motors was discovered to be faulty and the plane was forced to backtrack to the airport. Then after a stop in Newfoundland Gropius suddenly woke up in the night to realise the plane was on fire. 'I alarmed the crew,' as Gropius described the dramatic scene to Ise. The crew jumped up as if electrified. Life belts and parachute harnesses were hurriedly put on and the smouldering plane made it back to Newfoundland again. 'To my own surprise I was quite relaxed and calm while even the crew members were extremely nervous . . . With great effort the fire was kept under control until we finally landed again.' In the early afternoon the journey was continued: 'After ten hours' smooth flight over fairy cotton clouds we reached the Azores. Landing took an hour in thick fog. Midnight dinner during a rainstorm. European atmosphere, twice departure alarm, finally at four in the morning off to Europe. Ten flight hours to Frankfurt, rough and bumpy over France.' After a transfer to Tempelhof airport, he then travelled by bus through the 'indescribable misery' of war-devastated Berlin.

It has been estimated that between 1943 and 1945 Allied bombers destroyed at least a third of the city's 1.5 million buildings and laid waste to ten square miles of central Berlin. Russian forces, entering the city in 1945, had continued the destruction by turning their guns on the remaining buildings, reducing most of Unter den Linden to rubble, seriously damaging the Staatsoper, the Imperial Palace, the Adlon Hotel, the Romanische Café, familiar landmarks of his childhood and his youth.

For Gropius this was a traumatic return. 'Berlin is a has-been! A disintegrated corpse! Impossible to describe. The people bent down, bitter, hopeless. In the evening a meeting with Scharoun, Max Taut, Redslob, Lilly Reich – all so old-looking that I scarcely recognised them. Only Scharoun still has fire. I shall go to him tomorrow.' Hans Scharoun, one of the original members with Gropius of the progressive Zehnerring, the Ring of Ten, had managed to stay on in Germany, keeping a low profile, throughout the years of war.

Gropius was faced with a demanding schedule. Briefings, conferences, site inspections with army and military government officials. General Lucius Clay, notoriously impatient, annoyed him by demanding instant solutions, whereas Gropius could see that the replanning of the city and its surrounding mid-European areas would be dauntingly complex, a hugely ambitious reconstruction programme necessarily involving years of research. He was called upon to tour other German cities, travelling to Frankfurt, Bremen, Hanover, Stuttgart, Wiesbaden, Munich, appalled and depressed by the widespread scenes of ruin and human misery he found. Coming from the States, he was cross-examined closely about the Marshall Plan, in which General George C. Marshall, only months before, had proposed a European Recovery Programme involving the supply of food, medical supplies, industrial machinery and raw materials. Gropius now saw just how urgently practical American assistance was required.

He reported back to Sibyl Moholy-Nagy in Chicago: 'Conditions in Europe are appalling. People are like dry sponges clinging to everybody who comes from outside.' Some were prepared to make thirty-hour journeys from the Russian Zone to have half an hour's conversation with Gropius. People felt he could perform miracles in terms of city planning. He realised only too clearly he could not.

In an emotional letter to the Syrkuses he described his return to Germany as a harrowing experience:

Without seeing with one's own eyes the cities and the people, one cannot imagine with all one's fantasy what this war has done to Europe. I have seen all my people and many others, particularly the former Bauhaus members, and I came back exhausted. I gave advice to the Military Governor regarding reconstruction but I don't know how, under the conditions as they are, a really integrated planning and building should take place since everybody is thinking only of getting a roof over his head.

Gropius returned to the United States by way of England. He was travelling on his own since in the previous summer Ise had suffered a serious accident, a car crash that fractured her right ankle and broke her ribs. She would be in a wheelchair or else on crutches for another year. She was evidently frustrated at being left at home, grumbling about Walter travelling all over the world while she was stranded in Lincoln, Massachusetts, with little to do to entertain herself, not knowing his plans or how long letters would take to reach him once he arrived in England to attend the first post-war CIAM conference at Bridgwater. 'Where is Bridgeport?' Ise asked him, evidently confusing Bridgwater in Somerset with Bridport in Devon. Ise's confusion was forgivable since as the venue for a gathering of the world's leading international architects Bridgwater, a market town in rural Somerset, was hardly the most obvious choice. But attendance was high. Seventy or so architects assembled in England to take part in a conference whose theme was 'Reaffirmation of the Aims of CIAM' after the last ten years of struggle against Fascist domination of Europe, a time during which 'political, economic and social questions have taken on a new significance for everyone'.

A group photograph taken during a visit to the Bristol Airplane Company's aluminium temporary housing factory shows the predictable CIAM faces: Le Corbusier, Sigfried Giedion, Helena Syrkus (now one of the vice-presidents) and Josep Lluís Sert seated in the front row alongside a bow-tied Gropius. At this relatively local English congress there was a large British modernist contingent, including Philip Morton Shand, Maxwell Fry, Wells Coates and Jack Pritchard, almost amounting to a Lawn Road Flats reunion of those who had befriended Gropius when he first arrived in England in 1934. Gropius gave a keynote speech arising from his recent experiences in Germany, dwelling on the urgent need to replan society for all income groups and emphasising the importance of co-operative work by groups of architects, all with specialist knowledge. This was still the visionary Gropius proposing ideas of a new structure for architectural practice and speaking optimistically on post-war architecture's 'new conception of space'.

He criticised the 'misleading designation' of the International Style, which he equated with the soulless classicism of Soviet Socialist Realism. Instead he put a case for architectural decentralisation into neighbourhood units to be built in the country, a modernist version of English garden city thinking applied to the post-war resuscitation of Germany. Gropius argued that open spaces freed up in German cities by the diversion of housing to the country could then be used for parks, communal facilities and a 'basic network of traffic arteries'. It was a generous, imaginative vision, ending with the argument that the building of community centres connected to schools, as Gropius and

Fry themselves had done at Impington Village College, was a more urgent priority for post-war reconstruction than housing, 'for these centres represent a cultural breeding ground which enables the individual to attain his full stature within the community'.

At this point we see Gropius rise to the occasion. But his underlying mood of depression was obvious to Margarete Schütte-Lihotzky, who observed him closely as she sat beside him in Bristol waiting for the architects' group photograph to be taken. She had not seen Gropius for almost twenty years, since the 1929 CIAM conference in Frankfurt, and she was shocked by the change she found in him:

Externally Gropius was very little altered but looked pale and wretched and was extremely downcast. He had come from Germany where he'd been travelling for the first time since the war. The impact made on him by the cities destroyed by the war was resoundingly dreadful. 'Of course', he said to me, 'one can hear and read so much about the war. When you are far away from it you can choose to keep events at a distance, insulated from reality!'

Revisiting Berlin had been a shattering experience. Not once at the conference was Gropius seen to smile.

In 1947 Alma, too, returned to Europe. The visit was as traumatic for her as his return to Berlin had been for Gropius. 'Vienna was hell for me,' wrote Alma in her memoirs. 'The opera, the Burgtheater, St Stephen's – everything lay in ruins.' Her own once splendid house on the Hohe Warte was now uninhabitable, 'the roof gone, the top floor collapsed, the interior in ashes, heating plant, water and electricity ruined, the marble panelling torn out, used for officers' bathrooms in the neighbouring villas'. Alma stayed in a small rat-infested room in the Hotel Kranz, subsisting on the tinned food she had had the foresight to send ahead from California.

Alma was on a mission in Vienna to gain restitution of her property, in particular the beautiful, strange and mystical Edvard Munch painting *Summer Night by the Beach* (see plate 6) which Gropius had given her in 1916 to mark the birth of Manon. Alma had lent the painting together with four other works from her personal collection to the Österreichische Galerie in the Belvedere in 1937. After the Anschluss, once Alma and Werfel fled from Austria, her stepfather Carl Moll removed the painting and later sold it to the Austrian Gallery for 7,000 RM.

Alma now claimed that Moll was not authorised to sell her property. What she failed to mention was that in fact she had remained in contact with Moll, her half-sister Maria and Maria's husband Richard Eberstaller, all Nazis, during the years of Nazi rule, and that Alma's mother, before she died in 1938, had put Moll in charge of the administration of Alma's estate. As always with Alma the facts were less straightforward than she claimed.

By the time of her return in 1947 Moll and the Eberstallers were beyond interrogation. In 1945, just before the Red Army marched into

Vienna, they committed a triple suicide, all three of them taking poison in the house the two families shared. However, the Restitution Commission of the Regional High Court of Vienna was diligent in calling several witnesses who vouched for the continuing closeness of relations between Alma and the Moll family before and during the years of war. To Alma's lasting fury the case was dismissed. She never returned to Vienna, even boycotting the 1960 celebration of the centenary of Gustav Mahler's birth.

It was not until 2007, following the spirit of a new law making easier conditions for restitution of works of art unjustly acquired by the Nazis, that the painting originally given by Gropius to Alma was finally – grudgingly – returned to her granddaughter Marina Mahler by the Austrian Restitution Committee.

In August 1949 Alma's seventieth birthday was celebrated in grand style with sixty or so guests arriving for a party in the house in Beverly Hills. She was now a widow. After a series of heart attacks Franz Werfel had died in the summer of 1945, Alma sticking to her rule of not attending funerals. Alma, in parallel with Gropius, was now an American citizen. Photographs of the period show her looking like an ageing but still glamorous Hollywood celebrity with a well-permed swept-up hairstyle, exuding graciousness, expecting adoration. Amongst the guests who crowded in to be greeted by waiters serving glasses of champagne as well as Alma's staple Benedictine were Lion Feuchtwanger, the writer Carl Zuckmayer, Igor Stravinsky and the young British composer Benjamin Britten, who had been one of Mahler's earliest champions in England in the 1930s and who was now an acolyte of Alma's. At this lavish party a chamber orchestra played a 'birthday fugue' made up of Mahler themes.

The accolades were fulsome. Thomas Mann brought a copy of his latest book, inscribed 'To Alma, the personality, on her birthday, August 31, 1949, from her old friend and admirer'. The writer Willy Haas was even more effusive, assuring her that no one would possibly believe that she was now seventy. She would very well pass for thirty-five. But really 'you are timeless', he told Alma. 'And you are "blessed" amongst women, for you have beautified the lives of two great men and raised them on high.'

After the party we find Alma herself writing in her diary, 'Gustav Mahler and Franz Werfel were the essence and the substance of my life. The rest were clouds – some mighty thunderheads, others mere curls on the horizon.' Walter Gropius was increasingly becoming the forgotten, the deleted second husband both in Alma's and in other people's minds.

Gropius in fact sent Alma greetings for her birthday, which she acknowledged, saying, 'Dearest Walter I thank you most sincerely . . . I wish so much I could see you both again – but we always pass each other by.' She signed the letter Alma Maria, the name she had used at the height of their passion. Alma could never quite manage to let her old suitors – or indeed her one-time husbands – absolutely go.

For her birthday Alma also had a letter from Oskar Kokoschka, now married to Olda Palkovská and living in Britain. The hyper-emotional Kokoschka had suffered intensely in the war. Being anti-Nazi and out of sympathy with Austria's drift towards Fascism, he left Vienna for Prague in 1934, living there for four years until Germany occupied the Sudetenland. His return from Britain to a war-ravaged Prague in 1946, where he found his widowed sister desperately ill with leukaemia and alone in a badly damaged and isolated house, had been as deeply upsetting as Gropius's own recent journey back to Berlin.

'The span of time that we spent with each other', Kokoschka wrote to Alma in 1949, 'rises for me like a myth, distinctly above the events from the historical time in which world wars, disasters of all kinds, shattered society from the ground up.' Gropius and Kokoschka remained curiously linked, not just in the old, fierce, jealous rivalry of their love for Alma but in their responses to the tragic events of the Second World War, when the values they believed in were so totally destroyed.

———

In May 1948 Gropius himself was sixty-five. His once enormous stamina was dwindling. Later in the year he went into hospital for a bladder and prostate operation. When he emerged he weighed only 135 lbs, and Ise decided he needed to take things easy for a while. Once Walter recovered she herself would have to go back into hospital to have a graft made on her leg bone. The injury caused by the car crash still hampered her activity and she had to face another few months with her legs in plaster. Life at the Gropius House now inevitably quietened down.

Ati was no longer living with her parents. She was always apt to be wilful, unpredictable, and her relationship with Ise was never easy. She had left Black Mountain College a year early and had now moved to New York, turning down the offer of a job on American *Vogue* because she did not want a long-term commitment and taking less demanding work on a women's magazine. Ati was soon to marry her boyfriend Charles Forberg, a young architect who had been Gropius's student in the Graduate School of Design at Harvard. In 1948 Charles won a travelling scholarship to Europe, which enabled them to visit Scandinavia, Italy, France and Switzerland. In London she took Charles to Lawn Road Flats to meet the Pritchards, who had been so welcoming when Ati first arrived there in 1936, a bewildered child of ten.

The Gropiuses at Lincoln were increasingly aware of mounting political tensions. From August 1945, when the Americans dropped nuclear bombs first on Hiroshima, then on Nagasaki, they began to be haunted by new fears for the future. Ise claimed not to be able to read novels any more: 'Nothing seems to make much sense', she wrote, 'while we are sitting and waiting to have our bones glazed by the atomic bomb.'

In February 1947 Gropius had received a letter from Albert Einstein on behalf of the Emergency Committee of Atomic Scientists in Princeton, New Jersey, asking for his support in circulating information to the public on the simple facts of atomic energy and its implications for society. 'Through the release of atomic energy, our generation has brought into the world the most revolutionary force since prehistoric man's discovery of fire.' Gropius was already convinced by the grave dangers of the situation, having written a letter in March 1946 to US Senator Leverett Saltonstall expressing his alarm at the exploitation of nuclear research by the army and calling for civilian control. The tragic results of US nuclear policy were all too clear to him when Gropius himself visited Hiroshima in 1954.

426

In the immediate aftermath of war, efforts had been made to resuscitate the Bauhaus in Dessau. Gropius's original supporter Fritz Hesse was returned to office as mayor and a former Bauhaus student, Hubert Hoffmann, was appointed to run the school. Hoffmann's own war career was suspect in that he had worked as a planner on the redevelopment of Nazi-occupied Lithuania as a Third Reich colony, but he reputedly had the foresight to bury his Nazi uniform and his identification papers in a forest near Bismarck. Gropius himself rejected proposals that he should return to Dessau, but a number of his former Bauhaus colleagues were recruited.

However, this attempt to revive the Bauhaus was short-lived. In autumn 1946 the Soviet-backed, communist SED assumed political control and Hoffmann lost support. Hesse was removed from office and replaced by a Soviet sympathiser. Once the East/West division of Germany began in 1949 – the Federal Republic with Bonn as its capital, the GDR with East Berlin as its capital – the Bauhaus buildings in Weimar and Dessau were both stranded in the former Soviet Zone, objects of increasing hostility as Stalinist cultural policy took over. Avant-garde art was viewed as decadent by a regime dedicated to Socialist Realism. Gropius's Bauhaus now came under attack as self-indulgent and bourgeois, whereas Hannes Meyer's overtly communistic Bauhaus was lauded by the Soviets as having been in touch with the people's needs. Conflicting official attitudes towards the Bauhaus reflected the new East/West divide.

As tensions between the USA and the USSR escalated Gropius's personal position became the more invidious. Once the Cold War got underway in 1948 he became a powerfully symbolic figure, billed as the modernist hero of the West. Gropius filled the role of the admirable German who had played a crucial role in the development of European modernism in the years between the wars. He stood as a reminder of the humanistic, highly cultured people that, until subverted by the Nazis, the Germans really were. The international, cosmopolitan, idealistic nature of the Bauhaus as Gropius envisioned it was stressed by the Americans as a prime example of the indigenous German culture the Nazis had ruthlessly destroyed.

This heightened reputation put complex pressures on him as the naming and shaming of public figures suspected of having communist sympathies, the so-called 'Red Scare', started in America in 1948. Gropius now had reason to be cautious in reconsidering his past, playing down his early experimental Expressionist work, which called into question his purist reputation, dissociating himself from Hannes Meyer in spite of the fact it was Gropius himself who first appointed Meyer to the Bauhaus. How he squared the fact of his 1932 competition entry for the Palace of the Soviets in Moscow with his recent acquisition of American citizenship we do not precisely know. But it is quite clear that, as in Berlin in the 1930s, Gropius needed to be politically circumspect. And as before, this process of self-editing, so alien to his nature, inevitably took its toll.

The formation of TAC, The Architects Collaborative, gave Gropius a welcome new focus of attention. There were seven founder partners in the architectural firm alongside Walter Gropius himself: Louis McMillen, Robert McMillan and Ben Thompson and two married couples, John and Sally Harkness and Jean and Norman Fletcher. John was known as 'Chip' and Norman as 'Fletch'. All were in their thirties, half Gropius's own age. TAC became the largest architectural practice in America, employing hundreds, before its eventual closure in 1995. Doubts have often been cast as to whether, professionally speaking, co-founding TAC was a sensible decision for Gropius at this juncture. In some ways it was not. Unlike his partnership with Marcel Breuer this was far from being a partnership of equals. In many ways Gropius would need to make concessions. But it was idealistic and ambitious and emotionally it helped to anchor him.

TAC started informally. Chip Harkness, who had been Gropius's student at Harvard, was by this time working as his teaching assistant, the role that Breuer had once filled. He and Norman Fletcher, buoyed up by winning first and second prizes in a competition for a new residential building at Smith College, were already thinking about setting up an architectural practice. Rather on the spur of the moment Harkness went to see Gropius in his office and suggested he might join them.

When Gropius told his nephew Jochen that 'I picked out the best of the new crop for the first experiment' in forming a new office, this was not completely accurate. It was more a question of the group of younger architects enlisting Gropius, aware that his kudos and experience would be of huge value in gaining them commissions.

The partnership formalised in December 1945 was structured on consciously democratic lines instead of the more usual 'boss' and 'employees'. 'I have implemented my decision to give my 5 young partners exactly the same rights as myself,' Gropius reported in September 1946. (The figure 5 includes the husbands with their wives.) 'So far everything is going very smoothly and harmoniously.' It was a time of hope for all of them. The younger TAC partners were idealistic in their outlook, chastened by their experiences of war. Ben Thompson had served as a lieutenant on a US Navy destroyer. Chip Harkness, a conscientious objector, had joined the American Field Service. They were wide-ranging in their interests and ambitions. Fletcher, McMillen, McMillan and Thompson had been classmates in the architecture school at Yale, where they had already envisioned the formation of a so-called 'World Collaborative', an office embracing painting and sculpture as well as architecture. Sally Harkness defined the aim of TAC as nothing short of the remaking of the world.

The contrasts in style between TAC and the Bauhaus were in some ways striking. A picture of the partners assembled on the stairway of the Harvard Graduate Center, one of TAC's important early commissions, shows the men in suits and ties, Sally Harkness dressed in a flouncy all-American check cotton frock like someone in the chorus line in *Oklahoma*: a far cry from the outré dress code at the Bauhaus. But nevertheless the parallels are obvious. As the Bauhaus was founded by Gropius in response to the slaughter and the horrifying wastage of the earlier world war, TAC was now emerging from the debacle of another. Again there was a sense of common purpose, of the focusing of disparate talents towards the achievement of a common goal. Nobody would claim that Chip Harkness, Ben Thompson and the other young TAC members were on a comparable artistic or intellectual level to Albers,

Breuer, Kandinsky or Klee. But there were elements in the relationship that brought the aims and structure of the Bauhaus back.

Gropius's own considerable nostalgia for the Bauhaus was sharpened by the death of László Moholy-Nagy from a rare form of leukaemia in December 1946. Gropius, giving the address at his funeral in Chicago, could hardly hold himself together. Of all his Bauhaus colleagues Moholy had been the one to whom he was closest. 'The Bauhaus and what it has achieved cannot be thought of without bringing back into one's mind the fiery spirit of Moholy the great stimulator.' In writing to his widow Sibyl, Gropius told her he missed Moholy, his friend and most sensitive appreciative collaborator, more than he could say.

On Gropius's recommendation Serge Chermayeff was appointed to succeed Moholy in the running of the Chicago Institute of Design, but the appointment and indeed the institute itself would be short-lived. In going back over past ambitions and achievements Gropius was conscious not only of the Bauhaus but also of the early idealism that shaped his thinking as a radical young Berlin architect, a founder member of the Ring of Ten. In 1946, with the foundation of TAC, Gropius was sounding radical again in dismissing the appeal of the stand-alone star building, the concept of the architect as individual genius, and focusing instead on the rational, anonymous rebuilding of communities. As he explained to Jochen Burchard, 'For my part I'm increasingly interested in the big questions of urban planning. I'm just not interested any more in whether this or that building is balanced within itself, unless, that is, it is intended as part of a larger whole.'

'Teamwork' was the new mantra. 'Teamwork' was the great principle that motivated TAC, a concept already familiar to Gropius through the collaborative spirit of the Bauhaus, the communal enterprise of Lawn Road Flats. But here in America the context was quite new. To start with TAC's offices were unpompous, unimpressive, in a network of buildings around Harvard Square. Weekly assessment meetings involving all TAC partners were strictly non-hierarchical, with Gropius – 'Grope', as they called him – and the other partners sitting round the table, sharing frank discussion of all their projects.

'We at TAC knew Grope', remembered a later TAC partner, Perry King Neubauer, 'as a man of great design insight and a philosopher in his own right – but also an architect who faced the same design challenges we all struggled with. We honoured his past achievements, trusted his judgment, and were more than slightly awed by his presence in the firm.'

In spite of continuing rumours to the contrary Sally Harkness and Jean Fletcher were treated as completely equal partners, as Sally herself makes clear in a 2006 interview. Both had studied at the Cambridge School of Architecture and Landscape Architecture, the first degree-granting graduate school in the United States for women in these subjects. Since his arrival in the country Gropius had supported equal opportunities for women in architecture, giving his first public speech on the subject back in 1938.

At this point Gropius's arguments for teamwork were eloquent. But it could be argued, and very often has been, that this was the point at which his own architecture lost its way and that in TAC's pursuit of a worthy succession of hospitals, schools, civic administration buildings, large-scale urban projects a sameness took over. As Josep Lluís Sert maliciously commented, 'Walter would be all right, if only he would get rid of those fresh-faced young men.'

Frank Lloyd Wright, the original 'starchitect', had considerable reservations too. In July 1945 Gropius met him in Mexico City at a party at the house of the German-Mexican architect Max Cetto. The artist Diego Rivera was there as well. As Gropius described the episode:

I had just started a discussion on teamwork. [Wright] sat down at my side and listened with a grin on his face. When I had finished, he said, 'But Walter, when you want to make a child, you don't ask the help of your neighbour, or do you?' I answered, 'If the neighbour happens to be a woman, I might.'

There was a hippyish element in TAC as, in the 1950s, corduroys and jeans took over from the formal suits and ties worn by the partners in the early office photographs. This was the beginning of the Modern Neighbourhood developments in America, community experiments of which one of the first was Six Moon Hill in Lexington, a suburb to the west of Cambridge. Six Moon Hill was a consciously progressive settlement of twenty-eight houses designed by TAC partners Chip and Sally Harkness, Norman and Jean Fletcher, Bob McMillan and Ben Thompson to accommodate their families and a community of like-minded friends in a beautiful, optimistic, wooded, rocky landscape. The houses were ranged along a curving cul-de-sac with a communal pedestrian greensward down the centre. Built on half-acre sites, they varied in design and yet had a uniformity of style, reminiscent of Gropius's own house at Lexington in their combination of timber detailing and extensive use of glass. The element of light at Six Moon Hill was seen as all-important. These were houses directed to the sun, already exploiting what came to be known as green energy. Six Moon Hill was a concept way ahead of its time.

Ben and Mary Thompson raised five children at 40 Moon Hill Road, three boys and two girls. Their daughter Marina, who was four when they moved in, remembers the two-storey house being like one big playroom. The Six Moon Hill children in the 1950s were not 'parented'. They surged from house to house, flowing through the whole community, belonging everywhere and nowhere. The Thompsons' son Anthony describes the two-storey space 'illuminated by an Akari paper lantern hanging from the ceiling; a huge freestanding fireplace was the focal point of a house that was filled with modern paintings, modern sculptures. A Calder mobile swung silently in the air between stairway and chimney. You could reach out and touch it as you walked down the steps.' Ben Thompson, an enthusiast for Scandinavian design, built his own Finnish sauna in the basement. He often appeared naked at the breakfast table. This was a period when, according to Marina, where the men were concerned, 'big egos were OK'. Ben and Mary later parted and Ben married the architectural journalist Jane McCullough. This was not the only marital defection. There was certainly a downside to post-war paradise as conceived at Six Moon Hill.

Into this suburban site of many freedoms Gropius and Ise regularly arrived for Thanksgiving dinner and other occasions. Their visits to the

Thompsons had some of the formality of a royal progress. The impression tended to be given that Gropius had been the originator of the concept of Six Moon Hill. Mary Thompson was always thrown into a panic, especially anxious over how to deal with his allergy to garlic. What could she cook for him that was garlic-free? Gropius himself tended to be a bit withdrawn, 'very often fairly quiet', sitting on the sofa, bending over to talk to the Thompson boys, who called him Uncle Groggins. He always responded to the company of children. Ise was more generally sociable, vivacious in a still very continental manner. The child Marina was amazed by her appearance, especially the flame-red dyed hair which Ise wore swept up over her brow and then rolled back in an arrangement that struck Marina as 'sort of complicated'. She decided that Ise had 'a queenly air'.

At Christmas the Gropiuses would return to make another ceremonial visit bearing gifts for the children. One year they brought a Buckminster Fuller climbing frame, a 'DOME', for all the Six Moon Hill children to play on. Gropius and Ise were already friends with Bucky, the famous architect-inventor of the geodesic dome, who detected in Gropius something of his own enthusiasm for technological experiment, both of them seeing mastery of new materials and techniques as a means of entering new realms of psychological experience. After he had lunched with them at Lincoln Bucky wrote from Forest Hills, New York, telling Ise, 'Your husband is a great man . . . for he has effected an historical mutation in the extra corporeal evolution of man in universe. By his work man has begun to emerge from over introversion to balanced extroversion. SELFISHNESS – UN-SELF.' Buckminster Fuller identified with Gropius as a man in whom respect for art and science combined.

One of the central tenets in the founding of the Bauhaus was Gropius's belief in the spiritual power of the *Gesamtkunstwerk*, the total work of art. As he expressed it in the original Bauhaus Manifesto in those high-flown Germanic visionary terms, 'this great communal work of art, this cathedral of the future, will then shine with the fullness of light into the tiniest things of everyday life.' He still had not abandoned

Graduate Center, Harvard University, Walter Gropius and TAC, 1949.

the original idea that he developed at the Bauhaus of the gathering of talent, the working community of artists, the necessary fusion of art and architecture which saw a final flowering in the American post-war context of the Graduate Center at Harvard University.

In those early years after TAC was founded very few commissions came in. Gropius himself went to beg for work from the president of Harvard, James Conant, and the Dean of Fine Arts, Paul Buck, with the result that he and his partners were given the commission to design a group of seven three-storey residential blocks to accommodate 575 students alongside a single-storey student Commons Building with dining hall and sitting areas. The new building would occupy a wedge-shaped site at the northern edge of the university campus.

Gropius himself was lead architect for a project that involved almost all the partners in TAC. The design for Harvard obviously lacks the groundbreaking, attention-seeking quality of Gropius's Bauhaus building at Dessau, which was consciously designed to be a beacon of the new artistic thinking. But the Graduate Center has a well-thought-out coherence that shows TAC at its best. All the buildings are steel-framed but in the variations and the grouping around a central sunken garden there is a sense of informality and possibility. It was not just the buildings that were considered crucial. The spaces between them were equally important. The concept illuminates 'the new spatial experience', the idea of a building not being a magisterial stand-alone edifice but part of an accessible and democratic landscape, a sequence of interrelated visual experiences, which was one of Gropius's great themes of the time.

Such a blatantly modern intervention into a Harvard architectural setting where the prevailing style was English neo-Georgian proved predictably controversial. But Gropius stalwartly defended TAC's policy at Harvard in an article in the *New York Times*, maintaining that 'we cannot go on indefinitely reviving revivals . . . Neither medievalism nor colonialism can express the life of twentieth-century man. There is no finality in architecture – only continuous change.'

In commissioning works of art for the Harvard Graduate Center we see Gropius exercising his particular talent in matching the artist to the commission, a talent based on discrimination and experience. In a sense he had been doing this all his life. Not only did he see a work of art as the necessary completion of the architectural project, he also viewed it as an act of trust and friendship involving people he admired. From Josef Albers Gropius commissioned a large abstract brick relief for the recreation room in the Harkness Commons building. Herbert Bayer designed the coloured tile wall cladding that runs along one side of the pillared corridor as well as the mural for the small refectory that students irreverently titled 'Midday Nausea'. Another of the European exiles now working in the States, the Hungarian György (now Georg) Kepes, was commissioned to provide a sequence of maps of the world for the Graduate Center entrance halls.

Gropius went further afield in commissioning Joan Miró to contribute a six-metre-long oil painting for the larger Harkness Commons dining room. This big abstract mural, which is now in the Museum of Modern Art, New York, was later replaced by a Miró tile panel, a replica of the original. Two relief murals by Hans Arp in American redwood timber are still *in situ* in the dining room. These were given the title *Constellations*, pursuing Arp's interest in the endless variability of nature and the cosmic in an interplay of biomorphic forms. In developing this commission together Gropius and Arp were speaking the same language, a language that embraced an understanding of the rational and the mystical, the floating and the functional. In commissioning new works for Harvard from Arp Gropius was consciously enlarging the experience of the students thronging through the buildings. Education was not simply a matter of expanding the intellectual faculties. It involved appreciation of the visual as well.

Arp already had contacts and admirers in the States. Indeed Albers had invited him to come and teach at Black Mountain College in 1948, and although at this juncture Arp turned Albers down, he too kept in mind a new life in America as a future possibility. On his visit to discuss the commission at Harvard Arp came to stay with the Gropiuses at Lincoln. It seems likely that he and Gropius had known one another since the Deutscher Werkbund exhibition in Paris in 1930. 'I hope your magnificent buildings develop to your satisfaction,' Arp wrote in a friendly letter once he returned home. He added his greetings to Gropius's TAC partners, 'the lords of architects collaborators'. Remember-

436

TAC partners in acrobatic poses on Richard Lippold's sculpture at Harvard Graduate Center. Clockwise from bottom: Walter Gropius, Robert McMillan, Benjamin Thompson, Louis McMillen, Norman Fletcher, John ('Chip') Harkness.

ing the birdlife that was always such a feature of the Gropius House at Lincoln – the tits and bluebirds, woodpeckers and treecreepers that Ise loved to feed on pancakes and peanut butter – he asked Ise to greet her hummingbirds from him.

A further Harvard artwork, this time an outdoor one, was commissioned from American sculptor Richard Lippold. He had studied at the Art Institute of Chicago, graduating in 1937 in industrial design. Lippold now had a growing reputation for his geometric constructions in metal. For Harvard he conceived the abstract stainless-steel sculpture known as *World Tree*, almost ten metres high and sited on the lawn in front of Harkness Commons. A photograph taken at the time shows the five male TAC partners – McMillen, Thompson, McMillan, Fletcher,

Harkness – posed on the sculpture, with Gropius at the centre. The atmosphere is jokey, ebullient, triumphant, rather reminiscent of old Bauhaus group photographs. Gropius and his partners are grinning with delight. But the mood of triumphalism is misleading since it was now, in the early 1950s, that Gropius's official connections with Harvard came to a bitter and humiliating end.

———

Since the euphoria of his arrival at Harvard in the spring of 1937 relations between Gropius and Dean Joseph Hudnut had steadily deteriorated. Although Hudnut had taken the initiative in first appointing Gropius as chairman of the Department of Architecture, having at this point been committed to replacing the old Beaux Arts tradition of Harvard's architectural training with a much more modern Bauhaus-influenced approach, his attitude towards him then changed. Partly it seems that this was simple jealousy. With his fuddy-duddy, rather furtive personality Hudnut increasingly resented Gropius's charisma, his assumption of authority, his reputation on the international scene. As viewed by an inside commentator writing in the *Harvard Crimson* newspaper,

. . . when Hudnut realized that Gropius was receiving all the credit for the school's success and that the master was obscuring him more and more, it was natural for the dean to resent the other's presence. At times he would make statements such as 'learning should be a matter of experience rather than purely a matter of authority', and everyone knew, of course, who the authority was.

Ise later provided the further explanation that Hudnut had by this time lost his faith in modern architecture. He systematically blocked Gropius's attempts to introduce a Bauhaus-style Basic Design Course into the Harvard teaching programme. 'So they had a real battle, the two,' remembered Ise. The conflict between Gropius and Hudnut came to a head in 1948.

Hudnut was now operating a vendetta against Gropius, undermining his authority in dealing directly with members of his staff, bypassing the committees he established, cold-shouldering his associates in TAC.

Some of these attacks drove Gropius to near hysteria, as notes about Hudnut jotted down during a faculty meeting in 1948 attest. These include 'pathological jealousy', 'Sold me down the river', 'Rivalry set-up', 'Divide and rule', 'Shrouded in secrecy', 'Nobody trusts him'.

Meanwhile, in that same year Gropius received the surprising, shocking news that his post at Harvard would soon be at an end. When originally appointed chairman of the Department of Architecture he had, as we have seen, assumed that his tenure was for life. Now Harvard's president, James Conant, wrote to tell him he would reach retirement age in the following summer, on 30 June 1949. Gropius wrote back indignantly reminding Conant that he had originally been told that in his case the normal age limit was irrelevant since 'Harvard had only a few men of such distinction'. He pleaded that he had not been allowed time to build up his own architectural practice, since school duties had absorbed such a very high proportion of his time. Retirement from Harvard at this juncture would leave him in serious financial difficulties. Conant agreed to a revised retirement date of 30 June 1953, by which time Gropius would be seventy. But disagreements with Hudnut escalated and departmental staffing was reduced – Gropius's associates in TAC proving particularly vulnerable and having their teaching commitments scaled back. Finally, when departmental budgets were cut further Gropius lost all patience and handed in his resignation a year early, on 19 June 1952.

In writing formally to Conant expressing appreciation for Harvard's past support Gropius weighed in fiercely in criticising Hudnut. 'I have convinced myself', he wrote, 'that a good school must continuously develop its inner growth. For years the negative attitude of the Dean has had a demoralizing and frustrating influence on the entire staff, keeping such natural development from unfolding. Therefore, I do not want to share any longer the responsibility for the deterioration of a good school resulting from the Dean's pathological unreliability.' It would not be long before Joseph Hudnut himself retired.

Gropius's last official appearance at Harvard as professor took place on 25 March 1952, when he gave a lecture on 'The Architect in Industrial Society' to a large audience in Hunt Hall. The respectful, formal atmosphere was very different from the spontaneous outbursts of emotion when Gropius left the Bauhaus. Already recruitment had begun for his successor. Amongst several international candidates Gropius pushed the claims of the Milan-based Ernesto Rogers, uncle of the British architect Richard Rogers, and the Spanish CIAM member Josep Lluís Sert. It was Sert who was appointed in 1953.

Ise's subsequent analysis of Gropius's problems at Harvard is perceptive. She said in an interview:

Harvard was very difficult. See Gropius had been his own man all his life. He had an idea, the Bauhaus idea. He had gotten together a faculty of his liking and selection. And then he ran the school for nine years. When he came to Harvard he was a tiny bit of a huge outfit. The Bauhaus had at its best time no more than 150 students, and that was how he liked it. His belief was, and that was a very principled belief in him, that a small thing done really well has more influence on all the rest than a big thing done half well.

Ironically the Bauhaus-inspired Basic Design Course, which Hudnut had systematically resisted, was finally introduced in a small experimental way as a summer course at Harvard in 1948, when it was taught first by Naum Gabo and then by Josef Albers. As far as Gropius was concerned, this was too little too late.

23
Wandering Star: Japan, Paris, London, Baghdad, Berlin
1953–1959

Back in 1920, after his divorce from Alma and in love temporarily with Maria Benemann, Gropius in a new mood of fancy-freedom had described himself as a wandering star in the universe. Now at the age of seventy he was a wandering star indeed. After he was divested of responsibilities at Harvard, the next few years saw Gropius travelling the world, often on architectural assignments as TAC began receiving more important foreign commissions, or accepting international awards such as the Grand Prix d'Architecture of the Matarazzo Foundation in Brazil or his honorary doctorate from the University of Sydney, where he addressed an audience of a thousand people. The Sydney papers said that Gropius's speech meant as much to architects as a speech by Einstein would to physicists. Gropius thrived on these accolades, which to some extent compensated him for the knowledge that his rep-utation as a creative architect as opposed to an architectural pundit was being overshadowed by that of Corb, Mies and indeed the unstoppably productive Frank Lloyd Wright.

Travel as usual lifted his spirits, giving him a fresh sense of historical and political perspective and delighting him with the visual detail of every passing scene. The Gropiuses arrived in Tokyo on 19 May 1954 after a ten-hour flight from Manila, to be greeted by at least a dozen pho-tographers and a great crowd of people waving and cheering. The first press conference was held straight away in the airport waiting room. They were booked into Frank Lloyd Wright's Mayan revival Imperial Hotel, which had opened in 1923. 'Here we are at last,' reported Ise to Ati and Charles Forberg, 'sustained by F. L. Wright's ancient structure, surrounded by an ever changing stream of people who know more about us than we do about them and faced with so many commitments that our heads swirl.' It was Ise's view that the Imperial Hotel, 'which fascinated Walter in many respects, should be the domain of King Arthur and his knights'. But, she tells Ati, a fierce modernist, 'there is no doubt that there is a magnificent space conception and an incredible mastery of detail however repulsive it may be to you.'

Gropius was immediately attuned to the disciplined, minimalist Japanese approach to architecture and design, but what did the Japanese know about Gropius? There was already a considerable history of interconnections. A Japanese draughtsman, Bunzo Yamaguchi, had been in Gropius's Berlin office. They had a delighted reunion at dinner in a restaurant in Tokyo, during which Yamaguchi produced photographs of the staff at Potsdamer Privatstrasse in 1929, with himself in the centre of the group. A number of Japanese architects and artists had visited the Bauhaus in Weimar and Dessau. Iwao and Michiko Yamawaki, Bauhaus students from 1930 to 1931, had opened an architectural training centre in Ginza on returning to Japan, with a curriculum influenced by Albers. The school was closed down by the Japanese military government in 1936. The Bauhaus was still to some extent a name to conjure with. Among the incentives for Gropius's journey to Japan were plans for a Bauhaus exhibition in Tokyo, which he would be attending later in the trip.

Japanese attitudes to Gropius were complex. Post-war military occupation of Japan by the Allies only ended in 1952. Tokyo had been heavily bombed by the Americans and conditions in the city were still dire. 'The view from our hotel room', wrote Ise, 'is something else again. This part has been bombed out and, as far as the hotel goes, been reconstructed, but the neighbourhood is still rubble and it is a shocking sight to see the poorest of poor people trying to make a home there with no water supply or any sanitary facilities whatever.' Gropius was in Japan as the first delegate of the Rockefeller Foundation's programme to promote cultural exchanges between the East and West. Like the Japanese, Gropius the German belonged to a now defeated nation. But he was at the same time an American citizen, officially representing the United States. His position was, to say the least, ambivalent. Interestingly the German embassy in Tokyo made effusive overtures to Gropius while the American embassy ignored him. Ise commented sharply that this was typical.

'This country is like an onion; you peel and peel and there is always more underneath.' The Gropiuses' revelatory travels are recorded in Ise's diary and her long descriptive letters with a vividness of detail that shows what an exceptional experience this was for them both, a whole visual re-education that began with their very first sight of Mount Fuji from the plane, when the view they had always assumed to be artistic exaggeration turned out on the contrary to be 'the naked truth'.

In Tokyo they were allotted an official minder, Shigeharu Matsumoto, head of the International House cultural exchange centre, who at six foot three towered over many of his fellow Japanese. He arranged a hectic programme of official receptions and lectures. These included a lecture at the Kyoritsu Kodo auditorium, where an audience of 3,800, far beyond capacity, were crowded in. But Gropius was in an invidious position and younger Japanese architects in particular were suspicious of what they saw as American attempts to foist Western values on them. According to a hostile article in the architectural press,

There were two hidden intentions for the visit of Mr Gropius. One was to propagandize American culture, and the second was to relegate Japanese culture to history. The first was to demonstrate that the American culture is so superior to the Japanese that Japan cannot catch up easily; and the second was by parading the traditional low level of culture to order or restrict the rapid development of mechanical industrialization and pressure the Japanese system of handicraft so American control through colonialism might last longer.

Ironically Gropius the modernist was now coming under fire for his genuine appreciation of the traditional skills of Japanese folk art. The sheer breadth of his artistic sensibilities was suspect. When it came to the underlying politics his visit to Japan was not an easy ride.

But from time to time he and Ise were able to evade Mr Matsumoto and set off on their own, walking the streets of the crowded city, absorbing so many unexpected sights. At least a third of the Japanese women were still wearing kimonos and Japanese-style sandals. 'Walter loves this style', noted Ise, 'while I more or less pity them because it certainly is not very comfortable.' In a side street in Tokyo they came upon a group of children taking part in a festival gathering. The children all wore the same traditional clothes, which reminded Ise of the special visual quality of parties at the Bauhaus, with everybody following a common theme. But many of the sights they saw were anything but charming. Gropius was also taken on a tour of the slums which made him conscious more than ever that rehousing a fast-increasing urban population was as urgent a priority for Tokyo as it still was in Berlin.

After two weeks in Tokyo the Gropiuses set off for Kyoto, travelling through the countryside, admiring the indigenous peasant architecture of thick thatched roofs and simple practical interiors with their movable partitions of rice-paper and wood. Along the fronts of the houses he and Ise often spotted the family kimonos hung up for drying: 'They stick a bamboo pole through the arms and it looks as if a lot of open arms are welcoming you.' On many of the houses they also observed huge balloons in the form of fish, a Japanese tradition in celebration of Boys' Day. 'Each fish stands for one boy and it is a matter of pride to have so many. It looked gay and fantastic among the trees which surround every house.'

From the train they had 'the most heavenly views' of the lie of the land with its rice and tea plantations. As Ise described it:

I don't know how but the peasants have continued to turn agriculture into a veritable art form and the whole country looks like one gigantic 'basic design' course. One's eyes are caressed, stimulated, soothed, tickled on end and Walter was so enthused that he stood for fully three hours on the open back-platform to take photographs with his hair blowing wildly in the wind, trying to balance himself against the jolts of the train.

Gropius's great excitement in visiting Kyoto was seeing the Katsura Palace in reality. This imperial villa, built in the early seventeenth century on the south bank of the Katsura River by Prince Toshihito, apparently inspired by *The Tale of Genji*, had haunted Gropius's imagination for years. He had always regarded the Katsura Palace as the very purest example of architecture anywhere, but now the reality surpassed his highest expectations. 'I just want to tell you how moved we were seeing this rare example of complete balance and serenity,' Ise wrote in a long letter home to the TAC partners. 'It has a private character and its nobility shows itself in utter simplicity, not in regal splash and splendour.' There was directness in the architecture of the Katsura Palace, a negation of pomposity that reflected the basic tenets of the modernist principles Gropius espoused.

Though it rained for much of the time they were in Kyoto, the interplay of palaces, temples and gardens made a great impression. As they absorbed the meaning underpinning the Buddhist temples and the Shinto shrines Gropius became increasingly intrigued by the Zen philosophy, with its own subtle architectural concepts of illusion and abstraction, representing the continuing search for an alternative reality. In one of the Zen gardens they came upon an area giving the impression of a waterfall surrounded by rocks of tremendous size. It turned out that the water was simply simulated by the way in which the pebbles were arranged. They thought of Arp, Albers and Brancusi and wished they too could have seen all these places.

While he was in Japan Gropius was fascinated by the traditional tea ceremony, a ritual emanating from Zen philosophy which he saw as having had a profound influence on the grace and restraint of the country's architecture. He visited traditional Japanese potters and, after giving an appreciative address at the American Cultural Centre in Kyoto, Gropius was approached by the English potter Bernard Leach, who had been born and brought up in the Far East and who still had strong connections with Japan. He was involved as a young man in the *Shirakata* or White Birch movement, a group of Japanese idealists receptive to Western culture while preserving indigenous folk-based crafts. On moving to Britain Leach had become a kind of guru, revered for both his practice and philosophy of craftsmanship. He and Gropius shared a connection with Dartington in that Leach had been persuaded by the Elmhirsts to set up a pottery at Shinner's Bridge on their estate and was a leading figure in the World Craft Conference held at Dartington only two years earlier, in 1952.

Bernard Leach, a highly intellectual craftsman, would already have been familiar with ceramics at the Bauhaus. Now carried away by Gropius's Kyoto speech, he said that if he were younger he would 'try to join his outfit'. 'This was more than we had expected from a man who is so closely and exclusively linked to the crafts movement,' wrote Ise, and indeed there would surely have been a clash of egos if Gropius and Leach had managed to join forces. But, as Leach recognised, there was a definite connection in their views on an ideal internationalism in art.

From Kyoto the Gropiuses made a detour to visit Hiroshima. It was now eight years since the American bombing of the city. On the journey they were told about the continuing local flooding that was a result of the dropping of the H-bomb and the radioactive residue scientists had found in local fruit and vegetables. Soon after they arrived in an official party of architects Gropius and Ise were led to the top of a mountain behind the city. They stood for a moment in a state of near-paralysis surveying the scene that opened out before them. 'In all directions we saw mountain ridges staggered one behind the other, gently veiled by a haze and everywhere in the broad plain the curves of 6 arms of one big river melting into the enormous, multi-shaped port of Hiroshima. It is surpassed in its beauty only by the Rio de Janeiro,' judged Ise. 'I think if the world knew that one of the greatest beauty spots had been eradicated from the face of the earth the shock would have been even greater.' The city had now been largely reconstructed in a mode that Gropius considered to be as completely undistinguished as any modern commercial American or European city. The beautiful old Hiroshima had been flattened, though the bombed-out ruins remained.

Included in the party was Kenzo Tange, a Japanese architect of a younger generation influenced by Le Corbusier and already known to Gropius through CIAM. In 1949 Tange had won the competition for a Hiroshima Peace Memorial Park and two of his buildings were now almost completed, one an exhibition hall and museum, the other a community centre. Gropius praised his spare, restrained design as the visible symbol of a new mood of international reconciliation. An auditorium, also designed by Tange, was intended as the final building in the complex, but this had been supplanted by a mediocre building which Gropius found every opportunity to castigate as shamefully inappropriate for such an internationally sensitive site.

Further in the distance in the large memorial park they were able to view Tange's Memorial for the Dead, which was then under construction. This abstract concrete form consciously resembled early primitive Japanese houses of which small models, used as burial urns, had been unearthed from the debris of the bomb. Gropius, who must inevitably have compared it to his own Expressionist monument to the dead of the Kapp Putsch uprising, much admired Tange's understated but emotional memorial.

Before they left Hiroshima there was a final very arduous event: an afternoon lecture attended by eight hundred people, almost all men, many of whom had travelled significant distances to hear Gropius. As usual there were long introductory speeches of welcome and congratulation. Then Gropius spoke himself, a lengthy performance since his speech was translated paragraph by paragraph into Japanese. His position was politically precarious. Hiroshima had been flattened not so long before by the nation to which he now officially belonged. But this was after all a man whose life's work lay in the building of cities, not in their destruction, and he spoke convincingly and hopefully of a new unity of spirit arising from the 'hard fate' which befell Hiroshima during the war. It was a swelteringly hot day and Ise was aware of many members of the audience pulling their trousers up above their knees in desperation during Gropius's oration. To the Gropiuses' relief they were then invited to a quiet supper on a boat which took them down the river. The Hiroshima visit had been demanding in the extreme.

On their return to Tokyo Gropius was once again caught up in a rush of events. These included attending the traditional Japanese Noh plays, stylised and lengthy performances to which Gropius and Ise, used to Oskar Schlemmer's experimental productions at the Bauhaus, found themselves easily attuned. They were back in Tokyo to attend the opening of the Bauhaus exhibition at the Museum of Modern Art. To their great delight a number of Bauhaus objects were contributed by former Bauhaus students who had brought them back to Japan before the war. The Yamawakis, for example, still owned the original Marcel Breuer chairs they took with them when they left the Bauhaus thirty years before. The Tokyo exhibition was so beautifully designed and organised that Gropius was briefly tempted to start a new Bauhaus in Japan. He was by this time of the view that Japanese sensitivity to design alongside an inherent skill of craftsmanship was far in advance of that in other countries. He had begun to feel more and more at home.

While they were in Tokyo they fitted in a visit to their friend Charlotte Perriand, Le Corbusier's collaborator, in her Japanese house furnished with her own furniture designs. She herself was soon leaving to return to France. Perriand was in the process of preparing a book on the construction of the Japanese house, seen from a modern viewpoint. Here was another committed modernist designer exploring the creative relationship of East and West.

Gropius and Ise finally departed in early August, loaded up with silks and other textiles and the handmade shirts they had ordered for Walter in Kyoto. They travelled back in a leisurely fashion via Hong Kong, Calcutta, Karachi and Baghdad. They then stopped in Cairo, visiting the Pyramids and Luxor, before moving on to Athens, where they had arranged to meet Ati and Charles on the top of the Acropolis on 25 August 1954, punctually at midday.

They had also planned to meet Le Corbusier in Paris, but found he was away. Gropius left with the secretary in Corb's office what he called 'a very interesting carpenter's measure, used still today by the Japanese carpenters', which the Japanese architect Takamasa Yosizaka, a CIAM member, had given him in Tokyo to pass on. Gropius also left a photograph of the most beautiful seventh-century Japanese sculpture of the Miroku, the future Buddha, which he had seen so recently in Nara, knowing that Corb would appreciate it too.

They left Japan feeling that an important chapter in their life had come to an end. It had been a great and wonderful surprise for Gropius, 'at a time when he did not expect the world still had such wonders in readiness for us'. The visit had opened up his awareness of a whole new culture. As

Ise expressed it, 'The love and care and ritual that goes into everything is something unbelievable for Western eyes.' Gropius may have been well into old age but he was still excitedly receptive to new experiences.

Once finally back home he and Ise planted a Japanese garden outside the window of their dining room in Lincoln, Massachusetts.

———

Gropius returned to Paris often in the mid-1950s as a member of the committee appointed by the United Nations Educational, Scientific and Cultural Organisation to advise on the design of the UNESCO headquarters on the Place de Fontenoy. This was a gathering of five international architectural grandees: Le Corbusier from France, Ernesto Rogers from Italy, Sven Markelius from Sweden, Lúcio Costa from Brazil and Gropius himself representing the US. Gropius was appointed chairman once again.

The UNESCO committee's first responsibility was to choose the architect for such a significant post-war commission. Le Corbusier had himself initially coveted the job but lamented he had been vetoed by America because of his communist sympathies. After a false start in which French architect Eugène Beaudouin was appointed and his design was then turned down, the committee appointed Marcel Breuer, a somewhat unexpected candidate, to work on the new UNESCO building in collaboration with Pier Luigi Nervi, at the time the world's most expert structural engineer for reinforced concrete, and the French architect Bernard Zehrfuss. The Finnish-American Eero Saarinen was brought in as adviser to the scheme.

There is a story related by Breuer himself that he received the commission almost by accident. He was on holiday in Europe at a time when work in his New York office was slow and was strolling down the Boulevard St Germain in Paris at the very moment Gropius and the rest of the UNESCO advisory committee, with the exception of Le Corbusier, were sitting outside the Deux Magots café. Gropius called out to him to join them. In the course of conversation Breuer made it clear he was in need of new commissions and mentioned that he would be

Gropius, Le Corbusier, Marcel Breuer and Sven Markelius discussing the construction of the UNESCO building, Paris, in 1952.

leaving for Rome the next day. The committee made a quick decision and contacted Breuer with the news in Rome, where he was able to hold an initial meeting with Nervi. It is hard to believe that the possibility of appointing Breuer had not been in Gropius's mind already. Breuer had been with Gropius at the Bauhaus, had lived alongside him and worked with him in London, had taught with him at Harvard, had set up a partnership with him in Cambridge. In spite of some past bitter contretemps between them Gropius regarded Breuer as one of his own.

The UNESCO architecture is composed of two main elements: the central Secretariat Building and the wedge-shaped Conference Building alongside. The monumental Secretariat Building, set on seventy-two columns and curving round its site on the Place de Fontenoy, shows Breuer and Nervi working together to exploit the sculptural possibilities of concrete in an ambitious merging of technology with art. Like Gropius at Harvard, Breuer at UNESCO was closely involved in commissioning artworks for the buildings. This was an example of a *Gesamtkunstwerk* on an epic scale, which over the years included murals by Joan Miró, Alexander Calder's *Spirale* mobile, a relief for the library wall by Hans Arp, Picasso's politically controversial mural *The Fall of Icarus* and a cast of Giacometti's *Walking Man I*. A sculpture garden was commissioned from the Japanese sculptor Isamu Noguchi and a *Reclining Figure* in travertine marble from Henry Moore, Gropius's and Breuer's friend from pre-war London.

The spectacular success of the Paris commission took Breuer into a new architectural league of large-scale public buildings. Other important commissions in Europe as well as America followed. It is at this point we see Breuer overtaking and, in a sense with his collusion, outdoing Walter Gropius from the early 1960s as a leading modern architect on the international scene. Gropius had come to see the notable success of a one-time Bauhaus protégé as validating his own life's work.

———

Gropius returned to London in April 1956 to be presented with the Royal Gold Medal for Architecture by the Royal Institute of British Architects. This was not his first visit to London since leaving for the United States. He had, for instance, toured the Festival of Britain in 1951. But the presentation of such a prestigious medal by the institution he had addressed when he first arrived in England in 1934 made this an especially emotional return.

Before they departed Ise wrote to Molly Pritchard in a state of panic about London's current dress code. Would Walter need to bring a tuxedo for the celebration dinner? 'And what do the ladies do these days?' she enquired. 'Shall I bring a long evening dress or a short one, decolleté or buttoned up or medium? In the States, as you know, absolutely everything goes and there is practically no rule left.' With Gropius so

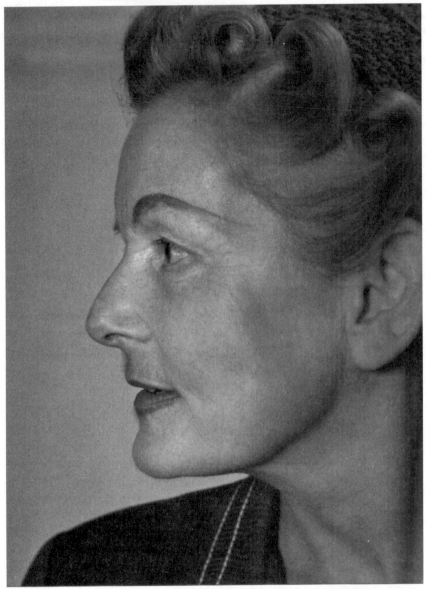

Ise Gropius photographed by Lotte Meitner-Graf in London in 1956.

often on the international presentation circuit she had got to know the pitfalls. It had, for example, been completely wrong not to take a long formal dress to Australia, whereas in Japan Ise had discovered that the only thing that mattered was to wear a wide skirt in order to squat gracefully. 'I hope England has stuck to its guns and still knows what to wear. So unless you want to see me turn up in skin-tight violet pants for cocktails – the rage here – you better give me a warning.'

Jack Pritchard was then planning a celebration dinner to follow the presentation and, in writing to Molly, Ise added the plea that Walter's former Bauhaus secretary, Hanna Lindemann, who was now living in London, should be asked. 'She has always been terribly helpful and loyal to him and we are quite indebted to her. Alas, she is no beauty, but she's just been made president of the Women's Guild of Golders Green which must be quite a distinction to come to a foreigner.' Miss Hanna Lindemann's name duly appears on the seating plan.

Ise Gropius also put in a word of warning about Lucia Moholy, who was still living in London, in case the Pritchards were considering asking her to attend the celebrations: 'I want to tell you that we are on unfriendly terms with her lately and that she has even brought or intends to bring a suit against Walter for having kept her Bauhaus photographs to himself.' Ise explained her side of the story: when Lucia left Germany in 1933, abandoning her many negatives, Moholy-Nagy gave them to the Gropiuses to keep safe. They were packed up with the rest of the Bauhaus records and shipped off eventually to the United States. According to Ise, 'We had no idea that Lucia had completely forgotten their whereabouts and assumed she was not interested in them any more.' But Lucia accused Gropius of having wilfully deprived her of records of her work which were hers by right.

Ise attributed this sudden interest in retrieving her old negatives to a current upsurge of interest in the Bauhaus.

The truth of the matter is that in those years, after the Nazis came in, everybody was glad to get rid of Bauhaus paraphernalia, while now she wants to sell copies of Bauhaus products etc. to magazines which is perfectly natural. We offered her immediately to send all the negatives over, but she demands recompensation [sic] and there are hard feelings on both sides.

It was a sad end to a brilliantly successful Bauhaus collaboration. Needless to say, Lucia Moholy was not included on the Gropius celebration invitation list.

Walter and Ise arrived in London on 7 April 1956, their trip being financed by the German government. The awards ceremony at the RIBA was held on 10 April, an occasion at which the *Manchester Guardian* registered the 'quality of passion' in Gropius's reception, and then two days later a formal dinner was given in Gropius's honour at the Ironmongers' Hall in the City of London, as a kind of coda to the banquet held at the Trocadero to mark his departure from England almost twenty years before. Some of the original dinner guests were dead: László Moholy-Nagy, H. G. Wells, Charles Reilly, for example. But many old friends and supporters now returned: Herbert Read (now knighted), Gordon Russell (also knighted), Ashley Havinden and Henry Moore.

Julian Huxley, who was in the chair as he had been at Gropius's farewell, ruminated on the many parallels between them as people involved both in science and in art. He recognised the meeting point, already present in the ideas of the Bauhaus, between ecology and the evolutionary practice of design:

I think it is Gropius's greatest achievement to have succeeded, as he has, in marshalling and mobilizing science and social planning, technology and art, awareness of beauty, all in the service of a truly living architecture . . . I feel that Walter Gropius is really one of the great creative figures of our time. He is creative in his own right, and he is creative in regard to the influence he has exerted in his profession.

Huxley took as a prime example Gropius's personal influence on him as secretary of London Zoo in establishing a modern architectural idiom. Without Gropius there would have been no Penguin Pool, no Elephant House at Whipsnade. Huxley was also eloquent on the UNESCO building under construction in Paris at the time, which he could already see was going to be the most exciting piece of modern architecture of the past two decades. Huxley, who was a member of the committee advising on the works of art, claimed that the UNESCO building project would not have been possible without Gropius's influence on the architects involved.

Henry Morris spoke as well, recollecting his experiences with Gropius at Impington, expressing the passionate regrets of many of those gathered that 'England did not seize the heaven-sent chance to get Gropius to stay in our country'. This was the prevailing mood of the event, one might almost say its *raison d'être*. Maxwell Fry, also placed at the top table, rose to his feet to deliver a typically whimsical effusion in free verse, going back over the days of his partnership with Gropius, saying this had been 'A windfall for the little race of Frys!'

The effusion continued:

> Just at the moment when a second wind was needed,
> When inspiration flagged and eloquence went unheeded
> And County Councils every job impeded
> Help came, and with it ravished melancholy;
> Came Gropius, Breuer and the brave, the gay, Moholy!
> Short was their stay and jobs were precious rare,
> Yet we were rich that had one job to spare
> – and who should care.
> When life was rich and gods walked with us here,
> What could we lack? What was there to fear?
> As then, so now, we have our Walter Gropius,
> And he is – what's the word? – he's cornucopious, Gropius!

Finally Gropius himself stood up and said, 'You must forgive me if I cannot quite bring myself to believe that all this is truly happening. It is more like one of those dreams when you go back to the scene of your former deeds and misdeeds to find everybody carry [sic] on as usual and trying to be quite casual about it.' He had never had serious regrets about leaving England but he was obviously deeply moved.

———

'Quick before the surf returns; it is morning and mist has settled over the Tigris.' This is Gropius's lyrical impression of Baghdad, a return to the romantic Mesopotamia he had dreamed of as a boy. In 1957 Gropius was given the grandiose commission of planning the new University of Baghdad, a complex of 273 buildings ranging from a five-thousand-seat auditorium to teaching blocks and faculty houses designed to accommodate twelve thousand students on a virgin site on a bend in the

Tigris, a whole progressive educational township rising on the southern edges of the city.

This was a point at which Iraq, then ruled by King Faisal II, was intent on inventing a new modern visual identity. It involved replacing the British colonial-style architects employed in Baghdad from the 1920s onwards with a whole galaxy of international modernists. As well as Gropius's university, a museum and arts centre was commissioned from Alvar Aalto, a public sports complex from Le Corbusier, a Ministry of Planning from Gio Ponti, an opera house from Frank Lloyd Wright.

Gropius's commissions came by way of Nizar Jawdat, a young architect who with his American wife Ellen had been a student of Gropius's at Harvard before returning to practise in Iraq. On their way back from Japan Gropius and Ise had stopped off to see them in Baghdad, where at a cocktail party given by the Jawdats they met a number of Baghdad University professors. Even more useful in securing the commission for Gropius was the fact that Nizar's father, Ali Jawdat al-Aiyubi, was prime minister of Iraq. 'This relation to the Jawdats is of the greatest importance to me', wrote Gropius at the beginning of this huge commission, 'and gives me a headstart everywhere. Nizar and Ellen are wonderfully helpful and everything seems to me toi, toi, toi.'

He was being too optimistic. Only a year into the commission there was a political upheaval. King Faisal, who had been enthusiastic in support of Baghdad's architectural transformation, was assassinated in a violent nationalist coup led by General Abd al-Karim Qasim. Ali Jawdat survived but lost all political influence. To keep the project running Gropius now needed to make overtures to the new regime, which he did successfully in the summer of 1959, meeting General Qasim in Baghdad. He and his TAC partner Louis McMillen managed not to be too daunted by the guards with machine guns who were also in the room. Ise reported to the Pritchards that Qasim had given his official blessings to Gropius's university plans 'but wants them bigger and quicker'.

It seems they need nothing more than education and training for their young people if they want to make a success of the new regime and so they have scrapped F. L.

Wright's opera house and even Aalto's Civic Centre was postponed because they intend to concentrate on the University and Corbu's stadium. Well, you can imagine what it means to build a university from scratch.

What did it mean? The new Baghdad was an enormously idealistic concept, a conscious merging of Eastern and Western influence, of modern technology and Arabic environmental detail, with date and eucalyptus trees planted along the broad approach roads, courtyards and pools, waterways and fountains. The plan for the new university was perhaps the ultimate expression of Gropius's architectural concept of unity and diversity, integration and difference. It drew on his now considerable experience of educational and community building, dating back to the Bauhaus of the 1920s, updated by his and TAC's experience of school and college buildings in the United States. In Baghdad, as in America, the interplay of buildings and outside open spaces was designed to facilitate sociability and understanding between students of different nationalities. The plan for Baghdad was ambitiously symbolic, with its towering Faculty Building, its futuristic mosque shaped like a Buckminster Fuller geodesic dome and an all too hopeful 'Open Mind' tower, gateway to knowledge, sited at the entrance to the university.

Gropius attempted to keep momentum going, travelling to and from Baghdad. In early 1960 the project appeared to be progressing well, with the finance sitting safely in a Swiss bank, while Gropius sent two of his TAC partners and fifteen architectural staff to Rome to recruit another ninety draughtsmen to undertake the working drawings. This was the most complex and ambitious commission of his life. The Italian art historian Giulio Carlo Argan wrote lyrically about the university developing in a 'far-away and fascinating country', comparing Gropius to Thomas Mann, 'another great German of the same generation', in the epic scope of his imagination. He saw Gropius's Baghdad as 'nothing less than the anti-Babel, the point where languages meet and unite', the embodiment of the principle of reason informing the building and the evolution of culture. 'Tomorrow', Argan suggested in a 1960 essay, 'the

Walter Gropius and TAC, entrance archway and corner of gatehouse, University of Baghdad.

University of Baghdad will be on everyone's lips, as Chandigarh was yesterday and Brasilia is today.'

This was not to be. With Iraq's endless political unrest Gropius's ambitious Baghdad concept foundered. Another coup took place in 1968, when the Iraqi Ba'ath Party took over. Only a few buildings were by now completed: the Faculty Tower, the Open Mind archway, a few of the teaching blocks. After Gropius's death the project teetered on but there were continuing changes of policy once Saddam Hussein came to power in 1979. The English-trained architect Rifat Chadirji, a leading light in the Iraqi architectural world who had originally supported the commissioning of TAC, was arrested in a clampdown by the Ba'athist regime and sentenced to twenty months in Abu Ghraib prison. A statue by Chadirji of the Unknown Soldier was replaced by a statue of Saddam, the very one that was eventually toppled by the regime's opponents in

2003. Chadirji was suddenly released from prison to supervise resumption of the project once Saddam Hussein himself became ambitious to make Baghdad an architectural marvel, another wonder of the world. Construction of the university began again in 1980, but the finances were never regulated and unpaid debts contributed to TAC's eventual closing down in bankruptcy in 1995. The Iran–Iraq War followed by the First Gulf War brought a sad end to Gropius's great dream of international enlightenment. Today only a few remnants of King Faisal's ambitious original scheme remain.

———

In the 1950s Gropius was frequently in Germany, officially and also on visits to his family. He was there for the opening in 1953 of the Hochschule für Gestaltung at Ulm, viewing it as the natural successor of the Bauhaus and giving the inaugural address. Henry van de Velde, now in his mid-nineties, supported the initiative, which was widely seen as an important factor in American–West German cultural relations after the war.

The Hochschule was sited on a hill above the heavily bombed city of Ulm in the former US Occupation Zone in southern Germany. It had a spotless pedigree. The idea had originally been conceived by Inge Scholl, a founder of the anti-Nazi resistance group in Munich, Die Weisse Rose (The White Rose), in memory of her brother and sister, both members of the group, who had been executed by the Nazis. The Hochschule, jointly financed by the American High Command in Germany and the West German government, was doubly important both as a reminder of courageous resistance to the Nazis and as the redemption of past German attitudes towards the Bauhaus. Paul Reilly, the old Hampstead friend of Gropius who would soon become director of the British Council of Industrial Design, voiced a widely held view when he described Ulm as 'a symbol for all that is anti-totalitarian in design, as much in contrast with the socialist realism of the East as the bygone blood and soil aesthetic of Nazism'. The tolerance and liberality of the new design school represented an atonement. The connection between the Bauhaus and the Hochschule was made the more emphatic by the appointment of Max Bill as the first director. Bill, a multi-talented Swiss designer who was a voluble spokesman for functionalist values, had been a Dessau student from 1927 to 1929.

Of course the ideology was never quite so simple. The HfG, as the Hochschule became known, could never have been a recreation of the Bauhaus. Times had changed. The philosophy behind the school quickly got bogged down in controversy as the school became more involved in corporate identity programmes and commercial product design, collaborating with Braun in developing a new design policy for electrical products which served as the basis for what became a widely marketed minimalist range by Braun's staff designer Dieter Rams. There were endless disputes over the issue of *Kommerzterror*. Should the HfG engage at all in capitalist commerce or should its policies be kept more strictly purist? In 1957 Max Bill resigned, to be succeeded by Tomás Maldonado, who vetoed Ulm's previous consumerist emphasis in favour of a more esoteric approach involving semiotics and systems thinking.

Although there are signs that Gropius himself became increasingly impatient with ructions at the HfG, he never quite lost faith in it. After all, the ideological arguments at Ulm were only a repeat of the endless Bauhaus controversies he had defended as part of the necessary processes of education. In 1968, with the school threatened by closure after financial crises and internal controversies, Gropius joined the protests. A photograph shows him marching in procession in his bow tie and his beret. But the HfG closed down that September anyway. Reyner Banham suggested in a *New Society* article that the closure hardly mattered since most serious design schools had by this time 'moved appreciably towards an Ulmish curriculum', and in this he was quite right.

Back in West Berlin Gropius was now involved in Interbau, a plan for an ambitious housing development in the Hansaviertel, a bombed-out area right in the centre of the city. Like UNESCO, Interbau was an example of post-war gesture architecture, a gathering of architects of different nationalities. The idea was to demonstrate Berlin's ability to reinvent itself and set an example internationally, and especially to

Gropius protesting against the closure of the Hochschule für Gestaltung at Ulm in 1968.

Eastern Europe, of the ideal post-war modern townscape. A competition was organised in which over sixty architects from fourteen countries took part. Gropius was on the committee appointed to oversee the project and select the architects, who predictably included Alvar Aalto, Sven Markelius, the Brazilian Oscar Niemeyer and Le Corbusier. The latter was characteristically intransigent, insisting on his own separate Interbau site on the edge of Berlin.

Gropius himself was among the chosen architects and in August 1955 he flew to Berlin to finalise arrangements for the apartment block he planned. As usual he was met at the airport by a reception committee, including two Berlin government officials and a number of photographers. In the evening he joined a number of the Bauhäusler for dinner at a cafe on the Kurfürstendamm. He was disconcerted to discover that the Am Zoo hotel in which he was staying incorporated what had at one time been the Gropius family's apartment. It was a strangely dreamlike return.

The Interbau building Gropius designed is a nine-storey apartment block containing sixty-four three-bedroom units for middle-class

Walter Gropius, block of flats for the Interbau International Building
exhibition in Berlin, 1957.

families and two larger penthouse apartments. It is a gently curving
concrete structure in which the wall fillings are composed of blocks
of bomb rubble, giving a sense of the phoenix rising from the ashes.
With its flexible planning and its children's play space this still seems
a welcoming and optimistic building, and it must have been yet more
so at a time when, as Gropius described it, Berlin was 'still a tragically
shocking sight, much more behind than the western cities'.

Gropius was once again received as the returning hero in Berlin.
When he delivered a public lecture on 19 September 1955 1,300 people packed the hall, with several hundred still attempting to get in and
causing such commotion that police were called. He was more than ever
being courted to take on larger building commissions for the city. 'Most
of all', as he told Ise, 'they would like to make me building dictator of
Berlin.' He resisted the majority of these proposals. Indeed when Konrad Adenauer, now the German Chancellor, contacted him personally

in 1951, asking him to give advice on housing construction, Gropius politely turned him down, while taking the opportunity to remind him of the interest he had shown in the Bauhaus when Ise went to see him in the years before the war. But in 1957 Gropius agreed to undertake a commission which reached him through the former Harvard president James B. Conant, who was now the US High Commissioner in Germany, to provide a masterplan for a giant housing development on a 650-acre site in the south-east sector of West Berlin.

For the next few years Gropius and TAC were occupied with the new township of Britz-Buckow-Rudow, envisioned to provide sixteen thousand housing units for forty-five thousand people. The plan was for the six hundred buildings that made up the new town to be ranged beside a wide public green along the U-Bahn running through the site. This would create visual unity as well as encouraging community activities, a concept that reminds one of the thinking behind TAC's Six Moon Hill community development, but on a giant European scale. In homage to Gropius the town was later renamed Gropiusstadt.

With Gropius now in his mid-seventies prestige awards kept coming. In 1957 he was in Hamburg to receive the Hanseatic Goethe Prize, which honoured him for 'the pedagogic achievement evidenced by the foundation of the Bauhaus' as well as for 'humanising an increasingly industrial society by means of his new concepts for living and for work'. Such a public association with Goethe pleased him greatly and inevitably brought back memories of Weimar. Bauhaus students processing in the park with its monument to Goethe. Klee's crowded and atmospheric studio alongside Goethe's garden house on the hill. For Gropius this was to be a decade of intense reconnections with the past.

But it was not a time for total self-congratulation. In spring 1958 an event occurred that shocked him and cut him down to size. Alma too had been working through her memories. Her autobiography was published in the States. The title, ominously, was *And the Bridge Is Love*. Alma's accounts of her relationship with Gropius, a man to whom she had after all been married, struck him as insultingly cursory. He simply did not recognise himself.

After Werfel's death the widowed Alma Mahler-Werfel, as she now styled herself when in the mood, had moved from Los Angeles to New York to occupy the top two floors of the house on 73rd Street in Manhattan that she had bought in 1945. The apartment was crowded with the trophies of her life. Paintings by her father, Emil Jakob Schindler, which Alma had succeeded in retrieving from Vienna. The studio photograph of Gustav Mahler in the place of honour on the Blüthner grand. The marvellous enigmatic portrait of Alma by Kokoschka, of which she had proudly informed Elias Canetti, 'And this is me as Lucrezia Borgia.' Six of the painted fans remaining after Gropius had destroyed the seventh in a rage. Alma and Kokoschka were still intermittently in touch, keeping up their crazily erotic correspondence, exchanging fantasies of bizarre sexual encounters into their old age. In one of these letters Kokoschka threatened to make a life-size wooden figure of himself with its penis in a position that Alma liked the most.

Alma Mahler's New York sitting room, with Oskar Kokoschka's
'Lucrezia Borgia' portrait above her writing bureau.

Here in this claustrophobic New York apartment, full of tangible evidence of her extraordinary *mouvementé* life, Alma and a co-author,

E. B. Ashton, worked spasmodically on *And the Bridge Is Love*. It is a strange book, anecdotal, rambling, veering from naive self-revelation to cautious self-defence. In comparison to her accounts of her relationships with Mahler, with Werfel, with Kokoschka, her love affair and marriage with Gropius hardly registers. She puts it over almost as a non-event. After the romantic encounter in Tobelbad with the handsome young German who reminds her of Wagner's Walther von Stolzing, Alma claims she rapidly loses interest in him. Soon she is complaining that her feelings for Gropius have given way to what she calls a tired twilight. In recounting the story of Gropius's discovery that the son she has just given birth to is in fact not his but Werfel's, Alma alludes to Gropius as a pitiful character who deserved a better fate. She admits a complete indifference to what she sarcastically refers to as his 'mission' in his high-flown ambitions for the Bauhaus, maintaining that his work was completely alien to her. She indignantly recounts their bitter scenes over custody of Manon. Most woundingly of all for a man as proud as Gropius, the picture she gives us of her one-time husband is of someone on the outer margins of her life.

He wrote to her in bitter indignation: 'The love story you connect with my name in the book was not ours. The memory of Mutzi should have prevented you from taking away the essential content of our *Erlebnis* [our personal experience] and its literary exposure is bound to kill also in me the blossoms of memory. The rest is silence.'

She replied in an attempt to mollify him, implying she had been unwell and muddled, putting the blame on her ghost writer and her publisher, who she claimed had ignored her instructions to send a draft of the book to Gropius so that he would have the chance to censor it. She said she had not realised this had not been done. Months later Alma wrote to Gropius again, saying, 'I beg your forgiveness . . . I am more guiltless than you think.' She piled on the pathos, telling him that following the death of Manon she was bereft and now totally alone. She told him reassuringly he was a great man and that she had always known it too.

Alma soon embarked on another autobiographical project, a rehash of the more romantic episodes of her life story. *Mein Leben* was published in German in 1960. This time she was more cautious in relation to Gropius, instructing her co-author, Willy Haas, to be discreet about still living persons, especially famous ones like Walter Gropius. Gropius was very shy, she warned him, and would not want their relationship to be shown in a harsh light.

But of course by this time the damage was done. Gropius was now registered in many people's minds as a man of not much interest, a Bauhaus-obsessed dullard, a subsidiary figure in the indefatigable celebrity-hunting Alma Mahler's world. This is how he appears in Tom Lehrer's satiric ditty 'Alma' in 1965:

> The loveliest girl in Vienna
> Was Alma, the smartest as well.
> Once you picked her up on your antenna,
> You'd never be free of her spell.
>
> Her lovers were many and varied,
> From the day she began her beguine.
> There were three famous ones that she married,
> And God knows how many between . . .
>
> While married to Gus she met Gropius,
> And soon she was swinging with Walter.
> Gus died, and her teardrops were copious.
> She cried all the way to the altar.
>
> But he would work late at the Bauhaus,
> And only come home now and then.
> She said: 'What am I running? A chowhouse?
> It's time to change partners again.'

Alma was now dead. Her funeral took place in New York in December 1964, after which her body was flown to Vienna, where she was buried in Grinzing cemetery alongside Manon. When Gropius eventually heard Tom Lehrer's take on him he is said to have just shrugged and moved on to other things.

Gropius's most controversial and, in my view, most resplendent post-war building, the Pan Am (later, MetLife) Building in New York, was constructed between 1958 and 1963. He worked closely with a young Yugoslavian architect, Alex Cvijanovic, who joined TAC in 1960. The two travelled almost weekly to New York to oversee the project, which placed extra pressure on its architects since the building occupied the airspace above Grand Central Terminal and it was not possible to stop the trains.

Cvijanovic later defined his relationship with Gropius: 'we had a connection. I was the son he never had, and he was the father I lost as a young boy.' Part of this connection was their shared background in an unstable, violent Europe. Cvijanovic's father was murdered in a communist purge of intellectuals and the family home was confiscated. Compared with the relatively settled and prosperous upbringings of Gropius's TAC partners, Cvijanovic's history had been perilous indeed. Another reason for their rapport was their shared foreignness. Both spoke American English with a distinctly European accent. They shared a common European culture, a love of music, a breadth of reading that included a deep knowledge of the Bible. Both professionally and emotionally it became a close companionship. Cvijanovic had been born on the same day of the same year as Gropius's adopted daughter Ati and he believed this was the reason for their quasi-familial relationship, which came to be resented by the all-American partners in TAC. The hyper-energetic perfectionist Gropius was evidently a hard taskmaster but his dedication was inspiring to the younger architect, and Cvijanovic spoke of him to me years later with enormous affection and gratitude.

Gropius stands proudly in front of the Pan Am Building, New York, 1963.

The Pan Am Building (see Plate 32) on Park Avenue was an unmistakeably commercial development, a tower block right in the centre of the city, fifty-nine storeys high and containing 2,350,000 square feet of office space. Joint architects were Gropius and the Italian Pietro Belluschi. Gropius, having the higher profile of the two, took the flak for a building that was vilified at the period when the modern movement was falling into disrepute. Jane Jacobs's book *The Death and Life of Great American Cities*, published in 1961 and critical of such high-rise developments, had considerable influence at the time. Criticism of Gropius's building focused on the way it blocked the view down Park Avenue, cast deep shadows over the surrounding area and ejected over twenty-five thousand office workers into already overcrowded streets. Amongst Gropius's most virulent critics were Sibyl Moholy and the ever-unpredictable Philip Johnson, who suggested that the site should instead be made into a green plaza. Gropius stalwartly dismissed such criticisms as urban sentimentality.

And indeed from today's perspective, now that the Pan Am Building is considerably smaller than many of the buildings that surround it, Gropius's concept has come into its own. The tower is an interesting shape, an elongated octagonal structure divided horizontally by two unglazed service colonnades at different levels. All of this gives it a lightness and an absence of monotony and bulk unusual for such a large, pre-cast concrete and glass structure. It could almost be read as a vast minimalistic sculpture. The choice of materials is opulent and marvellous: bronze and polished granite, textured glass. The specially commissioned artworks included Josef Albers's *The City* mural in formica (see Plate 33) and Richard Lippold's large wire sculpture. The urge to take a ride on the escalator down to the Grand Central Terminal, an old-time glamour scene of oyster bars and cocktail lounges, is almost irresistible.

With the Pan Am Building we are back with those old dreams of prismatic *Glasarchitektur*, the aspirational building in the centre of the city, celebrating its authority, defining its ambitions. One might see it as the compensation for Gropius's 1923 *Chicago Tribune* Tower competition entry that never saw the light of day. Much as Richard

Rogers's Lloyds Building sums up the feeling of 1980s London so Gropius's Pan Am Building exudes the capitalist confidence of 1960s New York.

Why did he do it? It's an interesting question. Why did Gropius ever get involved in work that was bound to attract accusations of a betrayal of his principles? Partly of course it was the usual reason. He was running a large office. TAC always needed work. But there was in his nature a certain contrariness, a kind of bloody-mindedness, and it is possible to view the Pan Am Building and the vehemence with which Gropius defended it as a conscious breakaway from the architecture of good intentions that defined the work of TAC.

Gropius's long rivalry with Mies van der Rohe was of course another factor. As we have seen, ever since their days of working together in Peter Behrens's office relations between them, though outwardly polite, had been distinctly strained. From 1938 onwards, when Mies too was living and working in the States, his private practice flourished to such an extent that we find Ise complaining of the success of his publicity machine in comparison to Gropius's. In 1958 Mies's superlatively elegant thirty-eight-storey Seagram Building opened on Park Avenue to a paean of praise. Peter Smithson, the young British Brutalist architect, judged that in comparison any other building looked like a jumped-up supermarket. This was patently unfair. But it has to be admitted that for all its architectural ambition and flair Gropius's Pan Am Building cannot quite compete with Mies's Seagram Building in its almost classical confidence and grace.

In the mid-1960s Gropius was drawn into a major scheme for London: the redevelopment of Piccadilly Circus. This was an initiative he should have steered well clear of since the developer concerned, Jack Cotton, was a leading figure in the now notorious English property boom of the 1950s onwards. Cotton was associated with an even more controversial developer, Charles Clore, whose speciality was the hostile takeover, whereby controlling shareholdings in a public company were bought out with the deliberate intention of ousting the company's management and board.

Cotton's plans for the Monico site in Piccadilly, named after the demolished Café Monico, began in 1955. Once the original proposals were turned down, Cotton's business partner Erwin Wolfson, president of the Pan Am Building, suggested that he should bring in Walter Gropius to give his proposals an aura of respectability. Cotton had invested $25 million in the Pan Am Building. Gropius was appointed design consultant in association with London establishment architects Richard Llewelyn Davies and John Weeks. It is easy to see what attracted Gropius to the Piccadilly project. He retained his romantic view of city centres, explaining in an interview, 'I asked myself what does Piccadilly represent? It became clear to me that every Englishman enjoys its gaiety, its boisterousness. The bursting life of the place had to be kept, its spirit undisturbed, by the building I designed. It would have to have advertising on the walls, just like the others, because that was part of Piccadilly.' But there were too many conflicting interests and the Monico site project was eventually dropped.

Gropius's involvement with Jack Cotton – an extrovert figure in his bow tie, a red carnation in his buttonhole – continued with schemes, once again abortive, for Birmingham city centre and their only successful collaboration, a relatively modest building on London's Park Lane containing apartments, offices and shops. Cotton at this time was living in the nearby Dorchester Hotel, occupying Suite 210. Working on this building Gropius was booked into the Dorchester as well. Evidently he found such proximity to Cotton a considerable strain, lamenting to Ise in September 1960, 'Spent yesterday and today recovering from Cotton . . . I am somewhat exhausted because Cotton has only numbers in his head and talks about nothing else. But he has a warm heart and makes an effort to treat me well.' Ise's own view was less generous. She wrote later, 'whether my husband could have kept Mr. Jack Cotton in check in the long run is still a question in my mind. He was much more dictatorial than any American client Gropius ever had.' Cotton died in 1964, after suffering a heart attack in the Bahamas. Gropius's building eventually became a Bunny Club, a fate at which he managed to raise a little smile.

Gropius's most prolonged and most successful collaboration through the 1960s was once again in Germany. The porcelain factory founded in 1879 by Philipp Rosenthal, who was Jewish, had its operations suspended by the Nazis and Rosenthal resigned its presidency in 1934. In 1937 he died. His son Philip, in exile in England through the war years, came back home to Germany in 1950 more English than the English. He was able to reclaim the family company, Rosenthal AG. It became committed to the modern, commissioning work from the best-known European and American designers. Philip Rosenthal and Gropius collaborated closely, went travelling together and became great friends.

The first of their joint projects, started in November 1963, was for a Rosenthal china factory in Selb, Bavaria, a building that would reflect the need of the workforce not just for efficient working conditions but for a culturally stimulating environment. At Selb Gropius initiated a library and concert hall. He also designed a spacious greenhouse filled with flowering plants and birds placed right in the centre of the working area, bringing a vestige of the outside inside. Alex Cvijanovic, who collaborated closely with Gropius for Rosenthal, remembered how he once asked Philip Rosenthal what the factory did to celebrate New Year. 'My workers chase a pig, catch it, and we have a pig roast,' Rosenthal replied. This practice struck Gropius as barbaric. He designed a special house for the pig, which he named Koko. A house made out of marble. 'Right there, next to the factory.'

The next commission for Philip Rosenthal was the Thomas Glass Factory in Amberg. Gropius's answer to the environmental problems of glassmaking was to design a large glass-blowing hall with a spectacularly high, steeply pitched roof. The building was popularly known as the Glass Cathedral. This was one of the most successful of Gropius's late works, his most impressive industrial building since the Faguswerk. Housing was designed for the workforce at subsidised rents.

The Rosenthal Glass Factory in Amberg, 1967, known as the Glass Cathedral. Porcelain teapot designed by Gropius with Louis McMillen and Katherine DeSousa of TAC, 1968.

Gropius was especially excited to be commissioned to design a china tea and coffee service for Rosenthal. He had been interested in the design of tableware since the early days of the Bauhaus pottery and his ongoing attempts to ally it more closely to industrial production. The Rosenthal design was a collaboration with Louis McMillen and Katherine DeSousa of TAC in which they made initial suggestions, with Gropius himself having the last word. The design for the teaset, which was produced in both white and black, has a great purity and elegance. It is still in production. Sixty years after it was launched it still looks modern. If one wants a design classic, this is it.

Gropius's work for Rosenthal had an unexpected repercussion. After decades of silence he heard from Maria Benemann again. She had read a newspaper article on Gropius and Rosenthal which had caused the memories to come flooding back. Maria had embarked on the writing of her own life story, in which Gropius features as the inspiring founder of the Bauhaus and as a passionate but evasive lover, the self-styled wandering star. Maria now addressed him:

Dear Walter Gropius!

It was with real joy that I discovered from the most recent issue of 'Die Zeit' that you are still visible. After all in recent years one has rarely read your name or heard of your continued existence in our earthly world. How happy I was to hear that, despite your advanced years, you are still capable of such fulfilling work. And in the same way that once, through your establishment of the Weimar Bauhaus, the working body of teachers and students found deep meaning in their human community, it seems that the owners of the new Rosenthal china factory in Selb are keen to realise the Bauhaus spirit. May those involved succeed, in the age of the 'conveyor belt', in communicating this to every last one of their workers.

I certainly hardly need say how much I personally would like to see you again. Specially in the last few weeks I was daily reminded of the years in and near Weimar, when one hope filled us all, that is, the hope of renewal, quietly from within, for each individual. For I am in the process of preventing something of my own memories from being forgotten, even if only for my children. And my thoughts also turn, with love, to you, as the great wandering star, which is how you passed through certain lives. How you, brightly gleaming, also long lingered above mine.

Wishing you and your loved ones all that is joyous and gratifying,

Your old Maria Benemann

It took Gropius many months to reply to her. We have no record that they ever met again.

———

The 1960s saw a reversal of the official policy of vilification of the Bauhaus by East Germany. The Bauhaus now came to be redefined as a socialist enterprise and Gropius treated as something of a hero. He was wary of invitations to visit East Germany in case this should be interpreted in America as support for the Communist regime. But in 1964 he agreed to a preparatory meeting in Berlin at which he expressed his willingness to visit Dessau and Weimar and take part in discussions about the restoration of the Bauhaus buildings. How could he resist it? He had invested so much in the creation of the Bauhaus. The reconstructed Bauhaus building in Dessau was finally opened in December 1976.

In this altered climate it was possible for East and West Germany to co-operate on an ambitious exhibition, *50 Years Bauhaus* (see Plate 34), which opened in Stuttgart in spring 1968, sponsored by the Federal Republic of Germany and the Bauhaus Archive, before moving to the Royal Academy in London in the autumn of that year. This was the Bauhaus story as Gropius liked to tell it, with the emphasis on the early years, the structure of basic courses and workshops, as well as individual artists and teachers whom Gropius had appointed. It was a tale of triumph. Hannes Meyer's regime was left out of this account.

As always with the Bauhaus there were battles of the egos, described by Herbert Bayer, who designed the exhibition: 'great trouble, as you have heard, with Albers, Nina Kandinsky, etc.' When he approached Mies van der Rohe to ask him to participate, the answer was 'I have absolutely nothing to do with the Bauhaus.' 'In spite of that', wrote Bayer, 'we will put him in the show and also Albers, unfortunately not as well represented as he would have been otherwise. I am certain we will not have any friends left after this exhibition.'

Gropius attended the openings in Stuttgart and in London, where *The Times* reported him as speaking in trombone tones and delivering an address full of combative matter. Attendance figures were high, total-

Herbert Bayer and Gropius collaborating on the Bauhaus exhibition, Stuttgart, 1968.
Abstract art work by Oskar Schlemmer, stereometric sculpture by Herbert Bayer.

ling around a hundred thousand in each place. This was the point at
which the Bauhaus began to acquire its legendary status, with Gropius
revered as a modernist pioneer. But some critics had their reservations.
In a year of student riots and intellectual turmoil, with so much up for
questioning – the once respected voices of authority, the traditional
aesthetic values – the Bauhaus was beginning to look old world.

———

On 18 May 1968 Gropius was eighty-five, and family and friends assembled for a whole succession of the birthday celebrations that had been
part of the Bauhaus tradition since the early days in Weimar. A great
party was held in Harvard Yard. There were flowers, balloons, straw-
berries, champagne. Well-wishers' hatbands bore the message 'Vote
Grope'. Students carried placards reading 'Total Scope with Grope'.

There were more intimate gatherings at the Gropius House. The family had grown. Ati had adopted a little German orphan girl, Sarina,

in 1957 and she also now had a daughter of her own. Erika Forberg was born in 1960. Ati had parted from Charles Forberg and was now remarried to the architect John Johansen. Like Forberg, Johansen had been a student of Gropius's at Harvard. Along with Marcel Breuer, Philip Johnson, Landis Gores and Eliot Noyes, all of whom designed distinguished modern houses in New Canaan, Johansen was one of the so-called Harvard Five.

Birthday congratulation cards and letters, many of them wonderfully illustrated, flooded in from Bauhäusler all over the world. Marianne Brandt sent a surreal photographic self-portrait. Julia Feininger sent Gropius a specially designed woodcut. Greetings came from Felix Klee in Bern, from the Bayers and the Breuers with affectionate messages. Josef Albers sent Gropius an inscribed copy of his new portfolio, *Homage to the Square*.

This was a decade in which Gropius's energies were focused on telling the Bauhaus story as he saw it. At a time of such worldwide recognition he put great effort into managing his legacy, an enterprise for

Gropius and Ise at his eighty-fifth birthday celebration at Harvard, 18 May 1968.

which – surely over-harshly – Gropius has been criticised. Telling one's life story in the way in which one saw it is surely one of the prerogatives of advancing age. The records retrieved from Nazi Germany were gradually sorted, together with later documents and correspondence, an enormous task which involved a total of around two hundred thousand items. This material needed reading and collating in preparation for a Bauhaus Archive which opened in Darmstadt before moving to Berlin, to a building originally planned by Gropius himself.

At a period in which the Bauhaus was perceived as part of history Gropius and Ise were besieged by researchers. As Ise complained to her old friend Peter Norton, 'perhaps the most time consuming thing is the steady inroad the past is making on the present. Art historians, architectural historians, educators, sociologists etc. have dug into the years before the first world war and after as if this were all dead history. The survivors of those days are at their mercy.' Gropius revived himself after these long sessions by watching westerns and detective stories on TV.

At the same time a biography of Gropius was claiming his and Ise's attention. He told his sister Manon: 'Somebody is writing a book about me and pokes into Ise and me for facts and dates. What seemed up to now unimportant to me, suddenly is made to seem important. And I admit that I begin to get interested to find out why I became who I am.'

The idea of a biography of Gropius was not a new one. Herbert Bayer had almost persuaded him to start an autobiography back in 1951. A small biography by Sigfried Giedion was published in 1954. A more critical assessment by Gropius's Bauhaus colleague Xanti Schawinsky was written but not published. Finally the task, something of a poisoned chalice, went to Reginald Isaacs, an architect who had studied under Gropius at Harvard and who was appointed Harvard's Professor of Regional Planning in 1953.

Work on the book started in 1962, within a framework of almost weekly meetings between Gropius and Isaacs. In that sense the biography, first published in German in 1983 under the title *Walter Gropius, Der Mensch und sein Werk*, then published in a shortened English version in 1991, was a work of collaboration in which the viewpoint was basically Gropius's own.

Ise was essential to the monumental enterprise of sorting the Bauhaus records and Gropius correspondence for posterity and providing translations from the German. She lamented in letters of the period that labours in the archive were keeping her up working till two in the morning and needing her to start again at seven. But it gave her a role in life. One senses she enjoyed it. She was the original keeper of the flame. How did Ise feel, one may wonder, as she sat at her Bauhaus-designed desk in New England, the double desk where she could work alongside Gropius, delving through her husband's love letters of the past: the letters of longing to his Lilychen, his Lily-cat; the 'wandering star' letters that he sent Maria Benemann? Did Ise not have qualms as she translated the letters of desperate passion which Herbert Bayer sent her in the early 1930s? Most likely not. The Bauhaus had been a joint venture, a true partnership in which her own role had been essential. She saw it as a duty to set the record straight.

If we regard Isaacs's book as an example of subject-controlled biography, which to some extent it obviously was, how should we view the picture of Gropius that emerges? In terms of Gropius's career path the book is never less than competent. His emotional development is quite another matter. We are given little understanding of the perils of being in love with Alma Mahler or of his longing for a closer relationship with his daughter Manon. Isaacs does not dwell on what the experience of exile meant to him or on the otherwise masterful Gropius's intermittent moments of self-doubt. Why was it that the Bauhaus and its history continued to be his great preoccupation and why did he cling to the little group of friends – Bayer and Breuer and Schawinsky – who had been with him at the Bauhaus, and who sometimes treated him with singular disloyalty, for the rest of his long life?

For a man of eighty-five Gropius's workload was enormous. He was still very much involved with TAC projects, which in the early 1960s included the John F. Kennedy Federal Building in Boston. Here Gropius continued with his policy of commissioning works of art from artists he admired: for instance a mural by Robert Motherwell and a sculpture, *Thermopylae*, by Dimitri Hadzi.

He and Ise were still indefatigable travellers. In December 1968 they went to Peru to view a new museum of Inca treasures, and on to Argentina to discuss plans for the new residence for the German ambassador that Gropius had been commissioned to design in Buenos Aires. On the way they stopped off in Brasilia 'because he was always interested in the development of this city, created from nothing,' as Ise told her friends the Nortons. 'Finally we came down in Trinidad to relish the tropical beauty of that island and then returned to have Christmas with us and Ati and her family . . . it was only when you were with Pius that you forgot the human limits.' Even for Ise Walter's zest for new experiences seemed almost unbelievable.

But there were now signs that even Gropius was flagging. His and Ise's visits to Arizona became more frequent. Arizona never lost its charm for him. It had a mythic quality as the land of the cactus and of cowboys and Indians, the dream of his youth come true. They stayed in the luxurious Castle Hot Springs Hotel. Gropius spent his days there riding and relaxing. A photograph taken in 1968 shows him on horseback, a grizzled old architect in a bright plaid shirt.

By the end of April 1969, after returning from Arizona, Gropius was complaining of feeling tired and he suffered from bouts of glandular pain in the chest. He was at last forced to cut down all his activities apart from his work at TAC's office, cancelling his foreign commitments. After his eighty-sixth birthday celebrations in May it became clear he was seriously ill and Gropius was admitted to the Pratt Diagnostic Hospital in Boston, where a virulent staphylococcus infection in the blood affecting one of his heart valves was diagnosed.

Gropius at first refused the recommended fitting of an artificial heart valve: 'why should I ask for more of life?' he said. But he was persuaded to change his mind and the operation took place on 25 June. He seemed to make good progress for a week or two. But his condition remained touch and go. The anxiety for Gropius's family was summed up by Ati in a letter to Jeremy Pritchard: 'The past four weeks have had that poor man in hospital, first with a critical staphylococcus infection. Then with a critical heart collapse, and subsequently a heart operation. He has survived all of this to date, but only just. And Ise and I have lived from day to day, week after week, in most terrible concern.'

One of the last people to see Gropius alive was his friend and fellow architect Richard Neutra. Although visitors apart from close family were banned, Neutra managed to bypass the nurses and sit and hold his hand. It was an emotional encounter. To Neutra Gropius had always been a person of great importance, not just as a fellow exile but as an influence on his own architectural development.

Walter Gropius died during the night of 4 July 1969. In his last few days he was already mostly absent and in no pain.

——

The messages of condolence started pouring in. The most effusive came from Maxwell Fry, who sent this telegram from London: 'Our hearts are with you at this end of Walter's wonderful great life. No man could have done more nor left a sweeter memory. His work will never die.' The British architect William Holford's wife Marjorie wept when she heard the news on the radio. The death of Walter Gropius stirred memories worldwide. Messages arrived from Alvar Aalto in Helsinki, Sven Markelius in Stockholm, Joan Miró in Majorca, the designer Sori Yanagi in Tokyo. There were tributes from L'Association de Henry van de Velde and the Taliesin Fellowship and Mrs Frank Lloyd Wright.

A message came from Willy Brandt, West Germany's Foreign Minister, soon to be Chancellor of the Federal Republic of Germany. Gropius's death prompted a flood of reminiscence. Serge Chermayeff, visiting Ise from Wellfleet, Massachusetts, recalled their wild parties together in the woods and the episode of Gropius and Xanti Schawinsky arriving very tipsy at 1 a.m. to haul the others out of bed for a moonlight swim.

There was no formal funeral for Gropius but a quiet gathering of his friends in one of TAC's meeting rooms. His closest associate, Alex Cvijanovic, read out the words Gropius had written more than thirty years before, shortly after Hitler seized power:

Testament April '33

Cremate me, but ask not for the ashes. The piety for cinders is a halfway thing.

Out with it.

Wear no signs of mourning.

It would be beautiful if all my friends of the present and the past would get together in a little while for a fiesta – à la Bauhaus – drinking, laughing, loving. Then I shall surely join in, more than in life. It is more fruitful than the graveyard oratory.

Love is the essence of everything.

Ise, you whom I have loved most, please put in order and manage my spiritual heritage; as to the property on hand, handle it as you see fit.

There was an addition, dated June 1948: 'Remember Ati, whom I love'. No doubt Manon was there in his heart too.

Almost half of his adult life had been lived in exile, without Gropius losing sight of the cause that he believed in: the pursuit of art and beauty. As one of his friends commented at the gathering, Gropius went out with 'protean fire'.

———

The 'fiesta à la Bauhaus' took place a year later, on 20 May 1970, a 'Grope Fest' staged at the TAC offices in Cambridge. It was a recreation of the legendary Metallic Festival held at the Bauhaus in 1929, just after Gropius's departure from Dessau. Admission was strictly 'by metallic decoration'. A thousand guests in shimmering, glittering, tinselly costume danced to two rock bands, watched a nude show by an experimental theatre group, marvelled at a multimedia slide and film show.

The predictable Bauhaus names were on the guest list: Albers, Breuer and Schawinsky. Ise arrived in a black and white gown wearing a tiara formed of aluminium discs. Ati wore a wig of curly metal shavings, Erika a crown of tinfoil flowers. Harvard students, younger artists and architects were present. There was plenty of 'drinking, laughing, loving' in what was not so much a wake as another spectacular Bauhaus celebration, showing how powerfully the past infused the present. It is easy to imagine Gropius joining in.

Afterword
Reverberations

In the summer of 1979 I met Ise Gropius for the first time. The visit was set up, as my earlier meeting with Walter Gropius had been organised, by the ubiquitous Jack Pritchard. Ise at the time was eighty-two. My husband was with me and we arrived at about eleven in the morning. Ise was dressed to the nines in a leopard-pattern housecoat. Her make-up was, as always, carefully applied, her hair spectacularly swept up above her forehead in its old-time film-star style. Ise was an architect's widow like no other, dedicated and phenomenally well informed.

She gave us the full guided tour of the house at Lincoln, which immediately struck us as a European house or, to be more precise, a Bauhaus house in its coolness and its confidence. Many items of furniture – the Marcel Breuer chairs in chrome and cane, the much-travelled double desk where Gropius and Ise used to sit working side by side, the circular dining table – were familiar already from photographs. Ise pointed out the many presents from their friends, works by Serge Chermayeff, László Moholy-Nagy, Herbert Bayer, besides Henry Moore's *Reclining Figure* in bronze.

Their years in Hampstead were remembered by the so-called Penguin Donkey designed by Egon Riss to accommodate Penguin books in its pair of panniers and by Marcel Breuer's Isokon Long Chair. Examples of pre-Columbian and Mexican folk art recalled their visit to Mexico in 1946. Above their bed hung a brilliantly coloured wool rug bought in Samarra, Iraq, by TAC partner Louis McMillen and given to the Gropiuses in the 1960s. In an alcove at the bottom of the stairs hung Ise's coats, wonderfully glamorous. For Ise the house contained the story of her life.

This was a house redolent of memories, the records of two lives lived with passionate conviction. As we have seen, Ise's contribution to the

Bauhaus had been vital. She liked to emphasise how the Bauhaus idea became her second self. Here she was in her old age still articulate in defence of its reputation and its values.

Soon after our visit she suffered a series of strokes. For the last few years of her life Ise was bedridden and it was at this point, in the early 1980s, that she wrote to her one-time lover Herbert Bayer, a letter in barely legible handwriting. She had not heard from him since Gropius's death fourteen years before. As Ati recalled it, 'Her letter spoke with immediacy and passion of long ago, and the certainty it had all been worthwhile. She regretted nothing in her reflections on her life. There was nothing to forget or forgive.' There is no record of whether Bayer responded. Ise Gropius died in 1983.

What in the end did the Bauhaus amount to? Gropius and Ise's joint creation affected generations to come. It was not just a style but a whole new way of being. In the view of Neil MacGregor, historian of German culture: 'Like the Weimar Republic, the Weimar Bauhaus would draw on the values of Germany's past to shape a new society. In fact, the Bauhaus reshaped the world. Our cities and houses today, our furniture and typography, are unthinkable without the functional elegance pioneered by Gropius and the Bauhaus.'

Successors of the Bauhaus included the Design Research furnishing stores founded in the States by Gropius's TAC partner Ben Thompson in the early 1950s, Terence Conran's Habitat shops of the 1960s onwards, with their mission of bringing good design to British high streets, and what has become the international flat-pack furniture phenomenon Ikea, which started in Sweden in 1943. Here it needs to be remembered that Gropius had designed his own series of simplified standardised furniture for middle-income families more than a decade earlier.

Everything in that New England home spoke of Gropius and Ise and their lives together. They had evolved a way of living that was fluent and flexible yet full of meaning. The selection of objects in their home was highly disciplined, with nothing contravening the high aesthetic standards of the things they chose to live with. But emotion came into it as well. Gropius's detractors have liked to stress his austereness, the absolute standards that ruled his life and his artistic choices. This is patently unfair. If he sometimes appeared inflexible, this was part of the Germanic discipline that was endemic in his upbringing and training. He remained to some extent the officer in the Hussars. We need to remember the strain on his emotions caused by his personal history: the turbulent affair and then disastrous marriage to Alma Mahler; the enforced separation from his daughter Manon and his grief at her tragic early death; the exigencies of exile, first to England, then in the USA.

But Gropius managed to surmount his own considerable personal disasters. He was a man of deep, if concealed, feeling. His reputation for doctrinaire rigidity, put about by Tom Wolfe in *From Bauhaus to Our House*, is a travesty of truth. His private life in New England allows us to glimpse a very different and much more sympathetic Gropius. Gropius at his morning ritual of feeding the birds. Gropius playing a ferocious game of ping-pong at the table erected in the porch. This was a man whose persona was also one of charm, generosity and imaginative outreach. His rapport with children and respect for their abilities had always been exceptional. He insisted on his granddaughters' art, and craftwork being displayed in the house alongside the work of Bayer and Moholy. The collage that Erika made him as a child is still on display in the Gropius House today. His belief in education was a species of religion. He would always argue that beyond functional practicality there must be 'the other, the aesthetic satisfaction of the human soul'.

After Gropius's death there were numerous obituaries, beginning with the *New York Times* and soon extending all over the world. There were some in particular that grasped his true importance, which was less that of the architect per se, like Le Corbusier in France or Aalto in Finland, more that of a great architectural thinker with a vision of the meaning of art in modern life. This view of Gropius was most lucidly expressed in the London *Observer* by Nikolaus Pevsner, his fellow exile, for whom Gropius remained a hero figure, with the Bauhaus as the summit of his achievement. 'It was his sterling human qualities', judged Pevsner, 'that held the Bauhaus together and it is through the Bauhaus that Gropius will live on in the history of twentieth-century art and architecture.' Or as Gropius's TAC colleague Sally Harkness later put it more succinctly: 'Everyone wants to think of him as one of the world's great architects; he wasn't. He was one of the world's great philosophers.'

It wasn't until I made that visit to Ise that I fully understood the significance of the Gropius way of living, the attitudes they promulgated at the Bauhaus, the freedoms they defended against all its detractors. The Bauhaus held out for experiment, delight and the meaning of our choices in the things we choose to live with. This was an attitude that affects us still today.

So who in the end was Walter Gropius? After five years' research and extended travels in Germany, England and America, viewing his buildings, searching out the people who had known or worked with Gropius, was I any nearer answering the question posed in Roger Graef's 1967 documentary? Beyond his belief in technological progress there was a romantic, idealistic undercurrent to all Gropius's endeavours. And here he was indeed like William Morris, imaginatively generous in his beliefs. All his life he continued to see art not as an adjunct to life but a necessity. Like Morris he believed that art is life itself. It was architectural soullessness, the despoliation of nature, the denial of community that brought out his fiercest critical opprobrium. In old age he poured scorn on the capitalist greed that had come to dominate the planning of cities in the United States.

'If I have a talent it is for seeing the relationship of things.' A statement made by Gropius towards the end of Graef's film reminds us that we can still learn from his ability to stand back and ruminate. He understood profoundly that man is not an island. In our age of ever-increasing fragmentation and specialisation his visions of connectedness make Walter Gropius worth listening to still.

Sources and References

Any modern biographer of Gropius needs to acknowledge Reginald Isaacs's pioneering *Walter Gropius*, begun in 1962 and drawing on weekly discussions with his subject. Gropius read and commented on early drafts of Isaacs's text before he died in 1969. His wife Ise was a continuing source of information and advice, organising the extensive Gropius archive and providing translations from the German of Gropius's correspondence in the years up to her own death in 1983.

Isaacs's biography originally ran to well over a million words, a length American publishers baulked at. It was, however, published in German in two volumes, under the title *Walter Gropius: Der Mensch und sein Werk* (Berlin, 1983–4) and an abridged version in English, edited by Gerard Van der Leun and Betty Childs, was eventually published in America in 1991. Although it has its limitations as an unashamedly partisan account by a Harvard friend and colleague, I have found Isaacs's book an invaluable resource, especially informative on Gropius's family background and his early years.

In my own pursuit of Walter Gropius I have been able to draw on a great deal of previously unpublished material, including Ise Gropius's account of her first meeting and whirlwind romance with Walter and her wonderfully detailed, frequently acerbic diary of the Bauhaus years in Weimar and Dessau.

The copious Gropius archives in Berlin and the United States have yielded fascinating letters from Gropius to his first wife Alma Mahler, to his later lovers Lily Hildebrandt and Maria Benemann, and to Ise herself, many of these in Ise Gropius's own translation. Isaacs's book was reticent on his personal life. I hope my own biography will redress the balance and reveal Gropius as a man of considerable passions and tenacity.

Rather than including an unwieldy list of secondary sources I have noted at the start of each chapter the specific books and essays I have found most interesting in the course of my research.

I should add that from the Bauhaus period onwards Gropius and his colleagues often followed Bauhaus rules in abolishing capital letters in their correspondence. For the sake of consistency I have reinstated the capitals.

The most frequently listed sources of quotations have been abbreviated as follows:

Hilmes	Oliver Hilmes, *Malevolent Muse, The Life of Alma Mahler*, translated by Donald Arthur (Boston, 2015)
Isaacs	Reginald Isaacs, *Gropius, An Illustrated Biography of the Creator of the Bauhaus* (Boston, 1991)
Mahler *Bridge*	Alma Mahler Werfel, *And the Bridge Is Love* (London, 1959)
Nerdinger	Winfried Nerdinger, *The Architect Walter Gropius*, catalogue of exhibition at Busch-Reisinger Museum, Harvard University and Bauhaus Archive, Berlin, 1985
Neumann	Eckhard Neumann (ed.), *Bauhaus & Bauhaus People* (New York, 1993)
Reidel	James Reidel, 'Walter Gropius, Letters to an Angel, 1927–35', letters between Walter Gropius and Manon Gropius, translated by James Reidel, *Journal of the Society of Architectural Historians* 69 (University of California Press, March 2010)
Whitford	Frank Whitford, *The Bauhaus, Masters and Students by Themselves* (London, 1992)

Archive Sources

AAA	Archives of American Art, Smithsonian Institution, Washington – Walter and Ise Gropius Papers – Ise Gropius Bauhaus diary 1924–8 – Herbert Bayer and Ise Gropius correspondence – Marcel Breuer and Ise Gropius correspondence
BHA	Bauhaus Archive, Berlin – Walter Gropius Papers
BRM	Busch-Reisinger Museum, Harvard University Art Museums – Architectural drawings, plans and photographs by Gropius and associates
DHA	Dartington Hall Archive, Exeter – Walter Gropius correspondence and plans
GRI	Getty Research Institute, Los Angeles – Lily and Hans Hildebrandt Papers
GSD	Graduate School of Design, Harvard University Archives – Walter Gropius Papers

HLH   Houghton Library, Harvard University
          – Walter Gropius Papers, MS Ger 208 Series III, letters to and from Walter Gropius
          – Ise Gropius Japan diary 1954
LCP   Fondation Le Corbusier, Paris
          – Walter Gropius correspondence with Le Corbusier
ONV   Österreichische Nationalbibliothek, Vienna, Ida Gebauer manuscript collection
          – Walter Gropius correspondence with Manon Gropius
UEA   University of East Anglia, Norwich
          – Pritchard Papers
          – Isokon Furniture Co. records and Lawn Road Flats correspondence
          – Maxwell Fry correspondence
UPP   University of Pennsylvania, Philadelphia
          – Mahler-Werfel Papers, Kislak Centre for Special Collections, Rare Books and
            Manuscripts
          – Alma Mahler's *Tagebuch* and draft of her memoir 'Der schimmernde Weg'
ZBZ   Zentralbibliothek, Zurich
          – Alma Mahler and Oskar Kokoschka Papers

Note: the personal archive of Walter Gropius was divided into two sections after his death
by his widow Ise Gropius. Originals of papers to end 1936 were consigned to the Bauhaus
Archive, Berlin (BHA), with photocopies to the Houghton Library, Harvard (HLH).
Originals of papers relating to 1937 onwards are at Harvard, with photocopies in Berlin.

Preface: The Silver Prince

4   'the Silver Prince' Felix Klee, quoted Neumann, p. 44
7   'Nobody's baby' Walter Gropius, speech at RIBA Gold Medal Presentation, London,
    12 April 1956
7   'the creation of beautiful proportions' Walter Gropius, *Apollo in the Democracy* (New
    York, 1968), p. 10
8   'I knew that face' Christopher Isherwood, *Prater Violet* (London, 1946), p. 12
8   'As a man' Joseph Rykwert, *Times Literary Supplement*, 2 May 1986

1: Berlin 1883–1907

The main sources for Walter Gropius's early life are the letters he wrote to his mother and
occasionally his father, translated from the German by his wife Ise for Reginald Isaacs's
biography. The originals are now in the Bauhaus Archive in Berlin. There is a perceptive
account of his background and childhood in the chapter on Gropius in Peter Gay's *Art and
Act* (New York, 1976). For the architectural evolution of the city, see the collected essays
in *Metropolis Berlin 1880–1940*, edited by Iain Boyd Whyte and David Frisby (Berkeley,
2012).

11   'when I was' Walter Gropius, *The Scope of Total Architecture* (London, 1956), p. 13
12   'And every time' Walter Benjamin, *Berlin Childhood Around 1900* (New York, 2000),
     p. 43
14   'the only really *kind*' Ise Gropius to Manon Burchard Gropius, 20 August 1925, BHA
14   'had wonderful constructions' Peter Gay, *Art and Act* (New York, 1976), p. 166

14 'had *Kultur*' ibid., p. 159

16 'Everything in the courtyard' Benjamin, *Berlin Childhood*, p. 39

16 'the caryatids and atlantes' ibid., p. 53

16 'I have made an effort' ibid., p. 38

19 'My uniforms fit me' Walter Gropius to Manon Burchard Gropius, 29 September 1904, BHA, quoted Isaacs, p. 12

20 'a very nice person' Walter Gropius to Manon Burchard Gropius, 9 October 1904, BHA

20 'very beautiful girls' Walter Gropius to Walther Gropius, 5 January 1905, BHA, quoted Isaacs, p. 13

20 'After this year' Walter Gropius to Manon Burchard Gropius, 7 November 1904, BHA, quoted Isaacs, p. 17

22 'I cannot follow' Walter Gropius to Manon Burchard Gropius, 26 June 1906, BHA, quoted Isaacs, p. 16

22 'push forward' Walter Gropius to Manon Burchard Gropius, n/d, BHA

2: Spain 1907–1908

23 'not even the most wonderful' Walter Gropius to his parents, 2 October 1907, BHA, quoted Isaacs, p. 17

25 'with its thousand pinnacles' Walter Gropius to Manon Burchard Gropius, 21 October 1907, BHA, quoted Isaacs, p. 18

26 'the two most beautiful girls' Walter Gropius to Manon Burchard Gropius, 8 January 1908, BHA, quoted ibid.

28 'a strong thread' Walter Gropius to his parents, 16 December 1907, BHA, quoted ibid.

29 'had instilled in him' Ise Gropius, 'First Encounter' typescript, *c*.1970, AAA

29 'Some of the Sagrada Família walls' *El Propagador de la Devoción a San José*, vol. LXVI, 1 June 1932

3: Berlin 1908–1910

Indispensable background on Gropius the architect, from his early beginnings in Peter Behrens's office, is given in Winfried Nerdinger's *The Architect Walter Gropius*, a comprehensive catalogue of the exhibition held at the Busch-Reisinger Museum, Harvard University, and the Bauhaus Archive, Berlin, in 1985–6. For Gropius and Behrens, see Alan Windsor, *Peter Behrens, Architect and Designer* (London, 1981) and the authoritative chapter in Peter Gay's *Art and Act* (New York, 1976). Reyner Banham's *Theory and Design in the First Machine Age* (London, 1960) is still as combative and stimulating as it must have appeared when first published.

For the Fagus factory, see Annemarie Jaeggi's *Fagus: Industrial Culture from Werkbund to Bauhaus* (New York, 2000). Jaeggi's analysis of Gropius's relations with his architectural partner Adolf Meyer and their evolution of collaborative working methods published in *Archithese* 4, July/August 1995, is illuminating. The Fagus factory in Alfeld is now a UNESCO World Heritage Site.

31 'Everything here' Robert Walser, 'Berlin W', *Berlin Stories* (New York, 2012), p. 17

31 'In Berlin' Alfred Hermann Fried, 1908, quoted in catalogue *Vienna–Berlin*, Berlinische Galerie, 2013, p. 116

32 'he took a fresh unprejudiced start' Walter Gropius, 'Peter Behrens, a testimonial', 24 April 1960, *Apollo in the Democracy* (New York, 1968), p. 165

32 'the first foundation' ibid., p. 166

34 'who was not only' Ise Gropius, 'First Encounter' typescript, *c*.1970, AAA

34 'based on respect' quoted Alan Windsor, *Peter Behrens* (London, 1981), p. 92

34 'Professor Behrens's factotum' Walter Gropius to Herta Hesse, 8 May 1969, quoted Nerdinger, p. 29

35 'a landmark' Walter Gropius, BBC statement on Crystal Palace, 5 December 1936, BHA

36 'sing the great song' quoted Windsor, *Peter Behrens*, p. 91

37 'the most vexatious dampness' Karl Ernst Osthaus to Peter Behrens, 4 February 1910, quoted ibid., p. 112

38 'latterly differences between' Walter Gropius to Karl Ernst Osthaus, 6 March 1910, quoted ibid., p. 115

40 'I would like to build' Walter Gropius to Alma Mahler, n/d, quoted Annemarie Jaeggi, *Fagus* (New York, 2000), p. 50

42 'ethereal material' Walter Gropius, lecture at Hagen, 1911, quoted ibid., p. 51

42 'one of the classic' Reyner Banham, *A Concrete Atlantis: US Industrial Building and European Modern Architecture 1900–1925* (Cambridge, 1986), p. 198

43 'what a pity' Ise Gropius diary, October 1924, AAA

4: Vienna and Alma Mahler 1910–1913

Crucial source material for the next two chapters is the interchange of letters between Walter Gropius and Alma Mahler now in the Bauhaus Archive in Berlin. Alma Mahler's dating of her letters is either erratic or non-existent and I have gratefully accepted the dating proposed by Jörg Rothkamm, who carried out detailed research at the suggestion of Henry-Louis de La Grange, author of a monumental biography of Mahler.

Besides Alma Mahler's own riveting but unreliable memoirs I have drawn on de La Grange's biography (vol. 4, Oxford, 2008) and Oliver Hilmes's authoritative *Malevolent Muse, The Life of Alma Mahler* (Boston, 2015), first published in German in 2004.

Background to the affair between Alma and Oskar Kokoschka comes mainly from Kokoschka's *My Life* (London, 1974) and *Oskar Kokoschka Letters 1905–1976* (London, 1992), and from Alfred Weidinger's *Kokoschka and Alma Mahler* (Munich, 1996), a beautifully detailed analysis of the interactions of their life and art. I have also been dependent on the catalogue of Richard Calvocoressi's exhibition *Oskar Kokoschka 1886–1980*, held at Tate Britain in 1986.

An illuminating account of Vienna at the period when Gropius first met Alma is given in Peter Vergo's *Art in Vienna 1898–1918* (London, 1975) and in Richard Calvocoressi and Keith Hartley's essay 'Vienna 1908–1918' in the catalogue of the exhibition *Century City*, held at Tate Modern in 2001. *Rebel Modernists: Viennese Architecture since Otto Wagner* by Liane Lefaivre (London, 2017) provides an interesting overview.

44 'Barefoot, clothed in' Mahler *Bridge*, p. 52

44 'Feeling responsible' ibid.

44 'by the tempestuous wooing' ibid., p. 53

46 'I remember one night' Alma Mahler Werfel typescript, *c*.1914, UPP, quoted Henry-Louis de La Grange, *Gustav Mahler*, vol. 4 (Oxford, 2008), p. 838

46 'I am the daughter' Mahler *Bridge*, p. 10

49 'We had some odd scenes' ibid., p. 17

49 'strikingly good-looking' ibid.

49   'a hideous gnome' ibid., p. 18

49   'childhood crush' ibid., p. 19

50   'stood in the kind of vacuum' ibid., p. 20

51   'I love in you' Alma Mahler to Walter Gropius, n/d, probably late August/early September 1910, BHA

51   'In this strange world' Mahler *Bridge*, p. 26

52   'The soup' ibid., p. 30

52   'only in part' ibid., p. 31

53   'I was really sick' ibid., p. 32

53   'Did you ever see Gropius?' Elias Canetti, *The Play of the Eyes* (London, 1990), p. 53

54   'much fresher and stronger' Gustav Mahler to Anna Moll, n/d, postmarked 1910, quoted de La Grange, *Gustav Mahler*, vol. 4, p. 838

54   'noble humanity' Walter Gropius to Anna Moll, 17 July 1910, BHA

55   'the young stranger's infatuation' Mahler *Bridge*, p. 52

55   'I feel dreadfully sorry' Alma Mahler to Walter Gropius, n/d, *c.* late July 1910, BHA

55   'Mahler was seated' Alma Mahler, *Gustav Mahler, Memories and Letters* (London, 1946), p. 145

55   'Just think' Alma Mahler to Walter Gropius, n/d, probably 31 July 1910, BHA

55   'I am now' Alma Mahler to Walter Gropius, n/d, probably 3 August 1910, BHA

56   'Gustav is like' ibid.

56   'I'll go out of my mind' Walter Gropius to Alma Mahler, n/d, probably early August 1910, BHA

57   'Whatever you do' Mahler *Bridge*, p. 52

57   'Why should I' Alma Mahler to Walter Gropius, n/d, probably 11 August 1910, BHA

57   'churned to the very bottom' Alma Mahler, *Gustav Mahler, Memories and Letters*, p. 145

57   'These songs are good' Mahler *Bridge*, p. 55

58   'Have mercy' Gustav Mahler annotations, quoted Hilmes, p. 69

58   'I feel trapped' Gustav Mahler to Alma Mahler, 17 August 1910, quoted Hilmes, p. 70

58   'this idolatrous love' Alma Mahler to Walter Gropius, n/d, probably 23 August 1910, BHA

58   'He felt his visit' Theodor Reik, *Dreissig Jahre mit Sigmund Freud* (Munich, 1976), quoted Hilmes, p. 70

58   'How dared a man' Alma Mahler, *Gustav Mahler, Memories and Letters*, p. 147

59   'you owned it' Alma Mahler to Walter Gropius, 27 August 1910, BHA

59   'I feel that' ibid.

59   'when will be the time' Alma Mahler to Walter Gropius, n/d, probably early September 1910, BHA

59   'G's music moved my heart' Walter Gropius to Alma Mahler, n/d, *c.* September 1910, BHA

60   'My life's happiness' Walter Gropius to Alma Mahler, 21 September 1910, BHA

61   'Rendez-vous would be' Alma Mahler to Walter Gropius, 12 October 1910, BHA

61   'The days in Paris' Alma Mahler to Walter Gropius, 8 November 1910, BHA

62   'The more you accomplish' Alma Mahler to Walter Gropius, n/d, BHA

62   'I shall try' Alma Mahler to Walter Gropius, 8 November 1910, BHA

62   'to cling to' Walter Gropius to Alma Mahler, 23 January 1911, BHA

63   'It is a recurring' Alma Mahler to Walter Gropius, 25 March 1911, BHA

64   'Gustav's death, too' Alma Mahler Werfel, *Tagebuch*, 27 July 1920, UPP, quoted Hilmes, p. 69

64   'I knew him still' Walter Gropius to Alma Mahler, n/d, probably late May 1911, BHA

65 'A hot feeling of shame' Walter Gropius to Alma Mahler, 18 September 1911, BHA

66 'Aren't we human beings?' Alma Mahler to Walter Gropius, 21 November 1911, BHA

66 'I was glad' Walter Gropius to Alma Mahler, 3 December 1912, BHA

66 'Soon I was surrounded' Mahler *Bridge*, p. 66

66 'after a decent interval' ibid., p. 67

66 'roaming in souls' ibid., p. 68

67 'When I reported' ibid., p. 70

67 'one fierce battle' ibid., p. 72

68 'I loved a woman' Oskar Kokoschka to Anna Kallin, September 1921, *Oskar Kokoschka Letters 1905–1976* (London, 1992), p. 77

68 'He was tall and slender' Mahler *Bridge*, p. 74

68 'I shall never' Oskar Kokoschka to Alma Mahler, 14 May 1913, *Oskar Kokoschka Letters 1905–1976*, p. 40

70 'He painted me' Mahler *Bridge*, p. 73

70 'Later he perpetually' Alma Mahler Werfel, 'Aus der Zeit meiner Liebe zu Oskar Kokoschka', quoted Hilmes, p. 93

71 'fiery red pyjamas' Alma Mahler Werfel, *Mein Leben*, quoted Alfred Weidinger, *Kokoschka and Alma Mahler* (Munich, 1996), p. 28

5: Gropius at War 1914–1918

72 'the architectural elements' quoted Nerdinger, p. 40

72 'something quite good' Walter Gropius to Manon Burchard Gropius, April 1914, BHA, quoted Isaacs, p. 31

74 '*enfant terrible*' Walter Gropius, letter to *Architectural Review* 134, July–December 1963, p. 6

75 'an unpleasant man' ibid.

76 'they decided the day' Walter Gropius to Manon Burchard Gropius, 19 September 1914, BHA, quoted Isaacs, p. 39

78 'much pleasanter' Walter Gropius to Manon Burchard Gropius, 11 November 1914, BHA, quoted Isaacs, p. 41

78 'hellish dance' Walter Gropius to Manon Burchard Gropius, early January 1914, BHA

79 'the nightmares' Ise Gropius, 'First Encounter', typescript, *c.*1970, AAA

79 'I try to visualise' Walter Gropius to Manon Burchard Gropius, 16 January 1915, BHA, quoted Isaacs, p. 42

70 'a kindred spirit' Alma Mahler to Walter Gropius, 26 July 1913, BHA

80 'There is a young architect' Mahler *Bridge*, p. 82

81 'In his early thirties' ibid., p. 83

82 'Our wildness' Alma Mahler to Walter Gropius, n/d, probably May 1915, BHA, quoted Isaacs, p. 42

82 'Alma Gropius!' Alma Mahler to Walter Gropius, n/d, probably June 1915, BHA, quoted Isaacs, p. 43

82 'the embattled days' Manon Burchard Gropius to Walter Gropius, 7 June 1915, BHA, quoted Isaacs, p. 43

82 'tried in a *young* life' Walter Gropius to Manon Burchard Gropius, 3 July 1915, BHA, quoted Isaacs, p. 43

82 'this beautiful name' Manon Burchard Gropius to Alma Mahler, 7 July 1915, BHA, quoted Isaacs, p. 43

83 'this person' Alma Mahler Werfel, *Tagebuch*, 8 April 1915, UPP, quoted Hilmes, p. 106

83   'he is just tepid' ibid., 8 June 1915, quoted Hilmes, p. 108

83   'beloved name' Alma Mahler to Walter Gropius, n/d, BHA

83   'my desire' Alma Mahler Werfel, *Tagebuch*, 26 September 1915, UPP, quoted Hilmes, p. 110

85   'sackfuls' Oskar Kokoschka, *My Life* (London, 1974), p. 74

86   'If you are able' Oskar Kokoschka to Hermine Moos, 20 August 1918, quoted Alfred Weidinger, *Kokoschka and Alma Mahler* (Munich, 1996), p. 89

87   'What is my idol' Oskar Kokoschka to Adolf Loos, 25 April 1918, *Oskar Kokoschka Letters 1905–1976* (London, 1992), p. 72

87   'Alma, I have in front' Oskar Kokoschka to Alma Mahler, 27 May 1921, ibid., p. 77

87   'so wonderfully beautiful' Alma Mahler to Walter Gropius, n/d, *c.* early September 1915, BHA, quoted Isaacs, p. 44

88   'My marriage' Mahler *Bridge*, p. 86

88   'She is very greedy' Alma Mahler to Walter Gropius, *c.* late September 1915, BHA, quoted Isaacs, p. 48

88   'You wrote today' Alma Mahler to Walter Gropius, n/d, 1915, BHA

89   'The first time' Alma Mahler to Walter Gropius, n/d, 1915, BHA

89   'the mark of Cain' Walter Gropius to Manon Burchard Gropius, 3 January 1916, BHA, quoted Isaacs, p. 48

90   'This position' Alma Mahler to Walter Gropius, n/d, *c.* late autumn 1915, BHA

91   '"Has the porch"' Alma Mahler to Walter Gropius, n/d, *c.* March 1916, BHA, quoted Isaacs, p. 49

92   'a rare and fine' Manon Burchard Gropius to Walter Gropius, 2 June 1916, BHA

92   'I am very sensual' Alma Mahler to Walter Gropius, n/d, probably summer 1916, BHA, quoted Isaacs, p. 49

92   'livid with rage' Walter Gropius to Manon Burchard Gropius, 17 August 1916, BHA, quoted Isaacs, p. 51

93   'embrace the world' Walter Gropius to Manon Burchard Gropius, n/d, probably early October 1916, BHA

93   'he just had not found' Mahler *Bridge*, p. 87

93   'When I saw him' ibid., p. 89

95   'she is lying' Walter Gropius to Manon Burchard Gropius, 26 March 1917, BHA, quoted Isaacs, p. 53

95   'turnips and so-called liverwurst' Walter Gropius to Manon Burchard Gropius, n/d, probably August/September 1917, BHA

95   'totally unable' Alma Mahler to Walter Gropius, n/d, *c.* summer 1917, BHA

96   'My school has become' Walter Gropius to Manon Burchard Gropius, 11 November 1917, BHA, quoted Isaacs, p. 54

96   'The strong odour' Mahler *Bridge*, p. 85

97   'I know the entire' ibid., p. 90

97   'a bowlegged, fat Jew' Alma Mahler Werfel, *Tagebuch*, November 1917, UPP, quoted Hilmes, p. 120

97   'a bored loathing' ibid., quoted Hilmes, p. 121

98   'the grey world' Walter Gropius to Manon Burchard Gropius, 7 January 1918, BHA, quoted Isaacs, p. 54

98   'We can fight battles' Walter Gropius to Manon Burchard Gropius, n/d, *c.* January/February 1918, BHA, quoted Isaacs, p. 54

99   'entirely forgotten' Walter Gropius to Karl Ernst Osthaus, 19 December 1917, BHA, quoted Isaacs, p. 54

99   'one where I myself' Walter Gropius to Manon Burchard Gropius, 10 April 1918
       BHA, quoted Isaacs, p. 55

99   'I was in the middle' Walter Gropius to Manon Burchard Gropius, May 1918, BHA,
       quoted Isaacs, p. 55

100   'I did not spare her' 'The Diary of Franz Werfel' in Mahler *Bridge*, p. 101

100   'Werfel and I' Alma Mahler Werfel, *Tagebuch*, n/d, UPP, quoted Hilmes, p. 122

100   'She has a great' Walter Gropius to Manon Burchard Gropius, 17 August 1918,
       BHA, quoted Isaacs, p. 58

100   'crumpled as though struck' Mahler *Bridge*, p. 119

101   'I am here to love you' 'The Diary of Franz Werfel' in Mahler *Bridge*, p. 116

101   'without the least sensation' Alma Mahler Werfel, *Tagebuch*, 24 October 1918, UPP,
       quoted Hilmes, p. 124

101   'a few thoughtful' Mahler *Bridge*, p. 119

6: Bauhaus Weimar and Lily Hildebrandt 1919–1920

The essential source for Gropius's relationship with Lily Hildebrandt is the sequence of
letters from Gropius to Lily now in the Bauhaus Archive in Berlin. Later correspondence
between them, which continued until Gropius's death in 1968, is in the Houghton Library
at Harvard University and the main archive for both Hans and Lily Hildebrandt is held at
the Getty Research Institute, Los Angeles.

Particularly interesting in relation to Lily Hildebrandt's own art are the catalogues of two
retrospective exhibitions, *Lily Hildebrandt 1887–1974*, held at Galerie Schlichtenmaier,
Grafenau, in 1988 and a show under the same title held at Das Verborgene Museum, Berlin,
in 1997.

For background on the Bauhaus at this formative period Hans M. Wingler's *The
Bauhaus* is an invaluable full documentation by the then director of the Bauhaus Archive,
first published in German with Gropius's support and approval in 1962 and revised
and expanded in successive English editions (Cambridge, Mass., from 1969). Another
compendious volume, *Bauhaus*, edited by Jeannine Fiedler and Peter Feierabend
(Potsdam, 2013), contains historical background, lavish illustrations and critical essays.
With popular paperbacks, scholarly analyses and exhibition catalogues the Bauhaus
literature has recently been growing to an almost unmanageable extent.

In preparing these chapters I have found most useful Frank Whitford's succinct *Bauhaus*
(London, 1984), Marcel Franciscono's *Walter Gropius and the Creation of the Bauhaus in
Weimar* (Urbana, 1971) and Gillian Naylor's *The Bauhaus Reassessed: Sources and Design
Theory* (London, 1985), particularly informative on the conflicting ideologies of those early
years. A term-by-term summary of Bauhaus developments in Weimar and Dessau, compiled
by Barry Bergdoll and Leah Dickerman, is included in the impressive catalogue of the
exhibition *Bauhaus 1919–1933: Workshops for Modernity* (Museum of Modern Art, New
York, 2009).

For more detailed background on the socio-political scene, see John V. Maciuika's
Before the Bauhaus, Architecture, Politics and the German State, 1890–1920 (New York,
2005), John Willett's *The New Sobriety: Art and Politics in the Weimar Period, 1917–1933*
(London, 1978) and Jeremy Aynsley's *Designing Modern Germany* (London, 2009), a
study which relates the beginnings of the Bauhaus to post-Second World War German
reconstruction in a very interesting way.

What was being at the Bauhaus actually like? The impressions and memories of the
Masters and the students, including their own varied attitudes to Gropius, have been

assembled in two fascinating collections: Eckhard Neumann's *Bauhaus and Bauhaus People* (New York, 1993) and Frank Whitford's *The Bauhaus, Masters and Students by Themselves* (London, 1992). The views of the Bauhaus Master Oskar Schlemmer are especially perceptive and very amusingly expressed. These have been published in an edition selected by his wife Tut Schlemmer as *The Letters and Diaries of Oskar Schlemmer* (Evanston, 1990). Nicholas Fox Weber's *The Bauhaus Group, Six Masters of Modernism* (Knopf, 2009), his wittily incisive Bauhaus histories of Gropius, Klee, Kandinsky, Josef and Anni Albers and Mies van der Rohe, has been essential reading for these and for my later Bauhaus chapters.

On Gropius's architecture once again Winfried Nerdinger's comprehensive catalogue and commentary *Walter Gropius*, accompanying the exhibition in Harvard and Berlin in 1985–6, has been a major resource. For Gropius's stylistic transition from Expressionist to modern, Wolfgang Pehnt's article 'Gropius the Romantic', published in *Art Bulletin*, vol. 53, 1971, and Joseph Rykwert's 'The Dark Side of the Bauhaus', published in *The Necessity of Artifice*, London, 1982, are particularly stimulating. Rosemarie Haag Bletter's lucid and scholarly introduction to *The Modern Functional Building: Adolf Behne* (Santa Monica, 1996) gives valuable background on Gropius's involvement with the German radical architectural scene.

102   'as in a flash' Walter Gropius, quoted Isaacs, p. 61
102   'I am here to participate' Walter Gropius to Karl Ernst Osthaus, 23 December 1918, quoted Whitford, p. 25
103   'all come to the meetings' Walter Gropius to Manon Burchard Gropius, 31 March 1919, BHA, quoted Isaacs, p. 64
103   'to build us' Mahler *Bridge*, p. 122
103   'The little boy' Alma Mahler to Manon Burchard Gropius, November 1918, BHA, quoted Isaacs, p. 62
103   'storming through Berlin' Walter Gropius to Karl Ernst Osthaus, 23 December 1918, quoted Whitford, p. 25
104   'They are excessive' Walter Gropius to Manon Burchard Gropius, late January 1919, BHA, quoted Isaacs, p. 63
104   'But I wanted both' Walter Gropius, letter to *Architectural Review* 134, July–December 1963, p. 6
104   'The ultimate aim' Walter Gropius, quoted Hans M. Wingler, *The Bauhaus* (Cambridge, 1969), p. 31
106   'Glass brings in' Paul Scheerbart, quoted Reyner Banham, *Theory and Design in the First Machine Age* (London, 1962), p. 266
106   'I imagine Weimar' Walter Gropius to Ernst Hardt, 14 April 1919, Thüringisches Staatsarchiv, Weimar
107   'the beginning' Lyonel Feininger to Walter Gropius, quoted in Gropius's funeral address for Feininger, 1955, HLH
108   'finely modelled face' Mahler *Bridge*, p. 123
109   'young men and women' Helmut von Erffa, 'Bauhaus: First Phase', *Architectural Review* 132, August 1957, p. 103
109   'a gradual condensation' Anni Albers, catalogue of exhibition *Ein Museum für das Bauhaus?*, Bauhaus Archive, 1979, p. 33
111   'If only I had died' Mahler *Bridge*, p. 126
111   'grandiose plan' ibid., p. 127
111   'In him and her' Lyonel Feininger to Julia Feininger, 30 May 1919, quoted Isaacs, p. 79

112 'What do I care?' Alma Mahler Werfel, *Tagebuch*, 3 July 1919, UPP, quoted Hilmes, p. 128

112 'Your splendid nature' Walter Gropius to Alma Mahler, 18 July 1919, BHA, quoted Isaacs, p. 81

112 'was it Lady Music?' Mahler *Bridge*, p. 128

112 'their impassioned modernism' ibid., p. 134

113 'Workers spat' ibid., p. 135

114 'Franz first admitted' Alma Mahler Werfel, *Tagebuch*, 16 June 1919, UPP, quoted Hilmes, p. 128

114 'horribly dissolute trait' ibid., 4 June 1920, quoted Hilmes, p. 131

114 'I long for a companion' Walter Gropius to Alma Mahler, 18 July 1919, BHA, quoted Isaacs, p. 82

116 'She did not want' Rainer Hildebrandt, introduction to *Lily Hildebrandt* exhibition catalogue, Galerie Schlichtenmaier, Schloss Dätzingen, 1988

116 'Nobody will believe' Walter Gropius to Lily Hildebrandt, 15 October 1919, BHA, quoted Isaacs, p. 83

116 'rush into each other' Walter Gropius to Lily Hildebrandt, 14 October 1919, BHA

116 'Our union' Walter Gropius to Lily Hildebrandt, late October/early November 1919, BHA, quoted Isaacs, p. 85

116 'My darling' Walter Gropius to Lily Hildebrandt, 15 October 1919, BHA

116 'Lilychen my darling' Walter Gropius to Lily Hildebrandt, n/d, *c*.1920, BHA

116 'My Lily-cat' Walter Gropius to Lily Hildebrandt, 1920, BHA

116 'I have a great longing' Walter Gropius to Lily Hildebrandt, 13 December 1919, BHA

117 'Your hair lotion' Walter Gropius to Lily Hildebrandt, 1920, BHA

117 'enchanted eyes' ibid.

117 'Now I am more' Walter Gropius to Lily Hildebrandt, late October 1920, BHA

117 'full of traditions' George Adams, 'Memories of a Bauhaus Student', *Architectural Review* 144, September 1968, p. 192

118 'wonderful party' Gunta Stölzl diary, 18 October 1919, *Gunta Stölzl: A Bauhaus Master*, ed. Moniker Stadler and Yael Aloni (Museum of Modern Art, New York, 2009), p. 45

119 'delightfully different' T. Lux Feininger, quoted Neumann, p. 183

120 'As though in paradise' Lydia Driesch-Foucar, quoted Whitford, p. 115

121 'When we meet' Lothar Schreyer, quoted Neumann, p. 74

121 'So that is Morris' Nikolaus Pevsner, 'From William Morris to Walter Gropius', *The Listener*, 17 March 1949, p. 439

121 'in order to have' William Morris, Arts and Crafts circular letter, Longmans, London, 1898

122 'their calm' Rolf Bürgi, quoted *The Private Klee*, exhibition catalogue, National Galleries of Scotland, 2000

123 'We were permitted' Hans Fischli, quoted Whitford, p. 76

124 'old world politeness' Adams, 'Memories of a Bauhaus Student', p. 193

124 'No, I am not in love' Walter Gropius to Lily Hildebrandt, November 1919, BHA, quoted Isaacs, p. 85

125 'Everywhere I try' Walter Gropius to Lily Hildebrandt, 1920, BHA

126 'I am in the terrible vortex' Walter Gropius to Lily Hildebrandt, 1 February 1920, BHA

126 'a big Bauhaus battle' Walter Gropius to Lily Hildebrandt, 13 December 1919, BHA

127 'without any bathing costumes' Staatsrat Rudolph, 4 September 1920, quoted Whitford, p. 115

Sources and References

128 'This was the first opportunity' Walter Gropius, letter to *Architectural Review* 134, July–December 1963, p. 6

129 'so Teutonic Robert Hughes, *The Shock of the New* (London, 1980), p. 194

7: Bauhaus Weimar and Maria Benemann 1920–1922

Crucial material for this chapter is the sequence of twenty-one letters and three postcards from Walter Gropius to Maria Benemann, dating from the beginning of their love affair in 1920. These letters were given to the Bauhaus Archive in Berlin by Benemann herself shortly before her death in 1980. One of them was quoted, and Maria Benemann herself named with a short reference to their relationship, in Reginald Isaacs's biography of Gropius in its 1983 German edition. But in the 1991 English edition, presumably after family protests, Maria had become anonymous, simply referred to as 'an attractive young widow'. This is the first time the correspondence has been drawn on fully, with translations by Fiona Elliott made especially for this book.

Maria Benemann's own memoirs, which include her account of her first meeting with Gropius, at the time still married to Alma Mahler, were published privately in 1978 under the title *Leih mir noch einmal die leichte Sandale* – 'Bestow on me once again the light sandal', a reference to poetic inspiration. The foreword to these memoirs was written by Maria's son Joachim Benemann, whose widow I discovered in 2017 to be living, aged one hundred, in a retirement home in Tiverton. Barbara Benemann's distant memories of Maria and her family have been of great value and interest to me.

131 'In the classical sense' Maria Benemann, *Leih mir noch einmal die leichte Sandale*, privately printed in Germany, 1978, p. 236

131 'I too am married' ibid., p. 238

132 'Maria Benemann speaks' ibid., p. 263

133 'It suddenly brought back' Rainer Maria Rilke, quoted ibid., p. 260

133 'dear letter' Walter Gropius to Maria Benemann, *c*. March 1920, BHA

134 'I am a wandering star' Walter Gropius to Maria Benemann, 19 April 1920, BHA

134 'In a flash' Walter Gropius to Maria Benemann, 30 April 1920, BHA

135 'The two poems' Walter Gropius to Maria Benemann, 26 July 1920, BHA

136 'You are suffering' Walter Gropius to Maria Benemann, n/d 1920, BHA

136 'You shy away' ibid.

136 'I am striving' Walter Gropius to Lily Hildebrandt, n/d 1921, BHA, quoted Isaacs, p. 92

136 'a firm bond' Walter Gropius to Lily Hildebrandt, n/d 1922, BHA

137 'The Bauhaus peels' Walter Gropius to Lily Hildebrandt, late October 1920, BHA

137 'He looked like a priest' Felix Klee, 'My Memories of the Weimar Bauhaus', quoted Neumann, p. 40

139 'uncooked mush' Mahler *Bridge*, p. 134

139 'he was in his office' Herbert Bayer, poem written for Gropius celebration, Columbia University, 1961, quoted Neumann, p. 141

140 'so Itten and Gropius' *The Letters and Diaries of Oskar Schlemmer*, ed. Tut Schlemmer (Evanston, 1990), p. 114

140 'He was certainly' Walter Gropius to Jack Pritchard, 15 February 1946, UEA

140 'At Weimar' Theo van Doesburg, quoted Joost Baljeu, *Theo van Doesburg* (London, 1974), p. 41

141 'manifest itself' Statement in *De Stijl*, vol. 1

141 'an arrogant and narrow' Walter Gropius, letter to *Architectural Review* 134, July–

December 1963, p. 6

141   'while his wife' Helmut von Erffa, 'Bauhaus: First Phase', *Architectural Review* 132, August 1957, p. 105

141   'scribbles sickly dreams' Vilmos Huszár, 'Bauhaus', *De Stijl*, September 1922

142   'art as the collective' 'The will to style', *De Stijl*, vol. 5

142   'enchanting, sympathetic' Lothar Schreyer, quoted Nikolaus Pevsner, 'Gropius and van de Velde', *Architectural Review* 133, March 1963, p. 167

142   'The Bauhaus philosophy' Walter Gropius, *Architectural Review* 134, July–December 1963, p. 6

143   'definitely would not' Walter Gropius to Morton Frank, 20 March 1958, HLH

8: Bauhaus Weimar and Ise Gropius 1923–1925

A major source for my account of Gropius at the Bauhaus in Weimar is Ise Gropius's typescript diary for 1924–8. Her detailed, witty and perceptive day-to-day record is illuminating on Bauhaus events and personalities and on Gropius's responses to the growing political antagonism towards the Bauhaus. It also shows the central role that Ise – who came to be known as 'Frau Bauhaus' – took in the development of the school.

Ise Gropius's diary was transported from Berlin to the States with their many other Bauhaus records after the Gropiuses left Germany. It was only rediscovered in the early 1960s, while Ise was searching through old files. The original German version, typed by Ise with handwritten amendments, is now in the Bauhaus Archive in Berlin, along with Gropius's early letters to Ilse Frank, as she then was, and Gropius's replies. My quotations are taken from Ise Gropius's translation of the diary, containing some later additions and amendments, a copy of which is in the American Archives of Art at the Smithsonian Institution in Washington.

Further crucial biographical details can be found in Ise Gropius's 'First Encounter', her retrospective account written in the early 1970s of her dramatic courtship and early married life. A good, brief account of her life with interesting personal insights is given in *Ise Gropius* by the Gropiuses' adopted daughter Ati Gropius Johansen, published by Historic New England for the Gropius House at Lincoln, Mass.

145   'The Bauhaus Week' Gerhard Marcks, memorandum to the Bauhaus Council of Masters, 22 September 1922, Thuringisches Staatsarchiv, Weimar, quoted Whitford, p. 141

147   'the Cubist idol' Paul Westheim, review in *Das Kunstblatt*, 1923, quoted Whitford, p. 153

148   'Abstract shapes' George Adams, 'Memories of a Bauhaus Student', *Architectural Review* 144, September 1968, p. 194

149   'a world that was being reborn' Sigfried Giedion, 'Bauhaus Week in Weimar', quoted Neumann, p. 84

150   'Leonardian' Walter Gropius, draft of funeral address for László Moholy-Nagy, 1946, HLH

152   'Yesterday I looked' Walter Gropius to Gerhard Marcks, 5 April 1923, Thuringisches Staatsarchiv, Weimar, quoted Whitford, p. 141

153   'he approached me' Lyonel Feininger to Julia Feininger, 1 August 1923, quoted Hans M. Wingler, *The Bauhaus* (Cambridge, Mass., 1969), p. 69

153   'a companion who loves me' Walter Gropius to Alma Mahler, 18 July 1919, BHA, quoted Isaacs, p. 82

153   'The Bauhaus idea' Ise Gropius, 'First Encounter', typescript, *c*.1970, AAA

154   'Unfortunately' Walter Gropius to the Frank sisters, 28 May 1923, BHA, quoted Isaacs, p. 104

154 'a very enjoyable evening' Ise Gropius, 'First Encounter'

155 'You have come' ibid.

156 'He looked at me' ibid.

156 'as if this were all happening' ibid.

156 'I am not a man' Walter Gropius to Ise Gropius, 10 July 1923, BHA, quoted 'First Encounter'

157 'generous and noble gesture' Ise Gropius, 'First Encounter'

157 'I arrived at his door' ibid.

158 'We were left free' ibid.

159 *Mon cul!*' Yvonne Le Corbusier, quoted Nicholas Fox Weber, *Le Corbusier, A Life* (New York 2008), p. 15. The story is attributed to Sigfried Giedion

160 'inspired by madness' Ise Gropius, 'First Encounter'

161 'My ability to type' ibid.

161 'I believe finally' Walter Gropius to Ise Gropius, March 1924, BHA

161 'Yesterday morning' Walter Gropius to Lieutenant General Hasse, 24 November 1923, BHA, quoted Isaacs, p. 110

162 'learned a lot' Ise Gropius, 'First Encounter'

162 'I am already' Walter Gropius to Ise Gropius, March 1924, BHA

162 'you know whenever' Ise Gropius to Walter Gropius, April 1924, BHA

162 'decisive years' ibid.

163 'I am happy' Walter Gropius to Ise Gropius, April 1924, quoted 'First Encounter'

163 'erotically still' Ise Gropius, 'First Encounter'

163 'in a fantastic mood' Ise Gropius to Manon Burchard Gropius, 18 May 1924, BHA

164 'a bad character' Ise Gropius, 'First Encounter'

164 'All the mechanical games' *Weimarer Zeitung*, quoted Whitford, p. 205

165 'a black morning!' Walter Gropius to Ise Gropius, probably September 1924, BHA

166 'showed to him' Ise Gropius, 'First Encounter'

168 'Well, I simply' ibid.

168 'We accuse the Government' ibid.

168 'Nobody will believe' Ise Gropius diary, 27 December 1924, AAA

169 'the charms' ibid.

169 'this teeming, lively, dirty' ibid.

170 'Oh, you don't know' Ise Gropius to Walter Gropius, 2 October 1924, BHA

170 'made this fortuitous encounter' Ise Gropius, 'First Encounter'

171 'The devil has entered' Ise Gropius diary, 11 March 1925, AAA

171 'If characters like' ibid., 19 March 1925

171 'Big relief' ibid., 23 March 1925

172 'The apartment is empty' Ise Gropius diary, 29 May 1925, AAA

172 'a lovely get-together' ibid., 22 June 1925

172 'Nina Kandinsky' Oskar Schlemmer to Tut Schlemmer, *The Letters and Diaries of Oskar Schlemmer* (Evanston, 1990), p. 172

172 'experiences of the stormy' Xanti Schawinsky, 'bauhaus metamorphosis', quoted Neumann, p. 156

9: Bauhaus Dessau 1925–1926

Ise Gropius's Bauhaus diary and her later account of the Bauhaus years in 'First Encounter' have once again been invaluable sources. An interesting summing up of reasons behind Gropius's decision to leave the Bauhaus in 1928 is given in a letter from

Ise Gropius to Reyner Banham written in 1970 and now in the Gropius Papers in the Houghton Library at Harvard.

On Manon ('Mutzi'), Walter Gropius and Alma Mahler's daughter, I have found particularly useful James Reidel's subtle, sensitive account in 'Walter Gropius, Letters to an Angel, 1927–35', published in the *Journal of the Society of Architectural Historians*, no. 69, March 2010, and drawing on the letters from Gropius to Manon in the Ida Gebauer Papers in the Österreichische Nationalbibliothek in Vienna. Ida Gebauer was Manon's nanny and remained as Alma's devoted companion for almost all her life. James Reidel has generously given me permission to use his translations of Gropius's letters to his daughter. In the originals Gropius follows Bauhaus practice in eliminating capital letters. However, for ease of reading I have reverted to capitals in quoting from this correspondence.

I have also found illuminating Werner David Feist's personal account of student life in Dessau, *My Years at the Bauhaus*, published in 2012 by the Bauhaus Archive, Berlin.

Bauhaus Conflicts, 1919–2009, Controversies and Counterparts, edited by Philipp Oswalt (Ostfildern, 2009), contains some stimulating retrospective essays on Gropius and the Bauhaus. Especially relevant to the next two chapters is Magdalena Droste's reassessment of the conflict between Gropius and his successor Hannes Meyer. See also Gillian Naylor, *The Bauhaus Reassessed: Sources and Design Theory* (London, 1985).

174   'If one regarded' Tut Schlemmer, lecture published 1962, quoted Neumann, p. 169
175   'more of an ivory tower' Walter Gropius, letter to *Architectural Review* 134, July–December 1963, p. 6
177   'an entirely new kind' Walter Gropius, 'Dessau Bauhaus principles of Bauhaus production', Bauhaus publication, March 1926
178   'He is such an able' Ise Gropius diary, 27 June 1925
178   'Visit with Frau Neufert' ibid., 29 September 1925
178   'under thunder and lightning' ibid., 17 October 1925
178   'Ground plans!' ibid., 22 April 1925
179   'In reality' ibid., 20 May 1925
181   'The first Bauhaus books' ibid., 10 October 1925
182   'The Bauhaus has now' ibid., 18 September 1925
182   'Like wandering journeymen' Ise Gropius, 'First Encounter', typescript, *c*.1970, AAA
182   'he struggles to keep' Ise Gropius diary, 21 May 1925
182   'We advance now' ibid., 22 September 1925
182   'The whole mess' Ise Gropius to Walter Gropius, 10 August 1925, quoted 'First Encounter'
183   'My dearest heart' Walter Gropius to Ise Gropius, September 1925, quoted 'First Encounter'
184   'a man of extraordinary beauty' Ise Gropius, 'First Encounter'
184   'They try to persuade' Ise Gropius diary, 6 November 1925
184   'We do not respond' ibid., 10 December 1925
185   'a very healthy' ibid., 18 December 1925
185   'His influence' ibid.
186   'in hottest preparation' ibid., 2 November 1926
186   'as though this' ibid., 3 November 1926
187   'What a difference' ibid., 4 December 1926
187   'The interest is astonishing' ibid., 6 December 1926
188   'such a dear, enchanting person' ibid., 12 October 1927

189   'for balancing exercises' Marianne Brandt, letter 13 May 1966, quoted Neumann, p. 107
189   'and there was this beautiful' Wilfred Franks, talk given in Liverpool, 6 November 1999, World Socialist website
190   'I was overawed' Werner David Feist, *My Years at the Bauhaus* (Berlin, 2012), p. 22
192   'two near menopausal Swiss ladies' ibid., p. 44
192   'casts light on aspects' Reyner Banham, *Theory and Design in the First Machine Age* (London, 1960), p. 288

10: Bauhaus Dessau 1927–1928

193   'They are located' Tadeusz Peiper, 'Im Bauhaus', 1927, quoted Wolfgang Thöner, *Life and Work in the Masters' House Estate in Dessau* (Dessau, 2003), p. 4
193   'freed of unnecessary burdens' Walter Gropius, quoted Nerdinger, p. 76
195   'The size of the room' Felix Klee, quoted Whitford, p. 211
196   'I'm sitting on our terrace' Lyonel Feininger to Julia Feininger, 2 August 1926, quoted Whitford, p. 209
196   'longed for' Ise Gropius, 'First Encounter', typescript, *c*.1970, AAA
197   'We have of course' Ise Gropius to Manon Burchard Gropius, n/d 1925, BHA
197   'When Frau Gropius' Konrad Wünsche, quoted Thöner, *Life and Work in the Masters' House Estate*, p. 26
197   'some very indignant' Ise Gropius diary, 11 October 1925, AAA
198   'They have probably' ibid.
198   'I was shocked' Oskar Schlemmer, quoted Nerdinger, p. 76
198   'strange surroundings' Alma Mahler, quoted Isaacs, p. 136
200   'Alma acted' Ise Gropius diary, 8 November 1927
200   'We are getting along' ibid., 15 November 1927
202   'The introduction' ibid., 26 April 1926
202   'also pointed to' ibid., 14 January 1927
203   'Personally he is very nice' ibid., 1 February 1927
204   'Hannes Meyer and family' ibid., 1 April 1927
204   'Meyer seems to force' ibid., 23 June 1927
204   'What did I discover' Hannes Meyer, quoted E. A. Seemann, *The Bauhaus Masters* (Leipzig, 2016), p. 35
204   'I believe' Walter Gropius, letter to *Architectural Review* 134, July–December 1963, p. 6
205   'quite beside himself' Ise Gropius diary, 7 January 1927
205   'You are uninformed' Walter Gropius to Wassily Kandinsky, 7 February 1927, quoted Whitford, p. 254
205   'looking wan' Ise Gropius diary, 20 June 1926
205   'the artistically inclined' ibid., 19 February 1927
206   'Hesse now strikes' ibid., 5 December 1927
206   'Cold weather' ibid., 20 February 1925
206   'beside himself' ibid., 13 January 1928
207   'For the sake of' Fritz Kuhr, February 1924, quoted Hans Wingler, *Bauhaus* (Cambridge, Mass., 1969), p. 136
208   'He suffers' Ise Gropius diary, 21 February 1928
208   'Everyone except Moholy-Nagy' Walter Gropius, letter to *Architectural Review* 134, July–December 1963, p. 6
208   'a treacherous character' ibid.

209 'The longing and joy' Ise Gropius diary, 21 January 1928
209 'Gropius, the organiser' Grete Dexel, *Frankfurter Zeitung*, 17 March 1928, quoted
       Whitford, p. 257
210 'Clear light' Lou Scheper, 1964, quoted Neumann, p. 125

11: America 1928

Besides the good detailed account of the Gropiuses' travels in America given in the
German edition of Reginald Isaacs's biography of Gropius there are valuable insights in the
catalogue of the exhibition *Walter Gropius: American Journey 1928*, held at the Bauhaus
Archive in Berlin in 2008. Many of the four hundred photographs taken in America by
Walter and Ise Gropius are included in this catalogue, with a foreword by Gerda Breuer and
Annemarie Jaeggi.

211 'Sommerfeld has a plan' Ise Gropius diary, 2 March 1928, AAA
212 'I think every single' Ise Gropius, 'Small but perfect things', interview recorded
       *c.*1980, transcribed in 1984, BHA
215 'the nakedness of the girls' Walter Gropius, quoted Isaacs, p. 145
215 'separate standards' ibid., p. 148
216 'The closer we get' Ise Gropius, 'In the Land of Singing Frogs and Sky-blue
       Waterfalls', typescript article, 1934, BHA
216 'the most overwhelming' Walter Gropius, quoted Isaacs, p. 148
218 'My dear Mutzi' Walter Gropius to Manon Gropius, 10 May 1928, quoted Reidel, p. 93
218 'Gropius here' Richard Neutra, *Life and Shape* (Los Angeles, 2009), p. 264
220 'Everything original' Walter Gropius, quoted Isaacs, p. 149

12: Berlin 1928–1932

The following chapter covers Gropius's return from Dessau to an increasingly unwelcoming
Berlin. His anxieties at this period are clear from the letters he wrote to his daughter
Manon, and here again I gratefully acknowledge James Reidel's permission to use his
translations of this correspondence, the originals of which are in the Österreichische
Nationalbibliothek, Vienna.

I have also made use of previously unpublished letters from Herbert Bayer to Ise
Gropius charting the course of their love affair, the cause of considerable disruption to
Gropius's marriage. Copies of these letters, translated by Ise herself, are in the Archives of
American Art, Smithsonian Institution, Washington.

For background on the city of Berlin in the 1920s and early 1930s I have found most
useful John Willett's *The New Sobriety, Art and Politics in the Weimar Period, 1917–1933*
(London, 1978), Rainer Metzger's cultural survey *Berlin in the Twenties* (London, 2007)
and, once again, *Metropolis Berlin 1880–1940*, a collection of contemporary texts on the
visual aspects of the city edited by Iain Boyd Whyte and David Frisby (Berkeley, 2012).

221 'The ideas of the new architecture' Max Osborn, *Berlins Aufstieg zur Weltstadt*
       (Berlin, 1929), quoted *Metropolis Berlin*, ed. Iain Boyd Whyte and David Frisby
       (Berkeley, 2012), p. 412
221 'Paris has become' Count Harry Kessler, 19 May 1930, *The Diaries of a
       Cosmopolitan, 1918–37* (London, 1971), p. 388
222 'a secluded, quiet life' Ise Gropius, 'First Encounter', typescript, *c.*1970, AAA

222   'Discipline and integrity' Nikolaus Pevsner, 'The Work of Walter Gropius, Royal Gold Medallist 1956', *RIBA Journal* 63, April 1956

224   'sitting forlornly' Ise Gropius to Hannah Arendt, February 1967, HLH

224   'G. is always dissatisfied' Ise Gropius diary, 11 April 1926, AAA

225   'He isn't a great conversationalist' ibid., 27 July 1925

225   'a compelling speaker' J. M. Richards, *Memoirs of an Unjust Fella* (London, 1980), p. 202

226   'the indubitable bird' ibid., p. 197

226   'The *basic requirements*' Walter Gropius, 'Large Housing Estates', article in *Zentralblatt der Bauverwaltung* 50 (1930), quoted Boyd Whyte and Frisby (eds), *Metropolis Berlin*, p. 484

227   'new forms' Walter Gropius, 'The Sociological Foundations of the Minimum Dwelling', quoted Eric Mumford, *The CIAM Discourse on Urbanism, 1928–1960* (Cambridge, Mass., 2002), p. 37

227   'The architect' Franz Hessel, 'I Learn', essay in *Ein Flaneur in Berlin*, 1929, quoted Boyd Whyte and Frisby (eds), *Metropolis Berlin*, p. 386

229   'bear witness' Walter Gropius, catalogue introduction 1930, quoted Nerdinger, p. 142

229   'we need casual' ibid.

230   'space and light' *Journal des débats*, quoted Nerdinger, p. 142

230   'In the afternoon' Count Harry Kessler, 30 May 1930, *Diaries of a Cosmopolitan*, p. 389

230   'As I recognized' Walter Gropius to Roger D. Sherwood, 9 August 1963, HLH, quoted Isaacs, p. 165

231   'the insignificant follower' Hannes Meyer, 'My Ejection from the Bauhaus', open letter to Mayor Hesse, 1930, quoted Whitford, p. 283

231   'Gropius was a man' Oskar Schlemmer to Willi Baumeister, 8 April 1929, *The Letters and Diaries of Oskar Schlemmer* (Evanston, 1990), p. 241

232   'I remember three students' Wilfred Franks, talk given in Liverpool, 6 November 1999, World Socialist website

232   'Marxist teaching methods' L. Pazitnov, *Das schöpferische Erbe des Bauhauses, 1919–1933* (East Berlin, Institut für Angewandte Kunst, 1963), quoted Isaacs, p. 165

233   'Then we heard' Wilfred Franks, Liverpool talk, 6 November 1999

233   'My dearest Mutzi' Walter Gropius to Manon Gropius, 26 February 1930, quoted Reidel, p. 94

234   'fancy chateau' Walter Gropius to Manon Gropius, 5 March 1931, quoted Reidel, p. 94

234   'won top prizes' Walter Gropius to Manon Gropius, 5 July 1931, quoted Reidel, p. 96

234   'Hitler's power' Sibyl Moholy-Nagy, *Moholy-Nagy, Experiment in Totality* (New York, 1950), p. 57

235   'you can hardly imagine' Walter Gropius to Manon Gropius, 5 July 1931, quoted Reidel, p. 96

237   'a theatre of mass events' Walter Gropius, quoted Nerdinger, p. 154

237   'The Soviet Palace' ibid., p. 160

239   'the poet Nebel' Oskar Schlemmer to Otto Meyer, 18 August 1927, *Letters and Diaries of Oskar Schlemmer*, p. 208

239   'the place where brows' Xanti Schawinsky, quoted Isaacs, p. 167

241   'the attachment' Ati Gropius Johansen, *Ise Gropius* (Historic New England, 2013), p. 8

241   'Oh zatt Hehr-bert' Anni Albers, quoted Nicholas Fox Weber, *The Bauhaus Group* (New York, 2009), p. 77

241   'Bayer was an immaculate' Werner David Feist, *My Years at the Bauhaus* (Berlin, 2012), p. 60

242 'brief but delightful' Walter Gropius to Manon Gropius, 23 December 1930, quoted Reidel, p. 94

242 'Shocking! Tonight no letter' Walter Gropius to Ise Gropius, *c.* late summer 1931, BHA, quoted Isaacs, p. 167

243 'perhaps it is not right' Herbert Bayer to Ise Gropius, January 1932, AAA

244 'You know that we want' Herbert Bayer to Ise Gropius, 2 June 1932, AAA

244 'I know how you feel' Walter Gropius to Ise Gropius, BHA, quoted Isaacs, p. 169

244 'I let him go ahead' Walter Gropius to Ise Gropius, July 1932, BHA, quoted Isaacs, p. 170

245 'Pius was deeply concerned' Herbert Bayer to Ise Gropius, 2 June 1932, AAA

245 'Yesterday we had' Walter Gropius to Ise Gropius, 5 July 1932, BHA, quoted Isaacs, p. 170

245 'his feeling of guilt' Walter Gropius to Ise Gropius, 23 July 1932, BHA

246 'will you let us' Ise Gropius to Walter Gropius, quoted Isaacs, p. 173

246 'But things are so difficult' Walter Gropius to Manon Burchard Gropius, 25 December 1932, HLH

247 'grey, depressed and frustrated' Unnamed architect, quoted Isaacs, p. 176

248 'horrified and shaken' Oskar Beyer (ed.), *Eric Mendelsohn: Letters of an Architect* (London, 1967), p. 126

248 'I am very sad' Walter Gropius to Manon Gropius, 1 January 1933, quoted Reidel, p. 98

13: Berlin 1933–1934

Besides Gropius's authorised biographer Reginald Isaacs's account of these politically problematic years I have taken into account Jonathan Petropoulos's important reassessment of Gropius in his book *Artists Under Hitler: Collaboration and Survival in Nazi Germany* (New Haven, 2014).

Also crucial in considering the degree of Gropius's involvement with the Nazi regime is Winfried Nerdinger's 'Bauhaus Architecture in the Third Reich', originally published in German in 1993 and included in translation in *Bauhaus Culture: From Weimar to the Cold War*, edited by Kathleen James-Chakraborty (Minneapolis, 2006).

There have been many detailed reconsiderations of the Bauhaus, the Bauhäusler and the Nazis in the fifty years since the publication of Barbara Miller Lane's pioneering *Architecture and Politics in Germany, 1918–1945* (Harvard, 1968). Particularly pertinent to Gropius is the essay by Peter Hahn, 'Bauhaus and Exile: Bauhaus architects and designers between the old world and the new', in the catalogue of the exhibition *Exiles and Emigrés: The Flight of European Artists from Hitler* (Los Angeles County Museum of Art, 1997) and the essay by Paul Betts, 'The Bauhaus and National Socialism – a Dark Chapter of Modernism', in *Bauhaus*, edited by Jeannine Fiedler and Peter Feierabend (Potsdam, 2013).

Michael Tymkiw's *Nazi Exhibition Design and Modernism* (University of Minnesota Press, 2018) gives interesting insights into Gropius and Joost Schmidt's design for the *Deutsche Volk – deutsche Arbeit* exhibition of 1934.

Gropius's personal commentary on life in Nazi Germany in letters to his daughter has been invaluable, and here again I have been reliant on the correspondence now in the Österreichische Nationalbibliothek as quoted by James Reidel in 'Walter Gropius, Letters to an Angel, 1927–35', *Journal of the Society of Architectural Historians* 69, March 2010.

249 'I suffer very much' Walter Gropius to Manon Gropius, 17 May 1933, quoted Reidel, p. 98

249 'News that Hitler' Klaus Mann, diary entry 30 January 1933, quoted Rainer Metzger, *Berlin in the Twenties* (London, 2007), p. 365

250 'Whether Gropius is a Jew' Rudolf Paulsen, 'Culturally Bolshevik Attacks', *Völkischer Beobachter*, 30 March 1932

251 'I flee Germany' Oskar Beyer (ed.), *Eric Mendelsohn: Letters of an Architect* (London, 1967), p. 125

251 'A uniformed Nazi patrol' Walter Gropius, discussion notes, Cambridge, Mass., September 1968, quoted Isaacs, p. 175

254 'glorious, a great success' Annemarie Wilke to Julia Feininger, 21 February 1933, quoted Whitford, p. 300

255 'Mies also stood' Frank Trudel, 'The end of the Bauhaus', *c.*1980, quoted Whitford, p. 302

256 'In other states' Adolf Hitler, speech at the topping-out ceremony for the new Reich Chancellery, Berlin, 2 August 1938, quoted Iain Boyd Whyte and David Frisby (eds), *Metropolis Berlin 1880–1940* (Berkeley, 2012), p. 603

257 'the outlook is bad' Walter Gropius to Manon Gropius, 17 June 1933, quoted Reidel, p. 99

258 'but it seems quite plain' Nancy Ross to Leonard Elmhirst, 30 December 1932, Dartington Papers, Devon Archives

258 'and to spend the time' Gropius quoted in letter from William Slater to Walter Gropius, 3 May 1933, Dartington Papers, Devon Archives

259 'We at Dartington' ibid.

259 'My knowledge' Walter Gropius to William Slater, 17 May 1933, Dartington Papers, Devon Archives

259 'An ancient gothic palace' Walter Gropius to Manon Gropius, 11 September 1933, quoted Reidel, p. 99

260 'many details' Walter Gropius to Leonard Elmhirst, 21 July 1933, Dartington Papers, Devon Archives

260 'the spiritual roots' Walter Gropius to Leonard Elmhirst, 5 September 1933, Dartington Papers, Devon Archives

260 'the harsh reality' Herbert Bayer to Walter Gropius, 9 March 1933, AAA

261 'Unfortunately the present state' Walter Gropius to William Slater, 29 September 1933, Dartington Papers, Devon Archives

262 'circus-like building' quoted Nerdinger, p. 100

263 'I feel a special kinship' Walter Gropius to Manon Gropius, 11 September 1933, quoted Reidel, p. 99

265 'destructive Marxist-Judaic' Oskar Schlemmer to Willi Baumeister, 2 April 1933, *The Letters and Diaries of Oskar Schlemmer*, ed. Tut Schlemmer (Evanston, 1990), p. 309

265 'ancestors, party, Jew' Oskar Schlemmer to Gunta Stölzl, 16 June 1933, ibid., p. 311

265 'Deeply shaken' Oskar Schlemmer to Minister Goebbels, 25 April 1933, ibid., p. 310

266 'Shall this strong' Walter Gropius to Eugen Hönig, 27 March 1934, BHA, quoted Isaacs, p. 180

267 'which would eclipse' Walter Gropius and Martin Wagner to the President of East Prussia, 1 February 1934, BHA, quoted Isaacs, p. 179

267 'The Houses of German work' Walter Gropius to Hans Weidemann, January 1934, quoted Jonathan Petropoulos, *Artists Under Hitler* (New Haven, 2014), p. 79

269 'I could see' Ise Gropius to Jack and Molly Pritchard, 15 October 1973, UEA

14: London, Berlin, Rome 1934

A major source for the following chapters on the three years Gropius spent living in England is the Pritchard Papers at the University of East Anglia. As well as correspondence between Walter and Ise Gropius and Jack and Molly Pritchard this archive includes exchanges with Maxwell Fry and Philip Morton Shand and background on Isokon.

Relevant memoirs are Jack Pritchard's *View from a Long Chair, the Memoirs of Jack Pritchard* (London, 1984) and Maxwell Fry's *Autobiographical Sketches* (London, 1975). Also indispensable have been *Gropius in England, a Documentation 1934–1937* by David Elliott, published by the Building Centre Trust in London in 1974, and Alastair Grieve's *Isokon* (London, 2004), an expanded version of his essay in the catalogue of the exhibition *Hampstead in the Thirties: A Committed Decade* (Camden Arts Centre, London, 1974). There is also useful background in Alan Powers's article 'Britain and the Bauhaus', *Apollo*, 1 May 2006.

On Dartington, Michael Young's *The Elmhirsts of Dartington: The Creation of an Utopian Community* (London, 1982) gives a good overview and *Going Modern and Being British* (Exeter, 1998), a collection of essays on local Devon architecture edited by Sam Smiles, provides an interesting commentary. The main source for Gropius's Dartington connection is the Dartington Archive in the Devon Record Office in Exeter.

For Gropius's correspondence with Manon I am again indebted to James Reidel's 'Walter Gropius, Letters to an Angel, 1927–35', published in the *Journal of the Society of Architectural Historians* 69, March 2010. I have also made use of Erich Rietenauer's memoir *Alma, meine Liebe* (Vienna, 2008). Rietenauer, a young family friend and a confidant of Manon and her nurse Ida Gebauer, gives a revealing account of Manon's final illness.

273 'Dearest Mutzili' Walter Gropius to Manon Gropius, 6 May 1934, quoted Reidel, p. 100
274 'with a heavy heart' Ise Gropius to Manon Gropius, May 1934, quoted Reidel, p. 101
274 'ex-Etonian' Maxwell Fry, *Building*, 31 October 1975, p. 53
275 'an entertaining contrast' *Journal of the RIBA*, 19 May 1934, pp. 667–8
275 'During the late twenties' R. D. Best, 'Postscript to Pevsner', *Design and Industries Yearbook* 1965–6, p. 96
275 'this highly nervous lion' Maxwell Fry, *Autobiographical Sketches* (London, 1975), p. 146
276 'filled us with a fervour' ibid., p. 147
276 'I have such a wild veneration' Nikolaus Pevsner to Lola Pevsner, 16 May 1934, quoted Susie Harries, *Nikolaus Pevsner: The Life* (London, 2011), p. 162
276 'I can imagine' Ise Gropius to Walter Gropius, May 1934, BHA
277 'never to get involved' ibid.
278 'Every morning Ali' ibid.
278 'a Puck-like figure' Maxwell Fry, *Autobiographical Sketches*, p. 138
279 'All the same' Jack Pritchard, *View from a Long Chair* (London, 1984), p. 57
279 'I am very pleased' Walter Gropius to Philip Morton Shand, 7 June 1934, UEA
280 'those with special qualifications' RIBA Council to Ministry of Labour, December 1933, quoted Anthony Jackson, *The Politics of Architecture: A History of Modern Architecture in Britain* (London, 1970), p. 42
280 'I feel very honoured' Maxwell Fry to Walter Gropius, 15 June 1934, UEA
281 'I had never' Maxwell Fry to Walter Gropius, 3 July 1934, UEA
281 'or whatever time' ibid.

281 'Do you think' Walter Gropius to Maxwell Fry, 23 June 1934, UEA

283 'Your becoming Catholic' Walter Gropius to Manon Gropius, 17 May 1933, quoted Reidel, p. 98

286 'I regard you' Eugen Hönig to Walter Gropius, 4 October 1934, BHA, quoted Isaacs, p. 183

286 'It is difficult' Ise Gropius to Jack Pritchard, 26 November 1973, UEA

286 'we sit in a dreadful' Walter Gropius to Manon Gropius, 1 October 1933, quoted Reidel, p. 102

287 'Walter, on the other hand' Ise Gropius to Jack Pritchard, 26 November 1973, UEA

288 'Building Theatres' For full text of Gropius's Rome address see *Apollo in the Democracy* (New York, 1968), pp. 153–63

290 'Why this hysterical fear' Walter Gropius quoted *Convegno di lettere, Tema: Il teatro drammatico* (Rome, 1935), p. 176

290 'I believe I can' ibid., insert p. 174

290 'The crucial moment' Ise Gropius to Jack Pritchard, 26 November 1973, UEA

291 'I am not only' Walter Gropius to Manon Gropius, 11 September 1933, quoted Reidel, p. 99

291 'I am curious' Walter Gropius to Manon Gropius, 1 October 1934, quoted Reidel, p. 102

15: London 1934

For my account of Gropius in London I have drawn on the following studies of émigrés in Britain: Daniel Snowman, *The Hitler Emigrés: The Cultural Impact on Britain of Refugees from Nazism* (London, 2002); John Willett, 'Exile in Great Britain, The Emigration and the Arts', an interesting chapter in *Exile in Britain: Refugees from Hitler's Germany*, ed. Gerhard Hirschfeld (Leamington Spa, 1984); and *A Different World: Emigré Architects in Britain 1928–1958*, edited by Charlotte Benton, catalogue of a RIBA Heinz Gallery exhibition held in London in 1995. There is also much useful background in *Exiles and Emigrés: The Flight of European Artists from Hitler*, especially Peter Hahn's essay 'Bauhaus and Exile', in the catalogue of the exhibition at Los Angeles County Museum of Art, 1997. For Hampstead in particular see *Hampstead in the Thirties: A Committed Decade*, catalogue of a memorable exhibition held at Camden Arts Centre in London in 1974, when many of the Hampstead residents included were still alive.

On Lawn Road Flats and Wells Coates see Sherban Cantacuzino, *Wells Coates, a Monograph* (London, 1978), and Laura Cohn, *The Door to a Secret Room: A Portrait of Wells Coates*, a memoir by his daughter (Aldershot, 1999). David Burke's *The Lawn Road Flats: Spies, Writers and Artists* (Woodbridge, 2014) gives a fascinating if sometimes over-excited account of the Soviet agents who were residents in Lawn Road Flats.

For the context of British architecture at this period, see Anthony Jackson, *The Politics of Architecture: A History of Modern Architecture in Britain* (London, 1970) and two surveys by Alan Powers, *Britain* (London, 2007) and *Modern: The Modern Movement in Britain* (London, 2005).

292 'We had come' Ise Gropius to Jack Pritchard, 29 April 1970, UEA

292 'we were used' ibid.

294 'After having experienced' Ise Gropius to Jack Pritchard, 28 February 1955, draft text celebrating twenty-first anniversary of Lawn Road Flats, HLH

296 'a fine tall girl' Jack Pritchard, *View from a Long Chair* (London, 1984), p. 71

297 'must have warmed' J. M. Richards, 'Wells Coates 1893–1958', in *The Rationalists,*

     Theory and Design in the Modern Movement, ed. Dennis Sharp (London, 1978), p. 93

297 'this idea of property' Wells Coates to Jack Pritchard, 13 July 1930, UEA

300 'You are now entering' Pritchard, *View from a Long Chair*, p. 102

300 'We're giving' John Betjeman, fragment of poetry given to John Gloag, quoted Bevis Hillier, *Young Betjeman* (London, 1988), p. 260

301 '"nest" of gentle artists' Herbert Read, *Apollo*, September 1962, quoted 'Art in Britain 1930–40', Marlborough Fine Art catalogue (London, 1965), p. 8

301 'the best of the living' Walter Gropius to Jack Pritchard, 24 January 1942, UEA

301 'When I left Hitler's Germany' Walter Gropius, 'On Herbert Read', *Herbert Read, A Memorial Symposium* (London, 1970), p. 27

302 'Europe, in the shape' J. M. Richards, *Memoirs of an Unjust Fella* (London, 1980), p. 121

303 'how immensely' Ise Gropius to Jack Pritchard, 28 February 1955, HLH

303 'it was foreign' Maxwell Fry, *Autobiographical Sketches* (London, 1975), p. 148

305 'We do not understand' Quoted Jack Pritchard, 'Gropius, the Bauhaus and the Future', address to Royal Society of Arts, London, 13 November 1968

306 'when I say' Nicholas Pevsner, *Industrial Art in England* (London, 1937), acknowledgements page

307 'There would be no leaving' Henry Morris Memorandum, 'The Village College', quoted David Rooney, *Henry Morris, The Cambridgeshire Village Colleges* (Sawston, Cambridge, 2013), p. 18

307 'orgasm!' Jack Pritchard in conversation with the author, *c.*1980

308 'They have offered' Walter Gropius to Martin Wagner, 26 December 1934, BHA

308 'a sort of English "Bauhaus"' ibid.

309 'the mills in England' ibid.

309 'with my three words' Walter Gropius to C. H. van der Leeuw, 19 September 1935, BHA, quoted Isaacs, p. 200

310 'Don't you remember?' Ise Gropius to Jack Pritchard, 16 December 1948, UEA

310 'a guest' Stefan Zweig, *The World of Yesterday* (London, 1943), p. 295

310 'only spatially' ibid., p. 298

16: London 1935

For an entertaining if inaccurate account of Manon Gropius's funeral, see Elias Canetti, *The Play of the Eyes* (London, 1990). There is an interesting investigation of the background to Berg's Violin Concerto 'To the memory of an angel' in Chris Walton's *Lies and Epiphanies* (Rochester, 2014).

    A detailed account of Gropius's failed relationship with the Royal College of Art is given in Christopher Frayling's history *The Royal College of Art, One Hundred and Fifty Years of Art and Design* (London, 1987).

311 'a magnificent building' Walter Gropius to Manon Gropius, 3 February 1935, quoted Reidel, p. 104

312 'had been presented' Elias Canetti, *The Play of the Eyes* (London, 1990), p. 200

312 'looked quite regal' Mahler *Bridge*, p. 207

314 'All Vienna' Canetti, *The Play of the Eyes*, p. 200

314 'She blossomed' Johannes Hollnsteiner, funeral oration, April 1935, quoted Chris Walton, *Lies and Epiphanies* (Rochester, 2014), p. 65

315 'a wondrous creature' Ludwig Karpath, 'Manon Gropius', *Wiener Sonn- und Montags-zeitung*, 29 April 1935

316   'For my husband' Ise Gropius, 'First Encounter', typescript, *c.*1970, AAA

316   'in bringing Mutzi' Alma Mahler to Walter Gropius, 19 June 1935, BHA, quoted
      Isaacs, p. 196

316   'the father' Alma Mahler, *Tagebuch*, quoted Reidel, p. 105

317   'I am ashamed' Walter Gropius to Jack Pritchard, 7 April 1935, BHA, quoted Isaacs,
      p. 195

317   'You will think me' Jack Pritchard to Walter Gropius, 31 July 1935, BHA, quoted
      Isaacs, p. 199

317   'You, no doubt, know' William Lescaze to W. B. Curry, 19 January 1935, quoted
      David Jeremiah, 'Dartington – A Modern Adventure', in *Going Modern and Being
      British*, ed. Sam Smiles (Exeter, 1998), p. 62

318   'a bigger work' Walter Gropius to William Slater, 6 January 1935, Dartington
      Archive, Exeter

319   'advocated by Walter Gropius' Madge Garland, *The Indecisive Decade* (London,
      1968), p. 11

319   'The Englishman in general' Anthony Blunt, 'Art: The English Home', *Spectator* 158,
      15 January 1937, p. 84

319   'Bauhaus balls' Bevis Hiller, *Young Betjeman* (London, 1988), p. 261

319   'with the rejected design' Evelyn Waugh, *Decline and Fall* (London, 2001), p. 110

320   'At a time' *Architects' Journal* LXXIX, 1934, p. 244

321   'He was one of the leaders' Frank Pick to the Board of Education, 10 December 1934

321   'but of course' Percy Jowett to the Board of Education, 29 March 1935

322   'As I explained' Walter Gropius to George Nelson, 14 September 1935, quoted
      Isaacs, p. 231

322   'After the Furtwängler affair' Walter Gropius to Martin Wagner, 26 December 1934,
      BHA

17: London 1935–1936

For Ati Gropius Johansen's own account of her arrival in London as a suddenly motherless child in 1936 a typescript memoir in the possession of her family has been invaluable, together with the memories of Jonathan Pritchard, her fellow pupil at Dora Russell's Beacon Hill school.

Correspondence and reviews relating to Gropius's *The New Architecture and the Bauhaus* are in the Faber & Faber Archive.

Good accounts of the experiences of former Bauhaus staff and students under the Nazis appear in *Bauhaus Women* by Ulrike Müller (Paris, 2009).

For Marcel Breuer, see Alastair Grieve's *Isokon* (London, 2004) and Jack Pritchard's memoir *View from a Long Chair* (London, 1984), in addition to Christopher Wilk's *Marcel Breuer, Furniture and Interiors* (Museum of Modern Art, New York, 1981), Robert McCarter's comprehensive *Breuer* (London, 2016) and the interesting insights in Breuer's almost lifelong correspondence with Ise Gropius, now in the American Archives of Art at the Smithsonian Institution, Washington.

For Moholy-Nagy in England, see Sibyl Moholy-Nagy, *Moholy-Nagy: Experiment in Totality* (New York, 1950), and a valuable essay, 'Moholy-Nagy: The Transitional Years' by Terence A. Senter, in the catalogue of the exhibition *Albers and Moholy-Nagy: From the Bauhaus to the New World* (Tate London, 2006).

On Gropius's architecture, besides David Elliott's *Gropius in England* (London, 1974) I am indebted to Louise Campbell for her research on the Levy House in London; see her essay 'Gropius in London: Modernism and Tradition' in *Proceedings of the Second International Docomomo Conference* (Dessau, 1992).

For background on the Wood House I am grateful to Rose Deakin, daughter of Gropius's clients Jack and Frances Donaldson, and the current owners Richard and Jane Everett. For Impington I have drawn on Harry Rée's *Educator Extraordinary: The Life and Achievement of Henry Morris 1889–1961* (London, 1973) and my own many conversations with Jack Pritchard. A full account of Gropius's rejection by Christ's College, Cambridge, is given by Alan Powers in *Oxford and Cambridge* in *Twentieth Century Architecture Series 11* (The Twentieth Century Society, London, 2013).

324   'I have no other' Herbert Read, *Art and Industry* (London, 1934), p. 63
325   'a great man' Philip Morton Shand, 'Scenario for a Human Drama', *Architectural Review*, August 1934
325   'typical products' Walter Gropius, *The New Architecture and the Bauhaus* (London, 1935), p. 26
325   'its sparkling insubstantiality' ibid., p. 23
327   'metaphysical abracadabra' Sybil Morton Shand to F. V. Morley, 3 April 1935, Faber Archive
327   'Quite between ourselves' Philip Morton Shand to F. V. Morley, 15 March 1935, Faber Archive
327   'I should like' Walter Gropius to Richard de la Mare, 23 October 1935, Faber Archive
327   'the best man' Philip Morton Shand to F. V. Morley, 1 May 1935, Faber Archive
328   'Professor Gropius' J. M. Richards, *Burlington Magazine*, November 1935
328   'the new spatial vision' Raymond McGrath, *The Listener*, 30 October 1935
328   'everyday objects' John Betjeman, 'The Ten Storey Town', *Sunday Express*, 24 August 1935
328   'has to his credit' Anthony Blunt, *Spectator*, 2 August 1935
329   'Why Not a City?' Robins Millar, *Glasgow Evening News*, 12 July 1935
329   'one of the most remarkable' Review in *New English Weekly*, 25 July 1935
330   'a happy, if all too brief, time' Marianne Brandt, 'Letter to the younger generation', 13 May 1966, quoted Neumann, p. 105
331   'heavy German cult' Sibyl Moholy-Nagy, *Moholy-Nagy: Experiment in Totality* (New York, 1950), p. 117
331   'where all the doors' Sibyl Moholy-Nagy to Jack Pritchard, 11 December 1970, UEA
332   'at the end of which' Jack Pritchard, *View from a Long Chair* (London, 1984), p. 124
333   'alas, the project' Richard Carline, *Draw They Must* (London, 1968), p. 268
333   'Walter, how marvellous' Ashley Havinden, biographical typescript, Havinden Archive, Scottish National Gallery of Modern Art, National Galleries of Scotland
333   '*liebe pia*' Marcel Breuer to Ise Gropius, 28 December 1933, AAA
333   'there is a fog' Marcel Breuer to Ise Gropius, 11 May 1934
333   'Your letter sounds' Marcel Breuer to Ise Gropius, 25 December 1934
333   'hated diatribe' Sibyl Moholy-Nagy to Jack Pritchard, 11 December 1970, UEA
334   'I always liked that girl' Marcel Breuer to Jack and Molly Pritchard, summer 1955, quoted Pritchard, *View from a Long Chair*, p. 97
334   'altogether on the loose' Herbert Bayer to Ise Gropius, 3 November 1935, AAA
334   'Gropius is a bad job' Walter Gropius to Jack Pritchard, 17 October 1935, BHA, quoted Isaacs, p. 200
334   'You must not worry' Jack Pritchard to Walter Gropius, 22 October 1935, BHA, quoted Isaacs, ibid.

Sources and References

335 'that any object' Marcel Breuer, article in *Das neue Frankfurt* magazine, 1927, quoted Hans M. Wingler, *The Bauhaus* (Cambridge, Mass., 1963), p. 454

337 'The sky was leaden' Ati Gropius Johansen, 'An English Education', typescript memoir

338 'hopelessly clogged' Ise Gropius, 'First Encounter', typescript, *c.*1970, AAA

338 'Jack and the boys' Ati Gropius Johansen, 'An English Education'

339 'My own belief' Bertrand Russell, quoted ibid.

339 'a child's garden' ibid.

340 'a charming man' Constance Cummings to Louise Campbell, 9 September 1992, personal correspondence

342 'a perfect example' Theo Crosby, quoted 'Goodbye Gropius Again – or How to Become Unstucco'd', *Building Design*, 27 July 1973, p. 13

343 'the modern form' Quoted *Timber and Plywood*, report on All Timber House Competition, 11 January 1936, BHA

343 'inharmonious with' Quoted H. Dalton Clifford, 'A Gropius House in Kent', *Country Life*, 17 July 1958, p. 132

343 'sort of lion-like approach' Maxwell Fry, interview in *Building*, 31 October 1975, p. 54

344 'capitalists with faces' Henry Morris, quoted Pritchard, *View from a Long Chair*, p. 48

344 'powerful combination' John Maynard Keynes and others to Henry Morris, 4 April 1936, letter later published in *New Statesman*

344 'I am afraid' John Maynard Keynes to Walter Gropius, 11 February 1937, HLH

345 'Gropius's plans' Henry Morris to Charles Fenn, quoted Pritchard, *View from a Long Chair*, p. 47

345 'I think from that time' Henry Moore, 'Farewell Night, Welcome Day', BBC broadcast, 4 January 1963

18: London 1936–1937

There is interesting background on Gropius, Peter Norton and the London Gallery in the Tate Archive, London; on Ashley Havinden in the Havinden Archive, Scottish National Gallery of Modern Art, National Galleries of Scotland; and on Pevsner and Gropius in Susie Harries's biography *Nikolaus Pevsner: The Life* (London, 2011).

347 'I ask you to realise' Walter Gropius to the Erfurt Court, 30 November 1936, BHA, quoted Isaacs, p. 215

348 'She is a little nervous' Walter Gropius to Herbert Bayer, 20 February 1937, HLH

349 'I asked Mrs. Norton' Lily Hildebrandt to Walter Gropius, 20 January 1937, HLH

350 'or worse, the presence' London Gallery prospectus, 1936, Tate Gallery Archive

353 'There is something sublime' Nikolaus Pevsner, *Pioneers of the Modern Movement: From William Morris to Walter Gropius* (London, 1936), p. 206

353 'was not entirely' Jack Pritchard to Walter Gropius, 1 December 1936, quoted Isaacs, p. 217

354 'The same man' Walter Gropius, farewell dinner speech, Trocadero, London, 9 March 1937, UEA

354 'Albers appears' Marcel Breuer to Ise Gropius, 25 December 1934, AAA

355 'for professional' Walter Gropius to Joseph Hudnut, 9 December 1936, quoted Isaacs, p. 218

355 'cultural Bolshevist' Walter Gropius to Ernst Jaeckh, 4 February 1937, HLH

355 'as I do so often' Herbert Bayer to Walter Gropius, 25 January 1937, AAA

356 'triumphantly, aboundingly' Edward Sackville-West to E. M. Forster, 7 January 1928, quoted Michael De-la-Noy, *Eddy: The Life of Edward Sackville-West* (London, 1988), p. 124

357 'this feature' Walter Gropius, farewell dinner speech, 9 March 1937

357 'as a ghost' Martin Wagner to Walter Gropius, 27 February 1937, HLH

19: Harvard 1937–1939

For this and the following chapters on Walter and Ise Gropius in America a valuable source has been the interchange of letters with Jack and Molly Pritchard in the Pritchard Archive at the University of East Anglia. Ati Johansen Gropius's memories of her New England upbringing have also been revealing in their detailed account of her adoptive parents' domestic life. 'Small but Perfect Things', two uninhibited recorded interviews given by Ise Gropius in her old age, one in 1977, the other *c*.1980, transcripts of which are in the Bauhaus Archive, throw interesting new light on the Harvard years.

On Gropius's architecture in America I have once again depended on Winfried Nerdinger's *Walter Gropius* (Busch-Reisinger Museum, Harvard and Bauhaus Archive, Berlin, 1985). On the Gropius House Ise Gropius's own *History of the Gropius House in Lincoln, Massachusetts*, written in 1977 for the Society for the Preservation of New England Antiquities, provided background to my own visits to the house, guided first by Ise Gropius in 1979 and by Gropius's granddaughter Erika Pfammatter in 2016.

Regina Bittner's *A Desk in Exile: A Bauhaus Object Traversing Different Modernities*, Bauhaus Taschenbuch No. 20, published for the Bauhaus Dessau Foundation, 2017, gives fascinating insights into the travels of Gropius's own working desk across the continents.

On Gropius, his friends and his followers' connections with the Cape Cod area, which became increasingly important as an outpost of modernism, see *Cape Cod Modern: Midcentury Architecture and Community on the Outer Cape* by Peter McMahon and Christine Cipriani (New York, 2014).

On Marcel Breuer, see Christopher Wilk, *Marcel Breuer: Furniture and Interiors* (Museum of Modern Art, New York, 1981), *Breuer Houses* by Joachim Driller (London, 2000) and Robert McCarter's massively comprehensive survey *Breuer* (London, 2016).

On Gropius at Harvard and his fraught relationship with Joseph Hudnut I have been dependent on Jill Pearlman's illuminating *Inventing American Modernism: Joseph Hudnut, Walter Gropius, and the Bauhaus Legacy at Harvard* (Virginia, 2007) and the recordings of her interviews with former Harvard students of Gropius's which she generously shared with me.

On Gropius's connections with the Museum of Modern Art and the 1938 Bauhaus exhibition, see David A. Hanks's chapter 'The Bauhaus: Mecca of Modernism' and Barry Bergdoll's 'Modern Architecture: International Exhibition' in *Partners in Design: Alfred H. Barr Jr. and Philip Johnson*, edited by David A. Hanks (New York, 2015).

There is useful background in *The Bauhaus and America, First Contacts 1919–1936* by Margret Kentgens-Craig (Cambridge, Mass., 1999) and in the catalogue *Exiles and Emigrés: The Flight of European Artists from Hitler*, edited by Stephanie Barron (Los Angeles County Museum of Art, 1997).

There is a good essay, 'Black Mountain College, NC' by Paul Betts, stressing the links between the Bauhaus and Black Mountain, in *Bauhaus*, edited by Jeannine Fiedler and Peter Feierabend (Berlin, 2013). On Black Mountain College in general I have relied on the catalogue of the exhibition *Black Mountain College: Experiment in Art*, edited by Vincent Katz (Cambridge, Mass., 2013), and *Leap Before You Look, Black Mountain College 1933–1957*, a generously illustrated survey by Helen Molesworth (Yale and Boston, 2015).

361 'This will then' Walter Gropius to Adolf Sommerfeld, 15 November 1936, BHA, quoted Isaacs, p. 216

361 'gorgeous half-castes' Walter Gropius to Marcel Breuer, 17 April 1937, HLH

361 'there were more and higher' Ise Gropius to Jack and Molly Pritchard, 19 April 1937, UEA

362 'This inexhaustible melting-pot' *Bertolt Brecht: Poems 1913–56*, eds John Willett and Ralph Manheim (London, 1976), p. 167

362 'Hitler is my best friend' Walter Cook, quoted Sibyl Moholy-Nagy, 'Hitler's Revenge', *Art in America*, 1968

363 'Welcome to America' Joseph Hudnut to Mr and Mrs Walter Gropius, radio telegram, 18 March 1937, HLH

364 'Dear Vi' Walter Gropius to Joseph Hudnut, 9 June 1937, HLH

364 'we could not be better' Ise Gropius to Jack and Molly Pritchard, 19 April 1937, HLH

364 'the least modern' Leopold Arnaud to James Stewart Polshek, 8 June 1980, quoted Jill Pearlman, *Inventing American Modernism* (Virginia, 2007), p. 1

364 'She fell in love' Jean Paul Carlhian, interview with Jill Pearlman, 12 May 1988

365 'characteristic old American' Walter Gropius, *Harvard Crimson*, 1 April 1937

365 'to create independently' Walter Gropius, address to dinner of Harvard Visiting Committee, Harvard Club, Boston, 30 March 1937

365 'the often primitive' Walter Gropius to Marcel Breuer, 17 April 1937, HLH

366 'Oh my God' Ise Gropius, 'Small but Perfect Things', transcript of interview *c*.1980, BHA

367 'The meals were merry' Ati Gropius Johansen, 'The Adolescent Years', typescript memoir

368 'Some generous old lady' Ise Gropius to Jack and Molly Pritchard, 29 November 1937, UEA

369 'an almost moral meaning' Ati Gropius Johansen, '68 Baker Bridge Road', *Architecture Boston*, 'American Gropius' issue, Summer 2013, p. 64

370 'Hail to the most indigenous' Lewis Mumford, Gropius House Visitors' Book, 18 November 1939

370 'The family lives in them' Ise Gropius to Jack and Molly Pritchard, 27 February 1938, UEA

372 'My father was no disciplinarian' Ati Gropius Johansen, '68 Baker Bridge Road'

372 'The expression in his eyes' Ati Gropius Johansen, 'The Adolescent Years'

372 'What is Isobar?' Ise Gropius to Jack and Molly Pritchard, 29 November 1937, UEA

373 'The newest excitement' Marcel Breuer to Dorothea Ventris, 16 November 1938, quoted Joachim Driller, *Breuer Houses* (London, 2000), p. 125

373 'He was tireless' Harvard alumnus, quoted Reginald Isaacs, 'Gropius at Harvard', 1983, BHA

373 'I like the human body' Walter Gropius, quoted Jean Paul Carlhian, interview with Jill Pearlman, 12 May 1988

375 'new and impressive' 'A House in Pittsburgh, Pa.', *Architectural Forum*, March 1941

376 'a background' Marcel Breuer, quoted Joachim Driller, ibid., p. 137

377 'merely a belated wreath' Alfred H. Barr, preface to catalogue *Bauhaus 1919–1928*, Museum of Modern Art, New York, 1938

378 'Bayer got the commission' Ise Gropius, 'Small but Perfect Things'

378 'I shall leap' Oskar Schlemmer to Ida Bienert, 25 October 1937, *The Letters and Diaries of Oskar Schlemmer*, ed. Tut Schlemmer (Evanston, 1990), p. 365

379 'In 1938 the Museum' Ferdinand Kramer, quoted Neumann, p. 83

381   'Many Americans' Alfred H. Barr to Walter Gropius, 10 December 1938, HLH
382   'It might be well' Walter Gropius to Alfred H. Barr, 15 December 1938, HLH
382   'the already terrific' Alfred H. Barr to Walter Gropius, 3 March 1939, HLH
383   'We all feel' Philip C. Johnson to Walter Gropius, 30 April 1951, HLH
385   'To open eyes' Josef Albers, quoted *Black Mountain College: Experiment in Art*, ed. Vincent Katz (Cambridge, Mass., 2013), p. 32
387   'I'm on the luckier side' Walter Gropius to Arthur Korn, 9 December 1937, HLH
388   'there is such a rush' Walter Gropius to Lily Hildebrandt, 14 November 1937, HLH
388   'I realise that something' Walter Gropius to Hans Hildebrandt, 19 January 1939, HLH
388   'I think democracy' Walter Gropius to Jack Pritchard, 3 December 1939, UEA

20: Harvard and the Second World War 1940–1944

In her autobiography *And the Bridge Is Love* (London, 1959) Alma Mahler gives a vivid description of her flight from France to America with Franz Werfel and of their subsequent life in Los Angeles, by then almost a colony of highly cultured European refugees. For a more sober analysis, see Ehrhard Bahr, *Weimar on the Pacific: German Exile Culture in Los Angeles and the Crisis of Modernism* (Berkeley, 2007).

The Gropius House at Lincoln was another port of call for European émigrés, especially ex-members of the Bauhaus, as the Gropius House Visitors' Book, still kept at the house, shows.

The continuing correspondence between the Gropiuses and Jack and Molly Pritchard, whose sons were evacuated from England and lived with the Gropiuses, shows clearly their anxious responses to the escalation of the war.

On the rift between Gropius and Breuer that resulted in the break-up of their architectural partnership there is a revealing interchange of letters in the Gropius Papers at the Houghton Library at Harvard.

392   'a wild, blond wench' Erich Maria Remarque, diary, 13 August 1942, quoted Hilmes p. 226
392   'safe from German presents' Walter Gropius to Maxwell Fry, 19 March 1940, HLH
392   'Now the heavenly islands' Herbert Bayer to Ise and Walter Gropius, 2 May 1940, HLH
393   'There was a close inner circle' Ati Gropius Johansen, '68 Baker Bridge Road', *Architecture Boston*, 'American Gropius' issue, Summer 2013, p. 64
393   'They seemed like family' Ati Gropius Johansen, 'The Adolescent Years', typescript memoir
394   'I am sorry' Jack Pritchard to Walter Gropius, 28 May 1940, HLH
394   'We get along' Ise Gropius to Jack Pritchard, 7 January 1941, UEA
394   'a definite part' Walter Gropius to Jack Pritchard, 8 August 1942, HLH
395   'Pour Madame et Monsieur' Joan Miró, Gropius House Visitors' Book, 24 May 1959
395   'cher *ami*' Le Corbusier, Gropius House Visitors' Book, 15 November 1959
395   'with old but not aged' Georg Kepes, Gropius House Visitors' Book, 21 January 1968
395   'When Wright had dinner' Walter Gropius to Vincent Scully, 31 January 1962, HLH
396   'romantic and explosive' Walter Gropius, statement on death of Frank Lloyd Wright, *Architectural Forum*, 12 April 1959
396   'A fine man' Sibyl Moholy-Nagy to Ise Gropius, 29 September 1948, HLH
397   'We both owe' Walter Gropius, 'Igor Stravinsky', *Apollo in the Democracy* (New York, 1968), p. 173

398   'the spirit of economising' Ati Gropius Johansen, '68 Baker Bridge Road'
399   'During our jury meeting' Marcel Breuer to Walter Gropius, 23 May 1941, HLH
399   'Dear Pius' Marcel Breuer to Walter Gropius, 23 May 1941, HLH
399   'Dear Lajkó' Walter Gropius to Marcel Breuer, 25 May 1941, HLH
399   'a bust-up' Walter Gropius to Herbert Bayer, July 1941, HLH
400   'He feels hampered' Ise Gropius diary, 27 November 1926, AAA
400   'His ambition grows' ibid., 10 February 1927
401   'he doesn't need me' Walter Gropius to Herbert Bayer, July 1941, HLH
403   'introverted technologist' Peter Blake, *No Place Like Utopia* (New York, 1993), p. 95
404   'Pearl Harbor' Walter Gropius to Jack Pritchard, 24 January 1942, UEA
405   'Hudnut wants' Walter Gropius, quoted Isaacs, p. 251
405   'Here are quite some changes' Walter Gropius to László Moholy-Nagy, 15 June 1942, HLH
405   'I found a pretty great' Martin Wagner to Walter Gropius, 8 November 1940, HLH
406   'I found in his teaching' Paul Rudolph, *Perspecta* 3 (Yale University, 1952)
406   'When I first came' I. M. Pei, speech at Gropius's eightieth birthday celebration, 18 May 1963, quoted Isaacs, p. 299
407   'The horizon' Walter Gropius to Maxwell Fry, 22 September 1944, HLH

21: Return to Berlin 1945–1947

For this chapter I am grateful for background information supplied by Gropius's great-nephew Dr Wolf Burchard and his family, and to Fiona Elliott for her translations of Gropius family correspondence.

409   'A lot of my past acquaintances' Walter Gropius to Manon Burchard, 16 September 1945, HLH
410   'There are no linen ties' Ise Gropius to Manon Burchard, 31 October 1946, HLH
412   'Whenever I read' Walter Gropius to Manon Burchard, 31 October 1946, HLH
412   'quite miraculously' Ise Gropius to Jack and Molly Pritchard, 29 October 1945, UEA
412   'Still waiting' Helena Syrkus, telegram to Walter Gropius, 6 June 1945, HLH
413   'He was forced to work' C. R. Mathewson to Walter Gropius, 8 October 1945, HLH
413   'a *great* many difficult experiences' Lily Hildebrandt to Walter Gropius, 30 January 1946, HLH
414   'Your letter' Walter Gropius to Lily Hildebrandt, 10 June 1946, HLH
414   'in spite of the trying' Margaret Leischner to Walter Gropius, 4 October 1946, HLH
415   'the misery and unspeakable sufferings' Lyonel Feininger to Walter Gropius, 22 June 1948, HLH
416   'Our desks are piled high' Ise Gropius to Maxwell Fry, 3 March 1947, HLH
416   'that terrible sense' Ise Gropius to Jack Donaldson, 18 March 1948, Donaldson family collection
416   'Don't you think?' Ise Gropius to Philip Johnson, 8 September 1947, HLH
417   'I got out' Margarete Schütte-Lihotzky, 'Frankfurt, the Bauhaus and Walter Gropius', Schütte-Lihotzky papers, University of Applied Arts, Vienna
417   'My post at Harvard' Walter Gropius to Joachim Burchard, 21 September 1946, HLH
418   'I alarmed the crew' Walter Gropius to Ise Gropius, 5 August 1947, HLH
420   'Conditions in Europe' Walter Gropius to Sibyl Moholy-Nagy, 8 October 1947, HLH
420   'Without seeing' Walter Gropius to Helena and Szymon Syrkus, 20 April 1948, HLH
420   'Where is Bridgeport?' Ise Gropius to Walter Gropius, 3 September 1947, HLH

421   'Reaffirmation of the Aims' Eric Mumford, *The CIAM Discourse on Urbanism, 1928–1960* (Massachusetts Institute of Technology, 2002), p. 172

421   'new conception of space' Walter Gropius, 'Urbanism', *Architects' Journal*, 25 September 1947, pp. 277–81

422   'Externally Gropius' Margarete Schütte-Lihotzky, 'Memories of Walter Gropius', Schütte-Lihotzky Papers, University of Applied Arts, Vienna

22: Harvard and TAC 1948–1952

Valuable insights into post-war political attitudes to the Bauhaus are given in articles by Paul Betts, 'The Bauhaus and National Socialism – A Dark Chapter of Modernism' and 'The Bauhaus in the German Democratic Republic – Between Formalism and Pragmatism', in *Bauhaus*, eds Jeannine Fiedler and Peter Feierabend (Potsdam, 2013). See also *Cold War Modern: Design 1945–1970*, catalogue of exhibition at the Victoria & Albert Museum, eds David Crowley and Jane Pavitt (London, 2008).

For a reassessment of Gropius's professorship at Harvard, see Jill Pearlman's *Inventing American Modernism: Joseph Hudnut, Walter Gropius, and the Bauhaus Legacy at Harvard* (Virginia, 2007).

A useful illustrated survey of TAC's origins and output up to the mid-1960s is given in *The Architects Collaborative Inc.* (Barcelona, 1966), with commentaries by Gropius and other founding partners. For a later reassessment and interesting recollections, see the 'American Gropius' issue of *Architecture Boston*, Summer 2013. I have also found illuminating the documentary film *Still Standing*, directed by TAC partner Perry King Neubauer and featuring his interviews with John and Sally Harkness and Norman Fletcher. My own meetings with John Harkness in the 1970s and in 2016 with Alex Cvijanovic, the late Jane Thompson and a phone interview with Marina Thompson provided invaluable background to this later phase of Gropius's life in America.

423   'Vienna was hell' Mahler *Bridge*, p. 274

424   'To Alma' Thomas Mann, quoted Mahler *Bridge*, p. 277

424   'you are timeless' Willy Haas, Birthday Book for Alma Mahler, quoted Hilmes, p. 259

425   'Gustav Mahler' Mahler *Bridge*, p. 277

425   'Dearest Walter' Alma Mahler to Walter Gropius, September 1949, HLH

425   'The span of time' Oskar Kokoschka, Birthday Book for Alma Mahler, quoted Hilmes, p. 260

426   'Nothing seems' Ise Gropius to Jack and Molly Pritchard, 29 October 1945, UEA

426   'Through the release' Albert Einstein to Walter Gropius, 10 February 1947, HLH

429   'I picked out the best' Walter Gropius to Joachim Burchard, 21 September 1946, HLH

430   'The Bauhaus' Walter Gropius, draft funeral address for László Moholy-Nagy, December 1946, HLH

430   'For my part' Walter Gropius to Joachim Burchard, 21 September 1946, HLH

431   'We at TAC' Perry King Neubauer, letter in *Architecture Boston*, Fall 2013

431   'Walter would be all right' Josep Lluís Sert, quoted Joseph Rykwert, *Times Literary Supplement*, 2 May 1986

431   'I had just started' Walter Gropius to J. M. Richards, 5 October 1953, HLH

432   'illuminated by an Akari' Anthony Thompson, '40 Moon Hill Road', *Architecture Boston*, Spring 2011, p. 17

432 'big egos were OK' Marina Thompson, interview with the author, 26 September 2016

433 'Your husband' R. Buckminster Fuller to Ise Gropius, 27 January 1950, HLH

433 'this great communal work' Bauhaus Manifesto 1919, quoted Marcel Franciscono, *Walter Gropius and the Creation of the Bauhaus of Weimar* (Urbana, 1971), p. 142

435 'we cannot go on' Walter Gropius, *New York Times*, 1949, quoted Gilbert Lupfer and Paul Sigel, *Gropius* (Cologne, 2006), p. 81

436 'I hope your magnificent' Hans Arp to Walter and Ise Gropius, 11 June 1950, HLH

438 'when Hudnut realized' Michael Maccoby, *Harvard Crimson*, 11 December 1952

438 'So they had a real battle' Ise Gropius, 'Small but perfect things', interview recorded *c.*1980, transcribed in 1984, BHA

439 'pathological jealousy' Walter Gropius notes, *c.*June 1948, quoted Isaacs, p. 263

439 'Harvard had only' Walter Gropius to James B. Conant, 27 March 1948, HLH

439 'I have convinced myself' Walter Gropius to James B. Conant, 19 June 1952, HLH

440 'Harvard was very difficult' Ise Gropius, 'Small but perfect things'

23: Wandering Star: Japan, Paris, London, Baghdad, Berlin 1953–1959

For Gropius's 1954 journey to Japan, see Ise Gropius's typescript Travel Diary in the Houghton Library at Harvard and her vividly detailed letters to Ati and Charles Forberg and to the partners in TAC in the Pritchard Papers at the University of East Anglia.

For Marcel Breuer, see Robert McCarter, *Breuer* (London, 2016). A perceptive commentary on the later development of Breuer's work is given in Barry Bergdoll's *Marcel Breuer: Bauhaus Tradition, Brutalist Invention* (New York, 2016).

For background on Ulm, see Jeremy Aynsley, *Designing Modern Germany* (London, 2009), Paul Betts, 'The Bauhaus as a Cold War Weapon', in *Bauhaus Conflicts, 1919–2009* (Ostfildern, 2009), and Jane Pavitt's essay 'Design and the Democratic Ideal' in the catalogue *Cold War Modern: Design 1945–1970* (London, 2008).

441 'Here we are' Ise Gropius to Ati and Charles Forberg, 22 May 1954, UEA

442 'The view' ibid.

443 'There were two' Masataka Ogawa in article 'Gropius and Japanese Culture', quoted Isaacs, p. 275

443 'Walter loves this style' Ise Gropius to Ati and Charles Forberg, 22 May 1954, UEA

444 'the most heavenly views' Ise Gropius to TAC, 16 June 1954, UEA

446 'try to join' Ise Gropius to TAC, 18 July 1954, UEA

446 'In all directions' Ise Gropius to TAC, 30 June 1954, UEA

447 'hard fate' Walter Gropius, draft of speech to be given in Hiroshima, HLH

448 'a very interesting' Walter Gropius to Le Corbusier, 12 September 1954, LCP

448 'at a time' Ise Gropius to TAC, 23 August 1954, UEA

449 'The love and care' Ise Gropius to Ati and Charles Forberg, 2 June 1954, UEA

451 'And what do the ladies do' Ise Gropius to Molly Pritchard, 23 February 1956, UEA

454 'quality of passion' *Manchester Guardian*, report on Gropius dinner held on 12 April 1956, UEA

454 'I think it is' Julian Huxley, speech at Gropius dinner, 12 April 1956, UEA

455 'England did not seize' Henry Morris, speech at Gropius dinner, 12 April 1956, UEA

455 'A windfall' Maxwell Fry verses at Gropius dinner, 12 April 1956, UEA

455 'You must forgive me' Walter Gropius speech at Gropius dinner, 12 April 1956, UEA

455 'Quick before the surf' Walter Gropius to Ise Gropius, 19 February 1960, quoted Isaacs, p. 281

456   'This relation to the Jawdats' Walter Gropius to Ise Gropius, 6 November 1957, quoted Isaacs, p. 281

456   'but wants them bigger' Ise Gropius to Jack and Molly Pritchard, 2 July 1959, UEA

457   'far-away and fascinating' Giulio Carlo Argan, typescript essay, 1960, HLH

459   'a symbol' Paul Reilly, *Design* 55, July 1953, p. 16

460   'moved appreciably' Reyner Banham, *Design* 234, June 1968, p. 21

462   'still a tragically shocking' Walter Gropius to Ise Gropius, 23 September 1955, BHA

462   'Most of all' ibid.

463   'the pedagogic achievement' Citation for the 1956 Hanseatic Goethe Prize, Hamburg, 5 June 1957, quoted Isaacs, p. 280

464   'And this is me' Elias Canetti, *The Play of the Eyes* (London, 1990), p. 52

465   'The love story' Walter Gropius to Alma Mahler, 17 August 1958, quoted Isaacs, p. 283

465   'I beg your forgiveness' Alma Mahler to Walter Gropius, 6 April 1960, quoted Isaacs, p. 283

466   'The loveliest girl' Tom Lehrer, *That Was the Year That Was*, Reprise Records, San Francisco, 1965

24: New England 1960–1969

Prime sources for this chapter have been my conversations with Gropius's granddaughter Erika Pfammater and his TAC colleague Alex Cvijanovic. I also had illuminating discussions with Fred Noyes and Perry King Neubauer.

On the Pan Am Building, Meredith L. Clausen, *The Pan Am Building and the Shattering of the Modernist Dream* (Cambridge, Mass., 2005).

On the background to Jack Cotton and the British property developers, Richard Davenport-Hines, *The English Affair: Sex, Class and Power in the Age of Profumo* (London, 2013).

On John Johansen, William D. Earls, *The Harvard Five in New Canaan* (New York, 2006) and Peter McMahon and Christine Cipriani, *Cape Cod Modern* (New York, 2014).

On Gropius's last illness I have used the accounts given by Ise Gropius in letters to Jack and Molly Pritchard (UEA) and to Peter Norton (Tate Gallery Archive).

467   'we had a connection' Alex Cvijanovic, *Architecture Boston*, Summer 2013, p. 29

471   'I asked myself' Walter Gropius, interview in *Think*, September 1962

471   'Spent yesterday' Walter Gropius to Ise Gropius, 1 September 1960, HLH

471   'whether my husband' Ise Gropius to David Elliott, 24 February 1973, David Elliott personal correspondence

472   'My workers chase' Alex Cvijanovic, *Architecture Boston*, Summer 2013, p. 29

474   'Dear Walter Gropius!' Maria Benemann to Walter Gropius, 17 October 1967, BHA

475   'great trouble' Herbert Bayer to Walter Gropius, 8 December 1967, HLH

478   'perhaps the most time consuming' Ise Gropius to Peter Norton, 21 April 1960, Tate Gallery Archive

478   'Somebody is writing' Walter Gropius to Manon Burchard, 16 February 1963, quoted Isaacs, p. xiii

480   'because he was always' Ise Gropius to Peter and Clifford Norton, 30 October 1969, Tate Gallery Archive

480   'why should I ask' Walter Gropius to Ise Gropius, June 1969, quoted Isaacs, p. 311

480   'The past four weeks' Ati Johansen to Jeremy Pritchard, n/d, UEA

481   'Our hearts are with you' Maxwell Fry to Ise Gropius, 8 July 1969, HLH

Sources and References

482   'Testament April '33' Walter Gropius, BHA
482   'protean fire' Quoted Ise Gropius to Peter Norton, 21 April 1969, Tate Gallery
      Archive
482   'by metallic decoration' Robert Reinhold, 'Grope Fest Honors Gropius', *New York Times*, 20 May 1970

Afterword: Reverberations

On Ise Gropius and the Gropius House in Lincoln, see Ati Gropius Johansen, *Ise Gropius* (Historic New England, 2013); Ise Gropius, *History of the Gropius House* (Society for the Preservation of New England Antiquities, 1977); 'The Things They Cherished', article in *Architecture Boston*, 'American Gropius' issue, Summer 2013. Also Ulrike Müller's appreciative chapter on Ise Gropius in *Bauhaus Women* (Paris, 2009).

484   'Her letter spoke' Ati Gropius Johansen, *Ise Gropius* (Historic New England, 2013), p. 23
484   'Like the Weimar Republic' Neil MacGregor, *Germany: Memories of a Nation* (London, 2014), p. 356
485   'the other' Walter Gropius, quoted Peter Gay, *Art and Act* (New York, 1976), p. 145
485   'It was his sterling' Nikolaus Pevsner, 'Gropius: A Moral Force in Architecture', obituary, *Observer*, 6 July 1969
486   'Everyone wants' Sally Harkness, quoted *Architecture Boston*, Summer 2013
486   'If I have a talent' Walter Gropius, quoted documentary *Who Is Walter Gropius?*, produced by Roger Graef for BBC Television, 1967

List of Illustrations

Illustrations in the text

15 Walter with his parents, sister Manon and younger brother Georg, *c*.1892. Photographer unknown. *Bauhaus-Archiv, Berlin.*

16 Gropius the architectural student at the Munich Technische Hochschule, 1903. *Imaging Department © President and Fellows of Harvard College. Harvard Art Museums/Busch-Reisinger Museum, gift of the Institute of Contemporary Art, BRGA.1.1.*

18 Gropius the cadet in the 15th Hussars Regiment, Wandsbeck, 1904. Photographer unknown. *Bauhaus-Archiv, Berlin.*

24 Gropius and Helmuth Grisebach travelling in Spain. Photographer unknown. *Bauhaus-Archiv, Berlin.*

33 Peter Behrens, Gropius's acknowledged architectural mentor. *Museum Folkwang Essen/ARTOTHEK.*

36 Peter Behrens's AEG Turbine Hall, Berlin, 1909. Photographer unknown. *Bauhaus-Archiv, Berlin.*

45 Alma Mahler photographed in 1908. *Photo by Fine Art Images/Heritage Images/Getty Images.*

50 Max Reinhardt, Gustav Mahler, Carl Moll, Hans Pfitzner in the garden of Carl Moll's villa in Vienna, 1905. Photograph Moritz Nähr, Vienna. *Hulton Archive © Getty Images/Imagno.*

73 Office building and factory for the Deutscher Werkbund exhibition, Cologne, 1914. Photographer unknown. Gelatin silver print. *Harvard Art Museums/Busch-Reisinger Museum, gift of Ise Gropius, BRGA.6.49. Photo: Imaging Department © President and Fellows of Harvard College. Work by Walter Gropius © DACS 2018.*

73 Sleeping car interior, 1914. Photographer unknown. Gelatin silver print, 22.4 x 17.2 cm. *Harvard Art Museums/Busch-Reisinger Museum, gift of Ise Gropius, BRGA.4.6. Photo: Imaging Department © President and Fellows of Harvard College. Work by Walter Gropius © DACS 2018.*

76 Gropius saw military service from 5 August 1914 with the 9th Wandsbeck Hussars. Photographer unknown. *Bauhaus-Archiv, Berlin.*

84 Oskar Kokoschka as a volunteer in the 15th Imperial Dragoons, 1915. Photograph H. Schieberth, Vienna. *Hulton Archive © Imagno/Getty Images.*

86 Oskar Kokoschka's *Doll*, made by Hermine Moos, Munich, 1919. Photographer unknown. Gelatin silver print, 30 x 40 cm. *© University of Applied Arts Vienna, Oskar Kokoschka Centre, Collection and Archive (Universität für angewandte Kunst Wien, Kunstsammlung und Archiv).*

94 Gropius, Alma and their daughter Manon, 1918. Photographer unknown. *Bauhaus-Archiv, Berlin.*

Illustrations in the plates

19. The six-storey Prellerhaus, designed to accommodate students and young Masters. Photograph Helen Mellor, 2016. *Courtesy Helen Mellor. Work by Walter Gropius © DACS 2018.*

20. Anni Albers, Wall Hanging WE 493/445, 1926. Cotton and synthetic silk. *Bauhaus-Archiv, Berlin. © The Josef and Anni Albers Foundation/Artists Rights Society (ARS), New York. Work by Anni Albers © DACS 2018.*

21. House for the Bauhaus Masters, 1925–26, built in pairs in the pinewood. Photograph Helen Mellor, 2016. *Courtesy Helen Mellor. Work by Walter Gropius © DACS 2018.*

22. Stairway of the semi-detached Bauhaus Master's house Wassily Kandinsky shared with Paul Klee. Photograph Helen Mellor, 2016. *Courtesy Helen Mellor. Work by Walter Gropius © DACS 2018.*

23. Oskar Schlemmer, *Bauhaustreppe* (Bauhaus Stairway), 1932. Oil on canvas, 162.3 x 114.3 cm. *Museum of Modern Art, New York, 597.1942. Digital Image © 2019 The Museum of Modern Art/Scala, Florence.*

24. Apartment house communal rooms for Deutscher Werkbund exhibition, Paris, 1930: Interior perspective, bar, 1930. Drawing Herbert Bayer. Transparent and opaque watercolour, black ink, over graphite on off-white wove paper, 42 x 57.1 cm. *Harvard Art Museums/Busch-Reisinger Museum, gift of Walter Gropius, BRGA.45.1. Photo: Imaging Department © President and Fellows of Harvard College. Work by Herbert Bayer © DACS 2018.*

25. Gropius's *Der neue Adler* (The new Adler), 1931. Design Herbert Bayer. Letterpress advertising brochure. Berlin: Dorland. Jan Tschichold Collection, gift of Philip Johnson. *Museum of Modern Art, New York, 542.1999. Digital Image © 2019 The Museum of Modern Art/Scala, Florence. Work by Herbert Bayer © DACS 2018. Work by Walter Gropius © DACS 2018.*

26. Non-ferrous metals section for 'German People–German Work' exhibition, Berlin, 1934. Design Walter Gropius. Isometric. Ink, wash, gouache, and collage elements on paper, 72.6 x 101.6 cm. *Harvard Art Museums/Busch-Reisinger Museum, gift of Walter Gropius, BRGA.74.2. Photo: Imaging Department © President and Fellows of Harvard College. Work by Walter Gropius © DACS 2018.*

27. Impington Village College, Cambridgeshire, designed by Gropius and Maxwell Fry, 1936–37. Photographed in 2006. Creative commons 2.0 Generic (CC BY-SA 2.0). *Work by Walter Gropius © DACS 2018.*

28. Menu card for dinner in honour of Gropius at the Trocadero restaurant, Piccadilly, London, 'on the occasion of his leaving England for Harvard University', 9 March 1937. Design László Moholy-Nagy. *RIBA Collections, CaE/2/3 recto, CaE/2/3 verso.*

29. The Gropius House, Lincoln, Massachusetts, 1938. View from south. Photographer Paul Davis. *Imaging Department © President and Fellows of Harvard College. Harvard Art Museums/Busch-Reisinger Museum, gift of Ise Gropius, BRGA.82.142. Work by Walter Gropius © DACS 2018.*

30. Gropius House Visitors' Book, entry by Joan Miró, 1959. *Courtesy of Historic New England. Work by Joan Miró © Successió / ADAGP, Paris and DACS London 2018.*

31. Ise's traditional lobster dinner at the Gropius House, Christmas 1952. *Photo courtesy Wolf Burchard.*

32. The Pan Am Building, New York, *c.*1958. Photographer unknown. Illustrated in *The Architects Collaborative* (1966), p. 121. *Work by Walter Gropius © DACS 2018.*

33. Formica mural, *The City*, Pan Am Building, New York, 1963. Design by Josef Albers. Formica panels, 8.1 x 16.8 m. *© 2018 The Josef and Anni Albers Foundation/Artists*

34. Book jacket, Bauhaus exhibition catalogue. London: Royal Academy Publishing,
    1968. Design Herbert Bayer. *Private Collection. Work by Herbert Bayer © DACS 2018.*

Text permissions

Acknowledgements

My thanks to Erika Pfammater for permission to quote from Gropius family correspondence, to Marina Mahler for Alma Mahler correspondence and to Jonathan Pritchard for Pritchard family correspondence. I am also grateful to Gropius's great-nephew Dr Wolf Burchard, his father Eike Burchard and his aunt Almut Faye for insights into Gropius family history; to James Reidel for allowing me to quote from his translations of Gropius's letters to his daughter Manon; and to Fiona Elliott for her sensitive translations of letters and documents from the original German for this book. Thanks too to Henry Isaacs for filling in the background to his father Reginald Isaacs's pioneering biography of Walter Gropius and for his interest and encouragement.

At the Bauhaus-Archiv Berlin particular thanks to Dr Annemarie Jaeggi, Director, and Nina Schönig, Archivist; at the Houghton Library, Harvard University, to Leslie A. Morris, Curator of Modern Books and Manuscripts, and her helpful staff; to Laura Muir, Research Curator, and Robert Wiesenberger at the Busch-Reisinger Museum at Harvard; to Dr Ruth Haüsler, Kokoschka Bequest at the Zentralbibliothek, Zurich; to Professor Patrick Werner at the Oskar Kokoschka Center, University of Applied Arts, Vienna; and to Bridget Gillies, Archivist, the Pritchard Papers at the University of East Anglia.

Research for this book involved extended travels in Germany, England and the United States, and I am grateful to the following people who spared the time for meetings, discussions and viewings of Gropius buildings, starting with his granddaughter Erika Pfammater, with whom I spent a memorable morning being guided round the Gropius House at Lincoln, Massachusetts. Thomas Abbott; Peter Agoos; Sana Al-Naimi; Stephen Bayley; Barbara Benemann; Professor

Acknowledgements

Barry Bergdoll; Professor Rosemarie Haag Bletter; Professor Iain Boyd Whyte; Professor Louise Campbell; the late Sherban Cantacuzino; Professor Harry Charrington; Alex and Maria Cvijanovic; Rose Deakin; David Elliott; Magnus Englund; Jane and Richard Everett; Martin Filler; Francesca Forty; Professor Hartmut Frank; Professor Sir Christopher Frayling; Michael Frayn; Professor Charles Jencks; Adèle Lewis; Renée Loth; Giles de la Mare; Peter McMahon; Wendy Moor; Richard Morphet; Dietrich Mueller; Perry King Neubauer; Fred Noyes; Jill Pearlman; Alan Powers; Jonathan and Maria Pritchard; Michael Ratcliffe; Nirvana Romell; Professor Joseph Rykwert; Deyan Sudjic; the late Jane Thompson; Maria Thompson; Edmund de Waal; Nicholas Fox Weber; the late Frank Whitford; Christopher Wilk; Susan Wright.

My own architect and designer friends have provided constant argument and stimulus and I thank the following in particular: Lucy Annan and Spencer de Grey; Dinah Casson and Alan Moses; Adrian and Audrey Gale; Birkin Haward and Joanna van Heyningen; Richard Hollis and Posy Simmonds; Michael and Patty Hopkins; Alan Irvine; Eva Jiricna; José Manser and the late Michael Manser.

Closer to home I am grateful to my daughter-in-law, photographer Helen Mellor, who took special colour pictures for this book. In 2016 my son Corin drove us on a memorable family expedition from Berlin to the Faguswerk building and the Bauhaus at Dessau, where my young grandsons were enthralled by the so-called 'Bauhaus Experience', staying overnight in one-time student rooms. My daughter, graphic designer Clare Mellor, has for many years shared my enthusiasm for the European avant-garde.

At Faber & Faber I have appreciated Laura Hassan's and Eleo Carson's perceptive editing. My thanks to Kate Ward and Eleanor Crow for designing a book so much in keeping with its subject; to Eleanor Rees for copyediting, Ian Bahrami for proofreading, Sarah Ereira for indexing, Jack Murphy for production work and Paddy Fox for artworking; to Robert Brown, Archivist at Faber, for providing many links between Gropius and my own publisher; and to Stephen Page for his constant interest and support.

My gratitude goes to my ever-encouraging and much-loved agent Michael Sissons who, alas, died before this book was finally completed; to Fiona Petheram, his successor as my agent at Peters Fraser and Dunlop; to Peter Matson, my agent in America and to the publications team at Harvard University Press.

In my own office Ruth Elliot has assisted with research and has performed miracles in transferring my handwritten manuscript onto computer.

Finally Richard Calvocoressi, expert in German and Viennese twentieth-century art and architecture and curator of the memorable Oskar Kokoschka centenary exhibition at the Tate in London, has contributed greatly in reading and commenting on my work in progress. I dedicate this book to him.

Index

Index